EMERGING

CONTEMPORARY READINGS FOR WRITERS

EMERGING

CONTEMPORARY READINGS FOR WRITERS

BARCLAY BARRIOS
Florida Atlantic University

BEDFORD/ST. MARTIN'S
Boston ◆ New York

For Bedford/St. Martin's

Senior Executive Editor: Leasa Burton
Executive Editor: John E. Sullivan III
Production Editor: Kendra LeFleur
Production Supervisor: Jennifer Peterson
Marketing Manager: Molly Parke
Editorial Assistant: Alicia Young
Copyeditor: Arthur Johnson
Senior Art Director: Anna Palchik
Text Design: Henry Rachlin
Cover Design: Sara Gates
Cover Art: Stefana McClure, *Map of the World*, 2005–06. Josée Bienvenu Gallery.
Composition: MPS Limited, A Macmillan Company
Printing and Binding: Haddon Craftsmen, Inc., an RR Donnelley & Sons Company

President: Joan E. Feinberg
Editorial Director: Denise B. Wydra
Editor in Chief: Karen S. Henry
Director of Marketing: Karen R. Soeltz
Director of Editing, Design, and Production: Marcia Cohen
Assistant Director of Editing, Design, and Production: Elise S. Kaiser
Managing Editor: Elizabeth M. Schaaf

Library of Congress Control Number: 2009934716

Manufactured in the United States of America.

5   4   3   2   1   0
f   e   d   c   b

For information, write: Bedford/St. Martin's, 75 Arlington Street, Boston, MA 02116 (617-399-4000)

ISBN-10: 0–312–47444–X
ISBN-13: 978–0–312–47444–7

Acknowledgments

Madeleine Albright, "Faith and Diplomacy." Chap. 5 from *The Mighty and the Almighty: Reflections on America, God, and World Affairs* by Madeleine Albright, pp. 65–78. Copyright © 2006 by Madeleine Albright. Reprinted by permission of HarperCollins Publishers.

Acknowledgments and copyrights are continued at the back of the book on pages 515–17, which constitute an extension of the copyright page. It is a violation of the law to reproduce these selections by any means whatsoever without the written permission of the copyright holder.

PREFACE FOR INSTRUCTORS

Emerging/Thinking

One of the fundamental facts of teaching writing is that when students leave our classrooms, they go back to their increasingly busy lives: They go to other classes, go to their jobs after school, go hang out with friends, go into their disciplines, go into their careers, go into the world. The challenge for us as instructors is to help students acquire the skills of critical reading, thinking, and writing that will allow them to succeed in these diverse contexts.

Emerging seeks to address this challenge. It offers sustained readings that present complex ideas in approachable language; it encourages critical thinking and writing skills by prompting students to make connections among readings; it draws from a broad cross section of disciplines in order to present students with numerous points of entry and identification; and it introduces emerging problems — such as globalization (in both its economic and its political dimensions), the impact of technology (from Wikipedia to brain science), and the dilemmas of ethics (including genetic engineering and the relations between religion and foreign politics) — that students, as agents in the public sphere, will be asked to address. More enduring issues are broached in this collection as well, such as concerns about aesthetics, community, race, and death.

The readings are organized alphabetically to showcase them and open up possibilities for connections. Because they consist of entire book chapters or complete articles, readings can stand on their own as originally intended. However, the readings in *Emerging* were chosen because they connect to each other in interesting and illuminating ways. The issues under discussion resonate across readings, prompting students to think about each selection in multiple dimensions. These resonant connections are shown through *tags*. About a half-dozen tags for each piece are listed in the table of contents, in each headnote, and for each assignment sequence — highlighting concepts such as *community, diversity, identity, culture,* and *technology*. The readings' central concepts are most prominent in the tags, with larger and darker type. Thus one can see at a glance the thematic connections among the readings and assignment sequences as well as the degree of those connections. Connections are also highlighted through the assignment sequences included at the back of the book (see p. 491). The assignment sequences suggest a succession of readings that are linked conceptually so that one assignment sequence provides the structure for an entire semester. (Sequences are further explained below.)

Emerging/Reading

Because students ultimately enter diverse disciplines, the readings are drawn from across fields of knowledge located both inside and outside the academy. Political science, sociology, anthropology, economics, and art are some of the disciplines one might expect to find in such a collection, but *Emerging* also includes readings from diplomacy, public health, psychology, business, technology, and law. The author of each selection addresses his or her concerns to an audience outside the discipline—a useful model for students who eventually will need to communicate beyond the boundaries of their chosen fields. Many of the readings also represent cross-disciplinary work—an economist thinking about politics, an anthropologist thinking about education—since the walls between departments in academia are becoming increasingly permeable.

Yet despite this disciplinary grounding, the readings, though challenging, are accessible, written as they are with a general, informed, and educated audience in mind. The readings thus demonstrate multiple ways in which complex ideas and issues can be presented in formal yet approachable language. The accessible nature of the essays also allows for readings longer than those typically seen in first-year composition anthologies, because the level of writing makes them comprehensible to students. Their length, moreover, means that these readings are substantive, providing greater opportunities for nuanced arguments—both in the readings themselves and in the writing students will in turn produce about them. Each essay serves as an opportunity for students to join important contemporary conversations.

Of course, in addition to referencing emerging issues, the title of this collection refers also to the students in first-year composition courses who themselves are emerging as readers, thinkers, and writers. By providing them with challenging texts along with the tools needed to decode, interpret, and deploy those texts, *Emerging* helps college readers to develop the skills they will need as they move into working with the difficult theoretical texts presented in their choice of majors—and ultimately into their twenty-first-century careers.

Beyond simply indexing developing sociocultural concerns, the title of the collection further refers directly to the concept of *emergence*. An idea taken from chaos/complexity theory, emergence pertains to the intricate and related patterns that materialize spontaneously from the interactions among independent, adaptive agents. In a famous example, emergence explains how a butterfly flapping its wings in China can cause a tornado in Texas; the concept also explains how individual neurons operating in the brain can produce consciousness. Though technically a branch of mathematics, complexity theory has been applied to multiple fields and phenomena, from economics to the Web. Indeed, it is present, implicitly or explicitly, in many of the readings gathered here.

Emerging/Writing

One of the philosophical tenets supporting *Emerging* is that students need to be prepared to deal with emerging issues in their jobs and lives, and to do so, they not only require information about those issues (since such information will continually change) but also must possess an ability to think critically in relation to them. The editorial apparatus in *Emerging* includes the following features that will help students develop the skills needed to become fluid, reflective, and critically self-aware writers:

▶ **General Introduction.** The introduction presents six key skills of academic success and global citizenship: the ability to read critically, think critically, synthesize, argue, support, and revise.

▶ **Assignment Sequences.** In order to stress the iterative processes of thinking and writing, ten assignment sequences are included in the back of the book, each of which uses multiple selections to engage students' thinking about a central theme, issue, or problem. Each sequence frames a project extensive enough for an entire semester's work and can be easily adapted for individual classes.

Additionally, apparatus accompanying each reading provides substantial help for students while featuring innovative approaches to understanding the essays and their relation to the world outside the classroom:

▶ **Headnotes.** A headnote before each reading selection provides biographical information about the author and describes the context of the larger work from which the reading has been taken.

▶ **Questions for Critical Reading.** These questions at the end of each reading direct students to central concepts, issues, and ideas from the essay in order to prompt a directed rereading of the text while providing a guide for the student's own interpretive moves.

▶ **Exploring Context.** In order to leverage students' existing literacies with digital technologies, these questions ask students to use the Web and other electronic sources to contextualize each reading further. Besides sites that might be familiar to students, such as Facebook or Wikipedia, these questions also feature emerging tools such as Twitter and Digg.

▶ **Questions for Connecting.** Because thinking across essays provides particular circumstances for critical thinking, these opportunities for writing ask students to make connections between essays and to apply and synthesize authors' ideas.

▶ **Language Matters.** The Language Matters questions are a unique feature of this reader. These questions address issues of grammar and writing through the context of the essays, presenting language not as a set of rules to be memorized but as a system of meaning-making that can also be used as a tool for analysis.

▶ **Assignments for Writing.** Each reading has three Assignments for Writing questions that ask students to build on the work they've done in the other questions of the apparatus and create a piece of writing with a sustained argument supported by textual engagement.

You Get More Choices with *Emerging*

Emerging doesn't stop with this book. Online, you'll find both free and affordable premium resources to help students get even more out of the book and your course. You'll also find convenient instructor resources, such as downloadable sample syllabi, classroom activities, and even a nationwide community of teachers. To learn more about or order any of the products below, contact your Bedford/St. Martin's sales representative, e-mail sales support (sales_support@bfwpub.com), or visit the Web site at bedfordstmartins.com/emerging/catalog.

Student Resources

Send students to free and open resources, upgrade to an expanding collection of innovative digital content, or package a stand-alone CD-ROM for free with *Emerging*.

Re:Writing, the best free collection of online resources for the writing class, offers clear advice on citing sources in *Research and Documentation Online* by Diana Hacker, thirty sample papers and designed documents, and over nine thousand writing and grammar exercises, with immediate feedback and reporting, in *Exercise Central*. Updated and redesigned, *Re:Writing* also features five free videos from *VideoCentral* and five new tutorials on visual analysis from our popular *ix visual exercises* by Cheryl Ball and Kristin Arola. *Re:Writing* is completely free and open (no codes required) to ensure access to all students.

VideoCentral is a growing collection of videos for the writing class that captures real-world, academic, and student writers talking about how and why they write. Writer and teacher Peter Berkow interviewed hundreds of people — from Michael Moore to Cynthia Selfe — to produce fifty brief videos about topics such as revising and getting feedback. *VideoCentral* can be packaged with *Emerging* at a significant discount. An activation code is required. To order *VideoCentral* packaged with the print book, use ISBN-10: 0–312–64258–X or ISBN-13: 978–0–312–64258–7.

Re:Writing Plus gathers all of Bedford/St. Martin's premium digital content for composition into one online collection. It includes hundreds of model documents, the first-ever peer review game, and *VideoCentral*. *Re:Writing Plus* can be purchased separately or packaged with the print book at a significant discount. An activation code is required. To order *Re:Writing Plus* packaged with the print book, use ISBN-10: 0–312–62463–8 or ISBN-13: 978–0–312–62463–7.

i-series on CD-ROM presents multimedia tutorials in a flexible CD-ROM format — because there are things you can't do in a book.

- **ix visual exercises** help students visualize and put into practice key rhetorical and visual concepts. To order *ix visual exercises* packaged with the print book, use ISBN-10: 0–312–62462–X or ISBN-13: 978–0–312–62462–0.

- **i·claim visualizing argument** offers a new way to see argument and includes six tutorials, an illustrated glossary, and over seventy multimedia arguments. To order *i·claim visualizing argument* packaged with the print book, use ISBN-10: 0–312–62453–0 or ISBN-13: 978–0–312–62453–8.

- **i·cite visualizing sources** brings research to life through an animated introduction, four tutorials, and hands-on source practice. To order *i·cite visualizing sources* packaged with the print book, use ISBN-10: 0–312–62452–2 or ISBN-13: 978–0–312–62452–1.

Instructor Resources

You have a lot to do in your course. Bedford/St. Martin's wants to make it easy for you to find the support you need and to get it quickly.

The **Resources for Teaching Emerging** is available in PDF files that can be downloaded from the Bedford/St. Martin's online catalog. In addition to chapter overviews and teaching tips, the Instructor's Manual includes sample syllabi, correlations to the Council of Writing Program Administrators' Outcomes Statement, and suggestions for classroom activities.

TeachingCentral offers the entire list of Bedford/St. Martin's print and online professional resources in one place. You'll find landmark reference works, sourcebooks on pedagogical issues, award-winning collections, and practical advice for the classroom — all free for instructors.

Bits collects creative ideas for teaching a range of composition topics in an easily searchable blog. A community of teachers — leading scholars, authors, and editors — discuss revision, research, grammar and style, technology, peer review, and much more. Take, use, adapt, and share the ideas. Then come back to the site to comment or to contribute your own suggestions.

Content cartridges for the most common course management systems — Blackboard, WebCT, Angel, and Desire2Learn — allow you to easily download Bedford/St. Martin's digital materials for your course.

Acknowledgments

This collection itself has been a long time emerging, and I would be remiss not to thank the many people who contributed their time, energy, feedback, and support throughout the course of this project.

I would first like to acknowledge past and current colleagues who have played a role in developing this text. Richard E. Miller and Kurt Spellmeyer, both of Rutgers University, through their mentorship and guidance laid the foundations for my approach to composition as reflected in this reader. My department chairs during my time here at Florida Atlantic University, Andrew Furman and Wenying Xu, provided reassurance and support as I balanced the work of this text and the work of serving as Director of Writing Programs. The members of the Writing Committee for Florida Atlantic University's Department of English — Jeff Galin, Joanne Jasin, Jennifer Low, Julia Mason, Daniel Murtaugh, and Magdalena Ostas — generously allowed me to shape both this reader and the writing program. The Dean's office of the Dorothy F. Schmidt College of Arts and Letters of Florida Atlantic University provided a Summer Teaching Development Award, which aided in the creation of the materials that form the core of the Instructor's Manual.

All the teachers in the writing program at Florida Atlantic University had a role to play in this text by teaching possible selections and offering feedback on what did or did not work in the classroom; I regret I cannot list them all. Some of these teachers deserve special mention, including Amy Letter and Brian Spears, who offered suggestions on readings as well as friendship and dinners, and those teachers who crafted assignments and sequences included in this edition, specifically Jennifer Brachfeld, Michael Buso, Skye Cervone, Daniel Creed, Ryan Dessler, Valorie Ebert, Margaret Feeley, Elizabeth Kelly, Gloria Panzera, Tracy Stone, Courtney Watson, and Scott Wood.

This project could not possibly have been completed without the relentless help of my assistant Alison Amato, who scanned essays into electronic format, edited and composed headnotes and assignments, handled all the details that threatened to overwhelm me, and kept me laughing all the while. Also deserving special mention: Paul Ardoin who brilliantly crafted much of the headnotes, Mike Shier who lifted my spirits and lent a keen eye to the manuscript proofs, and Mellissa Carr and Adam Berzak who helped proofread the manuscript.

I am grateful to the reviewers who examined the manuscript and provided valuable feedback: Sonja Andrus, Collin County Community College; Susan Bailor, Front Range Community College; Barbara Booker, Pasco-Hernando Community College; John Champagne, Penn State Erie, The Behrend College; Michael Cripps, York College/CUNY; Brock Dethier, Utah State University; Kimberly Harrison, Florida International University; Karen Head, the Georgia Institute of Technology; Virginia Scott Hendrickson, Missouri State University; Lindsay Lewan, Arapahoe Community College; April Lewandowski, Front Range Community College–Westminster; Gina Maranto, University of Miami; Erica Messenger, Bowling Green State University–Main Campus; Beverly Neiderman, Kent State University; Jill Onega, Calhoun Community College; Roberta Stagnaro, San Diego State University; Melora G. Vandersluis, Azusa Pacific University; and Patricia Webb Boyd, Arizona State University.

I cannot say enough about the support I have received from Bedford/St. Martin's. Joan Feinberg's enthusiasm for this project was always appreciated. Leasa Burton's ability to handle all the small details was essential. And my editor John Sullivan patiently pushed me to make the best book possible and provided vital encouragement whenever my spirits drooped. Thanks, too, to Alicia Young, for getting to me what I needed when I needed it. I am grateful to Sandy Schechter and Barbara Rodriguez for clearing text permissions and to Martha Friedman and Constance Gardner for obtaining art permissions. Kendra LeFleur expertly guided the manuscript through production, assisted by copyeditor Arthur Johnson. I appreciate their help.

Finally, a special thanks to those who kept me centered and strong, including Chris Larkin and Brian Ouellette but above all my partner Joseph Tocio, who offered not only love and support but a compelling reason to be in Boston so that I could meet with the publisher.

CONTENTS

THE READINGS

much of human ethics, a clear recognition of the principle that correlates greater knowledge and power with a greater need for moral responsibility serves as a key foundation. Until recently we could say that this principle had been highly effective."

▶ TAGS: *research*, *social changes*, *biotechnology*, *human dignity*, *ethics*

A noted essayist and novelist writes, "Nine months and five days ago, at approximately nine o'clock on the evening of December 30, 2003, my husband, John Gregory Dunne, appeared to (or did) experience, at the table where he and I had just sat down to dinner in the living room of our apartment in New York, a sudden massive coronary event that caused his death."

▶ TAGS: *loss*, *mourning*, *kinship*, *language*, *death*, *change*

A biologist and expert in public health examines a new approach to preventing AIDS: "LoveLife's media campaign . . . was positive and cheerful, and resembled the bright, persuasive modern ad campaigns that many South African kids were very much attracted to."

▶ TAGS: *community*, *research*, *conversation*, *technology*, *social change*, *media*

A Pulitzer Prize–winning journalist advances a novel geopolitical theory: "No two countries that are both part of a major global supply chain, like Dell's, will ever fight a war against each other as long as they are both part of the same global supply chain."

▶ TAGS: *politics*, *globalization*, *economics*, *knowledge*, *supply chains*, *collaboration*

A prominent political scientist says, "What the demand for equality of recognition implies is that when we strip all of a person's contingent and accidental characteristics away, there remains some essential human quality underneath that is worthy of a certain minimal level of respect — call it Factor X."

▶ TAGS: *civil rights*, *morality*, *human dignity*, *biotechnology*, *ethics*

much more fluid and ambiguous — something more like the social structures that have emerged in Hawaii as intermarriage has accelerated."

▶ TAGS: *research*, *race*, *community*, *diplomacy*, *diversity*, *ethnicity*, *bioethics*, *integration*

A historian notes that "Wikipedia has the potential to be the greatest effort in collaborative knowledge gathering the world has ever known, and it may well be the greatest effort in voluntary collaboration of any kind."

▶ TAGS: *diplomacy*, *groups*, *technology*, *community*, *collaboration*, *education*, *feedback*

An award-winning professor and journalist explains, "'Efficiency' is the term usually invoked to defend large-scale industrial farms, and it usually refers to the economies of scale that can be achieved by the application of technology and standardization. Yet Joel Salatin's farm makes the case for a very different sort of efficiency — the one found in natural systems, with their coevolutionary relationships and reciprocal loops."

▶ TAGS: *tradition*, *technology*, *collaboration*, *feedback*, *supply chains*, *biotechnology*

A writer on politics, economics, and culture contends, "Aesthetics may be a form of expression, but it doesn't enjoy the laissez-faire status accorded speech or writing. To the contrary, the more significant look and feel become, the more they tend to be restricted by law. The very power of beauty encourages people to become absolutists — to insist that other people's stylistic choices, or their trade-offs between aesthetics and other values, constitute environmental crimes."

▶ TAGS: *social change*, *identity*, *aesthetic boundaries*, *community*, *diplomacy*, *diversity*

A neurologist and brain expert suggests that "while biological and social factors, such as tool use, group hunting, and language, drove earlier brain changes, exposure to technology seems to be spurring the current alteration. One consequence of this change is that we face constant challenges to our ability to focus our attention."

▶ TAGS: *education, feedback, technology, creativity, multitasking*

A science writer says, "It is an unfortunate given of human trauma research that the things most likely to accidentally maim or kill people—things we most need to study and understand—are also the things most likely to mutilate research cadavers: car crashes, gunshots, explosions, sporting accidents. There is no need to use cadavers to study stapler injuries."

▶ TAGS: *research, surrogates, death, ethics, morality*

A noted advertising critic claims that "language experts know that America's language wouldn't be what it is—and certainly wouldn't pop as much—without black English."

▶ TAGS: *conversation, diversity, race, media, culture, language, collaboration, creativity*

An evolutionary and developmental biologist writes, "I would argue that the major reason that plastic surgeries, gastric bypasses, and sex reassignments are all given similar sensationalistic treatments is because the subjects cross what is normally considered an impenetrable class boundary: from unattractive to beautiful, from fat to thin, and in the case of transsexuals, from male to female, or from female to male."

▶ TAGS: *technology, gender, objectification, research, class, human dignity*

An expert in global commerce writes, "On one side are those who see adoption as a purely social interaction: It is about building families and rescuing children and assuaging the pain of missing people. . . . From the other side, however, adoption is not only a market but indeed a market of the worst possible sort. It is a market that sells innocent children, putting a price on their heads without any concern for their well-being or for the toll imposed by being treated as trade."

▶ TAGS: *community, family, culture, supply chains, human dignity, ethics, morality*

ASSIGNMENT SEQUENCES

Assignments

Life is filled with rites of passage—attending college, for example. Many such rites—as is the case with the quinceañera—are located at the intersection of the personal and the social, the individual and the community. These assignments explore the role that such rites play in the political sphere by exploring their relationship to rights.

▶ TAGS: *kinship*, *family*, *change*, *tradition*, *loss*, *religion*, *community*, *mourning*, *culture*, *death*, *identity*

Surviving Alone, Surviving Together: Ethical Conflict in a Global Economy

KWAME ANTHONY APPIAH, Making Conversation *and* The Primacy of Practice • HELEN EPSTEIN, AIDS, Inc • THOMAS FRIEDMAN, The Dell Theory of Conflict Prevention • DEBORA L. SPAR, Trading Places: The Practice and Politics of Adoption

Assignments

Living in a globalized world doesn't mean we all have to get along; it does mean, however, that we must learn how to mediate cultural differences in order to solve the problems we face in common with others. This sequence of assignments examines authors' writing and thinking about an array of global problems. The essays and assignments suggest tools and concepts needed to advocate for change not only globally but locally as well.

▶ TAGS: *international policy*, *globalization*, *ethics*, *terrorism*, *community*, *social change*

We tend to think of science as the neutral search for truth, but as the
readings in this sequence make clear, scientific endeavors are enmeshed
in political and ethical concerns. This sequence explores the relationship
between science and politics in order to foster conversations about the
ethics of a broad spectrum of scientific and technological research.

▶ TAGS: *diplomacy*, ***morality***, *biotechnology*, *knowledge and responsibility*,
human dignity, ***ethics***, *civil rights*

Psychotherapy is called the "talking cure" since it allows people to talk
through and resolve their inner conflicts with the help of a trained
professional. But can conversation function more generally as a kind
of social medicine? Can talking about things make them better? The
authors in this sequence all explore the value of conversation in a
variety of contexts. These assignments explore the potential for spoken
exchanges to create personal and social change.

▶ TAGS: ***conversation***, *social change*, ***technology***, *surrogates*

SEQUENCE 5   501

Wonderful Displays: Revelations of Art and Culture

MICHAEL KIMMELMAN, The Art of Collecting Lightbulbs • DIANA TAYLOR, False Identifications: Minority Populations Mourn Diana • VIRGINIA POSTREL, The Boundaries of Design • RICHARD RESTAK, Attention Deficit: The Brain Syndrome of Our Era

Assignments

We often think of art as rarefied and separated from our lives — that which hangs on a wall in a museum. But this sequence asks us to think about the ways in which art, performance, and aesthetics have very real effects on our lives and on culture. These effects force us to ask questions about the limits of creative expression, the rights of individuals and of communities in relation to art, and the future of aesthetics itself.

▶ TAGS: *culture, art, performance, aesthetic boundaries, censorship, creativity, technology*

SEQUENCE 6   504

Trouble with a Capital "C": Communities and Integration

REBEKAH NATHAN, Community and Diversity • KWAME ANTHONY APPIAH, Making Conversation *and* The Primacy of Practice • THOMAS FRIEDMAN, The Dell Theory of Conflict Prevention • MARSHALL POE, The Hive

Assignments

What role does diversity play in forming a community? This sequence explores the answer to that question by looking at diversity on college campuses and across the globe. It also considers the risks of diversity and the possibilities of community in the present and the future.

▶ TAGS: *community*, *globalization*, *diversity*, *education*, *supply chains*, *ethnic conflict*, *integration*, *cosmopolitanism*

We all use a variety of technologies every day—from computers to cell phones. This sequence considers the impact of technology not only on our world but also, more profoundly, on what it means to be human.

▶ TAGS: *politics*, *technology*, *knowledge*, *human dignity*, *multitasking*, *collaboration*, *economics*

What happens to the body when we see it as an object? This sequence considers the answers to that question by examining research on human cadavers, decision making, international adoption, and extreme body makeovers. It probes the ethical and economic implications of objectifying the body.

individual in these collaborative processes, using an examination of organic farming to understand the relationship between individuals and the group, or parts and the whole.

▶ TAGS: *holons, technology, groups, Wikipedia, knowledge, collaboration, supply chains*

EMERGING

CONTEMPORARY READINGS FOR WRITERS

INTRODUCTION
THINKING GLOBALLY, READING CRITICALLY

IN SOME CLASSES, such as biology, sociology, economics, or chemistry, what you learn and what you're tested on is content—a knowledge of terms and concepts. In contrast, what you need to learn in a composition class is a *process*—a process of reading and writing that you will practice with the essays of this book, in class discussions, and by responding to essay assignments. This class is not just about the readings in this book but also about what you can do with them. What you will do with them, of course, is write. And yet it's not entirely accurate to say you're here to learn how to write, either. After all, you already did a lot of writing in high school, and if you couldn't write you couldn't have gotten into college. But you will learn a particular *kind* of writing in this class, one which may be new to you: academic writing—researching, weighing, and incorporating what others say into your own work. It is the type of writing you'll be expected to do throughout your college career. The skills you learn in this class will also help you throughout your life. That's because academic writing involves critical thinking, and critical thinking is an essential skill no matter what career you choose. Thriving in a career—any career—is never about how much you know but about what you can do with the knowledge you have. College will prepare you for your career by providing you with knowledge (your job here is part memorization), but college will also help you learn how to evaluate knowledge, how to apply it, and how to create it; those are the skills of critical thinking.

The readings gathered here were all chosen to provide you fertile ground in which to practice critical thinking through academic writing. Each is a chapter from a current book, usually written by an expert in a particular field communicating to people outside that field. These readings are effective in a writing course because each contains a complex argument, which is why the readings might feel long and therefore why they might seem "hard" to you. You'll notice, though, that it's not the individual sentences that feel difficult. If you find these readings challenging, it's because you have to do a lot of thinking about what they say.

Take, for example, Thomas Friedman's chapter "The Dell Theory of Conflict Prevention" (p. 121), taken from his best-selling book *The World Is Flat*. Friedman is an expert in foreign relations, but he writes not to academics or economists or political theorists but to people like you and me. Yet his argument—that worldwide business supply chains bring political stability—requires a lot of thinking. Comprehension is not so much the issue. Friedman lays out his argument logically and supports it with many kinds of evidence (as you will learn to do as well). But the ideas he proposes about the relationship between economics and geopolitics, as well as his ideas about war, peace, and terrorism, will require you to think about the implications of his argument, and that kind of work is the start of critical thinking. Figuring out what's in the text is challenging, but even more challenging is figuring out what's not in the text: the examples that would challenge Friedman's argument, or new areas where his ideas have value, or modifications of his argument based on your experience or on other things you have read. That's critical thinking. *Emerging* will help you learn how to do it.

The headnotes that appear before each reading, for example, provide context. Besides finding out about the author, you'll learn about the larger argument of the book from which each reading is taken so that you can have a sense of the author's overall project. In reading the headnotes, you may find that you have already developed questions about the selection you're about to read, questions that can serve as the basis of your critical thinking. Your own questions can be supplemented by those at the end of each reading, which are more specifically designed to focus your reading and thinking in ways that will develop your critical thinking while helping you to produce the writing asked of you in this class. The Exploring Context questions use technology to deepen your understanding of the essay and its context in the world. These questions also underscore the fact that the readings have a life outside of this text where their ideas are discussed, developed, refuted, and extended—a life that you will contribute to through your work in this class. Questions for Critical Reading invite you to enter that process as well by returning you to key moments of the text and encouraging you to think more critically about specific aspects of the author's argument. Once you've flexed your critical thinking muscles in the context of the reading, Questions for Connecting then prompt you to apply those skills by relating the current reading to other selections in the book, and Assignments for Writing provide opportunities to join the conversation of these essays. All of these questions require you to use your skills with critical thinking.

The Language Matters questions ask you to do the same, but in the specific context of writing, grammar, and language. Academic writing is formal writing, and that means you need to pay attention to issues of grammar. Error-free writing should always be your goal. Proofreading is an important technique in meeting that goal, and you might also want to work with a handbook, which can give you specific guidance on issues of correctness. But in the end language is not about learning rules, though it might feel that way. Language is about creating meaning. The Language Matters questions at the end of each reading will help you practice skills with language and grammar by asking you to look at how meaning is made in these readings. Thinking critically about the language used by these authors will help you think critically about the language you use in your writing as well, so that you can take these insights back to your own writing.

But critical thinking is not just something you practice when you answer questions in response to texts like Friedman's. It's something we all do all the time. For instance, I asked one of the student workers in our department office, Sherline, about a recent problem she had to solve: buying a car. As a junior at our school Sherline was ready to move off campus, but that meant she needed a reliable means of transportation to make it to class and to work on time; relying on public transportation (especially in southern Florida) wouldn't be enough. The problem she needed to solve was which car to buy. *Whenever we solve problems or make decisions we use critical thinking because we gather, evaluate, and apply knowledge to the situation at hand.* So Sherline started by gathering information. She talked to friends and asked for recommendations about what car she should purchase, and she did some research on Web sites such as Cars.com and Kelly Blue Book. Then she applied that information to her specific context. For example, she had to work within a specific budget because she didn't want to finance. And, being a student, she knew she needed a car that wouldn't require a lot of expensive maintenance. In assessing the information she had gathered—discarding options she couldn't afford, deciding which of her friends had the best recommendation, assessing the value of what each Web site had to say—Sherline exercised critical thinking, and that helped her to make a decision and buy her car. (She got a 1999 Acura TL.)

> **Whenever we solve problems or make decisions we use critical thinking because we gather, evaluate, and apply knowledge to the situation at hand.**

Thinking about buying a car and thinking about geopolitical stability might seem like very different processes, but both involve very similar skills. And that's a key point: *The skills you need for academic writing are skills you already use in your life.* When you choose your career you use those skills. When you decide to help a disaster relief effort at home or abroad you use those skills. When you vote in an election you use those skills. And when you decide which cell phone plan is right for you, you use them too. Part of what you will gain through this class is an awareness of those skills. What you'll also gain is a translation of those skills into an academic context—taking everyday decision-making skills used for things like buying a car and applying them to things like the Friedman reading. As you refine those skills in an academic context, you also strengthen them for use in the rest of your life. Thus critical thinking is not simply a skill for college success; it's the cornerstone of the skills you will need to survive in the kind of globalized world that Friedman describes. You might call the skills of critical thinking the survival skills for global citizenship—not because you politically are a global citizen but because the world is now "flat." What makes the world flat for Friedman is not geography but the fact that economies are so interconnected that everyone everywhere is competing with everyone everywhere else. And as you enter the job market, that will include you too. But you're already participating in the global citizenship engendered by the flat world. If you need to consider gas mileage when buying a car or if you wince at the price of gas while filling up the car you own, you're reflecting what it means to live in a world where everyone competes for a limited resource. Similarly, if you chat online with someone who lives in another country, you're making connections through the global culture enabled by the flat world.

Skills for Global Citizenship and Academic Success

Fortunately, just as you've entered class with many writing skills, so too do you enter with skills in global citizenship and thus in critical thinking. Critical thinking, after all, is fully concerned with processing information, and we live in an information-rich world. So chances are many of the things you do every day involve some kind of critical thinking; this class will hone those skills and translate them into the academic realm.

For now, it might be helpful to focus on six skills you might already use that correspond to aspects of academic writing and that also will enable you to thrive in the world at large. Those skills are the abilities to search, to connect, to mash, to post, to sample, and to version. They are all familiar in some form to anyone living in a digital age. In academic terms, you will build them into the abilities to read critically, think critically, synthesize, argue, support, and revise.

Skills for Global Citizenship		Skills for Academic Success
Search	→	Read Critically
Connect	→	Think Critically
Mash	→	Synthesize
Post	→	Argue
Sample	→	Support
Version	→	Revise

Search, or Read Critically

We live in a world saturated with information — so much so that Richard Restak notes in "Attention Deficit: The Brain Syndrome of Our Era" (p. 332) that our brains are being rewired by the multiple and competing demands information makes on our attention. Mastering the ability to search is crucial to managing those demands since searching allows us to select just the information we're looking for. So basic is this skill to our survival today that we don't even think about it anymore. Indeed, you probably search for information on the Web every day, and you probably find what you need, too. Yet, while it seems intuitive, searching involves a kind of critical thinking. For starters, you have to do some thinking about what terms to use to find what you're looking for. And even then, Google and most other search engines return thousands or even millions of results when we search; we must evaluate those results in order to find the right one.

In an academic context, searching happens whenever you read critically. After all, reading is a way to find information. But you may find it difficult to locate information in these readings. They likely are not the kind of texts you've read previously in your life or educational career, and so they might feel very hard. That's OK; they're supposed to be hard because dealing with difficulty is the best way to develop your skills with critical thinking. In other words, if you didn't have to think about what you read in this class you wouldn't be doing any critical thinking at all.

Though these readings might seem hard they don't have to feel impossible. There are a number of strategies you can use to deal with their difficulty. The first step is to acknowledge the difficulty — recognizing it forces you to consciously activate your skills with critical thinking. The second step is just to keep reading, even if you feel you don't understand what you're reading. Often, the opening of an essay might be confusing or disorienting, but as you continue to read you start to see the argument emerge. Similarly, the author might repeat key points throughout the essay, and so by the time you complete the reading what seemed impossible to understand begins to make sense. After you've completed the reading, you might still feel confused. Write down what you *did* understand—no matter how little that might be and no matter how unsure you are of your understanding. Recognizing what you know is the best way to figure out what you need to learn. Identifying specific passages that you did not understand is an important strategy too. In locating any points of confusion, you can focus your critical thinking skills on those passages in order to begin to decode them. Make a list of specific questions you have, too, and then bring those questions to class as a way of guiding the class's discussion in ways that will enhance your understanding. The questions following the reading will give you some help, but your peers are another valuable resource. Discussing the reading with them allows you to pool your comprehension—the section you didn't understand might be the one your peer did, and vice versa. Finally, reread the essay. Reading, like writing, is an iterative process. We read and reread, just as we write and revise, and each time, we get a little more out of it.

DEALING WITH DIFFICULTY

- Acknowledge that the reading is hard.
- Keep reading the essay.
- Write down what you *did* understand.
- Identify specific passages that confused you.
- Make a list of specific questions.
- Use the questions that follow the reading.
- Discuss the reading with peers.
- Reread the essay at least once, or more.

Understand too that when you read the selections for this class, you'll be doing a kind of searching. As with the Web, you'll want to have some idea of what you're looking for before you start. The headnotes before each selection will guide you in that process by giving an overview of the author and the argument. While reading, one of the things you'll want to search for is the author's argument, the point he or she is trying to make in the selection. In addition, you'll want to search for concepts, terms, or ideas that are unique or central to the author's argument. Reading with a pen, highlighter, or sticky notes at hand will help you as you find this information. Marking places that strike you or that feel key to the author's argument is akin to bookmarking a Web site you want to find again—it shortcuts the search process when you return by making it easier to find the information again. In academic terms we

ANNOTATING THE TEXT

- Read with a pen, highlighter, or sticky notes at hand.
- Look for the author's argument.
- Mark key terms, concepts, and ideas.
- Mark information you will need again.
- Mark words you don't understand.
- Ask questions in reaction to the text.
- Summarize key points in the margin.

call this process annotating the text; it's the start of critical reading because it identifies the most important information in the essay, and that's exactly the information you need to think about.

Let's look at an example, an annotated excerpt from "What's Black, Then White, and Said All Over?" (p. 363), Leslie Savan's essay about the use of black slang in advertising and pop talk:

> Wannabe or crossover talk didn't begin with hip-hop, nor is lingo-lending from one group to another confined to blacks and whites in America. Whites talking some black is part of an apparently universal phenomenon that (sociolinguists) call covert prestige. This means that speakers of a "standard" language (whatever the language) "have favorable attitudes toward lower-class, nonstandard speech forms," explains the linguist Margaret Lee. "However, these attitudes are not always overtly expressed, and they may be subconscious, because they stray from mainstream—or overt—values about the perceived superior status of the standard forms." This occurs, she adds, "for the most part throughout the world—when new forms enter the mainstream, in fact, they usually come from nonstandard speech." (p. 377)

So then how is Savan's argument unique? Sounds like this happens all the time.

Note to self: look up this word

Definition of "covert prestige"

What would overt prestige look like? Could there be such a thing?

Again, if this happens all over, then how can Savan be making this argument?

In annotating the text, you will want to deploy several search strategies. The first of these involves marking information you will need again, such as the definition of "covert prestige," which is underlined in the passage above to lend it visual importance. You will also want to mark any terms you don't understand, such as *sociolinguist*. Another set of strategies, though, involves questions you have in reaction to the text, each of which can serve as a point for re-searching the text. Each question you ask during your initial reading of the text gives you a new direction for searching the text again—both for an answer to your question and for support for any alternative position you want to take.

That's because—just like when you are searching the Web—sometimes you don't find what you need the first time around. Returning to the text and reading it again refines your searching, helping you find what you missed the first time, and it provides an opportunity to briefly summarize key points. Rereading is not something we usually do if we're just reading for comprehension; generally we understand enough of what we read that we don't have to read it again. But in an academic context rereading is essential, because critical reading goes beyond comprehension to evaluation, and before we can evaluate we have to know the key points that need evaluation. The Questions for Critical Reading located at the end of each selection will help you in this process by focusing your rereading on a significant point in the essay—a particular term, concept, or idea that will allow you to read and think critically. Rereading Savan's essay with the above questions might cause you to pay attention to those parts of the essay where Savan explains why black talk uniquely impacts white language. For example, Savan talks about African American history in the United States, from slavery to minstrel shows and on through jazz and beyond. Taking note of those sections in rereading makes it clear why covert prestige is such a useful idea for Savan in making her argument: It explains how black talk "as the original flipside to the voice of the Man" enables "pop talk's crush on everything 'alternative' and 'outsider'" (p. 365).

It's important to note that searching is not *researching*. Searching finds what information is there; researching—in academic terms—means generating new knowledge. In this sense, researching a car purchase is very different from researching a paper topic. In the first case you're just using the information available; in the second you're applying the available information to create new information and ideas. Researching in an everyday context means gathering information, but researching in an academic context means producing new information. For instance, if a medical researcher only duplicated the information already available on a disease, no progress would be made toward a cure. At the same time, all research begins with a search because you need to know what information is available before you generate new knowledge. When you read these essays you will be searching, but when you write about them you will be doing a kind of research. Summarizing the reading won't be sufficient for this class since doing so only provides the search results, the information we already know. By thinking critically about what you found in your search of the text, you begin to move toward research because your critical thinking will generate something new, the unique product of your thoughts.

> **In an academic context rereading is essential, because critical reading goes beyond comprehension to evaluation.**

You'll be researching these essays when you respond to the Exploring Context questions, which often ask you to use the Web to elaborate your understanding of the text. However, before you use any Web site in an academic setting, you will want to make sure you evaluate it. You start that process by asking yourself how you want to use the site. Any site on the Web can be used as an example of your ideas or the ideas of any essay; thus, Savan uses Black People Love Us! (blackpeopleloveus.com) as an illustration of her ideas about how whites treat African Americans. What's clear in Savan's argument, though, is that the site is an example of her own idea—she doesn't use it to *provide* an idea. Whenever you take ideas or evidence from Web sites you need to be careful about which sites you use. Ask yourself questions about who wrote the material (a government organization? an individual?), what qualifications the source has, when the site was last updated, and how stable the address or URL is (is it hosted on a free site like geocities or through a domain name?). *Any Web site can be used as an example, but only those Web sites that establish their authority should be used for ideas or evidence.*

That's because research has such a specific meaning in the context of the academic world. When you generate new ideas in your writing for this class, you'll be doing a kind of research, but research also involves working with academic sources to support your points. For this class, those sources are largely provided for you by the essays in this book. If your argument needs support beyond that you will need to find valid and reliable evidence, and that will involve more than what you can find through Google or Wikipedia. Academic research demands academic sources, the kind you will find through the library in books and journals across the disciplines. You will need to move your Web-searching skills into the electronic interfaces that can help you find those sources. Once you do, you will need to search and re-search them through reading just as you would do with Savan's essay. This is what we mean when we say that academic writing is an iterative process—you do it, and then you do it again.

Connect, or Think Critically

Connecting is another skill that translates into an academic context. You already connect all the time because it too is an essential skill for surviving in the world today. In part, connecting means going online and connecting to static information on the Web, but it also means connecting to others, through the dynamic social networks you form through sites like Facebook or MySpace or through your friends, family, coworkers, and communities.

Connecting is also a method of critical thinking. Each of the essays you will read here is already connected to the rest of the book it originally appeared in and thus to that author's larger argument as well as to the conversation taking place around that author's particular topic. When you read, you will infer many of these connections, but as you think critically about these readings you will make new connections of your own, which is essential to critical thinking. You'll start by connecting what you read to your own life, to what you know and think and how you feel. Your instructor might ask you to keep a reading journal or a blog where you can record these initial connections.

These personal reactions will help you to think about the ideas of each essay. What will help you even more is connecting ideas *between* the essays. The strongest way to evaluate the information in an essay is to test it against other information, such as the ideas expressed in another essay. Connecting the readings might mean using a concept from one piece, such as Francis Fukuyama's idea of "Factor X," to explain another essay such as Mary Roach's "The Cadaver Who Joined the Army." But it might also mean using the ideas from one essay to modify the ideas in another: elaborating Michael Pollan's idea of the "holon" through Daniel Gilbert's concept of "super-replicators," for example. (See Figure 1.)

Connecting is a kind of critical thinking used by the authors of the essays in this book, too. We've already seen how Leslie Savan connects the concept of "covert prestige" to pop talk and black talk. In "AIDS, Inc." (p. 106), Helen Epstein does something similar in discussing HIV prevention programs in Africa:

> . . . Ugandans are more likely to know their neighbors and to live near members of their extended families. This in turn may have contributed to what sociologists call "social cohesion"—the tendency of people to talk openly with one another and form trusted relationships. Perhaps this may have facilitated more realistic and open discussion of AIDS, more compassionate attitudes toward infected people, and pragmatic behavior change. (p. 113)

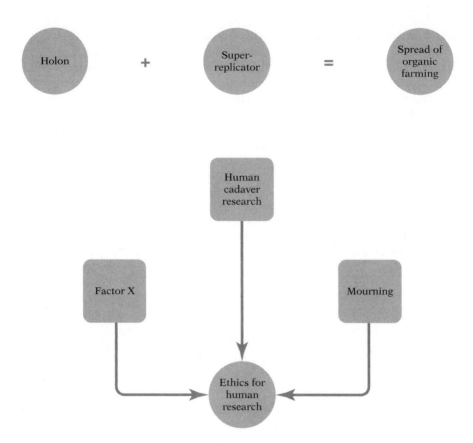

Figure 1   Clustering
Connecting and synthesizing are crucial ways of thinking critically about what you read.

Epstein, a molecular biologist and specialist in public health, connects a concept from sociology, "social cohesion," with HIV prevention in Uganda. In making that connection, she uses the idea to support her argument and to create
a new idea about what an effective prevention program should look like. It's
the connections between ideas that allow authors like Savan and Epstein—and
you—to make an argument.

In working with these readings you might feel like there simply are no
connections between them, that the topic of each essay is unique. But keep in
mind that a connection is not something you find; it's something you *make*. If
the connections were already sitting there in the essays, then there wouldn't be
much critical thinking involved because there wouldn't be much thinking involved at all. The process of making connections between disparate ideas is part
of critical thinking. Sociology and public health might not seem to have much
in common, but when we make connections between them we generate a new
understanding of how a search operates.

When making connections between the readings for this class, you might want to start by listing the important terms, concepts, and ideas from each essay. Once you've done that, you can literally draw lines between ideas that have some relation. You might also try a technique called *clustering*. Put the main concept of each essay in a circle on a sheet of paper. Draw other circles containing related or subsidiary ideas and connect them with lines to the circles containing the main ideas of the readings. When you find ways to connect the branches of these separate groups, you're locating relationships between the essays that you might want to pursue. Figuring out exactly what those relationships are not only utilizes critical thinking but also starts the process of forming your own ideas, which you will express in the writing of this class. The Questions for Connecting at the end of each reading will also help in this process by asking you to think specifically about one essay in terms of another. These questions, then, will give you a direction to think about both essays, using each to test the concepts and ideas of the other. The "tags" for each essay show key concepts, some of which overlap with the tags for other selections.

Mash, or Synthesize

Connecting defines relationships—in your life, between two people; in this class, between two ideas. Mashing—and its academic equivalent, synthesis—goes one step further by combining different sources of information to generate something new. In digital culture, mashing involves integrating two or more sources of information. For example, a DJ named Danger Mouse created quite a stir a few years back by taking music from The Beatles' *The White Album* and combining it with the vocals from Jay-Z's *The Black Album* to create *The Grey Album*, a new musical composition synthesized from the two sources. Similarly, the Kleptones use instrumentation from one source and vocals from another; the resulting mashup produces new music. Mashing happens on the Web, too, when different sources of data are combined into a new tool. You might have used mashups of Google Maps or Flickr. For example, Weather Underground's WunderMap (wunderground. com/wundermap) combines Google maps with National Weather Service data, satellite cloud images, and weather station information.

But mashing is not just a recreational activity for the digital world. It is a form of synthesis, a central component of critical thinking that you will use throughout your life and career. A doctor might combine test results, a patient's medical history, and her or his own knowledge to reach a diagnosis; a businessperson might use a marketing report, recent sales figures, a demographic study, and data on the current economic outlook to craft a business strategy. Whenever you combine multiple sources of information to create new information or ideas, you're mashing. When you do it in an academic context, you're synthesizing. Synthesis always creates something new; because you'll be using it in this class to create new ideas and thus new knowledge, you'll use it to show your critical thinking.

Steve Olson, for example, synthesizes information about genetics, history, and marriage in Hawaii to examine "The End of Race" (p. 250). In her essay

"The Boundaries of Design" (p. 296), Virginia Postrel synthesizes information about law and aesthetics to consider the boundary between the two. As we've seen, Helen Epstein synthesizes ideas from sociology and public health, while Leslie Savan synthesizes concepts from sociolinguistics with pop talk. All of the authors in this text use synthesis because all of them are working from what's already been said and written about a subject to say and write something new. You'll do the same. After you've read a piece and connected its ideas to other contexts, you will synthesize the ideas into a new idea, your own idea. That idea will form the center of the writing you do in this class.

There are several techniques you can use to synthesize the ideas of these readings. You might, for example, use ideas from two authors and combine them into a new concept that you use in your paper. Or you might use a concept from one essay to show the limitations of another author's argument. You might even invent a term all your own, defining and deploying it through the essays. When synthesizing or mashing, you want to ask yourself not simply how the two elements you're working with are alike but also how they're different. Paying attention to both similarities and differences allows you to find out how different ideas fit together in different ways.

Post, or Argue

All the processes we've discussed so far take place before you actually start writing in response to an assignment. You need to search (and re-search), connect, and mash in order to begin the process of critical thinking that forms the core of academic writing. Once you've done all that, it's time to post. If you've ever joined a discussion online or kept a blog, then you're familiar with posting. Posting involves joining a conversation, taking a stand, or making a point. When you write in this class you'll be doing all of those things.

In the academic world, making an argument is a form of posting—you take a position and defend it. But that sounds antagonistic, and academic arguments are not about fighting, or winning, really. After all, *argument* can mean several different things—an argument between lovers is quite different from an argument in a courtroom, which is also different from a scientific argument. Rather than thinking of a post as the position you defend, as an army would, it might be useful to think of it as the words you send out into the world, as in posting a letter in the mail. Posting in this sense has many academic equivalents: hypothesis, argument, thesis. In the sciences, for example, a hypothesis is an idea you test through an experiment, using the evidence from that experiment to prove the hypothesis true or false or, more generally, to modify the hypothesis in some way. In an academic sense, an argument is the primary point to be proven through evidence collected through research. *Thesis* might generally mean "theme," but it also has a similar meaning to *post*—the central point around which all the evidence is gathered. It is the claim you make, the point you want to prove. More generally, posts in the academic world and beyond have projects; when you post you're trying to *accomplish something*. Online, that might be trying to answer someone's questions about *World of Warcraft* in a discussion forum, but in this class it means making a specific contribution to the conversation around a subject.

Every paper you write is a post. You take a position in the paper and state that position in your argument or thesis. The point of the paper, your post, is to lay out your thinking regarding that position in order to persuade your reader of the validity of your ideas.

Sample, or Support

As you lay out your thinking, you'll need proof to support your point, which in academic writing happens through working with quotations from the texts. Using the text as support for your argument is similar to something you might know as sampling. In musical terms, sampling involves using part of one recording as an element in a whole new recording. For example, you're probably not familiar with James Brown's 1970 recording "Funky Drummer," but you may know its drum beat from songs by artists as diverse as Public Enemy, Dr. Dre, Big Daddy Kane, the Beastie Boys, Sinéad O'Connor, George Michael, and Dido. The "Amen Break," from the Winstons' 1960 song "Amen, Brother," is another famous drum loop used in a wide variety of songs today (see Figure 2). When artists sample music, they use a piece of another musical composition to support the music they want to make.

Figure 2   Sampling
Part of the waveform for the "Amen Break," including the cymbal crash at the end.

Quotation serves the same function in an academic context. When you use quotation in your writing, you support your words and ideas through the words and ideas of others. Quotation supports critical thinking in two ways. First, it provides evidence for your argument, thesis, or position, showing the reader how and why you thought that way and reached the conclusions that led to your argument. But beyond that, integrating quotation into your text itself requires some critical thinking.

That's the difference between "having" quotations in your paper and "using" them. It's not enough to drop in a quotation every now and then, just as it wouldn't make sense to have drum loops randomly sprinkled throughout a song.

> **When you use quotation in your writing, you support your words and ideas through the words and ideas of others.**

You need to think about the function of every quotation you use, its purpose in your paper: Is it defining a term? supporting an assertion? connecting ideas? To make that function clear, you will want to explain each quotation you use. That doesn't mean you should summarize or reiterate each quotation; it means you should write about what that piece of text does for your overall project. Think of it as connecting that text to your own text. You might also analyze the quotation in this process. Analyzing a quotation means explaining what it says and what it means.

Here's a pattern you can use to incorporate quotation into your paragraphs in ways that show your critical thinking through connection. Begin your paragraph with a sentence that contains the main idea you want to make or the connection you want to show between two essays. Introduce the first quotation, provide it, and then perhaps add a sentence that explains that quotation. After a brief transition, move to the second quotation. Then add several sentences that explain the connection you see between the quotations. These sentences should also explain how the relationship between the quotations supports your argument. These sentences record your critical thinking, allowing you to use the connection you've made between these two authors to support your project for the paper.

Crucially, as sampling has evolved as a musical technique, acknowledgment has become paramount. That is, artists can't take a sample without properly recognizing (and paying) the original artist. Similarly, it is absolutely essential that you acknowledge the words of others when you use them. In the real world, failure to do so can result in expensive lawsuits and ruined careers. In the academic world, failure to do so is considered plagiarism. Every time you use the words or ideas of another, you must provide a citation. Once you enter your major you'll learn a specific system for providing that citation—every discipline has its own system. In this class, the system you will likely use is MLA citation, developed through the Modern Language Association, the governing body for the discipline of English. You will probably spend time in class learning the intricacies of this system, but for now remember the basics: Every time you use a quotation or paraphrase, include the author's name and the page number in parentheses at the end of the sentence, just before the period. Publication information for all of your sources should be listed of the end of your paper.

Version, or Revise

So far we've discussed all the stages of critical thinking you'll need to exercise in order to produce a draft of your paper. Each stage relates to a skill you might already use, and each, too, will have value in your future career. Once you've written a draft, making an argument that contributes to the larger conversation and supporting it by working with quotation, there is still more work to be done, because *every good piece of writing goes through at least one revision.* This is the eighth draft of this introduction, for example.

Software goes through revision, too. Nearly every piece of software you use exists in multiple versions. Right now I'm writing what you're reading in Word 2008 for Mac, version 12.1.5, on a computer running Mac OS X version 10.5.6, while I listen to some music in iTunes 8.0.2 and chat online through Firefox 3.1b2 and Yahoo! Messenger version 3.0 beta 3. Most of the time we don't think about which version of a piece of software we're using — we just use it. But inevitably we will need to upgrade that software at some point, which involves moving to a new version. And when companies release a new version of software, they don't start from scratch — they begin with the previous version, adding what's needed, moving perhaps in a new direction with a novel feature, fixing what doesn't work.

When we write, we do the same thing: We produce new versions of our product through revision. Often students think of revision as "fixing" their papers — just correcting all the errors. But as with versions of software, that's only part of the process. Revision involves making substantive changes and should produce something new. Again, when we produce something new in the realm of ideas, we're doing critical thinking; revision, then, is also a form of critical thinking. Instead of thinking about the readings of the class, though, revision asks you to think critically about — to evaluate, test, and assess — your own writing.

When we discussed connecting, we said that it's easier to evaluate ideas against something else. The same is true with revision. Often when we write our initial draft looks fine to us; it seems like our best thinking. This is where connecting with others — in this case, through the process of peer revision — is again useful. As part of my job coordinating the writing classes at my university, I read the class evaluations for all of the writing courses, and one thing students say over and over is that they feel peer review is useless — *but really it's one of the most practical things you'll learn in this class.* In the rest of your life you won't be asked to write papers, but you will be asked to work with others on committees or teams again and again. Learning to work well with others — to recognize valuable feedback and to give it in turn — is essential, since, as James Surowiecki shows in "Committees, Juries, and Teams: The *Columbia* Disaster and How Small Groups Can Be Made to Work" (p. 440), the failure of small groups can lead to disaster.

Peer review gives you practice in testing your ideas with actual readers. Software makers don't just write some code and send it out into the world; they test it first (often through a "beta" version). And they test it with actual end users, the audience for the final product. Similarly, other students in your class—and not just your instructor—are actual end users for your writing. Every piece of writing has an audience, and your peers form part of that audience. Since the goal of each paper is to contribute to the conversation started in the texts, and since your classmates have also read and written about the texts, they are the interlocutors for your written conversation.

That process works in reverse, too. When you read your peers' writing you will want to bring all your critical thinking skills to bear. You might be tempted to just write "Good job!" no matter what you think about the writing, from fear of being critical, but that shows no critical thinking. Critical thinking is not the same as being critical. When you offer valuable feedback you're helping your classmates, no matter how strong that feedback is. Start by reading your peer's paper, using the same skills with search and research that you used when you read the texts of this class. Then think critically about what they are saying, using the skills you have with connection—connect what they say about the text to what you know about the text as well as to what you think and have written about the text. Then post your response.

Bringing It Together

It might be useful for you to see how this all comes together in an actual student paper. Let's start with the assignment, taken from one of my recent classes:

> In "What's Black, Then White, and Said All Over?" Leslie Savan explores the appropriation of black language into pop culture and its use in advertising and marketing. Locate your own example of a word or phrase that has entered pop culture from a racial, ethnic, or cultural group and then **write an essay in which you extend or complicate Savan's argument through this example.**
>
> Does your example participate in "cool"? Does it offer an alternative template for pop talk? Is it modeled on the dominant language or does it create a new model for others to follow? Has it been commercialized or does it resist that kind of appropriation? How? Does it participate in "covert prestige"?

You can apply your same skills with critical thinking to this assignment; treat it as you would one of the readings in this text. For starters, searching the assignment will help you locate key information in writing your response, and you should annotate it as you would a reading. Notice, for example, that the middle section is in bold, highlighting the main task of the assignment: "write an essay in which you extend or complicate Savan's argument through this example." That's the central task for your paper. If we search for the key terms in that core, we find *extend, complicate,* and *example.* You would need then to *use* the example you find to say something about Savan's argument. To do so you will need to mash the ideas from Savan and your own example, synthesizing them into a position that you will argue and support in the post that is your paper.

Here is one student's response to the assignment:

What's Geek, Then Sleek, and Read All Over?

In "What's Black, Then White, and Said All Over?" Leslie Savan argues that "African American vernacular" has been influencing pop culture for years, and recently, pop culture has been using this "black talk" in advertisements. Not only does black culture have a strong influence on pop culture, but — one could argue — it *defines* pop culture. Our society both knowingly and subconsciously uses words and phrases of African American origin on a regular basis. Just as African American vernacular has been infiltrating the English language for decades, Internet-inspired words and phrases are also beginning to influence our language, primarily with the help of video games and text messaging. It is undeniable that Internet-inspired words and phrases are becoming more and more popular. Internet slang is becoming more widespread, it is being used as a marketing tool, and it is even used by individuals to gain acceptance within certain communities.

As Savan points out in the text, black talk has proven to be an effective marketing tool for many products. When advertising for a video game system, the black talk might not appeal to the average video game consumer, so it seems that the geeks have created their own dialect. There are many popular initialisms used by nerds such as *ctf, ftw, orz, gg,* and *irl.* It is also common for nerds to substitute numbers for letters or even totally replace letters with numbers altogether. This mannerism is called 1337 5P34K (leet speak). It seems that in the gaming community, a gamer's coolness is directly proportional to how few letters he uses.

One form of leet speak has already been used as advertisement by Sony. Sony's Playstation has four main buttons on its controller: x, circle, triangle, and square. The Playstation slogan is "Live in your world. Play in ours," but some of the letters are cleverly replaced with the aforementioned shapes on the controller. This is an example of a major corporation using a form of Internet slang as a marketing tool. Savan says "at white society's major intersection with black language — that is, in entertainment — white society has gone from mocking black talk, as in minstrel shows, to marketing it, as in hip-hop" (Savan 48). Similarly, white society's major intersection with Internet talk is also in entertainment, with video games being a part of entertainment. Also, like black talk, society has gone from mocking geeks to using their language as advertisement.

Not all of the Internet slang words have nerdy connotations; some popular examples are *lol, bff, brb, g2g, idk,* and *ttyl.* These notations along with many other similar ones can be seen in just about any text message or instant message. They are widely used and accepted among America's youth, male and female, nerd and non-nerd. Some tech-savvy middle-aged adults might even recognize some of these notations. In early 2007 AT&T/Cingular released a commercial of a young girl who communicated with her mother solely using this jargon. Later in 2007 the company released a similar commercial. In both commercials there were subtitles translating the jargon and introducing many ignorant watchers to the phenomenon.

Even though I see many of these initialisms every day—and even hear them out loud occasionally—they are not words. Most of them are unpronounceable combinations of consonants. "Lol" is the only exception. It is always unexpected to hear "lol" in an out-loud or over-the-phone conversation, mainly because it is used to signify laughter. In a face-to-face conversation, it is just more natural to laugh out loud instead of saying "lol."

However, there are two words coined by video gamers that are both slowly gaining momentum in pop culture. One of them is "noob." It evolved from "newbie" and is sometimes spelled "newb." Thefreedictionary.com defines newbie as "one that is new to something, especially a novice at using computer technology or the Internet." Gamers have taken this definition a step further. Wikipedia accurately defines a noob as someone with "the sole purpose of annoying others." Wikipedia goes on to say that a noob is "someone who did something stupid, or asked an obvious question." Both of these definitions are applicable. Consequently, it is quite a degrading insult to be called a *noob* when playing an online game.

The second word to be adopted by video gamers is any variation of the word "own" (commonly misspelled and pronounced as "pwn"). Yes, this has always been a word, but video gamers have given it a new definition. To put things in perspective, our wallets are getting owned by gas prices. When my team wins a capture the flag game three to zero, that is an instance of *ownage.* Only *noobs* get *owned.*

As previously stated, both of these words are seeping into mainstream pop culture. I once saw someone wearing a shirt that simply said "GET OWNED" on it. At one point in time, only the hardcore computer nerds knew these words and how to use them. Slowly over time, as online gaming has boomed, these terms have become more widespread. Now, even casual video gamers call each other *noobs* and *own* each other. Even though it is uncommon, non-video gamers sometimes use these words in their nerdy contexts.

When playing a video game, it seems that the more nerdy lingo someone uses, the more accepted he will become. This is called covert prestige. As defined by Savan, covert prestige is when "speakers of a 'standard' language (whatever the language) have favorable attitudes toward lower-class, nonstandard speech forms'" (Savan 65). With black talk, covert prestige demonstrates coolness or toughness. When someone uses hip-hop language, it is easier to become accepted by the in-crowd whether the person is hip-hop or not. That is why Savan says that "it usually allows whites to feel good about themselves without having to do anything particularly worthwhile" (73). White people can put on a facade to appear hip-hop. The same is true with any community. Insecure individuals are willing to go great distances to feel accepted by people they admire. Although it's not the only reason, this might be part of the reason why Facebook walls, instant messages, and Internet forums are saturated with abbreviations and slang derived from Internet users. People imitate what they see in online communities to gain acceptance in that community. Savan observes that "a large number of male speakers, it seems, are more concerned with acquiring *covert prestige* than with obtaining social status" (65). This is true because often times, covert prestige has *become* social status. Many young people do not find themselves attractive or fun or cool, so they act like someone who *does* find himself cool and attractive and fun. If admired individuals use Internet-inspired initialisms on Facebook, then everyone who looks up to that person may start using the same initialisms. Also, if someone who is exceptionally good at Halo 3 uses words like *pwn* and *noob,* other Halo players will use those words.

As an avid gamer and Internet user, I enjoy seeing Internet lingo expand into pop culture. Because the Internet is such a vital part of our society, I think that Internet language has no choice but to become more popular. I expect to see more advertisements using Internet jargon in the coming years, and I expect that people will continue to use it as covert prestige.

Every paper needs an argument, the main point that the author is posting. This student makes that argument clear in the introduction: "Internet slang is becoming more widespread, it is being used as a marketing tool, and it is even used by individuals to gain acceptance within certain communities." Notice how the paper responds to the assignment: It *extends* Savan's argument through a new example. In order to reach that argument, the paper's author had to connect what Savan says about black language and pop talk to Internet talk. What's synthesized out of that is a new idea about how advertisers use Internet language to market products as well.

That argument, of course, needs to be proven through work with the text, and so the author uses quotations from Savan's text to support the argument. The third paragraph provides a particularly good example of this kind of work, showing how textual support can illustrate the kind of critical thinking that happens with connection and synthesis. The author begins with an example of Internet language in advertising and then uses a quotation from Savan to connect this ad to Savan's argument about companies using pop talk to sell products. Notice how the paragraph draws from the pattern described above in the discussion of sampling.

This is the second version of the paper — there was a prior initial draft — and though the author has improved many parts of the paper through revision, you may also notice that there are still some issues that could be resolved with additional revision to produce a new version of the paper. For instance, though there are several good examples of Internet language, not all of the examples are connected; that is, it's not clear how all of them support the argument. Some additional attention could also be paid to language matters; addressing those would make the argument stronger by making the meaning clearer.

Despite these shortcomings, this paper does demonstrate critical thinking through a clear argument supported with specific examples and quotations from the text. Your work in this class may look very different (in part because the writing prompts you work with may look very different), but the skills will remain the same. For, in the end, those skills are what matter — not just in this class and not just in college, but in your career and your life as well.

THE READINGS

MADELEINE ALBRIGHT

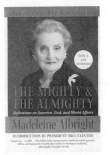

Madeleine Albright is the Mortara Distinguished Professor of Diplomacy at Georgetown University, but she is more widely known for being the first woman to serve as U.S. secretary of state, a position she held under President Bill Clinton from 1997 to 2001 and a role for which she was confirmed unanimously by the Senate. She has also served as the U.S. ambassador to the United Nations and as a member of the board of directors for the Council on Foreign Relations, a nonpartisan foreign policy think tank. Albright attended Wellesley College, Johns Hopkins University, and Columbia University, where she earned a Ph.D. in public law in government. She has written a number of books, including *The Mighty and the Almighty: Reflections on America, God, and World Affairs* (2006), from which the following chapter is taken, and, most recently, *Memo to the President Elect: How We Can Restore America's Reputation and Leadership* (2008).

The Mighty and the Almighty explores the role of religion in government affairs. As a former government official and a person whose identity was shaped dramatically by religion (she was raised Catholic but discovered her Jewish heritage when she was an adult), Albright is able to offer a unique perspective on the power and place of religion in politics.

In "Faith and Diplomacy," Albright suggests that religion's influence on world events is inherent and persistent. Our government, she argues, must recognize this reality and adjust its diplomatic strategy accordingly. Albright proposes concrete steps the government can take to prepare itself for the religious dimensions of inter- and intranational disputes, but she also advises that religiously informed diplomacy will not always solve the complicated problems of a complicated world.

Albright's aim, then, is to remind us that while dividing the religious from the political has fostered peace and stability here at home, we must keep in mind that religion often plays a much more central role in the affairs of nations abroad. Attending to that fact, Albright shows us, should be central to U.S. foreign policy.

▶ TAGS: *faith, diversity, conflict, religion, community, diplomacy*

Faith and Diplomacy

"This would be the best of all possible worlds if there were no religion in it!!" So wrote John Adams to Thomas Jefferson. The quotation, well known to proselytizing atheists, appears differently when placed in context. The full passage reads:

> Twenty times in the course of my late reading have I been on the point of breaking out, "This would be the best of all possible worlds if there were no religion in it!!" But in this exclamation I would have been . . .

fanatical. . . . Without religion this world would be something not fit to be mentioned in polite company, I mean hell.

In his song "Imagine," John Lennon urged us to dream of a world free of religious doctrines. For many nonbelievers, religion is not the solution to anything. For centuries, they argue, people have been making each other miserable in the name of God. Studies indicate that wars with a religious component last longer and are fought more savagely than other conflicts. As the acerbic liberal columnist I. F. Stone observed, "Too many throats have been cut in God's name through the ages, and God has enlisted in too many wars. War for sport or plunder has never been as bad as war waged because one man's belief was theoretically 'irreconcilable' with another."

The fault in such logic is that, although we know what a globe plagued by religious strife is like, we do not know what it would be like to live in a world where religious faith is absent. We have, however, had clues from Lenin, Stalin, Mao Zedong, and, I would also argue, the Nazis, who conjured up a soulless Christianity that denied and defamed the Jewish roots of that faith. It is easy to blame religion—or, more fairly, what some people do in the name of religion—for all our troubles, but that is too simple. Religion is a powerful force, but its impact depends entirely on what it inspires people to do. The challenge for policy-makers is to harness the unifying potential of faith, while containing its capacity to divide. This requires, at a minimum, that we see spiritual matters as a subject worth studying. Too often, as the Catholic theologian Bryan Hehir notes, "there is an assumption that you do not have to understand religion in order to understand the world. You need to understand politics, strategy, economics, and law, but you do not need to understand religion. If you look at standard textbooks of international relations or the way we organize our foreign ministry, there's no place where a sophisticated understanding of religion as a public force in the world is dealt with."

> **It is easy to blame religion . . . for all our troubles, but that is too simple.**

To anticipate events rather than merely respond to them, American diplomats will need to take Hehir's advice and think more expansively about the role of religion in foreign policy and about their own need for expertise. They should develop the ability to recognize where and how religious beliefs contribute to conflicts and when religious principles might be invoked to ease strife. They should also reorient our foreign policy institutions to take fully into account the immense power of religion to influence how people think, feel, and act. The signs of such influence are all around us in the lives of people of many different faiths. By way of illustration, I offer three stories.

In 1981, I visited Poland; it was during the second year of the uprising by the Solidarity movement against the communist government. I had long studied central and eastern Europe, where, for decades, very little had changed. Now   5 the entire region was awakening, as from a deep slumber. A large part of the reason was that Pope John Paul II had earlier returned for the first time to Poland, his native land. Formerly Karol Wojtyla, a teacher, priest, and bishop of Kraków, the pope exemplified the pervasive role that religion had played in the history of Poland. While communist leaders in Warsaw dictated what Poles could do, parish priests in every corner of the country still spoke to what Poles believed. The government, alarmed by the prospect of the pope's pilgrimage, sent a memorandum to schoolteachers identifying John Paul II as "our enemy" and warning of the dangers posed by "his uncommon skills and great sense of humor." The authorities nevertheless made a tactical mistake by allowing church officials to organize the visit, giving them a chance to schedule a series of direct contacts between the "people's pope" and the pope's people.

One of the titles of the bishop of Rome is pontifex maximus, or "greatest bridge-builder." In Poland, John Paul II helped construct a bridge that would ultimately restore the connection between Europe's East and West. For bricks, he used words carefully chosen to expose the void at the heart of the communist system, arguing that if people were to fulfill their responsibility to live according to moral principles, they must first have the right to do so. He made plain his conviction that the totalitarian regime could not survive if Poles had the courage to withhold their cooperation. Above all, he urged his countrymen not to be afraid—a simple request with enormous impact. Slowly at first, but with gathering momentum, the pope's listeners drew strength from one another. No longer were they separated into small, controllable groups; the communists' obsession with isolating dangerous ideas had met its match. Standing amid huge crowds, the listeners recognized in each other once again the qualities that made them proud to be Polish—faith in God and a willingness to run risks for freedom. The pope's visits—for he made more than one—sparked a revolution of the spirit that liberated Poland, brought down the Berlin Wall, reunited Europe, and transformed the face of the world.

The pope helped the people of Poland to overcome their fear. Bob Seiple, who served with me in the State Department as the first American ambassador-at-large for international religious freedom, tells a second story, this one about overcoming hate. It concerns Mary, a young Lebanese woman he encountered while working as the head of World Vision, a Christian relief and development agency. In the 1980s, Lebanon had been the scene of a destructive and multi-sided civil war. Mary lived in a mostly Christian village; and when a Muslim militia invaded it, everyone fled. Mary tripped on a root, plunging face-first to the ground. As she scrambled to her knees, a young man of no more than twenty pressed the barrel of a pistol into the side of her head and demanded, "Renounce the cross or die." Mary did not flinch. "I was born a Christian," she said. "I will die a Christian." The pistol fired, propelling a bullet through Mary's neck and spine. Remorselessly, the militiaman carved a cross on her chest with his bayonet, then left her to die.

The following day, the militia returned and prepared to occupy the village. As they carted off the dead, a few of them came across Mary, still alive but unable to move; she was paralyzed. Instead of finishing her off, the militiamen improvised a stretcher out of wood and cloth and took her to a hospital. Seiple continues:

> And I'm talking to Mary, sitting across from her, and I said, "Mary, this makes absolutely no sense. These are people who tried to kill you. Why in the world would they take you to the hospital the next day?"
>
> She says, "You know, sometimes bad people are taught to do good things."
>
> And I said, "Mary, how do you feel about the person who pulled the trigger? Here you are, an Arab woman in a land twice occupied at that time — the Israelis in the south, the Syrians every place else — strapped to a wheelchair, held hostage by your own body, a ward of the state for the rest of your life. How do you feel about the guy who pulled the trigger?"
>
> She said, "I have forgiven him."
>
> "Mary, how in the world could you forgive him?"
>
> "Well, I forgave him because my God forgave me. It's as simple as that."

In Seiple's view, there are two lessons in this story. The first is that there are people who are willing to die — and kill — for their faith. This was true thousands of years ago and is no less true today. The second lesson is that religion at its best teaches forgiveness and reconciliation, not only when those acts are relatively easy but also when they are almost unbelievably difficult. (Mary, I need hardly add, is a more forgiving person than most — including me.)

The third story involves a boy with haunted eyes whom I met on a blisteringly hot afternoon in December 1997 during my first trip to Africa as secretary of state. The youngster looked about five years old and spoke softly, in a voice drained of emotion. He told me that, two weeks earlier, the small village where his family lived had been attacked. His mother had thrown him to the ground, shielding him with her body. When it was quiet, he wriggled his way out from under her and looked. His mother was dead. The bodies of other women were nearby, more than a dozen, drenched in blood. The boy then heard an infant crying; it was his sister, lying among the corpses. He gathered the baby into his arms and started walking. For hours, as the youngster stumbled along over hills and rocks, the infant wailed. Eventually they came to a place where the boy knew from experience that they would be welcomed and kept safe.

That place was Gulu, a town in a remote part of northern Uganda. World Vision ran the camp and hospital there — a haven for local villagers, who were being terrorized by an outlaw militia group. During the previous decade, an estimated 8,000 children had been kidnapped; most were presumed dead. Boys who survived and did not escape were impressed into rebel units; girls were taken as servants or "wives."

Camp officials blamed rebel leaders who had twisted religion into something grotesque. The tragedy had begun in 1986, when a change in government threatened the privileges of a previously dominant tribe, the Acholi.

Fear is a powerful motivator, and the Acholi feared retribution for the many abuses they had committed while in power. A potential savior arrived in the unlikely form of a thirty-year-old woman, Alice Auma, who said that she was able to commune with spirits—a rare but by no means unique claim in her culture. She told her companions that she had been possessed by a deceased Italian military officer who had instructed her to organize an army and retake Kampala, the Ugandan capital. Once victory was achieved, commanded the spirit, the Acholi should cleanse themselves by seeking forgiveness. Auma's sacred campaign was launched but lacked the military clout to match its supernatural inspiration. After some initial successes, the movement—armed only with sticks, stones, and voodoo dolls—was crushed. Auma, her mind no longer host to the Italian officer, found refuge across the border in Kenya.

That would have ended the story had not Joseph Kony, Auma's nephew, decided to take up the cause of holy war. Piecing together a small force from various rebel groups, he assembled what came to be known as the Lord's Resistance Army (LRA). From 1987 on, the LRA has attacked villagers throughout the region, also targeting local governments and aid workers. Because Kony finds adults hard to control and reluctant to enlist, he kidnaps children as a means of procuring troops. Once captured, the children are forced to obey or be put to death; and obedience demands a willingness to kill anyone, including one another. Discipline is administered in the form of beatings, lashings, and amputations predicated on their leader's reading of the Old Testament. The LRA's professed goal is to overthrow the Ugandan government and replace it with one based on the Ten Commandments—or actually ten plus one. The eleventh, added by Kony to restrict the movements of adversaries, is "Thou shalt not ride a bicycle."

Itself a product of fear, the LRA has survived twenty years by instilling fear in others. The Ugandan government has veered between efforts to make peace with the LRA and efforts to destroy it, but officials lack the resources to protect those living in the vicinity of the rebel force. That task has been left to World Vision and similar groups whose resources are also limited, as I saw during my tour of the camp in Gulu. The surroundings reminded me of pictures I had seen of the Crimean War. The camp hospital smelled of disinfectant and human waste. Ancient IVs dripped. Mosquitoes were buzzing everywhere. There were hundreds of patients, most of them children, many covered with welts and scars, some missing a limb. I met a group of teenage girls sitting on mattresses, braiding each other's hair. They looked as if they belonged in junior high school, yet several were already mothers, their babies sired by LRA rapists. "Even if you are a very young girl," said one, who was wearing a Mickey Mouse T-shirt, "you would be given to a man who was the age of my father."

As I started to leave, a young man came up to me holding an infant. "This is the girl that little boy brought to us, his little sister. Her name is Charity." As I cradled the tiny orphan, I was told that the girl had been named for one of the volunteers at the mission. There were many such volunteers. It was a place filled with terrible suffering but also a resilient joy. Patients and volunteers laughed, sang, 15 played games, and cared for each other. The Italian doctor who ran the facility had been in Gulu for more than twenty years. What a contrast between the faith that manifests itself in such love and the twisted fantasies pursued by the LRA.*

One insight that is present in these stories and often in religious faith more generally is that we share a kinship with one another, however distant it may sometimes seem; we are all created in the image of God. This in turn places upon us a responsibility to our neighbors. That principle provides both a solid foundation for religion and a respectable basis for organizing the affairs of secular society. What complicates matters is that religion can be interpreted in ways that exclude large numbers of people from any claim to kinship. Those truly imbued with religious faith—such as Pope John Paul II, Bob Seiple's Mary, and the volunteers in Gulu—may affirm "We are all God's children"; but others may follow their convictions to a more argumentative conclusion—"I am right, you are wrong, go to hell!"

When I appeared on a panel with the Jewish writer and thinker Elie Wiesel, a survivor of the Holocaust, he recalled how a group of scholars had once been asked to name the unhappiest character in the Bible. Some said Job, because of the trials he endured. Some said Moses, because he was denied entry to the promised land. Some said the Virgin Mary, because she witnessed the death of her son. The best answer, Wiesel suggested, might in fact be God, because of the sorrow caused by people fighting, killing, and abusing each other in His name.

This is why so many practitioners of foreign policy—including me—have sought to separate religion from world politics, to liberate logic from beliefs that transcend logic. It is, after all, hard enough to divide land between two groups on the basis of legal or economic equity; it is far harder if one or both claim that the land in question was given to them by God. But religious motivations do not disappear simply because they are not mentioned; more often they lie dormant only to rise up again at the least convenient moment. As our experience in Iran reflected, the United States has not always understood this well enough. To lead internationally, American policy-makers must learn as much as possible about religion, and then incorporate that knowledge in their strategies. Bryan Hehir has compared this challenge to brain surgery—a necessary task, but fatal if not done well.

In any conflict, reconciliation becomes possible when the antagonists cease dehumanizing each other and begin instead to see a bit of themselves in their enemy. That is why it is a standard negotiating technique to ask each side to stand in the shoes of the other. Often this is not as difficult as it might seem. The very fact that adversaries have been fighting over the same issue or prize can furnish a common ground. For centuries, Protestants and Catholics competed for religious ascendancy in Europe. That was a point of similarity: wanting to be number one. For even longer, Christians, Muslims, and Jews have pursued

---

* In October 2005, the International Criminal Court issued arrest warrants for Joseph Kony and four other LRA leaders on the charge of crimes against humanity. The court does not, however, have any independent capacity to enforce those warrants.

rival claims in Jerusalem; that, too, is a point of similarity—wanting to occupy the same space. In parts of Asia and Africa, Christians and Muslims are fighting, but they share a desire to worship freely and without fear. When people are pursuing the same goal, each side should be able to understand what motivates the other. To settle their differences, they need only find a formula for sharing what both want—a tricky task, but one that can at least be addressed through an appeal to reason.

Not all conflicts lend themselves to this sort of negotiation. During World War II, the Axis and the Allies were fighting for two entirely different visions of the future. Today, Al Qaeda's lust for a war of vengeance fought with the tools of terror cannot be accommodated. Some differences are too great to be reconciled. In most situations, however, reconciliation will be eminently preferable to continued stalemate or war. But how is reconciliation achieved?

When participants in a conflict claim to be people of faith, a negotiator who has the credentials and the credibility to do so might wish to call their bluff. If the combatants argue the morality of their cause, how is that morality reflected in their actions? Are they allowing their religion to guide them or using it as a debating point to advance their interests? Has their faith instilled in them a sense of responsibility toward others or a sense of entitlement causing them to disregard the rights and views of everyone else?

> **Effective foreign policy requires that we comprehend why others act as they do.**

If I were secretary of state today, I would not seek to mediate disputes on the basis of religious principles any more than I would try to negotiate alone the more intricate details of a trade agreement or a pact on arms control. In each case, I would ask people more expert than I to begin the process of identifying key issues, exploring the possibilities, and suggesting a course of action. It might well be that my involvement, or the president's, would be necessary to close a deal, but the outlines would be drawn by those who know every nuance of the issues at hand. When I was secretary of state, I had an entire bureau of economic experts I could turn to, and a cadre of experts on nonproliferation and arms control whose mastery of technical jargon earned them a nickname, "the priesthood." With the notable exception of Ambassador Seiple, I did not have similar expertise available for integrating religious principles into our efforts at diplomacy. Given the nature of today's world, knowledge of this type is essential.

If diplomacy is the art of persuading others to act as we would wish, effective foreign policy requires that we comprehend why others act as they do. Fortunately, the constitutional requirement that separates state from church in the United States does not also insist that the state be ignorant of the church, mosque, synagogue, pagoda, and temple. In the future, no American ambassador should be assigned to a country where religious feelings are strong unless he or she has a deep understanding of the faiths commonly practiced there. Ambassadors and their representatives, wherever they are assigned, should establish relationships with local religious leaders. The State Department should hire or train a core of specialists in religion to be deployed both in Washington and in key embassies overseas.

In 1994, the Center for Strategic and International Studies published *Religion, the Missing Dimension of Statecraft.* The book makes a compelling case for recognizing the role of religion in affecting political behavior and for using spiritual tools to help resolve conflicts. Douglas Johnston, the book's coauthor, subsequently formed the International Center for Religion and Diplomacy (ICRD), which has continued to study what it calls "faith-based diplomacy" while also playing an important mediating role in Sudan and establishing useful relationships in Kashmir, Pakistan, and Iran. Johnston, a former naval officer and senior official in the Defense Department, believes that, ordinarily, everyone of influence in a given situation is not necessarily bad, and those who are bad aren't bad all the time. He argues that a faith-based mediator has means that a conventional diplomat lacks, including prayers, fasting, forgiveness, repentance, and the inspiration of scripture.

The ICRD is not alone in its efforts. After leaving the State Department, Bob Seiple founded the Institute for Global Engagement, which is working to improve the climate for religious liberty in such volatile nations as Uzbekistan and Laos. The institute's mantra is, "Know your faith at its deepest and richest best, and enough about your neighbor's faith to respect it."

While in office, I had occasion to work closely with the Community of Sant'Egidio, a lay movement that began in Rome in the 1960s, inspired by the Second Vatican Council of Pope John XXIII. Over a period of years, Sant'Egidio successfully brokered negotiations ending a long and bloody civil war in Mozambique. It has also played a constructive role in, among other places, Kosovo, Algeria, Burundi, and Congo. The community sees prayer, service to the poor, ecumenism, and dialogue as the building blocks of interreligious cooperation and problem solving.

Numerous other faith-based organizations, representing every major religion, are in operation. They are most effective when they function cooperatively, pooling their resources and finding areas in which to specialize. Some are most skilled at mediation; others are best at helping former combatants readjust to civilian life. Still others emphasize prevention, addressing a problem before it can explode into violence. Many are experts in economic development or building democracy, both insurance policies against war. Together, these activists have more resources, more skilled personnel, a longer attention span, more experience, more dedication, and more success in fostering reconciliation than any government.

The most famous example of faith-based peacemaking was orchestrated by President Jimmy Carter at Camp David in 1978. Most observers acknowledge that the peace agreement between Egypt and Israel would never have come about if not for Carter's ability to understand and appeal to the deep religious convictions of President Sadat and Prime Minister Begin. I recently asked the former president how policy-makers should think about religion as part of the foreign policy puzzle. He told me that it is not possible to separate what people feel and believe in the spiritual realm from what they will do as a matter of public policy. "This is an opportunity," he argued, "because the basic elements of the major religious faiths are so similar—humility, justice, and peace." He said that in the unofficial diplomacy he is often asked to conduct through the Carter Center, one of the first aspects he investigates is whether the parties to a dispute represent the same faith. He said it is often simpler to deal with people of completely different faiths than with those who share a religion but disagree about how it should be interpreted. As a moderate Baptist, Carter said he found it less complicated to have a conversation with a Catholic than with a Baptist fundamentalist; with the Catholic it was easier simply to accept the differences and not feel obliged to argue about them.

When I broached this same subject with Bill Clinton, he stressed two points. First, religious leaders can help to validate a peace process before, during, and after negotiations; through dialogue and public statements, they can make peace easier to achieve and sustain. Second, persuading people of different faiths to work cooperatively requires separating what is debatable in scripture from what is not. "If you're dealing with people who profess faith," he said, "they must believe there is a Creator; if they believe that, they should agree that God created everyone. This takes them from the specific to the universal. Once they acknowledge their common humanity, it becomes harder to kill each other; then compromise becomes easier because they've admitted that they are dealing with people like themselves, not some kind of Satan or subhuman species."

Faith-based diplomacy can be a useful tool of foreign policy. I am not arguing, however, that it can replace traditional diplomacy. Often the protagonists in a political drama are immune to, or deeply suspicious of, appeals made on religious or moral grounds. But if we do not expect miracles, little is lost in making the attempt. The resurgence of religious feeling will continue to influence world events. American policy-makers cannot afford to ignore this; on balance they should welcome it. Religion at its best can reinforce the core values necessary for people from different cultures to live in some degree of harmony; we should make the most of that possibility.   30

Questions for Critical Reading

1. According to Albright, does religion ultimately help or hinder diplomacy? Re-read Albright's text, searching for quotations that support your interpretation.

2. Although Albright closely examines the role religion should play in diplomacy she does not provide a clear picture of what a faith-inflected diplomacy would look like. Craft an argument about the role religion should play in foreign policy, locating quotations from her text that would support your argument.

3. Is faith-based diplomacy best pursued through the government or through private organizations? Reread Albright's text looking for passages that support your position.

Exploring Context

1. Using Flickr (flickr.com), search for images that illustrate Albright's argument. Paste these images into a document to create a visual montage of this essay.

2. Visit the Web site for the U.S. Department of State at state.gov. Explore the site, reading it critically to determine the role that religion currently plays in U.S. foreign policy. Does this Web site support your response to Question 3 of Questions for Critical Reading?

3. The International Center for Religion and Diplomacy (icrd.org) is an organization that seems to pursue Albright's goals of considering religion in diplomacy. Search through the center's Web site for evidence that would support Albright's arguments. Does it reflect your vision of faith-inflected diplomacy from Question 2 of Questions for Critical Reading?

Questions for Connecting

1. How would the primacy of practice, as described by Kwame Anthony Appiah in "Making Conversation" (p. 57) and "The Primacy of Practice" (p. 63), complicate Albright's vision of diplomacy? Would Appiah's understanding of cosmopolitanism enhance a faith-based diplomacy, or do political practices resist the kinds of changes Albright suggests? How can you synthesize their positions to argue for an effective diplomacy?

2. Is Kenji Yoshino's vision of civil rights in "Preface" (p. 479) and "The New Civil Rights" (p. 481) compatible with Albright's call for taking religion into consideration in foreign policy? Is the diplomacy described by Albright akin to a liberty or equality paradigm? Synthesize the ideas of these two authors and support your argument with quotations from both texts.

3. Which author provides a better strategy for reaching peace, Albright or Thomas Friedman in "The Dell Theory of Conflict Prevention" (p. 121)? Are their proposals concerning religion and economics and the roles each plays in global politics compatible? Is it possible to synthesize their ideas?

Language Matters

1. Varying your word choice adds interest for the reader, but it can be a particularly challenging task. Look back through Albright's essay. How does she vary her word choice to convey meaning? How many different words for "diplomacy" or "faith" does she use? How does she handle the implications of these terms? How might you vary your word choice in your own writing?

2. Select a key passage from Albright and replace all the verbs with blanks ("_____"). Working in small groups, fill in the blanks with verbs and then reflect on which verbs you chose and why. How does the context of each sentence determine which word to use? More important, how significant are verbs to the meaning of a sentence? Could you change Albright's entire argument by changing the verbs?

3. Constellations help us to make sense out of the stars — they give the stars meaning by grouping them into meaningful patterns. Examine how sentence

structure does the same with words. Select a key quotation from Albright's essay and then create a map of its different parts. How did you choose to break up the sentence? What relationships can you find between the parts? Are some connections more important than others? That is, if you took out certain parts of the sentence, would it still have the same meaning?

Assignments for Writing

1. Albright's essay makes it clear that faith can both unite and divide people. Write a paper in which you argue for faith's potential to enable political unification. Draw from your work on the role of religion in diplomacy from Question 1 in Questions for Critical Reading as well as the current political climate—both domestic and international—in your discussion. The goal of this assignment is for you to synthesize your experiences and observations of faith's function in current political climates with Albright's arguments. Consider, for example, what Albright says about a world without political doctrine; also, pay close attention to the stories she shares and the examples she offers the reader.

2. Albright finds a shared sense of humanity through religion, but the idea of a common sense of humanity extends to other fields of knowledge and experience. Write a paper in which you identify another avenue through which humans might find commonalities. Extend Albright's insights to those other instances of shared humanity, synthesizing her arguments with your examples. You may wish to use your work with one of the authors from Questions for Connecting in formulating your argument. To begin thinking critically about this assignment, consider these questions: In the end, is religion the only thing that binds humans together? Is religion the only thing that separates humans from everything else in existence?

3. Albright stresses that ignorance must be overcome in order for all of us to find common political ground. Although her essay focuses specifically on religious ignorance, her position could be the foundation for a much more comprehensive conversation on the matter. Write an essay in which you examine the possibilities of overcoming ignorance in relation to diplomacy. Must we overcome ignorance—religious or otherwise—in order to achieve productive international relations? If so, how do we overcome this ignorance? You may wish to incorporate the work you did in Question 3 of Exploring Context.

Julia Alvarez

Julia Alvarez was born in New York. Shortly afterward, her family returned to the Dominican Republic, where they lived under the infamous Trujillo dictatorship. Alvarez's father became involved with the underground resistance, and eventually the family was forced to flee the country and return to the United States, an experience which led Alvarez to write the 1994 novel *In the Time of the Butterflies.* She has written many other novels, including *How the Garcia Girls Lost Their Accents* (1991), as well as essays, poetry, and children's literature. She earned her B.A. from Middlebury College and an M.A. in creative writing from Syracuse University. Alvarez has received numerous awards and honors, including the Latina Leader Award in Literature from the Congressional Hispanic Caucus Institute in 2007. Her nonfiction book *Once Upon a Quinceañera: Coming of Age in the USA,* from which the following selection is taken, was a 2007 finalist for a National Book Critics Circle Award.

In *Once Upon a Quinceañera* Alvarez follows the female coming-of-age tradition known among Hispanic communities as quinceañera (or *quince,* for short). Throughout the book, Alvarez spends time with Monica, who is preparing for her quinceañera, as well as other teen girls and their families. Through her journey with these girls and their families Alvarez is able to explore the history and evolution of the quince tradition in the context of immigration, culture, class, and gender. In addition, Alvarez looks to the influences of religion, cultural tradition, and American consumerism for reasons this ritual is able to thrive throughout generations. Overall, while the book closely examines the motions and traditions of quinces, Alvarez pushes readers and herself to interrogate cultural perceptions of gender, as well as rituals and rites of passage, and how these perceptions might be influenced when crossing cultural boundaries.

In the following selections, Alvarez touches on various aspects of the quinceañera. While some view the quince as the initiation of a young girl into a community of womanhood and culture of responsibility, Alvarez wonders if such arguments merely provide an illusion of female power within a traditionally patriarchal system. Though Alvarez is continually skeptical of the quince craze, she often finds herself caught up in the excitement. Moments such as these lead Alvarez to a new stage of investigation in which she explores the social, familial, and economic implications of the quince tradition. Perhaps as Isabella, founder of bellaquinceanera.com, suggests, quinceañeras in the twenty-first century are an opportunity to offer young Latina women a sense of empowerment and individual importance. In order to do this, the tradition must be redefined in a way that reflects and embodies the values and desires of women today. Alvarez addresses the idea of whether and how this redefining might occur by leading readers and herself to consider the meaning of tradition and gender as they are practiced today. How can traditions be redefined in the spirit of these changing values and desires? Is it possible to redefine traditions without losing the original ties to them? How is it possible for traditions to offer a means of crossing cultural and social boundaries? What role does gender play in the preservation of cultural traditions, and how might these traditions differ according to gender? In what ways has consumerism affected the importance of quinceañeras and other traditions?

▶ TAGS: *tradition, rites, identity, culture, gender, race*

Selections from
Once Upon a Quinceañera

Every Girl Should Have One

I wish I'd had Isabella Martínez Wall to call up and talk to back when I was a young teen in need of rescue and an infusion of self-esteem.

Based in Los Angeles, Isabella is the founder of a one-stop quinceañera Web site cum advice column, bellaquinceañera.com. She's also an actress, a former Miss Dominican Republic, a successful fashion model, and founder of Someone Cares International, a nonprofit that is described on her Web site as "benefiting needy children" in her native country. Speaking by phone with this passionate and inspirational woman, I feel the same unsettling mixture of amazement, caution, and yearning that I feel toward televangelists. Can somebody really believe this? And if so, why can't I?

I learned about Isabella from a Dominican contact at Disney World, whom I had called to find out more about the Disney quince package. She described Isabella as an "awesome, full-bodied Latina" who is doing amazing things for young Hispanic girls. According to my contact, Isabella had actually found that young girls who had quinceañeras didn't drop out of school, didn't get pregnant, didn't get in trouble.

"Really? I mean, statistically?" I shot back. Here you go, I thought, peppering these kids with questions. But a quinceañera panacea seemed too good to be true. I'd just barely surfaced from *The State of Hispanic Girls** with a sense of dread in my heart, which was also making me want to grab for a cure.

"I don't know," my contact said. "Talk to Isabella, she'll tell you."

Ah, my people, I thought. Statistics are for the gringos. We trust testimonials, what our hearts and telenovelas tell us. I had just attended a lecture by Dr. James Martin titled "The Meaning of the 21st Century." Solutions to world problems didn't have to be costly or complex, the information technology guru

5

---

*A study published by the National Coalition of Hispanic Health and Human Services Organizations in 1999 that documented the high rates of teen pregnancy, substance abuse, school dropouts, and suicide attempts by young Latinas.

explained. In Mexico, a vanguard group of TV producers who understood the dangers of population explosion had started a campaign to bring down the birthrate by introducing female leads who practiced birth control into popular telenovelas. Initial results showed the campaign was working. Better than pamphlets or science classes or lectures like Dr. Martin's.

When I reached Isabella, after the initial honorifics, "So you're the author!" "So you're the beauty queen!" I asked her about this claim I'd heard that quinceañeras really turn girls around. Not that I wanted an analysis or anything academic, I added, thinking maybe I was sounding too much like a doubting-Thomas gringa. But with all those statistics still heavy in my heart, I wanted to hear why she thought quinceañeras were so effective. "Well, let me tell you." Isabella laughed right out. "There's nothing academic about a quinceañera!

"What I mean is there's no textbook about how you have to do a quinceañera," Isabella went on to explain. She hears from a lot of young ladies on her Web site, where she offers free advice, a kind of Ann Landers to Latina girls.

"They write me, and they ask, can I wear a short dress? Does it have to be white? Can I have a court with only my best friend and my sister? I tell them, listen, there are no rules. The most important thing is to make this celebration yours, totally yours. I try to educate them, I talk to them, the site is highly interactive. Quinceañeras are about creating strong women. Our girls need all the help we can give them."

The most important thing is to make this celebration yours, totally yours.

It's funny how you are sure you are going to end up on the other side of an opinion from someone, and it turns out you're in each other's court. Never would I have guessed that a former beauty queen promoting a princessy fantasy would turn out to be a crown-carrying feminist. But how on earth can this quasi beauty pageant cum mini wedding make an Amazon out of a stardust girl? 10

"I have seen it happen!" In fact, it happened to Isabella herself. As a teenager growing up in the Dominican Republic, she hit a wall. "I was smoking, drinking, I had body issues and identity problems." I'm dying to ask her to be specific, but she is on a roll. "When I turned fifteen, everybody started having quinceañeras. I mean everybody. Quinceañeras know no social or class boundaries. You might not have the money but you have a quinceañera for your daughter. The family is making that statement. We might not be rich but we value our daughter."

Isabella's quinceañera turned her around. "It made me feel so special." In fact, she credits it with leading her down the path to being crowned Miss Dominican Republic. "I've been there," Isabella says. "I had that moment. But how many women in the world get to feel like a queen? How many?"

Not this skinny, undersized Latina for sure, I have to agree.

"Well, that's the first reason to have a quinceañera," Isabella says. "To have that experience and not because you're marrying someone."

The second reason comes from her own experience. "Being fifteen, let's face it, it's a tough age. Your body is all over the map. You wonder who you are. Who 15 your friends are. Where you're going. You can get lost for sure. What better time in your life to have your family, friends, community come together and create a support system for you for the rest of your life?"

Isn't that asking an awful lot of a quinceañera?

But Isabella dismisses my skepticism. "About two years ago, I realized that I had a mission: to promote this important ritual. And yes, I've seen it turn girls around. I don't have statistics, this is not academic, like I said, but girls who have quinces, think about it, they're spending a lot of time with their moms, shopping, talking about life. Their friends are coming over to do rehearsals. I mean, a room full of fifteen-year-olds learning dance steps right under your nose. Parents are always complaining they don't know what to do when their daughters hit puberty. *Hel*-lo?! Here's something to do. Give her a wishing well.

"Of course, we've got to take the quinceañera a step forward," Isabella adds. Before, the whole quinceañera thing was about a girl being of marriageable age, goods to be displayed. But now we can invest this old tradition with new meaning.

"We can create a support platform for that young lady that she can have to look back upon for the rest of her life. That moment when she stands dressed like a queen with her mom beside her looking in the mirror, for that moment, if only that moment, she knows she is all right just as she is. She is the queen of her life if she can hold on to that feeling."

In fact, Isabella thinks quinces are so special, the tradition should come out　20 of its ethnic closet and become an American phenomenon. "I don't care what class or group you come from," Isabella claims. "Every girl should have one."

When I hang up I feel that uplifted feeling that must be why folks pick up the phone after watching a TV evangelist and put a donation on their charge card.

One-(Very Small)-Size-Fits-All Script

My first year at Abbot* did for me what Isabella Martínez Wall's year of going to quinceañeras and having her own quinceañera did for her. It gave me a new community to belong to, a narrative I could follow into adulthood. Instead of a family and community rallying around the quinceañera's transformation into a woman, planning and preparing sometimes for a year for that symbolic pageant marking her passage, I had a community of classmates and female teachers and coaches and housemothers honing my skills, encouraging my talents, preparing me for being what Isabella Martínez Wall would call "queen of my own life."

Incidentally, I was also turning from fourteen to fifteen, and, needless to say, away at a school where we were the only Latinas (the closest thing to us was a German girl whose parents lived in Guatemala and an American girl whose father was posted in Venezuela), I did not have a quinceañera. Nor was much made of my fifteenth birthday: a cake in the dorm, a phone call from my parents, a card with a check for twenty-five dollars. My older sister had already

---

*Abbot Academy: A private boarding school for girls in Massachusetts.

gotten my mother's ring, and away at school I could shave my legs and wear makeup without asking anyone for permission.

But although some psychological elements of the American quinceañera and my first Abbot year were the same—a community grooming a young lady for her entry into womanhood—the content of that grooming was significantly different. We Abbot girls were encouraged to develop our minds, not leave our brains parked at the door of our gender. In fact, the plaque at the front gate encouraged us to ENTER INTO UNDERSTANDING, SO YOU MAY GO FORTH TO NOBLER LIVING. Nobler living! True, many of my Abbot classmates would eventually marry and have children (this was, after all, the mid-sixties), but it was assumed we would all go to college first. (Out of a class of seventy-eight girls, only one, my room-mate, did not go to college, but married her longtime boyfriend instead.) And since many of our teachers were unmarried women, making their own way in the world, the subliminal message was clear: We were to be smart, resourceful, independent women.

This new narrative of female possibility was groundbreaking and bracing   25 even for my American classmates. "Although Columbus and Cabot never heard of Abbot," one of our school songs began. A good thing, too. Those old-world explorers would not have approved of young women taking over the helm of their journey through life and discovering their own new worlds.

In contrast, the typical quinceañera enacts a traditional narrative that is, let's face it, a one-(very small)-size-fits-all script corseting a full-bodied female life. The young Latina is dressed up in finery not unlike a bride, her father is changing her shoes, claiming that first waltz, then passing her on to a brother or uncle or grandfather, until finally she ends up in the arms of her escort to a round of applause. The quinceañera is like a rehearsal wedding without a groom, and it sends a clear message to the Latina girl: We expect you to get married, have children, devote **It's no wonder that girls end up getting pregnant soon after celebrating their quinces.** yourself to your family. It's no wonder that girls end up getting pregnant soon after celebrating their quinces. Jaider Sánchez, a hairdresser and dance coach for quinceañeras in Denver, mentioned in a recent interview that out of seven quinceañeras he instructed in 2005, four have already invited them to their baby showers.

And so, although it gives her a momentary illusion of power (the princess rhetoric, the celebration of her sexual power, her youth, her beauty), in fact, the ritual enacts an old paradigm of the patriarchy increasingly (in the U.S.A.) pumped up by a greedy market. In a fascinating book titled *Emerging from the Chrysalis: Studies in Rituals of Women's Initiations*, Bruce Lincoln, who teaches at the University of Chicago Divinity School, amplifies Arnold van Gennep's classic theory about rites of passage as they apply to females. According to van Gennep, who coined the term, rites of passage are ceremonies within cultures that enable an individual to pass from one well-defined role to another. Male initiation rites of passage involve the stripping, testing, and reintegration of the young man into the sociopolitical adult society.

But what Bruce Lincoln found was that female initiations follow a different pattern: The girl is decked in ceremonial finery, often layer on layer is piled on her, a magnification that confers on her cosmic status and participation in a mythic drama. "Rituals of women's initiation claim to transform a girl into a woman, [they] claim to renew society by providing it with a new productive member." During the ceremonies, the initiant is "regarded as having become a deity, a culture heroine, the link between past and future." So far so good, but Bruce Lincoln goes on to suggest that this mythic power is a substitution for actual power, a pie in the sky versus options and opportunities in the here and now:

> The strategy of women's initiation is to lead a woman's life . . . away from the sociopolitical arena, introducing her to the real or imagined splendors of the cosmos instead. To put it in different terms, women's initiation offers a religious compensation for a sociopolitical deprivation. Or to put it differently still, it is an opiate for an oppressed class. . . .
>
> Cosmic claims notwithstanding, the desired result of the ritual is to make a girl ready and willing to assume the traditional place of a woman as defined within a given culture. . . . The strategy is that of placing women on a pedestal, carried to its outermost possibilities: speak of her as a goddess to make of her a drudge.

Although the young quinceañera is being crowned queen, the ritual doesn't change anything. It merely casts its net of glittering meaning over what might be a dismal situation: "It is rare that a ritual can alter the basic ways in which a society is organized," Bruce Lincoln concludes. "Nor do rituals shape the way in which people live as much as they shape the way people understand the lives they would lead in any event."

Even if she is at the bottom of the American heap, if the young Latina girl can believe the fantasy—that her condition is temporary, that she is a Cinderella waiting for that fairy godmother or husband to endow her with their power—then she can bear the burden of her disadvantage. And as years go by, and the probability of her dream becoming true lessens, she can at least pass on the story to her daughter.

Maybe that is why I get tearful at quinceañeras. I'm watching the next   30 generation be tamed into a narrative my generation fought so hard to change. Why I feel like a snake in the garden, because here I sit in their living rooms or in their rented halls, eating their catered food, celebrating with la familia, and I am thinking, Why spend all this money enacting a fantasy that the hard numbers out there say is not going to come true?

Quinceañera Expo

At the Quinceañera Expo in the Airport Convention Center in San Antonio, little girls are walking around with tiaras in their hair, oohing and ahing at the fancy dresses, the pink balloons, the wedding-cake-size cakes, the last dolls encased in plastic, the fluffy pillows with straps for securing the heels in case the page trips as he bears them to the altar to be blessed by the priest.

At a cordoned-off area at the rear of the hall, Victoria Acosta, a fourteen-year-old local pop sensation, is singing into a microphone as she dances and gestures with her free hand. "Crazy, crazy, crazy, I think the world's gone crazy!" Her next song, "Once Upon a Time," is dedicated to "all of you out there who have had your hearts broken." "All of you out there" is a semicircle of pudgy pre-teens sitting on the floor, mesmerized by the slender, glamorous Victoria with her long mascara'd lashes, her glittery eye shadow, her slinky black outfit and sparkly silver tie. "You bet I'm going to have a quince," she tells me during a break between songs, although I don't see why. She seems to have already made her passage into womanhood quite successfully.

There isn't a male shopper in sight. In fact, the only men around are manning booths or working the floor:

> a couple of boy models, one in a white tuxedo with a pale pink vest, the other in a white suit with a yellow vest;
>
> a grown man in a military uniform, a popular escort outfit with some girls, he tells me;
>
> a dj in a cowboy hat who plays loud music while his sidekick, a skinny boy, hands out flyers;
>
> Seve, the clown (who come to think of it might be female under all that face paint and bulbous, attached nose);
>
> Dale of Awesome Ice Designs (for $350 you can have the "Fire & Ice Sculpture" with the quinceañera's picture embedded in a central medallion of ice);
>
> Ronny of VIP Chocolate Fountains, whose wife, Joanne, does most of the talking. (Did you know that you can run chili con queso through the fountains for a Mexican theme at your daughter's quinceañera? The young people still prefer chocolate, as you can imagine);
>
> and Tony Guerrero, the owner of Balloons Over San Antonio ("We Blow for u").

Add the two photographers at Tilde (Photography, Invitations, Videography), Mr. Acosta (Victoria's manager-dad), the guy with a Starbucks urn strapped to his back, and Manuel Villamil at the Primerica Financial Services booth—and that makes for just over a dozen men in a crowd of about three hundred women of all ages here to shop for some member of their family's quinceañera. The hall is so girl-packed that the discreetly curtained BABY CHANGING/NURSING booth seems extraneous. You could breast-feed your baby out in the open and still be within the strict bounds of modesty, like peeing without shutting your stall door in the ladies' room because everyone inside except the little toddler in Mommy's arms is female.

I feel as if I've wandered into the back room where the femaleness of the next generation of Latinas is being manufactured, displayed, and sold. A throwback vision, to be sure. Lots of pink-lacey-princessy-glittery-glitzy stuff. One little girl wheels a large última muñeca around while her mother follows, carting the baby sister, who has ceded her stroller to a doll bigger than she is. "How beautiful!" I bend down to admire the little girl's proud cargo. "Is that for your quince?" The little girl looks pleadingly toward her mom. "It's her cousin's," the mom says, gesturing with her head toward a chunky teenager carting a large shopping bag and lolling at Joanne and Ronny's booth, scooping her toothpick of cake into the chocolate fountain. The little girl looks forlorn. "I'm sure you'll have a last doll, too, when you have your quince," I console her. She gives me a weak smile in return. Why on earth am I encouraging her?

Crazy, crazy, crazy, I think the world's gone crazy.

It's not that. It's that after an hour roaming up and down the aisles, I fall in with the spirit of the expo. There is a contagious, evangelical air to the whole thing that sweeps you up and makes you want to be part of the almost religious fervor that surrounds this celebration. I half expect to find Isabella Martínez Wall here, addressing a crowd of wide-eyed teens.

In fact, my guide, Priscilla Mora, reminds me of Isabella. Both women share a crusading enthusiasm for a tradition they believe is one of the best things going for Latina womanhood. Plump and pretty with the sunny face of someone perennially in a good mood, Priscilla has organized six of these expos, and even though some have not been as well attended as she would have liked, her faith is undimmed. When not organizing these expos, she is a quinceañera planner, an author of the *Quinceañera Guide and Handbook,* and most of all a passionate promoter of the tradition. She actually thought up this business at a workshop where participants had to write down their dreams on little pieces of paper. Then they all put their pieces of paper in a fire and let their dreams go up to God. This isn't just a business, Priscilla explains, it's a calling, part of God's plan for her.

It's from Priscilla that I first hear that when the quinceañera makes her vow in the church, "it's about chastity. You're promising God that you're not going to have sex till you're back at the altar, getting married. That's why it's important that these girls learn all about the meaning," Priscilla insists. Otherwise, the quinceañera "is nothing but a party."

Priscilla's missionary zeal seems to be shared by many of the providers, who tell inspirational stories of why they got involved in quinces. Take Tony Guerrero of Balloons Over San Antonio. Tony grew up real poor in a family of four boys and four girls. ("Are you kidding?" he replies when I ask if the girls had quinceañeras.) A few years ago, Tony gave up his office job to do this because "I just wanted the opportunity to give back something to my community." He loves seeing people having fun, being happy, and hey, if nothing else, "I got myself another entry once I go over to the other side." "Another" because he already has a great-aunt over there. "She promised me she was going to have a spot waiting for me." Ruby of Great Expectations (a photography studio) thinks it's "a privilege" to share this special day with a girl. "I love the idea of rededicating your life to the Lord." (Echoes of Priscilla.) Curiously, the nuns' booth next to Ruby's is empty. "They told me they were coming." Priscilla looks momentarily nonplussed. But her sunny personality bounces back. "Maybe they'll be by later after Mass." This is Sunday, after all. The sisters, it turns out, are the Missionary

40

Catechists of Divine Providence, the first and only religious order of Mexican American women founded in the United States. Their focus on the quinceañera is part of their larger mission as "evangelizadoras del barrio and transmitters of a rich Mexican American faith to the universal Church."

The only heavy hitter at the expo is Sunita Trevino, who was born in Bombay but is married to a Hispanic. At her seminar on financing a quinceañera, Sunita gives us the opposite of the hard sell: the watch-your-financial-back-as-a-minority-woman talk that has me sitting at the edge of my chair. As she talks, Sunita paces up and down the raised platform stage like a lion trapped in a too-small cage.

Sunita works for Primerica Financial Services, but her training is in clinical psychology, which she ends up using a lot as she counsels families about their finances. "I'll tell you," she tells the audience of about a dozen, mostly grand-mothers, as this is the only area of the whole hall where there are chairs to sit down, "quinceañeras are high-stress times." A lot of couples come to see her for extra sessions. But the majority of Sunita's clients are single women who are in financial trouble. They don't budget. They overspend. They get into debt. She knows women in their seventies still paying off second mortgages they took out for their daughter's quinceañera. She finds this devastating.

"Nobody sits down to talk to us women! We are playing a money game but no one taught us the rules!" Sunita's own mother came from Bombay to America, thinking her husband would always be there to take care of her, and then her parents separated, and her mother was lost. She had no idea how to take care of herself. Sunita doesn't want to see this happen to any woman. We women are sinking into a hole of debt and the quinceañera is often where we get in over our heads.

Her recommendation to all of us sitting in the audience: pay cash. "If you budget eighteen hundred dollars for flowers, and what you pick amounts to double that, don't do it. DON'T DO IT! Stay within your budget. A lot of women get in trouble at the last minute. They think, oh, I'll go ahead, just this once."

If you end up borrowing money, "please," Sunita pleads with us, "read the terms, read them carefully. What the big print giveth, the small print taketh away. Educate yourselves! Don't think banks and savings accounts are there to do you a favor. Okay, let's see, who can tell me what banks do with your money?" she asks.

None of us grown women in the audience would dare hazard a guess. But a young girl about eleven years old raises her hand and says proudly, "They save it for you."

Sunita shakes her head fondly. "Out of the mouths of babes." She sighs. No-body laughs. Nobody seems to get the biblical reference that Sunita is misusing anyway. Out of the mouths of babes usually the truth comes. But this young girl is headed for that sinkhole of debt unless Sunita can steer her away from the dangers of borrowing. "No, honey, that's not what they do. They use your money to make money."

The girl sits back in her chair, a chastened, embarrassed expression on her face. Her tiara glints as Sunita explains to her that what she just said is what most people think. But that's why Sunita is here today. To tell us the truth no one else is going to tell us. To get us thinking about these things. "Two hundred fifty families declare bankruptcy every hour of every day in the U.S.A. I know a seventy-nine-year-old retired guy who is now bagging groceries. People don't plan to fail," Sunita explains. "They fail to plan. So, get mad. Get mad and learn the rules."

The girl squirms in her chair, as do the rest of us. After all, we came here in a party mood, not to feel that at the end of our adult lives we will end up as bag ladies, wishing we hadn't started down the road of debt with our own or our daughters' quinceañeras.

Throwing the House Out the Window

So, how much does a quinceañera cost? You ask any of the party planners and they'll tell you the same thing—anywhere from a hundred bucks for a cookout in the backyard and a stereo booming music for the young lady and her friends to fifty grand and up in a hall with a party planner, a limo, dinner for a hundred or more.

Everyone talks about this range, but after interviewing dozens of quinceañeras and talking to as many party planners, events providers, choreographers, caterers, I have to conclude that the cookout quinceañeras are becoming the exception. In the past, perhaps they were the rule. In the old countries, of course. In small homogenous pockets—a border town in Texas, a barrio composed solely of Central Americans; in other words, a group still largely out of the mainstream loop, perhaps. But now, as one quinceañera remarked, "If I had to be that cheap I just wouldn't have one. What for?" It is in the nature of the beast to be a splurge, an extravaganza. More than one person describing a recent quinceañera used the Spanish expression for an over-the-top expense: *throwing the house out the window.* They threw the house out the window for that girl's quinceañera.

They threw the house out the window. In a country where the rate of poverty is growing (12.7 percent of U.S. citizens were living below the poverty line in 2004, up from 11.3 percent in 2000), with Latinos forming a sizeable portion of those impoverished numbers (21.9 percent of the Hispanic population was living below the poverty line in 2004 according to a U.S. census survey). Sunita, it turns out, was not exaggerating.

They threw the house they probably didn't own out the window.

Monica's quinceañera was actually quite modest if her estimate of "maybe three thousand dollars" is correct. Why don't I have an exact number? Let me just come right out and say that talking to my people about money is not easy. Maybe if I were an Americana reporter with a stenographic notebook and only a sprinkling of classroom Spanish, I could get away with asking the parents how much they paid for the party. But I'm a Latina. I know the rules. They know I know the rules. To ask my host for the price tag of the fiesta would be una falta de vergüenza. And so, I learned any number of discreet ways to approach the topic. Aproximadamente, how much does a quinceañera cost in your experience? If someone were to throw a party not unlike this one, how much would that quinceañera cost them?

The one person I could openly ask this question turned out to be the quinceañera herself. But though fifteen-year-old girls are really good at knowing how much their dress or makeup session cost, they're not so good at knowing the charges for halls, or what it costs to have beef Wellington instead of Swedish meatballs for a hundred people, or what additional charge was made for the linen napkins and tablecloths or the chairs draped in white covers and tied with satin bows, which seem to be de rigueur for anything but the cheapest quinceañera. Fifteen-year-old girls like to throw out huge numbers to impress their friends, but they are not so good at addition—that is, if they paid $250 for a dress, and $250 for the limo, and the hall with a catered meal was $2,500 for one hundred people, not counting the cake made up of four cakes, which was no less than $300, and let's throw in another $100 to $200 for sessions at the beauty parlor, and at least $300 for the photographer and pictures, and because things always come up at the last minute and Mami definitely needs a new dress herself and Papi will probably have to rent a tux and some family members will need help with travel costs, another $500 to $1,000 more—anyhow, I've gone way over the low-end figure of $3,000 that Monica Ramos with uncharacteristic teenage understatement calculated.

And her father was not working.

They threw the rented apartment out the window. Why not? It's not theirs to keep anyhow, just as this American dream isn't as easy to achieve as it seems, so why not live it up, give your little girl a party she won't forget, enjoy the only thing you really have, tonight's good time, before the bills start rolling in.

When Abuelita Is No Longer a Resource

Will Cain is president and founder of *Quince Girl,* a new national magazine targeting the more than four hundred thousand Latinas in the United States who turn fifteen every year. Early in 2006, the magazine sent out a survey asking its readers how much they had spent or were planning to spend on their quinces. The resulting average was $5,000.

I confess to Will that I find that average low given the figures events planners and quinceañeras and their families have been quoting me. I'm thinking of Idalia's quinceañera, which cost her affluent Dominican family $80,000, not surprising given a guest list of more than five hundred and a fully choreographed performance by her court of twenty-eight couples (double the usual number so as not to leave out any friends or cousins) with special effects to rival a Broadway show and mermaid dresses for the girls designed by Leonel Lirio, renowned for Miss Universe Amelia Vega's gown. Granted that's the top end of the Q-scale, but the low end is rising. In Miami, Sofía's dad apologetically confessed that he was "only" spending about $12,000 on his daughter's quince, though his wife corrected him by appending, "Twelve thousand dollars not counting all the food and goodies we fed twenty-eight kids for three months of rehearsals."

"You have to remember that $5,000 takes into account the full spectrum," Will Cain reminds me about the *Quince Girl* average. "It includes the girl who is spending $25,000 with the one who might spend $1,000. The point is that even working-class folks who don't have a whole lot of purchasing power are going to devote a significant portion of their resources to this one tradition. It cuts across a wide range of strata."

Will himself did the numbers before he decided to launch his magazine. The Latino population is exploding, and it is mostly a young population. "I don't have to tell you about the demographics," Will tells me. "One out of every five teens is Hispanic. And that population is growing at the rate of 30 percent, while the non-Hispanic population rate is just 8 percent."

I'm trying to follow what Will is saying, but the question that keeps tugging at my curiosity is not about Hispanic demographics but about Will himself. Will Cain does not sound even close to a Hispanic name. How did "your run-of-the-mill white boy," as he describes himself when I ask him about his background, end up founding a magazine for young Latinas celebrating their quinceañeras?

Will, who is all of thirty-one—just over twice a quinceañera's age—grew up in Texas surrounded by Mexican Americans and has always been interested in the Hispanic culture. He was also interested in media. So, he decided to put the two things together and came up with the idea of *Quince Girl*. Though it's a shrewd economic decision, Will believes he's also providing an important service for Hispanics in this country.

"The Hispanic community is this very fractured community," he explains. "You have your Mexican Americans and your Puerto Ricans and your Cuban Americans. And the only thing that ties all these separate nationalities together—no, it's not Spanish," he says, anticipating what I might think, "in fact, many in the second and third generation don't even speak Spanish. What ties them together, the one single tie that binds all these cultures . . ."

As he drumrolls toward his conclusion, I'm thinking that Will Cain learned 65 something from growing up surrounded by a Hispanic community: a sense of drama.

". . . is this tradition celebrated across the whole diverse group: the quinceañera. I mean, it is big! And the rest of America is starting to pay attention to it."

"Amen," I say. I'm writing a whole book about it.

As if he can hear my mind thinking, Will adds, "We would not be having this conversation right now if this were not so."

What Will realized was that there was no magazine out there that these girls could consult about the tradition and trends and fashions. "Girls were in chat rooms asking each other about the ceremony, what to do. It used to be you could learn these things from your grandmother . . ." But with immigration and the amount of mobility in this country, la abuelita is not always a resource. Plus it's a different world from the one she grew up in. A different budget. Five thousand dollars is probably more than the grandparents earned in a year back in their home countries.

Does he think the tradition is becoming more popular here? 70

"Well." Will hesitates. He is rightly cautious about delivering opinions beyond what the numbers can tell him. "The quince tradition has always been important, but there's this retroculturation going on right now—"

"Retroculturation?" This is the first I've heard of the term.

"It's a pattern that's been happening with the Hispanic community," Will goes on to explain. "First generation comes to the United States, and they push to assimilate. They adopt the American culture and norms. Second generation, they want to be all-American. Many don't even speak Spanish. They aren't that familiar with the culture. By the third generation, they're born and bred here, but they have this special something that makes them unique, their Hispanic culture. They want to learn Spanish — many, in fact, speak more Spanish than the second generation. They make a concerted effort to hold on to their traditions, to establish cultural ties with their past."

Will quotes a study on Hispanic teens "just released today" by the Cheskin Group, an international consulting and marketing firm that has done a great deal of research on Hispanics. The study confirms Will's point that the up-and-coming generation of Hispanic teens is "predominantly bilingual and bicultural," celebrating its ethnic identity and combining it with mainstream teen culture. "They live on MySpace.com and shop at Abercrombie, but they listen to Spanish radio and embrace diversity," a summary of the study reads. Most important for businesses that are considering purchasing the full report with its $5,850 price tag — the cost of your average quinceañera — is that Hispanic teens are

> a bellwether for one of the most important trends shaping the future of the United States — the growth of the U.S. Hispanic population. Clearly, the future is theirs and they know it.

The future is ours and we know it. Meanwhile the present needs to be lived   75
through and paid for.

The Difference between Boys and Girls

How did the quinceañera get to be so expensive? Even the *Quince Girl* average of five thousand dollars is a lot of money to blow on a birthday party.

Kern's Nectar, which has developed a niche market of "untraditional" juices (guava, papaya, mango) popular among Latinos, sponsors a yearly Dulce Quinceañera Sweepstakes: "Fifteen lucky Quinceañeras will be awarded $1,000 each plus a year's supply of Kern's Nectars; the grand prize winner selected at random from this group takes home $15,000."

Why did Kern's Nectar single out this one tradition? "Next to marriage, a quinceañera is perhaps the most meaningful moment in a young woman's life," the press announcement reads. Given such claims, perhaps five thousand dollars is not a lot to spend on a girl's coming-of-age.

I decide to ask the girls themselves about such claims.

In the wood-paneled faculty lounge at Lawrence High School I speak with   80
a gathering of a dozen girls who have volunteered to be interviewed about the tradition. Light streams down from a magnificent stained-glass window, giving the room the hallowed feel of a chapel. At first glance, the robed scholar portrayed in the window could be Aristotle or Plato, but on closer inspection it turns out to be a woman. With one hand clutching a book, the other lifted, palm out, she seems to be setting the example of telling the truth, the whole truth,

and nothing but, which is precisely what I am after. Later I find out that this testifying woman is Emily Greene Weatherbee, the first female principal of the high school, in the 1880s.

A century and a quarter later, the room fills with the likes of students that Miss Emily could never have imagined. The young Latinas present are mostly of Dominican and Puerto Rican descent, though one junior varsity softball player in sweatpants and sweatshirt whom it's a stretch to imagine in the girly-girl getup of a quinceañera is of Ecuadorian parentage. Except for one girl who feels "really gypped" that she didn't have one (her mother said the expense was too high), the other eleven girls have all had or will be having quinceañeras before the year is out. A few days before my visit they were reminded to bring their albums along to school. They file in, lugging large pink or white wedding-type albums of what amounts to extensive photo shoots. A few of the empty-handed girls confess they left their albums at home so as not to have to haul such a heavy weight around all day.

After paging through several of these albums, I ask the girls if they consider their quinceañeras as important as their eventual marriages. "I mean if you get married," I add. I do not want to be pushing any assumptions on their life stories.

"That's the thing," Soraya pipes up. Hers is among the largest albums, borne in by her brother, who has carted it around all day for her. "You don't ever know if you're going to get married. I mean you hope you will, but that's not for sure. But you are going to turn fifteen no matter what." The other girls agree.

But if it's just about turning fifteen, boys turn fifteen, too. Why not give them a quinceañera?

"Boys don't need a quinceañera," Madeline, who left her heavy album at home, explains. "Boys are born men but girls turn into women."   85

I have pondered that statement many times in the last year. The comment highlights that very deep, heavily guarded (at least traditionally) divide in a young Latina's life when she goes from niña to señorita and becomes sexualized. In her memoir, *Silent Dancing: A Partial Remembrance of a Puerto Rican Childhood,* Judith Ortiz Cofer describes how when she became una señorita, she was watched closely as if she "carried some kind of time-bomb in [my] body that might go off any minute . . . Somehow my body with its new contours and new biological powers had changed everything: Half the world had now become a threat, or felt threatened by its potential for disaster."

"We never touch the girls," more than one male photographer told me when I interviewed them about the very popular photo shoots in Miami. The full package features young quinceañeras in a variety of provocative poses and outfits, including teensy bikinis. "We tell the mothers, 'Mami, there's a little masita that needs tucking in.' We let the mothers do it." Why was I being assured of this sexual delicacy over and over? Girls hitherto blithely living inside children's bodies turn into women with sexy, enticing cuerpos, and suddenly, it's open season. Meanwhile, boys, born men, who have been taught since day one to prove themselves as healthy machos, are going to prey on them.

When I make these observations to the Lawrence group, the roomful of young girls erupts into excited giggles. Obviously, I'm onto something.

All the girls admit that once they started developing, their parents, especially their papis, were like, *Who are you going out with? Who was that that just called? Whose parents will be there?*

These girls are on the receiving end of the ill effects of machismo, no arguing with that. But what of those poor boys having to perform from day one, if Madeline is to be believed? Often at quinceañeras, I'd spot some little tyke in a teensy tuxedo pushed and prodded to pick up some girl at a dance or given a shot of rum and encouraged to strut around. Contrary to how it's often described, machismo oppresses not just the girls but also the boys. And yet, understandably, would you want your pubescent daughter to be in the company of a grown version of this little macho, unsupervised? 90

"The quinceañera is the sanctioned way that a nice family says, okay, now my daughter may receive male attention," Gloria González, a Spanish professor at Middlebury College, explains to me about her experience growing up in Guadalajara, Mexico. "We are permitting this and we are monitoring it." That *is* a big moment. In fact, in his song "De Niña a Mujer," which is arguably *the* quinceañera anthem of all time, Julio Iglesias bewails how as a father he has been anticipating this moment when his little girl disappears forever inside a woman. The lament goes on for six pained stanzas. The song makes a daughter's growing up sound like something that's going to break her father's heart.

If so, then why celebrate this loss?

Enter the mothers.

If the father is losing his little girl, the mother is gaining a potential girlfriend. More than one girl in the Lawrence group mentions—and when she does the others agree—that planning their quinceañeras really brought them and their moms close together. "We were deciding about what dress and what decorations and addressing all the invitations. I'd say that I was spending most of my time when I wasn't in school with my mom," Soraya recalls about the months of preparations. "We were already close, but we got even closer."

Even if the ceremony itself focuses on the father-daughter transaction (he changes her flat shoes to heels, he dances her first grown-up dance in public with her), the months of preparations are intense mother-daughter time. Inevitably, this causes fights and disagreements, but even those moments offer opportunities for negotiation and bonding. And it's not just mothers and daughters, but the extended familia of tías, abuelitas, primas who often get involved. Sofía's mom in Miami, Consuelo, explained how in deciding each detail of her daughter's quinceañera her mother, her sisters, and Sofía's girl cousins would all vote. "We'd go into a store and try on dresses or pick out decorations and the whole gang would be giving their opinions." As her mom recounted how special it had been for her to share this experience with her only daughter, Sofía, who had been sitting quietly beside her, began to cry. 95

"Are you okay?" her father, who had come along for the interview, asked from the other end of the couch. "What's wrong?"

Consuelo, who had been distracted talking to me, turned to her daughter. In profile they were time-lapsed copies of each other. Consuelo understood.

Tears filled her own eyes as she reached over and the two women joined hands like little girls who were going to be best friends for life.

Remote Control

Another factor that has upped the price tag of this traditional celebration is that tricky word "traditional."

Más católico que el Papa, goes a Dominican saying, more Catholic than the pope. Our exported *tradiciones* mix and combine with those of other Latin American and Caribbean countries stateside and become more elaborate, more expensive, more traditional than they ever were back home.

In fact, to have a full-blown traditional quinceañera in our Pan-Hispanic United States is to have adopted every other Latino group's little traditions and then some. So that now, Cuban quinceañeras in Miami are hiring Mexican mariachis to sing the traditional "Las Mañanitas." The full court of fourteen *damas* and *chambelanes*, "each couple representing a year of the quinceañera's life," a mostly Mexican practice, is now a traditional must. As is the changing of the shoes to heels, which seems to originally have been a Puerto Rican embellishment. From the Puerto Ricans as well, though some say from the Mexicans, came the tradition of la última muñeca, a "last doll" dressed exactly like the quinceañera, which the girl cradles to symbolize the "end of her childhood" or "the child that she herself will be having in the not-too-distant future" (both explanations given to me by different events planners). The quinceañera might keep this last doll as a keepsake or give it away to a younger member of the family. In one celebration, perhaps inspired by the wedding bouquet, the quinceañera threw her last doll over her shoulder to be caught by a screaming group of little girls, anticipating their own future quinceañeras.

This symbol of bygone childhood is also mirrored in a Central American or Puerto Rican custom (I've heard both) of having a very little girl dress up in a minuscule version of the quinceañera's dress and be "the symbol of innocence." Sometimes she is accompanied by a little escort, though the tradition has now been further elaborated so that "the symbol of innocence" as well as a little prince and princess (slightly older) are part of a full traditional court.

There is also always some sort of photo session to commemorate the event. This is not a custom exclusive to quinceañeras. In our old countries every important life event is marked by a photograph. Your First Communion photo, your quince photo, your graduation photo, your wedding photo. Even in my husband's old German-Nebraskan family, there were the formal portraits shot in a studio, the principals in dress clothes, hair combed and tamped down: a wedding, a christening, a son shipping off to war. Of course, now there are whole albums of the young lady in different outfits, in different locations, a practice that seems to have started with the Cuban community in Miami, where girls sometimes just have the photo shoot and forego the party. Many girls also have videos made, recounting their lives since birth, with still shots and footage of themselves at different ages and credits rolling as if this were a real movie with the quinceañera playing the lead and her parents starring as "padre" and "madre" and Julio Iglesias's "De Niña a Mujer" as the score, of course. Clearly, the old-country portrait tradition has arrived stateside and, as one Cuban friend put it, "taken steroids."

The tradition of crowning the young girl is often ascribed to the Mexicans, who seem to be the group that has most ritualized the ceremony. But here in America, every quinceañera gets her tiara. The bouquet the quinceañera carries to put at the Virgin Mary's statue at the Mass is also part of the Mexican and Central American tradition, as is the Mass, which our more hedonistic Caribbean party-cultures dispensed with back home. But now the Mass and the Virgin's bouquet have become part of our Dominican and Puerto Rican and Cuban "tradition" in the United States.

One economically sensible and emotionally gratifying tradition that has not been picked up by other Hispanic groups is the Mexican custom of sponsorships by madrinas and padrinos. In a Mexican quince, every aspect of the fiesta from the cake to the dj has a sponsor, which spreads the cost of the celebration around. It is also a touching symbol of the emotional, spiritual, as well as financial investment of a whole community in this young person. Why aren't others adopting this custom?

"It's a point of pride not to go begging for your party," my Cuban friend Carmel confided. But in fact, a lot of informal sponsorships are going on. The grandmother who buys the quinceañera's earrings and necklace, the brother who gives her the birthday gift of paying for the limo, the sister who contributes to the dress. Still, when the twenty or more names of sponsors are read out in a Mexican-American quinceañera, there is a sense of public participation that is not lost on the young lady. "Everybody I knew contributed something," Verónica Fajardo remembers about her quinceañera fifteen years ago. "I felt like I received so many bendiciones, my whole community made it happen!" In actual fact, Verónica's family is from Nicaragua, but she grew up in a Mexican American neighborhood in Los Angeles, so though sponsorships were not part of the custom back home, by the time her quince came around, her family had adopted that tradition.

> They threw the house out the window for that girl's quinceañera.

Sometimes these cultural borrowings are not even coming from fellow Latinos. The tradition of lighting and dedicating candles, for example, seems to have been lifted from the Bar and Bat Mitzvah. In fact many critics see the quinceañera as going the same route as the Jewish celebration. Rabbi Jeffrey Salkin, author of *Putting God on the Guest List: How to Reclaim the Spiritual Meaning of Your Child's Bar or Bat Mitzvah*, compares this moment in time for the Hispanic community to the early 1960s for the Jewish community, when the Bar and Bat Mitzvah ceremonies became increasingly secular and extravagant. "These rites of passage are a way for a minority group to demonstrate that they have succeeded in America."

But given the statistics, our Hispanic community cannot yet lay claim to such wholesale success. For many, the quinceañera becomes an extravaganza that, as Sunita warned, puts the family further into the hole. Marie Arana of the *Washington Post* shared with me stories of visiting migrant camps in the Maryland and Virginia countryside where families with almost nothing would put out hundreds of dollars to throw their girls' quinceañeras. Perhaps these are the cookout parties everybody talks about, the ones that are under the radar because they are taking place in segregated, often undocumented populations? If you do the numbers, several hundred dollars for a migrant worker with no citizenship or papers or cushion of savings might as well be several thousand for a working-class family that owns a car and has access to unemployment benefits and credit cards.

"Today, it's all about supersizing," Nina Diaz, the executive producer of *My Super Sweet 16*, told *U.S. News & World Report*. (The price tag for a recent quince party featured in one of the episodes was $180,000.) One quince site I happened upon in cruising the Web for Q-lore—just Google "quinceañera" and you will get 8,230,000 hits (if you put the tilde over the "n") or 4,220,000 hits (if you dispense with the tilde)—urged providers to register with their site. "The Hispanic population's buying power is expected to reach $300 billion by 2006. Timing is prime to begin your Sweet 16 and Quinceañera advertising campaign. The demand for more vendors that cater to Latinos is of epic proportions."

Epic proportions; the house out the window; 8,230,000 hits and rising.

"Upholding this coming of age celebration is definitely expensive," Kimberly García concluded in her 1999 article: "Sweet 15: A Financial Affair." In the seven years since her article was published in *Hispanic Magazine*, the trend is growing. Her shocking high-end figure of $15,000 for a celebration would not raise an eyebrow now. More likely, it would elicit an apology, as with Sofía's dad. "Hispanics are likely to make a big spending decision no matter their income level," Lisa Holton reported in an article about quinceañeras for the *Chicago Sun-Times*. 110

At Disneyland, Denny Nicholas, manager of corporate and wedding sales, says he has seen anything from a modest $5,000 to $50,000 for a quinceañera, the average nowadays being about $12,000 to $15,000. When I ask Denny if he doesn't find this *average* shocking given that the poverty threshold for a family of three is $15,277, he laughs. "By the time families come to me, they've already made the decision that this is what they want. All I do is provide the elements they need to make their dreams come to life." It's just a different world, Denny reminds me. "Kids are growing up expecting so much more." He chuckles, sounding a lot more cheerful about this than I obviously feel. "I joke with my two boys that when I was growing up, the remote control was me standing by the TV and my dad saying, 'Change it to such and such a channel'!"

Dinero vs. Money

The supersizing of the tradition might well be blamed on U.S. consumerism, but the spending of money now instead of mañana seems to be our very own bagaje.

"Hispanics tend to make immediate use of their money," writes Rose Carbonell in her article "Dinero vs. Money." As part of her graduate research in Hispanic Marketing Communication at Florida State University, Carbonell studied the different attitudes of Hispanics toward money. She found that "capital accumulation is not a characteristic of Hispanics, especially because being wealthy has a negative connotation . . . as the masses of Hispanics have endured slavery and endemic poverty over the past 500 years, the meaning of wealth has been associated with the experience of others, not oneself."

Initially, I dismissed this as a kind of cultural profiling we do to ourselves as it hath been done unto us, until I found this point curiously echoed by none other than Octavio Paz, the seminal writer on Mexican identity and thought and the 1990 winner of the Nobel Prize in Literature. "Our poverty can be measured by the frequency and luxuriousness of our holidays. Fiestas are our only luxury," Paz writes in *The Labyrinth of Solitude*. "Wasting money and expending energy affirms the community's wealth in both. When life is thrown away it increases. What is sought is potency, life, health. In this sense the fiesta . . . is one of the most ancient economic forms."

Another way of understanding this phenomenon is an interesting term I 115 found bandied about in academic articles: "cultural capital." The term, originally coined by French social theorist Pierre Bourdieu, describes other kinds of assets, not monetary, that are important for status in a community. A family's throwing its daughter a lavish quinceañera represents a kind of cultural statement that counts for a lot more than the dollar cost. Thinking only of "how much it cost" in dollar amount is to simplify a much more complex and layered transaction. Patricia Saldarriaga, a professor of Spanish at Middlebury College, turned fifteen in 1975 in the port city of Talara, Peru, where her father was mayor. Although she did not want one, she was obligated to have a big quince party because of her father's position.

"*Somos decentes* is a very important concept in our communities," Eduardo Béjar, also a Spanish professor at Middlebury, explains. Eduardo, who grew up in Cuba in the forties and fifties, recalls how fiestas de quince años were a family's way of maintaining status. "Ser una familia decente. You work hard, you do things for the welfare of your family. La quinceañera reflects that: a way of saying we are decentes."

But why not have both? After all, being Latina/o is about being a hybrid, a made-in-the-U.S.A. sancocho of all our different cultures and races and histories and nationalities. Why not be una familia decente that celebrates a daughter's quinceañera without going into debt? Throw a fiesta, not the house, out the window? Our cultural habits and traditions can be revised to work better for us in the new realities we are facing right now.

But whenever I've suggested restraint to quinceañera parents and events providers, the refrain I often hear is, "We love to party!" That's the way we are.

This ethnic profiling persists both internally within our communities and without. It's a reductionist either/or way of thinking about ourselves that ill prepares us for this new millennium in which the world is shrinking and we are all becoming ever more permeable mixtures of traditions and cultures.

Mami, too, always maintained we couldn't have it both ways. We couldn't   120
be both girls from una familia decente and little Americanitas with minds (and
bodies) of our own.

"Why not?" I would challenge. "'I resist anything better than my own
diversity.'"

"Don't you answer me back!" she'd scold. "Don't you be fresh with me!"

"But that's Walt Whitman. We're reading him in English class."

That always made her stop.

"You live in this house, you respect our rules!" she'd grumble, more quietly   125
now. What monster had she created by sending her daughter to Abbot? "Who
do you think you are?"

"'I am large, I contain multitudes.'" I was finding a new way to defend myself. Technically, it was not "answering back" if I was reciting poetry.

Questions for Critical Reading

1. What is "retroculturation"? Reread Alvarez's text to locate passages that define
   the term. Can you think of additional examples? Do these examples support
   Alvarez's argument?

2. How does Alvarez feel about quinces? Search the texts for passages that reveal
   the author's stand on this cultural practice.

3. What is the value of tradition? Find quotations from Alvarez that support your
   position. Are the economic costs of traditions like quinces worth their cultural
   value?

Exploring Context

1. *My Super Sweet 16* is a television show chronicling a coming-of-age ritual similar
   to the quinceañera. Explore the Web site for the series at mtv.com/ontv/dyn/
   sweet_16/series.jhtml and connect what you find there to Alvarez's text. In what
   ways does the series reflect the issues and concerns about quinces that Alvarez
   explores? You might want to use your work on Alvarez's feelings about quinces
   from Question 2 of Questions for Critical Reading in making your response.

2. This selection opens with Alvarez's visit to Isabella Martínez Wall, who runs the
   Web site Bella Quinceañera (bellaquinceanera.com). How does the Web site, in
   its design and advertising, reflect the points that Alvarez wants to make about
   this ritual? Does the Web site reflect Alvarez's arguments about quinces? How
   does the Web site support or complicate your response to Question 3 of Questions for Critical Reading about the value of tradition?

3. What coming-of-age rituals exist in other cultures? Use the Web to search for
   information on another ritual, perhaps one from your own cultural, national,
   ethnic, or religious background. How is it preserved today? Does it have the
   same economic implications of the quince? In what ways is it connected to
   quinceañeras?

Questions for Connecting

1. Daniel Gilbert's essay "Reporting Live from Tomorrow" (p. 169) is about predicting our future happiness. How can his ideas help explain the features of quinces that Alvarez explores? Is the quinceañera a super-replicator? Does it function as a kind of cultural surrogate for womanhood? Is it possible to synthesize Gilbert's concepts with Alvarez's examples?

2. Retroculturation seems to promote diversity. How might colleges and universities promote retroculturation on their campuses? Would such a strategy solve the problems with community and diversity that Rebekah Nathan notes in "Community and Diversity" (p. 228)? Draw on your definition of the term from Question 1 in Questions for Critical Reading.

3. In "False Identifications: Minority Populations Mourn Diana" (p. 454), Diana Taylor examines the performance of grief by looking at how minority populations mourn celebrity figures such as Princess Diana. How do quinces also act as a cultural performance? Do they perform some sort of social drama? What is the "hauntology" of the quince? Synthesize these two cultural performances in order to argue for the function of social rituals. Support your argument with quotations from the texts.

Language Matters

1. Each discipline has a specific approach to evidence. Start by finding information on how research is done in your intended major or field. How would you pursue Alvarez's arguments through that field? How would that discipline make this argument?

2. In small groups, select a common grammatical error, such as sentence fragments or subject-verb agreement problems. Select a key quotation from Alvarez's text and then change it to represent the error. Share the original and altered quotations in small groups to create a list of error examples and corrections using this essay.

3. Spanish has a unique punctuation mark—an inverted question mark at the start of a question. In small groups, create your own punctuation marks and apply them to passages from Alvarez. What do you want your punctuation to do? What does any punctuation mark do?

Assignments for Writing

1. How do quinceañeras help to define self-identity in the Hispanic community? Write a paper in which you define the relationship between these rituals and self-identity. In making your argument you may want to use the other rituals you explored in Question 3 of Exploring Context or some of the concepts you synthesized in Questions for Connecting, such as super-replicators or cultural performance. To help you begin your critical thinking on this assignment, consider

these questions: How do traditions, both native and acquired, contribute to the development of identity? How does gender determine self-identity in the Hispanic community? Why do only girls receive quinceañeras? What part does retroculturation play in the establishing of self-identity? Is this rite of passage similar or different to rites of passage in other cultures? Does the commercialization of the quinceañera affect its overall value in establishing a girl's self-worth and self-identity? If so, how?

2. Alvarez examines the expanding marketplace emerging around the quinceañera. What role does business play in developing ideas of femininity? Write an essay in which you explore the intersection of commercialism and gender. In making your argument, draw not only from Alvarez's text but also from your work on the value of tradition in Question 3 of Questions for Critical Reading or your responses to the questions in Exploring Context. The following questions might help you locate a focus for your response; use them to think critically about this assignment: Does the quinceañera lend itself to the promotion of a specific view of femininity? What function does the Quinceañera Expo play in manufacturing femininity? How does the media shape perceptions of femininity in the Hispanic community? Is there still a generational gap in determining the social position of women?

3. Quinceañeras have an important role to play not simply in the lives of individuals but also, as Alvarez makes clear, in the lives of families and communities. Using Alvarez's text and your response to Question 3 of Questions for Critical Reading on the value of tradition and/or Question 3 of Questions for Connecting on cultural performances, determine the function of social rituals like the quinceañera in the lives of communities. Write a paper in which you specify the role of social ritual in community life, using Alvarez as well as your own experiences. Consider: What is the role of the individual in a community effort? What is the effect on a community when cultural events absorb outside cultural influences? How does retroculturation revitalize communities?

Kwame Anthony Appiah

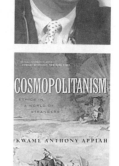

Kwame Anthony Appiah was born in London, grew up in Ghana, and earned a Ph.D. at Cambridge University. He is the Laurance S. Rockefeller University Professor of Philosophy and the University Center for Human Values at Princeton University. He has also taught at Duke, Harvard, Yale, Cornell, Cambridge, and the University of Ghana. He serves as an editor for *Transition Magazine* and has published numerous academic books and articles as well as three detective novels. In 2008, Appiah was recognized for his contributions to racial, ethnic, and religious relations when Brandeis University awarded him the first Joseph B. and Toby Gittler Prize.

Appiah's *Cosmopolitanism: Ethics in a World of Strangers* (2006) was one of the first books published in Henry Louis Gates Jr.'s "Issues of Our Time" series, which aims to tackle the important concerns of the information age. With *Cosmopolitanism*, Appiah examines the imaginary boundaries that have separated people around the world and the ways we can redraw those boundaries. Appiah claims with the book's title that we are all citizens of the world. In the time of al Qaeda, we can no longer afford to draw significant lines between different groups and regions. Humanity has fundamental commonalities, Appiah suggests, and we should embrace them.

The following selections, "Making Conversation" and "The Primacy of Practice," appear in *Cosmopolitanism* as the introduction and one of the book's chapters. Appiah first defines *cosmopolitanism* and its problems but ultimately determines that practicing a citizenship of the world is not only helpful in a post-9/11 world, but necessary. There is no divide between "us" and "them," he suggests, only a basic moral obligation we have to each other. It is not necessary for people to agree to behave morally for the right reason, or the right god, or the right country or custom. It is only necessary that they agree to behave morally. Conversation, Appiah writes, is the best starting point.

It's tempting to reduce what follows to something as simple as "We should all just get along," but Appiah is also challenging us to think about how we can make that happen. How primal is practice in your own life? Is what you do more important than why you do it?

▶ TAGS: *human dignity*, *community*, *globalization*, *identity*, *conversation*, *obligation*

Making Conversation

Our ancestors have been human for a very long time. If a normal baby girl born forty thousand years ago were kidnapped by a time traveler and raised in a normal family in New York, she would be ready for college in eighteen years. She would learn English (along with—who knows?—Spanish or Chinese), understand trigonometry, follow baseball and pop music; she would probably want a pierced tongue and a couple of tattoos. And she would be unrecognizably different from the brothers and sisters she left behind. For most of human history, we were born into small societies of a few score people, bands of hunters and gatherers, and would see, on a typical day, only people we had known most of our lives. Everything our long-ago ancestors ate or wore, every tool they used, every shrine at which they worshipped, was made within that group. Their knowledge came from their ancestors or from their own experiences. That is the world that shaped us, the world in which our nature was formed.

Now, if I walk down New York's Fifth Avenue on an ordinary day, I will have within sight more human beings than most of those prehistoric hunter-gatherers saw in a lifetime. Between then and now some of our forebears settled down and learned agriculture; created villages, towns, and, in the end, cities; discovered the power of writing. But it was a slow process. The population of classical Athens when Socrates died, at the end of the fifth century BC, could have lived in a few large skyscrapers. Alexander set off from Macedon to conquer the world three-quarters of a century later with an army of between thirty and forty thousand, which is far fewer people than commute into Des Moines every Monday morning. When, in the first century, the population of Rome reached a million, it was the first city of its size. To keep it fed, the Romans had had to build an empire that brought home grain from Africa. By then, they had already worked out how to live cheek by jowl in societies where most of those who spoke your language and shared your laws and grew the food on your table were people you would never know. It is, I think, little short of miraculous that brains shaped by our long history could have been turned to this new way of life.

Even once we started to build these larger societies, most people knew little about the ways of other tribes, and could affect just a few local lives. Only in the past couple of centuries, as every human community has gradually been drawn into a single web of trade and a global network of information, have we come to a point where each of us can realistically imagine contacting any other of our six billion conspecifics and sending that person something worth having: a radio, an antibiotic, a good idea. Unfortunately, we could also send, through negligence as easily as malice, things that will cause harm: a virus, an airborne pollutant, a bad idea. And the possibilities of good and of ill are multiplied beyond all measure when it comes to policies carried out by governments in our name. Together, we can ruin poor farmers by dumping our subsidized grain into their markets, cripple industries by punitive tariffs, deliver weapons that will kill thousands upon thousands. Together, we can raise standards of living by adopting new policies on trade and aid, prevent or treat diseases with vaccines and pharmaceuticals, take measures against global climate change, encourage resistance to tyranny and a concern for the worth of each human life.

And, of course, the worldwide web of information—radio, television, telephones, the Internet—means not only that we can affect lives everywhere but that we can learn about life anywhere, too. Each person you know about and can affect is someone to whom you have responsibilities: To say this is just to affirm the very idea of morality. The challenge, then, is to take minds and hearts formed over the long millennia of living in local troops and equip them with ideas and institutions that will allow us to live together as the global tribe we have become.

Under what rubric to proceed? Not "globalization"—a term that once referred to a marketing strategy, and then came to designate a macroeconomic thesis, and now can seem to encompass everything, and nothing. Not "multiculturalism," another shape shifter, which so often designates the disease it purports to cure. With some ambivalence, I have settled on "cosmopolitanism." Its meaning is equally disputed, and celebrations of the "cosmopolitan" can suggest an unpleasant posture of superiority toward the putative provincial. You imagine a Comme des Garçons–clad sophisticate with a platinum frequent-flyer card regarding, with kindly condescension, a ruddy-faced farmer in workman's overalls. And you wince.

Maybe, though, the term can be rescued. It has certainly proved a survivor. Cosmopolitanism dates at least to the Cynics of the fourth century BC, who first coined the expression cosmopolitan, "citizen of the cosmos." The formulation was meant to be paradoxical, and reflected the general Cynic skepticism toward custom and tradition. A citizen—a *politēs*—belonged to a particular *polis*, a city to which he or she owed loyalty. The cosmos referred to the world, not in the sense of the earth, but in the sense of the universe. Talk of cosmopolitanism originally signaled, then, a rejection of the conventional view that every civilized person belonged to a community among communities.

The creed was taken up and elaborated by the Stoics, beginning in the third century BC, and that fact proved of critical importance in its subsequent intellectual history. For the Stoicism of the Romans—Cicero, Seneca, Epictetus, and the emperor Marcus Aurelius—proved congenial to many Christian intellectuals, once Christianity became the religion of the Roman Empire. It is profoundly ironic that, though Marcus Aurelius sought to suppress the new Christian sect, his extraordinarily personal *Meditations*, a philosophical diary written in the second century AD as he battled to save the Roman Empire from barbarian invaders, has attracted Christian readers for nearly two millennia. Part of its appeal, I think, has always been the way the Stoic emperor's cosmopolitan conviction of the oneness of humanity echoes Saint Paul's insistence that "there is neither Jew nor Greek, there is neither bond nor free, there is neither male nor female: for ye are all one in Christ Jesus."[1]

Cosmopolitanism's later career wasn't without distinction. It underwrote some of the great moral achievements of the Enlightenment, including the 1789 "Declaration of the Rights of Man" and Immanuel Kant's work proposing a "league of nations." In a 1788 essay in his journal *Teutscher Merkur*, Christoph

Martin Wieland—once called the German Voltaire—wrote, in a characteristic expression of the ideal, "Cosmopolitans . . . regard all the peoples of the earth as so many branches of a single family, and the universe as a state, of which they, with innumerable other rational beings, are citizens, promoting together under the general laws of nature the perfection of the whole, while each in his own fashion is busy about his own well-being."[2] And Voltaire himself—whom nobody, alas, ever called the French Wieland—spoke eloquently of the obligation to understand those with whom we share the planet, linking that need explicitly with our global economic interdependence. "Fed by the products of their soil, dressed in their fabrics, amused by games they invented, instructed even by their ancient moral fables, why would we neglect to understand the mind of these nations, among whom our European traders have traveled ever since they could find a way to get to them?"[3]

So there are two strands that intertwine in the notion of cosmopolitanism. One is the idea that we have obligations to others, obligations that stretch beyond those to whom we are related by the ties of kith and kind, or even the more formal ties of a shared

> Cosmopolitanism is the name not of the solution but of the challenge.

citizenship. The other is that we take seriously the value not just of human life but of particular human lives, which means taking an interest in the practices and beliefs that lend them significance. People are different, the cosmopolitan knows, and there is much to learn from our differences. Because there are so many human possibilities worth exploring, we neither expect nor desire that every person or every society should converge on a single mode of life. Whatever our obligations are to others (or theirs to us) they often have the right to go their own way. As we'll see, there will be times when these two ideals—universal concern and respect for legitimate difference—clash. There's a sense in which cosmopolitanism is the name not of the solution but of the challenge.

A citizen of the world: How far can we take that idea? Are you really supposed to abjure all local allegiances and partialities in the name of this vast abstraction, humanity? Some proponents of cosmopolitanism were pleased to think so; and they often made easy targets of ridicule. "Friend of men, and enemy of almost every man he had to do with," Thomas Carlyle memorably said of the eighteenth-century physiocrat the Marquis de Mirabeau, who wrote the treatise L'Ami des hommes when he wasn't too busy jailing his own son. "A lover of his kind, but a hater of his kindred," Edmund Burke said of Jean-Jacques Rousseau, who handed each of the five children he fathered to an orphanage.

Yet the impartialist version of the cosmopolitan creed has continued to hold a steely fascination. Virginia Woolf once exhorted "freedom from unreal loyalties"— to nation, sex, school, neighborhood, and on and on. Leo Tolstoy, in the same spirit, inveighed against the "stupidity" of patriotism. "To destroy war, destroy patriotism," he wrote in an 1896 essay—a couple of decades before the tsar was swept away by a revolution in the name of the international working class. Some contemporary philosophers have similarly urged that the boundaries of nations are morally irrelevant—accidents of history with no rightful claim on our conscience.

But if there are friends of cosmopolitanism who make me nervous, I am happy to be opposed to cosmopolitanism's noisiest foes. Both Hitler and Stalin—who agreed about little else, save that murder was the first instrument of politics—launched regular invectives against "rootless cosmopolitans"; and while, for both, anti-cosmopolitanism was often just a euphemism for anti-Semitism, they were right to see cosmopolitanism as their enemy. For they both required a kind of loyalty to one portion of humanity—a nation, a class—that ruled out loyalty to all of humanity. And the one thought that cosmopolitans share is that no local loyalty can ever justify forgetting that each human being has responsibilities to every other. Fortunately, we need take sides neither with the nationalist who abandons all foreigners nor with the hardcore cosmopolitan who regards her friends and fellow citizens with icy impartiality. The position worth defending might be called (in both senses) a partial cosmopolitanism.

There's a striking passage, to this point, in George Eliot's *Daniel Deronda*, published in 1876, which was, as it happens, the year when England's first—and, so far, last—Jewish prime minister, Benjamin Disraeli, was elevated to the peerage as Earl of Beaconsfield. Disraeli, though baptized and brought up in the Church of England, always had a proud consciousness of his Jewish ancestry (given the family name, which his father spelled D'Israeli, it would have been hard to ignore). But Deronda, who has been raised in England as a Christian gentleman, discovers his Jewish ancestry only as an adult; and his response is to commit himself to the furtherance of his "hereditary people":

> It was as if he had found an added soul in finding his ancestry—his judgment no longer wandering in the mazes of impartial sympathy, but choosing, with the noble partiality which is man's best strength, the closer fellowship that makes sympathy practical—exchanging that bird's-eye reasonableness which soars to avoid preference and loses all sense of quality, for the generous reasonableness of drawing shoulder to shoulder with men of like inheritance.

Notice that in claiming a Jewish loyalty—an "added soul"—Deronda is not rejecting a human one. As he says to his mother, "I think it would have been right that I should have been brought up with the consciousness that I was a Jew, but it must always have been a good to me to have as wide an instruction and sympathy as possible." This is the same Deronda, after all, who has earlier explained his decision to study abroad in these eminently cosmopolitan terms: "I want to be an Englishman, but I want to understand other points of view. And I want to get rid of a merely English attitude in studies." [4] Loyalties and local allegiances determine more than what we want; they determine who we are. And Eliot's talk of the "closer fellowship that makes sympathy practical" echoes Cicero's claim that "society and human fellowship will be best served if we confer the most kindness on those with whom we are most closely associated." [5] A creed that disdains the partialities of kinfolk and community may have a past, but it has no future.

In the final message my father left for me and my sisters, he wrote, "Remember you are citizens of the world." But as a leader of the independence movement in what was then the Gold Coast, he never saw a conflict between local partialities and a universal morality—between being part of the place you were and a part of a broader human community. Raised with this father and an English mother, who was both deeply connected to our family in England and fully rooted in Ghana, where she has now lived for half a century, I always had a sense of family and tribe that was multiple and overlapping: Nothing could have seemed more commonplace.

Surely nothing *is* more commonplace. In geological terms, it has been a blink   15 of an eye since human beings first left Africa, and there are few spots where we have not found habitation. The urge to migrate is no less "natural" than the urge to settle. At the same time, most of those who have learned the languages and customs of other places haven't done so out of mere curiosity. A few were looking for food for thought; most were looking for food. Thoroughgoing ignorance about the ways of others is largely a privilege of the powerful. The well-traveled polyglot is as likely to be among the worst off as among the best off—as likely to be found in a shantytown as at the Sorbonne. So cosmopolitanism shouldn't be seen as some exalted attainment: It begins with the simple idea that in the human community, as in national communities, we need to develop habits of coexistence: conversation in its older meaning, of living together, association.

And conversation in its modern sense, too. The town of Kumasi, where I grew up, is the capital of Ghana's Asante region, and, when I was a child, its main commercial thoroughfare was called Kingsway Street. In the 1950s, if you wandered down it toward the railway yards at the center of town, you'd first pass by Baboo's Bazaar, which sold imported foods and was run by the eponymous Mr. Baboo—a charming and courteous Indian—with the help of his growing family. Mr. Baboo was active in the Rotary and could always be counted on to make a contribution to the various charitable projects that are among the diversions of Kumasi's middle class, but the truth is that I remember Mr. Baboo mostly because he always had a good stock of candies and because he was always smiling. I can't reconstruct the tour down the rest of the street, for not every store had bonbons to anchor my memories. Still, I remember that we got rice from Irani Brothers; and that we often stopped in on various Lebanese and Syrian families, Muslim and Maronite, and even a philosophical Druze, named Mr. Hanni, who sold imported cloth and who was always ready, as I grew older, for a conversation about the troubles of his native Lebanon. There were other "strangers" among us, too: In the military barracks in the middle of town, you could find many northerners among the "other ranks," privates and NCOs, their faces etched in distinctive patterns of ethnic scarification. And then there was the occasional European—the Greek architect, the Hungarian artist, the Irish doctor, the Scots engineer, some English barristers and judges, and a wildly international assortment of professors at the university, many of whom, unlike the colonial officials, remained after independence. I never thought to wonder, as a child, why these people traveled so far to live and work in my hometown; still, I was glad they did. Conversations across boundaries can be fraught, all the more so as the world grows smaller and the stakes grow larger. It's therefore worth remembering that they can also be a pleasure. What academics sometimes dub "cultural otherness" should prompt neither piety nor consternation.

Cosmopolitanism is an adventure and an ideal: But you can't have any respect for human diversity and expect everyone to become cosmopolitan. The obligations of those who wish to exercise their legitimate freedom to associate with their own kind—to keep the rest of the world away as the Amish do in the United States—are only the same as the basic obligations we all have: to do for others what morality requires. Still, a world in which communities are neatly hived off from one another seems no longer a serious option, if it ever was. And the way of segregation and seclusion has always been anomalous in our perpetually voyaging species. Cosmopolitanism isn't hard work; repudiating it is.

In the wake of 9/11, there has been a lot of fretful discussion about the divide between "us" and "them." What's often taken for granted is a picture of a world in which conflicts arise, ultimately, from conflicts between values. This is what we take to be good; that is what they take to be good. That picture of the world has deep philosophical roots; it is thoughtful, well worked out, plausible. And, I think, wrong.

I should be clear: This book is not a book about policy, nor is it a contribution to the debates about the true face of globalization. I'm a philosopher by trade, and philosophers rarely write really useful books. All the same, I hope to persuade you that there are interesting conceptual questions that lie beneath the facts of globalization. The cluster of questions I want to take up can seem pretty abstract. How real are values? What do we talk about when we talk about difference? Is any form of relativism right? When do morals and manners clash? Can culture be "owned"? What do we owe strangers by virtue of our shared humanity? But the way these questions play out in our lives isn't so very abstract. By the end, I hope to have made it harder to think of the world as divided between the West and the Rest; between locals and moderns; between a bloodless ethic of profit and a bloody ethic of identity; between "us" and "them." The foreignness of foreigners, the strangeness of strangers: These things are real enough. It's just that we've been encouraged, not least by well-meaning intellectuals, to exaggerate their significance by an order of magnitude.

As I'll be arguing, it is an error—to which we dwellers in a scientific age are peculiarly prone—to resist talk of "objective" values. In the absence of a natural science of right and wrong, someone whose model of knowledge is physics or biology will be inclined to conclude that values are not real; or, at any rate, not real like atoms and nebulae. In the face of this temptation, I want to hold on to at least one important aspect of the objectivity of values: that there are some values that are, and should be, universal, just as there are lots of values that are, and must be, local. We can't hope to reach a final consensus on how to rank and order such values. That's why the model I'll be returning to is that of conversation—and, in particular, conversation between people from different ways of life. The world is getting more crowded: In the next half a century the population of our once foraging species will approach nine billion. Depending on the circumstances, conversations across boundaries can be delightful, or just vexing: What they mainly are, though, is inevitable.

The Primacy of Practice

Local Agreements

Among the Asante, you will be glad to hear, incest between brothers and sisters and parents and children is shunned as *akyiwadeɛ*. You can agree with an Asante that it's wrong, even if you don't accept his explanation of why. If my interest is in discouraging theft, I needn't worry that one person might refrain from theft because she believes in the Golden Rule; another because of her conception of personal integrity; a third because she thinks God frowns on it. I've said that value language helps shape common responses of thought, action, and feeling. But when the issue is what to do, differences in what we think and feel can fall away. We know from our own family lives that conversation doesn't start with agreement on principles. Who but someone in the grip of a terrible theory would want to insist on an agreement on principles before discussing which movie to go to, what to have for dinner, when to go to bed?

Indeed, our political coexistence, as subjects or citizens, depends on being able to agree about practices while disagreeing about their justification. For many long years, in medieval Spain under the Moors and later in the Ottoman Near East, Jews and Christians of various denominations lived under Muslim rule. This modus vivendi was possible only because the various communities did not have to agree on a set of universal values. In seventeenth-century Holland, starting roughly in the time of Rembrandt, the Sephardic Jewish community began to be increasingly well integrated into Dutch society, and there was a great deal of intellectual as well as social exchange between Christian and Jewish communities. Christian toleration of Jews did not depend on express agreement on fundamental values. Indeed, these historical examples of religious toleration—you might even call them early experiments in multiculturalism—should remind us of the most obvious fact about our own society.

Americans share a willingness to be governed by the system set out in the U.S. Constitution. But that does not require anyone to agree to any particular claims or values. The Bill of Rights tells us, "Congress shall make no law respecting an establishment of religion, or prohibiting the free exercise thereof...." Yet we don't need to agree on what values underlie our acceptance of the First Amendment's treatment of religion. Is it religious toleration as an end in itself? Or is it a Protestant commitment to the sovereignty of the individual conscience? Is it prudence, which recognizes that trying to force religious conformity on people only leads to civil discord? Or is it skepticism that any religion has it right? Is it to protect the government from religion? Or religion from the government? Or is it some combination of these, or other, aims?

Cass Sunstein, the American legal scholar, has written eloquently that our understanding of Constitutional law is a set of what he calls "incompletely theorized agreements."[6] People mostly agree that it would be wrong for the Congress to pass laws prohibiting the building of mosques, for example, without agreeing exactly as to why. Many of us would, no doubt, mention the First Amendment (even though we don't agree about what values it embodies). But others would ground their judgment not in any particular law but in a conception, say, of democracy or in the equal citizenship of Muslims, neither of which is explicitly mentioned in the Constitution. There is no agreed-upon answer—and the point is there doesn't need to be. We can live together without agreeing on what the values are that make it good to live together; we can agree about what to do in most cases, without agreeing about why it is right.

I don't want to overstate the claim. No doubt there are widely shared values that help Americans live together in amity. But they certainly don't live together successfully because they have a shared theory of value or a shared story as to how to bring "their" values to bear in each case. They each have a pattern of life that they are used to; and neighbors who are, by and large, used to them. So long as this settled pattern is not seriously disrupted, they do not worry over-much about whether their fellow citizens agree with them or their theories about how to live. Americans tend to have, in sum, a broadly liberal reaction when they *do* hear about their fellow citizens' doing something that they would not do themselves: They mostly think it is not their business and not the government's business either. And, as a general rule, their shared Americanness matters to them, although many of their fellow Americans are remarkably unlike themselves. It's just that what they do share can be less substantial than we're inclined to suppose.

Changing Our Minds

It's not surprising, then, that what makes conversation across boundaries worthwhile isn't that we're likely to come to a reasoned agreement about values. I don't say that we can't change minds, but the reasons we exchange in our conversations will seldom do much to persuade others who do not share our fundamental evaluative judgments already. (Remember: The same goes, mutatis mutandis, for factual judgments.)

When we offer judgments, after all, it's rarely because we have applied well-thought-out principles to a set of facts and deduced an answer. Our efforts to justify what we have done—or what we plan to do—are typically made up after the event, rationalizations of what we have decided intuitively. And a good deal of what we intuitively take to be right, we take to be right just because it is what we are used to. If you live in a society where children are spanked, you will probably spank your children. You will believe that it is a good way to teach them right from wrong and that, despite the temporary suffering caused by a beating, they will end up better off for it. You will point to the wayward child and say, sotto voce, that his parents do not know how to discipline him; you will mean that they do not beat him enough. You will also, no doubt, recognize that there are people who beat their children too hard or too often. So you will recognize that beating a child can sometimes be cruel.

Much the same can be said about the practice of female genital cutting. . . . If you've grown up taking it for granted as the normal thing to do, you will probably respond at first with surprise to someone who thinks it is wrong. You will offer reasons for doing it—that unmodified sexual organs are unaesthetic; that the ritual gives young people the opportunity to display courage in their transition to adulthood; that you can see their excitement as they go to their ceremony, their pride when they return. You will say that it is very strange that someone who has not been through it should presume to know whether or not sex is pleasurable for you. And, if someone should try to force you to stop from the outside, you may decide to defend the practice as an expression of your cultural identity. But this is likely to be as much a rationalization as are the arguments of your critics. They say it is mutilation, but is that any more than a reflex response to an unfamiliar practice? They exaggerate the medical risks. They say that female circumcision demeans women, but do not seem to think that male circumcision demeans men.

I am not endorsing these claims, or celebrating the argumentative impasse, or, indeed, the poverty of reason in much discussion within and across cultures. But let's recognize this simple fact: A large part of what we do we do because it *is* just what we do. You get up in the morning at eight-thirty. Why *that* time? You have coffee and cereal. Why not porridge? You send the kids to school. Why not teach them at home? You have to work. Why that job, though? Reasoning—by which I mean the public act of exchanging stated justifications—comes in not when we are going on in the usual way, but when we are thinking about change. And when it comes to change, what moves people is often not an argument from a principle, not a long discussion about values, but just a gradually acquired new way of seeing things.

My father, for example, came from a society in which neither women nor men were traditionally circumcised. Indeed, circumcision was *akyiwadeε*; and since chiefs were supposed to be unblemished, circumcision was a barrier to holding royal office. Nevertheless, as he tells us in his autobiography, he decided as a teenager to have himself circumcised.

> As was the custom in those happy days, the young girls of Adum would gather together in a playing field nearby on moonlight nights to regale themselves by singing traditional songs and dancing from about 7 PM until midnight each day of the week.
>
> . . . On one such night, these girls suddenly started a new song that completely bowled us over: Not only were the words profane in the extreme, but they also constituted the most daring challenge to our manhood and courage ever flung at us. More than that, we were being invited to violate an age-old tradition of our ancestors, long respected among our people, namely the taboo on circumcision. Literally translated the words were:

"An uncircumcised penis is detestable, and those who are uncircumcised should come for money from us so that they can get circumcised. We shall never marry the uncircumcised."[7]

To begin with, my father and his friends thought the girls would relent. But
they were wrong. And so, after consultation with his mates, my father found
himself a *wansam*—a Muslim circumcision specialist—and had the operation
performed. (It was, he said, the most painful experience of his life and, if he'd
had it to do again, he would have refrained. He did not, of course, have the advantage of the preparation, the companionship of boys of his own age, and the
prestige of suffering bravely that would have come if the practice had been an
Akan tradition.)

My father offered a reason for this decision: He and his friends conceded
that "as our future sweethearts and wives, they were entitled to be heard in
their plea in favor of male circumcision, even though they were not prepared to
go in for female circumcision, which was also a taboo among our people." This
explanation invites a question, however. Why did these young women, in the
heart of Asante, decide to urge the young men of Adum to do what was not just
untraditional but taboo? One possibility is that circumcision somehow became
identified in their minds with being modern. If that was the point, my father
would have been sympathetic. He was traditional in some ways; but like many
people in Kumasi in the early twentieth century, he was also excited by a modern world that was bringing new music, new technology, new possibilities. To
volunteer for circumcision in his society he surely had not just to hear the plea
of the young women of Adum but to understand—and agree with—the impulse behind it. And, as I say, it may have been exactly the fact that it was untraditional that made it appealing. Circumcision—especially because it carried
with it exclusion from the possibilities of traditional political office—became a
way of casting his lot with modernity.

This new fashion among the young people of Adum was analogous to, if
more substantial than, the change in taste that has produced a generation of
Americans with piercings and tattoos. And that change was not simply the result of argument and debate, either (even though, as anyone who has argued
with a teenager about a pierced belly button will attest, people on both sides can
come up with a whole slew of arguments). There's some social-psychological
truth in the old Flanders & Swann song "The Reluctant Cannibal," about a
young "savage" who pushes away from the table and declares, "I won't eat
people. Eating people is wrong." His father has all the arguments, such as they
are. ("But people have always eaten people, / What else is there to eat? / If the Juju
had meant us not to eat people, / He wouldn't have made us of meat!") The son,
though, just repeats his newfound conviction: Eating people is wrong. He's just
sure of it, he'll say so again and again, and he'll win the day by declamation.

Or take the practice of foot-binding in China, which persisted for a thousand
years—and was largely eradicated within a generation. The anti-foot-binding
campaign, in the 1910s and 1920s, did circulate facts about the disadvantages
of bound feet, but those couldn't have come as news to most people. Perhaps

more effective was the campaign's emphasis that no other country went in for the practice; in the world at large, then, China was "losing face" because of it. Natural-foot societies were formed, with members forswearing the practice and further pledging that their sons would not marry women with bound feet. As the movement took hold, scorn was heaped on older women with bound feet, and they were forced to endure the agonies of unbinding. What had been beautiful became ugly; ornamentation became disfigurement. (The success of the anti-foot-binding campaign was undoubtedly a salutary development, but it was not without its victims. Think of some of the last women whose feet were bound, who had to struggle to find husbands.) The appeal to reason alone can explain neither the custom nor its abolition.

So, too, with other social trends. Just a couple of generations ago, in most of the industrialized world, most people thought that middle-class women would ideally be housewives and mothers. If they had time on their hands, they could engage in charitable work or entertain one another; a few of them might engage in the arts, writing novels, painting, performing in music, theater, and dance. But there was little place for them in the "learned professions"—as lawyers or doctors, priests or rabbis; and if they were to be academics, they would teach young women and probably remain unmarried. They were not likely to make their way in politics, except perhaps at the local level. And they were not made welcome in science. How much of the shift away from these assumptions is the result of arguments? Isn't a significant part of it just the consequence of our getting used to new ways of doing things? The arguments that kept the old pattern in place were not—to put it mildly—terribly good. If the *reasons* for the old sexist way of doing things had been the problem, the women's movement could have been done with in a couple of weeks. There are still people, I know, who think that the ideal life for any woman is making and managing a home. There are more who think that it is an honorable option. Still, the vast majority of Westerners would be appalled at the idea of trying to force women back into these roles. Arguments mattered for the women who made the women's movement and the men who responded to them. This I do not mean to deny. But their greatest achievement has been to change our habits. In the 1950s, if a college-educated woman wanted to go to law or business school, the natural response was "Why?" Now the natural response is "Why not?"

> **Reasoning . . . comes in not when we are going on in the usual way, but when we are thinking about change.**

Or consider another example: In much of Europe and North America, in places where a generation ago homosexuals were social outcasts and homosexual acts were illegal, lesbian and gay couples are increasingly being recognized by their families, by society, and by the law. This is true despite the continued opposition of major religious groups and a significant and persisting undercurrent of social disapproval. Both sides make arguments, some good, most bad, if you apply a philosophical standard of reasoning. But if you ask the social scientists what has produced this change, they will rightly not start with a story about reasons. They will give you a historical account that concludes with a sort of perspectival shift. The increasing presence of "openly gay" people in social life and in the media has changed our habits. Over the last thirty or so years, instead of thinking about the private activity of gay *sex*, many Americans started thinking about the public category of gay *people*. Even those who continue to think of the sex with disgust now find it harder to deny these people their respect and concern (and some of them have learned, as we all did with our own parents, that it's better not to think too much about other people's sex lives anyway).

Now, I don't deny that all the time, at every stage, people were talking, giving each other reasons to do things: accept their children, stop treating homosexuality as a medical disorder, disagree with their churches, come out. Still, the short version of the story is basically this: People got used to lesbians and gay people. I am urging that we should learn about people in other places, take an interest in their civilizations, their arguments, their errors, their achievements, not because that will bring us to agreement, but because it will help us get used to one another. If that is the aim, then the fact that we have all these opportunities for disagreement about values need not put us off. Understanding one another may be hard; it can certainly be interesting. But it doesn't require that we come to agreement.

Fighting for the Good

I've said we can live in harmony without agreeing on underlying values (except, perhaps, the cosmopolitan value of living together). It works the other way, too: We can find ourselves in conflict when we do agree on values. Warring parties are seldom at odds because they have clashing conceptions of "the good." On the contrary, conflict arises most often when two peoples have identified the same thing as good. The fact that both Palestinians and Israelis—in particular, that both observant Muslims and observant Jews—have a special relation to Jerusalem, to the Temple Mount, has been a reliable source of trouble. The problem isn't that they disagree about the importance of Jerusalem: The problem is exactly that they both care for it deeply and, in part, for the same reasons. Muhammad, in the first years of Islam, urged his followers to turn toward Jerusalem in prayer because he had learned the story of Jerusalem from the Jews among whom he lived in Mecca. Nor is it an accident that the West's fiercest adversaries among other societies tend to come from among the most Westernized of the group. *Mon semblable mon frère?* Only if the *frère* you have in mind is Cain. We all know now that the foot soldiers of al Qaeda who committed the mass murders at the Twin Towers and the Pentagon were not Bedouins from the desert; not unlettered fellahin.

Indeed, there's a wider pattern here. Who in Ghana excoriated the British and built the movement for independence? Not the farmers and the peasants. Not the chiefs. It was the Western-educated bourgeoisie. And when in the 1950s Kwame Nkrumah—who went to college in Pennsylvania and lived in London—created a nationalist mass movement, at its core were soldiers who had returned from fighting a war in the British army, urban market women who traded Dutch prints, trade unionists who worked in industries created by colonialism, and the so-called veranda boys, who had been to colonial secondary schools, learned English, studied history and geography in textbooks written in England. Who led the resistance to the British Raj? An Indian-born South African lawyer, trained in the British courts, whose name was Gandhi; an Indian named Nehru who wore Savile Row suits and sent his daughter to an English boarding school; and Muhammad Ali Jinnah, founder of Pakistan, who joined Lincoln's Inn in London and became a barrister at the age of nineteen.

In Shakespeare's *Tempest*, Caliban, the original inhabitant of an island commandeered by Prospero, roars at his domineering colonizer, "You taught me language and my profit on't / Is, I know how to curse." It is no surprise that Prospero's "abhorred slave" has been a figure of colonial resistance for literary nationalists all around the world. And in borrowing from Caliban, they have also borrowed from Shakespeare. Prospero has told Caliban,

> When thou didst not, savage,
> Know thine own meaning, but wouldst gabble like
> A thing most brutish, I endowed thy purposes
> With words that made them known.

Of course, one of the effects of colonialism was not only to give many of the natives a European language, but also to help shape their purposes. The independence movements of the post-1945 world that led to the end of Europe's African and Asian empires were driven by the rhetoric that had guided the Allies' own struggle against Germany and Japan: democracy, freedom, equality. This wasn't a conflict between values. It was a conflict of interests couched in terms of the same values.

The point applies as much within the West as elsewhere. Americans disagree about abortion, many vehemently. They couch this conflict in a language of conflicting values: They are pro-life or pro-choice. But this is a dispute that makes sense only because each side recognizes the very values the other insists upon. The disagreement is about their significance. Both sides respect something like the sanctity of human life. They disagree about such things as why human life is so precious and where it begins. Whatever you want to call those disagreements, it's just a mistake to think that either side doesn't recognize the value at stake here. And the same is true about choice: Americans are not divided about whether it's important to allow people, women and men, to make the major medical choices about their own bodies. They are divided about such questions as whether an abortion involves two people—both fetus and mother—or three people, adding in the father, or only one. Furthermore, no sane person on either side thinks that saving human lives or allowing people medical autonomy is the only thing that matters.

Some people will point to disputes about homosexuality and say that there, at least, there really is a conflict between people who do and people who don't regard homosexuality as a perversion. Isn't that a conflict of values? Well, no. Most Americans, on both sides, have the concept of perversion: of sexual acts that are wrong because their objects are inappropriate objects of sexual desire. But not everyone thinks that the fact that an act involves two women or two men makes it perverted. Not everyone who thinks these acts are perverse thinks they should be illegal. Not everyone who thinks they should be illegal thinks that gay and lesbian people should be ostracized. What is at stake, once more, is a battle about the meaning of perversion, about its status as a value, and about how to apply it. It is a reflection of the essentially contestable character of per- version as a term of value. When one turns from the issue of criminalization of gay sex—which is, at least for the moment, unconstitutional in the United States—to the question of gay marriage, all sides of the debate take seriously is- sues of sexual autonomy, the value of the intimate lives of couples, the meaning of family, and, by way of discussions of perversion, the proper uses of sex.

What makes these conflicts so intense is that they are battles over the mean- ing of the *same* values, not that they oppose one value, held exclusively by one side, with another, held exclusively by their antagonists. It is, in part, because we have shared horizons of meaning, because these are debates between people who share so many other values and so much else in the way of belief and of habit, that they are as sharp and as painful as they are.

Winners and Losers

But the disputes about abortion and gay marriage divide Americans bitterly 45 most of all because they share a society and a government. They are neigh- bors and fellow citizens. And it is laws governing all of them that are in dispute. What's at stake are their bodies or those of their mothers, their aunts, their sis- ters, their daughters, their wives, and their friends; those dead fetuses could have been their children or their children's friends.

We should remember this when we think about international human rights treaties. Treaties are law, even when they are weaker than national law. When we seek to embody our concern for strangers in human rights law and when we urge our government to enforce it, we are seeking to change the world of law in every nation on the planet. We have outlawed slavery not just domesti- cally but in international law. And in so doing we have committed ourselves, at a minimum, to the desirability of its eradication everywhere. This is no longer controversial in the capitals of the world. No one defends enslavement. But in- ternational treaties define slavery in ways that arguably include debt bondage; and debt bondage is a significant economic institution in parts of South Asia. I hold no brief for debt bondage, Still, we shouldn't be surprised if people whose income and whose style of life depend upon it are angry. Given that we have neighbors—even if only a few—who think that the fact that abortion is permit- ted in the United States turns the killing of the doctors who perform them into an act of heroism, we should not be surprised that there are strangers—even if only a few—whose anger turns them to violence against us.

I do not fully understand the popularity among Islamist movements in Egypt, Algeria, Iran, and Pakistan of a high-octane anti-Western rhetoric. But I do know one of its roots. It is, to use suitably old-fashioned language, "the woman question." There are Muslims, many of them young men, who feel that forces from outside their society—forces that they might think of as Western or, in a different moment, American—are pressuring them to reshape relations between men and women. Part of that pressure, they feel, comes from our media. Our films and our television programs are crammed with indescribable indecency. Our fashion magazines show women without modesty, women whose presence on many streets in the Muslim world would be a provocation, they think, presenting an almost irresistible temptation to men. Those magazines influence publications in their own countries, pulling them inevitably in the same direction. We permit women to swim almost naked with strange men, which is our business; but it is hard to keep the news of these acts of immodesty from Muslim women and children or to protect Muslim men from the temptations they inevitably create. As the Internet spreads, it will get even harder, and their children, especially their girls, will be tempted to ask for these freedoms too. Worse, they say, we are now trying to force our conception of how women and men should behave upon them. We speak of women's rights. We make treaties enshrining these rights. And then we want their governments to enforce them.[8]

Like many people in every nation, I support those treaties, of course; I believe that women, like men, should have the vote, should be entitled to work outside their homes, should be protected from the physical abuse of men, including their fathers, brothers, and husbands. But I also know that the changes that these freedoms would bring will change the balance of power between men and women in everyday life. How do I know this? Because I have lived most of my adult life in the West as it has gone through the latter phases of just such a transition, and I know that the process is not yet complete.

The recent history of America does show that a society can radically change its attitudes—and more importantly, perhaps, its habits—about these issues over a single generation. But it also suggests that some people will stay with the old attitudes, and the whole process will take time. The relations between men and women are not abstractions: They are part of the intimate texture of our everyday lives. We have strong feelings about them, and we have inherited many received ideas. Above all, we have deep *habits* about gender. A man and a woman go out on a date. Our habit is that, even if the woman offers, the man pays. A man and a woman approach an elevator door. The man steps back. A man and a woman kiss in a movie theater. No one takes a second look. Two men walk hand in hand in the high street. People are embarrassed. They hope their children don't see. They don't know how to explain it to them.

Most Americans are against gay marriage, conflicted about abortion, and amazed (and appalled) that a Saudi woman can't get a driver's license. But my guess is that they're not as opposed to gay marriage as they were twenty years ago. Indeed, twenty years ago, most Americans would probably just have thought the whole idea ridiculous. On the other hand, those Americans who are in favor of recognizing gay marriages probably don't have a simple set of reasons why. It just seems right to them, probably, in the way that it just seems wrong to those who disagree. (And probably they're thinking not about couples in the abstract but about Jim and John or Jean and Jane.) The younger they are, the more likely it is that they think that gay marriage is fine. And if they don't, it will often be because they have had religious objections reinforced regularly through life in church, mosque, or temple.

I am a philosopher. I believe in reason. But I have learned in a life of university teaching and research that even the cleverest people are not easily shifted by reason alone—and that can be true even in the most cerebral of realms. One of the great savants of the postwar era, John von Neumann, liked to say, mischievously, that "in mathematics you don't understand things, you just get used to them." In the larger world, outside the academy, people don't always even care whether they *seem* reasonable. Conversation, as I've said, is hardly guaranteed to lead to agreement about what to think and feel. Yet we go wrong if we think the point of conversation is to persuade, and imagine it proceeding as a debate, in which points are scored for the Proposition and the Opposition. Often enough, as Faust said, in the beginning is the deed: Practices and not principles are what enable us to live together in peace. Conversations across boundaries of identity—whether national, religious, or something else—begin with the sort of imaginative engagement you get when you read a novel or watch a movie or attend to a work of art that speaks from some place other than your own. So I'm using the word "conversation" not only for literal talk but also as a metaphor for engagement with the experience and the ideas of others. And I stress the role of the imagination here because the encounters, properly conducted, are valuable in themselves. Conversation doesn't have to lead to consensus about anything, especially not values; it's enough that it helps people get used to one another.

NOTES

1. Galatians 3:28. In quoting the Bible, I have used the King James version, except for the Pentateuch, where I have used Robert Alter's powerful modern translation, *The Five Books of Moses* (New York: Norton, 2004).
2. Christoph Martin Wieland. "Das Geheimniß des Kosmopolitenordens," *Teutscher Merkur*, August 1788, p. 107. (Where I give a reference only to a source that is not in English, the translation is mine.)
3. *Essai sur les mœurs et l'esprit des nations*, vol. 16 of *Oeuvres complètes de Voltaire* (Paris: L'Imprimerie de la Société Litteraire-Typographique, 1784), p. 241. Voltaire is speaking specifically here of "the Orient," and especially of China and India, but he would surely not have denied its more general application.
4. George Eliot, *Daniel Deronda* (London: Penguin, 1995), pp. 745, 661–62, 183.
5. Cicero, *De officiis* 1.50.
6. Cass R. Sunstein, "Incompletely Theorized Agreements," *Harvard Law Review* 108 (1995): 1733–72.
7. Joseph Appiah, *Joe Appiah: The Autobiography of an African Patriot* (New York: Praeger, 1990), p. 22.
8. I have put this complaint in the mouth of a Muslim. But the truth is you could hear it from non-Muslims in many places as well. It is less likely to be heard in non-Muslim Africa, because there, by and large (as Amartya Sen has pointed out), women have a less unequal place in public life. See Jean Drèze and Amartya Sen, *Hunger and Public Action* (Oxford: Clarendon Press, 1989).

Questions for Critical Reading

1. What does Appiah mean by "cosmopolitanism"? Use his text to create a definition, working with quotations from Appiah that support your interpretation. Then apply this definition to a current national or world situation. How does it show cosmopolitanism at work, or how might embracing this concept help resolve the situation?

2. According to Appiah, what are some crucial tools needed to enact his vision of cosmopolitanism? Reread his essay to locate quotations in which Appiah discusses these tools. How realistic is his vision? Based on the examples he offers, do you think these tools would be effective? Why or why not?

3. In order to make his argument Appiah includes some stories from his own life. How does he use these stories? What sort of evidence do they provide? What other forms of evidence does he use? Support your answers by searching for specific examples from the text.

Exploring Context

1. Appiah uses the term *cosmopolitanism* to describe an ability to get along with others in a globalized and deeply connected world, an ability he relates to having conversation. Locate a Web site that you think represents Appiah's understanding of "cosmopolitan." What makes it so? What kinds of conversations happen on this site? Locate passages from Appiah's text that support your interpretation of the Web site as an example of cosmopolitanism. Does the site fit the definition you created in Question 1 of Questions for Critical Reading?

2. Appiah looks at a number of culturally specific practices, including foot-binding in China and circumcision in African nations. Select one of Appiah's examples and use information from the Web to prepare a short report on how the practice has changed in its home culture. Are the reasons for these changes consistent with Appiah's arguments?

3. Visit a social networking site such as MySpace (myspace.com) or Facebook (facebook.com). If you don't currently have a profile on either site, create one. Explore the site and consider the role it might play in Appiah's vision of cosmopolitanism. Does it promote that ideal? What sorts of conversations does the site allow? Is it the kind of tool you described in Question 2 of Questions for Critical Reading?

Questions for Connecting

1. How do Appiah's insights about conversation confirm Helen Epstein's findings in "AIDS, Inc." (p. 106)? How can AIDS prevention be further promoted in Africa despite differences in values and practices? Synthesize the ideas of these authors to suggest strategies for halting the spread of HIV.

2. In "Community and Diversity" (p. 228), Rebekah Nathan explores the idea and the reality of community and diversity on college campuses. Can Appiah's ideas about cosmopolitanism be applied to educational settings to redress the problems that Nathan sees? Use your work on Appiah's concepts from Questions for Critical Reading or your findings from Exploring Context in composing your response.

3. What sorts of values are at play in the international adoption business as it is described by Debora L. Spar in "Trading Places: The Practice and Politics of Adoption" (p. 402)? Do these adoptions reflect cosmopolitanism or more local values?

Language Matters

1. Transition words or phrases help readers move from one idea or unit in an essay to another. In order to practice using transitions, locate a passage in Appiah that you found difficult or confusing. To clarify the thinking of your selected passages, write a short paragraph that could precede your selection using transitions to ease the difficulty of the passage from Appiah. Think about what Appiah is trying to do in that part of his essay and then clarify that purpose with transition words or phrases. How might the paragraph you write work as a transitional paragraph for Appiah's ideas? How can you more effectively use transitions in your own writing?

2. As an exercise in being concise, summarize Appiah's argument in a haiku, a Japanese form of nonrhyming poetry that has three lines with five syllables in the first line, seven syllables in the second line, and five in the third. For example:

> Language matters much.
> Working on a haiku can
> Clarify this text.

Use the haiku to express Appiah's argument in the fewest number of words.

3. Locate materials on simple sentences, then choose one of the key sentences of Appiah's text. Transform this sentence into a simple sentence or into a series of simple sentences. Does breaking down Appiah's sentence into simple sentences make his ideas easier to understand? When are simple sentences useful? Why didn't Appiah write this whole essay in simple sentences? When should you use these in your own writing? What makes them useful?

Assignments for Writing

1. For Appiah, cosmopolitanism is as much a challenge as a solution to the problems of a globalized world. Using Appiah's sense of the term *cosmopolitanism*, locate the challenges presented by the examples he uses to illustrate his arguments. Then write a paper in which you propose the best strategies for overcoming the challenges presented by cosmopolitanism. In what way does Appiah

offer a solution to facing these challenges in an increasingly diverse world? Is the solution Appiah finds in cosmopolitanism adequate in addressing these challenges in a way that respects the diversity of local populations? Use your work in Exploring Context to offer specific examples of successful strategies.

2. Appiah discusses his choice of cosmopolitanism as a rubric for moving forward. At the same time, he discusses the problems of realizing social change. Based on his discussion of the primacy of practice, how can we advocate for change in social practices? Write a paper in which you identify the best tools for achieving social change. In constructing and supporting your argument, you may wish to build on the cultural practice you explored in Question 2 of Exploring Context.

3. Appiah is invested in conversation as an engagement with others, but has this engagement been constructive in the ideological conflicts Appiah discusses? Using one of the examples Appiah describes in "Changing Our Minds" and "Fighting for the Good," write a paper in which you determine whether conversation has helped to resolve the conflict Appiah describes, and if so, how.

THE DALAI LAMA

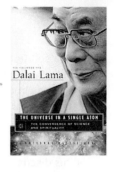

Tenzin Gyatso is the fourteenth Dalai Lama and the leader of the Central Tibetan Administration — the government-in-exile of Tibet. Gyatso was declared at two years old to be the reincarnation of an earlier Dalai Lama; at the age of fifteen he assumed the roles of religious and political leader of the Tibetan people. The only Dalai Lama to visit the West, Gyatso has become notable for gaining Western sympathy for the cause of a free Tibet and for authoring or coauthoring more than fifty books. Among his many honors are the Nobel Peace Prize (1989) and the U.S. Congressional Gold Medal (2006).

In *The Universe in a Single Atom* (2005), the Dalai Lama tries to reconcile religion with science, claiming that religion and science are parts of the same path to ultimate truth. Relying on just one, he suggests, is incomplete at best and "impoverishing" at worst. Simply following the rationale of science that everything "is reducible to matter and energy leaves out a huge range of human experience," and the opposite approach "can lock us into fundamentalist cages" that deny proven facts. According to the Dalai Lama, we must attempt to bridge this gap between our different ways of thinking.

In "Ethics and the New Genetics," a chapter from *The Universe in a Single Atom*, the Dalai Lama focuses on the field of genetic engineering. The potential benefits of this area of science are enormous, but the Dalai Lama reminds us to bear the potential costs in mind: "The higher the level of knowledge and power," he writes, "the greater must be our sense of moral responsibility." He argues that the speed of scientific progress in recent years has outpaced our society's ethical development, raising questions of what to do about possible breakthroughs in the future, when to trust our instinctual reactions, and what consequences science can have on culture and society.

In an age when stem cell research is passionately argued from both sides, the Dalai Lama urges us in this essay to craft ethical standards that can guide us in the complex decisions involved when technology intersects with life.

▶ TAGS: *research*, *social changes*, **biotechnology**, *human dignity*, **ethics**

Ethics and the New Genetics

Many of us who have followed the development of the new genetics are aware of the deep public disquiet that is gathering around the topic. This concern has been raised in relation to everything from cloning to genetic manipulation. There has been a worldwide outcry over the genetic engineering of foodstuffs. It is now possible to create new breeds of plants with far higher yields and far lower susceptibility to disease in order to maximize food production in a world where the increasing population needs to be fed. The benefits are obvious and wonderful. Seedless watermelons, apples that have longer shelf lives, wheat and

other grains that are immune to pests when growing in the field — these are no longer science fiction. I have read that scientists are even experimenting to develop farm products, such as tomatoes, injected with genes from different species of spiders.

But by doing these things, we are changing the genetic makeup, and do we really know what the long-term impact will be on the species of plants, on the soil, on the environment? There are obvious commercial benefits, but how do we judge what is really useful? The complex web of interdependence that characterizes the environment makes it seem beyond our capacity to predict.

Genetic changes have happened slowly over hundreds of thousands of years of natural evolution. The evolution of the human brain has occurred over millions of years. By actively manipulating the gene, we are on the cusp of forcing an unnaturally quick rate of change in animals and plants as well as our own species. This is not to say that we should turn our backs on developments in this area — it is simply to point out that we must become aware of the awesome implications of this new area of science.

The most urgent questions that arise have to do more with ethics than with science per se, with correctly applying our knowledge and power in relation to the new possibilities opened by cloning, by unlocking the genetic code and other advances. These issues relate to the possibilities for genetic manipulation not only of human beings and animals but also of plants and the environment of which we are all parts. At heart the issue is the relationship between our knowledge and power on the one hand and our responsibility on the other.

Any new scientific breakthrough that offers commercial prospects attracts tremendous interest and investment from both the public sector and private enterprise. The amount of scientific knowledge and the range of technological possibilities are so enormous that the only limitations on what we do may be the results of insufficient imagination. It is this unprecedented acquisition of knowledge and power that places us in a critical position at this time. The higher the level of knowledge and power, the greater must be our sense of moral responsibility.

If we examine the philosophical basis underlying much of human ethics, a clear recognition of the principle that correlates greater knowledge and power with a greater need for moral responsibility serves as a key foundation. Until recently we could say that this principle had been highly effective. The human capacity for moral reasoning has kept pace with developments in human knowledge and its capacities. But with the new era in biogenetic science, the gap between moral reasoning and our technological capacities has reached a critical point. The rapid increase of human knowledge and the technological possibilities emerging in the new genetic science are such that it is now almost impossible for ethical thinking to keep pace with these changes. Much of what is soon going to be possible is less in the form of new breakthroughs or paradigms in science than in the development of new technological options combined with the financial calculations of business and the political and economic calculations of governments. The issue is no longer whether we should or should not acquire knowledge and explore its technological potentials. Rather, the issue is how to use this new knowledge and power in the most expedient and ethically responsible manner.

The area where the impact of the revolution in genetic science may be felt most immediately at present is medicine. Today, I gather, many in medicine believe that the sequencing of the human genome will usher in a new era, in which it may be possible to move beyond a biochemical model of therapy to a genetically based model. Already the very definitions of many diseases are changing as illnesses are found to be genetically programmed into human beings and animals from their conception. While successful gene therapy for some of these conditions may be some way off, it seems no longer beyond the bounds of possibility. Even now, the issue of gene therapy and the associated question of genetic manipulation, especially at the level of the human embryo, are posing grave challenges to our capacity for ethical thinking.

A profound aspect of the problem, it seems to me, lies in the question of what to do with our new knowledge. Before we knew that specific genes caused senile dementia, cancer, or even aging, we as individuals assumed we wouldn't be afflicted with these problems, but we responded when we were. But now, or at any rate very soon, genetics can tell individuals and families that they have genes which may kill or maim them in childhood, youth, or middle age. This knowledge could radically alter our definitions of health and sickness. For example, someone who is healthy at present but has a particular genetic predisposition may come to be marked as "soon to be sick." What should we do with such knowledge, and how do we handle it in a way that is most compassionate? Who should have access to such knowledge, given its social and personal implications in relation to insurance, employment, and relationships, as well as reproduction? Does the individual who carries such a gene have a responsibility to reveal this fact to his or her potential partner in life? These are just a few of the questions raised by such genetic research.

To complicate an already intricate set of problems, I gather that genetic forecasting of this kind cannot be guaranteed to be accurate. It is sometimes certain that a particular genetic disorder observed in the embryo will give rise to disease in the child or adult, but it is often a question of relative probabilities. Lifestyle, diet, and other environmental factors come into play. So while we may know that a particular embryo carries a gene for a disease, we cannot be certain that the disease will arise.

People's life choices and indeed their very self-identity may be significantly affected by their perception of genetic risk, but those perceptions may not be correct and the risk may not be actualized. Should we be afforded such probabilistic knowledge? In cases where one member of the family discovers a genetic disorder of this type, should all the other members who may have inherited the same gene be informed? Should this knowledge be made available to a wider community — for instance, to health insurance companies? The carriers of certain genes may be excluded from insurance and hence even from access to health care all because there is a possibility of a particular disease manifesting itself. The issues here are not just medical but ethical and can affect the psychological well-being of the people concerned. When genetic disorders are detected in the embryo (as will increasingly be the case), should parents (or society) make the decision to curtail the life of that embryo? This question is further complicated by the fact that new methods of dealing with genetic disease and new medications are being found as swiftly as the genes carrying individual disease are identified. One can imagine a scenario in which a baby whose disease may manifest in twenty years is aborted and a cure for the disease is found within a decade.

Many people around the world, especially practitioners of the newly emerging discipline of bioethics, are grappling with the specifics of these problems. Given my lack of expertise in these fields, I have nothing concrete to offer in regard to any specific question — especially as the empirical facts are changing so rapidly. What I wish to do, however, is think through some of the key issues which I feel every informed person in the world needs to reflect upon, and to suggest some general principles that can be brought to bear in dealing with these ethical challenges. I believe that at heart the challenge we face is really a question of what choices we make in the face of the growing options that science and technology provide us.

> **At heart the challenge we face is really a question of what choices we make in the face of growing options that science and technology provide us.**

Attendant on the new frontiers of genetically based medicine there is a series of further issues which again raise deep and troubling ethical questions. Here I am speaking primarily of cloning. It has now been several years since the world was introduced to a completely cloned sentient being, Dolly, the famous sheep. Since then there has been a huge amount of coverage of human cloning. We know that the first cloned human embryos have been created. The media frenzy aside, the question of cloning is highly complex. I am told there are two quite different kinds of cloning — therapeutic and reproductive. Within therapeutic cloning, there is the use of cloning technology for the reproduction of cells and the potential creation of semi-sentient beings purely for the purpose of harvesting body parts for transplantation. Reproductive cloning is basically the creation of an identical copy.

In principle, I have no objection to cloning as such — as a technological instrument for medical and therapeutic purposes. As in all these cases, what must govern one's decisions is the question of compassionate motivation. However, regarding the idea of deliberately breeding semi-human beings for spare parts, I feel an immediate, instinctive revulsion. I once saw a BBC documentary which simulated such creatures through computer animation, with some distinctively recognizable human features. I was horrified. Some people might feel this is an irrational emotional reaction that need not be taken seriously. But I believe we must trust our instinctive feelings of revulsion, as these arise out of our basic humanity. Once we allow the exploitation of such hybrid semi-humans, what is to stop us from doing the same with our fellow human beings whom the whims of society may deem deficient in some way? The willingness to step across such natural thresholds is what often leads humanity to the commission of horrific atrocities.

Although reproductive cloning is not horrifying in the same way, in some respects its implications may be more far-reaching. Once the technology becomes feasible, there could be parents who, desperate to have children and unable to do so, may seek to bear a child through cloning. What would this practice do to the future gene pool? To the diversity that has been essential to evolution?

There could also be individuals who, out of a desire to live beyond biological possibility, may choose to clone themselves in the belief that they will continue to live in the new cloned being. In this case, I find it difficult to see any justifiable motives — from the Buddhist perspective, it may be an identical body, but there will be two different consciousnesses. They will still die.

One of the social and cultural consequences of new genetic technologies is their effect on the continuation of our species, through interference with the reproductive process. Is it right to select the sex of one's child, which I believe is possible now? If it is not, is it right to make such choices for reasons of health (say, in couples where a child is at serious risk of muscular dystrophy or hemophilia)? Is it acceptable to insert genes into human sperm or eggs in the lab? How far can we go in the direction of creating "ideal" or "designer" fetuses — for instance, embryos that have been selected in the lab to provide particular molecules or compounds absent in genetically deficient siblings in order that the children born from such embryos may donate bone marrow or kidneys to cure siblings? How far can we go with the artificial selection of fetuses with desirable traits that are held to improve intelligence or physical strength or specific color of eyes for instance?

When such technologies are used for medical reasons — as in the curing of a particular genetic deficiency — one can deeply sympathize. The selection of particular traits, however, especially when done for primarily aesthetic purposes, may not be for the benefit of the child. Even when the parents think they are selecting traits that will positively affect their child, we need to consider whether this is being done out of positive intention or on the basis of a particular society's prejudices at a particular time. We have to bear in mind the long-term impact of this kind of manipulation on the species as a whole, given that its effects will be passed on to following generations. We need also to consider the effects of limiting the diversity of humanity and the tolerance that goes with it, which is one of the marvels of life.

Particularly worrying is the manipulation of genes for the creation of children with enhanced characteristics, whether cognitive or physical. Whatever inequalities there may be between individuals in their circumstances — such as wealth, class, health, and so on — we are all born with a basic equality of our human nature, with certain potentialities; certain cognitive, emotional, and physical abilities; and the fundamental disposition — indeed the right — to seek happiness and overcome suffering. Given that genetic technology is bound to remain costly, at least for the foreseeable future, once it is allowed, for a long period it will be available only to a small segment of human society, namely the rich. Thus society will find itself translating an inequality of circumstance (that is, relative wealth) into an inequality of nature through enhanced intelligence, strength, and other faculties acquired through birth.

The ramifications of this differentiation are far-reaching — on social, political, and ethical levels. At the social level, it will reinforce — even perpetuate — our disparities, and it will make their reversal much more difficult. In political matters, it will breed a ruling elite, whose claims to power will be invocations of an intrinsic natural superiority. On the ethical level, these kinds of pseudo-nature-based differences can severely undermine our basic moral sensibilities insofar as these sensibilities are based on a mutual recognition of shared humanity. We cannot imagine how such practices could affect our very concept of what it is to be human.

When I think about the various new ways of manipulating human genetics, I can't help but feel that there is something profoundly lacking in our appreciation of what it is to cherish humanity. In my native Tibet, the value of a person rests not on physical appearance, not on intellectual or athletic achievement, but on the basic, innate capacity for compassion in all human beings. Even modern medical science has demonstrated how crucial affection is for human beings, especially during the first few weeks of life. The simple power of touch is critical for the basic development of the brain. In regard to his or her value as a human being, it is entirely irrelevant whether an individual has some kind of disability — for instance, Down syndrome — or a genetic disposition to develop a particular disease, such as sickle-cell anemia, Huntington's chorea, or Alzheimer's. All human beings have an equal value and an equal potential for goodness. To ground our appreciation of the value of a human being on genetic makeup is bound to impoverish humanity, because there is so much more to human beings than their genomes.

> **We cannot imagine how such practices could affect our very concept of what it is to be human.**

For me, one of the most striking and heartening effects of our knowledge of the genome is the astounding truth that the differences in the genomes of the different ethnic groups around the world are so negligible as to be insignificant. I have always argued that the differences of color, language, religion, ethnicity, and so forth among human beings have no substance in the face of our basic sameness. The sequencing of the human genome has, for me, demonstrated this in an extremely powerful way. It has also helped reinforce my sense of our basic kinship with animals, who share very large percentages of our genome. So it is conceivable if we humans utilize our newly found genetic knowledge skillfully, it could help foster a greater sense of affinity and unity not only with our fellow human beings but with life as a whole. Such a perspective could also underpin a much more healthy environmental consciousness.

In the case of food, if the argument is valid that we need some kind of genetic modification to help feed the world's growing population, then I believe that we cannot simply dismiss this branch of genetic technology. However, if, as suggested by its critics, this argument is merely a front for motives that are primarily commercial — such as producing food that will simply have a longer lasting shelf life, that can be more easily exported from one side of the world to the other, that is more attractive in appearance and more convenient in consumption, or creating grains and cereals engineered not to produce their own seeds so that farmers are forced to depend entirely upon the biotech companies for seeds — then clearly such practices must be seriously questioned.

Many people are becoming increasingly worried by the long-term consequences of producing and consuming genetically modified produce. The gulf between the scientific community and the general public may be caused in part by the lack of transparency in the companies developing these products. The onus should be on the biotech industry both to demonstrate that there are no long-term negative consequences for consumers of these new products and to adopt complete transparency on all the possible implications such plants may have for the natural environment. Clearly the argument that if there is no conclusive evidence that a particular product is harmful then there is nothing wrong with it cannot be accepted.

The point is that genetically modified food is not just another product, like a car or a portable computer. Whether we like it or not, we do not know the long-term consequences of introducing genetically modified organisms into the wider environment. In medicine, for instance, the drug thalidomide was found to be excellent for the treatment of morning sickness in pregnant women, but its long-term consequences for the health of the unborn child were not foreseen and proved catastrophic.

Given the tremendous pace of development in modern genetics, it is urgent now to refine our capacity for moral reasoning so that we are equipped to address the ethical challenges of this new situation. We cannot wait for a series of responses to emerge in an organic way. We need to confront the reality of our potential future and tackle the problems directly.

I feel the time is ripe to engage with the ethical side of the genetic revolution in a manner that transcends the doctrinal standpoints of individual religions. We must rise to the ethical challenge as members of one human family, not as a Buddhist, a Jew, a Christian, a Hindu, a Muslim. Nor is it adequate to address these ethical challenges from the perspective of purely secular, liberal political ideals, such as individual freedom, choice, and fairness. We need to examine the questions from the perspective of a global ethics that is grounded in the recognition of fundamental human values that transcend religion and science.

It is not adequate to adopt the position that our responsibility as a society is simply to further scientific knowledge and enhance our technological power. Nor is it sufficient to argue that what we do with this knowledge and power should be left to the choices of individuals. If this argument means that society at large should not interfere with the course of research and the creation of new technologies based on such research, it would effectively rule out any significant role for humanitarian or ethical considerations in the regulation of scientific development. It is essential, indeed it is a responsibility, for us to be much more critically self-aware about what we are developing and why. The basic principle is that the earlier one intervenes in the causal process, the more effective is one's prevention of undesirable consequences.

In order to respond to the challenges in the present and in the future, we need a much higher level of collective effort than has been seen yet. One partial solution is to ensure that a larger segment of the general public has a working grasp of scientific thinking and an understanding of key scientific discoveries, especially those which have direct social and ethical implications. Education needs to provide not only training in the empirical facts of science but also an examination of the relationship between science and society at large, including the ethical questions raised by new technological possibilities. This educational imperative must be directed at scientists as well as laypeople, so that scientists retain a wider understanding of the social, cultural, and ethical ramifications of the work they are doing.

Given that the stakes for the world are so high, the decisions about the course of research, what to do with our knowledge, and what technological possibilities should be developed cannot be left in the hands of scientists, business interests, or government officials. Clearly, as a society we need to draw some lines. But these deliberations cannot come solely from small committees, no matter how august or expert they may be. We need a much higher level of public involvement, especially in the form of debate and discussion, whether through the media, public consultation, or the action of grassroots pressure groups.

Today's challenges are so great — and the dangers of the misuse of technology so global, entailing a potential catastrophe for all humankind — that I feel we need a moral compass we can use collectively without getting bogged down in doctrinal differences. One key factor that we need is a holistic and integrated outlook at the level of human society that recognizes the fundamentally interconnected nature of all living beings and their environment. Such a moral compass must entail preserving our human sensitivity and will depend on us constantly bearing in mind our fundamental human values. We must be willing to be revolted when science — or for that matter any human activity — crosses the line of human decency, and we must fight to retain the sensitivity that is otherwise so easily eroded. 30

How can we find this moral compass? We must begin by putting faith in the basic goodness of human nature, and we need to anchor this faith in some fundamental and universal ethical principles. These include a recognition of the preciousness of life, an understanding of the need for balance in nature and the employment of this need as a gauge for the direction of our thought and action, and — above all — the need to ensure that we hold compassion as the key motivation for all our endeavors and that it is combined with a clear awareness of the wider perspective, including long-term consequences. Many will agree with me that these ethical values transcend the dichotomy of religious believers and nonbelievers, and are crucial for the welfare of all humankind. Because of the profoundly interconnected reality of today's world, we need to relate to the challenges we face as a single human family rather than as members of specific nationalities, ethnicities, or religions. In other words, a necessary principle is a spirit of oneness of the entire human species. Some might object that this is unrealistic. But what other option do we have?

I firmly believe it is possible. The fact that, despite our living for more than half a century in the nuclear age, we have not yet annihilated ourselves is what gives me great hope. It is no more coincidence that, if we reflect deeply, we find these ethical principles at the heart of all major spiritual traditions.

In developing an ethical strategy with respect to the new genetics, it is vitally important to frame our reflection within the widest possible context. We must first of all remember how new this field is and how new are the possibilities it offers, and to contemplate how little we understand what we know. We have now sequenced the whole of the human genome, but it may take decades for us fully to understand the functions of all the individual genes and their interrelationships, let alone the effects of their interaction with the environment. Too much of our current focus is on the feasibility of a particular technique, its immediate or short-term results and side effects, and what effect it may have on individual liberty. These are all valid concerns, but they are not sufficient. Their purview is too narrow, given that the very conception of human nature is at stake. Because of the far-reaching scope of these innovations, we need to examine all areas of human existence where genetic technology may have lasting implications. The fate of the human species, perhaps of all life on this planet, is in our hands. In the face of the great unknown, would it not be better to err on the side of caution than to transform the course of human evolution in an irreversibly damaging direction?

In a nutshell, our ethical response must involve the following key factors. First, we have to check our motivation and ensure that its foundation is compassion. Second, we must relate to any problem before us while taking into account the widest possible perspective, which includes not only situating the issue within the picture of wider human enterprise but also taking due regard of both short-term and long-term consequences. Third, when we apply our reason in addressing a problem, we have to be vigilant in ensuring that we remain honest, self-aware, and unbiased; the danger otherwise is that we may fall victim to self-delusion. Fourth, in the face of any real ethical challenge, we must respond in a spirit of humility, recognizing not only the limits of our knowledge (both collective and personal) but also our vulnerability to being misguided in the context of such a rapidly changing reality. Finally, we must all — scientists and society at large — strive to ensure that whatever new course of action we take, we keep in mind the primary goal of the well-being of humanity as a whole and the planet we inhabit.

The earth is our only home. As far as current scientific knowledge is concerned, this may be the only planet that can support life. One of the most powerful visions I have experienced was the first photograph of the earth from outer space. The image of a blue planet floating in deep space, glowing like the full moon on a clear night, brought home powerfully to me the recognition that we are indeed all members of a single family sharing one little house. I was flooded with the feeling of how ridiculous are the various disagreements and squabbles within the human family. I saw how futile it is to cling so tenaciously to the differences that divide us. From this perspective one feels the fragility, the vulnerability of our planet and its limited occupation of a small orbit sandwiched between Venus and Mars in the vast infinity of space. If we do not look after this home, what else are we charged to do on this earth?

Questions for Critical Reading

1. The Dalai Lama calls for an ethics to match our rapidly evolving technologies in areas such as genetic engineering. What might such an ethics look like? As you reread his essay to compose your response, locate quotations that support your proposed system of ethics.

2. What are the keys to developing an ethics apart from religion? Search the Dalai Lama's essay for quotations that support your position.

3. According to the Dalai Lama, when should we use genetic technologies? Reread his text for specific quotations that suggest the conditions necessary for the use of such technology.

Exploring Context

1. Visit the home page for the Human Genome Project (ornl.gov/sci/techresources/ Human_Genome/home.shtml). How does the project address the kinds of ethical problems that concern the Dalai Lama? Is it consistent with your proposed system of ethics from Question 1 of Questions for Critical Reading?

2. Explore the Web site for the President's Council on Bioethics (bioethics.gov). Are government organizations equipped to answer the Dalai Lama's call for a new ethics governing these technologies? Does the Council reflect your argument about a nonreligious ethics from Question 2 of Questions for Critical Reading?

3. London's Science Museum has an online exhibit about Dolly the sheep, the first cloned animal. Visit the site at sciencemuseum.org.uk/antenna/dolly/index.asp. In the aftermath of Dolly's life and death, what new ethical concerns should we consider?

Questions for Connecting

1. Francis Fukuyama's "Human Dignity" (p. 142) is also concerned about the potential of biotechnologies. How does Fukuyama's exploration of the matter complicate the Dalai Lama's call for a new ethics? What are their respective positions on genetic technologies? Does Fukuyama answer the Dalai Lama's call for a "moral compass"? You may wish to draw from your work on the use of genetic technologies from Question 3 of Questions for Critical Reading.

2. How can we apply the Dalai Lama's call for a new ethics to the use of human cadavers? Apply his concepts to Mary Roach's exploration of the subject in "The Cadaver Who Joined the Army" (p. 347). Can you synthesize their respective positions on ethics into a position of your own?

3. The Dalai Lama is a world religious figure. How can we account for his authority on the subject of genetics and ethics using the insights provided by Madeleine Albright in "Faith and Diplomacy" (p. 23)?

Language Matters

1. The Dalai Lama uses a clear, simple style of writing to discuss a very complex subject. Select a key quotation from his text and break down the parts of each sentence. How does he use language to express difficult concepts clearly? How can you do the same in your writing?

2. In a small group discuss what revision means. If you were going to revise this text, where would you start? What areas need more development?

3. If you were going to include images with this text, which ones would you choose? How would adding images change the meaning of the text? How does the visual support an argument?

Assignments for Writing

1. The Dalai Lama uses the complex ethical dilemma of genetic technologies to make his argument about the necessity for a moral compass to guide us in relation to knowledge and scientific discovery. Write a paper in which you extend the Dalai Lama's argument using your own example of a technology or discovery that demands a moral compass. You may want to use your example to discuss how to utilize new knowledge and power in the most expedient and ethically responsible manner. In composing your essay, consider the gap between moral reasoning and technological capacity. Should different approaches be taken when developing ethical standards for the two different types of cloning? Why? What are the implications of probabilistic knowledge?

2. In this essay the Dalai Lama discusses potential consequences of people being able to forecast genetic predispositions in their children and to alter their children's genetic makeup accordingly. Write a paper in which you propose a standard for when such forecasting should be used. Is such a technology ever ethical? Is it ever accurate? Why must relative probabilities be taken into consideration when thinking about genetic forecasting? To what degree must self-determination be considered a factor? You may wish to discuss the correlation of greater knowledge with a greater need for moral responsibility, and you may wish to draw from your exploration of the Web sites in Exploring Context and your understanding of the Dalai Lama's concepts from Questions for Connecting.

3. The possible consequences of genetic manipulation reach far beyond the sphere of science. Consider, for example, the role of national and global politics in relation to scientific breakthroughs that have the potential to literally change the face of humanity but will almost certainly not be available to everyone. Write a paper in which you examine the consequences of technology in terms of social and economic stability. How does the Dalai Lama characterize the relationship between knowledge and responsibility? In what ways does genetic engineering have the potential to perpetuate our disparities on social, political and ethical levels? Should new technologies be available to everyone?

Joan Didion

Joan Didion is a noted and versatile writer—a novelist, a screenwriter, an essayist, and a journalist. She began her career at *Vogue* magazine, where she worked as an associate features editor until the late 1960s. Since then, she has been a contributor to both the *New Yorker* and the *New York Review of Books*. However, she is perhaps best known for her collections of essays, including *Slouching Towards Bethlehem* (1968) and *The White Album* (1979). The following selection appeared in a different form in her nonfiction book *The Year of Magical Thinking* (2005), which won the National Book Award. Didion's memoir was later adapted into a one-woman show that ran on Broadway for twenty-four weeks and starred award-winning actress Vanessa Redgrave.

In *Magical Thinking*, Didion records the year after the death of her husband, John Gregory Dunne, with whom she wrote multiple screenplays, including 1996's *Up Close and Personal*. In December 2003, Didion's daughter Quintana fell into a coma, and just a few days later Didion's husband died from a massive heart attack. With this book, Didion details the "weeks and then months that cut loose any fixed idea I had ever had about death, about illness."

"After Life" deals with the immediate aftermath of Dunne's death. Didion recalls the moment his heart attack occurred (she first suspected he was joking), the arrival of the paramedics, and her realization that he was dead, which came when she met the social worker assigned to her at the hospital. In an instant, Didion finds herself answering questions about autopsies and funerals and deciding what to do with this bad news, whom to wake, and whom to leave undisturbed. And she deals with this grief while her daughter lies in a hospital room of her own. "You sit down to dinner and life as you know it ends," Didion writes. This, she adds, was not "the kind of conclusion [she] anticipated."

Grief and mourning are intensely personal and often private experiences. By inviting us in to these processes, Didion allows us to explore what happens to life in the wake of death.

▶ TAGS: *loss*, *mourning*, kinship, *language*, *death*, *change*

After Life

1

Life changes fast.
Life changes in the instant.
You sit down to dinner and life as you know it ends.
The question of self-pity.

Those were the first words I wrote after it happened. The computer dating on the   5
Microsoft Word file ("Notes on change.doc") reads "May 20, 2004, 11:11 PM,"
but that would have been a case of my opening the file and reflexively pressing
save when I closed it. I had made no changes to that file in May. I had made no
changes to that file since I wrote the words, in January 2004, a day or two or
three after the fact.

For a long time I wrote nothing else.

Life changes in the instant.

The ordinary instant.

At some point, in the interest of remembering what seemed most striking about what had happened, I considered adding those words, "the ordinary instant." I saw immediately that there would be no need to add the word
"ordinary," because there would be no forgetting it: The word never left my
mind. It was in fact the ordinary nature of everything preceding the event
that prevented me from truly believing it had happened, absorbing it, incorporating it, getting past it. I recognize now that there was nothing unusual
in this: Confronted with sudden disaster, we all focus on how unremarkable
the circumstances were in which the unthinkable occurred, the clear blue
sky from which the plane fell, the routine errand that ended on the shoulder
with the car in flames, the swings where the children were playing as usual
when the rattlesnake struck from the ivy. "He was on his way home from
work — happy, successful, healthy — and then, gone," I read in the account of
a psychiatric nurse whose husband was killed in a highway accident. In 1966 I
happened to interview many people who were living in Honolulu on the morning of December 7, 1941; without exception, these people began their accounts
of Pearl Harbor by telling me what an "ordinary Sunday morning" it had been.
"It was just an ordinary beautiful September day," people still say when asked
to describe the morning in New York when American Airlines 11 and United
Airlines 175 got flown into the World Trade towers. Even the report of the 9/11
Commission opened on this insistently premonitory and yet still dumbstruck
narrative note: "Tuesday, September 11, 2001, dawned temperate and nearly
cloudless in the eastern United States."

"And then — gone." *In the midst of life we are in death,* Episcopalians say at   10
the graveside. Later I realized that I must have repeated the details of what
happened to everyone who came to the house in those first weeks, all those
friends and relatives who brought food and made drinks and laid out plates

on the dining-room table for however many people were around at lunch or dinner, all those who picked up the plates and froze the leftovers and ran the dishwasher and filled our (I could not yet think *my*) otherwise empty apartment even after I had gone into the bedroom (our bedroom, the one in which there still lay on a sofa a faded terry-cloth XL robe bought in the 1970s at Richard Carroll in Beverly Hills) and shut the door. Those moments when I was abruptly overtaken by exhaustion are what I remember most clearly about the first days and weeks. I have no memory of telling anyone the details, but I must have done so, because everyone seemed to know them. At one point I considered the possibility that they had picked up the details of the story from one another, but immediately rejected it: The story they had was in each instance too accurate to have been passed from hand to hand. It had come from me.

Another reason I knew that the story had come from me was that no version I heard included the details I could not yet face, for example the blood on the living room floor that stayed there until José came in the next morning and cleaned it up.

José. Who was part of our household. Who was supposed to be flying to Las Vegas later that day, December 31, but never went. José was crying that morning as he cleaned up the blood. When I first told him what had happened he had not understood. Clearly I was not the ideal teller of this story, something about my version had been at once too offhand and too elliptical, something in my tone had failed to convey the central fact in the situation (I would encounter the same failure later when I had to tell our daughter Quintana), but by the time José saw the blood he understood.

I had picked up the abandoned syringes and ECG electrodes before he came in that morning but I could not face the blood.

In outline.

It is now, as I begin to write this, the afternoon of October 4, 2004.   15

Nine months and five days ago, at approximately nine o'clock on the evening of December 30, 2003, my husband, John Gregory Dunne, appeared to (or did) experience, at the table where he and I had just sat down to dinner in the living room of our apartment in New York, a sudden massive coronary event that caused his death. Our only child, Quintana, then 37, had been for the previous five nights unconscious in an intensive care unit at Beth Israel Medical Center's Singer Division, at that time a hospital on East End Avenue (it closed in August 2004), more commonly known as "Beth Israel North" or "the old Doctors' Hospital," where what had seemed a case of December flu sufficiently severe to take her to an emergency room on Christmas morning had exploded into pneumonia and septic shock. This is my attempt to make sense of the period that followed, weeks and then months that cut loose any fixed idea I had ever had about death, about illness, about probability and luck, about good fortune and bad, about marriage and children and memory, about grief, about the ways in which people do and do not deal with the fact that life ends, about the shallowness of sanity, about life itself.

I have been a writer my entire life. As a writer, even as a child, long before what I wrote began to be published, I developed a sense that meaning itself was resident in the rhythms of words and sentences and paragraphs, a technique for withholding whatever it was I thought or believed behind an increasingly impenetrable polish. The way I write is who I am, or have become, yet this is a case in which I wish I had instead of words and their rhythms a cutting room, equipped with an Avid, a digital editing system on which I could touch a key and collapse the sequence of time, show you simultaneously all the frames of memory that come to me now, let you pick the takes, the marginally different expressions, the variant readings of the same lines. This is a case in which I need more than words to find the meaning. This is a case in which I need whatever it is I think or believe to be penetrable, if only for myself.

2

December 30, 2003, a Tuesday.

We had seen Quintana in the sixth-floor ICU at Beth Israel North.

We had come home.

We had discussed whether to go out for dinner or eat in.

I said I would build a fire, we could eat in.

I built the fire, I started dinner, I asked John if he wanted a drink.

I got him a Scotch and gave it to him in the living room, where he was reading in the chair by the fire where he habitually sat.

The book he was reading was by David Fromkin, a bound galley of *Europe's Last Summer: Who Started the Great War in 1914?*

I finished getting dinner. I set the table in the living room where, when we were home alone, we could eat within sight of the fire. I find myself stressing the fire because fires were important to us. I grew up in California, John and I lived there together for twenty-four years, in California we heated our houses by building fires. We built fires even on summer evenings, because the fog came in. Fires said we were home, we had drawn the circle, we were safe through the night. I lighted the candles. John asked for a second drink before sitting down. I gave it to him. We sat down. My attention was on mixing the salad.

John was talking, then he wasn't.

At one point in the seconds or minute before he stopped talking he had asked me if I had used single-malt Scotch for his second drink. I had said no, I used the same Scotch I had used for his first drink. "Good," he had said. "I don't know why but I don't think you should mix them." At another point in those seconds or that minute he had been talking about why World War I was the critical event from which the entire rest of the twentieth century flowed.

I have no idea which subject we were on, the Scotch or World War I, at the instant he stopped talking.

I only remember looking up. His left hand was raised and he was slumped motionless. At first I thought he was making a failed joke, an attempt to make the difficulty of the day seem manageable.

I remember saying *Don't do that.*

When he did not respond my first thought was that he had started to eat and choked. I remember trying to lift him far enough from the back of the chair to give him the Heimlich. I remember the sense of his weight as he fell forward, first against the table, then to the floor. In the kitchen by the telephone I had taped a card with the New York–Presbyterian ambulance numbers. I had not taped the numbers by the telephone because I anticipated a moment like this. I had taped the numbers by the telephone in case someone in the building needed an ambulance.

Someone else.

I called one of the numbers. A dispatcher asked if he was breathing. I said *Just come.* When the paramedics came I tried to tell them what had happened but before I could finish they had transformed the part of the living room where John lay into an emergency department. One of them (there were three, maybe four, even an hour later I could not have said) was talking to the hospital about the electrocardiogram they seemed already to be transmitting. Another was opening the first or second of what would be many syringes for injection. (Epinephrine? Lidocaine? Procainamide? The names came to mind but I had no idea from where.) I remember saying that he might have choked. This was dismissed with a finger swipe: The airway was clear. They seemed now to be using defibrillating paddles, an attempt to restore a rhythm. They got something that could have been a normal heartbeat (or I thought they did, we had all been silent, there was a sharp jump), then lost it, and started again.

"He's still fibbing," I remember the one on the telephone saying.

"V-fibbing," John's cardiologist said the next morning when he called from Nantucket. "They would have said 'V-fibbing.' V for ventricular."

Maybe they said "V-fibbing" and maybe they did not. Atrial fibrillation did not immediately or necessarily cause cardiac arrest. Ventricular did. Maybe ventricular was the given.

I remember trying to straighten out in my mind what would happen next. Since there was an ambulance crew in the living room, the next logical step would be going to the hospital. It occurred to me that the crew could decide very suddenly to go to the hospital and I would not be ready. I would not have in hand what I needed to take. I would waste time, get left behind. I found my handbag and a set of keys and a summary John's doctor had made of his medical history. When I got back to the living room the paramedics were watching the computer monitor they had set up on the floor. I could not see the monitor, so I watched their faces. I remember one glancing at the others.

When the decision was made to move it happened very fast. I followed them to the elevator and asked if I could go with them. They said they were taking the gurney down first, I could go in the second ambulance. One of them waited with me for the elevator to come back up. By the time he and I got into the second ambulance the ambulance carrying the gurney was pulling away from the front of the building. The distance from our building to the part of New York–Presbyterian that used to be New York Hospital is six crosstown blocks. I have no memory of sirens. I have no memory of traffic. When we arrived at the emergency entrance to the hospital the gurney was already disappearing

35

into the building. A man was waiting in the driveway. Everyone else in sight was wearing scrubs. He was not. "Is this the wife?" he said to the driver, then turned to me. "I'm your social worker," he said, and I guess that is when I must have known.

"I opened the door and I seen the man in the dress greens and I knew. I immedi-   40
ately knew." This was what the mother of a nineteen-year-old killed by a bomb in Kirkuk said on an HBO documentary quoted by Bob Herbert in the *New York Times* on the morning of November 12, 2004. "But I thought that if, as long as I didn't let him in, he couldn't tell me. And then it—none of that would've happened. So he kept saying, 'Ma'am, I need to come in.' And I kept telling him, 'I'm sorry, but you can't come in.'"

When I read this at breakfast almost eleven months after the night with the ambulance and the social worker I recognized the thinking as my own.

Inside the emergency room I could see the gurney being pushed into a cubicle, propelled by more people in scrubs. Someone told me to wait in the reception area. I did. There was a line for admittance paperwork. Waiting in the line seemed the constructive thing to do. Waiting in the line said that there was still time to deal with this, I had copies of the insurance cards in my hand-bag, this was not a hospital I had ever negotiated—New York Hospital was the Cornell part of New York–Presbyterian, the part I knew was the Columbia part, Columbia-Presbyterian, at 168th and Broadway, twenty minutes away at best, too far in this kind of emergency—but I could make this unfamiliar hospital work, I could be useful, I could arrange the transfer to Columbia-Presbyterian once he was stabilized. I was fixed on the details of this imminent transfer to Columbia (he would need a bed with telemetry, eventually I could also get Quintana transferred to Columbia, the night she was admitted to Beth Israel North I had written on a card the beeper numbers of several Columbia doctors, one or another of them could make all this happen) when the social worker reappeared and guided me from the paperwork line into an empty room off the reception area. "You can wait here," he said. I waited. The room was cold, or I was. I wondered how much time had passed between the time I called the ambulance and the arrival of the paramedics. It had seemed no time at all (*a mote in the eye of God* was the phrase that came to me in the room off the reception area) but it must have been at the minimum several minutes.

I used to have on a bulletin board in my office, for reasons having to do with a plot point in a movie, a pink index card on which I had typed a sentence from *The Merck Manual* about how long the brain can be deprived of oxygen. The image of the pink index card was coming back to me in the room off the reception area: "Tissue anoxia for > 4 to 6 min. can result in irreversible brain damage or death." I was telling myself that I must be misremembering the sentence when the social worker reappeared. He had with him a man he introduced as "your husband's doctor." There was a silence. "He's dead, isn't he," I heard myself say to the doctor. The doctor looked at the social worker. "It's okay," the social worker said. "She's a pretty cool customer." They took me into the curtained cubicle where John lay, alone now. They asked if I wanted a priest. I said yes. A priest appeared and said the words. I thanked him. They gave me the silver clip in which John kept his driver's license and credit cards. They gave me the cash that had been in his pocket. They gave me his watch. They gave me his cell phone. They gave me a plastic bag in which they said I would find his clothes. I thanked them. The social worker asked if he could do anything more for me. I said he could put me in a taxi. He did. I thanked him. "Do you have money for the fare?" he asked. I said I did, the cool customer. When I walked into the apartment and saw John's jacket and scarf still lying on the chair where he had dropped them when we came in from seeing Quintana at Beth Is-rael North (the red cashmere scarf, the Patagonia windbreaker that had been the crew jacket on *Up Close and Personal*), I wondered what an uncool cus-tomer would be allowed to do. Break down? Require sedation? Scream?

> **I wondered what an uncool customer would be allowed to do. Break down? Require sedation? Scream?**

I remember thinking that I needed to discuss this with John.

There was nothing I did not discuss with John.

Because we were both writers and both worked at home our days were filled with the sound of each other's voices.

I did not always think he was right nor did he always think I was right but we were each the person the other trusted. There was no separation between our investments or interests in any given situation. Many people assumed that we must be, since sometimes one and sometimes the other would get the bet-ter review, the bigger advance, in some way "competitive," that our private life must be a minefield of professional envies and resentments. This was so far from the case that the general insistence on it came to suggest certain lacunae in the popular understanding of marriage.

That had been one more thing we discussed.

What I remember about the apartment the night I came home alone from New York Hospital was its silence.

In the plastic bag I had been given at the hospital there were a pair of cordu-roy pants, a wool shirt, a belt, and I think nothing else. The legs of the corduroy pants had been slit open, I supposed by the paramedics. There was blood on the shirt. The belt was braided. I remember putting his cell phone in the charger on his desk. I remember putting his silver clip in the box in the bedroom in which we kept passports and birth certificates and proof of jury service. I look now at the clip and see that these were the cards he was carrying: a New York State driver's license, due for renewal on May 25, 2004; a Chase ATM card; an Amer-ican Express card; a Wells Fargo MasterCard; a Metropolitan Museum card; a Writers Guild of America West card (it was the season before Academy voting, when you could use a WGAW card to see movies free, he must have gone to a movie, I did not remember); a Medicare card; a MetroCard; and a card issued by Medtronic with the legend "I have a Kappa 900 SR pacemaker implanted," the serial number of the device, a number to call for the doctor who implanted it, and the notation "Implant Date: 03 Jun 2003." I remember combining the cash that had been in his pocket with the cash in my own bag, smoothing the bills, taking special care to interleaf twenties with twenties, tens with tens, fives and ones with fives and ones. I remember thinking as I did this that he would see that I was handling things.

When I saw him in the curtained cubicle in the emergency room at New York Hospital there was a chip in one of his front teeth, I supposed from the fall, since there were also bruises on his face. When I identified his body the next day for the undertaker the bruises were not apparent. It occurred to me that masking the bruises must have been what the undertaker meant when I said no embalming and he said "in that case we'll just clean him up." The part with the undertaker remains remote. I had arrived to meet him so determined to avoid any inappropriate response (tears, anger, helpless laughter at the Oz-like hush) that I had shut down all response. After my mother died the undertaker who picked up her body left in its place on the bed an artificial rose. My brother had told me this, offended to the core. I would be armed against artificial roses. I remember making a brisk decision about a coffin. I remember that in the office where I signed the papers there was a grandfather clock, not running. John's nephew Tony, who was with me, mentioned to the undertaker that the clock was not running. The undertaker, as if pleased to elucidate a decorative element, explained that the clock had not run in some years but was retained as "a kind of memorial" to a previous incarnation of the firm. He seemed to be offering the clock as a lesson. I concentrated on Quintana. I could shut out what the undertaker was saying, but I could not shut out the lines I was hearing as I concentrated on Quintana: *Full fathom five thy father lies/Those are pearls that were his eyes.*

3

Eight months later I asked the manager of our apartment building if he still had the log kept by the doormen for the night of December 30. I knew there was a log, I had been for three years president of the board of the building, the door log was intrinsic to building procedure. The next day the manager sent me the page for December 30. According to the log, the doormen that night were Michael Flynn and Vasile Ionescu. I had not remembered that. Vasile Ionescu and John had a routine with which they amused themselves in the elevator, a small game, between an exile from Ceaucescu's Romania and an Irish Catholic from West Hartford, Connecticut, based on a shared appreciation of political posturing. "So where is bin Laden?" Vasile would say when John got onto the elevator, the point being to come up with ever more improbable suggestions: "Could bin Laden be in the penthouse?" "In the maisonette?" "In the fitness room?" When I saw Vasile's name on the log it occurred to me that I could not remember if he had initiated this game when we came in from Beth Israel North in the early evening of December 30. The log for that evening showed only two entries, fewer than usual, even for a time of the year when most people in the building left for more clement venues:

NOTE: Paramedics arrived at 9:20 PM for Mr. Dunne. Mr. Dunne was taken to hospital at 10:05 PM.

NOTE: Lightbulb out on A-B passenger elevator.

The A-B elevator was our elevator, the elevator in which the paramedics came up at 9:20 PM, the elevator in which they took John (and me) downstairs to the ambulance at 10:05 PM, the elevator in which I returned alone to our apartment at a time not noted. I had not noticed a lightbulb being out in the elevator. Nor had I noticed that the paramedics were in the apartment for forty-five minutes. I had always described it as "fifteen or twenty minutes." *If they were here that long does it mean that he was alive?* I put this question to a doctor I knew. "Sometimes they'll work that long," he said. It was a while before I realized that this in no way addressed the question.

The death certificate, when I got it, gave the time of death as 10:18 PM, December 30, 2003.

I had been asked before I left the hospital if I would authorize an autopsy. I had said yes. I later read that asking a survivor to authorize an autopsy is seen in hospitals as delicate, sensitive, often the most difficult of the routine steps that follow a death. Doctors themselves, according to many studies (for example, Katz, J., and Gardner, R., "The Intern's Dilemma: The Request for Autopsy Consent," *Psychiatry in Medicine* 3:197–203, 1972), experience considerable anxiety about making the request. They know that autopsy is essential to the learning and teaching of medicine, but they also know that the procedure touches a primitive dread. If whoever it was at New York Hospital who asked me to authorize an autopsy experienced such anxiety I could have spared him or her: I actively wanted an autopsy. I actively wanted an autopsy even though I had seen some, in the course of doing research. I knew exactly what occurs, the chest open like a chicken in a butcher's case, the face peeled down, the scale on which the organs are weighed. I had seen homicide detectives avert their eyes from an autopsy in progress. I still wanted one. I needed to know how and why and when it had happened. In fact I wanted to be in the room when they did it (I had watched those other autopsies with John, I owed him his own, it was fixed in my mind at that moment that he would be in the room if I were on the table) but I did not trust myself to rationally present the point so I did not ask.

If the ambulance left our building at 10:05 PM, and death was declared at 10:18 PM, the thirteen minutes in between were just bookkeeping, bureaucracy, making sure the hospital procedures were observed and the paperwork was done and the appropriate person was on hand to do the sign-off, inform the cool customer.

The sign-off, I later learned, was called the "pronouncement," as in "Pronounced: 10:18 PM."

I had to believe he was dead all along.

If I did not believe he was dead all along I would have thought I should have been able to save him.

Until I saw the autopsy report I continued to think this anyway, an example   60
of delusionary thinking, the omnipotent variety.

A week or two before he died, when we were having dinner in a restaurant,
John asked me to write something in my notebook for him. He always carried
cards on which to make notes, three-by-six-inch cards printed with his name
that could be slipped into an inside pocket. At dinner he had thought of something he wanted to remember but when he looked in his pockets he found no
cards. I need you to write something down, he said. It was, he said, for his new
book, not for mine, a point he stressed because I was at the time researching a
book that involved sports. This was the note he dictated: "Coaches used to go
out after a game and say, 'You played great.' Now they go out with state police,
as if this were a war and they the military. The militarization of sports." When I
gave him the note the next day he said "You can use it if you want to."

What did he mean?

Did he know he would not write the book?

Did he have some apprehension, a shadow? Why had he forgotten to bring
note cards to dinner that night? Had he not warned me when I forgot my own
notebook that the ability to make a note when something came to mind was
the difference between being able to write and not being able to write? Was
something telling him that night that the time for being able to write was running out?

One summer when we were living in Brentwood Park we fell into a pattern of   65
stopping work at four in the afternoon and going out to the pool. He would stand
in the water reading (he reread *Sophie's Choice* several times that summer, trying
to see how it worked) while I worked in the garden. It was a small, even miniature,
garden with gravel paths and a rose arbor and beds edged with thyme and san-
tolina and feverfew. I had convinced John a few years before that we should tear
out a lawn to plant this garden. To my surprise, since he had shown no previous
interest in gardens, he regarded the finished product as an almost mystical gift.
Just before five on those summer afternoons we would swim and then go into the
library wrapped in towels to watch *Tenko*, a BBC series, then in syndication, about
a number of satisfyingly predictable English women (one was immature and selfish, another seemed to have been written with *Mrs. Miniver* in mind) imprisoned
by the Japanese in Malaya during World War II. After each afternoon's *Tenko* segment we would go upstairs and work another hour or two, John in his office at
the top of the stairs, me in the glassed-in porch across the hall that had become
my office. At seven or seven thirty we would go out to dinner, many nights at
Morton's. Morton's felt right that summer. There was always shrimp quesadilla,
chicken with black beans. There was always someone we knew. The room was
cool and polished and dark inside but you could see the twilight outside.

John did not like driving at night by then. This was one reason, I later
learned, that he wanted to spend more time in New York, a wish that at the
time remained mysterious to me. One night that summer he asked me to drive
home after dinner at Anthea Sylbert's house on Camino Palmero in Hollywood.
I remember thinking how remarkable this was. Anthea lived less than a block
from the house on Franklin Avenue in which we had lived from 1967 until

1971, so it was not a question of reconnoitering a new neighborhood. It had occurred to me as I started the ignition that I could count on my fingers the number of times I had driven when John was in the car; the single other time I could remember that night was once spelling him on a drive from Las Vegas to Los Angeles. He had been dozing in the passenger seat of the Corvette we then had. He had opened his eyes. After a moment he had said, very carefully, "I might take it a little slower." I had no sense of unusual speed and glanced at the speedometer: I was doing 120.

Yet.

A drive across the Mojave was one thing. There had been no previous time when he asked me to drive home from dinner in town: This evening on Camino Palmero was unprecedented. So was the fact that at the end of the forty-minute drive to Brentwood Park he pronounced it "well driven."

He mentioned those afternoons with the pool and the garden and *Tenko* several times during the year before he died.

Philippe Ariès, in *The Hour of Our Death*, points out that the essential char- 70 acteristic of death as it appears in the *Chanson de Roland* is that the death, even if sudden or accidental, "gives advance warning of its arrival." Gawain is asked: "Ah, good my lord, think you then so soon to die?" Gawain answers: "I tell you that I shall not live two days." Ariès notes: "Neither his doctor nor his friends nor the priests (the latter are absent and forgotten) know as much about it as he. Only the dying man can tell how much time he has left."

You sit down to dinner.

"You can use it if you want to," John had said when I gave him the note he had dictated a week or two before.

And then — gone.

4

Grief, when it comes, is nothing we expect it to be. It was not what I felt when my parents died: My father died a few days short of his eighty-fifth birthday and my mother a month short of her ninety-first, both after some years of increasing debility. What I felt in each instance was sadness, loneliness (the loneliness of the abandoned child of whatever age), regret for time gone by, for things unsaid, for my inability to share or even in any real way to acknowledge, at the end, the pain and helplessness and physical humiliation they each endured. I understood the inevitability of each of their deaths. I had been expecting (fearing, dreading, anticipating) those deaths all my life. They remained, when they did occur, distanced, at a remove from the ongoing dailiness of my life. After my mother died I received a letter from a friend in Chicago, a former Maryknoll priest, who precisely intuited what I felt. The death of a parent, he wrote, "despite our preparation, indeed, despite our age, dislodges things deep in us, sets off reactions that surprise us and that may cut free memories and feelings that we had thought gone to ground long ago. We might, in that indeterminate period they call mourning, be in a submarine, silent on the ocean's bed, aware of the depth charges, now near and now far, buffeting us with recollections."

My father was dead, my mother was dead, I would need for a while to watch for mines, but I would still get up in the morning and send out the laundry. 75

I would still plan a menu for Easter lunch.

I would still remember to renew my passport.

Grief is different. Grief has no distance. Grief comes in waves, paroxysms, sudden apprehensions that weaken the knees and blind the eyes and obliterate the dailiness of life. Virtually everyone who has ever experienced grief mentions this phenomenon of "waves." Erich Lindemann, who was chief of psychiatry at Massachusetts General Hospital in the 1940s and interviewed many family members of those killed in the 1942 Cocoanut Grove fire, defined the phenomenon with absolute specificity in a famous 1944 study: "sensations of somatic distress occurring in waves lasting from twenty minutes to an hour at a time, a feeling of tightness in the throat, choking with shortness of breath, need for sighing and an empty feeling in the abdomen, lack of muscular power and an intense subjective distress described as tension or mental pain."

> **Grief, when it comes, is nothing we expect it to be.**

Tightness in the throat.

Choking, need for sighing. 80

Such waves began for me on the morning of December 31, 2003, seven or eight hours after the fact, when I woke alone in the apartment. I do not remember crying the night before; I had entered at the moment it happened a kind of shock in which the only thought I allowed myself was that there must be certain things I needed to do. There had been certain things I had needed to do while the ambulance crew was in the living room. I had needed for example to get the copy of John's medical summary, so I could take it with me to the hospital. I had needed for example to bank the fire, because I would be leaving it. There had been certain things I had needed to do at the hospital. I had needed for example to stand in the line. I had needed for example to focus on the bed with telemetry he would need for the transfer to Columbia-Presbyterian.

Once I got back from the hospital there had again been certain things I needed to do. I could not identify all of these things, but I did know one of them: I needed, before I did anything else, to tell John's brother Nick. It had seemed too late in the evening to call their older brother Dick on Cape Cod (he went to bed early, his health had not been good, I did not want to wake him with bad news) but I needed to tell Nick. I did not plan how to do this. I just sat on the bed and picked up the phone and dialed the number of his house in Connecticut. He answered. I told him. After I put down the phone, in what I can only describe as a new neural pattern of dialing numbers and saying the words, I picked it up again. I could not call Quintana (she was still where we had left her a few hours before, unconscious in the ICU at Beth Israel North), but I could call Gerry, her husband of five months, and I could call my brother, Jim, who would be at his house in Pebble Beach. Gerry said he would come over. I said there was no need to come over, I would be fine. Jim said he would get a flight. I said there was no need to think about a flight, we would talk in the morning. I was trying to think what to do next when the phone rang. It was John's and my agent, Lynn Nesbit, a friend since I suppose the late '60s. It was not clear to me at the time how she knew but she did (it had something to do with a mutual friend to whom both Nick and Lynn seemed in the last minute to have spoken), and she was calling from a taxi on her way to our apartment. At one level I was relieved (Lynn knew how to manage things, Lynn would know what it was that I was supposed to be doing) and at another I was bewildered: How could I deal at this moment with company? What would we do, would we sit in the living room with the syringes and the ECG electrodes and the blood still on the floor, should I rekindle what was left of the fire, would we have a drink, would she have eaten?

Had I eaten?

The instant in which I asked myself whether I had eaten was the first intimation of what was to come: If I thought of food, I learned that night, I would throw up.

Lynn arrived.   85

We sat in the part of the living room where the blood and electrodes and syringes were not.

I remember thinking as I was talking to Lynn (this was the part I could not say) that the blood must have come from the fall: He had fallen on his face, there was the chipped tooth I had noticed in the emergency room, the tooth could have cut the inside of his mouth.

Lynn picked up the phone and said that she was calling Christopher.

This was another bewilderment: The Christopher I knew best was in either Paris or Dubai and in any case Lynn would have said Chris, not Christopher. I found my mind veering to the autopsy. It could even be happening as I sat there. Then I realized that the Christopher to whom Lynn was talking was Christopher Lehmann-Haupt, who was the chief obituary writer at the *New York Times*. I remember a sense of shock. I wanted to say *not yet* but my mouth had gone dry. I could deal with "autopsy" but the notion of "obituary" had not occurred to me. "Obituary," unlike "autopsy," which was between me and John and the hospital, meant it had happened. I found myself wondering, with no sense of illogic, if it had also happened in Los Angeles. I was trying to work out what time it had been when he died and whether it was that time yet in Los Angeles. (Was there time to go back? Could we have a different ending on Pacific time?) I recall being seized by a pressing need not to let anyone at the *Los Angeles Times* learn what had happened by reading it in the *New York Times*. I called our closest friend at the *Los Angeles Times*. I have no memory of what Lynn and I did then. I remember her saying that she would stay the night, but I said no, I would be fine alone.

And I was.   90

Until the morning. When, only half awake, I tried to think why I was alone in the bed. There was a leaden feeling. It was the same leaden feeling with which I woke on mornings after John and I had fought. Had we had a fight? What about, how had it started, how could we fix it if I could not remember how it started?

Then I remembered.

For several weeks that would be the way I woke to the day.

I wake and feel the fell of dark, not day.

One of several lines from different poems by Gerard Manley Hopkins that John strung together during the months immediately after his younger brother committed suicide, a kind of improvised rosary.

> O the mind, mind has mountains; cliffs of fall
> Frightful, sheer, no-man-fathomed. Hold them cheap
> May who ne'er hung there.
> I wake and feel the fell of dark, not day.
> And I have asked to be
> Where no storms come.

I see now that my insistence on spending that first night alone was more complicated than it seemed, a primitive instinct. Of course I knew John was dead. Of course I had already delivered the definitive news to his brother and to my brother and to Quintana's husband. The *New York Times* knew. The *Los Angeles Times* knew. Yet I was myself in no way prepared to accept this news as final: There was a level on which I believed that what had happened remained reversible. That was why I needed to be alone.

After that first night I would not be alone for weeks (Jim and his wife would fly in from California the next day, Nick would come back to town, Tony and his wife would come down from Connecticut, José would not go to Las Vegas, our assistant Sharon would come back from skiing, there would never not be people in the house), but I needed that first night to be alone.

I needed to be alone so that he could come back.

5

Grief turns out to be a place none of us know until we reach it. We anticipate (we know) that someone close to us could die, but we do not look beyond the few days or weeks that immediately follow such an imagined death. We misconstrue the nature of even those few days or weeks. We might expect if the death is sudden to feel shock. We do not expect this shock to be obliterative, dislocating to both body and mind. We might expect that we will be prostrate, inconsolable, crazy with loss. We do not expect to be literally crazy, cool customers who believe that their husband is about to return. In the version of grief we imagine, the model will be "healing." A certain forward movement will prevail. The worst days will be the earliest days. We imagine that the moment to most severely test us will be the funeral, after which this hypothetical healing will take place.

When we anticipate the funeral we wonder about failing to "get through it," rise to the occasion, exhibit the "strength" that invariably gets mentioned as the correct response to death. We anticipate needing to steel ourselves for the moment: Will I be able to greet people, will I be able to leave the scene, will I be able even to get dressed that day? We have no way of knowing that this will not be the issue. We have no way of knowing that the funeral itself will be anodyne, a kind of narcotic regression in which we are wrapped in the care of others and the gravity and meaning of the occasion. Nor can we know ahead of the fact (and here lies the heart of the difference between grief as we imagine it and grief as it is) the unending absence that follows, the void, the very opposite of meaning, the relentless succession of moments during which we will confront the experience of meaninglessness itself.

As a child I thought a great deal about meaninglessness, which seemed at the time the most prominent negative feature on the horizon. After a few years of failing to find meaning in the more commonly recommended venues I learned that I could find it in geology, so I did. This in turn enabled me to find meaning in the Episcopal litany, most acutely in the words *as it was in the beginning, is now and ever shall be, world without end,* which I interpreted as a literal description of the constant changing of the earth, the unending erosion of the shores and mountains, the inexorable shifting of the geological structures that could throw up mountains and islands and could just as reliably take them away. I found earthquakes, even when I was in them, deeply satisfying, abruptly revealed evidence of the scheme in action. That the scheme could destroy the works of man might be a personal regret but remained, in the larger picture I had come to recognize, a matter of abiding indifference. No eye was on the sparrow. No one was watching me. *As it was in the beginning, is now and ever shall be, world without end.* On the day it was announced that the atomic bomb had been dropped on Hiroshima those were the words that came immediately to my ten-year-old mind. When I heard a few years later about mushroom clouds over the Nevada test site those were again the words that came to mind. I began waking before dawn, imagining that the fireballs from the Nevada test shots would light up the sky in Sacramento.

Later, after I married and had a child, I learned to find equal meaning in the repeated rituals of domestic life. Setting the table. Lighting the candles. Building the fire. Cooking. All those soufflés, all that crème caramel, all those daubes and albóndigas and gumbos. Clean sheets, stacks of clean towels, hurricane lamps for storms, enough water and food to see us through whatever geological event came our way. *These fragments I have shored against my ruins,* were the words that came to mind then. These fragments mattered to me. I believed in them. That I could find meaning in the intensely personal nature of my life as a wife and mother did not seem inconsistent with finding meaning in the vast indifference of geology and the test shots; the two systems existed for me on parallel tracks that occasionally converged, notably during earthquakes.

In my unexamined mind there was always a point, John's and my death, at which the tracks would converge for a final time. On the Internet I recently found aerial photographs of the house on the Palos Verdes Peninsula in which we had lived when we were first married, the house to which we had brought Quintana home from St. John's Hospital in Santa Monica and put her in her bassinet by the wisteria in the box garden. The photographs, part of the California

Coastal Records Project, the point of which was to document the entire California coastline, were hard to read conclusively, but the house as it had been when we lived in it appeared to be gone. The tower where the gate had been seemed intact but the rest of the structure looked unfamiliar. There seemed to be a swimming pool where the wisteria and box garden had been. The area itself was identified as "Portuguese Bend landslide." You could see the slumping of the hill where the slide had occurred. You could also see, at the base of the cliff on the point, the cave into which we used to swim when the tide was at exactly the right flow.

The swell of clear water.

That was one way my two systems could have converged.

We could have been swimming into the cave with the swell of clear water and the entire point could have slumped, slipped into the sea around us. The entire point slipping into the sea around us was the kind of conclusion I anticipated. I did not anticipate cardiac arrest at the dinner table.

Questions for Critical Reading

1. What does Didion mean by the "ordinary instant"? Develop a definition of that term supported with quotations from her text and then provide an example of an "ordinary instant" from your own life.

2. Grief plays a central role in Didion's essay. What does grief mean to Didion? Reread Didion's text, locating quotations that support your understanding of the term.

3. Didion examines death in this essay but she is also concerned with creating meaning in life. Locate passages that show how Didion believes meaning can be created despite — or perhaps even because of — death's inevitability.

Exploring Context

1. The book from which this essay was taken, *The Year of Magical Thinking*, was turned into a Broadway play. Visit the Web site for the play at magicalthinkingonbroadway.com/about.html. How does the design of the site reflect or complicate the meaning of Didion's text? Use your response to Question 3 of Questions for Critical Reading on creating meaning in life in making your response.

2. Research the stages of grief on the Web. Does Didion go through these stages as evidenced by this essay? Does the essay seem to suggest that Didion is stuck in a particular stage? How do these stages relate to the definition of grief you developed in your response to Question 2 of Questions for Critical Reading?

3. Using the Web, locate information on the decline in the number of autopsies. Why is Didion so insistent on having an autopsy? Why are autopsies occurring less frequently? Should they be performed more regularly?

Questions for Connecting

1. Daniel Gilbert's essay "Reporting Live from Tomorrow" (p. 169) is about the failure of our imaginations to predict our future happiness. Given Didion's essay, how well do our imaginations predict our future *unhappiness*? Use Gilbert's ideas to explore the process of grief documented by Didion.

2. How is an individual's response to death different from a community's response? Use Diana Taylor's "False Identifications: Minority Populations Mourn Diana" (p. 454) to examine the relationship between the mourning of individuals and the sorrowing of groups, synthesizing Taylor's ideas about grief and mourning with Didion's.

3. Mary Roach, in "The Cadaver Who Joined the Army" (p. 347), examines the ethics of using human cadavers. Expand her analysis by using Didion's experience. Is Didion concerned with medical knowledge when she asks for an autopsy to be performed on her husband? Does her experience of grief give us reason to avoid using cadavers in research? You may wish to use your research on autopsies from Question 3 of Exploring Context in composing your answer.

Language Matters

1. Ellipses and brackets are useful punctuation marks when using quotations. Select a long quotation from Didion that represents an important part of her essay. How would you use these punctuation marks to incorporate the quotation into your own writing? How might they be instead used, even unintentionally, to misrepresent the meaning of the quotation? How can you be sure you're using these punctuation marks correctly?

2. The most solid transitions come from a statement that directly ties together two paragraphs. Select two paragraphs from Didion's essay. Write a one-sentence summary of the first paragraph and then another one-sentence summary of the second paragraph. Then combine these two sentences into one to form a new transition between the paragraphs. How does it differ from Didion's transition? How can you use this skill in your own writing?

3. Using section headings or subtitles can help a reader understand the organization of your writing. Didion numbers her sections; provide descriptive subtitles for each section instead. Why might Didion have chosen numbers instead of subtitles? In what situations might you use these elements in your own writing?

Assignments for Writing

1. Given Didion's retelling of the events before and after her husband's death, write an essay that examines the relationship between trauma and memory. What does Didion remember about that night? About her husband? How does trauma shape those memories? You may want to use your response about mourning from Question 2 of Questions for Connecting to support your argument.

2. Didion authorized an autopsy of her husband because she needed to know more about her husband's death, so much so that she wanted to be present during the autopsy. Write a paper that evaluates Didion's decision to authorize an autopsy. Was she in the right frame of mind when she made her decision? What should she have considered that she did not when making her decision? Are autopsies immoral? Are they unethical? How does Didion justify her decision? Is there a need to justify such a decision? Does information beyond personal experience help the grieving process? Why is Didion more concerned about the obituary than the autopsy? Why do doctors feel anxiety about asking for an autopsy? You may want to use your research on autopsies from Question 3 of Exploring Context and your work with Roach's essay from Question 3 of Questions for Connecting in making your argument.

3. At times Didion wants to be alone—especially on the night of her husband's death—but at other times she seems surrounded by people. Using Didion's experience, write a paper in which you evaluate the need to be alone after a traumatic event such as the loss of a loved one. Consider: Why does Didion feel differently about the obituary than she does about the autopsy? What is the difference between grief as we imagine it and grief as it really is? Was Didion ever as alone as she really thought? Is grief strictly a private matter? Does it help to make grief public? What value is there in allowing others into our lives as we grieve?

HELEN EPSTEIN

After earning a Ph.D. in molecular biology from Cambridge University, **Helen Epstein** attended the London School of Hygiene and Tropical Medicine, where she earned an M.Sc. in public health in developing countries. In 1993, while working as a scientist for a biotechnology company in search of an AIDS vaccine, Epstein moved to Uganda, where she witnessed the suffering caused by the virus. Epstein still works in public health care in developing countries. She has had articles published in magazines such as the *New York Review of Books* and in 2007 published her book *The Invisible Cure: Africa, the West, and the Fight against AIDS*.

Epstein compiled the information she had gathered in her years as a scientist in Africa, along with her personal observations, to write *The Invisible Cure*. In it she explores the reasons behind the unprecedented AIDS epidemic in Africa and suggests ways to reduce infection rates on that continent. Along the way she corrects the misinformation and misconceptions that Westerners have been using as a guide for aiding Africans who suffer from or are at risk for AIDS/HIV. She points out that programs for prevention might need to be in the hands of Africans themselves in order to account for local cultures. For instance, while campaigns promoting condom usage might be successful in Western countries, this does not mean such campaigns will succeed within other cultures. Instead, listening to and understanding the traditions and customs of individual cultures might lead to more successful approaches to the AIDS epidemic.

In "AIDS, Inc," a chapter from *The Invisible Cure*, Epstein examines HIV and AIDS prevention programs in Africa. In South Africa, Epstein witnesses a government-run campaign that focuses on creating conversations about sexual activity among the nation's youth in order to help them create informed decisions about sex. However, many of the conversations stop there, leaving out any talk of people who already have AIDS. While the campaign may open up new avenues for youth in terms of sexual responsibility and respect, the lack of conversation surrounding AIDS perpetuates the social stigmas of infected peoples as well as an "out of sight, out of mind" attitude toward the virus. Perhaps, as Epstein points out, campaigns are only as successful as the conversations surrounding them. She points to Uganda—one of the few countries in Africa where the rate of infection has dropped precipitously—as an example of effective conversation. Open conversation among Ugandans about personal experiences with the virus has succeeded in preventing its spread by breaking the cycle of social stigmas surrounding those infected.

What social stigmas concerning HIV and AIDS exist locally and globally? How do these social stigmas interfere with campaigns to successfully prevent the spread of the virus? How might class, race, gender, and religion contribute to the way prevention is approached? While Epstein points out how important conversation is among communities, is it possible to create a global conversation about HIV and AIDS?

▶ TAGS: *community*, *research*, *conversation*, technology, *social change*, *media*

AIDS, Inc.

In response to government prevarication over HIV treatment, a vigorous AIDS activist movement emerged in South Africa and a fierce public relations battle ensued. The Treatment Action Campaign, or TAC, along with other activist groups, accused the South African health minister, Manto Tshabalala-Msimang, of "murder" for denying millions of South Africans access to medicine for AIDS. A spokesman from the ANC Youth League then called the activists "paid marketing agents for toxic AIDS drugs from America."[1] An official in the Department of Housing accused journalists who defended the AIDS activists of fanaticism, and quoted Lenin on how the "press in bourgeois society . . . deceive[s], corrupt[s], and fool[s] the exploited and oppressed mass of the people, the poor."

Meanwhile, across the nation thousands of people were becoming infected daily, from the rural homesteads of the former Bantustans to the peri-urban townships and squatter camps to the formerly all-white suburbs, now home to a growing black middle class. By 2005, the death rate for young adults had tripled.[2] Surveys showed that nearly everyone in South Africa knew that HIV was sexually transmitted and that it could be prevented with condoms, abstinence, and faithfulness to an uninfected partner. Children were receiving AIDS education in school and condoms were widely available, but these programs made little difference. In the din of the battle between the activists and the government, the deeper message, that HIV was everyone's problem, was lost.

In 1999, a group of public health experts sponsored by the U.S.-based Kaiser Family Foundation stepped into this fray. They were concerned about the worsening AIDS crisis in South Africa and wanted to launch a bold new HIV prevention program for young people. They also knew they had to take account of the South African government's attitudes toward AIDS and AIDS activists. Their program, called loveLife, would soon become South Africa's largest and most ambitious HIV prevention campaign. It aimed both to overcome the limitations of similar campaigns that had failed in the past and, at the same time, to avoid dealing with the issues of AIDS treatment and care that had become so controversial.

Could this work? I wondered. Was it possible to reduce the spread of HIV without involving HIV-positive people and the activists and community groups that supported them? LoveLife had been endorsed at one time or another by the archbishop of Cape Town; Nelson Mandela; the king of the Zulu tribe; Jacob

Zuma, South Africa's former deputy president; and even Zanele Mbeki, the wife of the president. In 2003, loveLife's annual $20 million budget was paid for by the South African government, the Kaiser Family Foundation, UNICEF, the Bill and Melinda Gates Foundation, and the Global Fund to Fight AIDS, Tuberculosis, and Malaria. At least South Africa's leaders were beginning to take AIDS seriously, I thought, but what kind of program was this?

"What we want to do is create a substantive, normative shift in the way young people behave," explained loveLife's director, David Harrison, a white South African doctor, when I met him in his Johannesburg office. The average age at which young South Africans lose their virginity—around seventeen—is not much different from the age at which teenagers in other countries do. What's different, Harrison said, was that many of the young South Africans who were sexually active were very sexually active. They were more likely to start having sex at very young ages, even below the age of fourteen—well below the national average. Those vulnerable young people were more likely to have more than one sexual partner, and they were less likely to use condoms. South African girls were more likely to face sexual coercion or rape, or to exchange sex for money or gifts, all of which placed them at greater risk of HIV infection. For Harrison, the trick was to "get inside the head-space of these young people . . . we have to understand what is driving them into sex—they know what HIV is, but they don't internalize it," he said.

LoveLife's aim was to get young people talking, to each other and to their parents, so they would really understand and act on what they knew. But to reach out to them, you had to use a special language that young people could relate to. According to Harrison, traditional HIV prevention campaigns were too depressing: They tried to scare people into changing their behavior, and this turned kids off. LoveLife's media campaign, on the other hand, was positive and cheerful, and resembled the bright, persuasive modern ad campaigns that many South African kids were very much attracted to.

In the past couple of years, nearly a thousand loveLife billboards had sprouted all along the nation's main roads. They were striking. For example, on one of them, the hands of four women of different races caressed the sculpted back and buttocks of a young black man as though they were appraising an antique newel post. The caption read, "Everyone he's slept with, is sleeping with you." On another, a gorgeous mixed-race couple—the boy looked like Brad Pitt, the girl like an Indian film star—lay in bed, under the caption "No Pressure." Some people told me they found these ads oversexualized and disturbing, but it is hard to see why. On the same roads, there are torsos advertising sexy underwear and half-naked actresses advertising romantic movies. Sex is a potent theme in marketing all sorts of products; loveLife, according to its creators, tries to turn that message around to get young people thinking and talking about sex in more responsible ways and convince them of the virtues of abstinence, fidelity, and the use of condoms.

Harrison calls loveLife "a brand of positive lifestyle." The sexy billboards and similar ads on TV and radio, as well as newspaper inserts that resemble teen gossip magazines, with articles and advice columns about clothes, relationships, and sexual health, were designed, Harrison says, to persuade young people to avoid sex in the same way a sneaker ad tries to seduce them into buying new sneakers, because the players in the ads look so cool. The idea is "to create a brand so strong that young people who want to be hip and cool and the rest of it want to associate with it," Harrison told an interviewer in 2001.[3]

The concept of a "lifestyle brand" originated with the rise of brand advertising in the 1960s, when ads for such products as Pepsi-Cola and Harley-Davidson began to promote not only soft drinks and motorcycles, but also a certain style or aesthetic. People were urged to "join the Pepsi generation" or ride a Harley-Davidson not just to get around, but to embrace a certain attitude. A Harley wasn't just a bike; it was a macho rebellion, an escape from the workaday world to the open road. In the 1970s, family-planning programs also tried to

> **Harrison calls loveLife "a brand of positive lifestyle."**

promote contraceptives in developing countries by tapping into poor people's aspirations for a glamorous Western lifestyle. Campaigns depicted small, well-dressed families surrounded by sleek new commodities, including televisions and cars. Harrison predicted that young South Africans would readily respond to this approach too.

"Kids have changed," Harrison explained. Today's young South Africans weren't like the activists who risked their lives in the anti-apartheid demonstrations at Sharpeville and Soweto. "Seventy-five percent of South African teenagers watch TV every day," Harrison informed me. "Their favorite program is *The Bold and the Beautiful*"—an American soap opera in which glamorous characters struggle with personal crises while wearing and driving some very expensive gear. "They are exposed to the global youth culture of music, fashion, pop icons, and commercial brands. They talk about brands among themselves, even if they can't afford everything they see."

The Kaiser Foundation's Michael Sinclair told me that loveLife drew much of its inspiration from the marketing campaign for the soft drink Sprite.[4] In the mid-1990s, sales of Sprite were flagging until the company began an aggressive campaign to embed Sprite in youth culture by sponsoring hip-hop concerts and planting attractive, popular kids in Internet chat rooms or college dormitories and paying them to praise or distribute Sprite in an unobtrusive way. Sprite is now one of the most profitable drinks in the world because it managed to exploit what marketing experts call "the cool effect"—meaning the influence that a small number of opinion leaders can have on the norms and behavior of large numbers of their peers. So far, corporate marketers had made the greatest use of the cool effect, but there was speculation that small numbers of trendsetters could change more complex behavior than shopping, such as criminality, suicide, and sexual behavior.[5]

For this reason, loveLife had established a small network of recreation centers for young people, known as Y-Centers, throughout the country. At Y-Centers, young people could learn to play basketball, volleyball, and other sports, as well as learn break dancing, radio broadcasting, and word processing. All Y-Center activities were led by "loveLife GroundBreakers"—older youths, usually in their early twenties, who, like the kids who made Sprite cool, were stylish and cheerful and enthusiastic about their product, in this case, loveLife and its program to encourage safer sexual behavior. If abstinence, monogamy, and condoms all happened to fail, each Y-Center was affiliated with a family-planning clinic that offered contraceptives and treatment for sexually transmitted diseases such as syphilis and gonorrhea. The centers offered no treatment for AIDS symptoms, however, and when I visited, none of them offered HIV testing either.

Any young person could become a Y-Center member, but in order to fully participate in its activities, he or she had to complete a program of seminars about HIV, family planning, and other subjects related to sexuality and growing up. The seminars emphasized the biological aspects of HIV and its prevention, but not the experience of the disease and its effects on people's lives. Members also received training to raise their self-esteem, because, as Harrison told an interviewer in 2001,

> there is a direct correlation between young people's sexual behavior and their sense of confidence in the future. Those young people who feel motivated, who feel that they have something to look forward to—they are the ones who protect themselves, who ensure that they do not get HIV/AIDS. . . . It's all about the social discount rates that young people apply to future benefits.[6]

Dr. Harrison arranged for me to visit a loveLife Y-Center in the archipelago of townships in the flat scrubland south of Johannesburg known as the Vaal Triangle. Millions of people live in these townships, many of them recent migrants from rural South Africa or from neighboring countries. The Vaal, once a patchwork of white-owned farms, is now a residential area for poor blacks. At first, only a few families moved here, because the apartheid government used the notorious pass laws to restrict the tide of impoverished blacks seeking a better life in Johannesburg. But when the apartheid laws were scrapped, people poured in. Today, the roads and other services in the area are insufficient for its huge and growing population, and many people have no electricity and lack easy access to clean water and sanitation. Unemployment exceeds 70 percent and the crime rate is one of the highest in South Africa.[7]

The loveLife Y-Center was a compound of two small lavender buildings surrounded by an iron fence and curling razor wire. Inside the compound, a group of young men in shorts and T-shirts were doing warm-up exercises on the outdoor basketball court, while girls and barefoot children looked on. Inside the main building, another group of boys in fashionably droopy jeans and dreadlocks practiced a hip-hop routine, and two girls in the computer room experimented with Microsoft Word.

Valentine's Day was coming up, and the Y-Center had organized a group discussion for some of its members. About thirty teenagers, most of them in school uniforms, sat around on the floor of a large seminar room and argued about who should pay for what on a Valentine's Day date. A GroundBreaker in a love-Life T-shirt and with a loveLife kerchief tied pirate-style on her head officiated. "I go with my chick and I spend money on her and always we have sex," said a husky boy in a gray school uniform. "And I want to know, what's the difference between my chick and a prostitute?" As we have seen, long-term transactional relationships—in which money or gifts are frequently exchanged—may not be the same as prostitution, but they nevertheless put many township youths at risk of HIV.[8]

"Boys, they are expecting too much from us. They say we are parasites if we don't sleep with them," said a plump girl in the uniform of a local Catholic school.

"The girls, they ask for a lot of things," another boy chimed in.

"Me, I think it is wrong. If most of the boys think Valentine's Day is about buying sex, the boys must stop," a girl said. "We girls must hold our ground."

These young people were certainly talking openly about sexual relation- 20 ships all right, just as Harrison prescribed. Nevertheless, I felt something was missing. "Do you ever talk about AIDS in those discussion groups?" I asked the GroundBreaker afterward. "We do it indirectly," she replied. "We know that if we just came out and started lecturing them about AIDS, they wouldn't listen. They would just turn off. So we talk about positive things, like making informed choices, sharing responsibility, and positive sexuality."

Was this true? Do young people in South Africa, like their politicians, really want to avoid the subject of AIDS? I wanted to meet young people outside the Y-Center and ask them what they thought about that. A few hundred yards away from the Y-Center stood the headquarters of St. Charles Lwanga, a Catholic organization that carries out a number of activities in the township. Their AIDS program, called Inkanyezi, meaning "star" in Zulu, provides counseling to young people about AIDS and also brings food and other necessities to some four hundred orphans and people living with AIDS in the Vaal.

St. Charles Lwanga was independent of loveLife, and its budget was modest, less than a tenth of what loveLife spent on its billboards alone. The Inkanyezi program was staffed almost entirely by volunteers, whose only compensation was that they were allowed to eat some of the food—usually rice and vegetables—that they prepared for the patients. Lack of funding greatly limited the help that Inkanyezi was able to provide. Although Inkanyezi nurses were able to dispense tuberculosis medicine, antiretroviral drugs were as yet unavailable. Indeed, many of the patients they visited lacked some of the most basic necessities for life and human dignity. Sometimes destitute patients had their water and electricity cut off. But the worst thing was that many of the patients were socially isolated and lived alone in flimsy shacks. The doors were easily broken down and at night neighborhood thugs sometimes came in and stole what little they had. Sometimes the patients were raped.

Justice Showalala, who ran Inkanyezi, organized a meeting for me with a group of about twenty-five young people from Orange Farm. The HIV rate in the area was not known, but several people explained to me how their lives had been changed by the virus. They said they had witnessed extreme prejudice and discrimination against people with AIDS, and they did not know where to turn when they learned that a relative or friend was HIV positive. "People say you shouldn't touch someone with HIV," said one girl. "I have a friend at school who disclosed she has HIV, and the others won't even walk with her." Justice explained how he had offered to introduce some teachers from a local school to some of his HIV-positive clients. "They said, 'If you want me to meet people with AIDS, you better give me a rubber suit.'"

The loveLife Y-Center did little to help young people deal with such confusion, stigma, and shame. "I learned basketball at the Y-Center," one girl told me, "and at meetings we talked about resisting peer pressure, [like when] your friends advise you to break your virginity, to prove you are girl enough. But I was afraid the people there would find out my sister had HIV. We talked about it as though it was someone else's problem."

In general, although sex was openly discussed at the Y-Center, the experience of AIDS was not. The Y-Center offered individual counseling for a small number of young people with HIV, but those who were hungry, homeless, or destitute, or were suffering from the symptoms of AIDS, were told to consult other organizations, including Inkanyezi. 25

It turns out that talking about the pain, both physical and emotional, that the disease creates is far more difficult than getting over the embarrassment of talking about sex. "I had heard about HIV before," said an Inkanyezi girl, wearing a bright blue T-shirt and matching headband. "But then I found out my mother was HIV positive. I was so shocked, so shocked. I even talked to my teacher about it. She said it can happen to anyone; it must have been from mistakes my mother made, and that I shouldn't make those mistakes in my own life."

"Sometimes, women have no choice," said the older woman sitting next to the girl in blue. She was thin, with intense dark eyes and a deep, wry smile. She was dressed entirely in black, except for a baseball cap with a red ribbon on it—the universal symbol of solidarity with HIV-positive people. "They get infected because of their husbands, and there's nothing they can do.

"It happened like this," the older woman went on. "It was back when we were living in Soweto, before we moved here. One day my daughter and I were washing clothes together," she said, nodding at the girl in blue. "She said she'd had a dream that I was so sick, that I had cancer and I was going to die. I waited until we were done with the washing, and then I told her that I was HIV positive. She said, 'I knew it, you were always sick and always going to support groups.' She was so down, she just cried all day and all night after that. I told her, 'Only God knows why people have this disease. Don't worry, I won't die right away.'

"Once I visited the loveLife Y-Center," the woman continued, "but I just saw children playing. I sat and talked with them, and they were shocked when I said I was HIV positive. I told them about what it was like, and one of them said she would ask the managers whether I could come and talk to a bigger group. But that was about six months ago and they haven't called me. I haven't moved and my number hasn't changed. I don't know why they haven't called."

"I think there should be more counseling and support groups for people   30
who find out their parents are HIV positive," the girl in blue said. "It puts you
down, it really gets to you, it haunts you. When you are standing in class and
you have to recite a poem or something, I find I can't get anything out of my
mouth. I can't concentrate. [The problem] here is ignorance. I didn't care about
HIV until I found out about my mother. Then I started to care about these
people. I wish many people in our country would also think like that."

In 2003, the only African country that had seen a nationwide decline in HIV
prevalence was Uganda. Since 1992 the HIV rate had fallen by some two-
thirds, a success that saved perhaps a million lives. The programs and policies
that led to this success [are discussed elsewhere], but the epidemiologists Rand
Stoneburner and Daniel Low-Beer have argued that a powerful role was played
by the ordinary, but frank, conversations people had with family, friends, and
neighbors—not about sex, but about the frightening, calamitous effects of
AIDS itself.[9] Stoneburner and Low-Beer maintain that these painful personal
conversations did more than anything else to persuade Ugandans to come to
terms with the reality of AIDS, care for the afflicted, and change their behavior.
This in turn led to declines in HIV transmission. The researchers found that
people in other sub-Saharan African countries were far less likely to have such
discussions.

In South Africa, people told Stoneburner and Low-Beer that they had heard
about the epidemic from posters, radio, newspapers, and clinics, as well as from
occasional mass rallies, schools, and village meetings; but they seldom spoke
about it with the people they knew. They were also far less likely to admit knowing someone with AIDS or to be willing to care for an AIDS patient. It may be
no coincidence that the HIV rate in South Africa rose higher than it ever did in
Uganda, and has taken far longer to fall.

When I was in Uganda during the early 1990s, the HIV rate was already
falling, and I vividly recall how the reality of AIDS was alive in people's minds.
Kampala taxi drivers talked as passionately about AIDS as taxi drivers elsewhere discuss politics or football. And they talked about it in a way that would
seem foreign to many in South Africa because it was so personal: "my sister,"
"my father," "my neighbor," "my friend."[10]

Ugandans are not unusually compassionate people, and discrimination
against people with AIDS persists in some families and institutions. But Ugandans do seem more willing to openly address painful issues in their lives. This
courage owes much to the AIDS information campaigns launched by the government of Uganda early on in the epidemic. But it may have other sources as
well. Maybe the difference between the ways South Africa and Uganda have
dealt with AIDS has historical roots. Both South Africa and Uganda have bitter
histories of conflict. But while Uganda was terrorized for decades by a series of
brutal leaders, they could not destroy the traditional rhythms of rural family
life. Uganda is one of the most fertile countries in Africa; there is enough land
for everyone, and most people live as their ancestors did, as peasant farmers
and herders. No large settler population displaced huge numbers of people or

set up a system to exploit and humiliate them, as happened in South Africa and in many other African countries. This means Ugandans are more likely to know their neighbors and to live near members of their extended families. This in turn may have contributed to what sociologists call "social cohesion"—the tendency of people to talk openly with one another and form trusted relationships. Perhaps this may have facilitated more realistic and open discussion of AIDS, more compassionate attitudes toward infected people, and pragmatic behavior change.

Perhaps many attempts to prevent the spread of HIV fail because those in charge of them don't recognize that the decisions people make about sex are usually a matter of feeling, not calculation. In other words, sexual behavior is determined less by what Dr. Harrison called "discount rates" that young people "apply to future benefits" than by emotional attachments. I thought of the South African girls who said they had lost a sister or a friend to AIDS. If one of them was faced with a persistent, wealthy seducer, what would be more likely to persuade her to decline? The memory of a loveLife billboard, with its flashy, beautiful models? Or the memory of a person she had known who had died?

On the morning before I left South Africa, I attended a loveLife motivational seminar at a school not far from Orange Farm. "These seminars help young people see the future, identify choices, and identify the values that underpin those choices," Harrison had told me. "We help them ask themselves, 'What can you do to chart life's journey and control it as much as possible?'" The seminars were based on Success by Choice, a series devised by Marlon Smith, a California-based African-American motivational speaker. How was Mr. Smith's message of personal empowerment translated to South Africa, I wondered, where children have to contend with poverty, the risk of being robbed or raped, and a grim future of likely unemployment?

About twenty-five children aged ten to fourteen were in the class, and the GroundBreaker asked them to hold their hands out in front of them, pretend they were looking in a mirror, and repeat the following words:

"You are intelligent!"

"You are gifted!"

"There is no one in the world like you!"

"I love you!"

The children spoke quietly at first, then louder, as though they were being hypnotized. The GroundBreaker urged them to talk more openly with their parents, to keep themselves clean, and to make positive choices in their lives, especially when it came to sexuality. There was little mention of helping other people, nor was there much advice about how to avoid being raped or harassed by other students as well as teachers, relatives, or strangers, or how to plan a future in a country where unemployment for township blacks was so high.

Then something really odd occurred. One of the GroundBreakers asked the children to stand up because it was time for an "Icebreaker." "This is a little song-and-dance thing we do, to give the children a chance to stretch. It improves their concentration," another GroundBreaker told me. The words of the song were as follows:

> *Pizza Hut*
> *Pizza Hut*
> *Kentucky Fried Chicken and a Pizza Hut*
> *McDonald's*
> *McDonald's*
> *Kentucky Fried Chicken and a Pizza Hut.*

In the dance, the children spread their arms out as though they were rolling out a pizza, or flapped their elbows like chickens.

What kinds of choices was Dr. Harrison really referring to? I wondered. The techniques of marketing attempt to impose scientific principles on human choices. But it seemed a mad experiment to see whether teenagers living through very difficult times could be persuaded to choose a new sexual lifestyle as they might choose a new brand of shampoo, or whether children could be trained to associate safe sex with pizza and self-esteem.

Afterward, I spoke to some of the children who had participated in the seminar. They all knew how to protect themselves from HIV, and they were eager to show off their knowledge about condoms, abstinence, and fidelity within relationships. But they all said they didn't personally know anyone with AIDS; nor did they know of any children who had lost parents to AIDS. They did mention Nkosi Johnson, the brave HIV-positive twelve-year-old boy who became world-famous in 2000 when he stood up at an International Conference on AIDS and challenged the South African president, Thabo Mbeki, to do more for people living with the virus.

In fact, their principal would tell me later, more than twenty children at the school were AIDS orphans, and many more had been forced to drop out because there was no one to pay their expenses after their parents died. The children I spoke to seemed not to know why some of their classmates wore ragged uniforms or had no shoes or stopped showing up at all.

The week before, I had met some teenage girls in Soweto and I had asked them the same question. They answered in the same way: The only person they knew with AIDS was Nkosi Johnson, the famous boy at the AIDS conference. Just as Harrison had warned me, these girls said they were tired of hearing about AIDS. The girls were orphans, although they said their parents had not died of AIDS. I later discovered that, in another part of that same orphanage, there was a nursery where thirty babies and small children, all of them HIV positive, all abandoned by their parents, lay on cots or sat quietly on the floor, struggling for life. No wonder those girls were tired of hearing about HIV. It was right in their midst, within earshot, but the world around them was telling them to look the other way.

A couple of years later, I would meet a group of primary-school students in Kigali, Rwanda. By then, the HIV infection rate in Rwanda had fallen steeply, just as it had in Uganda years earlier. The school was a typical single-story line of classrooms in one of the poorest sections of Kigali. I spoke to the principal first, and he showed me the government-issued manual used for teaching about AIDS, which contained the usual information about abstinence and condoms. The school day had just ended, and he went outside and asked a few students to stay behind and chat with me.[11]

The Rwandan students had no idea in advance what I wanted to talk to them about. But when I asked them the same question I had asked the South African children, "Do you know anyone with AIDS?" their answers floored me. Every one of them had a story about someone they knew who was HIV positive or suffering from AIDS. "I knew a man who had bad lips [sores] and tears all over his skin," said a fourteen-year-old boy. "People stigmatized him and he died because no one was caring for him." Another boy described a woman who was "so thin, she almost died." But then her relatives took her to the hospital, where she was given AIDS treatment. "She got better because people cared for her," he said.

When I asked the Rwandan children whether they had any questions for me, all they wanted to know was what they could do to help people with AIDS. The responses of the South African children were strikingly different. When I asked them if they had questions for me, they quickly changed the subject from AIDS and asked me what America was like and whether I knew any of the pop stars they admired on TV.

The persistent denial of AIDS in South Africa was deeply disturbing. People liked the colorful, frank advertising and the basketball games sponsored by loveLife. But its programs seemed to me to reinforce the denial that posed so many obstacles to preventing HIV in the first place. In 2005, the Global Fund to Fight AIDS, Tuberculosis, and Malaria would come to similar conclusions and terminate its multimillion-dollar grant to loveLife.[12]

> **The persistent denial of AIDS in South Africa was deeply disturbing.**

Epidemiologists are equivocal about whether loveLife had any effect on HIV transmission in South Africa, but during the program's first seven years, HIV infection rates continued to rise steadily.[13]

A more realistic HIV prevention program would have paid less attention to aspirations and dreams unattainable for so many young people, and greater attention to the real circumstances in people's lives that make it hard for them to avoid infection. It would also have been more frank about the real human consequences of the disease. But that would have meant dealing with some very painful matters that South Africa's policy-makers seemed determined to evade.

It was heartening that Western donors were now spending so much money on AIDS programs in Africa. But the problem with some large foreign-aid programs was that distributing the funds often involved negotiating with governments with a poor record of dealing with AIDS. In addition, the huge sums of money involved were often very difficult to manage, so that small community-based groups that need thousands of dollars, rather than millions—like Inkanyezi in Orange Farm—were often overlooked in favor of overly ambitious megaprojects, whose effectiveness had not been demonstrated and whose premises were open to question. It seemed clear to me that more could be learned from Inkanyezi's attempt to help people deal with the reality of AIDS than from loveLife's attempt to create a new consumerist man and woman for South Africa.

NOTES

1. Helen Schneider, "On the fault-line: The politics of AIDS policy in contemporary South Africa," *Afr Stud* 61:1 (July 1, 2002), 145–67; Samantha Power, "The AIDS Rebel," *New Yorker*, May 19, 2003, pp. 54–67.
2. Rob Dorrington et al., "The Impact of HIV/AIDS on Adult Mortality in South Africa" (Cape Town: Burden of Disease Research Unit, Medical Research Council of South Africa, September 2001); "Mortality and causes of death in South Africa, 2003 and 2004," Statistics South Africa, May 2006.
3. Richard Delate, "The Struggle for Meaning: A Semiotic Analysis of Interpretations of the loveLife His&Hers Billboard Campaign," November 2001, http://www.comminit.com/stlovelife/sld-4389.html.
4. Personal communication, February 2003.
5. For more about this, see Malcolm Gladwell, *The Tipping Point* (Boston: Little, Brown, 2000), and Everett Rogers, *Diffusion of Innovations* (New York: Free Press, 1983).
6. Delate, "Struggle for Meaning."
7. See Prishani Naidoo, "Youth Divided: A Review of loveLife's Y-Centre in Orange Farm" (Johannesburg: CADRE Report, 2003).
8. Nancy Luke and Kathleen M. Kurtz, "Cross-Generational and Transactional Sexual Relations in Sub-Saharan Africa: Prevalence of Behavior and Implications for Negotiating Safer Sexual Practices," International Center for Research on Women, 2002, http://www.icrw.org/docs/CrossGenSex_ Report_902.pdf; J. Swart-Kruger and L. M. Richter, "AIDS-related knowledge, attitudes and behaviour among South African street youth: Reflections on power, sexuality and the autonomous self," *Soc Sci Med* 45:6 (1997), 957–66; Editorial, "Reassessing priorities: Identifying the determinants of HIV transmission," *Soc Sci Med* 36:5 (1993), iii–viii.
9. Daniel Low-Beer and Rand Stoneburner, "Uganda and the Challenge of AIDS," in *The Political Economy of AIDS in Africa*, ed. Nana Poku and Alan Whiteside (London: Ashgate, 2004).
10. See Helen Epstein, "Fat," *Granta* 49 (1995). Low-Beer and Stoneburner make this observation, too, as do Janice Hogle et al. in *What Happened in Uganda? Declining HIV Prevalence, Behavior Change and the National Response* (USAID, 2002).
11. In 2006, the *Washington Post* reported that the HIV infection rate in Rwanda, once estimated to be 15 percent, was now estimated to be 3 percent. See Craig Timberg, "How AIDS in Africa Was Overstated: Reliance on Data from Urban Prenatal Clinics Skewed Early Projections," *Washington Post*, April 6, 2006, p. A1. Timberg attributed the downward revision to a new U.S. government survey and suggested that the earlier estimate, issued by the UNAIDS program, had been inflated, perhaps to raise money or appease AIDS activists. Although the old UNAIDS statistics were in need of correction, there clearly had been a decline in the true infection rate. A population-based survey carried out in

Rwanda in 1986 found that prevalence was 17.8 percent in urban areas and 1.3 percent in rural areas. (Rwandan HIV Seroprevalence Study Group, "Nationwide community-based serological survey of HIV-1 and other human retrovirus infections in a country," *Lancet* 1 (ii) (1989), 941–43.

12. A. E. Pettifor et al., "Young people's sexual health in South Africa: HIV prevalence and sexual behaviors from a nationally representative household survey," *AIDS* 19:14 (September 23, 2005), 1525–34; but see R. Jewkes, "Response to Pettifor et al.," *AIDS* 20:6 (April 4, 2006), 952–53; author reply, 956–58; and W. M. Parker and M. Colvin, "Response to Pettifor et al.," *AIDS* 20:6 (April 4, 2006), 954–55.

13. In 2005, an article in the prestigious medical journal *AIDS* reported that young people who had attended at least one loveLife program were slightly, but significantly, less likely to be HIV positive than those who had not. The author argued that this was consistent with the possibility that loveLife reduced risky sexual behavior. However, there could well be another explanation. From what I saw, loveLife attracted young people who would have been at lower risk of infection in the first place, either because they were wealthier or better educated or less vulnerable to abuse. (While the loveLife study attempted to control for education and wealth, it did not do so rigorously.) Indeed, the tendency to avoid the subject of AIDS would seem to discourage HIV-positive young people from attending loveLife's programs, and this could make it look as though loveLife protected young people when in fact it merely alienated those most at risk. Most loveLife materials were in English, and thus accessible only to young people with higher social status. This would have sent a clear signal to those—often marginalized and vulnerable young people—who could not speak English well that loveLife was not for them. The main author of the article reporting lower HIV rates among young people exposed to loveLife admitted to me in an interview that an anthropologist hired by loveLife itself had come to these same conclusions, but her results remain unpublished. See Pettifor et al., "A community-based study to examine the effect of a youth HIV prevention intervention on young people aged 15–24 in South Africa: results of the baseline survey," *Trop Med Int Health* 10:10 (October 2005), 971–80; but see also Jewkes, "Response to Pettifor et al.," author reply, and Parker and Colvin, "Response to Pettifor." Information re the loveLife anthropologist from Pettifor, personal communication, April 2006.

Questions for Critical Reading

1. What is a "lifestyle brand"? Define the term using Epstein's text. Then find an example of a lifestyle brand from popular culture. How might such an approach be used in health education? How effective might it be? How effective was it in South Africa?

2. Define *social cohesion* using Epstein's text. What role did it play in HIV infection rates in Uganda? How might that role be extended to other countries, including the United States?

3. Given Epstein's argument, what would an effective HIV prevention program look like in Africa? How about the United States? Would the same strategies be effective in those two different cultural contexts? Support your responses with passages from the essay.

Exploring Context

1. The (PRODUCT) RED campaign (joinred.com) pairs popular products with fundraising in the fight against AIDS in Africa. Explore the (PRODUCT) RED Web site. Given Epstein's argument, how successful might this campaign be? How does your work with lifestyle brands from Question 1 of Questions for Critical Reading inform your answer?

2. Use the Web to locate information on current HIV infection rates in Africa. Has the situation improved since Epstein wrote her essay, or is it continuing to get worse? What might account for this trend, given Epstein's argument?

3. One of Epstein's central arguments is the usefulness of conversation in combating HIV infection in Africa. How might social networking technologies like Facebook or MySpace help in such a campaign?

Questions for Connecting

1. Leslie Savan, in "What's Black, Then White, and Said All Over?" (p. 363), explores the role of black talk in mainstream advertising. How do her arguments help explain the loveLife campaign that Epstein examines? What are the limits of advertising? What role does race play in the production of cultural change? You may want to draw from your work on lifestyle brands from Question 1 of Questions for Critical Reading.

2. What role should religion play in HIV education in Africa and elsewhere? Use Madeleine Albright's arguments in "Faith and Diplomacy" (p. 23) to determine the best functions of religion in HIV prevention campaigns. You may want to use your work imagining a prevention program from Question 3 of Questions for Critical Reading in composing your response. Should faith be a determining factor when lives are at stake? Would taking religion into account produce better prevention campaigns? What do Epstein's experiences in Uganda and South Africa suggest?

3. Kenji Yoshino, in "Preface" (p. 479) and "The New Civil Rights" (p. 481), suggests that conversation has an important role to play in producing change around civil rights. How does Epstein's argument confirm or complicate Yoshino's ideas? What makes conversation useful in producing social change?

Language Matters

1. Periods are important marks of punctuation, denoting the units of meaning we call sentences. Select a key passage from Epstein's text and type it into a word processor without any capital letters or periods. In class, trade these never-ending sentences and work on replacing the missing punctuation marks. How can you tell when a period is needed in Epstein's text? How can you tell when one is needed in your own text?

2. Outlines can be helpful in creating organization before we start writing, but they can also help us see the organization of any existing piece of writing. Create a "postdraft outline" of Epstein's piece, using a one-sentence summary of each major move of her argument. What sections do you see in her essay? How do they relate to each other? How can you use postdraft outlines of your own papers to check your organization?

3. Because it is sexually transmitted, AIDS/HIV is a delicate issue for many people. What sort of tone and language does Epstein use to discuss the disease and its transmission? How do her choices reflect both her audience and the delicacy of the subject matter? When would you make similar choices in your own writing?

Assignments for Writing

1. Epstein explores the way children and families address the AIDS crisis in Africa. In a short paper, examine the generational response to HIV/AIDS using Epstein's essay. Here are some questions to help your critical thinking: How do adults handle the discussion of AIDS? Is this separate from the discussion of other sexually transmitted diseases? How do children and young adults handle this topic? How do *you* handle it? You might want to draw from your work on social cohesion from Question 2 of Questions for Critical Reading or your analysis of conversation's potential for combating HIV from Question 3 of Exploring Context.

2. Epstein evaluates a number of approaches to HIV prevention, both formal and informal campaigns. Write a paper in which you assess the role of government in the prevention of diseases like HIV. Consider: What should the role of the government be in addressing the HIV/AIDS crisis? Both loveLife and Inkanyezi are private organizations that address sexually transmitted diseases and HIV/AIDS; should there be a similar government outreach program? What role would that program play? Are ordinary people better at preventing disease? How can a government promote the kind of strategies that were effective in Uganda?

3. South Africa's loveLife relies heavily on an advertising campaign. Write an essay in which you evaluate the role of commercial culture in addressing national crises such as HIV/AIDS. What role should companies and advertisers take upon themselves? How does that differ from what they appear to do? Are they really just out for profit, or do companies have a conscience? Should or can they act on issues that affect national health? You might want to reference your work on Product (Red) from Question 1 in Exploring Context in making your argument.

THOMAS FRIEDMAN

Journalist and author **Thomas L. Friedman** holds a B.A. in Mediterranean studies from Brandeis University and an M.A. in Middle Eastern studies from Oxford University. Friedman joined the *New York Times* in 1981 and has won three Pulitzer Prizes since. His foreign affairs column appears in more than seven hundred newspapers, and his books *From Beirut to Jerusalem* (1989), *The Lexus and the Olive Tree: Understanding Globalization* (1999), *Longitudes and Attitudes: Exploring the World after September 11* (2002), *The World Is Flat: A Brief History of the Twenty-first Century* (2005), and *Hot, Flat, and Crowded: Why We Need a Green Revolution — and How It Can Renew America* (2008) have been national best-sellers.

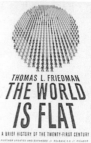

THOMAS L. FRIEDMAN
THE WORLD IS FLAT
A BRIEF HISTORY OF THE TWENTY-FIRST CENTURY

The World Is Flat examines the impact of the "flattening" of the globe, an international leveling of business competition enabled by increasing interconnectedness. Friedman argues that globalized trade, outsourcing, offshoring, supply-chaining, and six other economic, technological, and political forces have changed the world permanently. He examines the positive and negative effects flattening has had and will continue to have on global politics and business.

In "The Dell Theory of Conflict Prevention," which is the penultimate chapter in *The World Is Flat*, Friedman explores the future of war in a globalized economy. Updating a concept he first introduced in *The Lexus and the Olive Tree* — the "Golden Arches Theory of Conflict Prevention," which suggested that citizens in societies economically developed enough to support a McDonald's lose interest in fighting wars — Friedman proposes with the "Dell Theory of Conflict Prevention" that countries will hesitate to risk their place in the global supply chain by fighting a nonessential war. He warns, though, that his new theory does not apply to every kind of modern threat, for terrorists, too, have learned how to use global supply chains.

The flat world will have an impact on you directly as you compete for work with others around the world. This new business environment presents tremendous opportunities for us all; but what are the geopolitical consequences of this new economic reality, and will those consequences generate peace or more conflict?

▶ TAGS: *politics*, *globalization*, *economics*, knowledge, *supply chains*, *collaboration*

The Dell Theory of Conflict Prevention

> Free Trade is God's diplomacy. There is no other certain way of uniting
> people in the bonds of peace.
> —BRITISH POLITICIAN RICHARD COBDEN, 1857

Before I share with you the subject of this chapter, I have to tell you a little bit
about the computer that I wrote this book on. It's related to the theme I am
about to discuss. This book was largely written on a Dell Inspiron 600m notebook, service tag number 9ZRJP41. As part of the research for this book, I visited with the management team at Dell near Austin, Texas. I shared with them
the ideas in this book and in return I asked for one favor: I asked them to trace
for me the entire global supply chain that produced my Dell notebook. Here is
their report:

My computer was conceived when I phoned Dell's 800 number on April
2, 2004, and was connected to sales representative Mujteba Naqvi, who immediately entered my order into Dell's order management system. He typed in
both the type of notebook I ordered as well as the special features I wanted,
along with my personal information, shipping address, billing address, and
credit card information. My credit card was verified by Dell through its work
flow connection with Visa, and my order was then released to Dell's production system. Dell has six factories around the world—in Limerick, Ireland;
Xiamen, China; Eldorado do Sul, Brazil; Nashville, Tennessee; Austin, Texas; and
Penang, Malaysia. My order went out by e-mail to the Dell notebook factory in
Malaysia, where the parts for the computer were immediately ordered from the
supplier logistics centers (SLCs) next to the Penang factory. Surrounding every
Dell factory in the world are these supplier logistics centers, owned by the different suppliers of Dell parts. These SLCs are like staging areas. If you are a Dell
supplier anywhere in the world, your job is to keep your SLC full of your specific
parts so they can constantly be trucked over to the Dell factory for just-in-time
manufacturing.

"In an average day, we sell 140,000 to 150,000 computers," explained Dick
Hunter, one of Dell's three global production managers. "Those orders come in
over Dell.com or over the telephone. As soon as these orders come in, our suppliers know about it. They get a signal based on every component in the machine
you ordered, so the supplier knows just what he has to deliver. If you are supplying power cords for desktops, you can see minute by minute how many power
cords you are going to have to deliver." Every two hours, the Dell factory in
Penang sends an e-mail to the various SLCs nearby, telling each one what parts
and what quantities of those parts it wants delivered within the next ninety
minutes—and not one minute later. Within ninety minutes, trucks from the
various SLCs around Penang pull up to the Dell manufacturing plant and unload the parts needed for all those notebooks ordered in the last two hours. This
goes on all day, every two hours. As soon as those parts arrive at the factory, it
takes thirty minutes for Dell employees to unload the parts, register their bar

codes, and put them into the bins for assembly. "We know where every part in every SLC is in the Dell system at all times," said Hunter.

So where did the parts for my notebook come from? I asked Hunter. To begin with, he said, the notebook was codesigned in Austin, Texas, and in Taiwan by a team of Dell engineers and a team of Taiwanese notebook designers. "The customer's needs, required technologies, and Dell's design innovations were all determined by Dell through our direct relationship with customers," he explained. "The basic design of the motherboard and case—the basic functionality of your machine—was designed to those specifications by an ODM [original design manufacturer] in Taiwan. We put our engineers in their facilities and they come to Austin and we actually codesign these systems. This global teamwork brings an added benefit—a globally distributed virtually twenty-four-hour-per-day development cycle. Our partners do the basic electronics and we help them design customer and reliability features that we know our customers want. We know the customers better than our suppliers and our competition, because we are dealing directly with them every day." Dell notebooks are completely redesigned roughly every twelve months, but new features are constantly added during the year—through the supply chain—as the hardware and software components advance.

It happened that when my notebook order hit the Dell factory in Penang, one part was not available—the wireless card—due to a quality control issue, so the assembly of the notebook was delayed for a few days. Then the truck full of good wireless cards arrived. On April 13, at 10:15 AM, a Dell Malaysia worker pulled the order slip that automatically popped up once all my parts had arrived from the SLCs to the Penang factory. Another Dell Malaysia employee then took out a "traveler"—a special carrying tote designed to hold and protect parts—and started plucking all the parts that went into my notebook.

> This supply chain symphony . . . is one of the wonders of the flat world.

Where did those parts come from? Dell uses multiple suppliers for most of the thirty key components that go into its notebooks. That way if one supplier breaks down or cannot meet a surge in demand, Dell is not left in the lurch. So here are the key suppliers for my Inspiron 600m notebook: The Intel microprocessor came from an Intel factory either in the Philippines, Costa Rica, Malaysia, or China. The memory came from a Korean-owned factory in Korea (Samsung), a Taiwanese-owned factory in Taiwan (Nanya), a German-owned factory in Germany (Infineon), or a Japanese-owned factory in Japan (Elpida). My graphics card was shipped from either a Taiwanese-owned factory in China (MSI) or a Chinese-run factory in China (Foxconn). The cooling fan came from a Taiwanese-owned factory in Taiwan (CCI or Auras). The motherboard came from either a Korean-owned factory in Shanghai (Samsung), a Taiwanese-owned factory in Shanghai (Quanta), or a Taiwanese-owned factory in Taiwan (Compal or Wistron). The keyboard came from either a Japanese-owned company in Tianjin, China (Alps), a Taiwanese-owned factory in Shenzen, China (Sunrex), or a Taiwanese-owned factory in Suzhou, China (Darfon). The LCD display was made in either South Korea (Samsung or LG.Philips LCD), Japan (Toshiba or Sharp), or Taiwan (Chi Mei Optoelectronics, Hannstar Display, or AU Optronics). The wireless card came from either an American-owned factory in China (Agere) or Malaysia (Arrow), or a Taiwanese-owned factory in Taiwan (Askey or Gemtek) or China (USI). The modem was made by either a Taiwanese-owned company in China (Asustek or Liteon) or a Chinese-run company in China (Foxconn). The battery came from an American-owned factory in Malaysia (Motorola), a Japanese-owned factory in Mexico or Malaysia or China (Sanyo), or a South Korean or Taiwanese factory in either of those two countries (SDI or Simplo). The hard disk drive was made by an American-owned factory in Singapore (Seagate), a Japanese-owned company in Thailand (Hitachi or Fujitsu), or a Japanese-owned factory in the Philippines (Toshiba). The CD/DVD drive came from a South Korean–owned company with factories in Indonesia and the Philippines (Samsung); a Japanese-owned factory in China or Malaysia (NEC); a Japanese-owned factory in Indonesia, China, or Malaysia (Teac); or a Japanese-owned factory in China (Sony). The notebook carrying bag was made by either an Irish-owned company in China (Tenba) or an American-owned company in China (Targus, Samsonite, or Pacific Design). The power adapter was made by either a Thai-owned factory in Thailand (Delta) or a Taiwanese, Korean, or American-owned factory in China (Liteon, Samsung, or Mobility). The power cord was made by a British-owned company with factories in China, Malaysia, and India (Volex). The removable memory stick was made by either an Israeli-owned company in Israel (M-System) or an American-owned company with a factory in Malaysia (Smart Modular).

This supply chain symphony—from my order over the phone to production to delivery to my house—is one of the wonders of the flat world.

"We have to do a lot of collaborating," said Hunter. "Michael [Dell] personally knows the CEOs of these companies, and we are constantly working with them on process improvements and real-time demand/supply balancing." Demand shaping goes on constantly, said Hunter. What is "demand shaping"? It works like this: At 10 AM Austin time, Dell discovers that so many customers have ordered notebooks with 40-gigabyte hard drives since the morning that its supply chain will run short in two hours. That signal is automatically relayed to Dell's marketing department and to Dell.com and to all the Dell phone operators taking orders. If you happen to call to place your Dell order at 10:30 AM, the Dell representative will say to you, "Tom, it's your lucky day! For the next hour we are offering 60-gigabyte hard drives with the notebook you want—for only $10 more than the 40-gig drive. And if you act now, Dell will throw in a carrying case along with your purchase, because we so value you as a customer." In an hour or two, using such promotions, Dell can reshape the demand for any part of any notebook or desktop to correspond with the projected supply in its global supply chain. Today memory might be on sale, tomorrow it might be CD-ROMs.

Picking up the story of my notebook, on April 13, at 11:29 AM, all the parts had been plucked from the just-in-time inventory bins in Penang, and the computer was assembled there by A. Sathini, a team member "who manually screwed together all of the parts from kitting as well as the labels needed for Tom's system," said Dell in their production report to me. "The system was then sent down the conveyor to go to burn, where Tom's specified software was downloaded." Dell has huge server banks stocked with the latest in Microsoft, Norton Utilities, and other popular software applications, which are downloaded into each new computer according to the specific tastes of the customer.

"By 2:45 PM, Tom's software had been successfully downloaded, and [was]   10 manually moved to the boxing line. By 4:05 PM, Tom's system [was] placed in protective foam and a shuttle box, with a label, which contains his order number, tracking code, system type, and shipping code. By 6:04 PM, Tom's system had been loaded on a pallet with a specified manifest, which gives the Merge facility visibility to when the system will arrive, what pallet it will be on (out of 75+ pallets with 152 systems per pallet), and to what address Tom's system will ship. By 6:26 PM, Tom's system left [the Dell factory] to head to the Penang, Malaysia, airport."

Six days a week Dell charters a China Airlines 747 out of Taiwan and flies it from Penang to Nashville via Taipei. Each 747 leaves with twenty-five thousand Dell notebooks that weigh altogether 110,000 kilograms, or 242,500 pounds. It is the only 747 that ever lands in Nashville, except Air Force One, when the president visits. "By April 15, 2004, at 7:41 AM, Tom's system arrived at [Nashville] with other Dell systems from Penang and Limerick. By 11:58 AM, Tom's system [was] inserted into a larger box, which went down the boxing line to the specific external parts that Tom had ordered."

That was thirteen days after I'd ordered it. Had there not been a parts delay in Malaysia when my order first arrived, the time between when I phoned in my purchase, when the notebook was assembled in Penang, and its arrival in Nashville would have been only four days. Hunter said the total supply chain for my computer, including suppliers of suppliers, involved about four hundred companies in North America, Europe, and primarily Asia, but with thirty key players. Somehow, though, it all came together. As Dell reported: On April 15, 2004, at 12:59 PM, "Tom's system had been shipped from [Nashville] and was tenured by UPS shipping LTL (3-5-day ground, specified by Tom), with UPS tracking number 1Z13WA374253514697. By April 19, 2004, at 6:41 PM, Tom's system arrived in Bethesda, MD, and was signed for."

I am telling you the story of my notebook to tell a larger story of geopolitics in the flat world. To all the forces . . . that are still holding back the flattening of the world, or could actually reverse the process, one has to add a more traditional threat, and that is an outbreak of a good, old-fashioned, world-shaking, economy-destroying war. It could be China deciding once and for all to eliminate Taiwan as an independent state; or North Korea, out of fear or insanity, using one of its nuclear weapons against South Korea or Japan; or Israel and a soon-to-be-nuclear Iran going at each other; or India and Pakistan finally nuking it out. These and other classic geopolitical conflicts could erupt at any time and either slow the flattening of the world or seriously unflatten it.

The real subject of this chapter is how these classic geopolitical threats might be moderated or influenced by the new forms of collaboration fostered and demanded by the flat world — particularly supply-chaining. The flattening of the world is too young for us to draw any definitive conclusions. What is certain, though, is that as the world flattens, one of the most interesting dramas to watch in international relations will be the interplay between the traditional global threats and the newly emergent global supply chains. The interaction between old-time threats (like China *versus* Taiwan) and just-in-time supply chains (like China *plus* Taiwan) will be a rich source of study for the field of international relations in the early twenty-first century.

In *The Lexus and the Olive Tree* I argued that to the extent that countries tied their economies and futures to global integration and trade, it would act as a restraint on going to war with their neighbors. I first started thinking about this in the late 1990s, when, during my travels, I noticed that no two countries that both had McDonald's had ever fought a war against each other since each got its McDonald's. (Border skirmishes and civil wars don't count, because McDonald's usually served both sides.) After confirming this with McDonald's, I offered what I called the Golden Arches Theory of Conflict Prevention. The Golden Arches Theory stipulated that when a country reached the level of economic development where it had a middle class big enough to support a network of McDonald's, it became a McDonald's country. And people in McDonald's countries didn't like to fight wars anymore. They preferred to wait in line for burgers. While this was offered slightly tongue in cheek, the serious point I was trying to make was that as countries got woven into the fabric of global trade and rising living standards, which having a network of McDonald's franchises had come to symbolize, the cost of war for victor and vanquished became prohibitively high.

This McDonald's theory has held up pretty well, but now that almost every country has acquired a McDonald's, except the worst rogues like North Korea, Iran, and Iraq under Saddam Hussein, it seemed to me that this theory needed updating for the flat world. In that spirit, and again with tongue slightly in cheek, I offer the Dell Theory of Conflict Prevention, the essence of which is that the advent and spread of just-in-time global supply chains in the flat world are an even greater restraint on geopolitical adventurism than the more general rising standard of living that McDonald's symbolized.

The Dell Theory stipulates: No two countries that are both part of a major global supply chain, like Dell's, will ever fight a war against each other as long as they are both part of the same global supply chain. Because people embedded in major global supply chains don't want to fight old-time wars anymore. They want to make just-in-time deliveries of goods and services — and enjoy the rising standards of living that come with that. One of the people with the best feel for the logic behind this theory is Michael Dell, the founder and chairman of Dell.

"These countries understand the risk premium that they have," said Dell of the countries in his Asian supply chain. "They are pretty careful to protect the equity that they have built up or tell us why we should not worry [about their doing anything adventurous]. My belief after visiting China is that the change that has occurred there is in the best interest of the world and China. Once people get a taste for whatever you want to call it — economic independence, a better lifestyle, and a better life for their child or children — they grab on to that and don't want to give it up."

Any sort of war or prolonged political upheaval in East Asia or China "would have a massive chilling effect on the investment there and on all the progress that has been made there," said Dell, who added that he believes the governments in that part of the world understand this very clearly. "We certainly make clear to them that stability is important to us. [Right now] it is not a day-to-day worry for us . . . I believe that as time and progress go on there, the chance for a really disruptive event goes down exponentially. I don't think our industry gets enough credit for the good we are doing in these areas. If you are making money and being productive and raising your standard of living, you're not sitting around thinking, Who did this to us? or Why is our life so bad?"

There is a lot of truth to this. Countries whose workers and industries are   20 woven into a major global supply chain know that they cannot take an hour, a week, or a month off for war without disrupting industries and economies around the world and thereby risking the loss of their place in that supply chain for a long time, which could be extremely costly. For a country with no natural resources, being part of a global supply chain is like striking oil — oil that never runs out. And therefore, getting dropped from such a chain because you start a war is like having your oil wells go dry or having someone pour cement down them. They will not come back anytime soon.

"You are going to pay for it really dearly," said Glenn E. Neland, senior vice president for worldwide procurement at Dell, when I asked him what would happen to a major supply-chain member in Asia that decided to start fighting with its neighbor and disrupt the supply chain. "It will not only bring you to your knees [today], but you will pay for a long time — because you just won't have any credibility if you demonstrate you are going to go [off] the political deep end. And China is just now starting to develop a level of credibility in the business community that it is creating a business environment you can prosper in — with transparent and consistent rules." Neland said that suppliers regularly ask him whether he is worried about China and Taiwan, which have threatened to go to war at several points in the past half century, but his standard response is that he cannot imagine them "doing anything more than flexing muscles with each other." Neland said he can tell in his conversations and dealings with companies and governments in the Dell supply chain, particularly the Chinese, that "they recognize the opportunity and are really hungry to participate in the same things they have seen other countries in Asia do. They know there is a big economic pot at the end of the rainbow and they are really after it. We will spend about $35 billion producing parts this year, and 30 percent of that is [in] China."

If you follow the evolution of supply chains, added Neland, you see the prosperity and stability they promoted first in Japan, and then in Korea and Taiwan, and now in Malaysia, Singapore, the Philippines, Thailand, and Indonesia. Once countries get embedded in these global supply chains, "they feel part of something much bigger than their own businesses," he said. Osamu Watanabe, the CEO of the Japan External Trade Organization (JETRO), was explaining to me one afternoon in Tokyo how Japanese companies were moving vast amounts of low- and middle-range technical work and manufacturing to China, doing the basic fabrication there, and then bringing it back to Japan for final assembly. Japan was doing this despite a bitter legacy of mistrust between the two countries, which was intensified by the Japanese invasion of China in the last century. Historically, he noted, a strong Japan and a strong China have had a hard time coexisting. But not today, at least not for the moment. Why not? I asked. The reason you can have a strong Japan and a strong China at the same time, he said, "is because of the supply chain." It is a win-win for both.

Obviously, since Iraq, Syria, south Lebanon, North Korea, Pakistan, Afghanistan, and Iran are not part of any major global supply chains, all of them remain hot spots that could explode at any time and slow or reverse the flattening of the world. As my own notebook story attests, the most important test case of the Dell Theory of Conflict Prevention is the situation between China and Taiwan — since both are deeply embedded in several of the world's most important computer, consumer electronics, and, increasingly, software supply chains. The vast majority of computer components for every major company comes from coastal China, Taiwan, and East Asia. In addition, Taiwan alone has more than $100 billion in investments in mainland China today, and Taiwanese experts run many of the cutting-edge Chinese high-tech manufacturing companies.

It is no wonder that Craig Addison, the former editor of *Electronic Business Asia* magazine, wrote an essay for the *International Herald Tribune* (September 29, 2000), headlined "A 'Silicon Shield' Protects Taiwan from China." He argued that "Silicon-based products, such as computers and networking systems, form the basis of the digital economies in the United States, Japan, and other developed nations. In the past decade, Taiwan has become the third-largest information technology hardware producer after the United States and Japan. Military aggression by China against Taiwan would cut off a large portion of the world's supply of these products . . . Such a development would wipe trillions of dollars off the market value of technology companies listed in the United States, Japan, and Europe." Even if China's leaders, like former president Jiang Zemin, who was once minister of electronics, lose sight of how integrated China and Taiwan are in the world's computer supply chain, they need only ask their kids for an update. Jiang Zemin's son, Jiang Mianheng, wrote Addison, "is a partner in a wafer fabrication project in Shanghai with Winston Wang of Taiwan's Grace T.H.W. Group." And it is not just Taiwanese. Hundreds of big American tech companies now have R&D operations in China; a war that disrupted them could lead not only to the companies moving their plants elsewhere but also to a significant loss of R&D investment in China, which the Beijing government has been betting on to advance its development. Such a war could also, depending on how it started, trigger a widespread American boycott of Chinese goods — if China were to snuff out the Taiwanese democracy — which would lead to serious economic turmoil inside China.

The Dell Theory had its first real test in December 2004, when Taiwan   25
held parliamentary elections. President Chen Shui-bian's pro-independence
Democratic Progressive Party was expected to win the legislative runoff over
the main opposition Nationalist Party, which favored closer ties with Beijing.
Chen framed the election as a popular referendum on his proposal to write a
new constitution that would formally enshrine Taiwan's independence, ending the purposely ambiguous status quo. Had Chen won and moved ahead on
his agenda to make Taiwan its own motherland, as opposed to maintaining
the status quo fiction that it is a province of the mainland, it could have led to a
Chinese military assault on Taiwan. Everyone in the region was holding his or
her breath. And what happened? *Motherboards won over motherland.* A majority
of Taiwanese voted against the pro-independence governing party legislative
candidates, ensuring that the DPP would not have a majority in parliament.
I believe the message Taiwanese voters were sending was not that they never
want Taiwan to be independent. It was that they do not want to upset the status
quo right now, which has been so beneficial to so many Taiwanese. The voters
seemed to understand clearly how interwoven they had become with the mainland, and they wisely opted to maintain their de facto independence rather than
force de jure independence, which might have triggered a Chinese invasion and
a very uncertain future.

Warning: What I said when I put forth the McDonald's theory, I would repeat even more strenuously with the Dell Theory: It does not make wars obsolete. And it does not guarantee that governments will not engage in wars of
choice, even governments that are part of major supply chains. To suggest so
would be naive. It guarantees only that governments whose countries are enmeshed in global supply chains will have to think three times, not just twice,
about engaging in anything but a war of self-defense. And if they choose to go
to war anyway, the price they will pay will be ten times higher than it was a
decade ago and probably ten times higher than whatever the leaders of that
country think. It is one thing to lose your McDonald's. It's quite another to fight
a war that costs you your place in a twenty-first-century supply chain that may
not come back around for a long time.

While the biggest test case of the Dell Theory is China versus Taiwan, the fact is
that the Dell Theory has already proved itself to some degree in the case of India
and Pakistan, the context in which I first started to think about it. I happened
to be in India in 2002, when its just-in-time services supply chains ran into
some very old-time geopolitics—and the supply chain won. In the case of India
and Pakistan, the Dell Theory was working on only one party—India—but it
still had a major impact. India is to the world's knowledge and service supply
chain what China and Taiwan are to the manufacturing ones. By now readers
of this book know all the highlights: General Electric's biggest research center
outside the United States is in Bangalore, with seventeen hundred Indian engineers, designers, and scientists. The brain chips for many brand-name cell
phones are designed in Bangalore. Renting a car from Avis online? It's managed
in Bangalore. Tracing your lost luggage on Delta or British Airways is done

from Bangalore, and the backroom accounting and computer maintenance for scores of global firms are done from Bangalore, Mumbai, Chennai, and other major Indian cities.

Here's what happened: On May 31, 2002, State Department spokesman Richard Boucher issued a travel advisory saying, "We urge American citizens currently in India to depart the country," because the prospect of a nuclear exchange with Pakistan was becoming very real. Both nations were massing troops on their borders, intelligence reports were suggesting that they both might be dusting off their nuclear warheads, and CNN was flashing images of people flooding out of India. The global American firms that had moved their back rooms and R&D operations to Bangalore were deeply unnerved.

"I was actually surfing on the Web, and I saw a travel advisory come up on India on a Friday evening," said Vivek Paul, president of Wipro, which manages backroom operations from India of many American multinationals. "As soon as I saw that, I said, 'Oh my gosh, every customer that we have is going to have a million questions on this.' It was the Friday before a long weekend, so over the weekend we at Wipro developed a fail-safe business continuity plan for all of our customers." While Wipro's customers were pleased to see how on top of things the company was, many of them were nevertheless rattled. This was not in the plan when they decided to outsource mission-critical research and operations to India. Said Paul, "I had a CIO from one of our big American clients send me an e-mail saying, 'I am now spending a lot of time looking for alternative sources to India. I don't think you want me doing that, and I don't want to be doing it.' I immediately forwarded his message to the Indian ambassador in Washington and told him to get it to the right person." Paul would not tell me what company it was, but I have confirmed through diplomatic sources that it was United Technologies. And plenty of others, like American Express and General Electric, with back rooms in Bangalore, had to have been equally worried.

For many global companies, "the main heart of their business is now supported here," said N. Krishnakumar, president of MindTree, another leading Indian knowledge outsourcing firm based in Bangalore. "It can cause chaos if there is a disruption." While not trying to meddle in foreign affairs, he added, "What we explained to our government, through the Confederation of Indian Industry, is that providing a stable, predictable operating environment is now the key to India's development." This was a real education for India's elderly leaders in New Delhi, who had not fully absorbed how critical India had become to the world's knowledge supply chain. When you are managing vital back-room operations for American Express or General Electric or Avis, or are responsible for tracing all the lost luggage on British Airways or Delta, you cannot take a month, a week, or even a day off for war without causing major disruptions for those companies. Once those companies have made a commitment to outsource business operations or research to India, they expect it to stay there. That is a major commitment. And if geopolitics causes a serious disruption, they will leave, and they will not come back very easily. When you lose this kind of service trade, you can lose it for good.

"What ends up happening in the flat world you described," explained Paul, "is that you have only one opportunity to make it right if something [goes] wrong. Because the disadvantage of being in a flat world is that despite all the nice engagements and stuff and the exit barriers that you have, every customer has multiple options, and so the sense of responsibility you have is not just out of a desire to do good by your customers, but also a desire for self-preservation."

The Indian government got the message. Was India's central place in the world's services supply chain the only factor in getting Prime Minister Vajpayee to tone down his rhetoric and step back from the brink? Of course not. There were other factors, to be sure—most notably the deterrent effect of Pakistan's own nuclear arsenal. But clearly, India's role in global services was an important additional source of restraint on its behavior, and it was taken into account by New Delhi. "I think it sobered a lot of people," said Jerry Rao, who, as noted earlier, heads the Indian high-tech trade association. "We engaged very seriously, and we tried to make the point that this was very bad for Indian business. It was very bad for the Indian economy . . . [Many people] didn't realize till then how suddenly we had become integrated into the rest of the world. We are now partners in a twenty-four by seven by three-sixty-five supply chain."

Vivek Kulkarni, then information technology secretary for Bangalore's regional government, told me back in 2002, "We don't get involved in politics, but we did bring to the government's attention the problems the Indian IT industry might face if there were a war." And this was an altogether new factor for New Delhi to take into consideration. "Ten years ago, [a lobby of IT ministers from different Indian states] never existed," said Kulkarni. Now it is one of the most important business lobbies in India and a coalition that no Indian government can ignore.

"With all due respect, the McDonald's [shutting] down doesn't hurt anything," said Vivek Paul, "but if Wipro had to shut down we would affect the day-to-day operations of many, many companies." No one would answer the phones in call centers. Many e-commerce sites that are supported from Bangalore would shut down. Many major companies that rely on India to maintain their key computer applications or handle their human resources departments or billings would seize up. And these companies did not want to find alternatives, said Paul. Switching is very difficult, because taking over mission-critical day-to-day backroom operations of a global company takes a great deal of training and experience. It's not like opening a fast-food restaurant. That was why, said Paul, Wipro's clients were telling him, " 'I have made an investment in you. I need you to be very responsible with the trust I have reposed in you.' And I think that created an enormous amount of back pressure on us that said we have to act in a responsible fashion . . . All of a sudden it became even clearer that there's more to gain by economic gains than by geopolitical gains. [We had more to gain from building] a vibrant, richer middle class able to create an export industry than we possibly could by having an ego-satisfying war with Pakistan." The Indian government also looked around and realized that the vast majority of India's billion people were saying, "I want a better future, not more territory." Over and over again, when I asked young Indians working at call centers how they felt about Kashmir or a war with Pakistan, they waved me off with the same answer: "We have better things to do." And they do. America needs to keep this in mind as it weighs its overall approach to outsourcing. I would never advocate shipping some American's job overseas just so it will keep Indians and Pakistanis at peace with each other. But I would say that to the extent that this process happens, driven by its own internal economic logic, it will have a net positive geopolitical effect. It will absolutely make the world safer for American kids.

Each of the Indian business leaders I interviewed noted that in the event of some outrageous act of terrorism or aggression from Pakistan, India would do whatever it takes to defend itself, and they would be the first to support that—the Dell Theory be damned. Sometimes war is unavoidable. It is imposed on you by the reckless behavior of others, and you have to just pay the price. But the more India and, one hopes, soon Pakistan get enmeshed in global service supply chains, the greater disincentive they have to fight anything but a border skirmish or a war of words.

The example of the 2002 India-Pakistan nuclear crisis at least gives us some hope. That cease-fire was brought to us not by General Powell but by General Electric.

We bring good things to life.

Infosys versus al Qaeda

Unfortunately, even GE can do only so much. Because, alas, a new source for geopolitical instability has emerged only in recent years, for which even the updated Dell Theory can provide no restraint. It is the emergence of mutant global supply chains—that is, nonstate actors, be they criminals or terrorists, who learn to use all the elements of the flat world to advance a highly destabilizing, even nihilistic agenda. I first started thinking about this when Nandan Nilekani, the Infosys CEO, was giving me [a] tour . . . of his company's global videoconferencing center at its Bangalore headquarters. As Nandan explained to me how Infosys could get its global supply chain together at once for a virtual conference in that room, a thought popped into my head: Who else uses open-sourcing and supply-chaining so imaginatively? The answer, of course, is al Qaeda.

Al Qaeda has learned to use many of the same instruments for global collaboration that Infosys uses, but instead of producing products and profits with them, it has produced mayhem and murder. This is a particularly difficult problem. In fact, it may be the most vexing geopolitical problem for flat-world countries that want to focus on the future. The flat world—unfortunately—is a friend of both Infosys and al Qaeda. The Dell Theory will not work at all against these informal Islamo-Leninist terror networks, because they are not a state with a population that will hold its leaders accountable or with a domestic business lobby that might restrain them. These mutant global supply chains are formed for the purpose of destruction, not profit. They don't need investors, only recruits, donors, and victims. Yet these mobile, self-financing mutant supply chains use all the tools of collaboration offered by the flat world—open-sourcing to raise money, to recruit followers, and to stimulate and disseminate ideas; outsourcing to train recruits; and supply-chaining to distribute the tools and the suicide bombers to undertake operations. The U.S. Central Command has a name for this whole underground network: the Virtual Caliphate. And its leaders and innovators understand the flat world almost as well as Wal-Mart, Dell, and Infosys do.

In the previous chapter, I tried to explain that you cannot understand the rise of al Qaeda emotionally and politically without reference to the flattening of the world. What I am arguing here is that you cannot understand the rise of al Qaeda technically without reference to the flattening of the world, either. Globalization in general has been al Qaeda's friend in that it has helped to solidify a revival of Muslim identity and solidarity, with Muslims in one country much better able to see and sympathize with the struggles of their brethren in another country—thanks to the Internet and satellite television. At the same time, . . . this flattening process has intensified the feelings of humiliation in some quarters of the Muslim world over the fact that civilizations to which the Muslim world once felt superior—Hindus, Jews, Christians, Chinese—are now all doing better than many Muslim countries, and everyone can see it. The flattening of the world has also

> **In the flat world it is much more difficult to hide, but much easier to get connected.**

led to more urbanization and large-scale immigration to the West of many of these young, unemployed, frustrated Arab-Muslim males, while simultaneously making it much easier for informal open-source networks of these young men to form, operate, and interconnect. This certainly has been a boon for underground extremist Muslim political groups. There has been a proliferation of these informal mutual supply chains throughout the Arab-Muslim world today—small networks of people who move money through *hawalas* (hand-to-hand financing networks), who recruit through alternative education systems like the madrassas, and who communicate through the Internet and other tools of the global information revolution. Think about it: A century ago, anarchists were limited in their ability to communicate and collaborate with one another, to find sympathizers, and to band together for an operation. Today, with the Internet, that is not a problem. Today even the Unabomber could find friends to join a consortium where his "strengths" could be magnified and reinforced by others who had just as warped a worldview as he did.

What we have witnessed in Iraq is an even more perverse mutation of this mutant supply chain—the suicide supply chain. Since the start of the U.S. invasion in March 2002, more than two hundred suicide bombers have been recruited from within Iraq and from across the Muslim world, brought to the Iraqi front by some underground railroad, connected with the bomb makers there, and then dispatched against U.S. and Iraqi targets according to whatever suits the daily tactical needs of the insurgent Islamist forces in Iraq. I can understand, but not accept, the notion that more than thirty-seven years of Israeli occupation of the West Bank might have driven some Palestinians into a suicidal rage.

But the American occupation of Iraq was only a few months old before it started to get hit by this suicide supply chain. How do you recruit so many young men "off the shelf" who are ready to commit suicide in the cause of jihad, many of them apparently not even Iraqis? And they don't even identify themselves by name or want to get credit—at least in this world. The fact is that Western intelligence agencies have no clue how this underground suicide supply chain, which seems to have an infinite pool of recruits to draw on, works, and yet it has basically stymied the U.S. armed forces in Iraq. From what we do know, though, this Virtual Caliphate works just like the supply chains I described earlier. Just as you take an item off the shelf in a discount store in Birmingham and another one is immediately made in Beijing, so the retailers of suicide deploy a human bomber in Baghdad and another one is immediately recruited and indoctrinated in Beirut. To the extent that this tactic spreads, it will require a major rethinking of U.S. military doctrine.

The flat world has also been such a huge boon for al Qaeda and its ilk because of the way it enables the small to act big, and the way it enables small acts—the killing of just a few people—to have big effects. The horrific video of the beheading of *Wall Street Journal* reporter Danny Pearl by Islamist militants in Pakistan was transmitted by the Internet all over the world. There is not a journalist anywhere who saw or even just read about that who was not terrified. But those same beheading videos are also used as tools of recruitment. The flat world makes it much easier for terrorists to transmit their terror. With the Internet they don't even have to go through Western or Arab news organizations but can broadcast right into your computer. It takes much less dynamite to transmit so much more anxiety. Just as the U.S. Army had embedded journalists, so the suicide supply chain has embedded terrorists, in their own way, to tell us their side of the story. How many times have I gotten up in the morning, fired up the Internet, and been confronted by the video image of some masked gunman threatening to behead an American—all brought to me courtesy of AOL's home page? The Internet is an enormously useful tool for the dissemination of propaganda, conspiracy theories, and plain old untruths, because it combines a huge reach with a patina of technology that makes anything on the Internet somehow more believable. How many times have you heard someone say, "But I read it on the Internet," as if that should end the argument? In fact, the Internet can make things worse. It often leads to more people being exposed to crazy conspiracy theories.

"The new system of diffusion—the Internet—is more likely to transmit irrationality than rationality," said political theorist Yaron Ezrahi, who specializes in the interaction between media and politics. "Because irrationality is more emotionally loaded, it requires less knowledge, it explains more to more people, it goes down easier." That is why conspiracy theories are so rife in the Arab-Muslim world today—and unfortunately are becoming so in many quarters of the Western world, for that matter. Conspiracy theories are like a drug that goes right into your bloodstream, enabling you to see "the Light." And the Internet is the needle. Young people used to have to take LSD to escape. Now they just go online. Now you don't shoot up, you download. You download the precise point of view that speaks to all your own biases. And the flat world makes it all so much easier.

Gabriel Weimann, a professor of communication at Haifa University, Israel, did an incisive study of terrorists' use of the Internet and of what I call the flat world, which was published in March 2004 by the United States Institute of Peace and excerpted on YaleGlobal Online on April 26, 2004. He made the following points:

> While the danger that cyber-terrorism poses to the Internet is fre-
> quently debated, surprisingly little is known about the threat posed
> by terrorists' use of the Internet. A recent six-year-long study shows
> that terrorist organizations and their supporters have been using all of
> the tools that the Internet offers to recruit supporters, raise funds, and
> launch a worldwide campaign of fear. It is also clear that to combat
> terrorism effectively, mere suppression of their Internet tools is not
> enough. Our scan of the Internet in 2003–04 revealed the existence
> of hundreds of websites serving terrorists in different, albeit sometimes
> overlapping, ways . . . There are countless examples of how [terror-
> ists] use this uncensored medium to spread disinformation, to deliver
> threats intended to instill fear and helplessness, and to disseminate
> horrific images of recent actions. Since September 11, 2001, al Qaeda
> has festooned its websites with a string of announcements of an im-
> pending "large attack" on U.S. targets. These warnings have received
> considerable media coverage, which has helped to generate a wide-
> spread sense of dread and insecurity among audiences throughout the
> world and especially within the United States. . . .
>
> The Internet has significantly expanded the opportunities for ter-
> rorists to secure publicity. Until the advent of the Internet, terrorists'
> hopes of winning publicity for their causes and activities depended on
> attracting the attention of television, radio, or the print media. The
> fact that terrorists themselves have direct control over the content
> of their websites offers further opportunities to shape how they are
> perceived by different target audiences and to manipulate their image
> and the images of their enemies. Most terrorist sites do not celebrate
> their violent activities. Instead—regardless of their nature, motives,
> or location—most terrorist sites emphasize two issues: the restrictions
> placed on freedom of expression; and the plight of their comrades who
> are now political prisoners. These issues resonate powerfully with
> their own supporters and are also calculated to elicit sympathy from
> Western audiences that cherish freedom of expression and frown on
> measures to silence political opposition. . . .
>
> Terrorists have proven not only skillful at online marketing but
> also adept at mining the data offered by the billion-some pages of the
> World Wide Web. They can learn from the Internet about the schedules
> and locations of targets such as transportation facilities, nuclear power
> plants, public buildings, airports and ports, and even counterterrorism

measures. According to Secretary of Defense Donald Rumsfeld, an al Qaeda training manual recovered in Afghanistan tells its readers, "Using public sources openly and without resorting to illegal means, it is possible to gather at least 80 percent of all information required about the enemy." One captured al Qaeda computer contained engineering and structural architecture features of a dam, which had been downloaded from the Internet and which would enable al Qaeda engineers and planners to simulate catastrophic failures. In other captured computers, U.S. investigators found evidence that al Qaeda operators spent time on sites that offer software and programming instructions for the digital switches that run power, water, transportation, and communications grids.

Like many other political organizations, terrorist groups use the Internet to raise funds. Al Qaeda, for instance, has always depended heavily on donations, and its global fund-raising network is built upon a foundation of charities, nongovernmental organizations, and other financial institutions that use websites and Internet-based chat rooms and forums. The fighters in the Russian breakaway republic of Chechnya have likewise used the Internet to publicize the numbers of bank accounts to which sympathizers can contribute. And in December 2001, the U.S. government seized the assets of a Texas-based charity because of its ties to Hamas.

In addition to soliciting financial aid online, terrorists recruit converts by using the full panoply of website technologies (audio, digital video, etc.) to enhance the presentation of their message. And like commercial sites that track visitors to develop consumer profiles, terrorist organizations capture information about the users who browse their websites. Visitors who seem most interested in the organization's cause or well suited to carrying out its work are then contacted. Recruiters may also use more interactive Internet technology to roam online chat rooms and cyber cafes, looking for receptive members of the public, particularly young people. The SITE Institute, a Washington, D.C.–based terrorism research group that monitors al Qaeda's Internet communications, has provided chilling details of a high-tech recruitment drive launched in 2003 to recruit fighters to travel to Iraq and attack U.S. and coalition forces there. The Internet also grants terrorists a cheap and efficient means of networking. Many terrorist groups, among them Hamas and al Qaeda, have undergone a transformation from strictly hierarchical organizations with designated leaders to affiliations of semi-independent cells that have no single commanding hierarchy. Through the Internet, these loosely interconnected groups are able to maintain contact with one another — and with members of other terrorist groups. The Internet connects not only members of the same terrorist organizations but also members of different groups. For instance, dozens of sites supporting terrorism in the name of jihad permit terrorists in places as far-removed from one another as Chechnya and Malaysia to exchange ideas and practical information about how to build bombs, establish terror cells, and carry out attacks . . . Al Qaeda operatives relied heavily on the Internet in planning and coordinating the September 11 attacks.

For all of these reasons we are just at the beginning of understanding the geopolitical impact of the flattening of the world. On the one hand, failed states and failed regions are places we have every incentive to avoid today. They offer no economic opportunity and there is no Soviet Union out there competing with us for influence over such countries. On the other hand, there may be nothing more dangerous today than a failed state with broadband capability. That is, even failed states tend to have telecommunications systems and satellite links, and therefore if a terrorist group infiltrates a failed state, as al Qaeda did with Afghanistan, it can amplify its power enormously. As much as big powers want to stay away from such states, they may feel compelled to get even more deeply embroiled in them. Think of America in Afghanistan and Iraq, Russia in Chechnya, Australia in East Timor.

In the flat world it is much more difficult to hide, but much easier to get connected. "Think of Mao at the beginning of the Chinese communist revolution," remarked Michael Mandelbaum, the Johns Hopkins foreign policy specialist. "The Chinese Communists had to hide in caves in northwest China, but they could move around in whatever territory they were able to control. Bin Laden, by contrast, can't show his face, but he can reach every household in the world, thanks to the Internet." Bin Laden cannot capture any territory but he can capture the imagination of millions of people. And he has, broadcasting right into American living rooms on the eve of the 2004 presidential election.

Hell hath no fury like a terrorist with a satellite dish and an interactive Web site.

Too Personally Insecure

In the fall of 2004, I was invited to speak at a synagogue in Woodstock, New York, home of the famous Woodstock music festival. I asked my hosts how was it that they were able to get a synagogue in Woodstock, of all places, big enough to support a lecture series. Very simple, they said. Since 9/11, Jews, and others, have been moving from New York City to places like Woodstock, to get away from what they fear will be the next ground zero. Right now this trend is a trickle, but it would become a torrent if a nuclear device were detonated in any European or American city.

Since this threat is the mother of all unflatteners, this book would not be complete without a discussion of it. We can live with a lot. We lived through 9/11. But we cannot live with nuclear terrorism. That would unflatten the world permanently.

The only reason that Osama bin Laden did not use a nuclear device on 9/11 was not that he did not have the intention but that he did not have the capability. And since the Dell Theory offers no hope of restraining the suicide supply chains, the only strategy we have is to limit their worst capabilities. That means a much more serious global effort to stanch nuclear proliferation by limiting the supply—to buy up the fissile material that is already out there, particularly in the former Soviet Union, and prevent more states from going nuclear. Harvard University international affairs expert Graham Allison, in his book *Nuclear Terrorism: The Ultimate Preventable Catastrophe,* outlines just such a strategy for denying terrorists access to nuclear weapons and nuclear materials. It can be done, he insists. It is a challenge to our will and convictions, but *not to our capabilities.* Allison proposes a new American-led international security order to deal with this problem based on what he calls "a doctrine of the Three No's: No loose nukes, No new nascent nukes, and No new nuclear states." No loose nukes, says Allison, means locking down all nuclear weapons and all nuclear material from which bombs could be made—in a much more serious way than we have done up till now. "We don't lose gold from Fort Knox," says Allison. "Russia doesn't lose treasures from the Kremlin armory. So we both know how to prevent theft of those things that are super valuable to us if we are determined to do it." No new nascent nukes means recognizing that there is a group of actors out there who can and do produce highly enriched uranium or plutonium, which is nothing more than nuclear bombs just about to hatch. We need a much more credible, multilateral nonproliferation regime that soaks up this fissile material. Finally, no new nuclear states means "drawing a line under the current eight nuclear powers and determining that, however unfair and unreasonable it may be, that club will have no more members than those eight," says Allison, adding that these three steps might then buy us time to develop a more formal, sustainable, internationally approved regime.

It would be nice also to be able to deny the Internet to al Qaeda and its ilk, but that, alas, is impossible—without undermining ourselves. That is why limiting their capabilities is necessary but not sufficient. We also have to find a way to get at their worst intentions. If we are not going to shut down the Internet and all the other creative and collaborative tools that have flattened the world, and if we can't restrict access to them, the only thing we can do is try to influence the imagination and intentions that people bring to them and draw from them. When I raised this issue, and the broad themes of this book, with my religious teacher, Rabbi Tzvi Marx from Holland, he surprised me by saying that the flat world I was describing reminded him of the story of the Tower of Babel.

How so? I asked. "The reason God banished all the people from the Tower of Babel and made them all speak different languages was not because he did not want them to collaborate per se," answered Rabbi Marx. "It was because he was enraged at what they were collaborating on—an effort to build a tower to the heavens so they could become God." This was a distortion of the human capacity, so God broke their union and their ability to communicate with one another. Now, all these years later, humankind has again created a new platform for more people from more places to communicate and collaborate with less friction and more ease than ever: the Internet. Would God see the Internet as heresy?

"Absolutely not," said Marx. "The heresy is not that mankind works together — it is to what ends. It is essential that we use this new ability to communicate and collaborate for the right ends — for constructive human aims and not megalomaniacal ends. Building a tower was megalomaniacal. Bin Laden's insistence that he has the truth and can flatten anyone else's tower who doesn't heed him is megalomaniacal. Collaborating so mankind can achieve its full potential is God's hope."

Questions for Critical Reading

1. Much of Friedman's focus in this chapter is on collaboration. What role does collaboration play in economic and terroristic systems of production? You will need to analyze his text to determine a response; reread it to find supporting quotations.

2. What is the Dell Theory of Conflict Prevention? Reread Friedman's text to locate a quotation that defines this concept. Can you offer any examples from current events that show the Dell Theory's success or failure in relation to conflicts around the world?

3. What are mutant global supply chains? What makes them so successful and thus so dangerous? Locate passages from Friedman that support your answer.

Exploring Context

1. Friedman opens this chapter by tracing the assembly of his Dell notebook. Explore Dell's Web site (dell.com). Does it provide any sense of the global supply chains that are vital to the creation of its computers? Why would Dell highlight or obscure these global supply chains on its Web site? What global images and what national images are created? How does the site reflect your response to Question 1 of Questions for Critical Reading about collaboration?

2. Infosys, headquartered in Bangalore, India, is one of the companies that Friedman mentions. The Web site for Infosys has a special section about the flat world (infosys.com/flat-world/business/default.asp). How does the information on this site reflect Friedman's arguments?

3. Visit the Federal Bureau of Investigation's counterterrorism Web site at fbi.gov/terrorinfo/counterrorism/waronterrorhome.htm. Does it reflect the global nature of terror networks as explained by Friedman? How does Friedman propose we fight terrorism? Are such strategies being pursued by organizations like the FBI? You may want to draw from your work on collaboration and mutant global supply chains from Questions 1 and 3 of Questions for Critical Reading.

Questions for Connecting

1. Michael Pollan, in "The Animals: Practicing Complexity" (p. 281), describes a very different, very local economic system. What parallels can you find between

Pollan's and Friedman's ideas about the collateral effects of economic systems? Do "holons" have a role to play in the global supply chain? Are integrated and organic farming systems a kind of supply chain? Use your work defining Friedman's concepts from Questions for Critical Reading to help make your argument.

2. Like Friedman, James Surowiecki focuses on collaboration in "Committees, Juries, and Teams: The *Columbia* Disaster and How Small Groups Can Be Made to Work" (p. 440). How might some of the pitfalls of small groups noted by Surowiecki endanger the Dell Theory? Are small-group dynamics applicable to global collaborative systems? How can the lessons learned from Surowiecki's analysis help in the fight against mutant supply chains and terrorism? Use your work on collaboration from Question 1 of Questions for Critical Reading.

3. Leslie Savan examines the economic appropriation of black talk in "What's Black, Then White, and Said All Over?" (p. 363). Should there be limits on economic systems or global supply chains? Must we limit their effects? Or, based on the ideas of Friedman and Savan, is it in our best interests to give economic systems free reign? Drawing from your work in Exploring Context, can you use Dell or Infosys as an example for your argument?

Language Matters

1. Integrating the words of other authors into your writing is an essential skill. In small groups, select a key quotation from Friedman's text and then create three different sentences that integrate that quotation. Have different groups share their results. What general techniques or strategies did people use?

2. Systems of citation are a central aspect of academic writing. In this class, you may be asked to use MLA, APA, or some other format for in-text citations. Develop your own system and illustrate it by citing a quotation from Friedman's essay. What kind of information would it have to include? What does this then say about how citation systems work? Why are there so many citation systems?

3. Strong organization is self-evident. That is, when a paper is well organized each paragraph clearly has a place in the whole. Imagine a different order for Friedman's essay. What sections would you have placed first and why? What transitions would you need? Why do you think Friedman organized his essay the way he did?

Assignments for Writing

1. According to Friedman's theory, global supply chains promote geopolitical stability. But Friedman is careful to say that they do not guarantee peace. Write a paper in which you determine the limitations of Friedman's theory. What would cause the Dell Theory of Conflict Prevention to fail? Are there specific supply chains or commodities (oil, gas, natural resources) that fall outside this theory? You may want to build your argument using your work on the Dell Theory from Question 2 of Questions for Critical Reading.

2. Both Friedman's Dell Theory of Conflict Prevention and his earlier Golden Arches Theory seem to rely on the spread of American culture. Can we reap the benefits of globalized economics without sacrificing local culture? Write a paper in which you suggest strategies for balancing globalization with localization. You might want to draw from your work with Leslie Savan's essay from Question 3 of Questions for Connecting in making your argument. Consider, too, these questions: Are terrorist supply chains an attempt to preserve local cultures? Must global economics mean global culture?

3. As you learned in Question 1 of Questions for Critical Reading, collaboration is one of Friedman's central concerns in this essay. Write a paper in which you use Friedman's ideas to suggest the key factors for making collaboration a success. You might also want to draw from your work with James Surowiecki's essay from Question 2 of Questions for Connecting.

FRANCIS FUKUYAMA

Francis Fukuyama holds a B.A. in classics from Cornell University and a Ph.D. in political science from Harvard University. He is currently the Bernard L. Schwartz Professor in International Political Economy at Johns Hopkins University. As a prominent neoconservative thinker, Fukuyama signed letters to both President Bill Clinton (in 1998) and President George W. Bush (in 2001) advocating the overthrow of Saddam Hussein (at the time, the president of Iraq). However, Fukuyama ultimately disapproved of the 2003 invasion of Iraq, writing publicly that neoconservative ideas had changed and were no longer supportable. Fukuyama is the author of multiple books of political philosophy advocating liberal democracy, including his 2006 publication *America at the Crossroads*, which deals directly with his departure from the neoconservative agenda.

In *Our Posthuman Future: Consequences of the Biotechnology Revolution* (2002), Fukuyama updates an earlier proposal. Fukuyama had, in his book *The End of History and the Last Man* (1992), suggested that the history of humanity is an ideological struggle that is pretty much settled now, with liberal democracy as the eventual and destined end point, an argument he clarified in *America at the Crossroads*, stating that modernization is what wins the ideological struggle and that liberal democracy is merely one of the outcomes of modernization. In *Our Posthuman Future*, he reexamines this argument, taking into account the potential effects of biotechnology on liberal democracy. Now that human behavior can potentially be modified and DNA can be manipulated, Fukuyama asks, how will a political order based on natural equality survive?

In "Human Dignity," a chapter from *Our Posthuman Future*, Fukuyama examines the idea of "Factor X," an "essential human quality . . . that is worthy of a certain minimal level of respect" regardless of our varying individual characteristics, such as skin color, looks, or social class. Modern science, particularly the science of genetic engineering, Fukuyama claims, tends to disagree with the very idea of an essential human quality like Factor X. From this scientific perspective, human beings are the end result of genetic accidents and environmental influences. Fukuyama, however, finds merit in Pope John Paul II's assertion that science can't fully explain how human beings emerge from simple components. If that assertion is correct, Fukuyama speculates, what does this imply about science's ability to understand other complex systems? What does this mean for the future of human consciousness and political systems? With "Human Dignity," Fukuyama asks the reader to consider what happens to the idea of universal human equality when genetic engineering can be used to "improve" human genes.

Given the seemingly inevitable progress of science, which undoubtedly will influence you throughout your life, what does it mean to be human, and how can we preserve the qualities that make us so?

▶ TAGS: *civil rights*, *morality*, *human dignity*, *biotechnology*, *ethics*

Human Dignity

> Is it, then, possible to imagine a new Natural Philosophy, continually conscious that the "natural object" produced by analysis and abstraction is not reality but only a view, and always correcting the abstraction? I hardly know what I am asking for. . . . The regenerate science which I have in mind would not do even to minerals and vegetables what modern science threatens to do to man himself. When it explained it would not explain away. When it spoke of parts it would remember the whole. . . . The analogy between the *Tao* of Man and the instincts of an animal species would mean for it new light cast on the unknown thing, Instinct, by the inly known reality of conscience and not a reduction of conscience to the category of Instinct. Its followers would not be free with the words *only* and *merely*. In a word, it would conquer Nature without being at the same time conquered by her and buy knowledge at a lower cost than that of life.
>
> —C. S. LEWIS, *THE ABOLITION OF MAN* [1]

According to the Decree by the Council of Europe on Human Cloning, "The instrumentalisation of human beings through the deliberate creation of genetically identical human beings is contrary to human dignity and thus constitutes a misuse of medicine and biology." [2] Human dignity is one of those concepts that politicians, as well as virtually everyone else in political life, like to throw around, but that almost no one can either define or explain.

Much of politics centers on the question of human dignity and the desire for recognition to which it is related. That is, human beings constantly demand that others recognize their dignity, either as individuals or as members of religious, ethnic, racial, or other kinds of groups. The struggle for recognition is not economic: What we desire is not money but that other human beings respect us in the way we think we deserve. In earlier times, rulers wanted others to recognize their superior worth as king, emperor, or lord. Today, people seek recognition of their equal status as members of formerly disrespected or devalued groups—as women, gays, Ukrainians, the handicapped, Native Americans, and the like. [3]

The demand for an equality of recognition or respect is the dominant passion of modernity, as Tocqueville noted over 170 years ago in *Democracy in America*. [4] What this means in a liberal democracy is a bit complicated. It is not necessarily that we think we are equal in all important respects, or demand that our lives be the same as everyone else's. Most people accept the fact that a Mozart or an Einstein or a Michael Jordan has talents and abilities that they don't have, and receives recognition and even monetary compensation for what he accomplishes with those talents. We accept, though we don't necessarily like, the fact that resources are distributed unequally based on what James Madison called the "different and unequal faculties of acquiring property." But we also believe that people deserve to keep what they earn and that the faculties for working and earning will not be the same for all people. We also accept the fact that we look different, come from different races and ethnicities, are of different sexes, and have different cultures.

Factor X

What the demand for equality of recognition implies is that when we strip all of a person's contingent and accidental characteristics away, there remains some essential human quality underneath that is worthy of a certain minimal level of respect—call it Factor X. Skin color, looks, social class and wealth, gender, cultural background, and even one's natural talents are all accidents of birth relegated to the class of nonessential characteristics. We make decisions on whom to befriend, whom to marry or do business with, or whom to shun at social events on the basis of these secondary characteristics. But in the political realm we are required to respect people equally on the basis of their possession of Factor X. You can cook, eat, torture, enslave, or render the carcass of any creature lacking Factor X, but if you do the same thing to a human being, you are guilty of a "crime against humanity." We accord beings with Factor X not just human rights but, if they are adults, political rights as well—that is, the right to live in democratic political communities where their rights to speech, religion, association, and political participation are respected.

The circle of beings to whom we attribute Factor X has been one of the most contested issues throughout human history. For many societies, including most democratic societies in earlier periods of history, Factor X belonged to a significant subset of the human race, excluding people of certain sexes, economic classes, races, and tribes and people with low intelligence, disabilities, birth defects, and the like. These societies were highly stratified, with different classes possessing more or less of Factor X, and some possessing none at all. Today, for believers in liberal equality, Factor X etches a bright red line around the whole of the human race and requires equality of respect for all of those on the inside, but attributes a lower level of dignity to those outside the boundary. Factor X is the human essence, the most basic meaning of what it is to be human. If all human beings are in fact equal in dignity, then X must be some characteristic universally possessed by them. So what is Factor X, and where does it come from?

For Christians, the answer is fairly easy: It comes from God. Man is created in the image of God, and therefore shares in some of God's sanctity, which entitles human beings to a higher level of respect than the rest of natural creation. In the words of Pope John Paul II, what this means is that "the human individual cannot be subordinated as a pure means or a pure instrument, either to the species or to society; he has value per se. He is a person. With his intellect and his will, he is capable of forming a relationship of communion, solidarity, and self-giving with his peers . . . It is by virtue of his spiritual soul that the whole person possesses such dignity even in his body."[5]

Supposing one is not a Christian (or a religious believer of any sort), and doesn't accept the premise that man is created in the image of God. Is there a secular ground for believing that human beings are entitled to a special moral status or dignity? Perhaps the most famous effort to create a philosophical basis for human dignity was that of Kant, who argued that Factor X was based on the human capacity for moral choice. That is, human beings could differ in intelligence, wealth, race, and gender, but all were equally able to act according to moral law or not. Human beings had dignity because they alone had free will—not just the subjective illusion of free will but the actual ability to transcend natural determinism and the normal rules of causality. It is the existence of free will that leads to Kant's well-known conclusion that human beings are always to be treated as ends and not as means.

It would be very difficult for any believer in a materialistic account of the universe—which includes the vast majority of natural scientists—to accept the Kantian account of human dignity. The reason is that it forces them to accept a form of dualism—that there is a realm of human freedom parallel to the realm of nature that is not determined by the latter. Most natural scientists would argue that what we believe to be free will is in fact an illusion and that all human decision making can ultimately be traced back to material causes. Human beings decide to do one thing over another because one set of neurons fires rather than another, and those neuronal firings can be traced back to prior material states of the brain. The human decision-making process may be more complex than that of other animals, but there is no sharp dividing line that distinguishes human moral choice from the kinds of choices that are made by other animals. Kant himself does not offer any proof that free will exists; he says that it is simply a necessary postulate of pure practical reason about the nature of morality—hardly an argument that a hard-bitten empirical scientist would accept.

Seize the Power

The problem posed by modern natural science goes even deeper. The very notion that there exists such a thing as a human "essence" has been under relentless attack by modern science for much of the past century and a half. One of the most fundamental assertions of Darwinism is that species do not have essences.[6] That is, while Aristotle believed in the eternity of the species (i.e., that what we have been labeling "species-typical behavior" is something unchanging), Darwin's theory maintains that this behavior changes in response to the organism's interaction with its environment. What is typical for a species represents a snapshot of the species at one particular moment of evolutionary time; what came before and what comes after will be different. Since Darwinism maintains that there is no cosmic teleology guiding the process of evolution, what seems to be the essence of a species is just an accidental by-product of a random evolutionary process.

In this perspective, what we have been calling human nature is merely the species-typical human characteristics and behavior that emerged about 100,000 years ago, during what evolutionary biologists call the "era of evolutionary adaptation"—when the precursors of modern humans were living and breeding on the African savanna. For many, this suggests that human nature has no special status as a guide to morals or values because it is historically contingent. David Hull, for example, argues,

> I do not see why the existence of human universals is all that important. Perhaps all and only people have opposable thumbs, use tools, live in true societies, or what have you. I think that such attributions are either false or vacuous, but even if they were true and significant, the distributions of these particular characters is largely a matter of evolutionary happenstance.[7]

The geneticist Lee Silver, trying to debunk the idea that there is a natural order that could be undermined by genetic engineering, asserts,

> Unfettered evolution is never predetermined [toward some goal], and not necessarily associated with progress—it is simply a response to unpredictable environmental changes. If the asteroid that hit our planet 60 million years ago had flown past instead, there would never have been any human beings at all. And whatever the natural order might be, it is not necessarily good. The smallpox virus was part of the natural order until it was forced into extinction by human intervention.[8]

This inability to define a natural essence doesn't bother either writer. Hull, for example, states that "I, for one, would be extremely uneasy to base something as important as human rights on such temporary contingencies [as human nature]. . . I fail to see why it matters. I fail to see, for example, why we must all be essentially the same to have rights."[9] Silver, for his part, pooh-poohs fears about genetic engineering on the part of those with religious convictions or those who believe in a natural order. In the future, man will no longer be a slave to his genes, but their master:

> Why not seize this power? Why not control what has been left to chance in the past? Indeed, we control all other aspects of our children's lives and identities through powerful social and environmental influences and, in some cases, with the use of powerful drugs like Ritalin and Prozac. On what basis can we reject positive genetic influences on a person's essence when we accept the rights of parents to benefit their children in every other way?[10]

Why not seize this power, indeed?

Well, let us begin by considering what the consequences of the abandonment of the idea that there is a Factor X, or human essence, that unites all human beings would be for the cherished idea of universal human equality—an idea to which virtually all of the debunkers of the idea of human essences are invariably committed. Hull is right that we don't all need to be the same in order to have rights—but we need to be the same in some one critical respect in order to have *equal* rights. He for one is very concerned that basing human rights on human nature will stigmatize homosexuals, because their sexual orientation differs from the heterosexual norm. But the only basis on which anyone can make an argument in favor of equal rights for gays is to argue that whatever their sexual orientation, *they are people too* in some other respect that is more essential than their sexuality. If you cannot find this common other ground, then there is no reason not to discriminate against them, because in fact they are different creatures from everyone else.

Similarly, Lee Silver, who is so eager to take up the power of genetic engineering to "improve" people, is nonetheless horrified at the possibility that it could be used to create a class of genetically superior people. He paints a scenario in which a class called the GenRich steadily improve the cognitive abilities of their children to the point that they break off from the rest of the human race to form a separate species.

Silver is not horrified by much else that technology may bring us by way of unnatural reproduction — for example, two lesbians producing genetic offspring, or eggs taken from an unborn female fetus to produce a child whose mother had never been born. He dismisses the moral concerns of virtually every religion or traditional moral system with regard to future genetic engineering but draws the line at what he perceives as threats to human equality. He does not seem to understand that, given his premises, there are no possible grounds on which he can object to the GenRich, or the fact that they might assign themselves rights superior to those of the GenPoor. Since there is no stable essence common to all human beings, or rather because that essence is variable and subject to human manipulation, why not create a race born with metaphorical saddles on their backs, and another with boots and spurs to ride them? Why not seize *that* power as well?

The bioethicist Peter Singer, whose appointment to Princeton University   15 caused great controversy because of his advocacy of infanticide and euthanasia under certain circumstances, is simply more consistent than most people on the consequences of abandoning the concept of human dignity. Singer is an unabashed utilitarian: He believes that the single relevant standard for ethics is to minimize suffering in the aggregate for all creatures. Human beings are part of a continuum of life and have no special status in his avowedly Darwinian worldview. This leads him to two perfectly logical conclusions: the need for animal rights, since animals can experience pain and suffering as well as humans, and the downgrading of the rights of infants and elderly people who lack certain key traits, like self-awareness, that would allow them to anticipate pain. The rights of certain animals, in his view, deserve greater respect than those of certain human beings.

But Singer is not nearly forthright enough in following these premises through to their logical conclusion, since he remains a committed egalitarian. What he does not explain is why the relief of suffering should remain the only moral good. As usual, the philosopher Friedrich Nietzsche was much more clear-eyed than anyone else in understanding the consequences of modern natural science and the abandonment of the concept of human dignity. Nietzsche had the great insight to see that, on the one hand, once the clear red line around the whole of humanity could no longer be drawn, the way would be paved for a return to a much more hierarchical ordering of society. If there is a continuum of gradations between human and nonhuman, there is a continuum within the type human as well. This would inevitably mean the liberation of the strong from the constraints that a belief in either God or Nature had placed on them. On the other hand, it would lead the rest of mankind to demand health and safety as the only possible goods, since all the higher goals that had once been set for them were now debunked. In the words of Nietzsche's Zarathustra, "One has one's little pleasure for the day and one's little pleasure for the night: But one has a regard for health. 'We have invented happiness,' say the last men, and they blink."[11] Indeed, both the return of hierarchy and the egalitarian demand for health, safety, and relief of suffering might all go hand in hand if the rulers of the future could provide the masses with enough of the "little poisons" they demanded.

It has always struck me that one hundred years after Nietzsche's death, we are much less far down the road to either the superman or the last man than he predicted. Nietzsche once castigated John Stuart Mill as a "flathead" for believing that one could have a semblance of Christian morality in the absence of belief in a Christian God. And yet, in a Europe and an America that have become secularized over the past two generations, we see a lingering belief in the concept of human dignity, which is by now completely cut off from its religious roots. And not just lingering: The idea that one could exclude any group of people on the basis of race, gender, disability, or virtually any other characteristic

> **So what is Factor X, and where does it come from?**

from the charmed circle of those deserving recognition for human dignity is the one thing that will bring total obloquy on the head of any politician who proposes it. In the words of the philosopher Charles Taylor, "We believe it would be utterly wrong and unfounded to draw the boundaries any narrower than around the whole human race," and should anyone try to do so, "we should immediately ask what distinguished those within from those left out."[12] The idea of the equality of human dignity, deracinated from its Christian or Kantian origins, is held as a matter of religious dogma by the most materialist of natural scientists. The continuing arguments over the moral status of the unborn (about which more later) constitute the only exception to this general rule.

The reasons for the persistence of the idea of the equality of human dignity are complex. Partly it is a matter of the force of habit and what Max Weber once called the "ghost of dead religious beliefs" that continue to haunt us. Partly it is the product of historical accident: The last important political movement to explicitly deny the premise of universal human dignity was Nazism, and the horrifying consequences of the Nazis' racial and eugenic policies were sufficient to inoculate those who experienced them for the next couple of generations.

But another important reason for the persistence of the idea of the universality of human dignity has to do with what we might call the nature of nature itself. Many of the grounds on which certain groups were historically denied their share of human dignity were proven to be simply a matter of prejudice, or else based on cultural and environmental conditions that could be changed. The notions that women were too irrational or emotional to participate in politics, and that immigrants from southern Europe had smaller head sizes and were less intelligent than those from northern Europe, were overturned on the basis of sound, empirical science. That moral order did not completely break down in the West in the wake of the destruction of consensus over traditional religious values should not surprise us either, because moral order comes from within human nature itself and is not something that has to be imposed on human nature by culture.[13]

All of this could change under the impact of future biotechnology. The most clear and present danger is that the large genetic variations between individuals will narrow and become clustered within certain distinct social groups. Today, the "genetic lottery" guarantees that the son or daughter of a rich and successful parent will not necessarily inherit the talents and abilities that created conditions conducive to the parent's success. Of course, there has always been a degree of genetic selection: Assortative mating means that successful people will tend to marry each other and, to the extent that their success is genetically based, will pass on to their children better life opportunities. But in the future, the full weight of modern technology can be put in the service of optimizing the kinds of genes that are passed on to one's offspring. This means that social elites may not just pass on social advantages but embed them genetically as well. This may one day include not only characteristics like intelligence and beauty, but behavioral traits like diligence, competitiveness, and the like.

The genetic lottery is judged as inherently unfair by many because it condemns certain people to lesser intelligence, or bad looks, or disabilities of one sort or another. But in another sense it is profoundly egalitarian, since everyone, regardless of social class, race, or ethnicity, has to play in it. The wealthiest man can and often does have a good-for-nothing son; hence the saying "Shirtsleeves to shirtsleeves in three generations." When the lottery is replaced by choice, we open up a new avenue along which human beings can compete, one that threatens to increase the disparity between the top and bottom of the social hierarchy.

What the emergence of a genetic overclass will do to the idea of universal human dignity is something worth pondering. Today, many bright and successful young people believe that they owe their success to accidents of birth and upbringing but for which their lives might have taken a very different course. They feel themselves, in other words, to be lucky, and they are capable of feeling sympathy for people who are less lucky than they. But to the extent that they become "children of choice" who have been genetically selected by their parents for certain characteristics, they may come to believe increasingly that their success is a matter not just of luck but of good choices and planning on the part of their parents, and hence something deserved. They will look, think, act, and perhaps even feel differently from those who were not similarly chosen, and may come in time to think of themselves as different kinds of creatures. They may, in short, feel themselves to be aristocrats, and unlike aristocrats of old, their claim to better birth will be rooted in nature and not convention.

Aristotle's discussion of slavery in Book I of the *Politics* is instructive on this score. It is often condemned as a justification of Greek slavery, but in fact the discussion is far more sophisticated and is relevant to our thinking about genetic classes. Aristotle makes a distinction between conventional and natural slavery.[14] He argues that slavery would be justified by nature if it were the case that there were people with naturally slavish natures. It is not clear from his discussion that he believes such people exist: Most actual slavery is conventional—that is, it is the result of victory in war or force, or based on the wrong opinion that barbarians as a class should be slaves of Greeks.[15] The noble-born think their nobility comes from nature rather than acquired virtue and that they can pass it on to their children. But, Aristotle notes, nature is "frequently unable to bring this about."[16] So why not, as Lee Silver suggests, "seize this power" to give children genetic advantages and correct the defect of natural equality?

The possibility that biotechnology will permit the emergence of new genetic classes has been frequently noted and condemned by those who have speculated about the future.[17] But the opposite possibility also seems to be entirely plausible—that there will be an impetus toward a much more genetically egalitarian society. For it seems highly unlikely that people in modern democratic societies will sit around complacently if they see elites embedding their advantages genetically in their children.

Indeed, this is one of the few things in a politics of the future that people are likely to rouse themselves to fight over. By this I mean not just fighting metaphorically, in the sense of shouting matches among talking heads on TV and debates in Congress, but actually picking up guns and bombs and using them on other people. There are very few domestic political issues today in our rich, self-satisfied liberal democracies that can cause people to get terribly upset, but the specter of rising genetic inequality may well get people off their couches and into the streets.

If people get upset enough about genetic inequality, there will be two alternative courses of action. The first and most sensible would simply be to forbid the use of biotechnology to enhance human characteristics and decline to compete in this dimension. But the notion of enhancement may become too powerfully attractive to forgo, or it may prove difficult to enforce a rule preventing people from enhancing their children, or the courts may declare they have a right to do so. At this point a second possibility opens up, which is to use that same technology to raise up the bottom.[18]

This is the only scenario in which it is plausible that we will see a liberal democracy of the future get back into the business of state-sponsored eugenics. The bad old form of eugenics discriminated against the disabled and less intelligent by forbidding them to have children. In the future, it may be possible to breed children who are more intelligent, more healthy, more "normal." Raising the bottom is something that can only be accomplished through the intervention of the state. Genetic enhancement technology is likely to be expensive and involve some risk, but even if it were relatively cheap and safe, people who are poor and lacking in education would still fail to take advantage of it. So the bright red line of universal human dignity will have to be reinforced by allowing the state to make sure that no one falls outside it.

The politics of breeding future human beings will be very complex. Up to now, the Left has on the whole been opposed to cloning, genetic engineering, and similar biotechnologies for a number of reasons, including traditional humanism, environmental concerns, suspicion of technology and of the corporations that produce it, and fear of eugenics. The Left has historically sought to play down the importance of heredity in favor of social factors in explaining human outcomes. For people on the Left to come around and support genetic engineering for the disadvantaged, they would first have to admit that genes are important in determining intelligence and other types of social outcomes in the first place.

The Left has been more hostile to biotechnology in Europe than in North America. Much of this hostility is driven by the stronger environmental movements there, which have led the campaign, for example, against genetically modified foods. (Whether certain forms of radical environmentalism will translate into hostility to human biotechnology remains to be seen. Some environmentalists see themselves defending nature from human beings, and seem to be more concerned with threats to nonhuman than to human nature.) The Germans in particular remain very sensitive to anything that smacks of eugenics. The philosopher Peter Sloterdijk raised a storm of protest in 1999 when he suggested that it will soon be impossible for people to refuse the power of selection that biotechnology provides them, and that the questions of breeding something "beyond" man that were raised by Nietzsche and Plato could no longer be ignored.[19] He was condemned by the sociologist Jürgen Habermas, among others, who in other contexts has also come out against human cloning.[20]

On the other hand, there are some on the Left who have begun to make the case for genetic engineering.[21] John Rawls argued in *A Theory of Justice* that the unequal distribution of natural talents was inherently unfair. A Rawlsian should therefore want to make use of biotechnology to equalize life chances by breeding the bottom up, assuming that prudential considerations concerning safety, cost, and the like would be settled. Ronald Dworkin has laid out a case for the right of parents to genetically engineer their children based on a broader concern to protect autonomy,[22] and Laurence Tribe has suggested that a ban on cloning would be wrong because it might create discrimination against children who were cloned in spite of the ban.[23]

It is impossible to know which of these two radically different scenarios — one of growing genetic inequality, the other of growing genetic equality — is more likely to come to pass. But once the technological possibility for biomedical enhancement is realized, it is hard to see how growing genetic inequality would fail to become one of the chief controversies of twenty-first-century politics.

Human Dignity Redux

Denial of the concept of human dignity — that is, of the idea that there is something unique about the human race that entitles every member of the species to a higher moral status than the rest of the natural world — leads us down a very perilous path. We may be compelled ultimately to take this path, but we should do so only with our eyes open. Nietzsche is a much better guide to what lies down that road than the legions of bioethicists and casual academic Darwinians that today are prone to give us moral advice on this subject.

To avoid following that road, we need to take another look at the notion of human dignity, and ask whether there is a way to defend the concept against its detractors that is fully compatible with modern natural science but that also does justice to the full meaning of human specificity. I believe that there is.

In contrast to a number of conservative Protestant denominations that continue to hold a brief for creationism, the Catholic Church by the end of the twentieth century had come to terms with the theory of evolution. In his 1996 message to the Pontifical Academy of Sciences, Pope John Paul II corrected the encyclical *Humani generis* of Pius XII, which maintained that Darwinian evolution was a serious hypothesis but one that remained unproven. The pope stated, "Today, almost half a century after the publication of the Encyclical, new knowledge has led to the recognition of the theory of evolution as more than a hypothesis. It is indeed remarkable that this theory has been progressively accepted by researchers, following a series of discoveries in various fields of knowledge. The convergence, neither sought nor fabricated, of the results of work that was conducted independently is in itself a significant argument in favor of this theory."[24]

But the pope went on to say that while the church can accept the view that man is descended from nonhuman animals, there is an "ontological leap" that occurs somewhere in this evolutionary process.[25] The human soul is something directly created by God: Consequently, "theories of evolution which, in accordance with the philosophies inspiring them, consider the mind as emerging from the forces of living nature, or as a mere epiphenomenon of this matter, are incompatible with the truth about man." The pope continued, "Nor are they able to ground the dignity of the person."

The pope was saying, in other words, that at some point in the 5 million years between man's chimplike forebears and the emergence of modern human beings, a human soul was inserted into us in a way that remains mysterious. Modern natural science can uncover the time line of this process and explicate its material correlates, but it has not fully explained either what the soul is or how it came to be. The church has obviously learned a great deal from modern natural science in the past two centuries and has adjusted its doctrines accordingly. But while many natural scientists would scoff at the idea that they have anything to learn from the church, the pope has pointed to a real weakness in the current state of evolutionary theory, which scientists would do well to ponder. Modern natural science has explained a great deal less about what it means to be human than many scientists think it has.

Parts and Wholes

Many contemporary Darwinians believe that they have demystified the problem of how human beings came to be human through the classical reductionist methods of modern natural science. That is, any higher-order behavior or characteristic, such as language or aggression, can be traced back through the firing of neurons to the biochemical substrate of the brain, which in turn can be understood in terms of the simpler organic compounds of which it is composed. The brain arrived at its present state through a series of incremental evolutionary changes that were driven by random variation, and a process of natural selection by which the requirements of the surrounding environment selected for certain mental characteristics. Every human characteristic can thus be traced back to a prior material cause. If, for example, we today love to listen to Mozart or Beethoven, it is because we have auditory systems that were evolved, in the environment of evolutionary adaptation, to discriminate between certain kinds of sounds that were necessary perhaps to warn us against predators or to help us on a hunt.[26]

The problem with this kind of thinking is not that it is necessarily false but that it is insufficient to explain many of the most salient and unique human traits. The problem lies in the methodology of reductionism itself for understanding complex systems, and particularly biological ones.

Reductionism constitutes, of course, one of the foundations of modern natural science and is responsible for many of its greatest triumphs. You see before you two apparently different substances, the graphite in your pencil lead and the diamond in your engagement ring, and you might be tempted to believe that they were essentially different substances. But reductionist chemistry has taught us that in fact they are both composed of the same simpler substance, carbon, and that the apparent differences are not ones of essence but merely of the way the carbon atoms are bonded. Reductionist physics has been busy over the past century tracing atoms back to subatomic particles and thence back to an even more reduced set of basic forces of nature.

But what is appropriate for domains in physics, like celestial mechanics and fluid dynamics, is not necessarily appropriate for the study of objects at the opposite end of the complexity scale, like most biological systems, because the behavior of complex systems cannot be predicted by simply aggregating or scaling up the behavior of the parts that constitute them.* The distinctive and easily recognizable behavior of a flock of birds or a swarm of bees, for example, is the product of the interaction of individual birds or bees following relatively simple behavioral rules (fly next to a partner, avoid obstacles, and so on), none of which encompasses or defines the behavior of the flock or swarm as a whole. Rather, the group behavior "emerges" as a result of the interaction of the individuals that make it up. In many cases, the relationship between parts and wholes is nonlinear: That is, increasing input A increases output B up to a certain point, whereupon it creates a qualitatively different and unexpected output C. This is true even of relatively simple chemicals like water: H_2O undergoes a phase transition from liquid to solid at 32 degrees Fahrenheit, something that one would not necessarily predict on the basis of knowledge of its chemical composition.

*The determinism of classical Newtonian mechanics is based in large measure on the parallelogram rule, which says that the effects of two forces acting on a body can be summed as if each were acting independently of the other. Newton shows that this rule works for celestial bodies like planets and stars, and assumes that it will also work for other natural objects, like animals.

That the behavior of complex wholes cannot be understood as the aggregated behavior of their parts has been understood in the natural sciences for some time now,[27] and has led to the development of the field of so-called nonlinear or "complex adaptive" systems, which try to model the emergence of complexity. This approach is, in a way, the opposite of reductionism: It shows that while wholes can be traced back to their simpler antecedent parts, there is no simple predictive model that allows us to move from the parts to the emergent behaviors of the wholes. Being nonlinear, they may be extremely sensitive to small differences in starting conditions and thus may appear chaotic even when their behavior is completely deterministic.

This means that the behavior of complex systems is much more difficult to understand than the founders of reductionist science once believed. The eighteenth-century astronomer Laplace once said that he could precisely predict the future of the universe on the basis of Newtonian mechanics, if he could know the mass and motion of the universe's constituent parts.[28] No scientist could make this claim today—not just because of the inherent uncertainties introduced by quantum mechanics but also because there exists no reliable methodology for predicting the behavior of complex systems.[29] In the words of Arthur Peacocke, "The concepts and theories . . . that constitute the content of the sciences focusing on the more complex levels are often (not always) logically not reducible to those operative in the sciences that focus on their components."[30] There is a hierarchy of levels of complexity in the sciences, with human beings and human behavior occupying a place at the uppermost level.

Each level can give us some insight into the levels above it, but understanding the lower levels does not allow one to fully understand the higher levels' emergent properties. Researchers in the area of complex adaptive systems have created so-called agent-based models of complex systems, and have applied them in a wide variety of areas, from cell biology to fighting a war to distributing natural gas. It remains to be seen, however, whether this approach constitutes a single, coherent methodology applicable to all complex systems.[31] Such models may tell us only that certain systems will remain inherently chaotic and unpredictable, or that prediction rests on a precise knowledge of initial conditions that is unavailable to us. The higher level must thus be understood with a methodology appropriate to its degree of complexity.

We can illustrate the problematic relationship of parts to wholes by reference to one unique domain of human behavior, politics.[32] Aristotle states that man is a political animal by nature. If one were to try to build a case for human dignity based on human specificity, the capability of engaging in politics would certainly constitute one important component of human uniqueness. Yet the idea of our uniqueness in this regard has been challenged. . . . [C]himpanzees and other primates engage in something that looks uncannily like human politics as they struggle and connive to achieve alpha male status. They appear, moreover, to feel the political emotions of pride and shame as they interact with other members of their group. Their political behavior can also apparently be transmitted through nongenetic means, so that political culture would not seem to be the exclusive preserve of human beings.[33] Some observers gleefully cite examples like this to deflate human feelings of self-importance relative to other species.

But to confuse human politics with the social behavior of any other species is to mistake parts for wholes. Only human beings can formulate, debate, and modify abstract rules of justice. When Aristotle asserted that man is a political animal by nature, he meant this only in the sense that politics is a potentiality that emerges over time.[34] He notes that human politics did not begin until the first lawgiver established a state and promulgated laws, an event that was of great benefit to mankind but that was contingent on historical developments. This accords with what we know today about the emergence of the state, which took place in parts of the world like Egypt and Babylonia perhaps 10,000 years ago and was most likely related to the development of agriculture. For tens of thousands of years before that, human beings lived in stateless hunter-gatherer societies in which the largest group numbered no more than 50 to 100 individuals, most of them related by kinship.[35] So in a certain sense, while human sociability is obviously natural, it is not clear that humans are political animals by nature.

But Aristotle insists that politics is natural to man despite the fact that it did not exist at all in early periods of human history. He argues that it is human language that allows human beings to formulate laws and abstract principles of justice that are necessary to the creation of a state and of political order. Ethologists have noted that many other species communicate with sounds, and that chimpanzees and other animals can learn human language to a limited extent. But no other species has *human* language—that is, the ability to formulate and communicate abstract principles of action. It is only when these two natural characteristics, human sociability and human language, come together that human politics emerges. Human language obviously evolved to promote sociability, but it is very unlikely that there were evolutionary forces shaping it to become an enabler of politics. It was rather like one of Stephen Jay Gould's spandrels,* something that evolved for one reason but that found another key purpose when combined in a human whole.[36] Human politics, though natural in an emergent sense, is not reducible to either animal sociability or animal language, which were its precursors.

Consciousness

The area in which the inability of a reductionist materialist science to explain observable phenomena is most glaringly evident is the question of human consciousness. By consciousness I mean subjective mental states: not just the thoughts and images that appear to you as you are thinking or reading this page, but also the sensations, feelings, and emotions that you experience as part of everyday life.

---

*A spandrel is an architectural feature that emerges, unplanned by the architect, from the intersection of a dome and the walls that support it.

There has been a huge amount of research and theorizing about consciousness over the past two generations, coming in equal measure from the neurosciences and from studies in computer and artificial intelligence (AI). Particularly in the latter field there are many enthusiasts who are convinced that with more powerful computers and new approaches to computing, such as neural networks, we are on the verge of a breakthrough in which mechanical computers will achieve consciousness. There have been conferences and earnest discussions devoted to the question of whether it would be moral to turn off such a machine if and when this breakthrough occurs, and whether we would need to assign rights to conscious machines.

The fact of the matter is that we are nowhere close to a breakthrough; consciousness remains as stubbornly mysterious as it ever was. The problem with the current state of thinking begins with the traditional philosophical problem of the ontological status of consciousness. Subjective mental states, while produced by material biological processes, appear to be of a very different, nonmaterial order from other phenomena. The fear of dualism—that is, the doctrine that there are two essential types of being, material and mental—is so strong among researchers in this field that it has led them to palpably ridiculous conclusions. In the words of the philosopher John Searle,

> Seen from the perspective of the last fifty years, the philosophy of mind, as well as cognitive science and certain branches of psychology, present a very curious spectacle. The most striking feature is how much of mainstream philosophy of mind of the past fifty years seems obviously false . . . in the philosophy of mind, obvious facts about the mental, such as that we all really do have subjective conscious mental states and that these are not eliminable in favor of anything else, are routinely denied by many, perhaps most, of the advanced thinkers in the subject.[37]

An example of a patently false understanding of consciousness comes from one of the leading experts in the field, Daniel Dennett, whose book *Consciousness Explained* finally comes to the following definition of consciousness: "Human consciousness is *itself* a huge complex of memes (or more exactly, meme-effects in brains) that can best be understood as the operation of a *'von Neumannesque'* virtual machine *implemented* in the *parallel architecture* of a brain that was not designed for any such activities."[38] A naive reader may be excused for thinking that this kind of statement doesn't do much at all to advance our understanding of consciousness. Dennett is saying in effect that human consciousness is simply the by-product of the operations of a certain type of computer, and if we think that there is more to it than that, we have a mistakenly old-fashioned view of what consciousness is. As Searle says of this approach, it works only by denying the existence of what you and I and everyone else understand consciousness to be (that is, subjective feelings).[39]

Similarly, many of the researchers in the field of artificial intelligence sidestep the question of consciousness by in effect changing the subject. They assume that the brain is simply a highly complex type of organic computer that can be identified by its external characteristics. The well-known Turing test asserts that if a machine can perform a cognitive task such as carrying on a conversation in a way that from the outside is indistinguishable from similar activities carried out by a human being, then it is indistinguishable on the inside as well. Why this should be an adequate test of human mentality is a mystery, for the machine will obviously not have any subjective awareness of what it is doing, or feelings about its activities.* This doesn't prevent such authors as Hans Moravec [40] and Ray Kurzweil [41] from predicting that machines, once they reach a requisite level of complexity, will possess human attributes like consciousness as well.[42] If they are right, this will have important consequences for our notions of human dignity, because it will have been conclusively proven that human beings are essentially nothing more than complicated machines that can be made out of silicon and transistors as easily as carbon and neurons.

The likelihood that this will happen seems very remote, however, not so much because machines will never duplicate human intelligence—I suspect they will probably be able to come very close in this regard—but rather because it is impossible to see how they will come to acquire human emotions. It is the stuff of science fiction for an android, robot, or computer to suddenly start experiencing emotions like fear, hope, even sexual desire, but no one has come remotely close to positing how this might come about. The problem is not simply that, like the rest of consciousness, no one understands what emotions are ontologically; no one understands why they came to exist in human biology.

There are of course functional reasons for feelings like pain and pleasure. If we didn't find sex pleasurable we wouldn't reproduce, and if we didn't feel pain from fire we would be burning ourselves constantly. But state-of-the-art thinking in cognitive science maintains that the particular subjective form that the emotions take is not necessary to their function. It is perfectly possible, for example, to design a robot with heat sensors in its fingers connected to an actuator that would pull the robot's hand away from a fire. The robot could keep itself from being burned without having any subjective sense of pain, and it could make decisions on which objectives to fulfill and which activities to avoid on the basis of a mechanical computation of the inputs of different electrical impulses. A Turing test would say it was a human being in its behavior, but it would actually be devoid of the most important quality of a human being, feelings. The actual subjective form that emotions take are today seen in evolutionary biology and in cognitive science as no more than epiphenomenal to their underlying function; there are no obvious reasons this form should have been selected for in the course of evolutionary history.[43]

As Robert Wright points out, this leads to the very bizarre outcome that what is most important to us as human beings has no apparent purpose in the material scheme of things by which we became human.[44] For it is the distinctive human gamut of emotions that produces human purposes, goals, objectives,

*Searle's critique of this approach is contained in his "Chinese room" puzzle, which raises the question of whether a computer could be said to understand Chinese any more than a non-Chinese-speaking individual locked in a room who received instructions on how to manipulate a series of symbols in Chinese. See Searle (1997), p. 11.

wants, needs, desires, fears, aversions, and the like and hence is the source of human values. While many would list human reason and human moral choice as the most important unique human characteristics that give our species dignity, I would argue that possession of the full human emotional gamut is at least as important, if not more so.

The political theorist Robert McShea demonstrates the importance of human emotions to our commonsense understanding of what it means to be human by asking us to perform the following thought experiment.[45] Suppose you met two creatures on a desert island, both of which had the rational capacity of a human being and hence the ability to carry on a conversation. One had the physical form of a lion but the emotions of a human being, while the other had the physical form of a human being but the emotional characteristics of a lion. Which creature would you feel more comfortable with, which creature would you be more likely to befriend or enter into a moral relationship with? The answer, as countless children's books

> **We would regard a Mr. Spock who was truly devoid of any feelings as a psychopath and a monster.**

with sympathetic talking lions suggest, is the lion, because species-typical human emotions are more critical to our sense of our own humanness than either our reason or our physical appearance. The coolly analytical Mr. Spock in the TV series *Star Trek* appears at times more likable than the emotional Mr. Scott only because we suspect that somewhere beneath his rational exterior lurk deeply buried human feelings. Certainly many of the female characters he encountered in the series hoped they could rouse something more than robotic responses from him.

On the other hand, we would regard a Mr. Spock who was truly devoid of any feelings as a psychopath and a monster. If he offered us a benefit, we might accept it but would feel no gratitude because we would know it was the product of rational calculation on his part and not goodwill. If we double-crossed him, we would feel no guilt, because we know that he cannot himself entertain feelings of anger or of having been betrayed. And if circumstances forced us to kill him to save ourselves, or to sacrifice his life in a hostage situation, we would feel no more regret than if we lost any other valuable asset, like a car or a teleporter.[46] Even though we might want to cooperate with this Mr. Spock, we would not regard him as a moral agent entitled to the respect that human beings command. The computer geeks in AI labs who think of themselves as nothing more than complex computer programs and want to download themselves into a computer should worry, since no one would care if they were turned off for good.

So there is a great deal that comes together under the rubric of consciousness that helps define human specificity and hence human dignity, which nonetheless cannot currently be fully explicated by modern natural science. It is not sufficient to argue that some other animals are conscious, or have culture, or have language, for their consciousness does not combine human reason, human language, human moral choice, and human emotions in ways that are capable of producing human politics, human art, or human religion. All of the nonhuman precursors of these human traits that existed in evolutionary history, and all of the material causes and preconditions for their emergence, collectively add up to much less than the human whole. Jared Diamond in his book *The Third Chimpanzee* notes the fact that the chimpanzee and human genomes overlap by more than 98 percent, implying that the differences between the two species are relatively trivial.[47] But for an emergent complex system, small differences can lead to enormous qualitative changes. It is a bit like saying there is no significant difference between ice and liquid water because they differ in temperature by only 1 degree.

Thus one does not have to agree with the pope that God directly inserted a human soul in the course of evolutionary history to acknowledge with him that there was a very important qualitative, if not ontological, leap that occurred at some point in this process. It is this leap from parts to a whole that ultimately has to constitute the basis for human dignity, a concept one can believe in even if one does not begin from the pope's religious premises.

What this whole is and how it came to be remain, in Searle's word, "mysterious." None of the branches of modern natural science that have tried to address this question have done more than scratch the surface, despite the belief of many scientists that they have demystified the entire process. It is common now for many AI researchers to say that consciousness is an "emergent property" of a certain kind of complex computer. But this is no more than an unproven hypothesis based on an analogy with other complex systems. No one has ever seen consciousness emerge under experimental conditions, or even posited a theory as to how this might come about. It would be surprising if the process of "emergence" didn't play an important part in explaining how humans came to be human, but whether that is all there is to the story is something we do not at present know.

This is not to say that the demystification by science will never happen. Searle himself believes that consciousness is a biological property of the brain much like the firing of neurons or the production of neurotransmitters and that biology will someday be able to explain how organic tissue can produce it. He argues that our present problems in understanding consciousness do not require us to adopt a dualistic ontology or abandon the scientific framework of material causation. The problem of how consciousness arose does not require recourse to the direct intervention of God.

It does not, on the other hand, rule it out, either.   60

What to Fight For

If what gives us dignity and a moral status higher than that of other living creatures is related to the fact that we are complex wholes rather than the sum of simple parts, then it is clear that there is no simple answer to the question, What is Factor X? That is, Factor X cannot be reduced to the possession of moral choice, or reason, or language, or sociability, or sentience, or emotions, or consciousness, or any other quality that has been put forth as a ground for human dignity. It is all of these qualities coming together in a human whole that make up Factor X. Every member of the human species possesses a genetic endowment that allows him or her to become a whole human being, an endowment that distinguishes a human in essence from other types of creatures.

A moment's reflection will show that none of the key qualities that contribute to human dignity can exist in the absence of the others. Human reason, for example, is not that of a computer; it is pervaded by emotions, and its functioning is in fact facilitated by the latter.[48] Moral choice cannot exist without reason, needless to say, but it is also grounded in feelings such as pride, anger, shame, and sympathy.[49] Human consciousness is not just individual preferences and instrumental reason, but is shaped intersubjectively by other consciousnesses and their moral evaluations. We are social and political animals not merely because we are capable of game-theoretic reason, but because we are endowed with certain social emotions. Human sentience is not that of a pig or a horse, because it is coupled with human memory and reason.

This protracted discussion of human dignity is intended to answer the following question: What is it that we want to protect from any future advances in biotechnology? The answer is, we want to protect the full range of our complex, evolved natures against attempts at self-modification. We do not want to disrupt either the unity or the continuity of human nature, and thereby the human rights that are based on it.

If Factor X is related to our very complexity and the complex interactions of uniquely human characteristics like moral choice, reason, and a broad emotional gamut, it is reasonable to ask how and why biotechnology would seek to make us less complex. The answer lies in the constant pressure that exists to reduce the ends of biomedicine to utilitarian ones—that is, the attempt to reduce a complex diversity of natural ends and purposes to just a few simple categories like pain and pleasure, or autonomy. There is in particular a constant predisposition to allow the relief of pain and suffering to automatically trump all other human purposes and objectives. For this will be the constant trade-off that biotechnology will pose: We can cure this disease, or prolong this person's life, or make this child more tractable, at the expense of some ineffable human quality like genius, or ambition, or sheer diversity.

That aspect of our complex natures most under threat has to do with our emotional gamut. We will be constantly tempted to think that we understand what "good" and "bad" emotions are, and that we can do nature one better by suppressing the latter, by trying to make people less aggressive, more sociable, more compliant, less depressed. The utilitarian goal of minimizing suffering is itself very problematic. No one can make a brief in favor of pain and suffering, but the fact of the matter is that what we consider to be the highest and most admirable human qualities, both in ourselves and in others, are often related to the way that we react to, confront, overcome, and frequently succumb to pain, suffering, and death. In the absence of these human evils there would be no sympathy, compassion, courage, heroism, solidarity, or strength of character.* A person who has not confronted

65

---

*The Greek root of *sympathy* and the Latin root of *compassion* both refer to the ability to feel another person's pain and suffering.

suffering or death has no depth. Our ability to experience these emotions is what connects us potentially to all other human beings, both living and dead.

Many scientists and researchers would say that we don't need to worry about fencing off human nature, however defined, from biotechnology, because we are a very long way from being able to modify it, and may never achieve the capability. They may be right: Human germ-line engineering and the use of recombinant DNA technology on humans is probably much further off than many people assume, though human cloning is not.

But our ability to manipulate human behavior is not dependent on the development of genetic engineering. Virtually everything we can anticipate being able to do through genetic engineering we will most likely be able to do much sooner through neuropharmacology. And we will face large demographic changes in the populations that find new biomedical technologies available to them, not only in terms of age and sex distributions, but in terms of the quality of life of important population groups.

The widespread and rapidly growing use of drugs like Ritalin and Prozac demonstrates just how eager we are to make use of technology to alter ourselves. If one of the key constituents of our nature, something on which we base our notions of dignity, has to do with the gamut of normal emotions shared by human beings, then we are *already* trying to narrow the range for the utilitarian ends of health and convenience.

Psychotropic drugs do not alter the germ line or produce heritable effects in the way that genetic engineering someday might. But they already raise important issues about the meaning of human dignity and are a harbinger of things to come.

When Do We Become Human?

In the near term, the big ethical controversies raised by biotechnology will not be threats to the dignity of normal adult human beings but rather to those who possess something less than the full complement of capabilities that we have defined as characterizing human specificity. The largest group of beings in this category are the unborn, but it could also include infants, the terminally sick, elderly people with debilitating diseases, and the disabled.

This issue has already come up with regard to stem cell research and cloning. Embryonic stem cell research requires the deliberate destruction of embryos, while so-called therapeutic cloning requires not just their destruction but their deliberate creation for research purposes prior to destruction. (As bioethicist Leon Kass notes, therapeutic cloning is not therapeutic for the embryo.) Both activities have been strongly condemned by those who believe that life begins at conception and that embryos have full moral status as human beings.

I do not want to rehearse the whole history of the abortion debate and the hotly contested question of when life begins. I personally do not begin with religious convictions on this issue and admit to considerable confusion in trying to think through its rights and wrongs. The question here is, What does the natural-rights approach to human dignity outlined here suggest about the moral status of the unborn, the disabled, and so on? I'm not sure it produces a definitive answer, but it can at least help us frame an answer to the question.

At first blush, a natural-rights doctrine that bases human dignity on the fact that the human species possesses certain unique characteristics would appear to allow a gradation of rights depending on the degree to which any individual member of that species shares in those characteristics. An elderly person with Alzheimer's, for example, has lost the normal adult ability to reason, and therefore that part of his dignity that would permit him to participate in politics by voting or running for office. Reason, moral choice, and possession of the species-typical emotional gamut are things that are shared by virtually all human beings and therefore serve as a basis for universal equality, but individuals possess these traits in greater or lesser amounts: Some are more reasonable, have stronger consciences or more sensitive emotions than others. At one extreme, minute distinctions could be made between individuals based on the degree to which they possess these basic human qualities, with differentiated rights assigned to them on that basis. This has happened before in history; it is called natural aristocracy. The hierarchical system it implies is one of the reasons people have become suspicious of the very concept of natural rights.

There is a strong prudential reason for not being too hierarchical in the assignment of political rights, however. There is, in the first place, no consensus on a precise definition of that list of essential human characteristics that qualify an individual for rights. More important, judgments about the degree to which a given individual possesses one or another of these qualities are very difficult to make, and usually suspect, because the person making the judgment is seldom a disinterested party. Most real-world aristocracies have been conventional rather than natural, with the aristocrats assigning themselves rights that they claimed were natural but that were actually based on force or convention. It is therefore appropriate to approach the question of who qualifies for rights with some liberality.

Nonetheless, every contemporary liberal democracy does in fact differentiate rights based on the degree to which individuals or categories of individuals share in certain species-typical characteristics. Children, for example, do not have the rights of adults because their capacities for reason and moral choice are not fully developed; they cannot vote and do not have the freedom of person that their parents do in making choices about where to live, whether to go to school, and so on. Societies strip criminals of basic rights for violating the law, and do so more severely in the case of those regarded as lacking a basic human moral sense. In the United States, they can be deprived even of the right to life for certain kinds of crimes. We do not officially strip Alzheimer's patients of their political rights, but we do restrict their ability to drive and make financial decisions, and in practice they usually cease to exercise their political rights as well.

From a natural-rights perspective, then, one could argue that it is reasonable to assign the unborn different rights from those of either infants or children. A day-old infant may not be capable of reason or moral choice, but it already possesses important elements of the normal human emotional gamut—it can get upset, bond to its mother, expect attention, and the like, in ways that a day-old embryo cannot. It is the violation of the natural and very powerful bonding that takes place between parent and infant, in fact, that makes infanticide such a heinous crime in most societies. That we typically hold funerals after the deaths of infants but not after miscarriages is testimony to the naturalness of this distinction. All of this suggests that it does not make sense to treat embryos as human beings with the same kinds of rights that infants possess.

Against this line of argument, we can pose the following considerations, again not from a religious but from a natural-rights perspective. An embryo may be lacking in some of the basic human characteristics possessed by an infant, but it is also not just another group of cells or tissue, because it has the *potential* to become a full human being. In this respect, it differs from an infant, which also lacks many of the most important characteristics of a normal adult human being, only in the degree to which it has realized its natural potential. This implies that while an embryo can be assigned a lower moral status than an infant, it has a higher moral status than other kinds of cells or tissue that scientists work with. It is therefore reasonable, on nonreligious grounds, to question whether researchers should be free to create, clone, and destroy human embryos at will.

Ontogeny recapitulates phylogeny. We have argued that in the evolutionary process that leads from prehuman ancestor to human beings, there was a qualitative leap that transformed the prehuman precursors of language, reason, and emotion into a human whole that cannot be explained as a simple sum of its parts, and that remains an essentially mysterious process. Something similar happens with the development of every embryo into an infant, child, and adult human being: What starts out as a cluster of organic molecules comes to possess consciousness, reason, the capacity for moral choice, and subjective emotions, in a manner that remains equally mysterious.

Putting these facts together—that an embryo has a moral status somewhere between that of an infant and that of other types of cells and tissue, and that the transformation of the embryo into something with a higher status is a mysterious process—suggests that if we are to do things like harvest stem cells from embryos, we should put a lot of limits and constraints around this activity to make sure that it does not become a precedent for other uses of the unborn that would push the envelope further. To what extent are we willing to create and grow embryos for utilitarian purposes? Supposing some miraculous new cure required cells not from a day-old embryo, but tissue from a month-old fetus? A five-month-old female fetus already has in her ovaries all the eggs she will ever produce as a woman; supposing someone wanted access to them? If we get too used to the idea of cloning embryos for medical purposes, will we know when to stop?

If the question of equality in a future biotech world threatens to tear up the Left, the Right will quite literally fall apart over questions related to human dignity. In the United States, the Right (as represented by the Republican Party) is divided between economic libertarians, who like entrepreneurship and technology with minimal regulation, and social conservatives, many of whom are religious, who care about a range of issues including abortion and the family. The coalition between these two groups is usually strong enough to hold up during elections, but it papers over some fundamental differences in outlook. It is not clear that this alliance will survive the emergence of new technologies that, on the one hand, offer enormous health benefits and money-making opportunities for the biotech industry, but, on the other, require violating deeply held ethical norms.

We are thus brought back to the question of politics and political strategies. For if there is a viable concept of human dignity out there, it needs to be defended, not just in philosophical tracts but in the real world of politics, and protected by viable political institutions. . . .

NOTES

1. Clive Staples Lewis, *The Abolition of Man* (New York: Touchstone, 1944), p. 85.
2. Counsel of Europe, Draft Additional Protocol to the Convention on Human Rights and Biomedicine, On the Prohibiting of Cloning Human Beings, Doc. 7884, July 16, 1997.
3. This is the theme of the second part of Francis Fukuyama, *The End of History and the Last Man* (New York: Free Press, 1992).
4. For an interpretation of this passage in Tocqueville, see Francis Fukuyama, "The March of Equality," *Journal of Democracy* 11 (2000): 11–17.
5. John Paul II, "Message to the Pontifical Academy of Sciences," October 22, 1996.
6. Daniel C. Dennett, *Darwin's Dangerous Idea: Evolution and the Meanings of Life* (New York: Simon and Schuster, 1995), pp. 35–39; see also Ernst Mayr, *One Long Argument: Charles Darwin and the Genesis of Modern Evolutionary Thought* (Cambridge, Mass.: Harvard University Press, 1991), pp. 40–42.
7. Michael Ruse and David L. Hull, *The Philosophy of Biology* (New York: Oxford University Press, 1998), p. 385.
8. Lee M. Silver, *Remaking Eden: Cloning and Beyond in a Brave New World* (New York: Avon, 1998), pp. 256–57.
9. Ruse and Hull (1998), p. 385.
10. Silver (1998), p. 277.
11. Friedrich Nietzsche, *Thus Spoke Zarathustra*, First part, section 5, from *The Portable Nietzsche*, ed. Walter Kaufmann (New York: Viking, 1968), p. 130.
12. Charles Taylor, *Sources of the Self: The Making of the Modern Identity* (Cambridge, Mass.: Harvard University Press, 1989), pp. 6–7.
13. For a fuller defense of this proposition, see Francis Fukuyama, *The Great Disruption: Human Nature and the Reconstitution of Social Order*, part II (New York: Free Press, 1999).
14. Aristotle, *Politics* I.2.13, 1254b, 16–24.
15. Ibid., I.2.18, 1255a, 22–38.
16. Ibid., I.2.19, 1255b, 3–5.
17. See, for example, Dan W. Brock, "The Human Genome Project and Human Identity," in *Genes, Humans, and Self-Knowledge*, eds. Robert F. Weir and Susan C. Lawrence et al. (Iowa City: University of Iowa Press, 1994), pp. 18–23.
18. This possibility has already been suggested by Charles Murray. See his "Deeper into the Brain," *National Review* 52 (2000): 46–49.

19. Peter Sloterdijk, "Regeln für den Menschenpark: Ein Antwortschreiben zum Brief über den Humanismus," *Die Zeit*, no. 38, September 16, 1999.

20. Jürgen Habermas, "Nicht die Natur verbietet das Klonen. Wir müssen selbst entscheiden. Eine Replik auf Dieter E. Zimmer," *Die Zeit*, no. 9, February 19, 1998.

21. For a discussion of this issue, see Allen Buchanan and Norman Daniels et al., *From Chance to Choice: Genetics and Justice* (New York and Cambridge: Cambridge University Press, 2000), pp. 17–20. See also Robert H. Blank and Masako N. Darrough, *Biological Differences and Social Equality: Implications for Social Policy* (Westport, Conn.: Greenwood Press, 1983).

22. Ronald M. Dworkin, *Sovereign Virtue: The Theory and Practice of Equality* (Cambridge, Mass.: Harvard University Press, 2000), p. 452.

23. Laurence H. Tribe, "Second Thoughts on Cloning," *New York Times*, December 5, 1997, p. A31.

24. John Paul II (1996).

25. On the meaning of this "ontological leap," see Ernan McMullin, "Biology and the Theology of the Human," in Phillip R. Sloan, ed., *Controlling Our Desires: Historical, Philosophical, Ethical, and Theological Perspectives on the Human Genome Project* (Notre Dame, Ind.: University of Notre Dame Press, 2000), p. 367.

26. It is in fact very difficult to come up with a Darwinian explanation for the human enjoyment of music. See Steven Pinker, *How the Mind Works* (New York: W. W. Norton, 1997), pp. 528–38.

27. See, for example, Arthur Peacocke, "Relating Genetics to Theology on the Map of Scientific Knowledge," in Sloan, ed. (2000), pp. 346–50.

28. Laplace's exact words were: "We ought then to regard the present state of the universe [not just the solar system] as the effect of its anterior state and as the cause of the one which is to follow. Given an intelligence that could comprehend at one instant all the forces by which nature is animated and the respective situation of the beings who compose it — an intelligence sufficiently vast to submit these data [initial conditions] to analysis — it would embrace in the same formula the movements of the greatest bodies in the universe and those of the lightest atom; for it, nothing would be uncertain and the future, as the past, would be present to its eyes . . . The regularity which astronomy shows us in the movements of the comets doubtless exists also in all phenomena. The curve described by a simple molecule of air or vapor is regulated in a manner just as certain as the planetary orbits; the only difference between them is that which comes from our ignorance." Quoted in *Final Causality in Nature and Human Affairs*, ed. Richard F. Hassing (Washington, D.C.: Catholic University Press, 1997), p. 224.

29. Hassing, ed. (1997), pp. 224–26.

30. Peacocke, in Sloan, ed. (2000), p. 350.

31. McMullin, in Sloan, ed. (2000), p. 374.

32. On this question, see Roger D. Masters, "The Biological Nature of the State," *World Politics* 35 (1983): 161–93.

33. Andrew Goldberg and Christophe Boesch, "The Cultures of Chimpanzees," *Scientific American* 284 (2001): 60–67.

34. Larry Arnhart, *Darwinian Natural Right: The Biological Ethics of Human Nature* (Albany, N.Y.: State University of New York Press, 1998), pp. 61–62.

35. One exception to this appears to be the indigenous peoples of the American Pacific Northwest, a hunter-gatherer society that seems to have developed a

state. See Robert Wright, *Nonzero: The Logic of Human Destiny* (New York: Pantheon Books, 2000), pp. 31–38.

36. Stephen Jay Gould and R. C. Lewontin, "The Spandrels of San Marco and the Panglossian Paradigm: A Critique of the Adaptionist Programme," *Proceedings of the Royal Society of London* 205 (1979): 81–98.

37. John R. Searle, *The Mystery of Consciousness* (New York: New York Review Books, 1997).

38. Daniel C. Dennett, *Consciousness Explained* (Boston: Little, Brown, 1991), p. 210.

39. John R. Searle, *The Rediscovery of the Mind* (Cambridge, Mass.: MIT Press, 1992), p. 3.

40. Hans P. Moravec, *Robot: Mere Machine to Transcendent Mind* (New York: Oxford University Press, 1999).

41. Ray Kurzweil, *The Age of Spiritual Machines: When Computers Exceed Human Intelligence* (London: Penguin Books, 2000).

42. For a critique, see Colin McGinn, "Hello HAL," *New York Times Book Review,* January 3, 1999.

43. On this point, see Wright (2000), pp. 306–8.

44. Ibid., pp. 321–22.

45. Robert J. McShea, *Morality and Human Nature: A New Route to Ethical Theory* (Philadelphia: Temple University Press, 1990), p. 77.

46. Daniel Dennett makes the following bizarre statement in *Consciousness Explained:* "But why should it matter, you may want to ask, that a creature's desires are thwarted if they aren't conscious desires? I reply: Why would it matter more if they were conscious—especially if consciousness were a property, as some think, that forever eludes investigation? Why should a 'zombie's' crushed hopes matter less than a conscious person's crushed hopes? There is a trick with mirrors here that should be exposed and discarded. Consciousness, you say, is what matters, but then you cling to doctrines about consciousness that systematically prevent us from getting any purchase on *why* it matters" (p. 450). Dennett's question begs a more obvious one: What person in the world would care about crushing a zombie's hopes, except to the extent that the zombie was instrumentally useful to that person?

47. Jared Diamond, *The Third Chimpanzee* (New York: HarperCollins, 1992), p. 23.

48. The dualism between reason and emotion—that is, the idea that these are distinct and separable mental qualities—can be traced to Descartes (see *The Passions of the Soul,* Article 47). This dichotomy has been widely accepted since then but is misleading in many ways. The neurophysiologist Antonio Damasio points out that human reasoning invariably involves what he labels somatic markers—emotions that the mind attaches to certain ideas or options in the course of thinking through a problem—that help speed many kinds of calculations. Antonio R. Damasio, *Descartes' Error: Emotion, Reason, and the Human Brain* (New York: Putnam, 1994).

49. That is, the Kantian notion that moral choice is an act of pure reason overriding or suppressing natural emotions is not the way that human beings actually make moral choices. Human beings more typically balance one set of feelings against another and build character by strengthening the pleasurability of good moral choices through habit.

Questions for Critical Reading

1. What is "Factor X"? Reread Fukuyama to locate quotations where he defines this term and then provide a definition of the concept in your own words.

2. Do humans have an "essence"? Locate passages from Fukuyama that support your analysis. Does he think there is a human essence? What quotations make his position clear? You will need to read his text closely and critically to determine his position.

3. As the title of this selection suggests, Fukuyama is centrally concerned with the concept of human dignity in this chapter. Define human dignity, using quotations from Fukuyama that support your definition.

Exploring Context

1. Fukuyama opens this chapter by quoting from a decree from the Council of Europe. Visit the Council's Web site at coe.int and search for information on cloning. What else does the council have to say on the issue? How does its position reflect or complicate Fukuyama's argument?

2. Fukuyama turns to complexity theory to recuperate an understanding of the human essence. Conway's Game of Life is a classic mathematical model illustrating how simple rules governing individual parts can combine into very complex wholes. Play the Game of Life at bitstorm.org/gameoflife. Does it reflect the evolution of consciousness? How often does a stable pattern emerge in the game? How does it support or undercut Fukuyama's arguments about Factor X?

3. Fukuyama asks, "What is it that we want to protect from any future advances in biotechnology?" (p. 159). Visit the Web site of the *American Journal of Bioethics* at bioethics.net. In browsing through the site, what answers to Fukuyama's question can you find? How can we decide which biotechnologies should be pursued and which would cause us to lose our humanity?

Questions for Connecting

1. Michael Pollan's discussion of "holons" in "The Animals: Practicing Complexity" (p. 281) seems closely related to Fukuyama's use of complexity theory. In what ways are humans and organic farms similar? What insight does Pollan's essay provide on Fukuyama's argument?

2. In "The End of Race: Hawaii and the Mixing of Peoples" (p. 250), Steve Olson suggests that, as a result of intermarriage, race no longer has a genetic basis. Is race part of "Factor X"? How does Fukuyama's essay support or complicate Olson's argument about race? Is race part of being human? Is it part of human dignity? You may want to use the definition of human dignity you developed in Question 3 of Questions for Critical Reading in making your argument.

3. According to Richard Restak in "Attention Deficit: The Brain Syndrome of Our Era" (p. 332), our brains are being rewired to produce Attention Deficit Disorder. Is multitasking a threat to human dignity as well? If culture can change the wiring of our brains, then is that, too, a kind of biotechnology?

Language Matters

1. Select a key paragraph from the essay and then reduce each sentence of the paragraph down to a single subject and verb. What's lost by condensing the sentences in this way? What other grammatical constructions help carry the meaning of a sentence?

2. The best way to avoid awkward sentences in your own writing is to say what you mean. You can also use this technique when dealing with difficult readings like Fukuyama's. Select a particularly complex sentence from this essay. If you could make Fukuyama say what he meant, what would the sentence look like? Begin by breaking down his writing into several smaller sentences. Try substituting simpler vocabulary too. Once you've absorbed the ideas through this process, try stating out loud a summary of what Fukuyama is trying to communicate and then write down what you say. Try these same strategies in your own writing.

3. You're probably familiar with common parts of speech like nouns and verbs. Using Fukuyama's text, create new parts of speech from common combinations of the usual parts of speech. For example, a noun and a verb together might form a "quarplat," an adverb and an adjective might be a "jerbad." Create rules for your parts of speech. When does Fukuyama use the kinds of constructions you've named? When might you?

Assignments for Writing

1. Write a paper in which you explain what it means to be human. In making your argument, you should account for the fact that Fukuyama identifies many different qualities as being necessary to "Factor X." Why, then, does he call them collectively "Factor X"? How do you account for the seemingly infinite number of divergent views on what it is to be human? Use your definition of "Factor X" from Question 1 of Questions for Critical Reading.

2. Fukuyama acknowledges the difficulties that a vision of human equality presents when dealing with specific populations, including the elderly, disabled, and terminally ill. Write a paper in which you suggest standards for dealing with these boundary populations in relation to medical advances such as biotechnology. How might you change Fukuyama's working definitions of Factor X to be more inclusive? Consider using any specific examples you located from your work with the *American Journal of Bioethics* Web site in Question 3 of Exploring Context.

3. Fukuyama stresses the centrality of human nature in current political and ethical debate. Some environmentalists would consider his discussion anthropocentric. What about natural life beyond human beings? Write a paper in which

you extend Fukuyama's discussion of human dignity to account for the natural environment, ecosystems, and other forms of life. You may want to identify those parts of Fukuyama's essay that deal directly with the distinction between the "natural" and "human" worlds as a point of departure for this discussion. What happens when we extend the concept of dignity beyond humans? Would it change the way we acquire our food or what we eat? Consider your work with Michael Pollan from Question 1 of Questions for Connecting.

DANIEL GILBERT

Daniel Gilbert is a professor of psychology at Harvard University. He has won a Guggenheim fellowship, as well as the American Psychological Association's Distinguished Scientific Award for an Early Career Contribution to Psychology. In 2002, *Personality and Social Psychology Bulletin* named him one of the fifty most influential social psychologists of the decade. In addition to his book *Stumbling on Happiness* (2006) and his scholarly publications, Gilbert has published works of science fiction as well as contributed to the *New York Times*, the *Los Angeles Times*, *Forbes*, and *Time*.

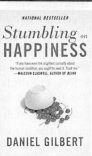

Stumbling on Happiness, a *New York Times* best-seller, applies Gilbert's expertise to the study of happiness itself. Gilbert argues that people are rarely able to predict with any accuracy how they will feel in the future, and so are often quite wrong about what will make them happy.

In "Reporting Live from Tomorrow," a chapter from *Stumbling on Happiness*, Gilbert suggests that beliefs, just like genes, can be "super-replicators," given to spreading regardless of their usefulness. Thus even beliefs that are based on inaccurate information can provide the means for their own propagation. Gilbert explains why humans, with our unreliable memories and imaginations, are so easily susceptible to such beliefs. Though "the best way to predict our feelings tomorrow is to see how others are feeling today," most people are unwilling to make use of the experiences of others because they mistakenly believe themselves to be unique.

The pursuit of happiness is central to our understanding of America—we all want to be happy. But this selection cautions us about predicting our future happiness and in the process provides the tools we need to correct our misapprehensions.

▶ TAGS: *research*, *happiness*, *surrogates*, *identity*, *decision making*

Reporting Live from Tomorrow

In Alfred Hitchcock's 1956 remake of *The Man Who Knew Too Much*, Doris Day sang a waltz whose final verse went like this:

> When I was just a child in school,
> I asked my teacher, "What will I try?
> Should I paint pictures, should I sing songs?"
> This was her wise reply:
> "*Que sera, sera*. Whatever will be, will be.
> The future's not ours to see. *Que sera, sera*."[1]

Now, I don't mean to quibble with the lyricist, and I have nothing but fond memories of Doris Day, but the fact is that this is *not* a particularly wise reply. When a child asks for advice about which of two activities to pursue, a teacher should be able to provide more than a musical cliché. Yes, of *course* the future is hard to see. But we're all heading that way anyhow, and as difficult as it may be to envision, we have to make *some* decisions about which futures to aim for and which to avoid. If we are prone to mistakes when we try to imagine the future, then how *should* we decide what to do?

Even a child knows the answer to that one: We should ask the teacher. One of the benefits of being a social and linguistic animal is that we can capitalize on the experience of others rather than trying to figure everything out for ourselves. For millions of years, human beings have conquered their ignorance by dividing the labor of discovery and then communicating their discoveries to one another, which is why the average newspaper boy in Pittsburgh knows more about the universe than did Galileo, Aristotle, Leonardo, or any of those other guys who were so smart they only needed one name. We all make ample use of this resource. If you were to write down everything you know and then go back through the list and make a check mark next to the things you know only because somebody told you, you'd develop a repetitive-motion disorder because almost *everything* you know is secondhand. Was Yury Gagarin the first man in space? Is *croissant* a French word? Are there more Chinese than North Dakotans? Does a stitch in time save nine? Most of us know the answers to these questions despite the fact that none of us actually witnessed the launching of *Vostok I*, personally supervised the evolution of language, hand-counted all the people in Beijing and Bismarck, or performed a fully randomized double-blind study of stitching. We know the answers because someone shared them with us. Communication is a kind of "vicarious observation"[2] that allows us to learn about the world without ever leaving the comfort of our Barcaloungers. The six billion interconnected people who cover the surface of our planet constitute a leviathan with twelve billion eyes, and anything that is seen by one pair of eyes can potentially be known to the entire beast in a matter of months, days, or even minutes.

The fact that we can communicate with one another about our experiences should provide a simple solution to the core problem with which this book has been concerned. Yes, our ability to imagine our future emotions is flawed — but that's okay, because we don't have to imagine what it would feel like to marry a lawyer, move to Texas, or eat a snail when there are so many people who have *done* these things and are all too happy to tell us about them. Teachers, neighbors, coworkers, parents, friends, lovers, children, uncles, cousins, coaches, cabdrivers, bartenders, hairstylists, dentists, advertisers — each of these folks has something to say about what it would be like to live in this future rather than that one, and at any point in time we can be fairly sure that one of these folks has actually *had* the experience that we are merely contemplating. Because we are the mammal that shows and tells, each of us has access to information about almost any experience we can possibly imagine — and many that we can't. Guidance counselors tell us about the best careers, critics tell us about the best restaurants, travel agents tell us about the best vacations, and friends tell us about the best travel agents. Every one of us is surrounded by a platoon of Dear Abbys who can recount their own experiences and in so doing tell us which futures are most worth wanting.

Given the overabundance of consultants, role models, gurus, mentors, yentas, and nosy relatives, we might expect people to do quite well when it comes to making life's most important decisions, such as where to live, where to work, and whom to marry. And yet, the average American moves more than six times,[3] changes jobs more than ten times,[4] and marries more than once,[5] which suggests that most of us are making more than a few poor choices. If humanity is a living library of information about what it feels like to do just about anything that can be done, then why do the people with the library cards make so many bad decisions? There are just two possibilities. The first is that a lot of the advice we receive from others is bad advice that we foolishly accept. The second is that a lot of the advice we receive from others is good advice that we foolishly reject. So which is it? Do we listen too well when others speak, or do we not listen well enough? As we shall see, the answer to that question is *yes*.

Super-Replicators

The philosopher Bertrand Russell once claimed that believing is "the most mental thing we do."[6] Perhaps, but it is also the most *social* thing we do. Just as we pass along our genes in an effort to create people whose faces look like ours, so too do we pass along our beliefs in an effort to create people whose minds think like ours. Almost any time we tell anyone anything, we are attempting to change the way their brains operate—attempting to change the way they see the world so that their view of it more closely resembles our own. Just about every assertion—from the sublime ("God has a plan for you") to the mundane ("Turn left at the light, go two miles, and you'll see the Dunkin' Donuts on your right")—is meant to bring the listener's beliefs about the world into harmony with the speaker's. Sometimes these attempts succeed and sometimes they fail. So what determines whether a belief will be successfully transmitted from one mind to another?

The principles that explain why some genes are transmitted more successfully than others also explain why some beliefs are transmitted more successfully than others.[7] Evolutionary biology teaches us that any gene that promotes its own "means of transmission" will be represented in increasing proportions in the population over time. For instance, imagine that a single gene were responsible for the complex development of the neural circuitry that makes orgasms feel so good. For a person having this gene, orgasms would feel . . . well, orgasmic. For a person lacking this gene, orgasms would feel more like sneezes—brief, noisy, physical convulsions that pay rather paltry hedonic dividends. Now, if we took fifty healthy, fertile people who had the gene and fifty healthy, fertile people who didn't, and left them on a hospitable planet for a million years or so, when we returned we would probably find a population of thousands or millions of people, almost all of whom had the gene. Why? Because a gene that made orgasms feel good would tend to be transmitted from generation to generation simply because people who enjoy orgasms are inclined to do the thing that transmits their genes. The logic is so circular that it is virtually inescapable: Genes tend to be transmitted when they make us do the things that transmit genes. What's more, even *bad* genes—those that make us prone to cancer or heart disease—can become super-replicators if they compensate for these costs by promoting their own means of transmission. For instance, if the gene that made orgasms feel delicious also left us prone to arthritis and tooth decay, that gene might still be represented in increasing proportions because arthritic, toothless people who love orgasms are more likely to have children than are limber, toothy people who do not.

The same logic can explain the transmission of beliefs. If a particular belief has some property that facilitates its own transmission, then that belief tends to be held by an increasing number of minds. As it turns out, there are several such properties that increase a belief's transmissional success, the most obvious of which is accuracy. When someone tells us where to find a parking space downtown or how to bake a cake at high altitude, we adopt that belief and pass it along because it helps us and our friends do the things we want to do, such as parking and bak-

> **Do we listen too well when others speak, or do we not listen well enough? As we shall see, the answer to that question is *yes*.**

ing. As one philosopher noted, "The faculty of communication would not gain ground in evolution unless it was by and large the faculty of transmitting true beliefs."[8] Accurate beliefs give us power, which makes it easy to understand why they are so readily transmitted from one mind to another.

It is a bit more difficult to understand why *inaccurate* beliefs are so readily transmitted from one mind to another—but they are. False beliefs, like bad genes, can and do become super-replicators, and a thought experiment illustrates how this can happen. Imagine a game that is played by two teams, each of which has a thousand players, each of whom is linked to teammates by a telephone. The object of the game is to get one's team to share as many accurate beliefs as possible. When players receive a message that they believe to be accurate, they call a teammate and pass it along. When they receive a message that they believe to be inaccurate, they don't. At the end of the game, the referee blows a whistle and awards each team a point for every accurate belief that the entire team shares and subtracts one point for every inaccurate belief the entire team shares. Now, consider a contest played one sunny day between a team called the Perfects (whose members always transmit accurate beliefs) and a team called the Imperfects (whose members occasionally transmit an inaccurate belief). We should expect the Perfects to win, right?

Not necessarily. In fact, there are some special circumstances under which the Imperfects will beat their pants off. For example, imagine what would happen if one of the Imperfect players sent the false message "Talking on the phone all day and night will ultimately make you very happy," and imagine that other Imperfect players were gullible enough to believe it and pass it on. This message is inaccurate and thus will cost the Imperfects a point in the end. But it may have the compensatory effect of keeping more of the Imperfects on the telephone for more of the time, thus increasing the total number of accurate messages they transmit. Under the right circumstances, the costs of this inaccurate belief would be outweighed by its benefits, namely, that it led players to behave in ways that increased the odds that they would share other accurate beliefs. The lesson to be learned from this game is that inaccurate beliefs can prevail in the belief-transmission game if they somehow facilitate their own "means of transmission." In this case, the means of transmission is not sex but communication, and thus any belief—even a false belief—that increases communication has a good chance of being transmitted over and over again. False beliefs that happen to promote stable societies tend to propagate because people who hold these beliefs tend to live in stable societies, which provide the means by which false beliefs propagate.

Some of our cultural wisdom about happiness looks suspiciously like a super-replicating false belief. Consider money. If you've ever tried to sell anything, then you probably tried to sell it for as much as you possibly could, and other people probably tried to buy it for as little as they possibly could. All the parties involved in the transaction assumed that they would be better off if they ended up with more money rather than less, and this assumption is the bedrock of our economic behavior. Yet, it has far fewer scientific facts to substantiate it than you might expect. Economists and psychologists have spent decades studying the relation between wealth and happiness, and they have generally concluded that wealth increases human happiness when it lifts people out of abject poverty and into the middle class but that it does little to increase happiness thereafter.[9] Americans who earn $50,000 per year are much happier than those who earn $10,000 per year, but Americans who earn $5 million per year are not much happier than those who earn $100,000 per year. People who live in poor nations are much less happy than people who live in moderately wealthy nations, but people who live in moderately wealthy nations are not much less happy than people who live in extremely wealthy nations. Economists explain that wealth has "declining marginal utility," which is a fancy way of saying that it hurts to be hungry, cold, sick, tired, and scared, but once you've bought your way out of these burdens, the rest of your money is an increasingly useless pile of paper.[10]

So once we've earned as much money as we can actually enjoy, we quit working and enjoy it, right? Wrong. People in wealthy countries generally work long and hard to earn more money than they can ever derive pleasure from.[11] This fact puzzles us less than it should. After all, a rat can be motivated to run through a maze that has a cheesy reward at its end, but once the little guy is all topped up, then even the finest Stilton won't get him off his haunches. Once we've eaten our fill of pancakes, more pancakes are not rewarding, hence we stop trying to procure and consume them. But not so, it seems, with money. As Adam Smith, the father of modern economics, wrote in 1776: "The desire for food is limited in every man by the narrow capacity of the human stomach; but the desire of the conveniences and ornaments of building, dress, equipage, and household furniture, seems to have no limit or certain boundary."[12]

If food and money both stop pleasing us once we've had enough of them, then why do we continue to stuff our pockets when we would not continue to stuff our faces? Adam Smith had an answer. He began by acknowledging what most of us suspect anyway, which is that the production of wealth is not necessarily a source of personal happiness.

> In what constitutes the real happiness of human life, [the poor] are in no respect inferior to those who would seem so much above them. In ease of body and peace of mind, all the different ranks of life are nearly upon a level, and the beggar, who suns himself by the side of the highway, possesses that security which kings are fighting for.[13]

That sounds lovely, but if it's true, then we're all in big trouble. If rich kings are no happier than poor beggars, then why should poor beggars stop sunning themselves by the roadside and work to become rich kings? If no one wants to be rich, then we have a significant economic problem, because flourishing economies require that people continually procure and consume one another's goods and services. Market economies require that we all have an insatiable hunger for *stuff*, and if everyone were content with the stuff they had, then the economy would grind to a halt. But if this is a significant *economic* problem, it is not a significant *personal* problem. The chair of the Federal Reserve may wake up every morning with a desire to do what the economy wants, but most of us get up with a desire to do what *we* want, which is to say that the fundamental needs of a vibrant economy and the fundamental needs of a happy individual are not necessarily the same. So what motivates people to work hard every day to do things that will satisfy the economy's needs but not their own? Like so many thinkers, Smith believed that people want just one thing—happiness—hence economies can blossom and grow only if people are deluded into believing that the production of wealth will make them happy.[14] If and only if people hold this false belief will they do enough producing, procuring, and consuming to sustain their economies.

> The pleasures of wealth and greatness . . . strike the imagination as something grand and beautiful and noble, of which the attainment is well worth all the toil and anxiety which we are so apt to bestow upon it. . . . It is this deception which rouses and keeps in continual motion the industry of mankind. It is this which first prompted them to cultivate the ground, to build houses, to found cities and commonwealths, and to invent and improve all the sciences and arts, which ennoble and embellish human life; which have entirely changed the whole face of the globe, have turned the rude forests of nature into agreeable and fertile plains, and made the trackless and barren ocean a new fund of subsistence, and the great high road of communication to the different nations of the earth.[15]

In short, the production of wealth does not necessarily make individuals happy, but it does serve the needs of an economy, which serves the needs of a stable society, which serves as a network for the propagation of delusional beliefs about happiness and wealth. Economies thrive when individuals strive, but because individuals will only strive for their own happiness, it is essential that they mistakenly believe that producing and consuming are routes to personal well-being. Although words such as *delusional* may seem to suggest some sort of shadowy conspiracy orchestrated by a small group of men in dark suits, the belief-transmission game teaches us that the propagation of false beliefs does not require that anyone be *trying* to perpetrate a magnificent fraud on an innocent populace. There is no cabal at the top, no star chamber, no master manipulator whose clever program of indoctrination and propaganda has duped us all into believing that money can buy us love. Rather, this particular false belief is a super-replicator because holding it causes us to engage in the very activities that perpetuate it.[16]

The belief-transmission game explains why we believe some things about happiness that simply aren't true. The joy of money is one example. The joy of children is another that for most of us hits a bit closer to home. Every human culture tells its members that having children will make them happy. When people think about their offspring — either imagining future offspring or thinking about their current ones — they tend to conjure up images of cooing babies smiling from their bassinets, adorable toddlers running higgledy-piggledy across the lawn, handsome boys and gorgeous girls playing trumpets and tubas in the school marching band, successful college students going on to have beautiful weddings, satisfy-

> **If parenting is such difficult business, then why do we have such a rosy view of it?**

ing careers, and flawless grandchildren whose affections can be purchased with candy. Prospective parents know that diapers will need changing, that homework will need doing, and that orthodontists will go to Aruba on their life savings, but by and large, they think quite happily about parenthood, which is why most of them eventually leap into it. When parents look back on parenthood, they remember feeling what those who are looking forward to it expect to feel. Few of us are immune to these cheery contemplations. I have a twenty-nine-year-old son, and I am absolutely convinced that he is and always has been one of the greatest sources of joy in my life, having only recently been eclipsed by my two-year-old granddaughter, who is equally adorable but who has not yet asked me to walk behind her and pretend we're unrelated. When people are asked to identify their sources of joy, they do just what I do: They point to their kids.

Yet if we measure the *actual* satisfaction of people who have children, a very different story emerges. As Figure 1 shows, couples generally start out quite happy in their marriages and then become progressively less satisfied over the course of their lives together, getting close to their original levels of satisfaction only when their children leave home.[17] Despite what we read in the popular press, the only known symptom of "empty nest syndrome" is increased smiling.[18] Interestingly, this pattern of satisfaction over the life cycle describes women (who are usually the primary caretakers of children) better than men.[19] Careful studies of how women feel as they go about their daily activities show that they are less happy when taking care of their children than when eating,

15

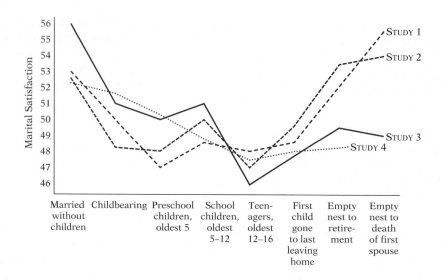

Figure 1

As the four separate studies in this graph show, marital satisfaction decreases dramatically after the birth of the first child and increases only when the last child leaves home.

exercising, shopping, napping, or watching television.[20] Indeed, looking after the kids appears to be only slightly more pleasant than doing housework.

None of this should surprise us. Every parent knows that children are a lot of work—a lot of really *hard* work—and although parenting has many rewarding moments, the vast majority of its moments involve dull and selfless service to people who will take decades to become even begrudgingly grateful for what we are doing. If parenting is such difficult business, then why do we have such a rosy view of it? One reason is that we have been talking on the phone all day with society's stockholders—our moms and uncles and personal trainers—who have been transmitting to us an idea that they *believe* to be true but whose accuracy is not the cause of its successful transmission. "Children bring happiness" is a super-replicator. The belief-transmission network of which we are a part cannot operate without a continuously replenished supply of people to do the transmitting, thus the belief that children are a source of happiness becomes a part of our cultural wisdom simply because the opposite belief unravels the fabric of any society that holds it. Indeed, people who believed that children bring misery and despair—and who thus stopped having them—would put their belief-transmission network out of business in around fifty years, hence terminating the belief that terminated them. The Shakers were a utopian farming community that arose in the 1800s and at one time numbered about six thousand. They approved of children, but they did not approve of the natural act that creates them. Over the years, their strict belief in the importance of celibacy caused their network to contract, and today there are just a few elderly Shakers left, transmitting their doomsday belief to no one but themselves.

The belief-transmission game is rigged so that we *must* believe that children and money bring happiness, regardless of whether such beliefs are true. This doesn't mean that we should all now quit our jobs and abandon our families. Rather, it means that while we *believe* we are raising children and earning paychecks to increase our share of happiness, we are actually doing these things for reasons beyond our ken. We are nodes in a social network that arises and falls by a logic of its own, which is why we continue to toil, continue to mate, and continue to be surprised when we do not experience all the joy we so gullibly anticipated.

The Myth of Fingerprints

My friends tell me that I have a tendency to point out problems without offering solutions, but they never tell me what I should do about it. In one chapter after another, I've described the ways in which imagination fails to provide us with accurate previews of our emotional futures. I've claimed that when we imagine our futures we tend to fill in, leave out, and take little account of how differently we will think about the future once we actually get there. I've claimed that neither personal experience nor cultural wisdom compensates for imagination's shortcomings. I've so thoroughly marinated you in the foibles, biases, errors, and mistakes of the human mind that you may wonder how anyone ever manages to make toast without buttering their kneecaps. If so, you will be heartened to learn that there *is* a simple method by which anyone can make strikingly accurate predictions about how they will feel in the future. But you may be disheartened to learn that, by and large, no one wants to use it.

Why do we rely on our imaginations in the first place? Imagination is the poor man's wormhole. We can't do what we'd really *like* to do—namely, travel through time, pay a visit to our future selves, and *see* how happy those selves are—and so we imagine the future instead of actually going there. But if we cannot travel in the dimensions of time, we can travel in the dimensions of space, and the chances are pretty good that somewhere in those other three dimensions there is another human being who is actually *experiencing* the future event that we are merely thinking about. Surely we aren't the first people ever to consider a move to Cincinnati, a career in motel management, another helping of rhubarb pie, or an extramarital affair, and for the most part, those who have already tried these things are more than willing to tell us about them. It is true that when people tell us about their past experiences ("That ice water wasn't really so cold" or "I love taking care of my daughter"), memory's peccadilloes may render their testimony unreliable. But it is also true that when people tell us about their *current* experiences ("How am I feeling right now? I feel like pulling my arm out of this freezing bucket and sticking my teenager's head in it instead!"), they are providing us with the kind of report about their subjective state that is considered the gold standard of happiness measures. If you believe (as I do) that people can generally say how they are feeling at the moment they are asked, then one way to make predictions about our own emotional futures is to find someone who is having the experience we are contemplating and ask them how they feel. Instead of remembering our past experience in order to simulate our future experience, perhaps we should simply ask other people to introspect on their inner states. Perhaps we should give up on remembering and imagining entirely and use other people as *surrogates* for our future selves.

This idea sounds all too simple, and I suspect you have an objection to it that goes something like this: *Yes, other people are probably right now experiencing the very things I am merely contemplating, but I can't use other people's experiences as proxies for my own because those other people are not me. Every human being is as unique as his or her fingerprints, so it won't help me much to learn about how others feel in the situations that I'm facing. Unless these other people are my clones and have had all the same experiences I've had, their reactions and my reactions are bound to differ. I am a walking, talking idiosyncrasy, and thus I am better off basing my predictions on my somewhat fickle imagination than on the reports of people whose preferences, tastes, and emotional proclivities are so radically different from my own.* If that's your objection, then it is a good one—so good that it will take two steps to dismantle it. First let me prove to you that the experience of a single randomly selected individual can sometimes provide a better basis for predicting your future experience than your own imagination can. And then let me show you why you—and I—find this so difficult to believe.

Finding the Solution

Imagination has three shortcomings, and if you didn't know that then you may be reading this book backward. If you did know that, then you also know that imagination's first shortcoming is its tendency to fill in and leave out without telling us (which we explored in the section on *realism*). No one can imagine every feature and consequence of a future event, hence we must consider some and fail to consider others. The problem is that the features and consequences we fail to consider are often quite important. You may recall the study in which college students were asked to imagine how they would feel a few days after their school's football team played a game against its archrival.[21] The results showed that students overestimated the duration of the game's emotional impact because when they tried to imagine their future experience, they imagined their team winning ("The clock will hit zero, we'll storm the field, everyone will cheer . . .") but failed to imagine what they would be doing afterward ("And then I'll go home and study for my final exams"). Because the students were focused on the game, they failed to imagine how events that happened *after* the game would influence their happiness. So what *should* they have done instead?

They should have abandoned imagination altogether. Consider a study that put people in a similar predicament and then forced them to abandon their imaginations. In this study, a group of volunteers (reporters) first received a delicious prize—a gift certificate from a local ice cream parlor—and then performed a long, boring task in which they counted and recorded geometric shapes that appeared on a computer screen.[22] The reporters then reported how they felt. Next, a new group of volunteers was told that they would also receive a prize and do the same boring task. Some of these new volunteers (simulators) were told what the prize was and were asked to use their imaginations to

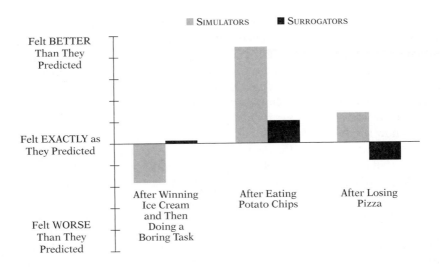

Figure 2
Volunteers made much more accurate predictions of their future feelings when they learned how someone else had felt in the same situation (surrogators) than when they tried to imagine how they themselves would feel (simulators).

predict their future feelings. Other volunteers (surrogators) were not told what the prize was but were instead shown the report of a randomly selected reporter. Not knowing what the prize was, they couldn't possibly use their imaginations to predict their future feelings. Instead, they had to rely on the reporter's report. Once all the volunteers had made their predictions, they received the prize, did the long, boring task, and reported how they actually felt. As the leftmost bars in Figure 2 show, simulators were not as happy as they thought they would be. Why? Because they failed to imagine how quickly the joy of receiving a gift certificate would fade when it was followed by a long, boring task. This is precisely the same mistake that the college-football fans made. But now look at the results for the surrogators. As you can see, they made extremely accurate predictions of their future happiness. These surrogators didn't know what kind of prize they would receive, but they did know that someone who had received that prize had been less than ecstatic at the conclusion of the boring task. So they shrugged and reasoned that they too would feel less than ecstatic at the conclusion of the boring task—and they were right!

Imagination's second shortcoming is its tendency to project the present onto the future (which we explored in the section on *presentism*). When imagination paints a picture of the future, many of the details are necessarily missing, and imagination solves this problem by filling in the gaps with details that it borrows from the present. Anyone who has ever shopped on an empty stomach, vowed to quit smoking after stubbing out a cigarette, or proposed marriage while on shore leave knows that how we feel now can erroneously influence how we *think* we'll feel later. As it turns out, surrogation can remedy this shortcoming too. In one study, volunteers (reporters) ate a few potato chips and reported how much they enjoyed them.[23] Next, a new group of volunteers was fed pretzels, peanut-butter cheese crackers, tortilla chips, bread sticks, and melba toast, which, as you might guess, left them thoroughly stuffed and with little desire for salty snack foods. These stuffed volunteers were then asked to predict how much they would enjoy eating a particular food the next day. Some of these stuffed volunteers (simulators) were told that the food they would eat the next day was potato chips, and they were asked to use their imaginations to predict how they would feel after eating them. Other stuffed volunteers (surrogators) were not told what the next day's food would be but were instead shown the report of one randomly selected reporter. Because surrogators didn't know what the next day's food would be, they couldn't use their imaginations to predict their future enjoyment of it and thus they had to rely on the reporter's report. Once all the volunteers had made their predictions, they went away, returned the next day, ate some potato chips, and reported how much they enjoyed them. As the middle bars in Figure 2 show, simulators enjoyed eating the potato chips more than they thought they would. Why? Because when they made their predictions they had bellies full of pretzels and crackers. But surrogators—who were equally full when they made their predictions—relied on the report of someone without a full belly and hence made much more accurate predictions. It is important to note that the surrogators accurately predicted their future enjoyment of a food despite the fact that they didn't even know what the food was!

Imagination's third shortcoming is its failure to recognize that things will look different once they happen—in particular, that bad things will look a whole lot better (which we explored in the section on *rationalization*). When we imagine losing a job, for instance, we imagine the painful experience ("The boss will march into my office, shut the door behind him . . .") without also imagining how our psychological immune systems will transform its meaning ("I'll come to realize that this was an opportunity to quit retail sales and follow my true calling as a sculptor"). Can surrogation remedy this shortcoming? To find out, researchers arranged for some people to have an unpleasant experience. A group of volunteers (reporters) was told that the experimenter would flip a coin, and if it came up heads, the volunteer would receive a gift certificate to a local pizza parlor. The coin was flipped and—*oh, so sorry*—it came up tails and the reporters received nothing.[24] The reporters then reported how they felt. Next, a new group of volunteers was told about the coin-flipping game and was asked to predict how they would feel if the coin came up tails and they didn't get the pizza gift certificate. Some of these volunteers (simulators) were told the precise monetary value of the gift certificate, and others (surrogators) were instead shown the report of one randomly selected reporter. Once the volunteers had made their predictions, the coin was flipped and—*oh, so sorry*—came up tails. The volunteers then reported how they felt. As the rightmost bars in Figure 2 show, simulators felt better than they predicted they'd feel if they lost the coin flip. Why? Because simulators did not realize how quickly and easily they would rationalize the loss ("Pizza is too fattening, and besides, I don't like that restaurant anyway"). But surrogators—who had nothing to go on except the report of another randomly selected individual—assumed that they wouldn't feel too bad after losing the prize, hence made more accurate predictions.

Rejecting the Solution

This trio of studies suggests that when people are deprived of the information that imagination requires and are thus *forced* to use others as surrogates, they make remarkably accurate predictions about their future feelings, which suggests that the best way to predict our feelings tomorrow is to see how others are feeling today.[25] Given the impressive power of this simple technique, we should expect people to go out of their way to use it. But they don't. When an entirely new group of volunteers was told about the three situations I just described—winning a prize, eating a mystery food, or failing to receive a gift certificate—and was then asked whether they would prefer to make predictions about their future feelings based on *(a)* information about the prize, the food, and the certificate; or *(b)* information about how a randomly selected individual felt after winning them, eating them, or losing them, virtually every volunteer chose the former. If you hadn't seen the results of these studies, you'd probably have done the same. If I offered to pay for your dinner at a restaurant if you could accurately predict how much you were going to enjoy it, would you want to see the restaurant's menu or some randomly selected diner's review? If you are like most people, you would prefer to see the menu, and if you are like most people, you would end up buying your own dinner. Why?

> **If you are like most people, then like most people, you don't know you're like most people.**

Because if you are like most people, then like most people, you don't know you're like most people. Science has given us a lot of facts about the average person, and one of the most reliable of these facts is that the average person doesn't see herself as average. Most students see themselves as more intelligent than the average student,[26] most business managers see themselves as more competent than the average business manager,[27] and most football players see themselves as having better "football sense" than their teammates.[28] Ninety percent of motorists consider themselves to be safer-than-average drivers,[29] and 94 percent of college professors consider themselves to be better-than-average teachers.[30] Ironically, the bias toward seeing ourselves as better than average causes us to see ourselves as less biased than average too.[31] As one research team concluded, "Most of us appear to believe that we are more athletic, intelligent, organized, ethical, logical, interesting, fair-minded, and healthy—not to mention more attractive—than the average person."[32]

This tendency to think of ourselves as better than others is not necessarily a manifestation of our unfettered narcissism but may instead be an instance of a more general tendency to think of ourselves as *different* from others—often for better but sometimes for worse. When people are asked about generosity, they claim to perform a greater number of generous acts than others do; but when they are asked about selfishness, they claim to perform a greater number of selfish acts than others do.[33] When people are asked about their ability to perform an easy task, such as driving a car or riding a bike, they rate themselves as better than others; but when they are asked about their ability to perform a difficult task, such as juggling or playing chess, they rate themselves as worse than others.[34] We don't always see ourselves as *superior,* but we almost always see ourselves as *unique.* Even when we do precisely what others do, we tend to think that we're doing it for unique reasons. For instance, we tend to attribute other people's choices to features of the chooser ("Phil picked this class because he's one of those literary types"), but we tend to attribute our own choices to features of the options ("But I picked it because it was easier than economics").[35] We recognize that our decisions are influenced by social norms ("I was too embarrassed to raise my hand in class even though I was terribly confused"), but fail to recognize that others' decisions were similarly influenced ("No one else raised a hand because no one else was as confused as I was").[36] We know that our choices sometimes reflect our aversions ("I voted for Kerry because I couldn't stand Bush"), but we assume that other people's choices reflect their appetites ("If Rebecca voted for Kerry, then she must have liked him").[37] The list of differences is long but the conclusion to be drawn from it is short: The self considers itself to be a very special person.[38]

What makes us think we're so darned special? Three things, at least. First, even if we aren't special, the way we know ourselves is. We are the only people in the world whom we can know from the inside. We *experience* our own thoughts and feelings but must *infer* that other people are experiencing theirs. We all trust that behind those eyes and inside those skulls, our friends and neighbors are having subjective experiences very much like our own, but that trust is an article of faith and not the palpable, self-evident truth that our own subjective experiences constitute. There is a difference between making love and reading about it, and it is the same difference that distinguishes our knowledge of our own mental lives from our knowledge of everyone else's. Because we know ourselves and others by such different means, we gather very different kinds and amounts of information. In every waking moment we monitor the steady stream of thoughts and feelings that runs through our heads, but we only monitor other people's words and deeds, and only when they are in our company. One reason why we seem so special, then, is that we learn about ourselves in such a special way.

The second reason is that we *enjoy* thinking of ourselves as special. Most of us want to fit in well with our peers, but we don't want to fit in too well.[39] We prize our unique identities, and research shows that when people are made to feel too similar to others, their moods quickly sour and they try to distance and distinguish themselves in a variety of ways.[40] If you've ever shown up at a party and found someone else wearing exactly the same dress or necktie that you were wearing, then you know how unsettling it is to share the room with an unwanted twin whose presence temporarily diminishes your sense of individuality. Because we *value* our uniqueness, it isn't surprising that we tend to overestimate it.

The third reason why we tend to overestimate our uniqueness is that we tend to overestimate everyone's uniqueness—that is, we tend to think of people as more different from one another than they actually are. Let's face it: All people are similar in some ways and different in others. The psychologists, biologists, economists, and sociologists who are searching for universal laws of human behavior naturally care about the similarities, but the rest of us care mainly about the differences. Social life involves selecting particular individuals to be our sexual partners, business partners, bowling partners, and more. That task requires that we focus on the things that distinguish one person from another and not on the things that all people share, which is why personal ads are much more likely to mention the advertiser's love of ballet than his love of oxygen. A penchant for respiration explains a great deal about human behavior—for example, why people live on land, become ill at high altitudes, have lungs, resist suffocation, love trees, and so on. It surely explains more than does a person's penchant for ballet. But it does nothing to distinguish one person from another, and thus for ordinary folks who are in the ordinary business of selecting others for commerce, conversation, or copulation, the penchant for air is stunningly irrelevant. Individual similarities are vast, but we don't care much about them because they don't help us do what we are here on earth to do, namely, distinguish Jack from Jill and Jill from Jennifer. As such, these individual similarities are an inconspicuous backdrop against which a small number of relatively minor individual differences stand out in bold relief.

Because we spend so much time searching for, attending to, thinking about, and remembering these differences, we tend to overestimate their magnitude and frequency, and thus end up thinking of people as more varied than they actually are. If you spent all day sorting grapes into different shapes, colors, and kinds, you'd become one of those annoying grapeophiles who talks endlessly about the nuances of flavor and the permutations of texture. You'd come to think of grapes as infinitely varied, and you'd forget that almost all of the really *important* information about a grape can be deduced from the simple fact of its grapehood. Our belief in the variability of others and in the uniqueness of the self is especially powerful when it comes to emotion.[41] Because we can *feel* our own emotions but must *infer* the emotions of others by watching their faces and listening to their voices, we often have the impression that others don't experience the same intensity of emotion that we do, which is why we expect others to recognize our feelings even when we can't recognize theirs.[42] This sense of emotional uniqueness starts early. When kindergarteners are asked how they and others would feel in a variety of situations, they expect to experience unique emotions ("Billy would be sad but I wouldn't") and they provide unique reasons for experiencing them ("I'd tell myself that the hamster was in heaven, but Billy would just cry").[43] When adults make these same kinds of predictions, they do just the same thing.[44]

Our mythical belief in the variability and uniqueness of individuals is the main reason why we refuse to use others as surrogates. After all, surrogation is only useful when we can count on a surrogate to react to an event roughly as we would, and if we believe that people's emotional reactions are more varied than they actually are, then surrogation will seem less useful to us than it actually is. The irony, of course, is that surrogation is a cheap and effective way to predict one's future emotions, but because we don't realize just how similar we all are, we reject this reliable method and rely instead on our imaginations, as flawed and fallible as they may be.

Onward

Despite its watery connotation, the word *hogwash* refers to the feeding—and not to the bathing—of pigs. Hogwash is something that pigs eat, that pigs like, and that pigs need. Farmers provide pigs with hogwash because without it, pigs get grumpy. The word *hogwash* also refers to the falsehoods people tell one another. Like the hogwash that farmers feed their pigs, the hogwash that our friends and teachers and parents feed us is meant to make us happy; but unlike hogwash of the porcine variety, human hogwash does not always achieve its end. As we have seen, ideas can flourish if they preserve the social systems that allow them to be transmitted. Because individuals don't usually feel that it is their personal duty to preserve social systems, these ideas must disguise themselves as prescriptions for individual happiness. We might expect that after spending some time in the world, our experiences would debunk these ideas, but it doesn't always work that way. To learn from our experience we must remember it, and for a variety of reasons, memory is a faithless friend. Practice and coaching get us out of our diapers and into our britches, but they are not enough to get us out of our presents and into our futures. What's so ironic about this predicament is that the information we need to make accurate predictions of our emotional futures is right under our noses, but we don't seem to recognize its aroma. It doesn't always make sense to heed what people tell us when they communicate their beliefs about happiness, but it does make sense to observe how happy they are in different circumstances. Alas, we think of ourselves as unique entities—minds unlike any others—and thus we often reject the lessons that the emotional experience of others has to teach us.

NOTES

1. J. Livingston and R. Evans, "Whatever Will Be, Will Be (Que Sera, Sera)" (1955).
2. W. V. Quine and J. S. Ullian, *The Web of Belief*, 2nd ed. (New York: Random House, 1978), 51.
3. Half of all Americans relocated in the five-year period of 1995–2000, which suggests that the average American relocates about every ten years; B. Berkner and C. S. Faber, *Geographical Mobility, 1995 to 2000* (Washington, D.C.: U.S. Bureau of the Census, 2003).
4. The average baby boomer held roughly ten jobs between the ages of eighteen and thirty-six, which suggests that the average American holds at least this many in a lifetime. Bureau of Labor Statistics, *Number of Jobs Held, Labor Market Activity, and Earnings Growth among Younger Baby Boomers: Results from More than Two Decades of a Longitudinal Survey*, Bureau of Labor Statistics news release (Washington, D.C.: U.S. Department of Labor, 2002).

5. The U.S. Census Bureau projects that in the coming years, 10 percent of Americans will never marry, 60 percent will marry just once, and 30 percent will marry at least twice. R. M. Kreider and J. M. Fields, *Number, Timing, and Duration of Marriages and Divorces, 1996* (Washington, D.C.: U.S. Bureau of the Census, 2002).

6. B. Russell, *The Analysis of Mind* (New York: Macmillan, 1921), 231.

7. The biologist Richard Dawkins refers to these beliefs as *memes*. See R. J. Dawkins, *The Selfish Gene* (Oxford: Oxford University Press, 1976). See also S. Blackmore, *The Meme Machine* (Oxford: Oxford University Press, 2000).

8. D. C. Dennett, *Brainstorms: Philosophical Essays on Mind and Psychology* (Cambridge, Mass.: Bradford/MIT Press, 1981), 18.

9. R. Layard, *Happiness: Lessons from a New Science* (New York: Penguin, 2005); E. Diener and M. E. P. Seligman, "Beyond Money: Toward an Economy of Well-Being," *Psychological Science in the Public Interest* 5: 1–31 (2004); B. S. Frey and A. Stutzer, *Happiness and Economics: How the Economy and Institutions Affect Human Well-Being* (Princeton, N.J.: Princeton University Press, 2002); R. A. Easterlin, "Income and Happiness: Towards a Unified Theory," *Economic Journal* 111: 465–84 (2001); and D. G. Blanchflower and A. J. Oswald, "Well-Being over Time in Britain and the USA," *Journal of Public Economics* 88: 1359–86 (2004).

10. The effect of declining marginal utility is slowed when we spend our money on the things to which we are least likely to adapt. See T. Scitovsky, *The Joyless Economy: The Psychology of Human Satisfaction* (Oxford: Oxford University Press, 1976); L. Van Boven and T. Gilovich, "To Do or to Have? That Is the Question," *Journal of Personality and Social Psychology* 85: 1193–1202 (2003); and R. H. Frank, "How Not to Buy Happiness," *Daedalus: Journal of the American Academy of Arts and Sciences* 133: 69–79 (2004). Not all economists believe in decreasing marginal utility: R. A. Easterlin, "Diminishing Marginal Utility of Income? Caveat Emptor," *Social Indicators Research* 70: 243–326 (2005).

11. J. D. Graaf et al., *Affluenza: The All-Consuming Epidemic* (New York: Berrett-Koehler, 2002); D. Myers, *The American Paradox: Spiritual Hunger in an Age of Plenty* (New Haven: Yale University Press, 2000); R. H. Frank, *Luxury Fever* (Princeton, N.J.: Princeton University Press, 2000); J. B. Schor, *The Overspent American: Why We Want What We Don't Need* (New York: Perennial, 1999); and P. L. Wachtel, *Poverty of Affluence: A Psychological Portrait of the American Way of Life* (New York: Free Press, 1983).

12. Adam Smith, *An Inquiry into the Nature and Causes of the Wealth of Nations* (1776), book 1 (New York: Modern Library, 1994).

13. Adam Smith, *The Theory of Moral Sentiments* (1759; Cambridge: Cambridge University Press, 2002).

14. N. Ashraf, C. Camerer, and G. Loewenstein, "Adam Smith, Behavorial Economist," *Journal of Economic Perspectives* 19: 131–45 (2005).

15. Smith, *The Theory of Moral Sentiments.*

16. Some theorists have argued that societies exhibit a cyclic pattern in which people do come to realize that money doesn't buy happiness but then forget this lesson a generation later. See A. O. Hirschman, *Shifting Involvements: Private Interest and Public Action* (Princeton, N.J.: Princeton University Press, 1982).

17. C. Walker, "Some Variations in Marital Satisfaction," in *Equalities and Inequalities in Family Life*, ed. R. Chester and J. Peel (London: Academic Press, 1977), 127–39.

18. D. Myers, *The Pursuit of Happiness: Discovering the Pathway to Fulfillment, Well-Being, and Enduring Personal Joy* (New York: Avon, 1992), 71.

19. J. A. Feeney, "Attachment Styles, Communication Patterns and Satisfaction Across the Life Cycle of Marriage," *Personal Relationships* 1: 333–48 (1994).

20. D. Kahneman et al., "A Survey Method for Characterizing Daily Life Experience: The Day Reconstruction Method," *Science* 306: 1776–80 (2004).

21. T. D. Wilson et al., "Focalism: A Source of Durability Bias in Affective Forecasting," *Journal of Personality and Social Psychology* 78: 821–36 (2000).

22. R. J. Norwick, D. T. Gilbert, and T. D. Wilson, "Surrogation: An Antidote for Errors in Affective Forecasting" (unpublished manuscript, Harvard University, 2005).

23. Ibid.

24. Ibid.

25. This is also the best way to predict our future behavior. For example, people overestimate the likelihood that they will perform a charitable act but correctly estimate the likelihood that others will do the same. This suggests that if we would base predictions of our own behavior on what we see others do, we'd be dead-on. See N. Epley and D. Dunning, "Feeling 'Holier Than Thou': Are Self-Serving Assessments Produced by Errors in Self- or Social Prediction?" *Journal of Personality and Social Psychology* 79: 861–75 (2000).

26. R. C. Wylie, *The Self-Concept: Theory and Research on Selected Topics*, vol. 2 (Lincoln: University of Nebraska Press, 1979).

27. L. Larwood and W. Whittaker, "Managerial Myopia: Self-Serving Biases in Organizational Planning," *Journal of Applied Psychology* 62: 194–98 (1977).

28. R. B. Felson, "Ambiguity and Bias in the Self-Concept," *Social Psychology Quarterly* 44: 64–69.

29. D. Walton and J. Bathurst, "An Exploration of the Perceptions of the Average Driver's Speed Compared to Perceived Driver Safety and Driving Skill," *Accident Analysis and Prevention* 30: 821–30 (1998).

30. P. Cross, "Not Can but Will College Teachers Be Improved?" *New Directions for Higher Education* 17: 1–15 (1977).

31. E. Pronin, D. Y. Lin, and L. Ross, "The Bias Blind Spot: Perceptions of Bias in Self versus Others," *Personality and Social Psychology Bulletin* 28: 369–81 (2002).

32. J. Kruger, "Lake Wobegon Be Gone! The 'Below-Average Effect' and the Egocentric Nature of Comparative Ability Judgments," *Journal of Personality and Social Psychology* 77: 221–32 (1999).

33. J. T. Johnson et al., "The 'Barnum Effect' Revisited: Cognitive and Motivational Factors in the Acceptance of Personality Descriptions," *Journal of Personality and Social Psychology* 49: 1378–91 (1985).

34. Kruger, "Lake Wobegon Be Gone!"

35. E. E. Jones and R. E. Nisbett, "The Actor and the Observer: Divergent Perceptions of the Causes of Behavior," in *Attribution: Perceiving the Causes of Behavior*, ed. E. E. Jones et al. (Morristown, N.J.: General Learning Press, 1972); and R. E. Nisbett and E. Borgida, "Attribution and the Psychology of Prediction," *Journal of Personality and Social Psychology* 32: 932–43 (1975).

36. D. T. Miller and C. McFarland, "Pluralistic Ignorance: When Similarity Is Interpreted as Dissimilarity," *Journal of Personality and Social Psychology* 53: 298–305 (1987).

37. D. T. Miller and L. D. Nelson, "Seeing Approach Motivation in the Avoidance Behavior of Others: Implications for an Understanding of Pluralistic Ignorance," *Journal of Personality and Social Psychology* 83: 1066–75 (2002).

38. C. R. Snyder and H. L. Fromkin, "Abnormality as a Positive Characteristic: The Development and Validation of a Scale Measuring Need for Uniqueness," *Journal of Abnormal Psychology* 86: 518–27 (1977).

39. M. B. Brewer, "The Social Self: On Being the Same and Different at the Same Time," *Personality and Social Psychology Bulletin* 17: 475–82 (1991).

40. H. L. Fromkin, "Effects of Experimentally Aroused Feelings of Undistinctiveness upon Valuation of Scarce and Novel Experiences," *Journal of Personality and Social Psychology* 16: 521–29 (1970); and H. L. Fromkin, "Feelings of Interpersonal Undistinctiveness: An Unpleasant Affective State," *Journal of Experimental Research in Personality* 6: 178–85 (1972).

41. R. Karniol, T. Eylon, and S. Rish, "Predicting Your Own and Others' Thoughts and Feelings: More Like a Stranger Than a Friend," *European Journal of Social Psychology* 27: 301–11 (1997); J. T. Johnson, "The Heart on the Sleeve and the Secret Self: Estimations of Hidden Emotion in Self and Acquaintances," *Journal of Personality* 55: 563–82 (1987); and R. Karniol, "Egocentrism versus Protocentrism: The Status of Self in Social Prediction," *Psychological Review* 110: 564–80 (2003).

42. C. L. Barr and R. E. Kleck, "Self-Other Perception of the Intensity of Facial Expressions of Emotion: Do We Know What We Show?" *Journal of Personality and Social Psychology* 68: 608–18 (1995).

43. R. Karniol and L. Koren, "How Would You Feel? Children's Inferences Regarding Their Own and Others' Affective Reactions," *Cognitive Development* 2: 271–78 (1987).

44. C. McFarland and D. T. Miller, "Judgments of Self-Other Similarity: Just Like Other People, Only More So," *Personality and Social Psychology Bulletin* 16: 475–84 (1990).

Questions for Critical Reading

1. What is a "super-replicator"? Develop a definition by rereading Gilbert's text and then offer an example not included in his essay. What function does this concept serve in Gilbert's argument?

2. What does Gilbert mean by *surrogate*? Gilbert never explicitly defines the term. Instead, you should read his text critically and construct a definition out of quotations you find that discuss the idea.

3. Using Gilbert's text, define *happiness*. As with *surrogate*, you will need to analyze Gilbert's text to construct this definition. What does it mean in the context of this essay, and what does it mean for you?

Exploring Context

1. Visit PikiStrips.com and make a comic strip that represents the argument of Gilbert's essay. Incorporate representations for your definitions of the terms in Questions for Critical Reading.

2. What is "happiness"? Put *happy*, *happiness*, and related terms into Google or another search engine. What sort of results do you get? What if you search for

images? What does "happiness" look like on the Web? Does it match the definition you developed in Question 3 of Questions for Critical Reading?

3. Gilbert suggests that if we want to know how happy we will be in the future
we should ask someone who's already living our goals. Use Yahoo! Answers
(answers.yahoo.com) to ask questions about possible plans for your future.
Can the Web function as a surrogate? Use the definition of *surrogate* that you
developed in Questions for Critical Reading in your answer.

Questions for Connecting

1. Gilbert examines the happiness produced by both money and children. How
does Debora L. Spar's discussion of adoption in "Trading Places: The Practice
and Politics of Adoption" (p. 402) challenge these findings? Can adopting children make people happy? You may want to use the definition of happiness you
developed in Questions for Critical Reading and Exploring Context.

2. What role does feedback play in the spread of super-replicators? Consider the
impact of Steven Johnson's ideas in "Listening to Feedback" (p. 191) on what
Gilbert has to say about both super-replicators and happiness, drawing from
the understanding of those terms that you developed in Questions for Critical
Reading.

3. Gilbert suggests that surrogates can help us predict our future happiness, but
can surrogates help us in dealing with other emotions as well? To what extent
does Joan Didion function as a surrogate in "After Life" (p. 88)? Does it match
your definition from Questions for Critical Reading?

Language Matters

1. Locate information on sentence diagrams. Then select a key sentence from
Gilbert's text and diagram the sentence. What are the different parts of the
sentence, and how are they related?

2. Locate a sentence in Gilbert's essay that uses *I* as the subject. When does
Gilbert use *I*? When doesn't he? When should you?

3. Take a key sentence from Gilbert. Summarize it and then paraphrase it. What's
the difference between a summary, a paraphrase, and a quotation? When would
you use each in your writing, and what citation does each need?

Assignments for Writing

1. According to Gilbert, surrogates can offer us an accurate sense of our future
happiness. Write a paper in which you assess the potential of the kind of surrogates that Gilbert describes. You will want to extend, complicate, or refute
Gilbert's argument for surrogates and their reliability in predicting the future.
Think about these questions: What role does individuality have in our future

happiness? Is Gilbert correct in claiming that we are not as unique as we believe? Can surrogates be used to examine all future events? How can surrogates be used to control social processes? If we are not unique, why do we see ourselves as individuals? Use your definition of *surrogate* from Question 2 of Questions for Critical Reading as well as your work with Yahoo! Answers from Question 3 of Exploring Context.

2. Write a paper in which you evaluate Gilbert's argument about surrogates and their reliability in predicting the future by finding an appropriate surrogate for you and your future happiness. You may wish to use your experience finding a surrogate on the Web from Question 3 of Exploring Context in making your argument. Also consider: What role does individuality have in our future happiness? Are surrogate examples more accurate than our imagination? What event in your life did you imagine was going to make you happier than it did?

3. Gilbert defines *super-replicators* as genes or beliefs that are given to transmission regardless of their usefulness. Write a paper in which you extend Gilbert's argument through your own example of a super-replicator that persists in society. How do we communicate our ideas to others? What super-replicators are we passing along to those we come into contact with? Does the validity of a belief correlate to its speed of transmission? What is the role of super-replicators in communicating cultural ideas? Use your definition of the term from Question 1 of Questions for Critical Reading.

STEVEN JOHNSON

Steven Johnson is currently serving as the Distinguished Writer in Residence in the journalism department at New York University. He has published five books: *Interface Culture: How New Technology Transforms the Way We Create and Communicate* (1997); *Emergence: The Connected Lives of Ants, Brains, Cities, and Software* (2001); *Mind Wide Open: Your Brain and the Neuroscience of Everyday Life* (2004); *Everything Bad Is Good For You: How Today's Popular Culture Is Actually Making Us Smarter* (2005); and *The Ghost Map: The Story of London's Most Terrifying Epidemic—and How it Changed Science, Cities, and the Modern World* (2006). Johnson has worked as a columnist for multiple magazines, and he is the founder of outside.in, a Web site that collects local information about individual neighborhoods.

Johnson calls *Emergence* "the story of bottom-up intelligence, from slime mold to Slashdot" and reports that it has influenced fields as far-ranging as "political campaigns, Web business models, urban planning, [and] the war on terror." In the book, Johnson explores the impact emergence theory already has had on the construction of neighborhoods, the World Wide Web, and media events, and he predicts that, fueled by the connectedness of the Internet, this power of self-organization will prompt further and fundamental revolutions, akin to those that followed the discovery of electricity.

"Listening to Feedback," an excerpt from *Emergence*, shows the impact of emergence theory in the world of television news media. Formerly structured in a hierarchical, top-down model, television news has increasingly transitioned into "a more bottom-up distributed model." Johnson uses the "positive feedback" model of local and national news outlets as a springboard into a discussion about the consequences of feedback loops and explores as well a different kind of feedback, one that can change "a complex system into a complex *adaptive* system." Johnson investigates the "lack of fatigue" detectable in television news feedback that seems to break the rules of natural feedback loops, the amplification of that same lack of fatigue through the Web, and the positive results that can come from a "mix of hierarchy and heterarchy." Ultimately, Johnson is concerned with finding the correct type and amount of feedback necessary to effectively regulate a complex system; the origins and potential of Slashdot.org and Amazon.com, Johnson suggests, might hold the answer. That answer has something to say to you, since through blogging and sites like YouTube, we all are playing a part in the larger systems of news and, through that, cultural power.

▶ TAGS: *collaboration*, **technology**, *social change*, *conversation*, **community**, *media*

Listening to Feedback

Late in the afternoon of January 23, 1992, during a campaign stop at the American Brush Company in Claremont, New Hampshire, the ABC political reporter Jim Wooten asked then-candidate Bill Clinton about allegations being made by an ex–cabaret singer named Gennifer Flowers. While rumors of Clinton's womanizing had been rampant among the press corps, Wooten's question was the first time the young Democratic front-runner had been asked about a specific woman. "She claims she had a long-standing affair with you," Wooten said with cameras running. "And she says she tape-recorded the telephone conversations with you in which you told her to deny you had ever had an affair."[1]

Wooten said later that Clinton took the question as though he'd been practicing his answer for months. "Well, first of all, I read the story. It isn't true. She has obviously taken money to change the story, a story she felt so strongly about that she hired a lawyer to protect her good name not very long ago. She did call me. I never initiated any calls to her. . . ." The candidate's denials went on for another five minutes, and then the exchange was over. Clinton had responded to the question, but was it news? Across the country, a furious debate on journalistic ethics erupted: Did unproven allegations about the candidate's sex life constitute legitimate news? And did it matter that the candidate himself had chosen to deny the allegations on camera? A cabaret singer making claims about the governor's adulterous past was clearly tabloid material—but what happened when the governor himself addressed the story?

After two long hours of soul-searching, all three major television networks —along with CNN and PBS's MacNeil/Lehrer show—chose not to mention Wooten's question on their national news broadcast, or to show any of the footage from the exchange. The story had emphatically been silenced by some of the most influential figures in all of mass media. The decision to ignore Gennifer Flowers had been unanimous—even at the network that had originally posed the question. Made ten or twenty years before, a decision of that magnitude could have ended a story in its tracks (assuming the *Washington Post* and the *New York Times* followed suit the next morning). For the story to be revived, it would need new oxygen—some new development that caused it to be reevaluated. Without new news, the Flowers story was dead.

And yet the following day, all three networks opened with Gennifer Flowers as their lead item. Nothing had happened to the story itself: None of the protagonists had revealed any additional information; even Clinton's opponents were surprisingly mute about the controversy. The powers that be in New York and Washington had decided the day before that there was no story—and yet here were Peter Jennings and Tom Brokaw leading their broadcasts with the tale of a former Arkansas beauty queen and her scandalous allegations.

How did such a reversal come to pass? It's tempting to resort to the usual hand-wringing about the media's declining standards, but in this case, the most powerful figures in televised media had at first stuck to the high road. If they had truly suffered from declining standards, the network execs would have put Jim

Wooten on the first night. Something pushed them off the high road, and that something was not reducible to a national moral decline or a prurient network executive. Gennifer Flowers rode into the popular consciousness via the *system* of televised news, a system that had come to be wired in a specific way.

What we saw in the winter of 1992 was not unlike watching Nixon sweat his way through the famous televised debate of 1960. As countless critics have observed since, we caught a first glimpse in that exchange of how the new medium would change the substance of politics: Television would increase our focus on the interpersonal skills of our politicians and diminish our focus on the issues. With the Flowers affair, though, the medium hadn't changed; the underlying system had. In the late eighties, changes in the flow of information—and particularly the raw footage so essential to televised news—had pushed the previously top-down system toward a more bottom-up, distributed model. We didn't notice until Jim Wooten first posed that question in New Hampshire, but the world of televised news had taken a significant first step toward emergence. In the hierarchical system of old, the network heads could willfully suppress a story if they thought it was best for the American people not to know, but that privilege died with Gennifer Flowers, and not because of lowered standards or sweeps week. It was a casualty of feedback.

It is commonplace by now to talk about the media's disposition toward feeding frenzies, where the coverage of a story naturally begets more coverage, leading to a kind of hall-of-mirrors environment where small incidents or allegations get amplified into Major Events. You can normally spot one of these feedback loops as it nears its denouement, since it almost invariably triggers a surge of self-loathing that washes through the entire commentariat. These self-critical waters seem to rise on something like an annual cycle: Think of the debate about the paparazzi and Princess Di's death, or the permanent midnight of "Why Do We Care So Much About O.J.?" But the feedback loops of the 1990s weren't an inevitability; they came out of specific changes in the underlying system of mass media, changes that brought about the first stirrings of emergence—and foreshadowed the genuinely bottom-up systems that have since flourished on the Web. That feedback was central to the process should come as no surprise: All decentralized systems rely extensively on feedback, for both growth and self-regulation.

Consider the neural networks of the human brain. On a cellular level, the brain is a massive network of nerve cells connected by the microscopic passageways of axons and dendrites. A flash of brain activity—thinking of a word, wrestling with a concept, parsing the syntax of the sentence you're reading now—triggers an array of neuronal circuits like traffic routes plotted on the map of the mind. Each new mental activity triggers a new array, and an unimaginably large number of possible neuronal circuits go unrealized over the course of a human life (one reason why the persistent loss of brain cells throughout our adult years isn't such a big deal). But beneath all that apparent diversity, certain circuits repeat themselves again and again.[2] One of the most tantalizing hypotheses in neuroscience today is that the cellular basis of learning lies in the repetition of those circuits. As neurologist Richard Restak explains, "Each thought and behavior is embedded within the circuitry of the neurons, and . . . neuronal activity accompanying or initiating an experience persists in the form of reverberating neuronal circuits, which become more   strongly defined with repetition. Thus habit and other forms of memory may consist of the establishment of permanent and semipermanent neuronal circuits." A given circuit may initially be associated with the idea of sandwiches, or the shape of an isosceles triangle—and with enough repetition of that specific circuit, it marks out a fixed space in the brain and thereafter becomes part of our mental vocabulary.[3]

Why do these feedback loops and reverberating circuits happen? They come into being because the neural networks of the brain are densely interconnected: Each individual neuron contains links—in the form of axons and synapses—to as many as a thousand other neurons. When a given neuron fires, it relays that charge to all those other cells, which, if certain conditions are met, then in turn relay the charge to their connections, and so on. If each neuron extended a link to one or two fellow neurons, the chance of a reverberating loop would be greatly reduced. But because neurons reach out in so many directions simultaneously, it's far more likely that a given neuron firing will wind its way back to the original source, thus starting the process all over again. The likelihood of a feedback loop correlates directly to the general interconnectedness of the system.[4]

By any measure, the contemporary mediasphere is a densely interconnected system, even if you don't count the linkages of the online world. Connected not just in the sense of so many homes wired for cable and so many rooftops crowned by satellite dishes, but also in the more subtle sense of information being plugged into itself in ever more baroque ways. Since Daniel Boorstin first analyzed the television age in his still-invaluable 1961 work, *The Image*, the world of media journalism has changed in several significant ways, with most of the changes promoting an increase of relays between media outlets. There are far more agents in the system (twenty-four-hour news networks, headline pagers, newsweeklies, Web sites), and far more repackagings and repurposings of source materials, along with an alarming new willingness to relay uncritically other outlets' reporting. Mediated media-critique, unknown in Boorstin's less solipsistic times, and formerly quarantined to early-nineties creations such as CNN's *Reliable Sources* and the occasional Jeff Greenfield segment on *Nightline*, is now regularly the lead story on *Larry King* and *Hardball*. The overall system, in other words, has shifted dramatically in the direction of distributed networks, away from the traditional top-down hierarchies. And the more the media contemplates its own image, the more likely it is that the system will start looping back on itself, like a Stratocaster leaning against the amp it's plugged into.

The upshot of all this is that—in the national news cycle at least—there are no longer any major stories in which the media does not eventually play an essential role, and in many cases the media's knack for self-reflection creates the story itself. You don't need much of an initial impulse to start the whole circuit reverberating. The Gennifer Flowers story is the best example of this process at work. As Tom Rosenstiel reported in a brilliant *New Republic* piece several years ago, the Flowers controversy blossomed because of a shift in the relationship between the national news networks and their local affiliates, a shift that made the entire system significantly more interconnected. Until the late eighties, local news (the six- and eleven-o'clock varieties) relied on the national network for thirty minutes of national news footage, edited according to the august standards of the veterans in New York. Local affiliates could either ignore the national stories or run footage that had been supplied to them, but if the network decided the story wasn't newsworthy, the affiliates couldn't cover it.

All this changed when CNN entered the picture in the mideighties. Since the new network lacked a pool of affiliates to provide breaking news coverage when local events became national stories, Ted Turner embarked on a strategy of wooing local stations with full access to the CNN news feed. Instead of a tightly edited thirty-minute reel, the affiliates would be able to pick and choose from almost anything that CNN cameras had captured, including stories that the executive producers in Atlanta had decided to ignore. The Flowers episode plugged into this newly rewired system, and the results were startling. Local news affiliates nationwide also had access to footage of Clinton's comment, and many of them **The system began calling the shots.** chose to jump on the story, even as the network honchos in New York and Washington decided to ignore it. "When NBC News political editor Bill Wheatley got home and turned on the eleven PM local news that night, he winced: The station NBC owned in New York ran the story the network had chosen not to air the same evening," Rosenstiel writes. "By the next afternoon, even Jim Lehrer of the cautious *MacNeil/Lehrer NewsHour* on PBS told the troops they had to air the Flowers story against their better judgment. 'It's out of my hands,' he said."[5]

The change was almost invisible to Americans watching at home, but its consequences were profound. The mechanism for determining what constituted a legitimate story had been reengineered, shifting from a top-down system with little propensity for feedback, to a kind of journalistic neural net where hundreds of affiliates participated directly in the creation of the story. And what made the circuit particularly vulnerable to reverberation was that the networks themselves mimicked the behavior of the local stations, turning what might have been a passing anomaly into a full-throttle frenzy. That was the moment at which the system began to display emergent behavior. The system began calling the shots, instead of the journalists themselves. Lehrer had it right when he said the Gennifer Flowers affair was "out of my hands." The story was being driven by feedback.

The Flowers affair is a great example of why emergent systems aren't intrinsically good. Tornadoes and hurricanes are feedback-heavy systems too, but that doesn't mean you want to build one in your backyard. Depending on their component parts, and the way they're put together, emergent systems can work toward many different types of goals: some of them admirable, some more destructive. The feedback loops of urban life created the great bulk of the world's most dazzling and revered neighborhoods—but they also have a hand in the self-perpetuating cycles of inner-city misery.[6] Slums can also be emergent phenomena. That's not an excuse to resign ourselves to their existence or to write them off as part of the "natural" order of things. It's reason to figure out a better system. The Flowers affair was an example of early-stage emergence—a system of local agents driving macrobehavior without any central authority calling the shots. But it was not necessarily *adaptive*.

Most of the time, making an emergent system more adaptive entails tinker-   15
ing with different kinds of feedback. In the Flowers affair, we saw an example of what systems theorists call positive feedback—the sort of self-fueling cycles that cause a note strummed on a guitar to expand into a howling symphony of noise.[7] But most automated control systems rely extensively on "negative feedback" devices. The classic example is the thermostat, which uses negative feedback to solve the problem of controlling the temperature of the air in a room. There are actually two ways to regulate temperature. The first would be to design an apparatus capable of blowing air at various different temperatures; the occupant of the room would simply select the desired conditions and the machine would start blowing air cooled or heated to the desired temperature. The problem with that system is twofold: It requires a heating/cooling apparatus capable of blowing air at precise temperatures, and it is utterly indifferent to the room's existing condition. Dial up seventy-two degrees on the thermostat, and the machine will start pumping seventy-two-degree air into the room—even if the room's ambient temperature is already in the low seventies.

The negative feedback approach, on the other hand, provides a simpler solution, and one that is far more sensitive to a changing environment. (Not surprisingly, it's the technique used by most home thermostats.) Instead of pumping precisely calibrated air into the room, the system works with three states: hot air, cool air, and no air. It takes a reading of the room's temperature, measures that reading against the desired setting, and then adjusts its state accordingly. If the room is colder than the desired setting, the hot air goes on. If it is warmer, the cool air flows out. The system continuously measures the ambient temperature and continuously adjusts its output, until the desired setting has been reached—at which point it switches into the "no air" state, where it remains until the ambient temperature changes for some reason. The system uses negative feedback to home in on the proper conditions—and for that reason it can handle random changes in the environment.

Negative feedback, then, is a way of reaching an equilibrium point despite unpredictable—and changing—external conditions. The "negativity" keeps the system in check, just as "positive feedback" propels other systems onward. A thermostat with no feedback simply pumps seventy-two-degree air into a room, regardless of the room's temperature. An imaginary thermostat driven by positive feedback might evaluate the change in room temperature and follow that lead: If the thermostat noted that the room had grown warmer, it would start pumping hotter air, causing the room to grow even warmer, causing the device to pump hotter air. Next thing you know, the water in the goldfish bowl is boiling. Negative feedback, on the other hand, lets the system find the right balance, even in a changing environment. A cold front comes in, a window is opened, someone lights a fire—any of these things can happen, and yet the temperature remains constant. Instead of amplifying its own signal, the system regulates itself.

We've been wrestling with information as a medium for negative feedback ever since Norbert Wiener published *Cybernetics* in 1949, and Wiener himself had been thinking about the relationship between control and feedback since his war-related research of the early forties. After the Japanese bombed Pearl Harbor and the United States joined the war in earnest, Wiener was asked by the army to figure out a way to train mechanical guns to fire automatically at their targets. The question Wiener found himself answering was this: Given enough information about the target's location and movement, could you translate that data into something a machine could use to shoot a V-2 out of the sky?

The problem was uniquely suited for the adaptability of negative feedback: The targets were a mixture of noise and information, somewhat predictable but also subject to sudden changes. But as it happened, to solve the problem Wiener also needed something that didn't really exist yet: a digital computer capable of crunching the flow of data in real time. With that need in mind, Wiener helped build one of the first modern computers ever created. When the story is told of Wiener's war years, the roots of the modern PC are usually emphasized, for legitimate reasons. But the new understanding of negative feedback that emerged from the ENIAC effort had equally far-reaching consequences, extending far beyond the vacuum tubes and punch cards of early computing.[8]

For negative feedback is not solely a software issue, or a device for your home furnace. It is a way of indirectly pushing a fluid, changeable system toward a goal. It is, in other words, a way of transforming a complex system into a complex *adaptive* system. Negative feedback comes in many shapes and sizes. You can build it into ballistic missiles or circuit boards, neurons or blood vessels. It is, in today's terms, "platform agonistic." At its most schematic, negative feedback entails comparing the current state of a system to the desired state, and pushing the system in a direction that minimizes the difference between the two states. As Wiener puts it near the outset of *Cybernetics*: "When we desire a motion to follow a given pattern, the difference between this pattern and the actually performed motion is used as a new input to cause the part regulated to move in such a way as to bring its motion closer to that given by the pattern."[9] Wiener gave that knack for self-regulation a name: homeostasis.[10]

Your body is a massively complex homeostatic system, using an intricate network of feedback mechanisms to keep itself stable in the midst of dynamically changing situations.[11] Many of those feedback mechanisms are maintained by the brain, which coordinates external stimuli received by sensory organs and responds by triggering appropriate bodily actions. Our sleep cycles, for instance, depend heavily on negative feedback. The body's circadian rhythms—accumulated after millions of years of life on a planet with a twenty-four-hour day—flow out of the central nervous system, triggering regular changes in urine formation, body temperature, cardiac output, oxygen consumption, cell division, and the secretions of endocrine glands. But for some reason, our body clocks are set a little slow: The human circadian cycle is twenty-five hours, and so we rely on the external world to reset our clock every day, both by detecting patterns of light and darkness, and by detecting the more subtle change in the earth's magnetic field, which shifts as the planet rotates. Without that negative feedback pulling our circadian rhythms back into sync, we'd find ourselves sleeping through the day for two weeks out of every month. In other words, without that feedback mechanism, it would be as though the entire human race were permanently trapped in sophomore year of college.

Understanding the body and the mind as a feedback-regulated homeostatic system has naturally encouraged some people to experiment with new forms of artificial feedback. Since the seventies, biofeedback devices have reported changes in adrenaline levels and muscle tension in real time to individuals wired up to special machines. The idea is to allow patients to manage their anxiety or stress level by letting them explore different mental states and instantly see the physiological effects. With a little bit of practice, biofeedback patients can easily "drive" their adrenaline levels up or down just by imagining stressful events, or reaching a meditative state. Our bodies, of course, are constantly adjusting adrenaline levels anyway—the difference with biofeedback is that the conscious mind enters into that feedback process, giving patients more direct control over the levels of the hormone in their system. That can be a means of better managing your body's internal state, but it can also be a process of self-discovery. The one time I tried conventional biofeedback, my adrenaline levels hovered serenely at the middle of the range for the first five minutes of the session; the doctor actually complimented me on having such a normal and well-regulated adrenal system. And then, in the course of our conversation, I made a joke—and instantly my adrenaline levels shot off the charts. At the end of my visit, the therapist handed me a printout of the thirty-minute session, with my changing adrenaline levels plotted as a line graph. It was, for all intents and purposes, a computer graph of my attempts at humor over the preceding half hour: a flat line interrupted by six or seven dramatic spikes, each corresponding to a witticism that I had tossed out to the therapist.

I walked away from the session without having improved myself in any noticeable way, and certainly I hadn't achieved more control over my adrenaline levels. But I'd learned something nonetheless: that without consciously realizing it, I'd already established a simple feedback circuit for myself years ago, when my body had learned that it could give itself a targeted adrenaline rush by making a passing joke in conversation. I thought of all those office meetings or ostensibly serious conversations with friends where I had found myself compulsively making jokes, despite the inappropriate context; I thought of how deeply ingrained that impulse is in my day-to-day personality—and suddenly it seemed closer to a drug addiction than a personality trait, my brain scrambling to put together a cheap laugh to secure another adrenaline fix. In a real sense, our personalities are partially the sum of all these invisible feedback mechanisms; but to begin to understand those mechanisms, you need additional levels of feedback—in this case, a simple line graph plotted by an ordinary PC.

If analyzing indirect data such as adrenaline levels can reveal so much about the mind's ulterior motives, imagine the possibilities of analyzing the brain's activity directly.[12] That's the idea behind the technology of neurofeedback: Rather than measure the *results* of the brain's actions, neurofeedback measures brain waves themselves and translates them into computer-generated images and sounds. Certain brain-wave patterns appear in moments of intense concentration; others in states of meditative calm; others in states of distraction, or fear. Neurofeedback—like so many of the systems we've seen—is simply a pattern amplification and recognition device: A series of EEG sensors applied to your skull registers changes in the patterns of your brain waves and transforms them into a medium that you can perceive directly, often in the form of audio tones or colors on a computer screen. As your brain drifts from one state to another, the tone or the image changes, giving you real-time feedback about your brain's EEG activity. With some practice, neurofeedback practitioners can more readily drive their brains toward specific states—because the neurofeedback technology supplies the brain with new data about its own patterns of behavior. Once you've reached a meditative state using neurofeedback, devotees claim, the traditional modes of meditation seem like parallel parking without a rearview mirror—with enough practice, you can pull it off, but you're missing a lot of crucial information.[13]

> Feedback, after all, is usually not a television thing. You need the Web to hear it wail.

Were he alive today, I suspect Wiener would be surprised to find that biofeedback and neurofeedback technology are not yet mainstream therapeutic practices. But Wiener also recognized that homeostasis was not exclusively the province of individual human minds and bodies. If systems of neurons could form elaborate feedback mechanisms, why couldn't larger human collectivities? "In connection with the effective amount of communal information," Wiener wrote, "one of the most surprising facts about the body politic is its extreme lack of efficient homeostatic processes."[14] He would have diagnosed the pathology of Gennifer Flowers in a heartbeat.[15] The Flowers episode was an instance of pure positive feedback, unchecked by its opposing force. Each agent's behavior encouraged more like-minded behavior from other agents. There was nothing homeostatic about the process, only the "ever-widening gyre" of positive feedback.

But if positive feedback causes such a ruckus in the media world, how can the brain rely so heavily on the reverberating circuits of neurons? One answer is a familiar term from today's media: *fatigue*. Every neuron in the brain suffers from a kind of regulated impotence: After firing for a stretch, the cell must go through a few milliseconds of inaction, the "absolute refractory period," during which it is immune to outside stimulation. Along with many other ingenious inhibiting schemes that the brain relies on, fatigue is a way of shorting out the reverberating circuit, keeping the brain's feeding frenzy in check.

It is this short circuit that is lacking in the modern media's vast interconnectedness. Stories generate more stories, which generate stories about the coverage of the stories, which generate coverage about the meta-coverage. (Here
the brain science seems wonderfully poetic: What better diagnosis for the 24/7
vertigo of media feedback than "lack of fatigue"?) A brain that can't stop reverberating is one way of describing what happens during an epileptic fit; the
media version is something like Steven Brill's epic critique of the Lewinsky coverage in the first issue of *Content*: a high-profile media critic launching a new
magazine with a high-profile indictment of the media's obsession with its own
reporting. If the problem stemmed from errors of judgment made by individual
reporters, then a media critique might make sense. But since the problem lies
in the media's own tendency for self-amplification, it only makes the problem
worse to cover the coverage. It's like firing a pistol in the air to stop a fusillade.
Once again, the Flowers affair illustrates the principle: The story wasn't "real
news" — according to the network wise men — until other outlets started covering it. The newsworthiness of a given story can't be judged by the play the
story is getting on the other channels. Otherwise the gravitational pull of positive feedback becomes too strong, and the loop starts driving the process, more
than the reporters *or* the event itself.

It's not overstating things to say that the story that emerged from this
loop was a milestone in American history. It's entirely possible that the Flowers controversy would have subsided had Clinton's answer to Jim Wooten been
ignored; the Clintons would never have gone on *60 Minutes,* and a whole series of tropes that appeared around the couple (Clinton's philandering, Hillary's
anti–Tammy Wynette feminism) might never have found their way into the
public mind. Without Gennifer Flowers in Clinton's past, would the Monica
Lewinsky affair have played out the same way? Probably not. And if that's the
case, then we must ask: What really brought this chain of events about? On
the one hand, the answer is simple: Individual life choices made by individual
people — Clinton's decision to have an affair, and to break it off, Flowers's decision to go public, Clinton's decision to answer the question — result in a chain of
events that eventually stirs up an international news story. But there is another
sine qua non here, which is the decision made several years before, somewhere in
an office complex in Atlanta, to share the entire CNN news feed with local affiliates. That decision was not quite a "pseudo event," in Boorstin's famous phrase.
It was a "system event": a change in the way information flowed through the
overall news system. But it was a material change nonetheless.

If you think that Clinton's remarks on Gennifer Flowers should never have
been a story, then who are the culprits? Whom do we blame in such a setting?
The traditional critiques don't apply here: There's no oak-paneled, cigar-smoke-
filled back room where the puppeteers pull their invisible strings; it's not that
the television medium is particularly "hot" or "cold"; there was a profit motive
behind CNN's decision to share more footage, but we certainly can't write off
the Flowers episode as just another tribute to the greed of the network execs.
Once again, we return to the fundamental laws of emergence: The behavior
of individual agents is less important than the overall system. In earlier times,

the channels that connected politicians, journalists, and ordinary citizens were one-way and hierarchical; they lacked the connections to generate true feedback; and too few agents were interacting to create any higher-level order. But the cable explosion of the eighties changed all that. For the first time, the system started to reverberate on its own. The sound was quiet during those initial years and may not have crossed into an audible range until Jim Wooten asked that question. And yet anyone who caught the nightly news on January 24, 1992, picked up its signal loud and clear.

Still, the top-heavy structure of mass media may keep those loops relatively   30
muted for the foreseeable future, at least where the tube is concerned. Feedback, after all, is usually not a television thing. You need the Web to hear it wail.

In June of 1962, a full year after the appearance of *The Death and Life of Great American Cities*, Lewis Mumford published a scathing critique of Jane Jacobs's manifesto in his legendary *New Yorker* column, "The Sky Line." In her prescriptions for a sidewalk-centric urban renewal, "Mother Jacobs"—as Mumford derisively called her—offered a "homemade poultice for the cure of cancer." The *New Yorker* critic had been an early advocate of Jacobs's work, encouraging her to translate her thoughts into a book while she was a junior editor at *Architecture Forum* in the midfifties. But the book she eventually wrote attacked Mumford's much-beloved Ebenezer Howard and his "garden cities," and so Mumford struck back at his onetime protégé with full fury.[16]

At over ten thousand words, Mumford's critique was extensive and wide-ranging, but the central message came down to the potential of metropolitan centers to self-regulate. Jacobs had argued that large cities can achieve a kind of homeostasis through the interactions generated by lively sidewalks; urban planning that attempted to keep people off the streets was effectively destroying the lifeblood of the urban system. Without the open, feedback-heavy connections of street culture, cities quickly became dangerous and anarchic places. Building a city without sidewalks, Jacobs argued, was like building a brain without axons or dendrites. A city without connections was no city at all, at least in the traditional sense of organic city life. Better to build cities that encouraged the feedback loops of sidewalk traffic by shortening the length of blocks and supporting mixed-use zoning.[17]

Mumford was no fan of the housing projects of the postwar era, but he had lost faith in the self-regulatory powers of massive urban systems. Cities with populations in the millions simply put too much stress on the natural homeostatic tendencies of human collectives. In *The City in History*, published around the same period, Mumford had looked back at the Greek city-states, and their penchant for founding new units once the original community reached a certain size—the urban equivalent of reproducing by spores. His attachment to Ebenezer Howard also stemmed from the same lack of confidence in metropolitan self-regulation: The Garden City movement—not entirely unlike the New Urbanist movement of today—was an attempt to provide the energy and dynamism of city life in smaller doses.[18] The Italian hill towns of the Renaissance had achieved an ideal mix of density and diversity while keeping their overall population within reasonable bounds (reined in largely by the walls that surrounded them). These were street-centric spaces with a vibrant public culture, but they remained knowable communities too: small enough to foster a real sense of civic belonging. That kind of organic balance, Mumford argued, was impossible in a city of 5 million people where the noise and congestion—the sensory overload of it all—drained out the "vitality" from the city streets. "Jacobs forgets that in organisms there is no tissue growth quite as 'vital' or 'dynamic' as cancer growths. . . . The author has forgotten the most essential characteristic of all organic growth—to maintain diversity and balance, the organism must not exceed the norm of its species. Any ecological association eventually reaches the 'climax stage,' beyond which growth without deterioration is not possible."[19]

Like many debates from the annals of urban studies, the Mumford/Jacobs exchange over the "climax stage" of city life mirrors recent developments in the digital realm, as Web-based communities struggle to manage the problems of runaway growth.[20] The first generation of online hangouts—dial-up electronic bulletin boards like ECHO or the Well—were the equivalent of those Italian hill towns: lively, innovative, contentious places, but also places that remained within a certain practical size. In their heyday before the Web's takeoff, both services hovered around five thousand members, and within that population, community leaders and other public characters naturally emerged: the jokers and the enablers, the fact checkers and the polemicists. These characters—many of them concealed behind playful pseudonyms—served as the equivalent of Jacobs's shopkeepers and bartenders, the regular "eyes on the street" that give the neighborhood its grounding and its familiarity.

These online communities also divided themselves into smaller units organized around specific topics. Like the trade-specific clusters of Savile Row and the Por Santa Maria, these divisions made the overall space more intelligible, and their peculiarities endowed each community with a distinctive flavor. (For the first few years of its existence, the Grateful Dead discussion area on the Well was larger than all the other areas combined.) Because each topic area attracted a smaller subset of the overall population, visiting each one felt like returning to an old block in a familiar part of town, and running into the same cast of characters that you had found there the last time you visited.

ECHO and the Well had a certain homeostatic balance in those early years—powerfully captured in Howard Rheingold's book *The Virtual Community*—and part of that balance came from the community's own powers of self-organization. But neither was a pure example of bottom-up behavior: The topic areas, for instance, were central-planning affairs, created by fiat and not by footprints; both communities benefited from the strong top-down leadership of their founders. That their overall populations never approached a "climax stage" reflected the slow modem-adoption curve of the general public, and the limited marketing budgets at both operations. More important, the elements of each community that did self-regulate had little to do with the underlying software. Anyone who spent any time on those services in the early nineties will tell you that community leaders and other recognizable figures emerged, but that status existed only in the perceptions of the users themselves. The software itself was agnostic when it came to status, but because the software brought hominid minds together—minds that are naturally inclined to establish hierarchies in social relationships—leaders and pariahs began to appear. The software did recognize official moderators for each discussion area, but those too were appointments handed down from above; you applied to the village chieftain for the role that you desired, and if you'd been a productive member of the society, your wish might be granted. The[re] were plenty of unofficial leaders, to be sure—but where the code was concerned, the only official moderators came straight from the top.

This mix of hierarchy and heterarchy was well suited to ECHO's and the Well's stage of growth. At five thousand members, the community was still small enough to be managed partially from above, and small enough that groups and recognizable characters naturally emerged. At that scale, you didn't need to solve the problem of self-regulation with software tools: All you needed was software that connected people's thoughts—via the asynchronous posts of a threaded discussion board—and the community could find its own balance. If something went wrong, you could always look to the official leaders for guidance. But even in those heady early days of the virtual community, the collective systems of ECHO and the Well fell short of achieving real homeostasis, for reasons that would become endemic to the next generation of communities then forming on the Web itself.

A threaded discussion board turns out to be an ideal ecosystem for that peculiar species known as the crank—the ideologue obsessed with a certain issue or interpretive model, who has no qualms about interjecting his or her worldview into any discussion, and apparently no day job or family life to keep him from posting voluminous commentary at the slightest provocation. We all know people like this, the ones grinding their ax from the back of the seminar room or the coffee shop: the conspiracy theorist, the rabid libertarian, the evangelist—the ones who insist on bringing all conversations back to their particular issue, objecting to any conversation that doesn't play by their rules. In real life, we've developed a series of social conventions that keep the crank from dominating our conversations. For the most pathological cases, they simply don't get invited out to dinner very often. But for the borderline case, a subtle but powerful mechanism is at work in any face-to-face group conversation: If an individual is holding a conversation hostage with an irrelevant obsession, groups can naturally establish a consensus—using words, body language, facial expressions, even a show of hands—making it clear that the majority of the group feels their time is being wasted. The face-to-face world is populated by countless impromptu polls that take the group's collective pulse. Most of them happen so quickly that we don't even know that we're participating in them, and that transparency is one reason why they're as powerful as they are. In the face-to-face world, we are all social thermostats: reading the group temperature and adjusting our behavior accordingly.

Some of those self-regulatory social skills translate into cyberspace—particularly in a threaded discussion forum or an e-mail exchange, where participants have the time and space to express their ideas in long form, rather than in the spontaneous eruptions of real-time chat. But there is a crucial difference in an environment like ECHO or the Well—or in the discussion areas we built at *FEED*. In a public discussion thread, not all the participants are visible. A given conversation may have five or six active contributors and several dozen "lurkers" who read through the posts but don't chime in with their own words. This creates a fundamental imbalance in the system of threaded discussion and gives the crank an opportunity to dominate the space in a way that would be much more difficult offline. In a threaded discussion, you're speaking both to the other active participants and to the lurkers, and however much you might offend or bore your direct interlocutors, you can always appeal to that silent majority out there—an audience that is both present and absent at the same time. The crank can cling to the possibility that everyone else tuning in is enthralled by his prose, while the active participants can't turn to the room and say, "Show of hands: Is this guy a lunatic or what?"

The crank exploits a crucial disparity in the flow of information: While we conventionally think of threaded discussions as two-way systems, for the lurkers that flow follows a one-way path. They hear us talking, but we hear nothing of them: no laughs, no hisses, no restless stirring, no snores, no rolling eyeballs. When you factor in the lurkers, a threaded discussion turns out to be less interactive than a traditional face-to-face lecture, and significantly less so than a conversation around a dinner table, where even the most reticent participants contribute with gestures and facial expressions. Group conversations in the real world have an uncanny aptitude for reaching a certain kind of homeostasis: The conversation moves toward a zone that pleases as much of the group as possible and drowns out voices that offend. A group conversation is a kind of circuit board, with primary inputs coming from the official speakers, and secondary inputs coming from the responses of the audience and other speakers. The primary inputs adjust their signal based on the secondary inputs of group feedback. Human beings . . . are exceptionally talented at assessing the mental states of other people, both through the direct exchanges of spoken language and the more oblique feedback mechanisms of gesture and intonation. That two-way exchange gives our face-to-face group conversations precisely the flexibility and responsiveness that Wiener found lacking in mass communications.

I suspect Wiener would immediately have understood the virtual community's problem with cranks and lurkers. Where the Flowers affair was a case of runaway positive feedback, the tyranny of the crank results from a scarcity of feedback: a system where the information flows are unidirectional, where the audience is present and at the same time invisible. These liabilities run parallel to the problems of one-way linking. . . . Hypertext links and virtual communities were supposed to be the advance guard of the interactive revolution, but in a real sense they only got halfway to the promised land. (Needless to say, the ants were there millions of years ago.) And if the cranks and obsessive-compulsives flourish in a small-scale online community of several thousand members, imagine the anarchy and noise generated by a million community members. Surely there is a "climax stage" on that scale where the online growth turns cancerous, where the knowable community becomes a nightmare of overdevelopment. If feedback couldn't help regulate the digital villages of early online communication, what hope can it possibly have on the vast grid of the World Wide Web?

The sleepy college town of Holland, Michigan, might seem like the last place you'd expect to generate a solution for the problem of digital sprawl, but the Web has never played by the rules of traditional geography. Until recent years, Holland had been best known for its annual tulip festival. But it is increasingly recognized as the birthplace of Slashdot.org—the closest thing to a genuinely self-organizing community that the Web has yet produced.

Begun as a modest bulletin board by a lifetime Hollander named Rob Malda, Slashdot came into the world as the ultimate in knowable communities: just Malda and his friends, discussing programming news, Star Wars rumors, video games, and other geek-chic marginalia. "In the beginning, Slashdot was small," Malda writes. "We got dozens of posts each day, and it was good. The signal was high, the noise was low."[21] Before long, though, Slashdot floated across the rising tsunami of Linux and the Open Source movement and found itself awash in thousands of daily visitors. In its early days, Slashdot had felt like the hill towns of ECHO and the Well, with strong leadership coming from Malda himself, who went by the handle Commander Taco. But the volume of posts became too much for any single person to filter out the useless information. "Trolling and spamming became more common," Malda says now, "and there wasn't enough time for me to personally keep them in check and still handle my other responsibilities."

Malda's first inclination was to create a Slashdot elite: twenty-five hand-picked spam warriors who would sift through the material generated by the community, eliminating irrelevant or obnoxious posts. While the idea of an elite belonged to a more hierarchical tradition, Malda endowed his lieutenants with a crucial resource: They could rate other contributions, on a scale of –1 to 5. You could browse through Slashdot.org with a "quality filter" on, effectively telling the software, "Show me only items that have a rating higher than 3." This gave his lieutenants a positive function as well as a negative one. They could emphasize the good stuff and reward users who were productive members of the community.

Soon, though, Slashdot grew too large for even the elites to manage, and Malda went back to the drawing board. It was the kind of thing that could only have happened on the Web. A twenty-two-year-old college senior, living with a couple of buddies in a low-rent house—affectionately dubbed Geek House One—in a nondescript Michigan town, creates an intimate online space for his friends to discuss their shared obsessions, and within a year fifty thousand people each day are angling for a piece of the action. Without anything resembling a genuine business infrastructure, much less a real office, Malda needed far more than his twenty-five lieutenants to keep the Slashdot community from descending into complete anarchy. But without the resources to hire a hundred full-time moderators, Slashdot appeared to be stuck at the same impasse that Mumford had described thirty years before: stay small and preserve the quality of the original community; keep growing and sacrifice everything that had made the community interesting in the first place. Slashdot had reached its "climax stage."

What did the Commander do? Instead of expanding his pool of special authorized lieutenants, he made *everyone* a potential lieutenant. He handed over the quality-control job to the community itself. His goals were relatively simple, as outlined in the Frequently Asked Questions document on the site:

1. Promote quality, discourage crap.
2. Make Slashdot as readable as possible for as many people as possible.
3. Do not require a huge amount of time from any single moderator.
4. Do not allow a single moderator a "reign of terror."

Together, these objectives define the parameters of Slashdot's ideal state. The question for Malda was how to build a homeostatic system that would naturally push the site toward that state without any single individual being in control. The solution that he arrived at should be immediately recognizable by now: a mix of negative and positive feedback, structured randomness, neighbor interactions, and decentralized control. From a certain angle, Slashdot today resembles an ant colony. From another, it looks like a virtual democracy. Malda himself likens it to jury duty.

Here's how it works: If you've spent more than a few sessions as a registered Slashdot user, the system may on occasion alert you that you have been given moderator status (not unlike a jury summons arriving in your mailbox). As in the legal analogy, moderators only serve for a finite stretch of time, and during that stretch they have the power to rate contributions made by other users, on a scale of –1 to 5.[22] But that power diminishes with use: Each moderator is endowed only with a finite number of points that he or she can distribute by rating user contributions. Dole out all your ratings, and your tenure as a moderator comes to an end.

Those ratings coalesce into something that Malda called karma: If your contributions as a user are highly rated by the moderators, you earn karma in the system, giving you special privileges. Your subsequent posts begin life at a higher rating than usual, and you are more likely to be chosen as a moderator in future sessions. This last privilege exemplifies meta-feedback at work, the ratings snake devouring its own tail: Moderators rate posts, and those ratings are used to select future moderators. Malda's system not only encouraged quality in the submissions to the site; it also set up an environment where community leaders could naturally rise to the surface. That elevation was specifically encoded in the software. Accumulating karma on Slashdot was not just a metaphor for winning the implicit trust of the Slashdot community; it was a quantifiable number. Karma had found a home in the database.

Malda's point system brings to mind the hit points of Dungeons & Dragons 50 and other classics of the role-playing genre. (That the Slashdot crowd was already heavily versed in the role-playing idiom no doubt contributed a great deal to the rating system's quick adoption.) But Malda had done something more ambitious than simply porting gaming conventions to the community space. He had created a kind of currency, a pricing system for online civics. By ensuring that the points would translate into special privileges, he gave them value. By making one's moderation powers expendable, he created the crucial property of scarcity. With only one or the other, the currency is valueless; combine the two, and you have a standard for pricing community participation that actually works.

The connection between pricing and feedback is itself more than a metaphor. As a character in Jane Jacobs's recent Socratic dialogue, *The Nature of Economies*, observes: "Adam Smith, back in 1775, identified prices of goods and rates of wages as feedback information, although of course he didn't call it that because the word *feedback* was not in the vocabulary at the time. But he understood the idea. . . . In his sober way, Smith was clearly excited about the marvelous form of order he'd discovered, as well he should have been. He was far ahead of naturalists in grasping the principle of negative feedback controls."[23]

Malda himself claims that neither *The Wealth of Nations* nor *The Dungeon Master's Guide* were heavy in his thoughts in Geek House One. "There wasn't really anything specific that inspired me," Malda says now. "It was mostly trial and error. The real influence was my desire to please users with very different expectations for Slashdot. Some wanted it to be Usenet: anything goes and unruly. Others were busy people who only wanted to read three to four comments a day."[24] You can see the intelligence and flexibility of the system firsthand: Visit the Slashdot site and choose to view all the posts for a given conversation. If the conversation is more than a few hours old, you'll probably find several hundred entries, with at least half of them the work of cranks and spammers. Such is the fate of any Web site lucky enough to attract thousands of posts an hour.

Set your quality threshold to four or five, however, and something miraculous occurs. The overall volume drops precipitously—sometimes by an order of magnitude—but the dozen or two posts that remain will be as stimulating as anything you've read on a traditional content site where the writers and the editors are actually paid to put their words and arguments together. It's a miracle not so much because the quality is lurking there somewhere in the endless flood of posting. Rather, it's a miracle because the community has collectively done such an exceptional job at bringing that quality to light. In the digital world, at least, there is life after the climax stage.

Slashdot is only the beginning. In the past two years, user ratings have become the kudzu of the Web, draping themselves across pages everywhere you look. Amazon had long included user ratings for all the items in its inventory, but in 1999 it began to let users rate the reviews of other users. An ingenious site called Epinions cultivates product reviews from its audience and grants "trust" points to contributors who earn the community's respect. The online auction system of eBay utilizes two distinct feedback mechanisms layered on top of each other: the price feedback of the auction bids coupled to the user ratings that evaluate buyers and sellers. One system tracks the value of stuff; the other tracks the value of people.

Indeed, the adoption rate for these feedback devices is accelerating so rapidly that I suspect in a matter of years a Web page without a dynamic rating system attached will trigger the same response that a Web page without hyperlinks triggers today: Yes, it's technically possible to create a page without these features, but what's the point? The Slashdot system might seem a little complex, a little esoteric for consumers who didn't grow up playing D&D, but think of the millions of people who learned how to use a computer for the first time in the past few years, just to get e-mail or to surf the Web. Compared to that learning curve, figuring out the rules of Slashdot is a walk in the park.

And rules they are. You can't think of a system like the one Malda built at Slashdot as a purely *representational* entity, the way you think about a book or a movie. It is partly representational, of course: You read messages via the Slashdot platform, and so the components of the textual medium that Marshall McLuhan so brilliantly documented in *The Gutenberg Galaxy* are on display at Slashdot as well. Because you are reading words, your reception of the information behind those words differs from what it would have been had that information been conveyed via television. The medium is still the message on Slashdot—it's just that there's another level to the experience, a level that our critical vocabularies are only now finding words for.

In a Slashdot-style system, there is a medium, a message, and an audience. So far, no different from television. The difference is that those elements exist alongside a set of rules that govern the way the messages flow through the system. "Interactivity" doesn't do justice to the significance of this shift. A button that lets you e-mail a response to a published author; a tool that lets you build your own home page; even a collection of interlinked pages that let you follow your own path through them—these are all examples of interactivity, but they're in a different category from the self-organizing systems of eBay or Slashdot. Links and home-page-building tools are cool, no question. But they are closer to a newspaper letters-to-the-editor page than Slashdot's collective intelligence.

First-generation interactivity may have given the consumer a voice, but systems like Slashdot force us to accept a more radical proposition: To understand how these new media experiences work, you have to analyze the message, the medium, *and the rules.* Think of those thousand-post geek-Dionysian frenzies transformed into an informative, concise briefing via the Slashdot quality filters. What's interesting here is not just the medium, but rather the rules that govern what gets selected and what doesn't. It's an algorithmic problem, then, and not a representational one. It is the difference between playing a game of Monopoly and hanging a Monopoly board on your wall. There are representational forces unleashed by a game of Monopoly (you have to be able

55

to make out the color coding of the various properties and to count your money) but what makes the game interesting—indeed, what makes it a game at all—lies in the instruction set that you follow while playing. Slashdot's rules are what make the medium interesting—so interesting, in fact, that you can't help thinking they need their own category, beyond message *and* medium.

Generically, you can describe those rules as a mix of positive and negative feedback pushing the system toward a particular state based on the activities of the participants. But the mix is different every time. The edge cities of Paul Krugman's model used feedback to create polycentric clusters, while other metropolitan systems collapse into a single, dense urban core. The networks in CNN-era television have engendered runaway positive feedback loops such as the Gennifer Flowers story, while a system like Slashdot achieves homeostatic balance, at least when viewed at level 5. Different feedback systems produce different results—even when those systems share the same underlying medium. In the future, every Web site may well be connected to a rating mechanism, but that doesn't mean all Web sites will behave the same way. There may be homeostasis at Slashdot's level 5, but you can always choose to read the unfiltered, anarchic version at level –1.

Is there a danger in moving to a world where all our media responds directly to user feedback? Some critics, such as *The Control Revolution's* Andrew Shapiro, worry about the tyranny of excessive user personalization, as in the old Nicholas Negroponte vision of the *Daily Me*, the newspaper perfectly custom-tailored to your interests—so custom-tailored, in fact, that you lose the serendipity and surprise that we've come to expect from reading the newspaper. There's no stumbling across a different point of view, or happening upon an interesting new field you knew nothing about—the *Daily Me* simply feeds back what you've instructed the software to find, and nothing more. It's a mind-narrowing experience, not a mind-expanding one. That level of personalization may well be around the corner. . . . But for now, it's worth pointing out that the Slashdot system is indifferent to your personal interests—other than your interest in a general level of quality. The "ideal state" that the Slashdot system homes in on is not defined by an individual's perspective; it is defined by the overall group's perspective. The collective decides what's quality and what's crap, to use Rob Malda's language. You can tweak the quality-to-crap ratio based on your individual predilections, but the ratings themselves emerge through the actions of the community at large. It's more groupthink than *Daily Me*.

Perhaps, then, the danger lies in too much groupthink. Malda designed his system to evaluate submissions based on the average Slashdot reader—although the karma points tend to select moderators who have a higher-than-average reputation within the community. It's entirely possible that Malda's rules have created a tyranny of the majority at Slashdot, at least when viewed at level 5. Posts that resonate with the "average" Slashdotter are more likely to rise to the top, while posts that express a minority viewpoint may be demoted in the system. (Technically, the moderation guidelines suggest that users should rate posts based purely on quality, not on whether they agree with the posts, but the line is invariably a slippery one.) From this angle, then, Slashdot bears a surprising resemblance to the old top-down universe of pre-cable network television. Both systems have a heavy center that pulls content toward the interests of the "average user"—like a planet pulling satellites into its orbit. In the days before cable fragmentation, the big three networks were competing for the entire television-owning audience, which encouraged them to serve up programming designed for the average viewer rather than for a particular niche. (McLuhan observed how this phenomenon was pushing the political parties toward the center as well.) The network decision to pursue the center rather than the peripheries was invariably made at the executive level, of course—unlike at Slashdot, where the centrism comes from below. But if you're worried about suppressing diversity, it doesn't really matter whether it comes from above or below. The results are the same, either way. Majority viewpoints get amplified, while minority viewpoints get silenced.

This critique showcases why we need a third term beyond *medium* and *message*. While it's true that Slashdot's filtering software creates a heavy center, that tendency is not inherent to the Web medium, or even the subset of online communities. You could just as easily build a system that would promote both quality *and* diversity, simply by tweaking the algorithm that selects moderators. Change a single variable in the mix, and a dramatically different system emerges. Instead of picking moderators based on the average rating of their posts, the new system picks moderators whose contributions have triggered the greatest range of responses. In this system, a member who was consistently rated highly by the community would be unlikely to be chosen as a moderator, while a member who inspired strong responses either way—both positive and negative—would be first in line to moderate. The system would reward controversial voices rather than popular ones. You'd still have moderators deleting useless spam and flamebait, and so the quality filters would remain in place. But the fringe voices in the community would have a stronger presence at level 5, because the feedback system would be rewarding perspectives that deviate from the mainstream, that don't aim to please everyone all the time. The cranks would still be marginalized, assuming their polemics annoyed almost everyone who came across them. But the thoughtful minorities—the ones who attract both admirers *and* detractors—would have a place at the table.

There's no reason why centrist Slashdot and diverse Slashdot can't coexist. If you can adjust the quality filters on the fly, you could just as easily adjust the diversity filters. You could design the system to track the ratings of both popular and controversial moderators; users would then be able to view Slashdot through the lens of the "average" user on one day, and through the lens of a more diverse audience the next. The medium and the message remain the same; only the rules change from one system to the other. Adjust the feedback loops, and a new type of community appears on the screen. One setting gives you Gennifer Flowers and cyclone-style feeding frenzies, another gives you the shapeless datasmog of Usenet. One setting gives you an orderly, centrist community strong on shared values, another gives you a multiculturalist's fantasy. As Wiener recognized a half century ago, feedback systems come in all shapes and sizes. When we come across a system that doesn't work well, there's no point in denouncing the use of feedback itself. Better to figure out the specific rules of the system at hand and start thinking of ways to wire it so that the feedback routines promote the values we want promoted. It's the old sixties slogan transposed into the digital age: If you don't like the way things work today, change the system.

BIBLIOGRAPHY

Dean, Katie. "Attention Kids: Play This Game." *Wired News*. December 19, 2000.

De Landa, Manuel. *A Thousand Years of Nonlinear History*. New York: Zone Books, Swerve Editions, 1997.

Edelman, Gerald M. *Bright Air, Brilliant Fire: On the Matter of Mind*. New York: Basic Books, 1992.

Jacobs, Jane. *The Death and Life of Great American Cities*. New York: Vintage, 1961.

———. *The Nature of Economies*. New York: Modern Library Original, 2000.

Kurzweil, Ray. *The Age of Spiritual Machines: When Computers Exceed Human Intelligence*. New York: Penguin Books, 1999.

Mumford, Lewis. *The City in History: Its Origins, Its Transformations and Its Prospects*. New York and London: Harcourt, Brace, Jovanovich, 1961.

Ridley, Matt. *Genome: The Autobiography of a Species in 23 Chapters*. New York: HarperCollins, 1999.

Rosenstiel, Tom. *Strange Bedfellows: How Television and the Presidential Candidates Changed American Politics, 1992*. New York: Hyperion, 1993.

Wiener, Norbert. *Cybernetics: or, Control and Communication in the Animal and the Machine*. Cambridge, Mass.: MIT Press, 1948.

Wright, Robert. *NonZero: The Logic of Human Destiny*. New York: Pantheon Books, 2000.

NOTES

1. Rosenstiel, 55–65.
2. This is true also for the interaction between the brain and the rest of the body. "Nervous system behavior is to some extent self-generated in loops; brain activity leads to movement, which leads to further sensation and perception and still further movement. The layers and the loops between them are the most intricate of any object we know, and they are dynamic; they continually change." Edelman, 1992, 29.
3. "What is learning? What changes occur to nerve cells when the brain (or the abdominal ganglion) acquires a new habit or a change in its behavior? The central nervous system consists of lots of nerve cells, down each of which electrical signals travel; and synapses, which are junctions between nerve cells. When an electrical nerve signal reaches a synapse, it must transfer to chemical agent, like a train passenger catching a ferry across a sea channel, before resuming its electrical journey. Kandel's attention quickly focused on these synapses between neurons. Learning seems to be a change in their properties. Thus when a sea slug habituates to a false alarm, the synapse between the

receiving, sensory neuron and the neuron that moves the gill is somehow weakened. Conversely, when the sea slug is sensitized to the stimulus, the synapse is strengthened." Ridley, 223.

4. Edelman has a far more precise variation on this theme, which he calls "reentry." "To explain how categorization may occur, we can use the workings of what I have called a 'classification couple' in the brain. This is a minimal unit consisting of two functionally different maps made up of neuronal groups and connected by reentry. Each map independently receives signals from other brain maps or from the world (in this example the signals come from the world). Within a certain time period, reentrant signaling strongly connects certain active combinations of neuronal groups in one map to different combinations in the other map." Edelman, 1992, 87.

5. Rosenstiel, 63.

6. Jacobs wrote about this in *Death and Life* as the tendency for successful cities to destroy themselves: "These forces, in the form that they work for ill, are: the tendency for outstandingly successful diversity in cities to destroy itself; the tendency for massive single elements in cities (many of which are necessary and otherwise desirable) to cast a deadening influence; the tendency for population instability to counter the growth of diversity; and the tendency for both public and private money either to glut or to starve development and change." Jacobs, 1961, 242.

7. . . . Positive feedback is also an important tool for understanding social or technological revolutions: "These meshworks of mutually supporting innovations (coal-iron-steam-cotton) are well-known to historians of technology. They existed long before the nineteenth century (e.g., the interlocking web formed by the horseshoe, the horse harness, and triennial rotation which was behind the agricultural intensification at the turn of the millennium), and they occurred afterward, as in the meshwork of oil, electricity, steel, and synthetic materials that contributed to the second industrial revolution. Nonetheless, as important as they were, autocatalytic loops of technologies were not complex enough to create a self-sustained industrial takeoff. Before the 1800s, as we noted, these intensifications often led back to depictions of resources and diminishing returns. Negative feedback eventually checked the turbulent growth generated by positive feedback." De Landa, 1997, 77.

8. As usual, Jane Jacobs was quick to adapt these new ideas to her understanding of the city: "The analogy that comes to mind is faulty feedback. The conception of electronic feedback has become familiar with the development of computers and automated machinery, where one of the end products of an act or series of acts by the machine is a signal which modifies and guides the next act. A similar feedback process, regulated chemically rather than electronically, is now believed to modify some of the behavior of cells. A report in the *New York Times* explains it thus:

> " 'The presence of an end product in the milieu of a cell causes the machinery that produces the end product to slow down or to stop. This form of cell behavior Dr. [Van R.] Potter [of the University of Wisconsin Medical School] characterized as "intelligent." In contrast, a cell that has changed or mutated behaves like an "idiot" in that it continues without feedback regulation to produce even materials that it does not require.'
>
> "I think that last sentence is a fair description of the behavior of city localities where the success of diversity destroys itself.

"Suppose we think of successful city areas, for all their extraordinary and intricate economic and social order, as faulty in this fashion. In creating city success, we human beings have created marvels, but we left out feedback. What can we do with cities to make up for this omission?" Jacobs, 1961, 251–52.

9. Wiener, 7.

10. "In short, our inner economy must contain an assembly of thermostats, automatic hydrogen-ion-concentration controls, governors, and the like, which would be adequate for a great chemical plant. These are what we know collectively as our homeostatic mechanism." Ibid., 115.

11. Ecosystems too abound with feedback systems. As one of the characters in Jane Jacobs's latest book says, "Here's a pleasing example of this category—a positive loop in a California coastal redwood forest. Mature redwoods require enormous amounts of water, about twice as much, on average, as rainfall delivers to their habitats. . . . A coastal redwood lives to an age of about two thousand years; quite a demonstration of successful survival. Here's how their seemingly inadequate supply situation is overcome. With their fine and luxuriant needles, the trees intercept fog and strip its moisture; in effect, they take water straight from clouds. During a dry but foggy night, each tall redwood douses the ground beneath it with as much water as if there had been a drenching rainstorm. This beneficent process works as a loop. The growth of the trees is fed in good part from the fog. Taller growth gives trees access to higher—hence additional—fog. Additional fog feeds still higher growth. And so on. Because of the height-fog loop, the trees themselves participate in keeping their environment stable." Jacobs, 2000, 93.

12. Dean.

13. "There is already one technology that appears to generate at least one aspect of a spiritual experience. This experimental technology is called Brain Generated Music (BGM), pioneered by NeuroSonics, a small company in Baltimore, Maryland, of which I am a director. BGM is a brain-wave biofeedback system capable of evoking an experience called the Relaxation Response, which is associated with deep relaxation. The BGM user attaches three disposable leads to her head. A personal computer then monitors the user's brain waves to determine her unique alpha wavelength. Alpha waves, which are in the range of eight to thirteen cycles per second (cps), are associated with a deep meditative state, as compared to beta waves (in the range of thirteen to twenty-eight cps), which are associated with routine conscious thought. Music is then generated by the computer, according to an algorithm that transforms the user's own brain-wave signal." Kurzweil, 157.

14. Wiener, 158.

15. ". . . One of the directions of work which the realm of ideas of the Macy meetings has suggested concerns the importance of the notion and the technique of communication in the social system. It is certainly true that the social system is an organization like the individual, that it is bounded together by a system of communication, and that it has a dynamics in which circular processes of a feedback nature play an important part." Ibid., 24.

16. "The program he proposed in 1898 was to halt the growth of London and also repopulate the countryside, where villages were declining, by building a new kind of town—the Garden City, where the city poor might again live close to

nature. So they might earn their livings, industry was to be set up in the Garden City, for while Howard was not planning cities, he was not planning dormitory suburbs either. His aim was the creation of self-sufficient small towns, really very nice towns if you were docile and had no plans of your own and did not mind spending your life among others who had no plans of their own. As in all Utopias, the right to have plans of any significance belonged only to the planners in charge." Jacobs, 1961, 17.

17. "Ebenezer Howard's vision of the Garden City would seem almost feudal to us. He seems to have thought that members of the industrial working classes would stay neatly in their class, and even at the same job within their class; that agricultural workers would stay in agriculture; that businessmen (the enemy) would hardly exist as a significant force in his Utopia; and that planners could go about their good and lofty work, unhampered by rude nay-saying from the untrained." Ibid., 289.

18. "Howard's greatest contribution was less in recasting the physical form of the city than in developing the organic concepts that underlay this form; for though he was no biologist like Patrick Geddes, he nevertheless brought to the city the essential biological criteria of dynamic equilibrium and organic balance: balance as between city and country in a larger ecological pattern, and balance between the varied functions of the city: above all, balance through the positive control of growth in the limitation in area, number, and density of occupation, and the practice of reproduction (colonization) when the community was threatened by such an undue increase in size as would lead only to lapse of function." Mumford, 1961, 516.

19. Mumford, 1962, 148–77.

20. Wiener had made the same connection a decade before in *Cybernetics*: "It has been commented on by many writers, such as D'Arcy Thompson, that each form of organization has an upper limit of size, beyond which it will not function. Thus the insect organization is limited by the length of tubing over which the spiracle method of bringing air by diffusion directly to the breathing tissues will function; a land animal cannot be so big that the legs or other portions of contact with the ground will be crushed by the weight; a tree is limited by the mechanism for transferring water and minerals from the roots to the leaves, and the products of photosynthesis from the leaves to the roots, and so on." Wiener, 150.

21. Posted on the Slashdot site: www.slashdot.org.

22. Technically, Slashdot moderators don't give each post a grade on the scale. Posts start out life at 0 or 1 (depending on whether their authors are registered users of the system). Moderators can then "spend" a moderation point rating a post either up or down. A post that starts life at 1, and receives three positive points and one negative point would be at Level 3, because 1 plus 3 minus 1 equals 3.

23. Jacobs, 2000, 154. A related idea is the pricing mechanism of market economies as an information-processing system, as described by the libertarian demigod Friedrich von Hayek. "Long before the fall of communism, Hayek identified its oft-overlooked weakness: Not only did it fail to offer an incentive to work hard; it forced signals connecting supply and demand to travel a tortuous path that invited distortion." Wright, 199.

24. Interview conducted with Rob Malda, April 2000.

Questions for Critical Reading

1. As Johnson's title might suggest, "feedback" plays a central role in this essay. What does Johnson mean by *feedback*? What definitions seem to be in operation in his text? Perform a critical reading of his text to develop a definition and provide citations to support your understandings of the term.

2. What is "homeostasis"? What role does it play in the media? in our bodies? Develop an understanding of the term by locating specific quotations from Johnson's text.

3. According to Johnson, what makes user-generated content systems like Slashdot successful? Can you think of other examples of self-regulating online communities?

Exploring Context

1. Spend some time exploring Slashdot (slashdot.org). Does it continue to exhibit the qualities that Johnson delineates? Is it still a successful self-regulating community? What makes it successful? Use your response to Question 3 of Questions for Critical Reading in evaluating the site.

2. The Stack tool of Digg Labs (labs.digg.com/stack) provides a real-time visual representation of the kind of feedback systems Johnson discusses in relation to the news and media. Based on what you see in the Stack, does Digg use a positive or negative feedback system? Does it reach homeostasis? Apply your definition of *homeostasis* from Question 2 of Questions for Critical Reading.

3. According to Johnson, CNN's decision to share its news feed with local affiliates changed the entire media system, making it more bottom-up than top-down. Visit CNN's Web site at cnn.com; does it suggest a bottom-up system?

Questions for Connecting

1. How can Johnson's insights about feedback help explain the success and failure of small groups, as explored by James Surowiecki in "Committees, Juries, and Teams: The *Columbia* Disaster and How Small Groups Can Be Made to Work" (p. 440)? Do groups achieve homeostasis? What happens when groups experience positive or negative feedback? Use your definition of *homeostasis* from Question 2 of Questions for Critical Reading.

2. Does Leslie Savan's description of advertising and pop talk in "What's Black, Then White, and Said All Over?" (p. 363) reflect a top-down or bottom-up system? How can systems like Slashdot change cultural practices like pop talk? Use your work with Slashdot from Question 3 of Questions for Critical Reading and Question 1 of Exploring Context as you consider these questions.

3. Marshall Poe in "The Hive" (p. 264) examines another popular Web publication, Wikipedia. In what ways is that site similar to Slashdot? What systems of

feedback are at work? What makes these sites so successful? Incorporate your responses about Slashdot from Questions for Critical Reading and Exploring Context.

Language Matters

1. At one point in this selection Johnson uses a sentence fragment (see if you can find it!). Why does Johnson use it? In what situations might a sentence fragment be acceptable?

2. Quotations in academic writing must be of appropriate length. Find a significant passage from the essay and choose the shortest and longest useful quotations from the passage. How short is *too* short? How long is too long? How might you use quotations of different lengths for different ends?

3. The classic rhetorical triangle is composed of receiver, sender, and message. Using this essay, design a new shape to explain this rhetorical situation: What additional elements should be considered? Would the inclusion of style make a rhetorical square? What elements would be in a rhetorical hexagon?

Assignments for Writing

1. Using Johnson's observations on the working rules of Slashdot, write a paper in which you propose strategies for incorporating feedback systems into news media. Incorporate your work with Slashdot from Questions for Critical Reading and Exploring Context, and consider these questions: Why is Slashdot "a virtual democracy," and why isn't the news media one? Is the news now a bottom-up system? Is it possible to incorporate feedback systems into the news?

2. Throughout this essay Johnson is concerned with making information networks successful. Drawing from Johnson's ideas, write a paper that determines the best practices for organizing and administering an information network. You may either choose a specific type of network, like a news organization or an online wiki, or write of practices that would work for many types of networks. What role should self-reflection play in an information network? What is the role of the individual in a decentralized system? How can a system promote a diverse perspective? You might want to construct your argument using your work with Wikipedia from Question 3 of Questions for Connecting.

3. What are the key factors to a successful collaboration? Write a paper in which you specify the crucial elements in the success of collaborative efforts, using Johnson's ideas about feedback in your argument. Consider: What is the function of a feedback loop? What is the role of self-regulation in a successful collaboration? You may want to use your response about feedback from Question 1 of Questions for Connecting in making your argument.

MICHAEL KIMMELMAN

Michael Kimmelman, the chief art critic for the *New York Times*, believes "art is too important and interesting to be left to the art world." A Harvard and Yale graduate and a Pulitzer Prize finalist, Kimmelman has contributed to *Egg: The Art Show* as well as the *New York Review of Books*, and in 1998 he published *Portraits: Talking with Artists at the Met, the Modern, the Louvre, and Elsewhere*. Kimmelman is currently working in Europe and writes the column "Abroad" for the *New York Times*, in which he explores culture and society all across Europe—from the cultural and societal ties of bullfighting in Spain to the anxieties of Russian artists and writers about artistic freedom under the current government. The selection printed here comes from his 2005 book, *The Accidental Masterpiece: On the Art of Life and Vice Versa*.

The Accidental Masterpiece

On the Art of Life and Vice Versa

Michael Kimmelman

As Kimmelman explains in the book's introduction, *The Accidental Masterpiece* is "about how creating, collecting, and even just appreciating art can make living a daily masterpiece," since "even the most ordinary daily affair . . . is enriched by the lessons that can be gleaned from art." He also offers the same argument in reverse—that the world of art can be enriched by even the most ordinary daily affair: There is an art to collecting lightbulbs. "Good art," Kimmelman said in a 2005 interview, is "about encouraging people to look more closely at what's around them."

"The Art of Collecting Lightbulbs" tells the story of Hugh Francis Hicks, a dentist who has assembled an astonishing collection of lightbulbs and lightbulb-related objects. Kimmelman examines more collectors of the ordinary and not-so-ordinary and the art that has emerged from their work. "Serious obsessives," motivated more by an appreciation of their objects than by the desire for fame and fortune often present in the professional art world, have made extraordinary contributions to art through their ordinary collections. Kimmelman proposes that all modern collections, whether lightbulbs in a basement or paintings in a museum, owe a debt to pioneers of the practice who assembled "wonder cabinets." These "cabinets of curiosities . . . meant to encapsulate the world in microcosm," composed order and art from the chaos of everyday life.

▶ TAGS: *technology,* **aesthetic boundaries,** **art,** *creativity*

The Art of Collecting Lightbulbs

A few years ago I met Hugh Francis Hicks, a dentist in downtown Baltimore with an office on the parlor floor of a big old brownstone just up the street from the Walters Art Museum. One afternoon he took me into his building's basement to show me a collection he has been putting together for nearly seventy years. Dr. Hicks, who died at the age of seventy-nine in 2002, collected lightbulbs.

He had 75,000 of them. You probably won't be surprised to learn that this was the largest collection of lightbulbs in the world. Dr. Hicks had officially turned it into a museum, the Mount Vernon Museum of Incandescent Lighting. It contained what used to be the world's biggest bulb (at 50,000 watts and four feet high, it was the size of a shrub) and also the smallest, which you could see only by looking through a microscope. Edison's early experimental bulbs were there, with their original Bristol-board filaments. One of them still worked. The bulbs were decoratively arranged in crowded glass-and-wood cases, like the ones that turn-of-the-previous-century museums used to have, the cases accompanied by yellowed typewritten labels full of arcane information, detailing the source of the name Mazda (a Zoroastrian sun god) and the history of tungsten filaments. Dr. Hicks had what lightbulb collectors evidently considered to be an incredible collection of "B" type Mazdas. He amassed a definitive variety of switches, sockets, and adapters, and he also had many one-of-a-kind, or nearly one-of-a-kind, treasures: the headlamps from Himmler's Mercedes and three lights from the *Enola Gay*. There were also joke bulbs shaped like Dick Tracy and Betty Boop, men's ties that lighted up, and a display documenting the history of Christmas lighting. A kind of rabbit warren, the basement included a room at the end with a big round table covered by a plastic flowered tablecloth where Dr. Hicks served cookies to visiting schoolchildren. Before visiting, I phoned ahead, and he met me in his office—there were no patients around—then took me downstairs and turned on the lights.

Why do people collect? The consolation of art comes in many forms. For some it is making, for others it is having. For Dr. Hicks, it was the hunting and gathering of illuminating trophies. For many of us it may simply be appreciating what people like Dr. Hicks have collected—it may be just looking at constellations of someone else's extraordinary things. Dr. Hicks said that his obsession began in the crib. His mother noticed one day that he was bored with his toys, so for some reason she gave him an old lightbulb to play with. He survived this brush with danger and began devising school projects entailing electricity. In time, he discovered other bulb enthusiasts and began to trade. He was not above thievery. Once, on vacation in Paris, he spotted a row of 1920s tungsten bulbs along a wall of a Metro station and hurriedly swiped one, whereupon the whole station went pitch-black because the bulbs were wired so that if one were removed, they would all go out. Unable to fit the stolen bulb back into the socket, he decided to flee. At his museum, he displayed his booty in a case marked "Hot Types."

Psychiatrists came to interview him about why he collected, and he told them about William J. Hammer, one of Edison's engineers, who before 1900 collected 130,000 different electric bulbs, which were evidently later dispersed. Hammer died the month that Dr. Hicks was born. "Do you believe in reincarnation?" he asked the psychiatrists. They seemed stupefied.

Some people collect because collecting can be a great art if earnestly engaged in. That is why we enjoy looking at great collections, even if we are not collectors. Collecting is a way to bring order to the world, which is what museums, our public collectors, do. It is also a way to define some idiosyncratic niche for the collector, as art does for an artist. There are people who collect candy wrappers without the candy, thimbles, and inedible food. If you look up Dr. Hicks's museum on the Internet, you will find links to various collections of technological artifacts, from slide rules to chopsticks to pocket calculators to mimeograph machines. Over the years, I have visited a museum of trash and the basement of a churchgoing teetotaler in New Jersey who had collected several thousand miniature liquor bottles and several dozen miniature Vargas pinups from old cigarette packs. (He didn't smoke, either.) I have toured the Nicholas Roerich Museum on the Upper West Side of Manhattan, an obscure shrine to a once-famous Russian mystic (or charlatan, depending on which accounts of him you read), which collects his eccentric paintings. I have seen a few of the cars and planes that James Turrell, the sculptor of light, has collected in Arizona. Turrell is like Donald Judd and Dan Flavin, archetypal American minimalists, purveyors of the sparest sort of modern art, who were in their private lives aspiring packrats. Like the teetotaler who loved liquor bottles, Turrell is the quintessential paradoxical collector. His art consists of the most ephemeral and insubstantial thing of all, light, while

> Collecting is a way to bring order to the world, which is what museums, our public collectors, do.

his collecting entails big bulky machines, which I must assume fill some private need, aside from the practical one of getting him from one place to another, and this other need may be partly aesthetic but is also, no doubt, psychological. Judd collected cars, modern furniture (a warehouse full of it), Indian crafts, and buildings along with books; Flavin, who also made art out of the light cast by colored fluorescent tubes, collected Stickley furniture, Rembrandt etchings, Asian pottery, Indian jewelry, nineteenth-century American drawings, Japanese prints, and sketches by modernists he admired, like Brancusi and Malevich.

It is taken for granted that Rembrandts are worth collecting because they are art and expensive, but collectors, as Dr. Hicks proves, will collect pretty much everything, without necessarily thinking that what they collect has aesthetic or monetary value. Prestige, like taste in art, is often in the eye of the collector, and true value may be greatest when the value is only symbolic. Collected objects become symbolic when they lose their utilitarian purpose. A former prisoner in a Stalinist labor camp, for example, collected keys to locks that were no longer in use. A key is no longer just a key if it belonged to the Bastille, nor a sewing kit just a sewing kit if Betsy Ross sewed with it. As Philipp Blom, a writer on collecting, has put it: "As often as not the objects collected are the cast-offs of society, overtaken by technological advance, used and disposable, outmoded, disregarded, unfashionable." Their uselessness becomes their asset: They turn into totems and fragments of the lost worlds they came from. So the arm of Teresa of Avila is prized not because it is practical to medical science as a specimen of muscle and bone but because it is connected, as Blom says, "with otherworldliness, as a key to heaven, to a world infinitely richer than our everyday existence." It becomes a holy relic.

Just as art promises wonderment—an access to a realm beyond the everyday, through the experience of which we may understand the everyday better—a collection of things, even everyday things, promises wonderment, too, as these things become no longer everyday, having been enshrined by a collector. Walter Benjamin, who collected books, said that "one of the finest memories of a collector is the moment when he rescued a book to which he might never have given a thought, much less a wishful look, because he found it lonely and abandoned on the marketplace and bought it to give it its freedom—the way the prince bought a beautiful slave girl in 'The Arabian Nights.'" He added, "To a book collector, you see, the true freedom of all books is somewhere on his shelves."

For Benjamin, collecting makes sense of a senseless world. Collectors take up "arms against dispersal. The great collector is touched to the core by the confusion and the dispersal in which things are found in this world." Collectors impose their own private rationale on what they own. They make order out of chaos. Albert C. Barnes made a fortune at the turn of the last century with an over-the-counter antiseptic remedy called Argyrol, and with the money he made put together one of the world's most spectacular and idiosyncratic collections: He amassed great Cézannes, Matisses, and African art, along with metal knickknacks and folk doodads like door locks and a tiny acorn sculpture in the shape of a cricket. Famously, he displayed these all together at a mansion outside Philadelphia, in odd, mixed-up arrangements, seemingly arbitrary to the uninitiated—arrangements he vigorously explained according to an elaborate private dogma of decoration, partly inspired by John Dewey, which he and his cultish disciples, at a school he founded on the premises specifically to perpetuate his artistic beliefs, preached with a kind of quasi-religious fervor through pamphlets and books. Pictures might be put together to convey a triangular or diagonal scheme that Dr. Barnes thought he perceived in their compositions. A great Seurat could thereby share real estate with *Balloon Man,* a painting by somebody Dr. Barnes came across named Liz Clark. Works that looked optimistically attributed to El Greco, along with dozens of pinheaded Renoirs, mostly awful but some great, hung with sublime landmarks of the most intelligent sort of modern art like the mural by Henri Matisse that Barnes, in a stroke of genius, commissioned. Matisse evidently enjoyed Barnes's eccentricity. He declared the weird juxtapositions a help to the public, since people could "understand a lot of things that the academics don't teach," which was true. Nobody else looked at art the way Barnes did. Self-taught in this regard, from a working-class background, having earned his way through medical school playing professional baseball, he developed a notorious chip on his shoulder toward what he considered the art establishment, and he feuded publicly with anyone he thought hoity-toity. His collection was only open to "the plain people, that is men and women who gain their livelihood by daily toil in shops, factories, schools, stores, and similar places." The eminent art historian Erwin Panofsky supposedly had to dress up like a chauffeur to sneak in.

Nine months before he died in 1951 at the age of seventy-nine, when his Packard collided with a ten-ton truck, Barnes decided, in another stroke of eccentric philanthropy, to bequeath everything to a small, historically black school in Chester County, Pennsylvania, called Lincoln University, which had little, if any, experience with art collecting. He stipulated that the school maintain the museum untouched where it was, ensuring years of legal wrangling, financial crisis, and limited access for almost everyone, including plain people, to some of the most important modern art in the world—that is, until 2004. Overriding Barnes's will, a judge ordered the straitened museum to be reconstituted in Philadelphia, as a partial simulacrum of itself, more convenient to tourists and with money from several local foundations that had made its move downtown a condition of their support. The decision would have horrified Dr. Barnes, who acted, you could say, like a jealous lover (the erotic aspect of collecting has always been much commented on): He wanted to control these objects of his desire, even beyond the grave.

He was not merely being perverse. His collection, he realized, was itself a novel expression of creativity. You might never have noticed a connection between Persian miniature painting and the early American modernist painter Marsden Hartley unless Barnes had put them together. His unorthodox installations, so unlike what other museums did, inclined you to look at his art fresh, which is what museums should do. Barnes imposed himself onto great works of Georges Seurat and Matisse by insisting they be viewed only as he saw fit, which meant that a colorful

> **Not all collectors are eccentrics, of course.**

and ornery former baseball player and medical entrepreneur declared a kind of aesthetic authority over cultural figures of enduring consequence—not a perfectly defensible position for advocates of serious art who believe art should really be as accessible as reasonably possible to the public. But Barnes (whose Argyrol, by the way, was a remedy for conjunctivitis in newborns, an aid to seeing) opened more than a few eyes with his display techniques while demonstrating that there was an art to collecting—and, by extension, to appreciating a great collection.

It is a fair question to ask whether collectors like Barnes devise their own museums because they are exhibitionists or promoters of some private philosophy or have a sense of civic responsibility, or all of the above. Not all collectors are eccentrics, of course. Most aren't, although the best often are: Out of passion and private conviction, they collect what may not yet be ratified, as opposed to what fashion and the market already prize, in the belief that public taste should someday catch up. The combination of public service and the strength of one's conviction is what defines an admirable collector. Like artists, collectors may also collect in a vain hope of achieving immortality. Collections, as Blom says (and this certainly pertains to Barnes's), "have always had overtones of burial and interment. Graves are filled with objects symbolic of future use, shoring up the deceased against irrevocable loss, allowing him a symbolic afterlife with all the comforts of the here and now. The greater a collection, the more precious its contents, the more it must be reminiscent of a mausoleum, left behind by a ruler determined not to be forgotten, not to have his memory squabbled over and his most immediate self disintegrate to dust."

This even applies to benign collectors like Dr. Hicks, whose museums of artifacts can have a fascination that is indistinguishable from that of art museums. I don't mean that, aesthetically, lightbulbs or slide rules are as compelling as paintings. I mean that the museum, whether it is a collection of art or something else, derives from the old *Kunst- und Wunderkammern*, or art and wonder cabinets, and it retains its original aspirations to wonderment.

Kunst- und Wunderkammern began to proliferate more or less in the sixteenth century, the result of humanist curiosity, technological advances in things like optics and engineering, a revival of interest in antique texts that were preoccupied with the marvelous, and global exploration, which exposed Europe to what seemed like a strange new world. Sophisticated banking systems also made the exchange of rare and precious worldly goods easier. Trading empires, like the Dutch and Venetian, fostered and facilitated rich collectors who sought the most wonderful objects. Wonderment in the sixteenth and seventeenth centuries came to be perceived as a kind of middle state between ignorance and knowledge, and wonder cabinets were theaters of the marvelous, museums of accumulated curiosities, proving God's ingenuity. They contained whatever was the biggest, the smallest, the rarest, the most exquisite, the most bizarre, the most grotesque. Art, astrolabes, armor—man-made wonders—were cheek by jowl with monkeys' teeth and pathological anomalies like human horns. A German doctor named Lorenz Hoffman had a typical *Kunst- und Wunderkammer*: He owned paintings by Albrecht Dürer and Lucas Cranach, a skeleton of a newborn, two dozen miniature spoons hidden within a cherry pit, an armband made of elks' hooves, mummies, and various rare musical instruments. In the middle of the sixteenth century the Dutch collector Hubert Goltzius could list 968 collections he knew of in the Low Countries, Germany, Austria, Switzerland, France, and Italy. In Amsterdam, nearly 100 private cabinets of curiosities were documented between 1600 and 1740. Calvinist propriety discouraged the Dutch from displays of wealth in public, but in the privacy of their homes they stuffed fancy mahogany cupboards with coins, cameos, and statues, capped off by precious porcelain, the archetype for modern bourgeois drawing rooms with their obligatory glass-fronted cabinet in which to show off the family china.

Wonder cabinets of the past were, in part, meant to encapsulate the world in microcosm: again, order from chaos. Blom reminds us about Philipp Hainhofer, the great Augsburg envoy and collector, who, in designing various cabinets for princes, devised one of the most extraordinary pieces of seventeenth-century furniture: a vast chest, topped by a huge rare Seychelle nut, in which objects were methodically arranged to represent the animal, plant, and mineral worlds, the four continents, and various human activities, with painted *vanitas* scenes on the front to remind everyone that death is part of life. The drawers contained exotica like bezoars, calcareous concretions from the stomachs of Persian goats, believed to be antidotes to poison, vastly expensive; musk pouches; cups of *lignum Guaiacum*, a West Indian wood of medicinal powers, and objects "for vexation," like gloves with no openings for the hands, fake fruit, and pictures that came into focus only when viewed through special mirrors.

CHARLES WILLSON PEALE, *The Artist in His Museum*

These early cabinets of wonderment became occasions for collectors to exercise their artistic skills at display. The art of museum exhibition has its roots in this impulse. Frederik Ruysch, a Dutch anatomist and famous collector, concocted wild tableaux made of flowers, skulls, kidney stones, and diseased organs in his *Wunderkammer* in Amsterdam. One of the first museums in the United States, which belonged to the Philadelphia artist Charles Willson Peale, was a kind of *Wunderkammer,* containing fossils and stuffed birds as well as paintings. In 1822, Peale did a painting of himself holding open a curtain onto his museum, like a carnival barker inviting visitors into the big top. Collecting, for Peale and the others, put the world together like pieces of a puzzle.

While driving to Dr. Hicks's in Baltimore, I noticed a sign on the highway for a museum of hunting decoys in Havre de Grace, Maryland, so I pulled off at the exit for a visit. Havre de Grace is a sleepy place on the Susquehanna Flats, where the Susquehanna River meets the Chesapeake Bay. It is duck hunter's nirvana, although a series of laws during the 1930s and '40s curtailed market-gunning or hunting ducks for restaurants. The Decoy Museum preserves hundreds of duck decoys by local carvers. Astonishingly, the carvers are also preserved behind glass, right there in life-size, full-length polyvinylacetate figures, like decoys, you might say, of the decoy makers. There's a big tableau that lights up when you press a button, à la Madame Tussaud's, showing local carvers sitting around a stove in one of the town's decoy shops in 1942. Display cases are dedicated to different expert decoy makers. At a glance, I couldn't always tell the difference between the works of R. Madison Mitchell, a local funeral director, who was evidently the Giotto of Havre de Grace, and the works of Bob McGaw, who perfected a way of decorating his decoys that, I learned, is called scratch painting. But no doubt the distinctions are obvious to the people who have looked at the decoys a lot longer than I did. Connoisseurship entails making distinctions through slow, comparative observation, whether it involves paintings or wooden ducks.

Partly it was a desire for a more methodical approach to collected objects, a system for spreading connoisseurship, that ushered in a new age of museums two centuries ago. Museums began to specialize. Elks' hooves went one way, paintings another. The balance tipped from delight toward instruction. The new museums set out more systematically to categorize things, to create order, or at least to imply that there is an order to life. René Descartes, who called wonderment the first of all the passions, also wrote that an excess of wonder can "pervert the use of reason." The age of wonder cabinets turned into the age of Descartes and the encyclopedists.

But the spirit of the wonder cabinets never altogether died. Art museums, and even modern collections of light bulbs, though they may not be true wonder cabinets, preserve what's marvelous to show us what is rare and what we can't see otherwise, and thereby help us see, with heightened curiosity, what is around us. Thomas Dent Mütter was a Philadelphia surgeon who went to Paris in the 1830s, when it was the medical mecca. There he saw hospital wards arranged according to diseases, so that doctors could compare the conditions of patients suffering from the same things; he also saw collections of tumors, aneurysms, bones, and so on. He returned to Philadelphia inspired by the systematic connection of morbid anatomy and clinical pathology. Soon he began to build his own teaching collection of anatomical and pathological specimens for the benefit of medical students. In the nineteenth century, medical students regularly learned about scientific anomalies like human horns or conjoined twins by looking at collections of dried dissections, wax models of skin diseases, and papier-mâché models of reproductive organs. To this end, Mütter accumulated hundreds of air-dried specimens, specimens preserved in alcohol, plaster casts, watercolors, and oil paintings—1,344 items—all of which he bequeathed in 1858 to the College of Physicians of Philadelphia, a private medical society with some of its own oddments whose founders included lettered men like Benjamin Rush, a signer of the Declaration of Independence.

Mütter understood novelty as a kind of collector's bait. So he also collected the bladder stones removed from Chief Justice John Marshall by Philip Syng Physick, the father of American surgery, in 1831, and the deformed skeleton of

> **The balance tipped from delight toward instruction.**

a woman whose rib cage had been compressed by tying her corset too tightly. In time, the college added to his oddments. The Mütter Museum, as it came to be called, now occupies part of a big, somewhat forbidding Georgian building behind a tall iron gate in the center of the city. A two-story anachronism of polished wood cases, thick burgundy curtains, and brass lamps, it looks much as one imagines Peale's museum to have looked. In recent years it has streamlined its display, making it more attractive to tourists but somewhat skewing the public's perception of the historic function of the museum by showing only what's most striking or unusual or catchy. The collection today boasts of having the connected livers of the Siamese twins Chang and Eng; a piece of the thorax of John Wilkes Booth; a tumor removed from the jaw of President Grover Cleveland; the skeleton of a seven-foot-six-inch man from Kentucky who suffered from a condition called acromegaly, a hyperactive pituitary gland; a bound foot from China; the remains of the so-called Soap Lady, whose corpse decomposed into a grayish white fatty, soapy wax substance called adipocere; and more than two thousand objects removed from choking victims, the objects carefully arranged in narrow drawers in a filing cabinet according to type: meat, nuts, pins, buttons, toy jacks. These last items came to the museum in 1924 from a pioneering bronchoesophagologist named Chevalier Jackson, who devised a technique for extracting them from patients' throats.

J. DENNIS WELSCH
Dr. Chevalier Jackson pointing to diagram of safety pin lodged in throat

In the collection is also a photograph of Dr. Jackson himself, looking a bit like Sigmund Freud, unsmiling, in bow tie and a white doctor's gown with natty trim, stiffly pointing to a large diagram on an easel showing a safety pin stuck in a throat.

It is now possible to see much of what the Mütter keeps on view as art: 20 Théodore Géricault, the great French Romantic artist, painted severed limbs; Kiki Smith, the contemporary artist, has made sculptures of flayed figures; Nayland Blake and Damien Hirst have in recent years devised artful arrangements of medical instruments; and to see the Soap Lady, her mouth wide open, is to be put in mind of the paintings by Zoran Music, a Holocaust survivor who became a painter in Paris, of screaming figures. The Mütter's dried skeleton of a newborn child, hanging by its outstretched arms, head back, can even make you think of some great crucifixion by Peter Paul Rubens, with Jesus's eyes upturned, as if in a state of spiritual ecstasy.

But I wouldn't want to push the connection too far; I only wish to stress how a place like the Mütter, notwithstanding its original medical function, can seem neatly to blur the distinction between science and art by dwelling in the marvelous. Its collection causes us to react in a way that, like art, goes beyond reason and touches our nerves. Was Dr. Mütter motivated merely by scientific inquiry? Maybe he was, but many collections, including his, suggest an obsession on the part of the collector that exceeds practicality. A Manhattan psychoanalyst, Werner Muensterberger, once wrote a book called *Collecting: An Unruly Passion*, in which he argued that collecting is, among other things, more or less a form of displaced childhood in which the collector longs for parental comfort, his or her collected objects becoming, like sucked thumbs, stand-ins for a mother's breast. They are the lightbulb in Dr. Hicks's crib. I am not a collector. I can't say. Collecting, the issue of financial investment aside, is clearly some form of consolation to many collectors, as is its appreciation by others. Beyond that, it can be a wonder and a mystery.

In his prologue to *Invisible Man*, Ralph Ellison wrote, "In my hole in the basement there are exactly 1,369 lights. I've wired the ceiling, every inch of it. And not with fluorescent bulbs, but with the older, more expensive-to-operate kind, the filament kind. . . . When I finish all four walls, then I'll start on the floor. Just how that will go, I don't know. Yet when you have lived invisible for as long as I have you develop a certain ingenuity."

Dr. Hicks, our lightbulb man with his basement museum, told me about those psychiatrists who came to interview him. "They were something," he said. "They didn't blink their eyes. They were interviewing collectors from all over the world. After spending $4 million, they concluded that collectors collect for the fascination of an object and for no other reason. Heck, I would have told them that for $1 million."

Questions for Critical Reading

1. In what ways is collecting an art form? You will need to reread this essay closely to form your response. Look for passages from the essay that illustrate Kimmelman's points about the connection between collecting and art to support your response.

2. According to Kimmelman, what is the connection between wonder cabinets and art? Can you locate any modern equivalent to the wonder cabinet? Is your example also a form of art?

3. What connection does Kimmelman suggest between medicine and art? Does such a connection still exist today? What makes art "art"? What connection does it have to science?

Exploring Context

1. Spend some time on eBay (ebay.com) browsing through the categories. Given all the objects collected there, could you argue that eBay is a kind of virtual museum? Locate passages from Kimmelman to support your position, and draw from your understanding of collecting as art from Question 1 of Questions for Critical Reading.

2. Visit a local museum, and then visit the Web site for that museum. How is collecting represented differently in the real and virtual spaces?

3. PostSecret (postsecret.blogspot.com) is a public art project in which people design postcards that reveal a secret about themselves. Review the most recent collection of postcards. How does each card function as art, and how does the collection as a whole function as art? Is the group of cards more of an art form than one individual postcard? Use Kimmelman's essay to support your position.

Questions for Connecting

1. Kimmelman discusses the Mütter Museum's display of medical anomalies. How can Kimmelman's analysis further explain people's fascination with before and after photos as explored by Julia Serano in "Before and After: Class and Body Transformations" (p. 392)? Do such photos function as a kind of art? Do collections like the Mütter Museum's participate in systems of class? Explain your responses. You may want to use your experience visiting a museum from Question 2 of Exploring Context.

2. What is the role of human dignity in collecting? Apply Francis Fukuyama's discussion of human dignity in his essay of the same title (p. 142) to Kimmelman's analysis. Does Fukuyama's discussion of complexity, in which the whole is greater than the sum of its parts, underscore the power of collecting as Kimmelman describes it?

3. The wonder cabinets that Kimmelman discusses seem related to the public display of Evita's corpse examined by Diana Taylor in "False Identifications: Minority Populations Mourn Diana" (p. 454). In what ways do art and mourning perform similar social functions? Extend Taylor's analysis to Kimmelman's essay. Use your work on wonder cabinets, medicine, and art from Questions 2 and 3 of Questions for Critical Reading.

Language Matters

1. Select a section of the essay and then locate and remove the topic sentence of each paragraph in that section. What strategies did you use to find the topic sentences? How does removing a paragraph's topic sentence affect the meaning of the paragraph?

2. Introductions do a lot of important work in your papers: They introduce the authors, the essays, and, most important, your position or argument. How does Kimmelman introduce this chapter? How effective is it as an introduction? Why would you want (or not want) to open your paper that way?

3. Photocopy a couple of pages from Kimmelman's essay and then cut out each individual paragraph with a pair of scissors. Trade these in small groups. Can everyone put the paragraphs back in the right order? How strong is Kimmelman's organization? What elements of the paragraphs indicate their order within the piece?

Assignments for Writing

1. Kimmelman states that the great collector is touched to the core by the confusion and dispersal in which things are found in this world. Locate your own example of a "wonder cabinet" and write an essay in which you extend or complicate Kimmelman's argument through this example. Does your example participate in finding order out of chaos? Can a collection of dissimilar objects in itself be considered ordered? What is the purpose of collecting? Does collecting make sense of a senseless world? In making your argument, consider using your exploration of eBay in Question 1 of Exploring Context.

2. In this essay Kimmelman states that a collection can blur the distinction between science and art by "dwelling in the marvelous." Write an essay exploring the role that a collection can play in science. Can a medical collection indeed serve to teach something to students? Can science be an art? Is there a place for art in science? You may want to incorporate your work on the relationship between medicine and art from Question 3 of Questions for Critical Reading in supporting your argument.

3. For Kimmelman, collecting art is itself an art form; his essay thus asks us to rethink what we mean by *art*. Working from Kimmelman's argument, write an essay in which you create a definition of *art* that encompasses collection and display. Consider these questions: Can a collection of ordinary objects be art? Why or why not? Is something artistic only after it loses its utilitarian or everyday purpose? Is a collection artistic only after it is displayed? What role does display have in art? In your response, draw from your work on collecting from Question 1 of Questions for Critical Reading.

REBEKAH NATHAN

Rebekah Nathan is a pseudonym for Cathy Small, an anthropology professor at North Arizona University. When Small went undercover to write her second book, *My Freshman Year: What a Professor Learned by Becoming a Student* (2005), she took on the pseudonym to protect the identity of her students and her university. Small previously published *Voyages: From Tongan Villages to American Suburbs* (1997), an ethnographical study of immigrants in their old and new homelands.

My Freshman Year is the result of a two-semester study by Small of all aspects of freshman life at her university. She applied to the university, enrolled in classes, moved into the student dorms, and even ate with students in the resident dining hall, hoping with her experiment to become a better teacher. After so long in the field, Small had found herself disconnected from the average student at her university, unable to understand why her students seemed so uninterested in and unprepared for class. She reveals in *My Freshman Year* that the demands on freshmen are much more varied and pressing than she had realized and that her initial assessment of her students had not been completely accurate.

"Community and Diversity," a chapter from *My Freshman Year*, deals with the difference between a university's stated goals for both community and diversity and their realization on campus, as well as the perpetual confusion among educators and administrators about why the image and the reality don't align. Small investigates low attendance at dorm events, patterns of freshman friendship, and the eating habits of ethnic and gender groups to reach some conclusions about the reality behind the lofty unmet intentions and the necessity of having such intentions at all.

As a student, you've undoubtedly encountered the call for community and diversity. It's likely, too, that you've seen this call go unanswered. You are in a unique position to continue Small's work on the possibilities of forming community and fostering diversity on the college campus.

▶ TAGS: *community*, *diversity*, *integration*, *research*, *education*, *conversation*

Community and Diversity

One would be hard-pressed to find words more widespread in university rhetoric than "community" and "diversity." As a student, one is immediately enlisted to join the group, to get involved, to realize that one has become a part of the AnyU "community."

It starts during Previews and Welcome Week. We sing the AnyU alma mater with leaders; we learn the AnyU cheer. At the convocation that commences our freshman year, we are welcomed to AnyU with some statistics about our class, and then an entertaining PowerPoint presentation with voice-over begins: "In the year that you were born . . ."—it goes back eighteen years and shows a baby—"Ronald Reagan was president, AnyU was building its South Campus, and the movie that won the Academy Award was *Out of Africa*." We see graphics of all this, and AnyU history, at least for the past eighteen years, is interspersed with the shared "history" of the audience, which consists primarily of movies, TV shows, and dramatic historical events. "In 1986," the story continues, "the Emmy goes to *L.A. Law*, and the explosion of the *Challenger* saddens the American public." The presentation takes us briefly through all eighteen years of the baby-who-is-us.

By 1991 we have torn down the Berlin Wall, constructed the new AnyU library, and arrived at the same year that *Seinfeld* begins. There is silence, clapping, or booing as the event being described moves us. Our history continues, year by year, to mention, among other things, the end of the TV series *Cheers* in 1993, the Monica Lewinsky scandal in 1998, the beginning of *Friends* in 1994 (to thunderous applause), and the September 11, 2001, attack. By 2002 we are eighteen and ready to go to college, and—the lights come on—here we are, part of the AnyU family.

The presentation works; it is relatively short, and students leave mildly entertained and energized, having experienced a compressed version of our joint heritage and our shared place at the starting line of something new. It is clear what the common heritage has been constructed to be. What holds students together, really, is age, pop culture, a handful of (recent) historical events, and getting a degree. No one ever remembers the institutional history or the never-sung alma mater.

How Community Works at AnyU

Youth, pop culture, and getting a degree are pretty accurately the ties that bind   5
together a public state university "community." Unless it offers a big-time (and winning) sports team that draws large attendance and loyalty, there is little in the way of shared first-year experiences that three thousand or so freshmen will have in common. AnyU did have a Freshman Colloquium course that was mandatory for all first-year students. It was designed to be just such a community builder, one that required students to complete a summer reading assignment—usually a provocative contemporary novel chosen collectively by the participating faculty—that would be discussed in small seminars before classes formally began.

The faculty had an ambitious, and what they thought exciting, intellectual agenda in mind. Students would read the same book, and then their academic career would start with a stimulating seminar-style discussion with only twenty or so participants. The entire freshman class would be engaged in the same reading, and thus have a common basis for debate and dialogue. Freshmen would then meet the book's author, who had been invited at great expense to give a talk following their small-group discussions. This experience would jump-start the colloquium that would follow: a small, seminar-based freshman course centered on readings about community and citizenship, diversity, environment, and technology, designed to help them explore their journeys as "thinking persons," including the purpose of the liberal education they had begun. For the administration, the course was also a way to build a sense of loyalty and community, and thus, according to official belief, to retain freshmen as paying students.

I was in one of the last freshman classes to take the course. It was nullified as a requirement because the university faculty and administration concluded that it wasn't working. For one thing, only about a third of the students actually did the summer reading. My own pre-course seminar was led by an impressive instructor who practically pulled teeth trying to get a response to questions raised by our reading: "Does a common enemy help to make people a community? What is a typical American or an ideal citizen? Can anyone think of places within America that seem like a different country? Does technology bring you closer to or farther away from other people—does it separate or connect?" She ended up letting us go a half-hour early because, I surmised, of our silence. Very few in my seminar had read the book, at least "all the way through," as one student qualified it.

According to student surveys, many disliked the course that followed, in particular the idea that they "had no choice and that they *had* to take it," but also because it was abstract and impractical, and they didn't learn anything "related to their interests." The requirement, designed as the only common academic experience the freshmen would have, was accordingly wiped from the books, leaving an elective course, chosen separately by each student, in its place.

One can learn from the fate of the freshman seminar. It is a good example of what happens nowadays when efforts at building community compete with the demand for choice. The freshman course had been designed and initiated at AnyU as part of a nationwide agenda, begun in the early 1990s, to engage students in their freshman year and quickly establish a "learning community." It was one local response to what educational policy analysts identified as a crisis in community that left the university to be experienced in "momentary and marginal ways." "Not only has cultural coherence faded," reads the thoughtful and influential 1990 report from the Carnegie Foundation for the Advancement of Teaching, "but the very notion of commonalities seems strikingly inapplicable to the vigorous diversity of contemporary life." Titled *Campus Life: In Search of Community*, the report called for a renewal of community in higher learning. Its authors wrote:

> It is of special significance, we believe, that higher learning institutions, even the big, complex ones, continue to use the familiar rhetoric of "community" to describe campus life and even use the metaphor of "family." Especially significant, 97 percent of the college and university presidents we surveyed said they "strongly believe in the importance

of community." Almost all the presidents agreed that "community is appropriate for my campus" and also support the proposition that "administrators should make a greater effort to strengthen common purposes and shared experiences."[1]

It is a cry that has been taken up in earnest by university presidents around the country. Because *requiring* common experiences is vastly unpopular, and efforts often meet the fate of the freshman seminar, AnyU, like many universities today, encourages community through elective participation. "If you don't see what you like," said one Welcome Week booster, "start your own club." The 158 registered student organizations on campus don't tell the full story of the options that confront a student in a single week, from salsa dancing night at a downtown club, to the regular pickup game of coed volleyball, to the Overeaters Anonymous meeting, to the self-defense lesson in the dorm, to the plethora of academic events that are part of lecture and film series.

Every week the hall bulletin boards are plastered with notices about new events to attend, new music groups in town, or organizations offering enthusiastic invitations to their open house. The proliferation of event choices, together with the consistent message to "get involved," and the ever available option of dropping out, creates a self-contradictory system. Students are confronted with an endless slate of activities vying for their time. Every decision not to join but to keep one's time for oneself is interpreted as "student apathy" or "program irrelevance," and ever more activities are designed to remedy them. Each decision to join something new pulls at another commitment, fragmenting the whole even further. Not only people but also community are spread thin.

> **AnyU, like many universities today, encourages community through elective participation.**

In my life as a student this process of community building through elective involvement was repeated numerous times and in numerous places within the university. On my dorm floor alone, where we had not done much together as a group during my first semester, the process worked like this. To begin our second semester and usher in a renewed spirit of community, our enthusiastic RA devised an "interest survey," which she administered at the first mandatory hall meeting of that period. (Since it was second semester, the turnout was decidedly sparse: Only six people attended.) "Let's do more things together," the RA suggested, and we agreed. It would be desirable, the collective thinking seemed to be, to have more "community" in the dorm.

"What would we like to do this semester?" she asked us. To find out, she distributed the survey with a written checklist that would assist her in launching new dorm programs that fit our interests and schedules. There were sixty-four activities suggested on the checklist in ten categories (community living, health/wellness, social awareness, employment skills, academic programs, relationship issues . . .), which ranged from presentation and panels, to group games and activities, to participatory workshops. We could write in activities if the ones presented did not suit. There was also an availability section of the form, where we were asked to check our preferred times—which evenings, which hours—for the activities. Because the showing at the meeting was so meager, our RA placed questionnaires under each of the doors on the wing, to be returned to her by a specified date. I asked whether I could see the final tallies.

A total of 304 selections were made by all hall mates, with eighteen of the sixty-four listed activities chosen by approximately half of all respondents. The most popular choice was not an activity at all but an expressed interest in buying floor T-shirts or boxer shorts. Among activities, several—including swing or salsa dancing and playing board games—were high on the list, but the RA decided to start her local "community" program with the biggest vote-getter, "Movie Night," endorsed by about three-quarters of the voting residents on the floor.

Movie Night was an activity whereby once every other week we would come to our RA's room, as in Welcome Week, to watch a movie on video while sharing popcorn and other snacks provided by the RA or anted up by the residents. The preferred time, according to the questionnaires, was 8 PM on Tuesday. And so Movie Night was instituted twice a month on Tuesday nights, and slips of paper appeared under our doors to announce the first movie. On the first Tuesday, two people showed, besides the RA. The second time nobody showed. The RA moved the night to Sunday. Still nobody showed. The program was canceled, leaving the RA wondering what she could do to "really involve" her corridor.

Two organizational levels up from the corridor was the dorm. Here RAs and dorm officers attempted more extensive full-dorm programs that would get the residents involved. There were dozens of them, in addition to the corridor or floor-level activities devised by individual RAs. The most residents I ever saw attend any single event in our dormitory, housing about four hundred people, was for the talent show, where there were about twenty-one people—mostly the talent—and the "How to Make Edible Underwear" program around Valentine's Day, which drew twenty-three people.

With varying degrees of success, this was the pattern of "community involvement" that operated at various levels of the university: a multiplicity of voluntary activities, a handful of participants at each, and renewed efforts to create new activities that were more relevant and attractive, resulting in an even greater proliferation of choices and fragmentation of the whole.

The American Way: The Individualism in Community

To university administrators my story of Movie Night would be yet one more example of failing involvement and community on the contemporary college campus. By 1990 it was already becoming clear that few students participate in campus events; 76 percent of college and university presidents called nonparticipation a moderate to major problem on campuses.[2] An RA might count Movie Night as a personal failure, and become dispirited by the apathy of residents, or perhaps hear a call to invent more and better activities.

Students, I imagine, would see it a little differently. The activities chosen were not the "wrong" ones, nor were their RAs remiss. Nor had students been insincere in their desire for more community life in the dorm. If you had asked most students what happened with Movie Night, they would have answered, "I wanted to go, but when the time came, I didn't," or "I forgot." They genuinely want to have a close community, while at the same time they resist the claims that community makes on their schedule and resources in the name of individualism, spontaneity, freedom, and choice.

This is exactly how many students talk about sororities and fraternities. Fewer than 10 percent of AnyU residents are members of either. When I asked students whether they'd considered "rushing," instead of mentioning the "elitism" or "conservative politics" that dominated Greek critique in my day, students complained about "conformity" and "control of my life." Judy explained that she had almost rushed but then changed her mind because "you become lost. It's hard to know all ninety girls in a sorority. You become the same rather than an individual in a group. It can get, you know, almost cult-like, and you spend all your time there. You can't live in other dorms, or meet new people." 20

I found that students' greatest objections to the Greek system were its steep demands—that it required so much time ("I can't give up that many nights a week to one organization") and so many resources ("Why should I pay all that money to a fraternity to have friends when I can make friends for free?"), all of them mandatory ("I don't want people telling me what to do and where I have to be all the time"; "I'm an individual, not a group person"). Yet, the one AnyU student in ten who did join a fraternity or sorority was, according to 2003 surveys conducted by the Office of Student Life, much less likely to drop out of school and much more likely to report the highest level of satisfaction with campus life.

There is a familiar dilemma here. "The very organizations that give security to students," concluded national policy analysts in 1990, "can also create isolation and even generate friction on the campus."[3] More than half of university presidents were reported to view Greek life as a problem, largely because it creates "little loyalties" that isolate students, removing them from the mainstream life of the university. It is not just Greek groups that operate this way. They are only illustrative of what one university president saw as "a great deal of 'orbital energy' among the many subgroups, a magnetism that tugs at these groups, pulling them away from any common agenda."[4]

Struggling with community in this way is, as observers of American life have pointed out, the American way.[5] The same things that make us feel connected and protected are the things that make us feel obligated and trapped as individuals and/or cut off from other groups with different agendas. For most students, as for most Americans in general, the "big community" has a dual connotation that includes both a warm and fuzzy side, all about "oneness" or "togetherness" or "common purpose," and a negative side that tends to surface with reference to government regulations, Big Brother images, and fears of conformity. When students talk about their educational community, these contradictory ideas of community are reproduced, bouncing between an entity that provides love and a sense of belonging and one that limits freedom and imposes new obligations.

I initially encountered student thoughts about community on "introduction sheets," tellingly titled "IT'S ALL ABOUT ME," that the RA had asked us to fill out and hang on our doors. Aimed at "community building," the sheets posed questions designed to acquaint others on the hall with our opinions and personality. After blanks for our major, hometown, and favorite color, and prompts to name our distinctive qualities, "the things I like to do for fun," and "what makes you unique," was the question, "What does community mean to you?"

For half the students, community was a somewhat naïve amalgam of love, belonging, sharing, and togetherness—all the things we would want community to do for us with none of its obligations. It was, in their words, "respect; caring, open people" who would be "sharing together, always there for me"; a place where there are "pillows on the floor" and "everybody leaves their door open," where you can "crash on your neighbor's floor if you're too tired to go home." My favorite answer in this category was "Community means being able to fart comfortably," because it so perfectly ignores the possibility of being the one at the other end of the farting freedom who has to put up with her flatulent neighbors. Only one person, in fact, mentioned any kind of responsibility when defining community, stating that she would "pick up garbage when I see it on the ground." 25

The downside of the community coin was also well represented, with some students balking at the idea of community or making jokes: "Community means Communism"; "Community means dirt—do you realize how many germs infest close-proximity living quarters?"; "Community means I can do whatever annoying habits I want and if my neighbors don't like it they can move out."

What I saw in student responses, as well as in student behavior, was a profound ambivalence about community life, resulting in a tentative, often conflicted relationship to the collective life of the university. Not only did campus participation suffer from this conflict, but also it was difficult to create mutual commitments and agreements among people whose connection to community was so hesitant.

One of the most interesting community ventures at AnyU came in the form of our second hall meeting in each semester, where we devised our "Community Living Agreement." Initiated by the RAs, these were to be the local agreements that each wing lived by, the "dos and don'ts" of hall life, fashioned by the residents themselves. The agreement for the first semester was drafted at a "mandatory" hall meeting at which seven people on the wing showed, one of whom left almost immediately because it was her birthday and she was too drunk to pay attention. After pizza, M&Ms, and yet another icebreaker game, the RA introduced our charge of creating a joint compact and handed out cards and pens, asking each person to write down something in the way of a rule or a "don't" that she would like to obtain for the hall. When we'd finished, the RA taped an enormous blank sheet of white paper to the wall, stood next to it with a marker, and said, "Tell me some of your items." Reluctantly and slowly, each person volunteered some rule. "Don't be too loud at night"; "Close the shower curtain so it doesn't flood the little anteroom"; "Don't leave your hair in the drain"; "Keep your door open when you're in your room (unless you're studying/sleeping)"; "Wipe your hair off of the shower walls"; "Don't take showers too long if there are people waiting."

There was no real discussion of any of the items. After everyone contributed, the RA took the sheet off the wall and left us to our candy. About one week later a large printed poster appeared on the hall, titled "Community Living Agreement," listing eight items, half of them pertaining to showers and a few to hair.

The same process occurred during the second semester, although shower   30
etiquette had a lower priority. Six items were posted in the hall for our second semester community agreement:

Keep hair off the shower walls.
Keep doors open while you're chillin'.
Sleepovers and parties on the hall are cool.
Yell "flushing" if there's someone in the shower [because the shower water turned scalding during the flush].
No writing on the bathroom stall walls [this was the RA's].
Say "hi" to people to be friendly.

Although the agreement no doubt reflected some important values held by the residents, including sociability, courtesy, and cleanliness, it was the relationship of the individuals to the community agreement that interested me most. There had been no road map for actually creating an agreement, no mechanism for turning individual opinions into a community document. No one, including the RA, was comfortable suggesting that we might modify, prioritize, or remove individuals' suggestions from the list. While the seven students in attendance were considered to "represent" the others, because the latter did not show up to participate, there was no means for making the "agreement" binding on hall residents. As a result, the list remained posted for a semester, but each student on the hall decided whether she would abide by the agreement or not.

I never once heard anyone yell "flushing" in the bathroom, nor did I ever see a "cool sleepover" or public party on the hall. It seemed to me that the same people who kept their doors open prior to the agreement, including me, were the ones who kept their doors open afterward. There was never any follow-up or discussion about whether our agreement was being honored.

Community in the American university is paradoxically a private and an individual decision. As Robert Putnam documents in his history of community in the United States, *Bowling Alone*, the private decision to participate in community life is one that individuals in recent U.S. history are making less and less. From civic and religious life to political participation and informal social connections, there is an increasing individualism in American life that is evident in our universities as well.[6]

In such a historical light, the trends in dormitory living are thought-provoking. The newest dormitories being built across the country are both higher in amenities and lower in density than those of the past. It is no longer considered a viable model of campus life to have a hall full of people sharing a communal bathroom, lounge, and washing machine. The old blueprint of collective living has given way to much more individualized and opulent arrangements. Put in student lingo, individualism "rules."

At AnyU, new dorms are all built "suite-style," with four students shar- 35 ing a huge apartment with four bedrooms and two bathrooms, as well as its own living room, kitchen, and washer-dryer units. The private bedrooms and semi-private bathrooms are more acceptable to contemporary students, who are no longer accustomed in childhood to sharing a room with a sibling. In fact, according to AnyU's Office of Residence Life, the number one reason why students move out of traditional dormitories is that they do not like sharing a communal bathroom. Dormitories, like campus life as a whole, are increasingly privatized, well appointed, and focused on an ever smaller network of people that constitutes the significant living community of the student.

These national trends bring into clearer focus the use of space in my own dormitory, a building constructed in the 1940s for a 1940s student. One can see how new students with new values have refashioned the existing space. The dormitory includes big, cushy public spaces filled with overstuffed furniture which appear to be expecting a crowd. There are lounges on each floor, one with a fireplace and some with large outside terraces; they have tables and chairs, community TVs and VCRs.

After using these spaces as a student, I began to realize something that I subsequently checked by monitoring more public lounges in my dorm and others: Fellow students didn't really use these areas as social space. With the exception of the cleaning staff on their lunch breaks, I never saw students bring food and eat together, sit and socialize together, or even watch television together in our local lounge. During the course of an entire semester, what could be called "community life" or even "social activity" was extremely sparse. I saw one or two card games in the lounge on my floor, one simulation game meeting, scattered study groups that assembled in the dorm to work on a class project, and a Christian group who occasionally used the space to work on volunteer projects.

My observations of lounges in other dormitories were not significantly different. These spaces often sat empty. During the day, no one used them at all. On most nights, the overstuffed couches and chairs in our largest lounge would be draped with one to three students who had positioned themselves as far as possible from one another. Interviews with the few students who *were* in the lounges during my observations revealed that the majority came there to "get away" — from a gathering in their room, music blasting on the hall, or a roommate with a guest. In other words, the community spaces were often a *retreat* from social interaction, a way to create more private options. They were no longer, as their builders had probably envisioned, primarily a place for people to come together and participate in joint activities.

One of my greatest epiphanies about community life in the dorm came on Super Bowl Sunday. I had sneaked home Saturday night, intending to stay at my own house until Sunday night, when I realized that on Sunday afternoon at 2 PM Super Bowl coverage would begin, and I needed to be at the dorm. The event had been advertised heavily in the hall for weeks. "Free Ticket," the flyers read, and the "ticket" entitled one to good company, free pizza, and drinks during the game. The large lobby had been set up with two big-screen TVs so as to accommodate viewers from any vantage point.

I arrived a little early to get a good seat and waited for the lobby lounge to   40 fill, but by game time there were only five other people in the space. One had tuned the second TV set to a different program, so I and four others watched the opening kickoff together. A couple of months earlier, when I had been the only one in the lounge for the World Series, I simply assumed that the event was under-advertised and that this generation had no love of baseball. When I saw that the same no-show pattern had occurred with the well-publicized football event, I decided to investigate further. Where were the other students? I left at halftime.

Many, I surmised, had gone to sports bars. But as I wandered the floors of my dorm, I could hear the game playing from numerous rooms. On my corridor alone, where there were two open doors, I could see clusters of people in each room eating and drinking as they watched the game together on their own sizable television sets. It seemed telling to me that so many dormitory residents were watching the same game in different places, the great majority preferring to pass the time with a carefully chosen group of personal friends in their own private space. It spoke in a more general way to how community really worked in the university.

Rather than being located in its shared symbols, meetings, activities, and rituals, the university for an undergraduate was more accurately a world of self-selected people and events. The university community was experienced by most students as a relatively small, personal network of people who did things together. This "individual community" was bolstered by a university system that honors student choice, as well as a level of materialism in the larger society that, by enabling students to own their own cars, computers, TV sets, and VCRs, renders collective resources and spaces superfluous. These characteristics of American university life—individualism, choice, and materialism—stand out even more clearly in chapter 4, where foreign students at AnyU describe and compare their own educational systems.

AnyU's Real Community: The Ego-Centered Network

When I asked students in interviews whether they felt they had a "community" at AnyU, most said yes. But what they meant by community were these personal networks of friends that some referred to as my "homeys." It was these small, ego-centered groups that were the backbone of most students' social experience in the university.

On a daily basis these personal networks were easily recognizable within the dorm and on campus. "Where are you now?" says the cell phone caller walking back to the dorm from class. "I'm on my way home, so ask Jeffrey and Mark to come, and I'll meet you at my room at 8." Such conversations are everywhere. In the dorm, residents can be heard discussing the timing and location of dinners and after-dinner plans, and message boards record the social negotiations: "Be home by 5:30. What about Mexican? Call me—P." Creating one's community involved very conscious choices to make one's leisure hours jibe with selected others'. There were few open invitations in these exchanges. Unless the RA had planned an activity, there was no general call to join in on dinner plans or come watch a video in someone's room.

Among members of the same network, however, there were constant inter-   45
actions, ranging from borrowing detergent and snacks, to arranging social and shopping trips, to watching TV or videos together, to working out. The commu-nications among network members occurred both publicly, like the planning just noted, and privately, as I saw in student diaries, where frequent cell phone contact and Instant Messaging sessions were the norm.

The intense reciprocity of ego-based groups helped explain a problem about campus traffic that had long puzzled me. As a professor, I could never under-stand why campus roads were so hopelessly jammed between classes. After all, AnyU had a campus bus system, and students had parking permits only for the lots adjacent to their dorms. They couldn't legally park at classroom building lots and would receive a hefty ticket if they did. When I pasted my student park-ing pass on my car, I found myself basically grounded—able to drive off campus and back to my dorm but nowhere else. Why, then, were the roads so crowded with cars seemingly traveling from dorms to classes?

It wasn't long before I saw message boards with reminders such as "Tara, don't forget to pick me up 10 AM at the Social Science building.—L." Or "Be out in the Education Parking Lot at 3:10—Nick." As I walked or took the bus to class, I began to pay more attention to the non-dormitory parking lots and real-ized that there was a vast web of personal relationships activated for dropping and picking up passengers. It was network reciprocity at work.

These personal networks grew in importance to me as I realized their salience in the life of my fellow students, and in the life of the university. I became increasingly interested in how friends are made, how groups are formed, and how activities are coordinated. I built these queries in to my interviews and discovered much that observation alone did not tell me.

Student networks, like family relations, are ego based. In a family, even your first cousin will have relatives that you don't have in common, and the same is true of two students who are in each other's networks. Pam and Terry are part of the same social network, but when they separately name their own closest friends, the names are not exactly the same. Pam includes her boyfriend and his roommate along with Alice and Marie in her close net-work, while Terry includes Alice, Marie, and Pam but also a friend from class whom Pam barely knows. And Pam's boyfriend shares only a few of Pam's friends. One student's network, although it may overlap with those of others, is essentially personal; no two people share the exact same group of friends. This is what is meant by ego based: Even these intimate forms of community are quite individual.

Most students, I found, had established a network of two to six friends who [50] formed their core university community. From the "native" point of view, they got together because "we like each other." Students regularly named personality traits and attitudes to explain their attraction to friends: "They're outspoken"; "We're all a little weird"; "We like to have fun"; they're "strong-minded and focused like me"; they're "up for anything, and pretty laid back"; "We're the same when it comes to school, not big party-ers"; or they're "real friendly, open, responsible people."

To an outsider, especially an outsider who is looking at the points of convergence among a number of students, student networks have less to do with personality than with shared circumstances and shared demographics. Kyle, a Christian student on the floor, had a network of close friends for whom being Christian was very important. They'd met while they were still in high school, after attending several retreats that happened to be held at AnyU. By the time they came to AnyU as freshmen, they were already friends. The close networks of five of the six minority students in my sample contained several other minority students. A number of them had met their closest friends in an intensive pre-college summer program for first-generation students, where there had been a sizable percentage of minority students. One of the most surprising findings to me was the discovery that eight of fourteen students interviewed about the subject of social networks had one or more people in their close personal networks whom they knew from high school or their hometown. In all, then, many of the networks that endured through college were based on experiences *before* college, and these were conditioned by demographic characteristics such as religion, race, ethnicity, and/or hometown (itself a function of race, ethnicity, religion, and class).

Once in school, it was also edifying to learn how early the enduring friendships occurred in students' college life, and how little they drew on academic interests and contacts. Most students whose friends were cultivated after college began had met their closest friends by virtue of living in the same freshman dorm or floor. Classroom contacts figured relatively little in the social networks of students; fewer than one-quarter of my interview students had met a member of their network in an academic class or in an activity or club related to their major, while almost as many had met a close friend through ROTC or work.

Despite the belief that college expands our social horizons and extends our experience to include new and different types of people, the findings suggest otherwise. The most significant relationships are formed either before college or very early in one's college career, most often in some shared affiliation, whether voluntary or not, such as freshman dorm assignment, special freshman summer program, ROTC, ethnic club, or sorority and fraternity rush.

Diaries and interviews confirmed that for many students, their social lives at the university consisted of repeated contacts with the same people, who constituted that student's personal network. Once networks were formed, usually by the end of the freshman year, students tended to stay with their groups, maintaining intense and frequent interactions with their network and more superficial and sparse contacts with others. The way that student social life is formed necessarily affects issues of diversity.

Diversity at AnyU?

Student networks may be able to explain, at least in part, the failed diversity   55
efforts at many universities, and certainly at AnyU. About 22 to 25 percent of AnyU students are considered "minority" by federal standards, and minority students appear approximately in these percentages in AnyU dorms and classes. What makes diversity a "success" in a state university, however, is not only that the university population reflects the diversity of the general population but also that students become more involved in the lives and issues of that diverse population. Part of that diversity ideal is the hope that all students will develop friends and have important conversations with those of backgrounds and ethnicities different from their own.

The National Survey of Student Engagement tries to capture this information by asking a student to self-report as to whether he or she has "had serious conversations with students of a different race or ethnicity than your own." In 2003, fifty percent of college seniors nationwide indicated

> **Most students, but white students predominantly, ended up becoming close friends with people of their own ethnicity.**

that they "often" or "very often" had such conversations, while only 13 percent said they did not.

This jibed with the information I initially was getting from my interviews about social networks, where I was finding that many students named someone from a different ethnic group within their close circle of friends. The interview information, though, did not match my direct observations, and this led me to probe further by fiddling with my interview questions and format. I soon realized that if I started, as I had, by asking informants whether they had close friends from other ethnic groups, the majority of students would say that they did. If I questioned them further, they would name that man from a class, or woman on the same intramural volleyball team, with whom they had close contact and describe how they met.

If, however, I started by asking informants to name their closest friends and then later asked them to identify the ethnicity of the named people, it turned out that most students, but white students predominantly, ended up becoming close friends with people of their own ethnicity. Since I thought that this "names first, ethnicity later" approach was more accurate, I changed the order of my questions and arrived at a very different picture. Five out of six white students I interviewed in this way about their networks had no members of another racial or ethnic group in their close social circle; the networks of five of the six minority students contained one or more minorities (more on the details of this later).

One can see from the descriptions of how networks form why this might be true. Many students are building on contacts developed before they entered college, contacts that have strong demographic and social components. If many student networks begin with hometown contacts, what is the likelihood that they will cross class, ethnic, race, or even religious lines when the United States is demographically divided along precisely these lines? Although there was one instance in my data of a cross-racial network pair with its origin in high school, the probabilities in this country work strongly the other way because of de facto neighborhood and school segregation. All other examples I found of high school or hometown friends in an AnyU network involved a woman or man of the same ethnicity as the person interviewed.

Even many relationships developed early in college contain a built-in bias. Although classes and interest clubs may be ethnically well mixed, this is not where students make their earliest school contacts. Freshman dorms are generally well integrated, but not several of the early programs and events that help introduce and acclimate new students, including Previews weekends designated for particular ethnic groups, pre-college "outdoor adventure" trips that cost extra money, a summer program for first-generation college students, or the opening round of sorority and fraternity mixers. Some institutional structures like these may encourage the early formation of same-ethnicity relationships.

There is no doubt that active racism also plays a part in the lack of diversity on college campuses. Yet, race or ethnicity is typically ignored as a topic of conversation in mainstream college culture, treated as an invisible issue and with silence. As Levine and Cureton (1998) found in their nationwide survey, students were "more willing to tell intimate details of their sex lives than discuss race relations on campus."[7] When the subject *is* raised, as in the occasional class, students of color report being continually expected to educate whites about minority issues or speak "as a representative of their race."

Despite the general invisibility of the subject of race in informal student culture, there was not a single minority student I interviewed who hadn't experienced racism.[8] Few openly complained, but everyone had at least one story to tell of comments made in class, rude remarks on the street, or just hostile looks. When I asked Pat, a Hispanic–Native American woman, whether she had ever considered rushing a sorority, she told me that she had in her freshman year, but "I could see that it wasn't really right for me, because I'd pass by all the sorority tables—you know how they call out to girls to come over and take a look—well, I saw they called out to other girls but not to me. They just kinda ignored me, not hostile or anything, but not interested either."

"It's just how it is," another female student explained. "There are some good people and some not so good people, and you deal with it."

Who Eats with Whom: A Study of Student Dining

My very small sample of student networks and interviews was suggestive to me but not convincing that diversity in student relationships was in serious question. So I decided to conduct a larger observational study of students' informal social behavior. I chose eating as the focus, one of my favorite social activities, and asked the research question "Who eats with whom?" This seemed a fair and appropriate inquiry into diversity, to determine the range of people with whom one breaks bread.

It was my most extensive and longest-running "mini-study" of campus life. For five months I directly observed and recorded the dining behavior of fellow students during randomly selected periods of the day at optional dining areas on campus.[9] Although some patrons carried out their food, returning to their dorms or outside benches to eat, many ate and drank singly or in groups at the various tables provided in one of five eating areas I surveyed. Sitting at a different table in the room, I would record who sat at each table by gender and, as much as outward appearances can signal, ethnicity.

It is always problematic to do research like this, because there is a wide range of appearances for all ethnicities, and many sticky issues. My interest, however, *was* in appearances, and in seeing to what extent students chose to share food and conversation with people who looked like them (or, more accurately, seemed to belong in the same broad ethnic category that an observer would attribute to them). Although there are other kinds of diversity (e.g., age), I recorded only the data reflecting each person's gender and, to the extent possible, his or her category of ethnicity such as white non-Hispanic, Hispanic, Asian, African American, Native American, and so on. These were not easy calls. Sometimes I could tell only that someone was not a white non-Hispanic but couldn't identify the more specific group to which she or he belonged; at other times I could not tell whether a person was white and non-Hispanic or something else.

In gathering this information I had these questions in mind: To what extent did informal university activities (e.g., eating together) convey diversity? Did students eat in same or mixed ethnic and gender groups? Were there differences in the eating patterns of dominant (defined as white non-Hispanic) and non-dominant (defined as people of color) ethnic groups? Did any ethnic group or category eat alone more often than others?

I analyzed the data with regard to these questions but took care to analyze by person rather than by table in order to try to see the data through the eyes of the particular diner. For instance, if there were a table consisting of four people—a white male, two white women, and one Hispanic woman—each would have a different reality at the table: The male is eating with a table of all women of mixed ethnicity; both white women are eating at a table of mixed gender and mixed ethnicity; and the Hispanic woman is eating at a mixed-gender table where everyone is of a different ethnicity from herself. I recorded the data, preserving the perspective of each diner, and then analyzed the data in ten different categories that allowed me to examine the relationship of each table diner to the rest.[10] In this way, I tracked almost 1,500 examples of dining behavior.

What I found was interesting. It showed not only an overall lack of diversity, as national studies report,[11] but also the existence of huge differences in the diversity experiences of dominant and non-dominant groups. Minorities (people of color) ate alone only slightly more often: one-quarter of minority women and more than one-third of minority men sitting in public spaces ate alone, a rate greater than that for white women and men by 3 percent and 5 percent, respectively. But of all those who ate with others, only 10 percent of white men and 14 percent of white women ate at a table where there was anyone of a different color from themselves. Only 2.6 percent and 3.5 percent of white men and women, respectively, ate at a table of two or more where they were the only white person. The statistics were strikingly different for people of color: 68 percent of women and 58 percent of men ate with "mixed groups." People of color were ten times more likely than whites to eat in a group in which they were the only person of a different race/ethnicity at the table.

The same patterns I saw in the dining spaces proved true in the composition   70
of personal networks when I compared a group of twelve students on my hall, six whites and six students of color. Although the networks of Caucasian students included more whites, and those of people of color more minorities, the total networks of minority students were primarily "mixed," comprising people of various ethnicities, including whites. One student of color was in an all-white network, while another had friends of only her own ethnicity. By contrast, five of the six white students had networks that were solidly white; only one white student had a mixed network, and none was the only Caucasian.

Seen in this context, minority ethnic clubs, dorms, and student unions have a clearer meaning. Ethnic-based groups are often clouded by perceptions that they, like the Greek system, remove their members from the mainstream and surround them with people of the same background. What the data suggest to me is that people of color are already heavily involved in interethnic and interracial relationships on campus. In fact, most of their informal dining contacts, as well as personal networks, included people who were ethnically different from them. Under these circumstances, an ethnic-based club—which half of the minorities in my sample thought was important in their lives—is better understood as a needed respite from difference, a chance to rest comfortably with others who share similar experiences in the world.

It was white students, most markedly males, whose social lives suffered from a lack of diversity. When white men *did* eat with those of different ethnicities, the majority of tables were "cross-gender." In other words, white men socialized at meals to a greater degree with nonwhite women or with groups that included nonwhite women. There was extremely little contact between white and nonwhite men. Only 4 of 489 white males, fewer than 1 percent, ate with (only) males of a different ethnicity, but 31 ate in different or mixed ethnic groups in which women were present. Men of color, while much more diverse in their dining, followed a similar pattern, tending to have fewer cross-ethnic male-only eating partners (7 of 79) while favoring cross-ethnic tables where women were eating too (24 of 79). The same pattern was not true of women. For both white women and women of color, their cross-color contact was primarily with other women.

One of the more disturbing but confusing findings was how few people of color, proportionally, used the common eating spaces. Only 13 percent of the entire dining sample was nonwhite, while 22 percent of full-time students were nonwhite. This left more than 40 percent of the minority population unaccounted for. There are certainly many ways to interpret what was going on. Perhaps this eyeballing approach to minority status simply fails to recognize many who are legal minorities. Perhaps there are economic factors at work that bear on having a meal ticket or buying food during the day that disadvantage some minority students. Perhaps the difference is explained by the larger percentage of minority students who enroll in off-campus programs. But there is another possibility that I entertained, which was related to my finding that more minority students eat alone.

My evidence is only anecdotal because I didn't formally monitor what I thought I was seeing, but this is what I noticed. I would observe the food court area as people got their food and stood in line to pay, watching each person leave the register to see where he or she went to sit in order to mark it in my book. I often found that instead of going to a table, however, a person of color would go to a condiment area, pack up a napkin and the food in a bag, and leave. It seemed to me that a greater proportion of minorities was leaving.

One day, as I was just finishing an observation session, an African American woman left the register and headed for a table. She would be the last diner to enter my monitored space in the set time period. I prepared to mark her table choice, but instead of sitting down, she readjusted her backpack, took her food, and left. Where is she going? I asked myself. To meet a friend in a different area? To eat outside? I felt a bit like a stalker as I followed her out of the dining area and out of the building. She passed the outdoor tables and kept walking until she entered one of the freshman dorms, went through the lobby, and up the stairs. My guess was that she had returned to eat in her dorm room. 75

I will never know for sure what lay behind that one observation, or what I perceived to be the larger proportion of students of color who did not stay to eat. But it left me with the uncomfortable feeling that I was witnessing the effect of a "white space" — which I had never noticed because I am white — where people of color could eat alone publicly, or eat with people different from themselves, or go home to their rooms. Perhaps, many times, the dorm room just seems the most comfortable option, and this may have explained some of the missing 40 percent of minority students in the dining areas.

The ideals of community and diversity are certainly in place at AnyU and remain important components of stated university policy. Yet neither is fully realized in university culture, as I believe I have illustrated in this chapter. What I also hope I've illustrated, though, is what anthropologists mean when they say that a culture cannot really be divided into its parts; one part of a culture cannot be understood in isolation from its other parts, and all must be contextualized within the larger whole. Culture, we argue, is both integrated and holistic.

In just this way "community" and "diversity" are parts of university culture, but they are not intelligible on their own. As the descriptions of student life attest, diversity is one part of college culture that is intimately tied to community, another part. And both parts are ultimately conditioned by structures in the larger American society — including values of individualism and choice, materialism, and the realities of U.S. demographics — that may seem, at first, to have little bearing on whether college diversity increases because freshmen Joe and Juan truly become friends, or whether Jane strengthens community by deciding to attend Movie Night. But they do. Not understanding this leads to a reality about diversity and community in university culture that does not match its rhetoric, and a persistent confusion about why this is so.

NOTES

1. Carnegie Foundation for the Advancement of Teaching 1990, 64, 63.
2. Ibid., 48.
3. Ibid., 49.
4. Ibid., 50
5. Varenne 1977.
6. Putnam 2000.
7. Levine and Cureton 1998, 72.
8. My brief section here hardly does justice to the urgency of race and ethnicity issues on campus or, for that matter, to the active discrimination experienced by gay and transgendered individuals. For more on the thoughts and experiences of minority and gay students, see Lesage et al. 2002 and Howard and Stevens 2000, and see Tusmith and Reddy 2002 for teachers' challenges with teaching diversity to students.
9. To mitigate such factors as meal plans and off-campus versus on-campus living, which may draw differentially on class and ethnicity, I confined my observations to tables shared in the optional dining areas on campus where either a meal plan card or cash was accepted. I made observations only during the day and from Monday to Friday, when most classes were in session, because these were the times and meals, I figured, that would be least affected by demographic and economic differences among students.
10. Each diner ("who," according to gender and ethnicity) and the number at the table (#) were recorded. Then each person sitting at the table was recorded by gender and specific ethnicity, where possible. The data were then sorted and analyzed by looking at the composition of the table from the diner's point of view and marked as to whether the diner was eating with: (1) no one (the person was sitting alone); (2) females of the same ethnic/power group (SF), males of the same ethnic/power group (SM), or a mixed-gender table of the same ethnic/power group (SX); (2) females (OF) or males (OM) of a different ethnic/power group, a mixed-gender table comprising members of a different ethnic/power group (OX); or (3) a mixed ethnic/power group that was all female (MxF), all male (MxM), or mixed gender (MxX). The term "ethnic/ power group" is used because, for purposes of this section, people's ethnicities were analyzed in two broad categories that are more than ethnic designations: dominant (white non-Hispanic) and minority (people of color) groups. More detailed ethnic information was recorded and reviewed, but the comparisons here focused on dominant and non-dominant groups.
11. "Walk into the cafeteria in most colleges and universities," write Levine and Cureton, "and the tables are separated by race and ethnicity. The larger the campus, the sharper the divisions" (1998, 86).

BIBLIOGRAPHY

Carnegie Foundation for the Advancement of Teaching. 1990. *Campus Life: In Search of Community.* Princeton: Carnegie Foundation for the Advancement of Teaching.

Howard, Kim, and Annie Stevens. 2000. *Out and About Campus: Personal Accounts by Lesbian, Gay, Bisexual, and Transgendered College Students.* Los Angeles: Alyson Books.

Lesage, Julia, Abby L. Ferber, Debbie Storrs, and Donna Wong. 2002. *Making a Difference: University Students of Color Speak Out.* Lanham, Md.: Rowman & Littlefield.

Levine, Arthur, and Jeanette S. Cureton. 1998. *When Hope and Fear Collide: A Portrait of Today's College Student.* San Francisco: Jossey-Bass.

Putnam, Robert D. 2000. *Bowling Alone: The Collapse and Revival of American Community.* New York: Simon & Schuster.

Tusmith, Bonnie, and Maureen T. Reddy, eds. 2002. *Race in the College Classroom: Pedagogy and Politics.* New Brunswick: Rutgers University Press.

Varenne, Hervé. 1977. *Americans Together: Structured Diversity in a Midwestern Town.* New York: Teachers College Press.

Questions for Critical Reading

1. What does Nathan mean by *ego-centered network*? Develop a definition of the term by locating passages where Nathan discusses this concept. What role do these networks play in community? Support your answer with examples from the essay.

2. Most of Nathan's essay is concerned with the failures of both community and diversity at AnyU. Reread her essay critically to locate passages in which Nathan indicates the main reasons for the lack of both at her school.

3. Submerged in Nathan's analysis are the requirements for successfully promoting community and diversity. Look back through her essay and find quotations that provide the tools needed to promote these ideals.

Exploring Context

1. In this selection Nathan is interested in exploring the gap between her school's stated goals for community and diversity and the actuality of these ideals in student life. What are your school's objectives in these two areas? Generate a sense of how your school approaches community and diversity by searching for these terms in your institution's Web site, and then prepare a short report on what you find in this search. Do you find the same gap between image and reality that Nathan finds at her institution? If not, what might account for the success of community and diversity in your school? How does your work on failures of community and diversity from Question 2 of Questions for Critical Reading apply to your school's Web site?

2. Nathan opens by recounting the time line presentation that students at AnyU watch during orientation. Use the Web to research significant national or world events that took place at different stages of your own life. Share these time lines in small groups. Do you and your classmates share the same historical sense?

Did you look up the same years or dates? How might such a time line produce community, and why might you and your classmates have different events listed? Do the differences in your apprehensions of the past create challenges to forming community? Does the diversity of your class play any role?

3. At the heart of Nathan's analysis are the very definitions of community and diversity. Search for blog entries on "community" and "diversity" using BlogPulse (blogpulse.com), a search engine for blogs. Based on the blog postings you read, what do these terms mean to people in general? How do they talk about them? Do they value them? How are they viewed differently in the blogosphere and at AnyU? What might account for this difference?

Questions for Connecting

1. How can Leslie Savan's analysis of pop talk in "What's Black, Then White, and Said All Over?" (p. 363) help explain the failure of diversity on college campuses? What role might "paying the dues" have in achieving true diversity? Relate your answer to your work on this issue from Questions for Critical Reading.

2. Given Steve Olson's argument in "The End of Race: Hawaii and the Mixing of Peoples" (p. 250) about the end of any genetic basis for race, how important is diversity? Does Hawaii serve as a model for college communities? Or does Nathan help explain why notions of race persist even without a genetic basis?

3. Michael Pollan examines the complex ecosystems of organic farming in "The Animals: Practicing Complexity" (p. 281). Might those ecosystems provide a model for community and diversity in education? How can individuals serve as holons on the college campus? Use your work on your school's Web site from Question 1 of Exploring Context in considering your own school as an ecosystem. What might be a holon for your campus?

Language Matters

1. Sentences can be written in either active or passive voice. If you're not sure what these terms mean, look up *active* and *passive voice* in a grammar handbook or reference guide. Then select a quotation from Nathan's essay that you think is key to her argument. Identify whether it is written in active or passive voice, noting how you know this to be the case. Then rewrite the sentence in the opposite voice. Is the argument weaker in passive voice or in active voice? Are concepts clearer in one voice or the other? Why or why not? Why might you choose active or passive voice in your own writing?

2. Word choice and tone are important in your writing. Select a significant quotation from Nathan's text, type it into a blank document in a word processor, and, using a thesaurus (the word processor's, one online, or a printed one), replace every significant word in the sentence with a synonym. Does the sentence still work? How does word choice influence tone and meaning? Why didn't Nathan

use "fancier" or more "academic" language in this text? Based on what you have discovered, what sort of tone do you think you should use in your writing for this class?

3. Drafting and revising are crucial components of the writing process. We often see a published piece of writing as perfect, but imagine earlier drafts of Nathan's text. How do you think she started this piece? What areas do you think Nathan revised the most? Where do you think you should do the most revision as you draft your own papers?

Assignments for Writing

1. Nathan notes that despite AnyU's best efforts to unite the university's population, students who make up the different communities within the school would rather bond within their own social groups than venture outside of them. Assess the situation Nathan talks about in her essay. Thinking beyond Nathan's findings, write a paper in which you examine the possibilities of communities becoming fully integrated. Is such integration even possible in a world made up of so many diverse and differing communities? The purpose of this essay is for you to apply the concepts in Nathan's essay to your own specific observations and experiences. Rather than simply writing a story about your own opinions, you should instead use your experiences and observations among diverse communities, on an academic campus or elsewhere, to explore the possibilities of a truly integrated community. You may also want to use your responses to Questions for Critical Reading and Exploring Context in supporting your argument.

2. Nathan decides going undercover is the only way to understand why university social life has not become what university presidents want. This reflects her belief that these leaders are out of touch with students' perspectives on community. So, although university presidents want the best for their schools, in fact it seems like their actions have had little impact. Write a paper in which you examine why it is important for university and college leaders to share the same outlook as their students in terms of community building. To help you complete your essay successfully, you may want to closely read specific passages from Nathan's essay that outline the perspectives university presidents and students have. Why is it so important to understand the differences in those perspectives?

3. How does individuality inhibit community building within diverse populations? Write a paper in which you assess the potential for balancing the needs of individuals and communities. Use your responses to Questions for Critical Reading as well as to Question 3 of Questions for Connecting to support your argument. Are ego-centered networks inevitable? Are diversity and community mutually exclusive goals?

STEVE OLSON

Journalist **Steve Olson**, who holds a B.S. in physics from Yale University, has reported for the *Atlantic Monthly, Science,* and *Scientific American* and has published multiple books, including *Mapping Human History: Discovering the Past through Our Genes* (2002), which was a finalist for the National Book Award, and *Count Down* (2004), about teens at the International Mathematical Olympiad.

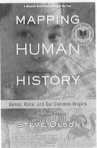

In *Mapping Human History,* the source of the following selection, Olson studies the path of our species through genes and continents, tracking all of humanity back to a small group that lived in eastern Africa, debunking racial myths along the way. Regardless of what appear to be differences among us, suggests Olson, biologically we are all basically the same. Our group origins and differences, which were superficial to begin with, lose importance as time goes by.

In "The End of Race: Hawaii and the Mixing of Peoples," Olson considers centuries of intermarriage between native and nonnative races in the Hawaiian islands. Although this extensive "mixing of peoples" has led some to propose Hawaii as an example of interracial harmony, Olson acknowledges that such claims are not entirely true. Though the majority of those born and raised in Hawaii come from a complex racial and ethnic makeup, social, political, and historical influences have contributed to deep cultural divides among the various island populations. Now, in the aftermath of European colonization, the preservation of Hawaiian culture as well as the definition of what it means to be a native Hawaiian are pressing questions with no easy genetic or biological answers. Thus Olson ultimately questions whether racial and cultural identity are rooted in biology or affiliation. The "end of race" is, perhaps, no end at all.

What defines race? And given how complicated such a definition must inevitably be, how can we end racism and promote racial harmony?

▶ TAGS: *research,* race, *community,* diplomacy, *diversity,* ethnicity, bioethics, *integration*

The End of Race: Hawaii and the Mixing of Peoples

> He loved everything, he was full of joyous love toward everything that
> he saw. And it seemed to him that was just why he was previously so
> ill—because he could love nothing and nobody.
>
> —HERMANN HESSE, *Siddhartha*

On the morning of November 26, 1778, the 100-foot-long, three-masted ship
Resolution, captained by the fifty-year-old Englishman James Cook, sailed
into view off the northeast coast of the Hawaiian island of Maui. The island's
Polynesian inhabitants had never seen a European sailing ship before. The
sight of the *Resolution* just beyond the fierce windward surf must have looked
as strange to them as a spaceship from another planet. Yet they responded
without hesitation. They boarded canoes and paddled to the ship. From atop
the rolling swells they offered the sailors food, water, and, in the case of the
women, themselves.

One can easily imagine the contrast: the European sailors—gaunt, dirty,
many bearing the unmistakable signs of venereal disease—and the Polynesians, a people who abided by strict codes of personal hygiene, who washed every
day and plucked the hair from their faces and underarms, whose women had
bodies "moulded into the utmost perfection," in the words of one early admirer.
At first Cook forbade his men to bring the women on board the ship "to prevent
as much as possible the communicating [of the] fatal disease [gonorrhea] to
a set of innocent people." In the weeks and months to come, as the *Resolution*
lingered offshore, Cook was far less resolute. Toward the end of 1779, the first of
what are today called *hapa haoles*—half European, half non-European—were
born on the island of Maui.

The nineteenth-century stereotype of the South Pacific as a sexual paradise owes as much to the feverish imaginations of repressed Europeans as to
the actions of the Polynesians. The young women who swam out to the ships in
Hawaii, Tahiti, and other South Pacific islands were from the lower classes, not
from the royalty, which carefully guarded its legitimacy. Many were training to
be dancers in religious festivals. They would rise in status by exchanging their
sexual favors for a tool, a piece of cloth, or an iron nail.

The Polynesians paid dearly for their openness. At least 300,000 people,
and possibly as many as 800,000, lived on the Hawaiian islands when Captain
Cook first sighted them (today the total population of the state is about 1.2 million). Over the course of the next century, diseases introduced by Europeans
reduced the native population to fewer than 50,000. By the time the painter
Paul Gauguin journeyed to the Pacific in 1891, the innocence that Europeans
had perceived among the Polynesians was gone. "The natives, having nothing,
nothing at all to do, think of one thing only, drinking," he wrote. "Day by day
the race vanishes, decimated by the European diseases. . . . There is so much
prostitution that it does not exist. . . . One only knows a thing by its contrary,

and its contrary does not exist." The women in Gauguin's paintings are beautiful yet defeated, without hope, lost in a vision of the past.

Today visitors to Maui land on a runway just downwind from the shore   5
where Captain Cook battled the surf eleven generations ago. Once out of the airport, they encounter what is probably the most genetically mixed population in the world. To the genes of Captain Cook's sailors and the native Polynesians has been added the DNA of European missionaries, Mexican cowboys, African American soldiers, and plantation workers from throughout Asia and Europe. This intense mixing of DNA has produced a population of strikingly beautiful people. Miss Universe of 1997 and Miss America of 2001 were both from Hawaii. The former, Brook Mahealani Lee, is a classic Hawaiian blend. Her ancestors are Korean and Hawaiian, Chinese and European.

Bernie Adair—who was selling candles at a swap meet in Kahului, Maui's largest town, when I met her—told me that her family's history was typical. Adair, whose ancestors came to Hawaii from the Philippines, married a Portuguese man in the 1960s. In the 1980s their daughter Marlene married a man of mixed Hawaiian, Chinese, and Portuguese descent. Adair's granddaughter Carly, peeking shyly at me from under a folding table, therefore embodies four different ethnicities. "These children have grandparents with so many different nationalities you can't tell what they are," Adair said.

> **Hawaii's high rates of intermarriage have fascinated academics for decades.**

Almost half the people who live in Hawaii today are of "mixed" ancestry. What it means to be mixed is not at all obvious genetically, but for official purposes it means that a person's ancestors fall into more than one of the four "racial" categories identified on U.S. census forms: black, white, Native American, and Asian or Pacific Islander. Intermarriage is a cumulative process, so once an individual of mixed ancestry is born, all of that person's descendants also will be mixed. As intermarriage continues in Hawaii—and already almost half of all marriages are between couples of different or mixed ethnicities—the number of people who will be able to call themselves pure Japanese, or pure Hawaiian, or pure white (*haole* in Hawaiian), will steadily decline.

Hawaii's high rates of intermarriage have fascinated academics for decades. The University of Hawaii sociologist Romanzo Adams wrote an article titled "Hawai'i as a Racial Melting Pot" in 1926, and many scholars since then have extolled Hawaii as a model of ethnic and racial harmony. The researchers have always been a bit vague about the reasons for all this intermarriage; explanations have ranged from the benign climate to the "aloha spirit" of the Native Hawaiians. But their lack of analytic rigor hasn't damped their enthusiasm. One of the goals of the former Center for Research on Ethnic Relations at the University of Hawaii was "to determine why ethnic harmony exists in Hawai'i" and "to export principles of ethnic harmony to the mainland and the world."

The rest of the United States has a smaller percentage of mixed marriages than does Hawaii. But given recent trends, one might wonder if the country as a whole is headed down a road Hawaii took long ago. According to the 2000 census, one in twenty children under the age of eighteen in the United States is mixed, in that their parents fall into more than one racial category. Between the 1990 and 2000 censuses, the number of interracial couples quadrupled. This number—about 1.5 million of 55 million married couples—is not yet high, but because of kinship ties, American families are already much more mixed than they look. Demographer Joshua Goldstein of Princeton University has calculated that about 20 percent of Americans are already in extended families with someone from a different racial group—that is, they or their parents, uncles and aunts, siblings, or children have married someone classified as a member of a different race.

The rapid growth of interracial marriages in the United States and else-   10 where marks a new phase in the genetic history of humanity. Since the appearance of modern humans in Africa more than 100,000 years ago, human groups have differentiated in appearance as they have expanded across the globe and have undergone some measure of reproductive isolation. This differentiation has always been limited by the recentness of our common ancestry and by the powerful tendency of groups to mix over time. Still, many human populations have remained sufficiently separate to develop and retain the distinctive physical characteristics we recognize today.

In Hawaii this process is occurring in reverse. It's as if a videotape of our species' history were being played backward at a fantastically rapid speed. Physical distinctions that took thousands of generations to produce are being wiped clean with a few generations of intermarriage.

The vision of the future conjured up by intermarriage in Hawaii can be seductive. When everyone is marrying everyone else, when the ethnic affiliation of most people can no longer be ascertained at a glance, one imagines that ethnic and racial tensions would diminish. But spending some time in Hawaii shows that the future will not be that simple. Despite the high rate of intermarriage here, ethnic and racial tensions haven't really disappeared. They have changed into something else, something less threatening, perhaps, but still divisive. Hawaii may well be a harbinger of a racially mixed future. But it won't be the future many people expect.

Many of the harshest conflicts in the world today are between people who are physically indistinguishable. If someone took a roomful of Palestinians and Israelis from the Middle East, or of Serbs and Albanians from the Balkans, or of Catholics and Protestants from Ireland, or of Muslims and Hindus from northern India, or of Dayaks and Madurese from Indonesia, gave them all identical outfits and haircuts, and forbade them to speak or gesture, no one could distinguish the members of the other group—at least not to the point of being willing to shoot them. The antagonists in these conflicts have different ethnicities, but they have been so closely linked biologically throughout history that they have not developed marked physical differences.

Yet one of the most perverse dimensions of ethnic thinking is the "racialization" of culture—the tendency to think of another people as not just culturally but genetically distinct. In the Yugoslavian war, the Croats caricatured their

Serbian opponents as tall and blond, while the Serbs disparaged the darker hair and skin of the Croats—even though these traits are thoroughly intermixed between the two groups. During World War II the countries of Europe fiercely stereotyped the physical attributes of their enemies, despite a history of inter-marriage and migration that has scrambled physical characteristics through-out the continent. In Africa the warring Tutsis and Hutus often call attention to the physical differences of their antagonists, but most observers have trouble distinguishing individual members of the two groups solely on the basis of appearance.

The flip side of this biological stereotyping is the elevation of one's own an-cestry. The Nazis were the most notorious believers in the purity of their past, but many other groups have similar beliefs. They proclaim themselves to be descended from ancient tribes of noble warriors, or from prominent families in the distant past, or even from famous individuals.

Genetics research has revealed the flaw inherent in any such belief. Every group is a mixture of many previous groups, a fleeting collection of genetic variants drawn from a shared genetic legacy. The Polynesian colonizers of the Hawaiian archipelago are a good example. In 1795 the German anatomist J. F. Blumenbach proposed that the "Malays"—a collection of peoples, including

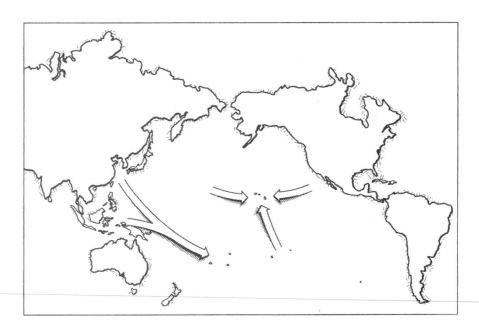

The Polynesian inhabitants of Hawaii are descended from people who lived both in southeastern Asia and in Melanesia, which includes New Guinea and nearby islands. The Polynesians migrated first to the South Pacific islands of Fiji, Tonga, and Samoa, with later migrations taking their descendants from the Marquesas islands to Hawaii. More recent migrants have included people from Asia, the Americas, and Europe.

the Polynesians, from southeastern Asia and Oceania—were one of the five races of humanity, in addition to Africans, Caucasians, Mongoloids, and Native Americans. But all of these groups (to the extent that they can be defined) are genetic composites of previous groups. In the case of the Polynesians, this mixing was part of the spread of humans into the Pacific. The last major part of the world to be occupied by humans was Remote Oceania, the widely separated islands scattered in a broad crescent from Hawaii to New Zealand. Before that, humans had been living only in Near Oceania, which includes Australia, Papua New Guinea, and the Bismarck Archipelago. The humans who settled these regions were adept at short ocean crossings, but they never developed the kinds of boats or navigation skills needed to sail hundreds of miles to Fiji, Samoa, and beyond.

Then, about 6,000 years ago, rice and millet agriculture made the leap across the Formosa Strait from the mainland of southeastern Asia to Taiwan. From there, agriculture began to spread, island by island, to the south and southeast. With it came two important cultural innovations. The first was the Austronesian language family, which eventually spread halfway around the world, from Madagascar to Easter Island. The second was a suite of new technologies—pottery, woodworking implements, and eventually the outrigger canoe and ways of using the stars to navigate across large expanses of open water. Archaeological evidence shows that people first reached the previously uninhabited island of Fiji about 3,000 years ago. They sailed to Easter Island, their farthest point east, in about AD 300 and to New Zealand, their farthest point south, in about 800.

One hypothesis, known as the express-train model of Polynesian origins, claims that both the knowledge of agriculture and Austronesian languages were carried into the Pacific by people descended almost exclusively from the first farmers who set sail from Taiwan. But genetic studies have revealed a much more complex picture. Mitochondrial and Y-chromosome haplotypes among today's Polynesians show that there was extensive mixing of peoples in Near Oceania, which eventually produced the groups that set sail for the remote islands. Though many of the mitochondrial haplotypes and Y chromosomes of the Polynesians do seem to have come from the mainland of southeastern Asia and Taiwan, others originated in New Guinea and its nearby islands—a geographic region known as Melanesia (named for the generally dark skin of its inhabitants). Geneticists Manfred Kayser and Mark Stoneking of the Max Planck Institute for Evolutionary Anthropology in Leipzig have dubbed the resulting synthesis the "slow-boat model." According to this model, today's Polynesians can trace their ancestry both to the Austronesian speakers who moved out of southeastern Asia and to the people who already occupied Melanesia.

The Polynesians first reached the Hawaiian islands around AD 400, probably in a migration from the Marquesas islands. A subsequent wave of people migrated to Hawaii from Tahiti between the twelfth and the fourteenth century. Then the islands saw no more newcomers until Captain Cook's arrival four centuries later.

The discovery of Hawaii by Europeans did not result in an immediate influx   20
of colonists. The early decades of the nineteenth century brought just a trickle
of settlers to the islands—washed-up sailors, retired captains, British and
Russian traders, missionaries. Large-scale migration began only after the first
sugar plantations were established around the middle of the century. In 1852,
three hundred Chinese men arrived to work the plantations. Over the next century nearly half a million more workers followed. They came from China, Japan,
Korea, Puerto Rico, Spain, Poland, Austria, Germany, Norway, and Russia.
Some of these groups have long since disappeared, blending into the genetic
background. Others still have a significant ethnic presence on the islands.

A few miles from the Honolulu airport is a vivid reminder of those times.
Hawaii's Plantation Village is one of the few tourist attractions designed as
much for the locals as for mainlanders. It meticulously recreates a camp town
of the type that once dotted the islands, housing the workers who toiled each
day in the sugar and pineapple fields. Each house along the main avenue reflects
the ethnicity of the workers who lived there: A large bread oven sits next to
the Portuguese house, rice cookers dominate the kitchen of the Chinese house,
crucifixes adorn the walls of the Puerto Rican house. A Japanese shrine is a few
doors away from the Chinese society building. Down the hill by the taro fields is
a *dohyo*, a sumo ring, where the workers wrestled every Sunday afternoon.

Mike Hama showed me around the day I was there. The descendant of
Japanese, German, Hawaiian, and Irish grandparents, Hama grew up on a plantation camp in the 1940s. "Kids of all different nationalities played together in
these camps," he told me. "We didn't know we were different." They communicated using a pidgin that combined words from many languages. The German
kids taught the other kids to polka in the camp social halls. The Japanese kids
taught their friends sumo wrestling. When the Japanese emperor visited Hawaii
after World War II, according to a widely told if hard-to-verify story, he was so
impressed to see wrestlers of all different nationalities in the *dohyo* that when he
returned to Japan he opened the country's sumo rings to foreigners.

When Hama was eighteen, he joined the military and was stationed in
California. "That was a real awakening for me," he recalls. "For the first time I
saw the bigotry that was going on outside Hawaii." He moved back to Hawaii as
soon as he could and married a woman of mixed ancestry. His four daughters
think of themselves as nothing other than local Hawaiians.

The camp towns disappeared decades ago in Hawaii, yet they have left a
remarkable legacy. Large-scale segregation in housing remains rare on the
islands. People of all ethnic backgrounds live side by side, just as they did in
the camp towns. The only people who live in ghettos are the soldiers on military bases and wealthy haoles who wall themselves off in gated communities.
Because neighborhoods are integrated in Hawaii, so are most of the schools.
Children of different ethnicities continue to grow up together and marry, just as
they did in the camps.

Integrated neighborhoods, integrated schools, high rates of intermarriage—the   25
islands sound as if they should be a racial paradise. But there's actually a fair

amount of prejudice here. It pops up in novels, politics, the spiels of standup comics. And it's especially prominent in everyday conversation—"talk stink" is the pidgin term for disrespecting another group.

Some of the prejudice is directed toward haoles, who continue to occupy many of the positions of social and economic prominence on the islands (though their days as plantation overlords are long gone). Nonwhites label haoles as cold, self-serving, arrogant, meddling, loud, and even that old stereotype—smelly (because, it is held, they still do not bathe every day). White kids say they'll get beat up if they venture onto certain nonwhite beaches. Occasionally a rumor sweeps through a school about an upcoming "Kill a Haole" day. The rumors are a joke meant to shock the prevailing sensibilities. But one would not expect such a joke where racial tensions are low.

Other groups come in for similarly rough treatment. The Japanese are derided as clannish and power-hungry, the Filipinos as ignorant and under-handed, the Hawaiians as fat, lazy, and fun-loving. And, as is true of stereotypes everywhere, the objects of them have a tendency to reinforce them, either by too vigorously denying or too easily repeating them.

"Intermarriage may indicate tolerance," says Jonathan Okamura, an anthropologist at the University of Hawaii, "but it doesn't mean we have an egalitarian society on a larger scale." Though he calls his viewpoint a "minority position," Okamura holds that racial and ethnic prejudice is deeply ingrained in the institutional structures of everyday life in Hawaii. For example, the integration of the public schools is deceptive, he says. Well-off haoles, Chinese, and Japanese send their children to private schools, and the public schools are underfunded. "We've created a two-tiered system that makes inequality increasingly worse rather than better," says Okamura. Meanwhile the rapid growth of the tourism industry in Hawaii has shut off many traditional routes to economic betterment. Tourism produces mostly low-paying jobs in sales, service, and construction, Okamura points out, so people have few opportunities to move up career ladders.

Of course, talented and lucky individuals still get ahead. "Students with parents who didn't go to college come to the university and do well—that happens all the time," Okamura says. "But it doesn't happen enough to advance socioeconomically disadvantaged groups in society."

Several ethnic groups occupy the lower end of the socioeconomic scale, but one in particular stands out: the people descended from the island's original inhabitants. Native Hawaiians have the lowest incomes and highest unemployment rates of any ethnic group. They have the most health problems and the shortest life expectancy. They are the least likely to go to college and the most likely to be incarcerated. 30

Then again, applying statistics like these to a group as large and diverse as Native Hawaiians is inevitably misleading. Individuals with some Hawaiian ancestry make up a fifth of the population in Hawaii. Some are successful; some are not. Some are consumed by native issues; others pay them no mind. And Native Hawaiians are much less marginalized in Hawaii than are, for example, Native Americans in the rest of the United States. Hawaiian words, names, and outlooks have seeped into everyday life on the islands, producing a cultural amalgam that is one of the state's distinct attractions.

Native Hawaiians should not be seen as simply another ethnic group, the leaders of their community point out. Other cultures have roots elsewhere; people of Japanese, German, or Samoan ancestry can draw from the traditions of an ancestral homeland to sustain an ethnic heritage. If the culture of the Native Hawaiians disappears, it will be gone forever. Greater recognition of the value and fragility of this culture has led to a resurgence of interest in the Hawaiian past. Schools with Hawaiian language immersion programs have sprung up around the islands to supplement the English that children speak at home. Traditional forms of Hawaiian dance, music, canoeing, and religion all have undergone revivals.

This Hawaiian Renaissance also has had a political dimension. For the past several decades a sovereignty movement has been building among Native Hawaiians that seeks some measure of political autonomy and control over the lands that the U.S. government seized from the Hawaiian monarchy at the end of the nineteenth century. Reflecting the diversity of the native population, several sovereignty organizations have carried out a sometimes unseemly struggle over strategies and goals. One radical faction advocates the complete independence of the islands from the United States. More moderate groups have called for the establishment of a Native Hawaiian nation modeled on the Indian tribes on the mainland. Native Hawaiians would have their own government, but it would operate within existing federal and state frameworks, and its citizens would remain Americans.

Native Hawaiian sovereignty faces many hurdles, and it is premature to harp on exactly how it would work. But whenever the topic comes up in discussion, a question quickly surfaces: Exactly who is a Native Hawaiian? "Pure" Hawaiians with no non-Hawaiian ancestors probably number just a few thousand. Many Native Hawaiians undoubtedly have a preponderance of Hawaiian ancestors, but no clear line separates natives from nonnatives. Some people who call themselves Native Hawaiians probably have little DNA from Polynesian ancestors.

Past legislation has waffled on this issue. Some laws define Native Hawaiians as people who can trace at least half their ancestry to people living in Hawaii before the arrival of Captain Cook. Others define as Hawaiian anyone who has even a single precontact Hawaiian ancestor. These distinctions are highly contentious for political and economic as well as cultural reasons. Many state laws restrict housing subsidies, scholarships, economic development grants, and other benefits specifically to Native Hawaiians.

As the study of genetics and history has progressed, an obvious idea has arisen. Maybe science could resolve the issue. Maybe a genetic marker could be found that occurs only in people descended from the aboriginal inhabitants of Hawaii. Then anyone with that marker could be considered a Native Hawaiian.

No one is better qualified to judge this idea than Rebecca Cann, a professor of genetics at the University of Hawaii. Cann was the young graduate student at the University of California at Berkeley who, with Mark Stoneking, did much of the work that led to the unveiling of mitochondrial Eve. She haunted hospital delivery rooms to obtain mitochondrion-rich placentas, which at that time was the only way to get enough mitochondrial DNA to sequence. She ran gels and compared nucleotides. Her faculty adviser, Allan Wilson, landed mitochondrial Eve on the cover of *Newsweek*, but Cann did the footwork.

She moved to Hawaii even before mitochondrial Eve made headlines, responding to an ad in *Science* magazine for a job. She's been here ever since, though her flat American accent still betrays a childhood spent in Iowa. She met me at the door of her office, in the foothills above Honolulu, dressed in sandals and a patterned Hawaiian dress. "I think we correctly anticipated many of the applications and potential problems of this research," she said, "right down to people wanting to clone Elvis from a handkerchief he'd used to wipe his brow. What we didn't understand was the degree to which religious and cultural beliefs would dictate attitudes toward genetic materials. In Hawaii, for instance, there's a very strong belief in *mana*, in the power of the spirit, which is contained in the remains of a person's ancestors. The absolute disgust that many people have toward the desecration of a grave—that was a cultural eye-opener for me."

Despite the occasional cultural difficulties, Cann has continued her study of human genetics in Hawaii and has played an important role in piecing together the prehistory of the Pacific. By comparing the mitochondrial

Exactly who is a Native Hawaiian?

DNA sequences of people on various islands, she has traced the gradual eastward spread of modern humans from southeastern Asia and Melanesia. She has discovered that men and women had different migration patterns into the Pacific and has even detected tantalizing evidence, still unconfirmed, of genetic contacts between Pacific Islanders and South Americans. "I'm convinced that our history is written in our DNA," she told me.

Yet she cautioned against using genetics to determine ethnicity. "I get people coming up to me all the time and saying, 'Can you prove that I'm a Hawaiian?'" She can't, she said, at least not with a high degree of certainty. A given individual might have a mitochondrial haplotype that is more common among Native Hawaiians. But the ancestors of the aboriginal Hawaiians also gave rise to other Pacific populations, so a mitochondrial sequence characteristic of Native Hawaiians could have come from a Samoan or Filipino ancestor.

Also, a person's mitochondrial DNA is not necessarily an accurate indication of ancestry. The only way for a person to have mitochondrial DNA from a woman who lived in Hawaii before the arrival of Captain Cook is for that person to have an unbroken line of grandmothers dating back to that woman. But because groups have mixed so much in Hawaii, mitochondrial lineages have become thoroughly tangled. People who think of themselves as Native Hawaiian could easily have had non-Hawaiian female ancestors sometime in the past eleven generations, which would have given them mitochondrial DNA from another part of the world.

These genetic exchanges are also common elsewhere in the world, even in populations that think of themselves as less mixed. Most native Europeans, for example, have mitochondrial DNA characteristic of that part of the world. But some have mitochondrial DNA from elsewhere—southern Africa, or eastern Asia, or even Polynesia—brought to Europe over the millennia by female immigrants. The British matron who has a mitochondrial haplotype found most often in southern Africans is not an African, just as the Native Hawaiian with mitochondrial DNA from a German great-great-grandmother does not automatically become German.

This confusion of genetic and cultural identities becomes even greater with the Y chromosome, given the ease with which that chromosome can insert itself into a genealogy. Most of the early migrants to Hawaii, for example, were males, especially the plantation workers. Those males mated with native women more often than native men mated with immigrant women, so nonnative Y chromosomes are now more common in mixed populations than nonnative mitochondrial DNA. In some populations in South America, virtually all the Y chromosomes are from Europe and all the mitochondrial DNA is from indigenous groups.

The mixing of genes can cause great consternation, but it is the inevitable consequence of our genetic history. Several years ago a geneticist in Washington, D.C., began offering to identify the homelands of the mitochondrial DNA and Y chromosomes of African Americans. The service foundered for several reasons, but one was that 30 percent of the Y chromosomes in African American males come from European ancestors.

Within a few years geneticists will be able to use DNA sequences from all the chromosomes to trace ancestry. But these histories will be just as convoluted as those of mitochondrial DNA and the Y. Granted, geneticists will be able to make statistical assessments. They will be able to say, for instance, that a given person has such and such a probability of descent from a Native Hawaiian population, and in some cases the probability will be very high. But probabilities don't convey the cold, hard certainties that people want in their genealogies.

Beyond the purely genetic considerations are the social ones. When children are adopted from one group into another, they become a member of that group socially, yet their haplotypes and those of their descendants can differ from the group norm. Rape is another way in which the genetic variants of groups mix. And sometimes people from one group make a conscious decision to join another and are gladly accepted, despite their different genetic histories.

"I get nervous when people start talking about using genetic markers to prove ethnicity," Cann told me. "I don't believe that biology is destiny. Allowing yourself to be defined personally by whatever your DNA sequence is, that's insane. But that's exactly what some people are going to be tempted to do."

When geneticists look at our DNA, they do not see a world of rigidly divided groups each going its own way. They see something much more fluid and ambiguous—something more like the social structures that have emerged in Hawaii as intermarriage has accelerated.

   The most remarkable aspect of ethnicity in Hawaii is its loose relation to biology. Many people have considerable latitude in choosing their ethnic affiliations. Those of mixed ancestry can associate with the ethnicity of a parent, a grandparent, or a more distant ancestor. They can partition their ethnic affiliations: They can be Chinese with their Chinese relatives; Native Hawaiian with their native kin; and just plain local with their buddies. The community of descent that a person associates with has become more like a professional or religious affiliation, a connection over which a person has some measure of control.

   People whose ancestors are from a single ethnic group have fewer options,   50
but they, too, can partake of at least some of Hawaii's ethnic flexibility. Young whites, for example, sometimes try to pass themselves off as mixed by maintaining an especially dark tan. Among many young people, dating someone from a different ethnic group is a social asset rather than a liability, in part because of the doors it opens to other communities. Many prospective students at the University of Hawaii simply mark "mixed" in describing their ethnicity on application forms, even if both parents have the same ethnic background. "My students say they don't want to be pigeonholed," says Okamura. "That way they can identify with different groups."

   Hawaii's high rates of intermarriage also contribute greatly to the islands' ethnic flux. Ethnicity is not defined just by who one's ancestors were. It also is defined prospectively—by the group into which one is expected to marry. For most young people in Hawaii, the pool of marriageable partners encompasses the entire population. Relations among groups are inevitably less fractious when their members view each other as potential mates.

   Of course, ethnic and even "racial" groups still exist in Hawaii, and they will for a long time. Despite the rapid growth of intermarriage in Hawaii and elsewhere, the mixing of peoples takes generations, not a few years or even decades. Most people around the world still choose marriage partners who would be classified as members of the same "race." In many parts of the world—the American Midwest, China, Iceland—few other options are available. Five hundred years from now, unless human societies undergo drastic changes, Asians, Africans, and Europeans still will be physically distinguishable.

   But the social effects of intermarriage are much more immediate than are the biological effects. Socially, intermarriage can quickly undermine the idea that culture has biological roots. When a substantial number of mixed individuals demonstrate, by their very existence, that choices are possible, that biology is not destiny, the barriers between groups become more permeable. Ethnicity in Hawaii, for example, seems far less stark and categorical than it does in the rest of the United States. The people of Hawaii recognize overlaps and exceptions. They are more willing to accept the haole who claims to have non-European ancestors or the Native Hawaiian who affiliates with Filipinos. It's true that people talk about the differences among groups all the time, but even talking about these differences, rather than rigidly ignoring them, makes them seem less daunting. Expressions of social prejudice in Hawaii are more like a form of social banter, like a husband and wife picking at each other's faults.

The logical endpoint of this perspective is a world in which people are free to choose their ethnicity regardless of their ancestry. Ethnicity is not yet *entirely* voluntary in Hawaii, but in many respects the islands are headed in that direction. State law, for example, is gradually coming to define a Native Hawaiian as anyone with a single Hawaiian ancestor. But at that point ethnicity becomes untethered from biology—it is instead a cultural, political, or historical distinction. People are no longer who they say they are because of some mysterious biological essence. They have chosen the group with which they want to affiliate.

Genetically, this view of ethnicity makes perfect sense. Our DNA is too tightly interconnected to use biology to justify what are essentially social distinctions. Our preferences, character, and abilities are not determined by the biological history of our ancestors. They depend on our individual attributes, experiences, and choices. As this inescapable conclusion becomes more widely held, our genetic histories inevitably will become less and less important. When we look at another person, we won't think Asian, black, or white. We'll just think: person.

In his novel *Siddhartha,* Hermann Hesse tells the story of a young man in ancient India, a disciple of an inspired teacher, who sets out to find the reality beneath the world of appearance. After years of study and wandering, Siddhartha becomes a ferryman, learning from his predecessor how to listen to the voices in the passing river. One day a childhood friend named Govinda comes to the river. Siddhartha and Govinda have a long conversation about the interdependence of illusion and truth, about the existence of the past and future in the present, about the need not just to think about the world but to love it. Finally Govinda asks Siddhartha how he has achieved such peace in his life. Siddhartha replies, "Kiss me on the forehead, Govinda." Govinda is surprised by the request, but out of respect for his friend he complies. When he touches Siddhartha's forehead with his lips, he has a wondrous vision:

> He no longer saw the face of his friend Siddhartha. Instead he saw other faces, many faces, a long series, a continuous stream of faces— hundreds, thousands, which all came and disappeared and yet all seemed to be there at the same time, which all continually changed and renewed themselves and which were all yet Siddhartha. . . . He saw the face of a newly born child, red and full of wrinkles, ready to cry. He saw the face of a murderer, . . . He saw the naked bodies of men and women in the postures and transports of passionate love. . . . Each one was mortal, a passionate, painful example of all that is transitory. Yet none of them died, they only changed, were always reborn, continually had a new face; only time stood between one face and another.

I began this book [*Mapping Human History*] by calling attention to the different appearances of human beings. I conclude it now by calling attention to the opposite. Throughout human history, groups have wondered how they are related to one another. The study of genetics has now revealed that we all are linked: the Bushmen hunting antelope, the mixed-race people of South Africa, the African Americans descended from slaves, the Samaritans on their mountain stronghold, the Jewish populations scattered around the world, the Han Chinese a billion strong, the descendants of European settlers who colonized the New World, the Native Hawaiians who look to a cherished past. We are members of a single human family, the products of genetic necessity and chance, borne ceaselessly into an unknown future.

Questions for Critical Reading

1. What is a "community of descent"? Develop a definition by rereading Olson's text to locate quotations that define the concept. Offer, too, an example of a community of descent from your own experience.

2. How does Olson define *race*? Create a definition and support it using quotations from Olson's essay. To do so, you will need to reread his essay critically, paying close attention to what Olson has to say about the concept of race.

3. If race no longer has a biological basis, as Olson claims, why do ethnicities continue to function in society? Use Olson's text to propose reasons why race persists.

Exploring Context

1. Read the U.S. Census Bureau's explanation of the racial categories used in the census taken every ten years: census.gov/population/www/socdemo/race/racefactcb.html. How do these categories relate to Olson's argument? Relate your response to your work on the persistence of race from Question 3 of Questions for Critical Reading.

2. Visit Hawaii's official state government Web site at hawaii.gov and then visit the official Hawaii tourism Web site at gohawaii.com. How is race represented on these sites? What races do you see in the images? Is the representation of race the same for residents and for tourists? Why might there be differences? Use the definition of race you developed in Question 2 of Questions for Critical Reading to support your position.

3. One place that race persists in Hawaii, according to Olson, is in schools. Locate the Web site for some schools in Hawaii. Do you find evidence to support Olson's argument or to complicate it?

Questions for Connecting

1. If Olson is right in discounting the genetic basis of race, why do racial categories persist? Does Leslie Savan's analysis of the economic value of pop talk and its relation to black talk in "What's Black, Then White, and Said All Over?" (p. 363) offer some reasons? Apply your analysis of race from Question 3 of Questions for Critical Reading in making your response.

2. How does the quinceañera reflect a "community of descent"? Using your defini-tion of the term from Question 1 of Questions for Critical Reading as well as Olson's other concepts, explain the widespread popularity of quinces as demon-strated by Julia Alvarez in "Selections from *Once Upon a Quinceañera*" (p. 35). Is retroculturation a hindrance to the end of race?

3. Does Hawaii offer a model for the new civil rights that Kenji Yoshino advocates in "Preface" (p. 479) and "The New Civil Rights" (p. 481)? Given the end of race, should we pursue a liberty or an equality paradigm?

Language Matters

1. Choose a key quotation from Olson. Revise it to make it less effective but still grammatically correct. Would making it a question blunt its force? What about changing it to passive voice? Draw some general conclusions from this experi-ment. What makes a sentence effective?

2. Locate materials in a reference book or online on writing a résumé and then make a résumé for this essay. What would be this essay's "career objective"? What would be its "experience"? Who would it list for references?

3. How would you "grade" Olson's essay? In small groups, develop a set of grading criteria and then apply those criteria to Olson's text. What does your group value in writing? What does this class value in writing?

Assignments for Writing

1. Can there be an end to race? Engage Olson's essay by writing a paper in which you examine the possibility of an end to race. Why does race persist? Can or should we move beyond concepts of race? Would something replace the idea of race, or has something replaced it already? You may want to draw on your responses to the Questions for Critical Reading as well as your examination of the census from Question 1 of Exploring Context in making your argument.

2. Olson's argument is based in part on advances in genetic technologies. Write a paper in which you evaluate the relationship between technology and race. Consider: Is race itself a kind of technology? Can technology move us beyond race? You may want to use the definition of race you developed in Question 2 of Questions for Critical Reading in making your argument.

3. Race is not the only factor in determining group identity; Olson discusses com-munities of descent as well. Using Olson's essay, write a paper in which you determine the relationship between race and cultural identity. Does the history of a particular race dictate its importance as a cultural identity? Can a particular race have ownership over its cultural aspects? Can an individual choose a racial or cultural identity? In making your argument, you may want to use the defini-tion of communities of descent that you developed in Questions for Critical Reading.

MARSHALL POE

Marshall Poe, a historian who has published numerous books on Russian and Soviet history and has held fellowships at Harvard and Columbia universities, is currently associate professor of history at the University of Iowa. In addition to his work in history, Poe is also interested in the intersections of technology, publishing, and memory. He is the creator of MemoryArchive (memoryarchive.org), a Wikipedia-modeled "encyclopedia of memories," where users can post their memories of personal or historical events and others can read them. As a journalist, Poe worked for the *Atlantic Monthly,* where he published the following article, "The Hive," in September 2006.

"The Hive" tells a number of stories about Wikipedia (wikipedia.org), the collaboratively written and edited online encyclopedia, in order to tell a larger story about collaborative knowledge in general. Poe details his embarrassing attempt to add his own biography to the site's archives, the early role-playing game and discussion-board lives of the site's founders, and the fate of Wikipedia's predecessor. He also documents the site's birth pangs, revealing the influences and motivating factors behind its rapid growth and rapidly growing importance.

"Wikipedia," Poe claims, "has the potential to be the greatest effort in collaborative knowledge gathering the world has ever known, and it may well be the greatest effort in voluntary collaboration of any kind." The epistemological questions offered by "The Hive" go beyond merely what people know to whether collective knowledge is valid, what motivates people to share their knowledge, and what can be gained from what Poe calls "the wisdom of crowds."

Each of you has the opportunity to contribute or edit entries in Wikipedia. But what is the ultimate value of Wikipedia's collective knowledge, and what are the keys to Wikipedia's success?

▶ TAGS: *diplomacy*, **groups**, *technology*, *community*, *collaboration*, *education*, *feedback*

The Hive

Several months ago, I discovered that I was being "considered for deletion." Or rather, the entry on me in the Internet behemoth that is Wikipedia was.

For those of you who are (as uncharitable Wikipedians sometimes say) "clueless newbies," Wikipedia is an online encyclopedia. But it is like no encyclopedia Diderot could have imagined. Instead of relying on experts to write articles according to their expertise, Wikipedia lets anyone write about anything. You, I, and any wired-up fool can add entries, change entries, even propose that entries be deleted. For reasons I'd rather not share outside of therapy, I created a one-line biographical entry on "Marshall Poe." It didn't take long for my tiny article to come to the attention of Wikipedia's self-appointed guardians. Within a week, a very active—and by most accounts responsible—Scottish Wikipedian named "Alai" decided that . . . well, that I wasn't worth knowing about. Why? "No real evidence of notability," Alai cruelly but accurately wrote, "beyond the proverbial average college professor."

Wikipedia has the potential to be the greatest effort in collaborative knowledge gathering the world has ever known, and it may well be the greatest effort in voluntary collaboration of any kind. The English-language version alone has more than a million entries. It is consistently ranked among the most visited Web sites in the world. A quarter century ago it was inconceivable that a legion of unpaid, unorganized amateurs scattered about the globe could create anything of value, let alone what may one day be the most comprehensive repository of knowledge in human history. Back then we knew that people do not work for free; or if they do work for free, they do a poor job; and if they work for free in large numbers, the result is a muddle. Jimmy Wales and Larry Sanger knew all this when they began an online encyclopedia in 1999. Now, just seven years later, everyone knows different.

The Moderator

Jimmy Wales does not fit the profile of an Internet revolutionary. He was born in 1966 and raised in modest circumstances in Huntsville, Alabama. Wales majored in finance at Auburn, and after completing his degree enrolled in a graduate program at the University of Alabama. It was there that he developed a passion for the Internet. His entry point was typical for the nerdy set of his generation: fantasy games.

In 1974, Gary Gygax and Dave Arneson, two gamers who had obviously read *The Lord of the Rings*, invented the tabletop role-playing game Dungeons & Dragons. The game spread largely through networks of teenage boys, and by 1979, the year the classic *Dungeon Master's Guide* was published, it seemed that every youth who couldn't get a date was rolling the storied twenty-sided die in a shag-carpeted den. Meanwhile, a more electronically inclined crowd at the University of Illinois at Urbana-Champaign was experimenting with moving fantasy play from the basement to a computer network. The fruit of their labors was the unfortunately named MUD (Multi-User Dungeon). Allowing masses of players to create virtual fantasy worlds, MUDs garnered a large audience in the 1980s and 1990s under names like Zork, Myst, and Scepter of Goth. (MUDs came to be known as "Multi-Undergraduate Destroyers" for their tendency to divert college students from their studies.)

Wales began to play MUDs at Alabama in the late 1980s. It was in this context that he first encountered the power of networked computers to facilitate voluntary cooperation on a large scale. He did not, however, set up house in these fantasy worlds, nor did he show any evidence of wanting to begin a career in high tech. He completed a degree in finance at Auburn, received a master's in finance at the University of Alabama, and then pursued a Ph.D. in finance at Indiana University. He was interested, it would seem, in finance. In 1994, he quit his doctoral program and moved to Chicago to take a job as an options trader. There he made (as he has repeatedly said) "enough."

Wales is of a thoughtful cast of mind. He was a frequent contributor to the philosophical "discussion lists" (the first popular online discussion forums) that emerged in the late '80s as e-mail spread through the humanities. His particular passion was objectivism, the philosophical system developed by Ayn Rand. In 1989, he initiated the Ayn Rand Philosophy Discussion List and served as moderator—the person who invites and edits e-mails from subscribers. Though discussion lists were not new among the technorati in the 1980s, they were unfamiliar territory for most academics. In the oak-paneled seminar room, everyone had always been careful to behave properly—the chairman sat at the head of the table, and everyone spoke in turn and stuck to the topic. E-mail lists were something altogether different. Unrestrained by convention and cloaked by anonymity, participants could behave very badly without fear of real consequences. The term for such poor comportment—*flaming*—became one of the first bits of net jargon to enter common usage.

Wales had a careful moderation style:

> First, I will frown—very much—on any flaming of any kind whatsoever. . . . Second, I impose no restrictions on membership based on my own idea of what objectivism really is. . . . Third, I hope that the list will be more "academic" than some of the others, and tend toward discussions of technical details of epistemology. . . . Fourth, I have chosen a "middle-ground" method of moderation, a sort of behind-the-scenes prodding.

Wales was an advocate of what is generically termed "openness" online. An "open" online community is one with few restrictions on membership or posting—everyone is welcome, and anyone can say anything as long as it's generally on point and doesn't include gratuitous ad hominem attacks. Openness fit not only Wales's idea of objectivism, with its emphasis on reason and rejection of force, but also his mild personality. He doesn't like to fight. He would rather suffer fools in silence, waiting for them to talk themselves out, than confront them. This patience would serve Wales well in the years to come.

Top-Down and Bottom-Up

In the mid-1990s, the great dream of Internet entrepreneurs was to create *the* [10] entry point on the Web. "Portals," as they were called, would provide everything: e-mail, news, entertainment, and, most important, the tools to help users find what they wanted on the Web. As Google later showed, if you build the best "finding aid," you'll be a dominant player. In 1996, the smart money was on "Web directories," man-made guides to the Internet. Both Netscape and Yahoo relied on Web directories as their primary finding aids, and their IPOs in the mid-1990s suggested a bright future. In 1996, Wales and two partners founded a Web directory called Bomis.

Initially, the idea was to build a universal directory, like Yahoo's. The question was how to build it. At the time, there were two dominant models: top-down and bottom-up. The former is best exemplified by Yahoo, which began as *Jerry's Guide to the World Wide Web.* Jerry — in this case Jerry Yang, Yahoo's cofounder — set up a system of categories and began to classify Web sites accordingly. Web surfers flocked to the site because no one could find anything on the Web in the early 1990s. So Yang and his partner, David Filo, spent a mountain of venture capital to hire a team of surfers to classify the Web. Yahoo ("Yet Another Hierarchical Officious Oracle") was born.

Other would-be classifiers approached the problem of Web chaos more democratically. Beginning from the sound premise that it's good to share, a seventeen-year-old Oregonian named Sage Weil created the first "Web ring" at about the time Yang and Filo were assembling their army of paid Web librarians. A Web ring is nothing more than a set of topically related Web sites that have been linked together for ease of surfing. Rings are easy to find, easy to join, and easy to create; by 1997, they numbered 10,000.

Wales focused on the bottom-up strategy using Web rings, and it worked. Bomis users built hundreds of rings — on cars, computers, sports, and especially "babes" (e.g., the Anna Kournikova Web ring), effectively creating an index of the "laddie" Web. Instead of helping all users find all content, Bomis found itself positioned as the *Playboy* of the Internet, helping guys find guy stuff. Wales's experience with Web rings reinforced the lesson he had learned with MUDs: Given the right technology, large groups of self-interested individuals will unite to create something they could not produce by themselves, be it a sword-and-sorcery world or an index of Web sites on Pamela Anderson. He saw the power of what we now call "peer-to-peer," or "distributed," content production.

> **Wales is of a thoughtful cast of mind.**

Wales was not alone: Rich Skrenta and Bob Truel, two programmers at Sun Microsystems, saw it too. In June 1998, along with three partners, they launched GnuHoo, an all-volunteer alternative to the Yahoo Directory. (GNU, a recursive acronym for "GNUs Not Unix," is a free operating system created by the über-hacker Richard Stallman.) The project was an immediate success, and it quickly drew the attention of Netscape, which was eager to find a directory capable of competing with Yahoo's index. In November 1998, Netscape acquired GnuHoo (then called NewHoo), promising to both develop it and release it under an "open content" license, which meant anyone could use it. At the date of Netscape's acquisition, the directory had indexed some 100,000 URLs; a year later, it included about a million.

Wales clearly had the open-content movement in mind when, in the fall of 1999, he began thinking about a "volunteer-built" online encyclopedia. The idea — explored most prominently in Stallman's 1999 essay "The Free Universal Encyclopedia and Learning Resource" — had been around for some time. Wales says he had no direct knowledge of Stallman's essay when he embarked on his encyclopedia project, but two bits of evidence suggest that he was thinking of Stallman's GNU free documentation license. First, the name Wales adopted for his encyclopedia—Nupedia.org—strongly suggested a Stallman-esque venture. Second, he took the trouble of leasing a related domain name, GNUpedia.org. By January 2000, his encyclopedia project had acquired funding from Bomis and hired its first employee: Larry Sanger.

The Philosopher

Sanger was born in 1968 in Bellevue, Washington, a suburb of Seattle. When he was seven, his father, a marine biologist, moved the family to Anchorage, Alaska, where Sanger spent his youth. He excelled in high school, and in 1986 he enrolled at Reed College. Reed is the sort of school you attend if you are intelligent, are not interested in investment banking, and wonder a lot about truth. There Sanger found a question that fired his imagination: What is knowledge? He embarked on that most unremunerative of careers, epistemology, and entered a doctoral program in philosophy at Ohio State.

Sanger fits the profile of almost every Internet early adopter: He'd been a good student, played Dungeons & Dragons, and tinkered with PCs as a youth—going so far as to code a text-based adventure game in BASIC, the first popular programming language. He was drawn into the world of philosophy discussion lists and, in the early 1990s, was an active participant in Wales's objectivism forum. Sanger also hosted a mailing list as part of his own online philosophy project (eventually named the Association for Systematic Philosophy). The mission and mien of Sanger's list stood in stark contrast to Wales's Rand forum. Sanger was far more programmatic. As he wrote in his opening manifesto, dated March 22, 1994:

> The history of philosophy is full of disagreement and confusion. One reaction by philosophers to this state of things is to doubt whether the truth about philosophy can ever be known, or whether there is any such thing as the truth about philosophy. But there is another reaction: One may set out to think more carefully and methodically than one's intellectual forebears.

Wales's Rand forum was generally serious, but it was also a place for philosophically inclined laypeople to shoot the breeze: Wales permitted discussion of "objectivism in the movies" or "objectivism in Rush lyrics." Sanger's list was more disciplined, but he soon began to feel it, too, was of limited philosophical worth. He resigned after little more than a year. "I think that my time could really be better spent in the real world," Sanger wrote in his resignation letter, "as opposed to cyberspace, and in thinking to myself, rather than out loud to a bunch of other people." Sanger was seriously considering abandoning his academic career.

As the decade and the century came to a close, another opportunity arose, one that would let Sanger make a living away from academia, using the acumen he had developed on the Internet. In 1998, Sanger created a digest of news reports relating to the "Y2K problem." *Sanger's Review of Y2K News Reports* became a staple of IT managers across the globe. It also set him to thinking about how he might make a living in the new millennium. In January 2000, he sent Wales a business proposal for what was in essence a cultural news blog. Sanger's timing was excellent.

The Cathedral

Wales was looking for someone with good academic credentials to organize Nupedia, and Sanger fit the bill. Wales pitched the project to Sanger in terms of Eric S. Raymond's essay (and later book) "The Cathedral and the Bazaar." Raymond sketched two models of software development. Under the "cathedral model," source code was guarded by a core group of developers; under the "bazaar model," it was released on the Internet for anyone to tinker with. Raymond argued that the latter model was better, and he coined a now-famous hacker aphorism to capture its superiority: "Given enough eyeballs, all bugs are shallow." His point was simply that the speed with which a complex project is perfected is directly proportional to the number of informed people working on it. Wales was enthusiastic about Raymond's thesis. His experience with MUDs and Web rings had demonstrated to him the power of the bazaar. Sanger, the philosopher, was charier about the wisdom-of-crowds scheme but drawn to the idea of creating an open online encyclopedia that would break all the molds. Sanger signed on and moved to San Diego.

According to Sanger, Wales was very "hands-off." He gave Sanger only the loosest sketch of an open encyclopedia. "Open" meant two things: First, anyone, in principle, could contribute. Second, all of the content would be made freely available. Sanger proceeded to create, in effect, an online academic journal. There was simply no question in his mind that Nupedia would be guided by a board of experts, that submissions would be largely written by experts, and that articles would be published only after extensive peer review. Sanger set about recruiting academics to work on Nupedia. In early March 2000, he and Wales deemed the project ready to go public, and the Nupedia Web site was launched with the following words: 20

> Suppose scholars the world over were to learn of a serious online encyclopedia effort in which the results were not proprietary to the encyclopedists, but were freely distributable under an open content license in virtually any desired medium. How quickly would the encyclopedia grow?

The answer, as Wales and Sanger found out, was "not very." Over the first several months little was actually accomplished in terms of article assignment, writing, and publication. First, there was the competition. Wales and Sanger had the bad luck to launch Nupedia around the same time as *Encyclopedia Britannica* was made available for free on the Internet. Then there was the real problem: production. Sanger and the Nupedia board had worked out a multistage editorial system that could have been borrowed from any scholarly journal. In a sense, it worked: Assignments were made, articles were submitted and evaluated, and copyediting was done. But, to both Wales and Sanger, it was all much too slow. They had built a cathedral.

The Bazaar

In the mid-1980s, a programmer named Ward Cunningham began trying to create a "pattern language" for software design. A pattern language is in essence a common vocabulary used in solving engineering problems—think of it as best practices for designers. Cunningham believed that software development should have a pattern language, and he proposed to find a way for software developers to create it.

Apple's Hypercard offered inspiration. Hypercard was a very flexible database application. It allowed users to create records ("cards"), add data fields to them, and link them in sets. Cunningham created a Hypercard "stack" of software patterns and shared it with colleagues. His stack was well liked but difficult to share, since it existed only on Cunningham's computer. In the 1990s, Cunningham found himself looking for a problem-solving technique that would allow software developers to fine-tune and accumulate their knowledge collaboratively. A variation on Hypercard seemed like an obvious option.

Cunningham coded and, in the spring of 1995, launched the first "wiki," calling it the "WikiWikiWeb." (*Wiki* is Hawaiian for "quick," which Cunningham chose to indicate the ease with which a user could edit the pages.) A wiki is a Web site that allows multiple users to create, edit, and hyperlink pages. As users work, a wiki can keep track of all changes; users can compare versions as they edit and, if necessary, revert to earlier states. Nothing is lost, and everything is transparent.

The wiki quickly gained a devoted following within the software community. And there it remained until January 2001, when Sanger had dinner with an old friend named Ben Kovitz. Kovitz was a fan of "extreme programming." Standard software engineering is very methodical—first you plan, then you plan and plan and plan, then you code. The premise is that you must correctly anticipate what the program will need to do in order to avoid drastic changes late in the coding process. In contrast, extreme programmers advocate going live with the earliest possible version of new software and letting many people work simultaneously to rapidly refine it.

Over tacos that night, Sanger explained his concerns about Nupedia's lack of progress, the root cause of which was its serial editorial system. As Nupedia was then structured, no stage of the editorial process could proceed before the previous stage was completed. Kovitz brought up the wiki and sketched out "wiki magic," the mysterious process by which communities with common interests work to improve wiki pages by incremental contributions. If it worked for the rambunctious hacker culture of programming, Kovitz said, it could work for any online collaborative project. The wiki could break the Nupedia bottleneck by permitting volunteers to work simultaneously all over the project. With Kovitz in tow, Sanger rushed back to his apartment and called Wales to share the idea.

Over the next few days he wrote a formal proposal for Wales and started a page on Cunningham's wiki called "WikiPedia."

Wales and Sanger created the first Nupedia wiki on January 10, 2001. The initial purpose was to get the public to add entries that would then be "fed into the Nupedia process" of authorization. Most of Nupedia's expert volunteers, however, wanted nothing to do with this, so Sanger decided to launch a separate site called "Wikipedia." Neither Sanger nor Wales looked on Wikipedia as anything more than a lark. This is evident in Sanger's flip announcement of Wikipedia to the Nupedia discussion list. "Humor me," he wrote. "Go there and add a little article. It will take all of five or ten minutes." And, to Sanger's surprise, go they did. Within a few days, Wikipedia outstripped Nupedia in terms of quantity, if not quality, and a small community developed. In late January, Sanger created a Wikipedia discussion list (Wikipedia-L) to facilitate discussion of the project. At the end of January, Wikipedia had seventeen "real" articles (entries with more than 200 characters). By the end of February, it had 150; March, 572; April, 835; May, 1,300; June, 1,700; July, 2,400; August, 3,700. At the end of the year, the site boasted approximately 15,000 articles and about 350 "Wikipedians."

Setting the Rules

Wikipedia's growth caught Wales and Sanger off guard. It forced them to make quick decisions about what Wikipedia would be, how to foster cooperation, and how to manage it. In the beginning it was by no means clear what an "open" encyclopedia should include. People posted all manner of things: dictionary definitions, autobiographies, position papers, historical documents, and original research. In response, Sanger created a "What Wikipedia Is Not" page. There he and the community defined Wikipedia by exclusion—not a dictionary, not a scientific journal, not a source collection, and so on. For everything else, they reasoned that if an article could conceivably have gone in *Britannica*, it was "encyclopedic" and permitted; if not, it was "not encyclopedic" and deleted.

Sanger and Wales knew that online collaborative ventures can easily slide into a morass of unproductive invective. They had already worked out a solution for Nupedia, called the "lack of bias" policy. On Wikipedia it became NPOV, or the "neutral point of view," and it brilliantly encouraged the work of the community. Under NPOV, authors were enjoined to present the conventionally acknowledged "facts" in an unbiased way, and, where arguments occurred, to accord space to both sides. The concept of neutrality, though philosophically unsatisfying, had a kind of everybody-lay-down-your-arms ring to it. Debates about what to include in the article were encouraged on the "discussion" page that attends every Wikipedia article.

The most important initial question, however, concerned governance. When Wikipedia was created, wikis were synonymous with creative anarchy. Both Wales and Sanger thought that the software might be useful, but that it was no way to build a trusted encyclopedia. Some sort of authority was assumed to be essential. Wales's part in it was clear: He owned Wikipedia. Sanger's role was murkier.

Citing the communal nature of the project, Sanger refused the title of "editor   30
in chief," a position he held at Nupedia, opting instead to be "chief organizer."
He governed the day-to-day operations of the project in close consultation with
the "community," the roughly two dozen committed Wikipedians (most of them
Nupedia converts) who were really designing the software and adding content
to the site. Though the division of powers between Sanger and the community
remained to be worked out, an important precedent had been set: Wikipedia
would have an owner, but no leader.

The Cunctator

By October 2001, the number of Wikipedians was growing by about fifty
a month. There were a lot of new voices, among them a user known as "The
Cunctator" (Latin for "procrastinator" or "delayer"). "Cunc," as he was called,
advocated a combination of anarchy (no hierarchy within the project) and radical openness (few or no limitations on contributions). Sanger was not favorably
disposed to either of these positions, though he had not had much of a chance to
air his opposition. Cunc offered such an opportunity by launching a prolonged
"edit war" with Sanger in mid-October of that year. In an edit war, two or more
parties cyclically cancel each other's work on an article with no attempt to find
the NPOV. It's the wiki equivalent of "No, *your* mother wears combat boots."

With Cunc clearly in mind, Sanger curtly defended his role before the
community on November 1, 2001:

> I need to be granted fairly broad authority by the community—by you,
> dear reader—if I am going to do my job effectively. Until fairly recently,
> I was granted such authority by Wikipedians. I was indeed not infre-
> quently called to justify decisions I made, but not constantly and nearly
> always respectfully and helpfully. This place in the community did not
> make me an all-powerful editor who must be obeyed on pain of ousting;
> but it did make me a leader. That's what I want, again. This is my job.

Seen from the trenches, this was a striking statement. Sanger had so far said he
was primus inter pares; now he seemed to be saying that he was just primus.
Upon reading this post, one Wikipedian wrote: "Am I the only person who
detects a change in [Sanger's] view of his own position? Am I the only person
who fears this is a change for the worse?"

On November 4, the Sanger-Cunc contretemps exploded. Simon Kissane, a
respected Wikipedian, accused Sanger of capriciously deleting pages, including
some of Cunc's work. Sanger denied the allegation but implied that the excised
material was no great loss. He then launched a defense of his position in words
that bled resentment:

> I do reserve the right to permanently delete things—particularly when
> they have little merit and when they are posted by people whose main
> motive is evidently to undermine my authority and therefore, as far as
> I'm concerned, damage the project. Now suppose that, in my experi-
> ence, if I make an attempt to justify this or other sorts of decisions, the

people in question will simply co-opt huge amounts of my time and will never simply say, "Larry, you win; we realize that this decision is up to you, and we'll have to respect it." Then, in order to preserve my time and sanity, I have to act like an autocrat. In a way, I am being trained to act like an autocrat. It's rather clever in a way—if you think college-level stunts are clever. Frankly, it's hurting the project, guys—so stop it, already. Just write articles—please!

The blowup disturbed Wales to no end. As a list moderator, he had tried hard to keep his discussants out of flame wars. He weighed in with an unusually forceful posting that warned against a "culture of conflict." Wikipedia, he implied, was about building an encyclopedia, not about debating how to build or govern an encyclopedia. Echoing Sanger, he argued that the primary duty of community members was to contribute—by writing code, adding content, and editing. Enough talk, he seemed to be saying: We know what to do, now let's get to work. Yet he also seemed to take a quiet stand against Sanger's positions on openness and on his own authority:

> Just speaking off the top of my head, I think that total deletions seldom make sense. They should be reserved primarily for pages that are just completely mistaken (typos, unlikely misspellings), or for pages that are nothing more than insults.

Wales also made a strong case that anyone deleting pages should record his or her identity, explain his or her reasons, and archive the entire affair.

Within several weeks, Sanger and Cunc were at each other's throats again. Sanger had proposed creating a "Wikipedia Militia" that would deal with issues arising from sudden massive influxes of new visitors. It was hardly a bad idea: Such surges did occur (they're commonly called "slash-dottings"). But Cunc saw in Sanger's reasonable proposition a very slippery slope toward "central authority." "You start deputizing groups of people to do necessary and difficult tasks," he wrote, "fast-forward two/three years, and you have pernicious cabals."

Given the structure of Wikipedia there was little Sanger could do to defend himself. The principles of the project denied him real punitive authority: He couldn't ban "trolls"—users like Cunc who baited others for sport—and deleting posts was evidence of tyranny in the eyes of Sanger's detractors. A defensive strategy wouldn't work either, as the skilled moderator's tactic for fighting bad behavior—ignoring it—was blunted by the wiki. On e-mail lists, unanswered inflammatory posts quickly vanish under layers of new discussion; on a wiki, they remain visible to all, often near the tops of pages. Sanger was trapped by his own creation.

The "God-King"

Wales saw that Sanger was having trouble managing the project. Indeed, he seems to have sensed that Wikipedia really needed no manager. In mid-December 2001, citing financial shortfalls, he told Sanger that Bomis would be cutting its staff and that he should look for a new job. To that point, Wales and his partners had supported both Nupedia and Wikipedia. But with Bomis suffering in the Internet bust, there was financial pressure. Early on, Wales had said that advertising was a possibility, but the community was now set against any commercialization. In January 2002, Sanger loaded up his possessions and returned to Ohio.

Cunc responded to Sanger's departure with apparent appreciation:

> I know that we've hardly been on the best of terms, but I want you to know that I'll always consider you one of the most important Wikipedians, and I hope that you'll always think of yourself as a Wikipedian, even if you don't have much time to contribute. Herding cats ain't easy; you did a good job, all things considered.

Characteristically, Sanger took this as nothing more than provocation: "Oh, how nice and gracious this was. Oh, thank you SO much, Cunctator. I'm sure glad I won't have to deal with you anymore, Cunctator. You're a friggin' piece of work." The next post on the list is from Wales, who showed a business-as-usual sangfroid: "With the resignation of Larry, there is a much less pressing need for funds."

Sanger made two great contributions to Wikipedia: He built it, and he left it. After forging a revolutionary mode of knowledge building, he came to realize—albeit dimly at first—that it was not to his liking. He found that he was not heading a disciplined crew of qualified writers and editors collaborating on authoritative statements (the Nupedia ideal), but trying to control an ill-disciplined crowd of volunteers fighting over ever-shifting articles. From Sanger's point of view, both the behavior of the participants and the quality of the scholarship were wanting. Even after seeing Wikipedia's explosive growth, Sanger continued to argue that Wikipedia should engage experts and that Nupedia should be saved.

Wales, though, was a businessman. He wanted to build a free encyclopedia, and Wikipedia offered a very rapid and economically efficient means to that end. The articles flooded in, many were good, and they cost him almost nothing. Why interfere? Moreover, Wales was not really the meddling kind. Early on, Wikipedians took to calling him the "God-King." The appellation is purely ironic. Over the past four years, Wales has repeatedly demonstrated an astounding reluctance to use his power, even when the community has begged him to. He wouldn't exile trolls or erase offensive material, much less settle on rules for how things should or should not be done. In 2003, Wales diminished his own authority by transferring Wikipedia and all of its assets to the nonprofit Wikimedia Foundation, whose sole purpose is to set general policy for Wikipedia and its allied projects. (He is one of five members of the foundation's board.) 40

Wales's benign rule has allowed Wikipedia to do what it does best: grow. The numbers are staggering. The English-language Wikipedia alone has well more than a million articles and expands by about 1,700 a day. (*Britannica*'s online version, by comparison, has about 100,000 articles.) As of mid-February 2006, more than 65,000 Wikipedians—registered users who have made at least ten edits since joining—had contributed to the English-language Wikipedia. The number of registered contributors is increasing by more than 6,000 a month; the number of unregistered contributors is presumably much larger. Then there are the 200-odd non-English-language Wikipedias. Nine of them already have more than 100,000 entries each, and nearly all of the major-language versions are growing on pace with the English version.

What Is Wikipedia?

The Internet did not create the desire to collect human knowledge. For most of history, however, standardizing and gathering knowledge was hard to do very effectively. The main problem was rampant equivocation. Can we all agree on what an apple is exactly, or the shades of the color green? Not easily. The wiki offered a way for people to actually decide in common. On Wikipedia, an apple is what the contributors say it is *right now*. You can try to change the definition by throwing in your own two cents, but the community—the voices actually negotiating and renegotiating the definition—decides in the end. Wikipedia grew out of a natural impulse (communication) facilitated by a new technology (the wiki).

The power of the community to decide, of course, asks us to reexamine what we mean when we say that something is "true." We tend to think of truth as something that resides in the world. The fact that two plus two equals four is written in the stars—we merely discovered it. But Wikipedia suggests a different theory of truth. Just think about the way we learn what words mean. Generally speaking, we do so by listening to other people (our parents, first). Since we want to communicate with them (after all, they feed us), we use the words in the same way they do. Wikipedia says judgments of truth and falsehood work the same way. The community decides that two plus two equals four the same way it decides what an apple is: by consensus. Yes, that means that if the community changes its mind and decides that two plus two equals five, then two plus two does equal five. The community isn't likely to do such an absurd or useless thing, but it has the ability.

The Internet did not create the desire to collect human knowledge.

Early detractors commonly made two criticisms of Wikipedia. First, unless experts were writing and vetting the material, the articles were inevitably going to be inaccurate. Second, since anyone could edit, vandals would have their way with even the best articles, making them suspect. No encyclopedia produced in this way could be trusted. Last year, however, a study in the journal *Nature* compared *Britannica* and Wikipedia science articles and suggested that the former are usually only marginally more accurate than the latter. *Britannica* demonstrated that *Nature*'s analysis was seriously flawed ("Fatally Flawed" was the fair title of the response), and no one has produced a more authoritative study of Wikipedia's accuracy. Yet it is a widely accepted view that Wikipedia is comparable to *Britannica*. Vandalism also has proved much less of an issue than originally feared. A study by IBM suggests that although vandalism does occur (particularly on high-profile entries like "George W. Bush"), watchful members of the huge Wikipedia community usually swoop down to stop the malfeasance shortly after it begins.

There are, of course, exceptions, as in the case of the journalist John Seigenthaler, whose Wikipedia biography long contained a libel about his supposed complicity in the assassinations of John F. and Robert Kennedy. But even this example shows that the system is, if not perfect, at least responsive. When Seigenthaler became aware of the error, he contacted Wikipedia. The community (led in this instance by Wales) purged the entry of erroneous material, expanded it, and began to monitor it closely. Even though the Seigenthaler entry is often attacked by vandals, and is occasionally locked to block them, the page is more reliable precisely because it is now under "enough eyeballs." The same could be said about many controversial entries on Wikipedia: The quality of articles generally increases with the number of eyeballs. Given enough eyeballs, all errors are shallow.

Common Knowledge

In June 2001, only six months after Wikipedia was founded, a Polish Wikipedian named Krzysztof Jasiutowicz made an arresting and remarkably forward-looking observation. The Internet, he mused, was nothing but a "global Wikipedia without the end-user editing facility." The contents of the Internet—its pages—are created by a loose community of users, namely those on the Web. The contents of Wikipedia—its entries—are also created by a loose community of users, namely Wikipedians. On the Internet, contributors own their own pages, and only they can edit them. They can also create new pages as they see fit. On Wikipedia, contributors own *all* of the pages collectively, and each can edit nearly every page. Page creation is ultimately subject to community approval. The private-property regime that governs the Internet allows it to grow freely, but it makes organization and improvement very difficult. In contrast, Wikipedia's communal regime permits growth *plus* organization and improvement. The result of this difference is there for all to see: Much of the Internet is a chaotic mess and therefore useless, whereas Wikipedia is well ordered and hence very useful.

Having seen all of this in prospect, Jasiutowicz asked a logical question: "Can someone please tell me what's the end point/goal of Wikipedia?" Wales responded, only half jokingly, "The goal of Wikipedia is fun for the contributors." He had a point. Editing Wikipedia *is* fun, and even rewarding. The site is huge, so somewhere on it there is probably something you know quite a bit about. Imagine that you happen upon your pet subject, or perhaps even look it up to see how it's being treated. And what do you find? Well, this date is wrong, that characterization is poor, and a word is mispelled. You click the "edit" tab and make the corrections, and you've just contributed to the progress of human knowledge. All in under five minutes, and at no cost.

Yet Wikipedia has a value that goes far beyond the enjoyment of its contributors. For all intents and purposes, the project is laying claim to a vast region of the Internet, a territory we might call "common knowledge." It is the place where all nominal information about objects of widely shared experience will be negotiated, stored, and renegotiated. When you want to find out *what something is*, you will go to Wikipedia, for that is where common knowledge will, by convention, be archived and updated and made freely available. And while you are there, you may just add or change a little something, and thereby feel the pride of authorship shared by the tens of thousands of Wikipedians.

Keeper

One of the objects of common knowledge in Wikipedia, I'm relieved to report, is "Marshall Poe." Recall that the Scottish Wikipedian Alai said that I had no "notability" and therefore couldn't really be considered encyclopedic. On the same day that Alai suggested my entry be deleted, a rather vigorous discussion took place on the "discussion" page that attended the Marshall Poe entry. A Wikipedian who goes by "Dlyons493" discovered that I had indeed written an obscure dissertation on an obscure topic at a not-so-obscure university. He gave the article a "Weak Keep." Someone with the handle "Splash" searched Amazon and verified that I had indeed written books on Russian history, so my claim to be a historian was true. He gave me a "Keep." And finally, my champion and hero, a Wikipedian called "Tupsharru," dismissed my detractors with this:

> Keep. Obvious notability. Several books published with prestigious academic publishers. One of his books has even been translated into Swedish. I don't know why I have to repeat this again and again in these deletion discussions on academics, but don't just use Amazon when the Library of Congress catalogue is no farther than a couple of mouse clicks away.

Bear in mind that I knew none of these people, and they had, as far as I   50
know, no interest other than truth in doing all of this work. Yet they didn't stop with verifying my claims and approving my article. They also searched the Web for material they could use to expand my one-line biography. After they were done, the Marshall Poe entry was two paragraphs long and included a good bibliography. Now that's wiki magic.

Questions for Critical Reading

1. What makes Wikipedia so successful? Reread Poe's text to locate quotations that demonstrate the key qualities of Wikipedia's success.

2. Poe examines top-down and bottom-up systems. Find passages from his text that show the advantages of each system. Is one inherently better than the other? In what contexts does each work best?

3. Poe spends time discussing the conflict between Cunc and Larry Sanger. Is such conflict beneficial or detrimental to the kind of system Wikipedia represents? Locate quotations from Poe's text that support your position.

Exploring Context

1. This essay is about the collaborative process behind the creation of entries in the online encyclopedia Wikipedia (wikipedia.org). Visit Wikipedia and find an entry you feel qualified to write about. Register at the site and participate in the authorship process by editing your selected entry. What's the process like? Is it consistent with Poe's description? Relate your experience to your work on the key factors in Wikipedia's success from Question 1 of Questions for Critical Reading.

2. Poe is the creator of MemoryArchive (memoryarchive.org), whose wiki-like format allows users to create an encyclopedia of memories. Explore the site and perhaps contribute a memory of your own. Does this site harness the same collective power that Poe locates in Wikipedia? What makes it different? Use your response on Wikipedia's success from Question 1 of Questions for Critical Reading to support your answer.

3. Poe opens this essay by discussing his own entry in Wikipedia. Visit his entry on the site at en.wikipedia.org/wiki/Marshall_Poe and then examine the history of changes to the entry by clicking on the history tab at the top of the page. How has his entry changed? What reasons can you find for those changes? Does the entry reflect the success of the kind of process Poe describes?

Questions for Connecting

1. In what ways is Wikipedia like Slashdot? What systems of feedback are needed for Wikipedia's success? Apply Steven Johnson's ideas in "Listening to Feedback" (p. 191) to Poe's discussion of collaborative knowledge. You may want to use your experience with wikis from Exploring Context in composing your response.

2. In "Ethics and the New Genetics" (p. 76), the Dalai Lama argues for a moral compass to guide us around scientific developments such as genetic technologies, but how can we develop a system of ethics when knowledge itself is coming to be socially constituted? Is ethics possible without transcendent truths? Does Wikipedia threaten the idea of "truth," or can its collaborative model be used to create the ethical system the Dalai Lama calls for?

3. James Surowiecki outlines the many dangers of small groups in "Committees, Juries, and Teams: The *Columbia* Disaster and How Small Groups Can Be Made to Work" (p. 440). Are the same dangers present in a large-scale group project like Wikipedia? How can the pitfalls that Surowiecki details be avoided? Use your responses from Questions for Critical Reading and Exploring Context to support your position.

Language Matters

1. Select a key quotation from Poe's text and then translate it into another language using an online tool such as Babel Fish (babelfish.yahoo.com) or Google's Language Tools (google.com/language_tools). You might even choose

to translate it several times (from English to French to German to Chinese). Then translate it back into English. The resulting sentence will probably make little sense. Describe what happened to the sentence. Did translation change parts of speech? Verb tense? The sentence structure? What elements of the sentence are key to transmitting Poe's meaning? Do they survive translation? What parts of your own sentences should you then pay attention to the most?

2. Draw the argument of Poe's essay, either by hand or with a graphics program on your computer. How would the inclusion of this drawing affect Poe's text? What elements of visual argument do you use to convey Poe's meaning?

3. Locate a key passage from Poe's text and then revise the quotation you've selected using more informal language or slang. How does this revision change the meaning of the quotation? What audience would be most receptive to your revision? Why did Poe choose the tone he used in this essay, and what tone might you choose in your own writing for this class?

Assignments for Writing

1. Write a paper in which you determine the role of collaboration in the production of knowledge. Does a consensus determine the truth? Is knowledge created by individuals? Does society have the right to determine that "two plus two equals five," as noted in the selection from Poe? Use your experience with wikis in Exploring Context and your work with Poe's concepts from Questions 1 and 3 of Questions for Connecting in making your argument.

2. Though Poe's explicit concern is Wikipedia, his essay is also concerned with the circulation of knowledge. Write a paper in which you determine who owns knowledge. Can knowledge be owned? Is it common property or the property of academics or other experts? Consider the ethical implications by drawing from your work with the Dalai Lama's essay from Question 2 of Questions for Connecting.

3. What is the power of experts? Does a consensus determine the truth? Poe's essay asks us to consider these questions, since the collaborative authorship of Wikipedia suggests that experts are not vital in the creation of knowledge. Write a paper in which you suggest the proper boundaries between experts and nonexperts in relation to knowledge. What role does technology play in this process? Should experts be granted special status in relation to knowledge? What makes an expert "expert" anyway?

MICHAEL POLLAN

Michael Pollan is Knight Professor of Journalism at the University of California at Berkeley as well as the author of five books: *Second Nature: A Gardener's Education* (1991), *A Place of My Own* (1997), *The Botany of Desire: A Plant's-Eye View of the World* (2001), *The Omnivore's Dilemma: A Natural History of Four Meals* (2006), and *In Defense of Food: An Eater's Manifesto* (2008). A graduate of Bennington College and Columbia University, Pollan has won multiple journalism awards, and his writing has appeared in *The Norton Book of Nature Writing* (1990), *Best American Essays* (1990 and 2003), and *Best American Science Writing* (2004). Pollan's work can often be seen in the *New York Times*, where he is a contributing writer.

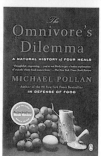

The *Omnivore's Dilemma*, declared by the *New York Times* to be one of 2006's best nonfiction books, traces three different food chains—the industrial, the pastoral, and the personal—from nature to table. Ultimately, the book is about the politics of eating: what we should eat, why we should eat it, and what impact our eating decisions have.

In "The Animals: Practicing Complexity" from *The Omnivore's Dilemma*, Pollan writes about an alternative to traditional agribusiness and profiles farmer Joel Salatin. With few outside raw materials, Salatin is able to run an incredibly productive farm that mimics a natural ecosystem in which nothing goes to waste. Pollan shows how order arises from the complex system of Salatin's farm, where everything plays a part, from a tree to a cow to the cow's manure, in a system—described as "holon"-based—in which each element is simultaneously an individual whole and an active part in a complex system.

For Pollan, the omnivore's dilemma is one we face each day: what to have for dinner? This selection suggests that providing a healthy and sustainable answer to that question might come not from rejecting agribusiness entirely for an idealized agrarian past but from rethinking the intersection of business, farming, and food.

▶ TAGS: *tradition, technology, collaboration, feedback, supply chains, biotechnology*

The Animals: Practicing Complexity

1. Tuesday Morning

It's not often I wake up at six in the morning to discover I've overslept, but by the time I had hauled my six-foot self out of the five-foot bed in Lucille's microscopic guest room, everyone was already gone and morning chores were nearly done. Shockingly, chores at Polyface commence as soon as the sun comes up (five-ish this time of year) and always before breakfast. Before coffee, that is, not that there was a drop of it to be had on this farm. I couldn't recall the last time I'd even attempted to do anything consequential before breakfast, or before caffeine at the very least.

When I stepped out of the trailer into the warm early morning mist, I could make out two figures—the interns, probably—moving around up on the broad shoulder of hill to the east, where a phalanx of portable chicken pens formed a checkerboard pattern on the grass. Among other things, morning chores consist of feeding and watering the broilers and moving their pens one length down the hillside. I was supposed to be helping Galen and Peter do this, so I started up the path, somewhat groggily, hoping to get there before they finished.

As I stumbled up the hill, I was struck by how very beautiful the farm looked in the hazy early light. The thick June grass was silvered with dew, the sequence of bright pastures stepping up the hillside dramatically set off by broad expanses of blackish woods. Birdsong stitched the thick blanket of summer air, pierced now and again by the wood clap of chicken pen doors slamming shut. It was hard to believe this hillside had ever been the gullied wreck Joel had described at dinner, and even harder to believe that farming such a damaged landscape so intensively, rather than just letting it be, could restore it to health and yield this beauty. This is not the environmentalist's standard prescription. But Polyface is proof that people can sometimes do more for the health of a place by cultivating it rather than by leaving it alone.

By the time I reached the pasture Galen and Peter had finished moving the pens. Fortunately they were either too kind or too timid to give me a hard time for oversleeping. I grabbed a pair of water buckets, filled them from the big tub in the center of the pasture, and lugged them to the nearest pen. Fifty of these pens were spread out across the damp grass in a serrated formation that had been calibrated to cover every square foot of this meadow in the course of the fifty-six days it takes a broiler to reach slaughter weight; the pens moved ten feet each day, the length of one pen. Each ten-by-twelve, two-foot-tall floorless pen houses seventy birds. A section of the roof is hinged to allow access, and a five-gallon bucket perched atop each unit fed a watering device suspended inside.

Directly behind each pen was a perfectly square patch of closely cropped grass resembling a really awful Jackson Pollock painting, thickly spattered with chicken crap in pigments of white, brown, and green. It was amazing what a mess seventy chickens could make in a day. But that was the idea: Give them twenty-four hours to eat the grass and fertilize it with their manure, and then move them onto fresh ground.

Joel developed this novel method for raising broiler chickens in the 1980s and popularized it in his 1993 book, *Pastured Poultry Profit$*, something of a cult classic among grass farmers. (Joel has self-published four other how-to books on farming, and all but one of them has a $ stepping in for an S somewhere in its title.) Left to their own devices, a confined flock of chickens will eventually destroy any patch of land, by pecking the grass down to its roots and poisoning the soil with their extremely "hot," or nitrogenous, manure. This is why the typical free-range chicken yard quickly winds up bereft of plant life and hard as brick. Moving the birds daily keeps both the land and the birds healthy; the broilers escape their pathogens and the varied diet of greens supplies most of their vitamins and minerals. The birds also get a ration of corn, toasted soybeans, and kelp, which we scooped into long troughs in their pens, but Joel claims the fresh grass, along with the worms, grasshoppers, and crickets they peck out of the grass, provides as much as 20 percent of their diet—a significant savings to the farmer and a boon to the birds. Meanwhile, their manure fertilizes the grass, supplying all the nitrogen it needs. The chief reason Polyface Farm is completely self-sufficient in nitrogen is that a chicken, defecating copiously, pays a visit to virtually every square foot of it at several points during the season. Apart from some greensand (a mineral supplement to replace calcium lost in the meadows), chicken feed is the only important input Joel buys, and the sole off-farm source of fertility. ("The way I look at it, I'm just returning some of the grain that's been extracted from this land over the last 150 years.") The chicken feed not only feeds the broilers but, transformed into chicken crap, feeds the grass that feeds the cows that, as I was about to see, feeds the pigs and the laying hens.

After we had finished watering and feeding the broilers, I headed up to the next pasture, where I could hear a tractor idling. Galen had told me Joel was moving the Eggmobile, an operation I'd been eager to watch. The Eggmobile, one of Joel's proudest innovations, is a ramshackle cross between a henhouse and a prairie schooner. Housing four hundred laying hens, this rickety old covered wagon has hinged nesting boxes lined up like saddlebags on either side, allowing someone to retrieve eggs from the outside. I'd first laid eyes on the Eggmobile the night before, parked a couple of paddocks away from the cattle herd. The hens had already climbed the little ramp into the safety of the coop for the night, and before we went down to dinner Joel had latched the trapdoor behind them. Now it was time to move them into a fresh paddock, and Joel was bolting the Eggmobile to the hitch of his tractor. It wasn't quite 7:00 AM yet, but Joel seemed delighted to have someone to talk to, holding forth being one of his greatest pleasures.

"In nature you'll always find birds following herbivores," Joel explained, when I asked him for the theory behind the Eggmobile. "The egret perched on the rhino's nose, the pheasants and turkeys trailing after the bison—that's a symbiotic relationship we're trying to imitate." In each case the birds dine on the insects that would otherwise bother the herbivore; they also pick insect larvae and parasites out of the animal's droppings, breaking the cycle of infestation and disease. "To mimic this symbiosis on a domestic scale, we follow the cattle in their rotation with the Eggmobile. I call these gals our sanitation crew."

Joel climbed onto the tractor, threw it into gear, and slowly towed the rickety contraption fifty yards or so across the meadow to a paddock the cattle had vacated three days earlier. It seems the chickens eschew fresh manure, so he waits three or four days before bringing them in—but not a day longer. That's because the fly larvae in the manure are on a four-day cycle, he explained. "Three days is ideal. That gives the grubs a chance to fatten up nicely, the way the hens like them, but not quite long enough to hatch into flies." The result is prodigious amounts of protein for the hens, the insects sup-

> **I began to understand just how radically different this sort of farming is from the industrial models I'd observed before.**

plying as much as a third of their total diet—and making their eggs unusually rich and tasty. By means of this simple little management trick, Joel is able to use his cattle's waste to "grow" large quantities of high-protein chicken feed for free; he says this trims his cost of producing eggs by twenty-five cents per dozen. (Very much his accountant father's son, Joel can tell you the exact economic implication of every synergy on the farm.) The cows further oblige the chickens by shearing the grass; chickens can't navigate in grass more than about six inches tall.

After Joel had maneuvered the Eggmobile into position, he opened the trapdoor, and an eager, gossipy procession of Barred Rocks, Rhode Island Reds, and New Hampshire Whites filed down the little ramp, fanning out across the pasture. The hens picked at the grasses, especially the clover, but mainly they were all over the cowpats, doing this frantic backward-stepping break-dance with their claws to scratch apart the caked manure and expose the meaty morsels within. Unfolding here before us, I realized, was a most impressive form of alchemy: Cowpatties in the process of being transformed into exceptionally tasty eggs.

"I'm convinced an Eggmobile would be worth it even if the chickens never laid a single egg. These birds do a more effective job of sanitizing a pasture than anything human, mechanical, or chemical, and the chickens love doing it." Because of the Eggmobile, Joel doesn't have to run his cattle through a headgate to slather Ivomectrin, a systemic paraciticide, on their hides or worm them with toxic chemicals. This is what Joel means when he says the animals do the real work around here. "I'm just the orchestra conductor, making sure everybody's in the right place at the right time."

That day, my second on the farm, as Joel introduced me to each of his intricately layered enterprises, I began to understand just how radically different this sort of farming is from the industrial models I'd observed before, whether in an Iowa cornfield or an organic chicken farm in California. Indeed, it is so different that I found Polyface's system difficult to describe to myself in an orderly way. Industrial processes follow a clear, linear, hierarchical logic that is fairly easy to put into words, probably because words follow a similar logic: First this, then that; put this in here, and then out comes that. But the relationship between cows and chickens on this farm (leaving aside for the moment the other creatures and relationships present here) takes the form of a loop rather than a line, and that makes it hard to know where to start, or how to distinguish between causes and effects, subjects and objects.

Is what I'm looking at in this pasture a system for producing exceptionally tasty eggs? If so, then the cattle and their manure are a means to an end. Or is it a system for producing grass-fed beef without the use of any chemicals, in which case the chickens, by fertilizing and sanitizing the cow pastures, comprise the means to that end. So does that make their eggs a product or a by-product? And is manure—theirs or the cattle's—a waste product or a raw material? (And what should we call the fly larvae?) Depending on the point of view you take—that of the chicken, cow, or even the grass—the relationship between subject and object, cause and effect, flips.

Joel would say this is precisely the point, and precisely the distinction between a biological and industrial system. "In an ecological system like this everything's connected to everything else, so you can't change one thing without changing ten other things.

"Take the issue of scale. I could sell a whole lot more chickens and eggs than I do. They're my most profitable items, and the market is telling me to produce more of them. Operating under the industrial paradigm, I could boost production however much I wanted—just buy more chicks and more feed, crank up that machine. But in a biological system you can never do just one thing, and I couldn't add many more chickens without messing up something else. 15

"Here's an example: This pasture can absorb four hundred units of nitrogen a year. That translates into four visits from the Eggmobile or two passes of a broiler pen. If I ran any more Eggmobiles or broiler pens over it, the chickens would put down more nitrogen than the grass could metabolize. Whatever the grass couldn't absorb would run off, and suddenly I have a pollution problem." Quality would suffer, too. Unless he added more cattle, to produce more grubs for the chickens and to keep the grass short enough for them to eat it, those chickens and eggs would not taste nearly as good as they do.

"It's all connected. This farm is more like an organism than a machine, and like any organism it has its proper scale. A mouse is the size of a mouse for a good reason, and a mouse that was the size of an elephant wouldn't do very well."

Joel likes to quote from an old agricultural textbook he dug out of the stacks at Virginia Tech many years ago. The book, which was published in 1941 by a Cornell Ag professor, offers a stark conclusion that, depending on your point of view, will sound either hopelessly quaint or arresting in its gnomic wisdom: "Farming is not adapted to large-scale operations because of the following reasons: Farming is concerned with plants and animals that live, grow, and die."

"Efficiency" is the term usually invoked to defend large-scale industrial farms, and it usually refers to the economies of scale that can be achieved by the application of technology and standardization. Yet Joel Salatin's farm makes the case for a very different sort of efficiency—the one found in natural systems, with their coevolutionary relationships and reciprocal loops. For example, in nature there is no such thing as a waste problem, since one creature's waste becomes another creature's lunch. What could be more efficient than turning cow pies into eggs? Or running a half-dozen different production systems—cows, broilers, layers, pigs, turkeys—over the same piece of ground every year?

Most of the efficiencies in an industrial system are achieved through sim- 20 plification: doing lots of the same thing over and over. In agriculture, this usually means a monoculture of a single animal or crop. In fact, the whole history of agriculture is a progressive history of simplification, as humans reduced the biodiversity of their landscapes to a small handful of chosen species. (Wes Jackson calls our species "homo the homogenizer.") With the industrialization of agriculture, the simplifying process reached its logical extreme—in monoculture. This radical specialization permitted standardization and mechanization, leading to the leaps in efficiency claimed by industrial agriculture. Of course, how you choose to measure efficiency makes all the difference, and industrial agriculture measures it, simply, by the yield of one chosen species per acre of land or farmer.

By contrast, the efficiencies of natural systems flow from complexity and interdependence—by definition the very opposite of simplification. To achieve the efficiency represented by turning cow manure into chicken eggs and producing beef without chemicals you need at least two species (cows and chickens), but actually several more as well, including the larvae in the manure and the grasses in the pasture and the bacteria in the cows' rumens. To measure the efficiency of such a complex system you need to count not only all the products it produces (meat, chicken, eggs) but also all the costs it eliminates: antibiotics, wormers, paraciticides, and fertilizers.

Polyface Farm is built on the efficiencies that come from mimicking relationships found in nature, and layering one farm enterprise over another on the same base of land. In effect, Joel is farming in time as well as in space—in four dimensions rather than three. He calls this intricate layering "stacking" and points out that "it is exactly the model God used in building nature." The idea is not to slavishly imitate nature, but to model a natural ecosystem in all its diversity and interdependence, one where all the species "fully express their physiological distinctiveness." He takes advantage of each species' natural proclivities in a way that not only benefits that animal but other species as well. So instead of treating the chicken as a simple egg or protein machine, Polyface honors—and exploits—"the innate distinctive desires of a chicken," which include pecking in the grass and cleaning up after herbivores. The chickens get to do, and eat, what they evolved to do and eat, and in the process the farmer and his cattle both profit. What is the opposite of zero-sum? I'm not sure, but this is it.

Joel calls each of his stacked farm enterprises a "holon," a word I'd never encountered before. He told me he picked it up from Allan Nation; when I asked Nation about it, he pointed me to Arthur Koestler, who coined the term in *The Ghost in the Machine.* Koestler felt English lacked a word to express the complex relationship of parts and wholes in a biological or social system. A holon (from the Greek *holos*, or whole, and the suffix *on*, as in proton, suggesting a particle) is an entity that from one perspective appears a self-contained whole, and from another a dependent part. A body organ like the liver is a holon; so is an Eggmobile.

At any given time, Polyface has a dozen or more holons up and running, and on my second day Joel and Daniel introduced me to a handful of them. I visited the Raken House, the former toolshed where Daniel has been raising rabbits for the restaurant trade since he was ten. ("Raken?" "Half rabbit, half chicken," Daniel explained.) When the rabbits aren't out on the pasture in portable hutches, they live in cages suspended over a deep bedding of woodchips, in which I watched several dozen hens avidly pecking away in search of earthworms. Daniel explained that the big problem in raising rabbits indoors is their powerful urine, which produces so much ammonia that it scars their lungs and leaves them vulnerable to infection. To cope with the problem most rabbit farmers add antibiotics to their feed. But the scratching of the hens turns the nitrogenous rabbit pee into the carbonaceous bedding, creating a rich compost teeming with earthworms that feed the hens. Drugs become unnecessary and, considering how many rabbits and chickens lived in it, the air in the Raken was, well, tolerable. "Believe me," Daniel said, "if it weren't for these chickens, you'd be gagging right about now, and your eyes would sting something awful."

Before lunch I helped Galen and Peter move the turkeys, another holon.   25 Moving the turkeys, which happens every three days, means setting up a new "feathernet"—a paddock outlined by portable electric fencing so lightweight I could carry and lay out the entire thing by myself—and then wheeling into it the shademobile, called the Gobbledy-Go. The turkeys rest under the Gobbledy-Go by day and roost on top of it at night. They happily follow the contraption into the fresh pasture to feast on the grass, which they seemed to enjoy even more than the chickens do. A turkey consumes a long blade of grass by neatly folding it over and over again with its beak, as if making origami. Joel likes to run his turkeys in the orchard, where they eat the bugs, mow the grass, and fertilize the trees and vines. (Turkeys will eat much more grass than chickens, and they don't damage crops the way chickens can.) "If you run turkeys in a grape orchard," Joel explained, "you can afford to stock the birds at only seventy percent of normal density, and space the vines at seventy percent of what's standard, because you're getting two crops off the same land. And at seventy percent you get much healthier birds and grapevines than you would at one hundred percent. That's the beauty of stacking." By industry standards, the turkey and grape holon are each less than 100 percent efficient; together, however, they produce more than either enterprise would yield if fully stocked, and they do so without fertilizer, weeding, or pesticide.

I had witnessed one of the most winning examples of stacking in the cattle barn during my first visit to Polyface back in March. The barn is an unfancy open-sided structure where the cattle spend three months during the winter, each day consuming twenty-five pounds of hay and producing fifty pounds of manure. (Water makes up the difference.) But instead of regularly mucking out the barn, Joel leaves the manure in place, every few days covering it with another layer of woodchips or straw. As this layer cake of manure, woodchips, and straw gradually rises beneath the cattle, Joel simply raises the adjustable feed gate from which they get their ration of hay; by winter's end the bedding, and the cattle, can be as much as three feet off the ground. There's one more secret ingredient Joel adds to each layer of this cake: a few bucketfuls of corn. All winter long the layered bedding composts, in the process generating heat to warm the barn (thus reducing the animals' feed requirements), and fermenting the corn. Joel calls it his cattle's electric blanket.

Why the corn? Because there's nothing a pig enjoys more than forty-proof corn, and there's nothing he's better equipped to do than root it out with his powerful snout and exquisite sense of smell. "I call them my pigaerators," Salatin said proudly as he showed me into the barn. As soon as the cows head out to pasture in the spring, several dozen pigs come in, proceeding systematically to turn and aerate the compost in their quest for kernels of alcoholic corn. What had been an anaerobic decomposition suddenly turns aerobic, which dramatically heats and speeds up the process, killing any pathogens. The result, after a few weeks of pigaerating, is a rich, cakey compost ready to use.

> These were the happiest pigs I'd ever seen.

"This is the sort of farm machinery I like: never needs its oil changed, appreciates over time, and when you're done with it you eat it." We were sitting on the rail of a wooden paddock, watching the pigs do their thing—a thing, of course, we weren't having to do ourselves. The line about the pigaerators was obviously well-worn. But the cliché that kept banging around in my head was "happy as a pig in shit." Buried clear to their butts in composting manure, a bobbing sea of wriggling hams and corkscrew tails, these were the happiest pigs I'd ever seen.

I couldn't look at their spiraled tails, which cruised above the earthy mass like conning towers on submarines, without thinking about the fate of pigtails in industrial hog production. Simply put, there *are* no pigtails in industrial hog production. Farmers "dock," or snip off, the tails at birth, a practice that makes a certain twisted sense if you follow the logic of industrial efficiency on a hog farm. Piglets in these CAFOs* are weaned from their mothers ten days after birth (compared with thirteen weeks in nature) because they gain weight faster on their drug-fortified feed than on sow's milk. But this premature weaning leaves the pigs with a lifelong craving to suck and chew, a need they gratify in confinement by biting the tail of the animal in front of them. A normal pig would fight off his molester, but a demoralized pig has stopped caring. "Learned helplessness" is the psychological term, and it's not uncommon in CAFOs, where tens of thousands of hogs spend their entire lives ignorant of earth or straw or

*CAFOs: Confined Animal Feeding Operations.

sunshine, crowded together beneath a metal roof standing on metal slats suspended over a septic tank. It's not surprising that an animal as intelligent as a pig would get depressed under these circumstances, and a depressed pig will allow his tail to be chewed on to the point of infection. Since treating sick pigs is not economically efficient, these underperforming production units are typically clubbed to death on the spot.

Tail docking is the USDA's recommended solution to the porcine "vice" of tail chewing. Using a pair of pliers and no anesthetic, most—but not quite all—of the tail is snipped off. Why leave the little stump? Because the whole point of the exercise is not to remove the object of tail biting so much as to render it even more sensitive. Now a bite to the tail is so painful that even the most demoralized pig will struggle to resist it. Horrible as it is to contemplate, it's not hard to see how the road to such a hog hell is smoothly paved with the logic of industrial efficiency.

A very different concept of efficiency sponsors the hog heaven on display here in Salatin's barn, one predicated on what he calls "the pigness of the pig." These pigs too were being exploited—in this case, tricked into making compost as well as pork. What distinguishes Salatin's system is that it is designed around the natural predilections of the pig rather than around the requirements of a production system to which the pigs are then conformed. Pig happiness is simply the by-product of treating pigs as pigs rather than as "a protein machine with flaws"—flaws such as pigtails and a tendency, when emiserated, to get stressed.

Salatin reached down deep where his pigs were happily rooting and brought a handful of fresh compost right up to my nose. What had been cow manure and woodchips just a few weeks before now smelled as sweet and warm as the forest floor in summertime, a miracle of transubstantiation. As soon as the pigs complete their alchemy, Joel will spread the compost on his pastures. There it will feed the grasses, so the grasses might again feed the cows, the cows the chickens, and so on until the snow falls, in one long, beautiful, and utterly convincing proof that in a world where grass can eat sunlight and food animals can eat grass, there is indeed a free lunch.

2. Tuesday Afternoon

After our own quick lunch (ham salad and deviled eggs), Joel and I drove to town in his pickup to make a delivery and take care of a few errands. It felt sweet to be sitting down for a while, especially after a morning taken up with loading the hay we'd baled the day before into the hayloft. For me this rather harrowing operation involved attempting to catch fifty-pound bales that Galen tossed in my general direction from the top of the hay wagon. The ones that didn't completely knock me over I hoisted onto a conveyor belt that carried them to Daniel and Peter, stationed up in the hayloft. It was an assembly line, more or less, and as soon as I fell behind (or just fell, literally) the hay bales piled up fast at my station; I felt like Lucille Ball at the candy factory. I joked to Joel that, contrary to his claims that the animals did most of the real work on this farm, it seemed to me they'd left plenty of it for us.

On a farm, complexity sounds an awful lot like hard work, Joel's claims to the contrary notwithstanding. As much work as the animals do, that's still us humans out there moving the cattle every evening, dragging the broiler pens across the field before breakfast (something I'd pledged I'd wake up in time for the next day), and towing chicken coops hither and yon according to a schedule tied to the life cycle of fly larvae and the nitrogen load of chicken manure. My guess is that there aren't too many farmers today who are up for either the physical or mental challenge of this sort of farming, not when industrializing promises to simplify the job. Indeed, a large part of the appeal of industrial farming is its panoply of labor- and thought-saving devices: machines of every description to do the physical work, and chemicals to keep crops and animals free from pests with scarcely a thought from the farmer. George Naylor works his fields maybe fifty days out of the year; Joel and Daniel and two interns are out there every day sunrise to sunset for a good chunk of the year.

Yet Joel and Daniel plainly relish their work, partly because it is so varied from day to day and even hour to hour, and partly because they find it endlessly interesting. Wendell Berry has written eloquently about the intellectual work that goes into farming well, especially into solving the novel problems that inevitably crop up in a natural system as complex as a farm. You don't see much of this sort of problem-solving in agriculture today, not when so many solutions come ready-made in plastic bottles. So much of the intelligence and local knowledge in agriculture has been removed from the farm to the laboratory, and then returned to the farm in the form of a chemical or machine. "Whose head is the farmer using?" Berry asks in one of his essays. "Whose head is using the farmer?"

"Part of the problem is, you've got a lot of D students left on the farm today," Joel said, as we drove around Staunton running errands. "The guidance counselors encouraged all the A students to leave home and go to college. There's been a tremendous brain drain in rural America. Of course that suits Wall Street just fine; Wall Street is always trying to extract brainpower and capital from the countryside. First they take the brightest bulbs off the farm and put them to work in Dilbert's cubicle, and then they go after the capital of the dimmer ones who stayed behind, by selling them a bunch of gee-whiz solutions to their problems." This isn't just the farmer's problem, either. "It's a foolish culture that entrusts its food supply to simpletons."

It isn't hard to see why there isn't much institutional support for the sort of low-capital, thought-intensive farming Joel Salatin practices: He buys next to nothing. When a livestock farmer is willing to "practice complexity"—to choreograph the symbiosis of several different animals, each of which has been allowed to behave and eat as they evolved to—he will find he has little need for machinery, fertilizer, and, most strikingly, chemicals. He finds he has no sanitation problem or any of the diseases that result from raising a single animal in a crowded monoculture and then feeding it things it wasn't designed to eat. This is perhaps the greatest efficiency of a farm treated as a biological system: health.

I was struck by the fact that for Joel abjuring agrochemicals and pharmaceuticals is not so much a goal of his farming, as it so often is in organic agriculture, as it is an indication that his farm is functioning well. "In nature health is the default," he pointed out. "Most of the time pests and disease are just nature's way of telling the farmer he's doing something wrong."

At Polyface no one ever told me not to touch the animals, or asked me to put on a biohazard suit before going into the brooder house. The reason I had to wear one at Petaluma Poultry is because that system—a monoculture of chickens raised in close confinement—is inherently precarious, and the organic rules' prohibition on antibiotics puts it at a serious disadvantage. Maintaining a single-species animal farm on an industrial scale isn't easy without pharmaceuticals and pesticides. Indeed, that's why these chemicals were invented in the first place, to keep shaky monocultures from collapsing. Sometimes the large-scale organic farmer looks like someone trying to practice industrial agriculture with one hand tied behind his back.

By the same token, a reliance on agrochemicals destroys the information   40
feedback loop on which an attentive farmer depends to improve his farming. "Meds just mask genetic weaknesses," Joel explained one afternoon when we were moving the cattle. "My goal is always to improve the herd, adapt it to the local conditions by careful culling. To do this I need to know: Who has a propensity for pinkeye? For worms? You simply have no clue if you're giving meds all the time."

"So you tell me, who's really *in* this so-called information economy? Those who learn from what they observe on their farm, or those who rely on concoctions from the devil's pantry?"

Of course the simplest, most traditional measure of a farm's efficiency is how much food it produces per unit of land; by this yardstick too Polyface is impressively efficient. I asked Joel how much food Polyface produces in a season, and he rattled off the following figures:

30,000 dozen eggs
10,000 broilers
800 stewing hens
50 beeves (representing 25,000 pounds of beef)
250 hogs (25,000 pounds of pork)
1,000 turkeys
500 rabbits

This seemed to me a truly astonishing amount of food from one hundred acres of grass. But when I put it that way to Joel that afternoon—we were riding the ATV up to the very top of the hill to visit the hogs in their summer quarters—he questioned my accounting method. It was far too simple.

"Sure, you can write that we produced all that food from a hundred open acres, but if you really want to be accurate about it, then you've got to count the four hundred and fifty acres of woodlot too." I didn't get that at all. I knew the woodlot was an important source of farm income in the winter—Joel and Daniel operate a small sawmill from which they sell lumber and mill whatever wood they need to build sheds and barns (and Daniel's new house). But what in the world did the forest have to do with producing food?

Joel proceeded to count the ways. Most obviously, the farm's water supply depended on its forests to hold moisture and prevent erosion. Many of the farm's streams and ponds would simply dry up if not for the cover of trees. Nearly all of the farm's 550 acres had been deforested when the Salatins arrived; one of the first things Bill Salatin did was plant trees on all the north-facing slopes.

"Feel how cool it is in here." We were passing through a dense stand of oak and hickory. "Those deciduous trees work like an air conditioner. That reduces the stress on the animals in summer."

Suddenly we arrived at a patch of woodland that looked more like a savanna than a forest: The trees had been thinned and all around them grew thick grasses. This was one of the pig paddocks that Joel had carved out of the woods with the help of the pigs themselves. "All we do to make a new pig paddock is fence off a quarter acre of forest, thin out the saplings to let in some light, and then let the pigs do their thing." Their thing includes eating down the brush and rooting around in the stony ground, disturbing the soil in a way that induces the grass seed already present to germinate. Within several weeks, a lush stand of wild rye and foxtail emerges among the trees, and a savanna is born. Shady and cool, this looked like ideal habitat for the sunburn-prone pigs, who were avidly nosing through the tall grass and scratching their backs against the trees. There is something viscerally appealing about a savanna, with its pleasing balance of open grass and trees, and something profoundly heartening about the idea that, together, farmer and pigs could create such beauty here in the middle of a brushy second-growth forest.

But Joel wasn't through counting the benefits of woodland to a farm; idyllic pig habitat was the least of it.

"There's not a spreadsheet in the world that can measure the value of maintaining forest on the northern slopes of a farm. Start with those trees easing the swirling of the air in the pastures. That might not seem like a big deal, but it reduces evaporation in the fields—which means more water for the grass. Plus, a grass plant burns up fifteen percent of its calories just defying gravity, so if you can stop it from being wind whipped, you greatly reduce the energy it uses keeping its photovoltaic array pointed toward the sun. More grass for the cows. That's the efficiency of a hedgerow surrounding a small field, something every farmer used to understand before 'fencerow to fencerow' became USDA mantra."

Then there is the water-holding capacity of trees, he explained, which on a north slope literally pumps water uphill. Next was all the ways a forest multiples a farm's biodiversity. More birds on a farm mean fewer insects, but most birds won't venture more than a couple hundred yards from the safety of cover. Like many species, their preferred habitat is the edge between forest and field. The biodiversity of the forest edge also helps control predators. As long as the weasels and coyotes have plenty of chipmunks and voles to eat, they're less likely to venture out and prey on the chickens.

There was more. On a steep northern slope trees will produce much more biomass than will grass. "We're growing carbon in the woods for the rest of the farm—not just the firewood to keep us warm in the winter, but also the wood-chips that go into making our compost." Making good compost depends on the proper ratio of carbon to nitrogen; the carbon is needed to lock down the more volatile nitrogen. It takes a lot of woodchips to compost chicken or rabbit waste. So the carbon from the woodlots feeds the fields, finding its way into the grass and, from there, into the beef. Which it turns out is not only grass fed but tree fed as well.

These woods represented a whole other order of complexity that I had failed to take into account. I realized that Joel didn't look at this land the same way I did, or had before this afternoon: as a hundred acres of productive grassland patchworked into four hundred and fifty acres of unproductive forest. It was all of a biological piece, the trees and the grasses and the animals, the wild and the domestic, all part of a single ecological system. By any conventional accounting, the forests here represented a waste of land that could be put to productive use. But if Joel were to cut down the trees to graze more cattle, as any conventional accounting would recommend, the system would no longer be quite as whole or as healthy as it is. *You can't just do one thing.*

For some reason the image that stuck with me from that day was that slender blade of grass in a too big, wind-whipped pasture, burning all those calories just to stand up straight and keep its chloroplasts aimed at the sun. I'd always thought of the trees and grasses as antagonists—another zero-sum deal in which the gain of the one entails the loss of the other. To a point, this is true: More grass means less forest; more forest less grass. But either-or is a construction more deeply woven into our culture than into nature, where even antagonists depend on one another and the liveliest places are the edges, the in-betweens or both-ands. So it is with the blade of grass and the adjacent forest as, indeed, with all the species sharing this most complicated farm. Relations are what matter most, and the health of the cultivated turns on the health of the wild. Before I came to Polyface I'd read a sentence of Joel's that in its diction had struck me as an awkward hybrid of the economic and the spiritual. I could see now how characteristic that mixing is, and that perhaps the sentence isn't so awkward after all: "One of the greatest assets of a farm is the sheer ecstasy of life."

Questions for Critical Reading

1. What makes Polyface so successful? Locate passages where Pollan describes the key features of this farm, reading this essay critically to abstract the key factors to the farm's success.

2. What is a "holon"? Use Pollan's text to define this term and to offer examples. Then apply the concept to another area by locating your own example of a holon.

3. Pollan subtitles this essay "Practicing Complexity." Use his text to explain what this means, referring to specific quotations or passages that show complexity in practice. You will need to read critically to determine your answer since Pollan never explains the relationship between this subtitle and his essay.

Exploring Context

1. Learn more about Polyface Farm by visiting its Web site at polyfacefarms.com. Look under "Products" for pictures of the Eggmobile and the Gobbledygo. You can also learn more about the farm by checking the sections on "Principles" and "Our Story." How do you see the ideas that Pollan discusses at work in the farm's Web site? Use your work on the success of Polyface from Question 1 of Questions for Critical Reading in making your response.

2. Visit the Web site for the U.S. Department of Agriculture's National Organic Program at ams.usda.gov/nop. What differences can you locate between the philosophy of organic farming at Polyface and that of the U.S. government? Which seems like a better standard for "organic," and why?

3. Spend some time at Michael Pollan's home page, michaelpollan.com. How does this essay fit into Pollan's other writing? What biases do you think he might have based on the information you find on his site? Do these biases make a difference in this essay?

Questions for Connecting

1. Pollan's description of Polyface Farm reveals a complex economic and ecological system. In what ways is this system consistent with the global supply chains that Thomas Friedman explores in "The Dell Theory of Conflict Prevention" (p. 121)? Can local and global economic systems work together?

2. What role does feedback play in ecological systems? Use Steven Johnson's ideas about feedback in "Listening to Feedback" (p. 191) to explain the success of Polyface Farm. Connect your response to the work you did on Polyface and complexity in Questions 1 and 3 of Questions for Critical Reading.

3. Michael Kimmelman explores collections in "The Art of Collecting Lightbulbs" (p. 216). How can we view farming as a kind of art? What sort of collection is necessary for a successful organic farm like Polyface?

Language Matters

1. Find a passage in Pollan's text that you think is central to his argument. Identify each of the verbs in your selected passage. What are the key verbs? What is the *action* of these sentences? Are there more verbs used in clauses? What are the implications of where each verb is located and what kind of verb is used? How can you apply these insights to your own writing?

2. Knowing your audience is a crucial factor in the success of any piece of writing. Looking at Pollan's writing, what audience do you think he has in mind? How do you know that? What audience should you keep in mind when writing in this class? How can you make sure that your writing reflects that audience?

3. Conjunctions are words that join nouns, phrases, or clauses. Find two quotations that seem to have some relation in Pollan's essay (or choose one from Pollan and one from another essay you've read for this class). Express the relationship between the two quotations using only one conjunction. When might you want to use this same conjunction in your own writing?

Assignments for Writing

1. Pollan reviews farmer Joel Salatin's alternative farming methods, in the process prompting us to question the very nature of farming. By attempting to simplify and sanitize farming, have we moved away from the health and efficiency inherent in a natural system? Can the benefits of biotechnology outweigh the benefits of symbiosis and nature? As biotechnology pushes science and food toward new frontiers, will we find that the old ways of farming are the better, more healthful ways, or is technologically engineered food simply a measurement of healthy progress, no different than progress in any other arena? Using Pollan's essay, formulate an argument on the relationship between food production methods and health. To support your position, consider the alternatives to Salatin's farming methods, the effect of farming practices on our health, and how the interdependence among the different parts of the farming process affects not only the farmer, the animals, and the farm's products but the consumer as well. Use your work with complexity from Question 3 of Questions for Critical Reading.

2. Using Pollan's essay, write a paper in which you evaluate the efficiency of nature-based farming methods versus the efficiency of biotechnology-based farming methods in food production. What does Pollan mean when he describes Salatin's methods as "holon"-based? Why don't we all still farm in the traditional, interdependent manner practiced by Salatin? What are the benefits and disadvantages to "alternative," natural farming? What are the benefits and disadvantages to farming with biotechnology? Do complexity and multiculture lead to better efficiency? Are complexity and multiculture more or less efficient than simplicity and monoculture? Use your work with Pollan's essay from Questions for Critical Reading to support your argument.

3. As agribusiness continues to expand in a global economy, will we find that the old ways of farming are the more effective ways, or will we find current monoculture practices are needed to keep up with the demands of an ever-expanding world population? Using Pollan's essay, write a paper in which you evaluate the advantages of monoculture-based farming methods versus multiculture-based farming methods in food production. What are the benefits and disadvantages to "alternative," natural farming, or what Pollan calls "coevolutionary

relationships"? What are the benefits and disadvantages to farming with biotechnology in the form of vaccines, disease-resistant crop varieties, chemical
fertilizers, and genetically modified seeds? Are complexity and multiculture
necessary to feed the modern world? Are complexity and multiculture more or
less efficient than simplicity and monoculture? Draw from your work on complexity from Question 3 of Questions for Critical Reading.

Virginia Postrel

Virginia Postrel, who holds a B.A. in English literature from Princeton University, is a writer on politics, economics, and culture. She regularly contributes to the "Culture & Commerce" column in the *Atlantic Monthly* and has also written for *Forbes,* the *New York Times,* and the *Wall Street Journal.* Known for her libertarian philosophy, Postrel served as editor of *Reason* magazine for more than a decade, during which she won a Free Press Association Mencken Award. She also serves on the board of directors of the Foundation for Individual Rights in Education (FIRE), an organization concerned with civil liberties on college campuses.

Postrel has published two books: *The Future and Its Enemies: The Growing Conflict over Creativity, Enterprise, and Progress* (1998) and *The Substance of Style: How the Rise of Aesthetic Value Is Remaking Commerce, Culture, and Consciousness* (2003), from which "The Boundaries of Design" is drawn. In *The Substance of Style*, Postrel argues that aesthetic value is growing in importance and is changing the personal and professional lives of Americans. This growth, though, is not something to fear—it is a symptom of a vibrant, dynamic society. This outlook reflects Postrel's similarly forward-looking philosophy, dynamism, which she examined in her first book.

"The Boundaries of Design" addresses the role of aesthetics in public life and, more important, the role of the public in shaping aesthetics. The democratization of taste has created a nation of experts, argues Postrel, each of whom holds an opinion about the design of public buildings, a neighbor's house, even a neighbor's outfit. Postrel also addresses the issues facing a society in which others—from community organizations to government agencies—impose taste on individuals.

Few of us consider the impact aesthetics has had on our everyday lives. But Postrel suggests that it is an essential component of our world, one closely tied to systems of cultural and political power, making it an important concern for us all.

▶ TAGS: *social change*, *identity*, *aesthetic boundaries*, *community*, *diplomacy*, *diversity*

The Boundaries of Design

Los Angeles artist Mike McNeilly was up high on the wall of a ten-story Westwood office building, painting a mural, when a building inspector showed up and ordered him to stop.[1] McNeilly, who had permission from the building owner but no permit from the city, kept going. Then the cops showed up. "I was told in no uncertain terms from LAPD, 'You either stop painting or you're going to jail,'" he later recalled. With no desire to spend his weekend in the slammer, McNeilly quit working. He was charged with five misdemeanors.

For more than a year thereafter, a striking monument stared west down Wilshire Boulevard: a jaggedly incomplete Statue of Liberty, her face vanishing below her eyes. McNeilly had inadvertently created a graphic symbol of the intensifying conflicts between aesthetic expression and aesthetic control.

When "design is everywhere, and everywhere is now designed," whoever determines look and feel controls a great deal of economic and personal value. As our surroundings get more aesthetically pleasing, the things we find ugly or disconcerting stand out. We demand better design, and that demand inevitably generates conflict. "Design" implies a single set of purposes served by a coherent aesthetic. But not everyone has the same purposes or finds the same elements enjoyable. Identities differ and so do tastes, including the taste for variety versus consistency. Depending on its boundaries, then, design can be satisfying or tyrannical. It ranges from the individualistic, expressing one identity among many possibilities, to the totalitarian, subordinating all particulars to a unitary vision.

Does the aesthetic imperative mean letting all of us pursue our individual aesthetic dreams? Or does it demand that we eliminate stylistic oddities to maintain a consistent theme? Both approaches generate meaning and pleasure. Both create aesthetic value. The challenge is to keep each in its place. To avoid design tyranny, we need to find the right boundaries—to discover rules that preserve aesthetic discovery and diversity, accommodating plural identities and tastes, while still allowing the pleasures of consistency and coherence.

Aesthetics may be a form of expression, but it doesn't enjoy the laissez-faire status accorded speech or writing. To the contrary, the more significant look and feel become, the more they tend to be restricted by law. The very power of beauty encourages people to become absolutists—to insist that other people's stylistic choices, or their trade-offs between aesthetics and other values, constitute environmental crimes. Individuals may expect more expressive freedom for themselves, but they often feel affronted and victimized by the aesthetic choices of others. This is particularly true for places, the touchstone category of our aesthetic era.

The desire for attractive, controlled, immersive environments extends beyond the walls of shopping malls or restaurants. When designer Karim Rashid says, "Our entire physical landscape has improved, and that makes people more critical as an audience," he's thinking of the market for products like his. But that critical audience doesn't just shop for trash cans and furniture. It buys houses and drives down city streets. And it has opinions about how the landscape should look, opinions that increasingly shape not only personal choices but the rules governing the built environment. Instead of tolerating sights they don't like, from tacky porch furniture to innovative architecture, more and more people are demanding a world free of "visual pollution."

Home owners take offense at their neighbors' paint colors, their window frames, even their kids' play equipment. "The 'not in my backyard' creed, so deftly applied to public works, has been given a new kicker: 'and not in yours either,'" wrote a *New York Times* reporter after her backyard neighbors objected to the swing set she and her husband had put up for their young son.[2] Following zoning regulations, the couple had placed the swing set well inside their yard, shielded by trees and bushes. But the neighbors complained they could see it from their bathroom window. "We like to think of your yard as an extension of ours," they said, voicing an increasingly common attitude. "People are definitely less tolerant than they used to be," says a suburban New York building inspector.

Over the past two decades, master-planned communities with standardized styles and prescriptive "pattern books" have become the norm for large-scale home developments. These communities sell predictability. While old-line suburbs started out fairly uniform to keep down construction costs, owners could (and did) dramatically transform their homes over time. Master-planned developments, by contrast, seek to control changes. Buyers are bound by contract to abide by rules designed to preserve a certain look and feel.

The Highlands Ranch community in Colorado, for instance, limits house numbers to no more than six inches tall and kids' backyard clubhouses to no more than twenty-four square feet.[3] No white picket fences are allowed in most neighborhoods. An enforcement team cruises the streets looking for such offenses as deviant home colors. (A light purple house got neighbors particularly riled up.) A competing community, Prospect New Town, takes a contrasting tack, going so far as to require striking colors on its houses—no Highlands Ranch neutrals allowed. Prospect, too, tightly regulates its environment. The developers require changes on 95 percent of the new house plans submitted for their approval. "It sounds harsh," says one. "But somebody's taste has to prevail, or else it would be anarchy."

No white picket fences are allowed.

In this case, the taste enforcement occurs within a voluntary profit-sensitive development that has to compete with nearby alternatives offering radically different design philosophies. Home buyers select the design regime that fits their personalities and lifestyles, and business success depends on design rules that please potential residents. But design restrictions aren't limited to competing contractual communities. The public sector has jumped into the act, bringing similarly uniform standards to property owners who don't necessarily want them.   10

Building appearance is getting the sort of government scrutiny once reserved for public health and safety. A 1993 survey found that 83 percent of American cities and towns had some form of design review to control building looks, usually on purely aesthetic (as opposed to historic preservation) grounds.[4] Three-quarters of these regulations, covering 60 percent of cities and towns, were passed after 1980, an adoption rate survey author Brenda Case Scheer compares to "zoning in the 1930s." The trend appears to have accelerated in the late nineties.

Some communities prescribe design rules in detailed *dos* and *don'ts*. Others use general terms like *appropriate* and *compatible*, illustrated with drawings showing acceptable and unacceptable examples. Scheer recalls a suburb that had no specific rules at all, allowing the design review board to outlaw whatever members happened to dislike. The result was an ad hoc checklist of idiosyncratic no-nos — "the *strangest* things," she says, "like they didn't want to have any windows with round tops on them. The decking on a deck couldn't run diagonally. If you had shutters, your shutters had to be able to close."[5]

This town isn't an isolated example. Architectural review boards, planning commissions, and city councils often have broad discretion to determine and enforce taste standards, from mandating rooflines and window styles to specifying what kinds of trees can be planted. Minutes of routine meetings record officials opining that the red leaves of ornamental bushes will clash with the brick of a shopping center sign and instructing a housing developer to build more single-story homes on certain streets.[6] In one town, a city council member praised the beauty of Bradford pear trees, while in another an official condemned them as an "epidemic."

In Eden Prairie, Minnesota, authorities ordered a Caribbean restaurant to cut down its summertime palm trees because they undercut the downtown's "visual theme."[7] Savannah, Georgia, told a hotel's owners they could not use a half-inch brick veneer to remodel the building but would have to use full-size bricks, reducing the size of the rooms.[8] Mequon, Wisconsin, ordered McDonald's to keep its building beige and tan, rejecting the restaurant's plan to adopt a retro look with the chain's original red, yellow, and white color scheme.[9] In Fairfax, Virginia, the owner of a golf driving range spent ninety-seven days in jail after refusing to plant nearly three hundred trees and shrubs ordered by local zoning officials.[10]

In Portland, Oregon, you can no longer build a new home whose front is less than 15 percent windows and doors or whose garage takes up more than half the façade.[11] The front door must be within eight feet of the longest street-facing wall. The goal of the ordinance, said a local official in response to critics, was to "put a stop to the ugly and stupid houses that we see going up."[12] Environmental policy is not just about clean air and water anymore. It is, increasingly, about legislating tastes.

"To feel secure in a changing and diverse society, we seem to need consistency, neatness, and 'quality,' wrapped in a reassuring, even sentimental typology," writes Scheer, an architect and urban planning professor who has grown skeptical of the design-review process she once championed.[13] "We are tired of ravaged commercial corridors, garish billboards, the ubiquitous and ever-changing steel-framed buildings coated in the flavor of the month. We want our neighbor to mow his lawn and keep his whirligigs out of sight in his own backyard."

Neither environmental aesthetics nor aesthetic conflict is limited to the outdoors, however. Personal appearance also sparks disputes, particularly within the workplace. Today's tolerance for divergent styles makes conflict more apparent. With less social consensus to dictate the proper appearance, workers sometimes expect more expressive freedom than the boss's standards allow. When style is strategy and hotels have "casting directors," how employees look can be as much a part of the atmosphere as the grain of the furniture or the beat of the background music. To create its signature environment, Starbucks not only controls the look, feel, sound, and smell of its stores. It also gives employees a uniform and requires them to cover tattoos and remove most piercings—a rule whose existence demonstrates how common those once-transgressive adornments have become. "I just take it as a protocol," says a seven-year Starbucks veteran who hides his tattoos under wristbands. "It's a business."[14]

Not all workers are so agreeable. Today's dress codes may be more about interior decorating than authority and conformity, but they can still provoke rebellion. Employees take their appearance as seriously as employers do, and they're especially likely to protest when the rules change. When Harrah's casino in Reno, Nevada, began requiring female employees to sign a promise to wear mascara, blush, powder, and lipstick to work, one bartender refused, was fired, and sued.[15] When the Dallas Police Department began enforcing a long-ignored hairstyle policy, two officers refused to cut their dreadlocks and were fired.[16] One filed a complaint with the Equal Employment Opportunity Commission; the other sued, alleging wrongful discharge.

At first glance, it may seem that only the employees in these cases are arguing for free expression, objecting to rules that violate their sense of identity. In fact, both sides want the freedom to establish an aesthetic personality. For the employee, that identity is personal; for the employer it's organizational. The employer is using how employees look to create a particular atmosphere or suggest what sort of place it is.

The two sides may even agree on what employees' appearance should signal and disagree only on the interpretation. To the cops who wouldn't cut their hair, dreadlocks are natural, practical hairstyles that represent honesty and strength. To the police department, by contrast, dreadlocks signify insensitivity and insubordination, violating the department's need to present a "neutral and uniform image, to effectively relate to all segments of the population." A significant minority of the public sees locked hair as a sign of rebellion or racial separatism, inappropriate messages for a police officer to send. The problem is that dreadlocks do mean all these different, contradictory things. Both sides are right. Even more than beauty, meaning is in the eye of the beholder.

The policy question isn't whether freedom of expression is good but where the design boundaries should be. Who gets to decide which aesthetic matches which purposes? Forcing an employer to accept an unwanted style is in some sense like forcing a newspaper to publish articles that disagree with its editorial viewpoint, or like redesigning a magazine or reediting a film against the will of its owners. Authors, graphic designers, and movie directors have freedom of expression, but they can't require businesses to use their work. They have to compete with others offering different visions and talents, and they often have to alter their creations to suit their clients, or to quit jobs they believe are making unreasonable demands. And, of course, they're free to raise a public fuss about their would-be employers' bad judgment.

Such disputes are more amenable to the give-and-take of negotiation than to the black and white of law, which must operate without the parties' intimate knowledge of particulars. Successful managers will avoid driving off valued

20

employees simply on the basis of looks, one reason for the spread of "business casual" dress and for the adoption of more stylish and personalizable uniforms everywhere from McDonald's to upscale hotels. Still, some conflicts are inevitable. As more lines of work incorporate aesthetic aspects, claims of expressive freedom and disputes over "creative differences" will spread into new areas.

Choosing employees may itself be partly a design decision, often a subliminal one: Who seems to match the place? Who will appeal to customers? The most important considerations are, of course, qualities of personality and character. But like casting a play, "casting" a work role may mean considering appearance as well—not just how employees dress or wear their hair but how they look to begin with. When such considerations are overt, they, too, can provoke controversy. Given the history of legally enforced racial and gender discrimination, we tend to condemn any hiring choices that seem to reflect similarly superficial preferences.

In Britain, it may be all right for a personnel manager to tell an interviewer that his hotel hires "young, very friendly . . . people that look the part . . . [and] fit in with the whole concept of the hotel."[17] American employers who look for a certain type, however, can find themselves in trouble with the law, which rarely recognizes design as a valid reason for favoring one job applicant over another. After celebrity hotelier Ian Schrager took over the Mondrian Hotel in Los Angeles, his new management fired the bell staff and hired a new "cool-looking" crew.[18] All of the new staff was white, compared to only one of the fired employees. The EEOC filed a suit, which the hotel settled, paying each former bellman $120,000.

"Cool" comes in all colors, of course, which casts doubt on the Mondrian's rationale. But what if the hotel had fired its old bellmen and hired a cool-looking multiethnic staff? That probably wouldn't fly either. A jury made up of uncool regular folks would sympathize with the dismissed workers, says a plaintiff's lawyer.[19] To avoid discrimination charges, warns an attorney who represents employers, the new staff "would also have to be multiage. If you think 'cool' means young folks, you've got a problem."[20] The EEOC's lawyer in the Mondrian case goes further, arguing that hiring only "lithe" or "athletic-looking" people would violate the Americans With Disabilities Act, which would also protect anyone with "a limb impairment, or a facial impairment, or a disfigurement."[21]

"It's one thing to have to have somebody who's slender and athletic and young-looking playing Tinkerbell in a Broadway production of *Peter Pan*," she says. "It's something entirely different if the job is to wait on tables, or if the essence of the job is to carry bags, or to check people in and make sure to get the correct information and assign the correct room."

Looks and personal style, which vary with the individual, are more like personality, strength, or initiative than they are like the status categories of race and gender. If a charming or intelligent person can have an edge in the job market, why not a handsome or stylish one? Neither charm nor intelligence is distributed any more equally than good looks. But in the lawyer's view, personal appearance is simply not a legitimate source of value outside a few conventionally artistic fields like theater. The "essence of the job" in a hotel, she insists, must have nothing to do with look and feel, which are extraneous considerations. A hotel shouldn't use its staff to create an aesthetically pleasing environment or send signals about what sort of place it is. Form is not part of function, goes this reasoning, so the law should not recognize an aesthetic imperative.

Fitness clubs feature beautiful bodies in their advertising and in their hiring. These businesses sell aesthetic aspiration; the boom in gym memberships reflects not just health concerns but heightened competition to look good. So it's not surprising that Jazzercise Inc. declined to certify a 240-pound woman as an aerobics instructor, telling her that "a Jazzercise applicant must have a higher muscle-to-fat ratio and look leaner than the public."[22] At five feet eight inches tall, Jennifer Portnick was about one hundred pounds overweight. If she wanted to lead Jazzercise classes, the company said, she would have to develop a "more fit appearance."

Portnick filed a complaint with the San Francisco Human Rights Commission. Her argument was the same as the EEOC lawyer's: An aerobic instructor's form isn't part of her function. The "essence of the job" is to lead exercise classes, not to look trim doing so, and the essence is all that counts. Jazzercise, Portnick charged, had illegally discriminated against her. Under San Francisco's "fat and short ordinance" she had a strong case. The ordinance

> **Jazzercise Inc. declined to certify a 240-pound woman as an aerobics instructor.**

puts the burden on employers to prove that weight is a "bona fide occupational qualification" and declares that "weight may not be used as a measure of health [or] fitness." It flatly prohibits considering whether obese employees might turn off customers: "The wishes, tastes, or preferences of other employees or customers may not be asserted to justify discrimination." Under legal pressure, Jazzercise revised its rules.

More interesting than the legal result was the media's almost entirely sympathetic treatment of Portnick's cause. Beautiful bodies create anxiety as well as pleasure and aspiration, and the commentary on the case reflected that anxiety. What a relief it was to think that looks might be irrelevant even to leading aerobics classes! To argue that Portnick's obesity really made no difference at all to the job, however, commentators couldn't justify San Francisco's regulation on humanitarian grounds. They couldn't just say Jazzercise was cruel or unfair. They had to declare the law cost-free, even beneficial to the employer. So they insisted that Jazzercise's aesthetic strategy made no business sense—that, contrary to its understanding of its market, the company would actually be better off with fat instructors. Again and again, outside observers second-guessed the company's judgment and identity, declaring that obese fitness teachers would attract customers.

"Don't tell me her 'appearance' is a turnoff.[23] The large, muscular, and graceful woman was the first fitness teacher I ever had who didn't embody some impossible physical dream," wrote syndicated columnist Ellen Goodman after attending a Portnick class. The hosts of ABC's daytime talk show *The View* took the same line.[24] "A skinny broad is going to annoy me," said the show's famously hefty Star Jones. "Surely, there must be room for all types of fitness teachers," editorialized the *San Francisco Chronicle*, concluding, "We hope Portnick gets her wish."[25]

Behind these arguments is a testable business hypothesis: that Jazzercise is leaving money on the table by not providing fat-friendly aerobics classes. Nothing stops these commentators, or those who agree with them, from pitting their aesthetic theory against Jazzercise's. The business is fairly easy to enter, and many nonprofit groups also offer potential venues. Portnick herself teaches at a local YMCA. A chain of Star Jones aerobics centers would even have celebrity selling power.

Experience, however, suggests that the commentators are wrong. Despite an easy-to-enter marketplace and intense competition for new clients, the world is not full of fat aerobics instructors (although some niche classes do exist). Apparently most potential customers really do prefer teachers with trim bodies, whether because thin instructors inspire greater effort, because they're simply more enjoyable to look at, or because people who identify with fat instructors won't actually take aerobics classes.

The commentary also ignores the crucial issue of design boundaries, seeking to impose the commentators' aesthetic preferences—a range of body types—on every exercise studio. If "there must be room for all types of fitness teachers," that room does not have to be under the same roof. Jazzercise is one operator among many. Its rules do not dictate a uniform aesthetic to the entire marketplace any more than Star Jones's straightened hair means all women must wear their hair straight. In a diverse exercise marketplace, some chains might want to establish their identities around slim instructors, others might prefer fit but fat role models, and some might hire both. Just as master-planned communities can offer competing ideals that attract different sorts of home buyers—Highlands Ranch conservatism versus Prospect New Town avant-garde—so not all health clubs need to be the same. Forcing every organization into a single design strategy because that identity suits some potential customers is both intolerant and unnecessary.

But the temptation to second-guess other people's aesthetic choices is nearly irresistible. Everyone, after all, has opinions about what looks good (or bad) and when aesthetics is, or is not, a legitimate concern. Those convictions determine how we make our own world special and how we use look and feel to signal who we are. We enjoy having—and sharing—our opinions of other people's aesthetic choices, a habit that can, of course, be quite unpleasant when we're subject to those judgments ourselves: *Can you believe that hideous tie? . . . What a beautiful garden. . . . He obviously spends way too much time on his hair. . . . That's a cool car. . . . I like that house, but the green trim is too bright. . . . Bell-bottoms were ugly in the 1970s, and they're still ugly. . . . She'd look better if she colored her gray hair. . . .* Even without professional critics, the world would buzz with aesthetic judgments. They are a normal part of human social interaction, a sign of the importance we "visual, tactile creatures" place on look and feel.

Our eagerness to make aesthetic judgments can blind us, however, to the differing aesthetic values of other people. Rather than trust the trial and error of experimentation and experience, we presume we can deduce in advance what's best, dismissing or ignoring contrary theories and opposing tastes. If our aesthetic preferences are good for us, we often assume they're good for everyone. Although we live in an age of aesthetic plenitude, we sometimes forget that our tastes may not be universal. The right house or neighborhood layout for me is not necessarily the right house or neighborhood layout for you; our identities, as well as our lifestyles, are different. Myopic aesthetic judgments become particularly problematic when the judges have the political power to enforce their tastes, all the more so when the law establishes no clear stopping point for that interference.

Consider these passages from the minutes of the design review board in Mount Pleasant, South Carolina, a suburb of Charleston.[26] An architect is presenting plans for a restaurant to be built in the Towne Centre shopping center. Among other details, he explains: "The restaurant has a very nice back bar of custom designed mahogany and glass shelves. They have incorporated a nice area of glass block there instead of storefront windows to give texture and light and visual interest." After the planning staff comments on the design, board members weigh in:

> [The first board member said] they may have to get rid of the ceramic tile band, but brick detailing could be just as nice. The brick color should be uniform to allow the detail to be read rather than the brick texture. . . .
> He asked about the glass block. [The architect] said it is incorporated into the design of the bar itself to allow light through the bar. [The board member] said he cannot recall if any glass block was used in Towne Centre at all; but, he feels it is out of place. Glass block at a door tends to be uninviting. [Another board member] said it looks good. . . .
> [A third board member said] his three concerns are the glass block on either side of the door, the left elevation has no detail from the back of the window on, and the rear elevation is a big green box. . . . Green is probably better than silver, but it would not be his choice.

These criticisms, expressing board members' personal feelings about tile, brick, glass block, and green paint, are a long way from straightforward rules like "plant trees and hide the garbage cans" meant to avoid imposing a nuisance on the neighbors.

Mount Pleasant does have lots of explicit design rules—no neon, for instance—but the board's critique is open-ended. If members don't like glass block or ceramic tile, they say so, even if the city has no law against either material. An architect who wants his plans approved will bend his client's budget, tastes, and aesthetic identity to suit the board, all the more so if he expects to submit future plans to the same board.

"Design review turns architectural designers into legal strategists and political conspirators; it suppresses artistry and innovation; and like other forms of absolute power, it corrupts those who wield it and compromises the processes they preside over," writes architect Denise Scott Brown.[27] In the process, the goals of the original design are likely to be lost, overridden by outsiders' aesthetic judgments. Instead of glass block to "give texture and light and visual interest," you wind up with a standard plate-glass window, inoffensive but uninteresting. "In short," says Scott Brown, "design review is a lawyer's, not an artist's, solution to the problem of obtaining quality in design."

Such forced homogenization is what made Brenda Scheer begin to doubt the wisdom of many design review laws. As a planner in Boston, she and her staff used their regulatory power to reward developers who matched their idea of good design, sending back for revisions the plans they disliked. Over time, local architects got the message. "Projects submitted were more and more acceptable and similar, responding to the developing sense of what my staff would accept," she writes.[28] "After several years, I was pleased: My view of the urban landscape became solidified and official."

But Scheer began to wonder whether a city of "acceptable and similar" buildings was such a good thing after all. Planners were implicitly turning the city into a single design project, reflecting a uniform vision. Intended to avoid bad architecture, design review had become an open-ended invitation to demand revisions, substituting the reviewer's judgments and priorities for the builder's. The process was stamping out variety and squelching architectural creativity. "One day," writes Scheer,

> I sat in on a review of a simple housing project. One of the staff reviewers, a recent architecture-school grad, was marking up a set of drawings— drawings that in the early days of mediocrity would have been greeted with pleasure because of their sense of context and originality. He didn't like the porch or the roof detail. The size of the brick was "wrong." A bulb clicked in my head, and the long process of questioning began.

When aesthetic experiments require official permission, even slightly unusual ideas tend to get screened out. (Hence the objection to glass block.) Innovations may offend conventional sensibilities or, just as likely, simply be hard to explain in advance. The result, writes Scheer, is that "all over the country, in every state and most cities, adventurous design is being smoothed out or blocked outright.[29] At issue here is not the freedom of the 'prima donna' architects, but the potential of the city, of any designed environment, to be a sharp and stimulating place."

Even when planning authorities don't enjoy limitless power to revise and fiddle, they tend to overreach the boundaries of their knowledge. They don't have the building owner's understanding of or concern for the structure's organizational context and purposes. They haven't gone through the thinking to figure out how to solve specific problems of site, use, and budget. They may not share the owner's tastes or tacit understanding of what effects the design is trying to achieve. And, of course, they don't bear the costs, financial or otherwise, of the changes they dictate. The result can be absurd, as in the strange case of the Frist Campus Center at Princeton University.

When the school decided to establish a full-service student center in the late 1990s, it hired Venturi, Scott Brown and Associates, who had already designed four new buildings for the campus and renovated many others. Robert Venturi, a Princeton graduate, and Denise Scott Brown had won plaudits for integrating the forms, colors, and decorative enthusiasm of the campus's traditional Gothic styles with the starker, machine-made geometries of contemporary architecture. Their buildings, concludes a critic, "demonstrated that a modern architect did not have to turn his back on history."[30]

The campus center demanded that ability to integrate past and present. It would begin with a three-story Tudor Gothic building opened in 1909 to house the physics department. The old Palmer Hall had the modest doors and leaded windows typical of Princeton's older classroom buildings. It was substantial but essentially private. Along with extensive remodeling inside, the architects sought to turn the building into a campus focal point and obviously public place, giving new meaning to the old structure without doing violence to the original design. An extension at the rear would be transparent, with a two-story graphic of the Princeton shield etched in the rectangular wall of paned glass. Along the path in front of the building, a freestanding arcade—a row of rectangular columns topped by a horizontal beam—would invite entry through ten different openings. Across the 215-foot-long arcade's top, FRIST CAMPUS CENTER would be carved in letters two to three feet square. Each letter would project about a foot above the lintel.

"It is the outer layer which is saying, 'This building is very open,'" explains Venturi.[31] "It does not have one single door in the center for four hundred students and physicists a day. You go through the arcade, and there are several openings that you slide into. That makes it a civic building, a community building in the campus, open and inviting."

For all the architect's thoughtful design, even his fans admit the arcade looked weird in models, "a little Potemkin façade," says one.[32] But the university trusted Venturi's judgment. "We have a long experience with Bob that is extremely reassuring," says an official. "He knows what he's doing. He's good at this." A student activist wasn't so trusting, though. When the local planning board invited comment, he made a passionate argument against "that big ugly thing." Although board members can't regulate aesthetics directly, they found another tool. What Venturi saw as an inviting outer building layer, an "iconographic frieze" integral to the overall design, the board declared an illegally large "accessory sign." Local regulations limit signs to 16 square feet and, by the planning department's calculations, the Frist carving was a 334-square-foot sign.

With a typical combination of anger and humor, Venturi vented his protests in a memo to the university titled "Why the Tasteful Frieze on the Front of the Frist Campus Center Is Not a Vulgar Sign but a Tasteful Frieze—Designed Also by a Highfalutin' Architect."[33] He cited historical precedents, from Elizabethan manor houses to Princeton's own campus architecture "teeming" with symbolic decoration. His arguments failed. The board refused to grant a sign variance. Rather than abandon the arcade altogether, as opponents hoped, the university came up with a novel solution. It erected the structure without any carving, but with room to add the letters later. The shapes of the absent words' tops still rise above the lintel. Like the partly finished Lady Liberty in Los Angeles, the odd humps serve as a monument to the ongoing conflict over look and feel.

Even without the offending sign (or frieze), the design worked. The arcade, 50 which matches the old building's brick and limestone exterior, does create an attractive and inviting entrance that marks Frist as an important, if less clearly labeled, campus gathering place. The space between the arcade and the building forms an implicit outdoor vestibule. Campus visitors who see the mysterious humps and hear their story tend to think the town's rules absurd. These visitors aren't quibbling over the meaning of *sign*. They're wondering why off-campus authorities got to decide anything at all about a structure that is barely visible from the road. If design review can reach inside a university campus, where does it stop?

As Princeton's primary physics building, Palmer Hall was long ago obsolete. But it took a novel architectural solution to adapt the building to its new use, a solution no one had thought of before. The campus center's unfamiliar arcade challenged the imaginations of people looking at models, and it fit uneasily into existing planning categories. Only because the university and the architects were stubborn and wily did the arcade survive.

Without the right design boundaries, we risk turning the aesthetic imperative into a justification for homogeneity and stasis, blocking experimentation and crushing the sources of new pleasure and meaning. The aesthetic discovery process is too unpredictable for fixed, uniform standards. Even individuals with settled tastes and identities want some variety over time, as the enduring power of fashion demonstrates. New technologies, from air-conditioning to computer-assisted design, make new styles possible, while cultural and ideological changes generate new identities demanding new aesthetic expressions. There is no one best way, and a static model of "good design" threatens the process through which aesthetic meaning and pleasure evolve. Trying to avoid all aesthetic mistakes can be as damaging as mistakes themselves.

"If you go to Germany or you go to Switzerland and you go through the countryside, there are all these houses that are exactly the same, [only] a little variation.[34] Sometimes they even have coordinated geranium flowers. It looks beautiful—a great place for a vacation," says Logitech founder Pierluigi Zappacosta. The landscape is tightly regulated in these countries, curbing individuality and experimentation in the name of good design.

Things are different in Italy, which also happens to be famous for its wildly creative design industries. "If you go to the Italian countryside where people really live and work, you cannot find two houses that look the same. It's continuous experimentation. And 99 percent of them are *ugly*, but ugly—ugly, ugly, ugly," says Zappacosta. But, he suggests, the culture that allows that experimentation, tolerating failures, is the same culture that produces aesthetic breakthroughs. He quotes a design professor friend: "It is tolerance for the ugliness that is the basis for the greatness of Italian design."

Of course, somebody enjoys those coordinated geraniums, and German 55 design is famous for qualities of its own. No single standard, *even the standard that allows maximum variety and experimentation*, can please everyone. Again, the challenge is not to eliminate design but to get the boundaries right. We don't want to force everyone into the world of "anything goes" (itself a particular design choice) but to match design with audience, to align coherent aesthetic with shared purpose. Overstretching the bounds of design implies two unappealing alternatives: too *little* design, offering "something for 'everyone' but nothing specifically for anyone," like the department stores young people shun for their lack of identity, or too *narrow* design, imposing a single well-defined aesthetic on people it doesn't suit.[35]

When legal authorities seek to avoid conflict by eliminating distinctive aesthetic identities—whether that means banning glass block or requiring aerobics instructors who represent all body types—we find ourselves in the homogeneous world of too little design. No one is offended, but no one is pleased. Narrow design, by contrast, excludes all but a limited range of styles, imposing a single clear identity. Thus Portland's ordinance essentially dictates a New Urbanist ideal adapted from early-twentieth-century neighborhoods, excluding many modern designs.

Such sweeping bans spring from the belief that "ugly and stupid houses" are an offense against the community, a form of visual pollution. Invoking pollution is a way of taking aesthetics out of the realm of expression, where liberal societies generally err on the side of freedom, and prescribing a single design for a large territory. But fighting aesthetic "pollution" isn't as straightforward as reducing air or water pollution, because the harms are entirely subjective. While air or water pollution may also have some subjective effects, at least in theory we can base regulatory standards on objective risks to health and safety.[36]

There are no epidemiological standards for good design. As a result, regulation tends to rely on assertions of raw power, reflecting personal quirks rather than predictable rules.[37] While design review boards made up of lay citizens drive architects crazy with their "offend no one" blandness dictates (too little design), expert reviewers can just as easily use their power to enforce their favorite professional dogmas (too narrow design). The Washington Fine Arts Commission even vetoed a headquarters proposed by the American Institute of Architects, apparently because its postmodern style offended the commission's modernist views.[38]

This problem does not mean that aesthetic spillovers cause no harms. If look and feel can be subjectively valuable, they can also be subjectively detrimental. Economists talk about pollution in terms of "externalities," which impose involuntary costs on third parties who don't reap the benefits; to the person bearing them, those costs are real regardless of whether some expert can measure an objective harm.

When Bard College proposed a performing arts center designed by Frank Gehry, neighbors in its Hudson Valley community protested.[39] Glimpses of the flashy stainless-steel building, they argued, would spoil the views from hiking trails and from an 1804 mansion preserved as a historic site. To avoid lengthy court battles, the college moved the building site farther inside campus, raising construction costs by about $10 million. When I mentioned the case in a column on aesthetic conflicts, my editor responded with a note excoriating Gehry's design: "The Bard development was a modernist monstrosity that would have damaged property values in a fifteen-mile radius.[40] Isn't there an externality here that has to be addressed? And if [Bard president and symphony conductor Leon] Botstein can force me to look at something like this, the next thing you know he will force me to listen to Schoenberg in the Grand Central waiting room."

The fifteen-mile radius is hyperbole—it's hard to imagine any building whose architecture alone could affect such a wide area—but the general point is legitimate: Aesthetic choices create spillovers. They impose costs on people with different sensibilities. Not surprisingly, most aesthetic conflicts arise from externalities.[41] We don't care that much about aesthetic choices we never experience. Your ugly house bothers your neighbors; your ugly sofa does not.

But just about everything people do in society—from the way they raise their children to the way they worship God—creates spillovers, many of them subjectively harmful. Only an isolated hermit has no effect on other people. And to some onlookers, negative aesthetic externalities would include not only peeling paint, cluttered billboards, or strange architecture but bad skin, thunderous thighs, or a penchant for plaid. Taste is subjective, and aesthetic identity is often personal. Are spillovers really a sort of criminal assault, or are they something more ambiguous? Should we really ban, tax, or otherwise deter any activity that has unpleasant effects on third parties?

Economist Ronald Coase asked that provocative question in a famous 1960 article, "The Problem of Social Cost," which helped win him the 1991 Nobel Prize.[42] He began with an important but counterintuitive point: Pollution is not a simple matter of physical invasion or evildoing. It is a by-product of valuable actions. Simply eliminating the pollution at its source would require harms of its own, by eliminating or reducing that value. The self-professed pollution victim is asking to reap benefits by inflicting harms, to create a mirror image of the original problem. Seeing the Gehry building may damage observers who find it a monstrosity, but denying Bard its stainless-steel building would damage the college.

The policy issue is one of trade-offs—costs and benefits, not good and evil. "The problem which we face in dealing with actions which have harmful effects is not simply one of restraining those responsible for them," observes Coase. "What has to be decided is whether the gain from preventing the harm is greater than the loss which would be suffered elsewhere as a result of stopping the action which produced the harm."

If a Portland resident builds a house with a big garage door facing the street, people who find that façade unfriendly are harmed. But if the city forbids that design, making two-car garages impossible to fit on many lots or forcing builders to design homes with less living space, home buyers who want garages are harmed. The question from a Coasean perspective is, Which is the greater harm, and how should we avoid it? It's incorrect simply to assert that intruding on someone's line of sight is the action that should be prevented. We have to consider the costs and benefits for both sides.

Thinking of the problem as one of reciprocal harms and benefits, Coase realized that if making deals in the marketplace costs nothing, the final level of pollution will be the same regardless of how the law assigns liability. If a factory has the right to operate even if it pollutes, then people who don't want to breathe stinky air can pay the owner not to pollute. If, on the other hand, the neighbors have the legal right not to suffer pollution, the factory can pay them to waive that right. In either case, the pollution will be set at the level that makes everyone as happy as possible.[43] This insight came to be known as the Coase Theorem.

In the Bard case, chances are good that the offended neighbors would have been satisfied with less than $10 million in exchange for letting the building stay put. But an enforceable agreement would have been hard to put together, perhaps impossible. As Coase would be the first to point out, we don't live in a world where deals are free. Gathering information, rounding up all the affected parties, negotiating contracts, monitoring compliance, and so on are all costly. Transaction costs can make agreements difficult, especially when a lot of people are involved.[44] That's why air pollution that harms many dispersed people can't be controlled through simple bargaining. In the real world, the way rights are assigned does matter. We want to mitigate significant harms, but we don't want to deter activities that create more value than they subtract.

The couple won the case in court.

In that cause, Coase argued that it's essential not only to consider both the offense and the personal and social value of the activity that gives rise to it but also to look at all the options, on both sides, for ameliorating the harms. Imagine, he proposed, that a factory spews smoke that causes $100 in damage. Traditional economics might suggest that the government put a $100 tax on the factory to compensate for the pollution. That gives the company an incentive to eliminate the pollution by, for instance, installing a $90 device.

But, noted Coase, the $90 device may not be the only way to avoid $100 in damage, or the most efficient. Again, you have to consider both sides. The harm exists not only because the factory creates smoke but because neighbors are there to be damaged. Suppose instead of eliminating the pollution at the source, the neighbors could avoid it for just $40, by either installing some other technology or perhaps even moving. (Coase obviously chose these figures to illustrate the mathematics of the choice, not as realistic cost estimates.) That would be an even better approach, because it would keep the overall harms to a minimum. If the neighbors had the right not to breathe smoke, the factory would presumably pay them the $40. But the government would have to recognize that the harm had disappeared, even though the smoke had not.

In many cases, if we consider all costs, all benefits, and all possible remedies, it turns out that the least costly way to deal with aesthetic conflicts is what we might call the Italian solution—to look away from the stuff we don't like. The small cost to us is dwarfed by the large benefit to the owner and, in some cases, to other people as well. This is particularly true since the costs of aesthetic tolerance tend to decline over time, another difference from more objective types of pollution. Our senses detect changes in our surroundings more keenly than the ongoing levels of stimuli; we unconsciously adjust our expectations to the background. That's why we don't notice bad smells after a while and why we come out of loud concerts to find ordinary speech seemingly muffled. In the built environment, once-discordant elements tend to become part of the background, going largely unnoticed. And there is a systemic advantage. By tolerating minor negative spillovers from other people's aesthetic choices, we, too, enjoy the advantages of personal expression and aesthetic innovation.

These sorts of calculations, done less explicitly, help explain why home owners generally have had broad freedom to decorate their yards and home exteriors to their own taste—a large benefit to them, at a small cost to neighbors who disagree but can look away. Even when harms are too substantial for the "look away" approach to work, it's often less costly to ameliorate spillovers than to abolish otherwise valuable activities. Because the social value of mobile phone service is so high, for instance, U.S. law prohibits communities from completely banning cell-phone towers.[45] Phone companies don't have the right to build a tower anywhere they want, but the towers can't be kept out altogether. Towns have to find less costly ways to deal with spillovers, requiring disguises on towers, locating them in less intrusive places, or demanding reasonable compensation to nearby residents.

For the cell-phone towers or the Portland garage regulation, the conflict is between aesthetic considerations and other values. If the towers didn't provide a nonaesthetic benefit, no one would want them. Similarly, hardly anybody thinks houses look better with big garage doors facing the street; that design is simply an efficient way to fit a house on a lot. Like smoke from a factory, we can generally agree that a cell-phone tower or a "snout house" does create a negative spillover. That assessment is subjective, but widely shared. In a world without technical or financial constraints, pretty much everyone would agree on what to do. The dispute is about relative costs and benefits, not about what's ideal.

Because of that underlying agreement, it's often possible to find a compromise solution, incrementally improving aesthetics while preserving most nonaesthetic benefits. A big-box store whose architecture is cheap but plain can assuage the neighbors' concerns by spending somewhat more for landscaping or architectural detail, as Wal-Mart has begun to do as it moves into urban locations where neighbors are closer by.[46] Like the cell-tower solutions, these approaches generally work only if the store has a right to operate, subject to reasonable accommodations to the neighbors' sensibilities (the political version of a Coasean bargain). If offended neighbors can block the store altogether, or if a single objector can tie up the issue in court, the store may not be built, even at the cost of making the public at large worse off. Where there's enough flexibility, however, both sides can often find an agreeable solution when aesthetics conflicts with other values.

In other cases, the dispute is more fundamental. There is no agreement on what would be ideal in a world without financial or technical constraints. Tastes simply clash, making trade-offs difficult, if not impossible. When Portland bans houses without many front windows, it's outlawing modern architecture that some people like very much. Critics of the Portland rule usually cite Frank Lloyd Wright's work as something that would be illegal, but the same is true of many midcentury styles, including the Eichler tract homes that today enjoy cultlike devotion and command a price premium. By contrast to the garage rule, this taste conflict wouldn't go away if resources were unlimited. When aesthetics oppose aesthetics, one design regime or another has to win.

In an older neighborhood in Louisville, Kentucky, an art therapist and a graphic designer shocked traditionalist neighbors by building a high-style contemporary house with a façade of plastic, corrugated metal, and concrete tiling. Trying to address neighbors' concerns, the home owners changed some exterior colors, but tastes differed so radically that a satisfactory compromise wasn't possible. Neighbors sued, charging that the house violated deed restrictions. "They want us essentially to tear the house down or dramatically change the exterior," said the couple's lawyer.[47] "I don't see there's a middle ground." The couple won the case in court. The judge ruled that the neighbors couldn't pick and choose when to apply design rules that had been flouted for decades. That the house "is not in keeping with their neighborhood's traditional aesthetics cannot be a basis to selectively enforce the deed restrictions," he said.

When aesthetic preferences are diametrically opposed, the spillovers are not entirely negative. To the contrary, some third parties reap benefits. Some people in Louisville are thrilled with the unusual home; local architects have included it in special tours, and one neighbor calls it "a beautiful addition to the neighborhood."[48] The conflict isn't just between the owner and third parties but between different groups of third parties. Toting up the costs and benefits of an aesthetic spillover, we have to include not only the benefits to the owner, which are generally high, but the dispersed benefits to bystanders who share the same tastes.

Ultimately, the only way to mitigate aesthetic conflicts is to establish design boundaries that recognize the wide variety of people and the impossibility of deducing from aesthetic principles what individuals will, or should, value. We have to return to Adam Smith: to accept the importance of specialization and to understand that a *large market* of many people need not be a *mass market* of homogeneous goods. Good design boundaries won't try to find the one best way to dress, to run an aerobics class, to design a restaurant, or to build a neighborhood. They'll embrace pluralism. They'll allow competition and discovery, including discovery of how big the boundaries should be. A niche design that pleases many people will expand over time. A niche that loses popularity will shrink.

Design boundaries can surround an organization (a restaurant chain's signage and interior design, a company's dress code, a religious order's habit), an informal group (friends' costume echoes a subculture's adornment, a fan group's team logos), or a geographic area (a neighborhood, a shopping district, an office park). Boundaries work best when the rules are clear and members have voluntarily accepted them, when the units are small enough for members to exit without extraordinary cost, and when different design regimes compete.

In the built environment, the need for small units means thinking of an area not as a single design but as a collection of small, self-governing districts with their own design rules—whether prescriptive details, generic structures, or no restrictions at all. If you don't like the rules, you can move without disrupting the rest of your life.[49] The area's overall order emerges from the decentralized decisions of those competing units and the individuals who choose them. Over time, new sets of design rules develop to satisfy previously unmet demands.

In liberal societies, we take such pluralism and competition for granted in most aesthetic realms. Only repressive societies try to dictate dress by law. Only centrally planned economies try to decide without competition what furniture or dishes people should want. If you don't like the green-dominated Starbucks, you can go to the blue-dominated Starbucks two blocks away—or to the bright-green-and-orange tea bar or the Populuxe diner down the street. You can decorate your living room with distressed furniture and folk art, antiques and Persian rugs, or subdued modern couches and chocolate-and-oatmeal walls. Unless you've enlisted in a cable TV makeover show, you don't have to accept what a design czar decrees, and you can change or mix styles at will. Despite some well-publicized disputes, employee dress codes are mostly no big deal, because there are many employers and professions, with many different views of dress; one of the dreadlocked cops quickly got a job in a neighboring police department, while the other became a schoolteacher.

It's hard, however, to fully embrace the idea that there are many good ways to make a neighborhood. In Louisville, some of the most eloquent advocates of architectural freedom sneered at the neighbors' "German 'cave-style'" houses and mocked their affection for brick.[50] While the legal dispute hinged on technical questions, the public debate was between those who declared that the iconoclastic home owners "have no sense of place" and those who said they "should be applauded for trying to be different"—between those who believe continuity is good and those, including the home owners, who believe in "questioning tradition." Like the question of what dreadlocks "really" mean, this dispute can't be settled on the facts. It's a clash of values.

Such ideologically charged disputes are typical. Critiques of the built environment commonly seek not to make incremental improvements, or to offer another choice among many, but to redesign the world into someone's vision of the single right way to live. Designers often believe that the right environment will make people better, with "better" defined by the designer's vision of the good society. If we build suburbs with yards and cul de sacs, away from the smoke and crowds of the city, as the twentieth-century Garden City movement advocated, labor and capital will live in peace. If we build new houses with porches, goes today's New Urbanist reasoning, we'll be neighborly like in the good old days. (Never mind that air-conditioning makes hanging out on the porch less necessary or desirable.) If we outlaw big garages, people will abandon their automobiles. If we build unusual houses, people will be tolerant. If we make a city exactly the way I want to live, everyone will be like me.

When it comes to the built environment, a genuine design pluralist is hard to find. Certainly, the last place I expected to meet one was in an urban-planning firm in Irvine, California. The Orange County town is the epitome of tightly controlled design, a squeaky-clean Edge City of office parks and master-planned neighborhoods, a place without billboards or whirligigs. It's so tidy that when my husband started teaching at the University of California campus there he couldn't find a gas station.

On a bright April day, I've come to Irvine to talk with Steve Kellenberg, who creates master plans for large-scale developments that sell more than a thousand homes a year. These "high-production, high-velocity" businesses represent the present and future of American home construction, supplying homes for the booming suburbs of the Sunbelt.[51] I'd heard Kellenberg tell an audience of developers about survey data showing that 63 percent of buyers in master-planned communities want more diversity, while only 32 percent want their neighborhood to look consistent.

That was what I wanted to hear. Like many variety-loving city dwellers, I'm leery of master-planned communities, even though I know they're extremely popular. It's bad enough that even my little eighteen-unit town-house complex has ridiculously conformist rules—no plants by the front door, no non-neutral window coverings, no door decorations except around Christmas—but at least our homes are literally connected to each other, making the cost of spillovers high. I can't imagine wanting to live in a whole neighborhood of similar uniformity.

But people really are different.

Over and over again, Kellenberg comes back to that message, expressing a tolerance that arises as much from relentless pragmatism as from liberal idealism. If you're in the business of designing environments people will pay money to live in, you can't kid yourself about what they value. You can't design your idea of utopia and force everyone to conform to it; if you try, everyone who isn't just like you will go elsewhere to find a home.

Unlike me, some people really do prefer uniformity to variety, regardless of cost. Not everybody thinks it's bad if every house on the street looks pretty much like every other one, or if people can't change their houses much over time. Some people *like* that sort of predictability. It makes them feel secure, at home in their neighborhood. Even if cost were no object, not everybody would want the same thing I'd pick.

"We have this incredible tendency to overgeneralize about the population and to say, 'Everybody wants this—everybody wants to live in a community where you can't paint your house unless it's the right color and you have to close your garage door,'" says Kellenberg. "Well, the fact is that there really are a lot of people who want that kind of controlled, predictable environment," often because they've had bad experiences in deteriorating neighborhoods. "And there are others that find that an incredibly repressive regime and wouldn't live there if you *gave* them a house, because they believe there should be an organic, fluid, self-expressive environment."

People are different. 90

"You have people in Irvine that love living in Irvine," he says. "And you have people that moved to Irvine and leave after five years because they hate it, and they move to Seal Beach or Santa Ana," nearby towns with few design restrictions. In a diverse society, some people will indeed want a lot of rules, "but it clearly isn't something that *is the right way* of doing it for everybody." Neither is the alternative.

People are different.

Even those survey statistics are misleading aggregates. Some people care a lot about diversity; others really, really want consistency. A lot are in the middle. Some people want to be sure to run into their neighbors. Others just want to stay in with their big-screen TVs or to socialize with the friends they already have. Some people want to be able to walk to the store without seeing a car. Others want to be able to drive in and out easily. The difference isn't one of demographics—age, income, education, and so on—but of identity and attitude. In the same price range, for the same size families, you can find people who want all sorts of different neighborhood designs.

What the survey numbers actually say is that part of the housing market has been underserved. For years, large-scale developers have focused so much on those home buyers who want a predictable environment and the most house for the money that they've ignored other groups. Offer the long-ignored groups a different sort of design, and they'll reward you handsomely. This pragmatic, trial-and-error process of discovering new sources of aesthetic value is less grandiose, and perhaps less inspiring, than the ideological search for the one best way to live. But it is also less divisive and venomous.

You can see its latest products in the spanking-new streets of Ladera Ranch, 95 a huge new development about a half-hour drive southeast of Irvine. A blue-gray Cape Cod home, with the deeply sloping roof of its saltbox ancestors, sits next to an updated beige and brown Craftsman with a low-pitched roof. Down the street is a Spanish Colonial with a red-tile roof and around the corner a stuccoed house whose turret recalls the fantasy homes of 1920s Los Angeles. Although many garages face the street, violating the Portland prescription, most are recessed so they don't dominate the landscape. You see porches and yards and sidewalks—social space. And between the sidewalk and street is something no new Southern California community has gotten in a generation: a small parkway planted with trees, spindly today but promising charm and shade as the neighborhood ages.

These are mass-produced homes, with metal windows and Hardiboard concrete siding rather than wood. They'd never pass purists' tests of authenticity. But they offer something genuine and rare—variation in more than façade, rooflines and massing that match their styles, a street of different colors and different forms. Built on the empty hillsides of what once really was a ranch, Ladera Ranch is turning the previously unfulfilled desire for varied and sociable neighborhoods into extraordinary profits. The development sells twelve hundred houses a year for prices 10 percent to 14 percent higher per square foot than in the more conventional community right next door. The landscaping and construction quality cost more, acknowledges Kellenberg, but even accounting for those costs, "it still appears that there's a 7 to 10 percent lift in the base values that can only be explained by people being willing to pay more to live there."

People are different.

Specialization pays. "There really is a lot of the market that doesn't want everything to look the same, that does want to have individuality in their home, that does want a diversity of neighborhoods, that wants [the design] to feel like it grew out of the heritage of the place, that are interested in meeting their neighbors, that would enjoy having the street designed as a social space, that would like to have other social spaces and social opportunities that they could participate in," he says.

Ladera Ranch's design owes much to the New Urbanism, with its emphasis on community and its understanding of streets as social spaces. But Kellenberg dismisses the New Urbanism's one-size-fits-all doctrines, its "singular mission" that "rejects everything other than New Urbanism." Lots of beloved neighborhoods, he notes, don't conform to New Urbanist prescriptions. The design for Ladera Ranch isn't New Urbanism. It's specialization—specialization within specialization, in fact. The development includes four different neighborhood styles, each crafted to suit a different personality and lifestyle. And if you want something different, you don't have to buy a place in Ladera Ranch. You can go next door. There's something for everyone and, if there isn't, a smart developer will figure out how to fill in the gaps.

The seeming homogeneity of master-planned communities—the planning that gives them a bad name among intellectuals—turns out to be real-world pluralism once you realize that everyone doesn't have to live within the same design boundaries. Community designs and governance structures are continuously evolving, offering new models to compete with the old. This pluralist approach may overturn technocratic notions of how city planning should work, but it's the way towns are in fact developing in the United States, suggesting that these institutions offer real benefits to residents. From 1970 to 2002, the number of American housing units in home-owner associations, including condominiums and cooperatives, rose from 1 percent to 17 percent, with more than half of all new units in some areas in these associations.[52]

As an alternative or supplement to large-scale local government, some economists and legal scholars have begun debating ways to let home owners who aren't in private associations form them, whether for whole neighborhoods or just a few blocks. Some proposals envision the privatization of former city services like garbage collection and of zoning-style regulations.[53] Others want only a specialized complement to city governance, with special fees to cover services that people in that small area particularly value. For instance, suggests a legal scholar, "if artists were to concentrate their studios on a particular city block, their [Block Improvement District] could make unusually heavy expenditures on street sculptures.[54] Indeed, the prospect of forming a Block Improvement District might encourage artists to cluster together in the first place."

Some of these plans would require unanimous agreement, others a supermajority. The question of whether new boundaries can be drawn around residents without their individual consent is a difficult one. If unanimous agreement is necessary, a single holdout can make everyone worse off. But retroactively limiting what property owners can do with their homes raises the same problems of pluralism that allowing small districts is supposed to avoid.

This problem is especially great when the new district isn't truly self-governing. Many cities, for instance, allow a supermajority of home owners to petition to make their neighborhood a historic district subject to special aesthetic controls—potentially a good model of specialized design boundaries. Unfortunately, historic districts usually have to conform to procedures established by a higher level of government. They can't create processes and rules tailored to the wishes of those they govern. In Los Angeles, for instance, a Historic Preservation Overlay Zone is regulated by a five-member board.[55] Unlike a home-owner association board, members are appointed by city officials and other board members, and only three of the five must be residents of the area they govern. Since residents don't have a direct vote, they can't easily predict, or check, the board's actions.

Even some preservation activists admit to concerns. A San Fernando Valley resident who's campaigning to make her neighborhood a historic zone says she isn't looking to crush individual home owners' self-expression, only to raise awareness of the history and value of the neighborhood's midcentury Eichler homes.[56] But some local preservationists are sticklers for architectural authenticity, narrowly defined. If the board is captured by purists, she admits, it might even outlaw the pistachio-green siding she and her husband chose to match their vintage car. "I don't think we'd like that too much ourselves," she says.

Even in the best of circumstances, small, self-governing districts wouldn't eliminate aesthetic conflict. Neither do master-planned communities. As anyone who's lived in a small condo complex knows, even small groups of people disagree. Governance rules simply provide processes for resolving disputes. And they help people know what to expect, avoiding the nasty surprises and bitter conflicts that result when aesthetic rules are imposed after the fact. The best we can hope for isn't perfection but fairness, predictability, and a reasonable chance of finding rules that suit our individual preferences. The advantage of narrow boundaries is that if all else fails, we can vote with our feet, not only improving our own situation but sending a signal that the competition is offering a better design package.

The more difficult it is for people to enter and exit—to find design rules to their liking—the more general the rules need to be. A four-block special district can have very prescriptive rules that would be inappropriate for an entire city. A metropolitan area like Orange County that is made up of many smaller cities can offer a range of city-level design regimes.

In larger areas, one way to accommodate different tastes within an overall sense of structure is to make the rules fairly generic. Consider the difference between a work uniform, a requirement to wear black, and a general prescription for "business casual." All three establish an organizational identity, but each allows more individual choice and flexibility than the previous one, accommodating a wider range of appearance and personality. To attract a diverse group of employees, to avoid turning off independent or creative individuals, or simply to stay up-to-date as fashions change, it may be better to keep the dress code as general as possible.

Along similar lines, Brenda Scheer suggests that urban-design regulations should pay more attention to the urban forms that are hard to change and concentrate less on the stylistic details that are easily altered. It's easy enough to ignore a single building you don't like, especially once it's been around awhile. But street widths, setbacks, and lot sizes affect the whole experience of being in a particular neighborhood. They establish the underlying structure that creates the sense of place. "If you get the lots right and the blocks right and the street right and the setbacks right, somebody can build a crummy house and it will sit there for thirty years, and somebody will tear it down and build a nice one," she says.[57] "There's a kind of self-healing process that's available if the structure is fine."

This model allows for flexibility, personal expression, and change, while still preserving a coherent underlying design. It echoes the pattern identified by Stewart Brand in *How Buildings Learn*, which examines how buildings are adapted to new uses over time.[58] Brand explores what makes architecture resilient and capable of "learning" as its purposes change. A building, he notes, contains six nested systems: Site, Structure (the foundation and load-bearing elements), Skin (the exterior), Services (wiring, plumbing, heating, etc.), Space plan (the interior layout), and Stuff. The further out the nested system, the more permanent. Moving around furniture (Stuff) is easy; altering a foundation (Structure) is difficult. In a building:

> the lethargic slow parts are in charge, not the dazzling rapid ones. Site dominates Structure, which dominates the Skin, which dominates the Services, which dominate the Space plan, which dominates the Stuff. How a room is heated depends on how it relates to the heating and cooling Services, which depend on the energy efficiency of the Skin, which depends on the constraints of the Structure. . . . The quick processes provide originality and challenge, the slow provide continuity and constraint.

A well-designed, adaptable building, Brand argues, respects the different [110] speeds and different functions of these nested layers. It keeps them separate, allowing "slippage" so that the quick inner layers can change without disrupting the more permanent systems. (You don't have to tear up the foundation to fix the plumbing.)

Scheer's proposal applies a similar model to the surrounding environment. She essentially adds a seventh layer we can call the Street. By limiting design restrictions to the Street, Site, and possibly Structure, rather than the usual obsession with Skin, she makes room for evolution and learning. Like Brand, she emphasizes the effects of time. Given enough slippage between outer and inner layers, we can correct flaws and adapt to changing circumstances while preserving some underlying sense of order. A city, she says, is "a living thing, it's a changing thing, and it has to adapt or it dies. A city that is not having a continuous renewal is a dying place."

A dynamic model of city life recognizes that not just purposes or technologies change over time. So do tastes. Like Capri pants and stiletto heels, aesthetic spillovers go in and out of fashion, flipping from positive to negative and back again. Hard as it is to believe today, from the end of World War II until the 1980s, the Art Deco hotels of Miami Beach were considered "tacky, in bad taste, and old fashioned."[59] When the Miami Design Preservation League was formed in 1976, recalled one of its founders a decade later, South Beach "was considered a disgrace to the city, because of its cheap neon lights, 'funny-shaped' buildings, and the signs along Ocean Drive blaring 'rooms $5 a week.'"

Similarly, American tastemakers have for decades condemned neon signs as the epitome of commercial tackiness, and many cities continue to ban neon. Others, however, have rediscovered the lively pleasures of the lights. While some neighboring cities such as Santa Monica have been forcing businesses to take down their neon signs, Los Angeles has spent about half a million dollars helping building owners restore and relight historic neon signs.[60] The city's Museum of Neon Art not only preserves vintage signs but lends them to the popular Universal CityWalk outdoor shopping area. Commercial neon has slowly regained its 1920s status as a source of public pleasure.

The built environment is filled with examples of once-scorned designs that have become architectural touchstones or popular icons. When it was new, a critic called the Golden Gate Bridge an "eye-sore to those living and a betrayal of future generations."[61] *Architectural Record* critic Suzanne Stephens provides a wide-ranging tour of similar examples:

> Because of his idiosyncratic Baroque architecture, Francesco Borromini was criticized by his [seventeenth-century] contemporary, the writer Giovanni Bellori, as "a complete ignoramus, the corrupter of architecture, the shame of our century."[62] John Vanbrugh's early-18th-century Blenheim Palace was panned for its unclassical Elizabethan corner towers, and his work reviled by his influential client, the Duchess of Marlborough.
>
> Other buildings were judged harshly in their time as well. The works of Frank Furness and his followers in Philadelphia were too contrived and too awkward for critics in [*Architectural*] RECORD a hundred or so years ago. In 1889 artists, architects, and writers, including Charles Garnier and Guy de Maupassant, called the Eiffel Tower "useless and monstrous." Frank Lloyd Wright's Larkin Building in Buffalo was deemed "ugly" by eminent critic Russell Sturgis in [*Architectural*] RECORD in 1908, and in 1959 his Guggenheim Museum was dismissed by visionary architect Frederick Kiesler.
>
> In 1931 Lewis Mumford charged that New York's Chrysler Building by William Van Alen was full of "inane romanticism" and

"void symbolism," while Douglas Haskell felt Howe and Lescaze's International Style PSFS Building of 1932 was just a "filing cabinet." . . . Will Michael Graves' 1983 Portland Building—along with recent work by Eric Moss, Bernard Tschumi, Michael Hopkins, and Frank Gehry, which have received criticism (even in these pages)—be subject to a revised perspective as time goes by? We will have to wait.

Tolerating strange styles can create significant value over time, as the unfamiliar becomes familiar, leading to aesthetic appreciation. As Stephens also suggests, however, the test of time works both ways. Sometimes, we indeed come to love, or at least to ignore, once-controversial artifacts. In other cases, we look back and wonder, "What were we thinking?" Did people really believe architecture called Brutalist could be *good*? Acclaimed twenty years earlier, the Portland Building made a 2002 *Metropolis* magazine list of "The Twentieth Century's Worst Design Ideas," an assessment that itself may be subject to future revision.[63] A generation from now, we may regard Frank Gehry's buildings as beautiful art or hideous folly. Or we may find them something altogether different: nostalgic reminders of turn-of-the-century enthusiasms, regardless of their formal merits.

Time adds meaning to form. After the Twin Towers were destroyed, many news reports revisited the critical revulsion that had greeted the World Trade Center.[64] *New York Times* critic Paul Goldberger had called the buildings "blandness blown up to a gigantic size," opining in 1979:

> By now the twin towers are icons, as familiar in souvenir shops as those little miniatures of the Empire State Building. We have all come to some sort of accommodation with the towers, God help us, and there have even been moments when I have seen them from afar and admitted to some small pleasure in the way the two huge forms, when approached from a distance, play off against each other like minimal sculpture. But the buildings remain an occasion to mourn: They never should have happened, they were never really needed, and if they say anything at all about our city, it is that we retreat into banality when the opportunity comes for greatness.

Shortly after September 11, I heard a radio interview in which Goldberger recalled his harsh words somewhat sheepishly. He acknowledged that the buildings had grown on New Yorkers over time and, of course, that their destruction had given their memory a permanent emotional resonance.

As the now-lost towers testify, personally and communally we come to cherish landmarks we associate with significant places and experiences. This value itself often creates conflict, because those special places are often owned by other people. "Let's face it," says a Los Angeles activist trying to preserve the exuberant Populuxe-era architecture called Googlie.[65] "Our public spaces in Los Angeles are *private* public spaces—Ships coffee shop affected more people than any city building or the Los Angeles Museum of Art." That's true not only of L.A. but of most of the United States, a nation whose most notable landmarks include office buildings, hotels, theaters, churches, mansions, and university halls with private, often commercial, owners. Even Mount Vernon remained a private home belonging to the Washington family until 1858, when a woman appalled by its disrepair organized the Mount Vernon Ladies' Association to buy and restore the estate.[66] (The private association continues to own and support the property, which receives no government funding.)

In an influential examination of aesthetic regulation, legal scholar John J. Costonis argues that emotional attachment, not formal beauty, properly drives public efforts to preserve iconic buildings. Aesthetic regulations, he writes, "respond to our perception of the environment as a stage, rich in icons that infuse our lives with constancy, self-confirmation, eroticism, nostalgia, and fantasy."[67] Costonis's psychological insight seems sound, but his analysis offers little reassurance to building owners, for whom time often has just the opposite effect, reducing value and increasing costs. Third parties enjoy the heightened emotional benefits of continuity without bearing the escalating maintenance expense or forgoing the profits of alternative uses.

Consider Oklahoma City's Gold Dome, a 1958 bank building featuring a gold-plated geodesic dome.[68] After Bank One acquired the dome in a merger with another bank, it estimated that the building needed about $2 million in renovations, including new air-conditioning, roof repairs, and asbestos removal. With twenty-seven thousand square feet, the building was nearly six times too big for Bank One's purposes. In the era of ATMs and branches in supermarkets, banks no longer want giant showcases.[69] But locals were horrified when Bank One announced plans to demolish the dome and replace it with a small branch and a chain drugstore. Like San Francisco's Transamerica pyramid or Seattle's Space Needle, the Gold Dome had come to represent Oklahoma City. As a symbol, the dome's communal value was large, even though its private benefits had dwindled and its private costs increased.

> Like Capri pants and stiletto heels, aesthetic spillovers go in and out of fashion.

"It may be financial folly to restore the dome, but it would be a great gesture to Oklahoma City if Bank One could find a way to do so," wrote a local columnist, acknowledging the uneven distribution of costs and benefits.[70] "The dome is a community focal point, a serendipitous little inner-city oddity. Look at it and you're momentarily transported back to 'The Jetsons.' . . . The dome—along with the elegant, modern tower that's paired with it—is a rarity in Oklahoma City. It is an architectural landmark."

The columnist got his wish, minus the financial folly. The uproar delayed the demolition, encouraging the company to put the building on the market. At the last minute, the bank found a buyer. A local optometrist plans to convert the dome to professional offices, retail space, and an Asian cultural center. The bank will build a small building next door. The $1.1 million sales price wasn't as high as the company wanted but, said a bank official, "All things being equal, we'd rather not tear the dome down."[71]

It's easy to say something is precious if you can enjoy it at someone else's expense. Talk is cheap. Like review boards redrawing building plans, preservation authorities sometimes exercise almost unlimited power to require property owners to maintain old buildings without compensation for their troubles. One result is that the buildings don't have to be widely valued for either their pleasures or their meaning. They just have to appeal to somebody with more political influence than the owner.

Over the past decade, the Charleston, South Carolina, Board of Architectural Review has expanded its jurisdiction from a relatively small area of antebellum mansions into some of the poorest parts of town. At particular issue are four-room "freedman's cottages," believed to have been built by emancipated slaves.[72] The freedman's cottages are often in terrible shape and, even if restored, would be too small to command rents high enough to recoup the expense. One owner who was denied permission to tear down four freedman's cottages estimated they'd cost $100,000 each to repair and would still rent for only $200 to $300 a month. In another case, a man unfortunate enough to inherit a freedman's cottage spent four years fighting for permission to tear it down after Hurricane Hugo damaged the place beyond habitability. The city offered a mere $4,000 for the dilapidated structure, a ninth of its assessed value for tax purposes. Officials frequently fined the owner for not maintaining the property before finally giving him permission to demolish it.

The tiny homes do reveal something about Charleston's history, but as useful houses they're obsolete. Black Charlestonians fortunately have better housing options in the twenty-first century than they had in the nineteenth; they don't want to live in tiny, run-down houses, however historic. That makes the review board's preservationist zeal quite costly to the people who happen to own the cottages. If a freedman's cottage is of interest to historians but not to potential residents, then historians should buy and preserve it as a research site, demonstrating its value by paying the owner. Otherwise, their cheap talk just encourages neglect and, in this case, perpetuates a history of injustice.

Oklahoma City, by contrast, had to put its money where its mouth was, demonstrating that the Gold Dome really was a cherished icon. Activists couldn't force Bank One to maintain the building as a free architectural museum for their pleasure. Saving the dome required finding someone to buy it, compensating the bank. Given the value locals attach to the Gold Dome, preservationists conceivably could have put together $1.1 million from private sources, or the city could have used tax funds to buy the building. Fortunately, neither step was necessary, since the structure captured a commercial buyer's imagination, and no authenticity-oriented law hampered its conversion to new uses.

Giving the public a voice, making time for counteroffers (or, in predesignated cases, giving a city or preservation group the right of first refusal), and providing funds to buy or maintain particularly meaningful structures, while leaving the ultimate decision to the building owner, seems to strike the best long-term balance of rights in dealing with icons.[73] In Oklahoma City, the delay was crucial, because it gave the public a chance to let Bank One know how much people cared about the dome. A commercial establishment that draws its customers from the local area has a strong business motive to honor their aesthetic values, whether by improving the landscaping of a parking lot or preserving a beloved building. (An individual owner with eccentric tastes may be less susceptible to public pressure, since eccentric tastes and caring what the neighbors think don't tend to go together.)

There's no perfect solution to such conflicts, of course. If owners have to be compensated to preserve icons, there's always the danger that they'll pretend to threaten their buildings in order to extract payment. And sometimes icons will fall to the wrecking ball, lacking adequate support to save them. Even so, the greater danger lies in fostering what Scheer calls "the culture of aesthetic poverty," depriving the urban landscape of beauty, inventiveness, and meaning.[74] If building or preserving a potential icon makes it subject to de facto confiscation, property owners will erect and maintain only boring buildings. Or they'll be sure to tear down their buildings before public sentiment can interfere with their freedom of action. Or builders will limit the aesthetic details to the inside, with no free benefits to the general public.

Even without such perverse incentives, cost-conscious building owners often avoid investing in positive spillovers. "All the beauty, all the marble, all the stuff is put on the inside," laments Scheer, angry about the "fabulous internal environments" of malls and hotels that look like giant boxes from the outside. "An old hotel from the nineteenth century would die before they would do that. It would have been considered rude." Nineteenth-century hotel owners could count on controlling their building's fate, however. If they erected a showcase only to find it no longer useful, they could sell it for new purposes or raze it without punishment. Putting up a building that the public could enjoy didn't invite the public to assume control of that building's design or destiny. And those nineteenth-century hotels were special places, catering to a wealthy elite that expected aesthetic quality inside and out. When the general public began to stay in hotels more often, plain function—"the best surprise is no surprise"—was good enough.

Now, however, the quality-demanding elite is no longer so elite. It includes most of us. That means Scheer's lament about the culture of aesthetic poverty need not continue indefinitely. In the postwar era of function and convenience, the general public was relatively insensitive to aesthetics, tolerating an ugly environment in exchange for other benefits. Aesthetic regulation might have improved the landscape, but it was politically unpopular, because on the margin most people preferred low-cost function.

Now that people increasingly care about look and feel in their private choices, aesthetic regulation is less necessary to control blatant public ugliness. The same taste shift that has made the spread of design review politically viable is slowly but surely changing the definition of what's commercially necessary. If owners have the freedom to create, alter, and destroy them if necessary, fabulous external environments are sure to follow their interior counterparts. Our greatest fears of the aesthetic future are not of too little design but of too much.

NOTES

1. The building has continuously displayed patriotic murals since February 1999. McNeilly eventually won his case in a state appellate court, and the original charges were dropped. He continued to illegally erect patriotic murals on the spot, including one honoring firefighters and rescue workers after September 11. When the city charged him with new offenses for the September 11 mural, the American Civil Liberties Union filed a federal lawsuit on his behalf, citing his First Amendment right to engage in noncommercial political speech. The building's owner, who gave McNeilly permission to erect the murals, has also sued the city. Mike McNeilly, interviews with the author, July 1999 and June 13, 2002. Gary Mobley, attorney for Mike McNeilly, interviews with the author, July 1999 and October 6, 1999. Daniel Hienerfeld, interview with the author, July 1999. Virginia Postrel, "The Esthetics Police," *Forbes*, November 1, 1999, p. 174. Bob Pool, "Yearning to Paint Freely, Artist Battles the City," *Los Angeles Times*, May 17, 2000, p. B1. Bob Pool, "Ruling Will Allow Trial of Artist over Building Mural," *Los Angeles Times*, May 18, 2000, p. B5. Lawrence Ferchaw, "Painter Places Canvas over Mural for Holiday," *Daily Bruin*, May 30, 2000, p. 1. *Michael McNeilly v. City of Los Angeles*, complaint for injunctive and declaratory relief, U.S. District Court for the Central District of California, October 23, 2001.
2. Kathryn Shattuck, "Beware the Cry of 'Niyby': Not in Your Backyard!" *New York Times*, May 11, 2000, p. F1. The official quoted is Adolph M. Orlando, a building inspector in Scarsdale, New York.
3. Ron Lieber, "Is This *Your* Beautiful House?" *Fast Company*, July 2001, pp. 124–40.
4. Brenda Case Scheer, "The Debate on Design Review," in *Design Review: Challenging Urban Aesthetic Control*, ed. Brenda Case Scheer and Wolfgang F. E. Preiser (New York: Chapman & Hall, 1994), p. 1. Brenda Scheer, e-mail to the author, February 7, 2001. The survey includes only laws, not private covenants. Note that 83 percent of all cities and towns does not mean 83 percent of all people, since many municipalities are fairly small and some of the largest cities don't have design review.
5. Brenda Scheer, interview with the author, July 18, 2002.
6. Gladstone, Missouri, City Council meeting minutes, March 27, 2000. Roswell, Georgia, Design Review Board minutes, February 1, 2000.
7. Chuck Haga, "Do Palm Trees Distort the 'Image' of Eden Prairie?" *Star Tribune*, July 8, 2001, p. 1A. After a spate of bad publicity, the city reached a compromise with the restaurant, allowing it to keep the palm trees for the summer, provided they were replaced with more traditional shade trees in the fall. James Lileks, "Eden Prairie's Parrot Is in a Pickle over Palms," *Star Tribune*, July 13, 2001, p. 3B. Stuart Sudak, "Restaurant's Palm Trees Get Reprieve from City," *Eden Prairie News*, July 11, 2001, http://www.edenprairienews.com/main.asp?Search=1&ArticleID=2021&SectionID=18&SubSectionID=79&S=1.
8. Vernon Mays, "Historic Savannah Says No to Fake Bricks," *Architecture*, December 2000, p. 25.
9. Mike Johnson, "McDonald's Retro Colors Have Some Seeing Red," *Milwaukee Journal Sentinel*, July 23, 2000, http://www.jsonline.com/news/wauk/jul00/mcdon24072300a.asp.
10. Tom Jackman, "Freedom Has Its Price in Fairfax," *Washington Post*, May 25, 2001, p. B1. Leef Smith, "Landscapers Storm Driving Range Early," *Washington Post*, May 26, 2001, p. B1.

11. City of Portland, "Base Zone Design Standards: City Council Adopted Report," July 27, 1999.
12. Charlie Hales, commissioner, City of Portland, letter to Jane M. Leo, governmental affairs director, Portland Metro Association of Realtors, January 11, 1998.
13. Brenda Case Scheer, "When Design Is Against the Law," *Harvard Design Magazine*, Winter/Spring 1999, p. 47.
14. Mary Jo Feldstein, "Piercing, Tattoos Create Workplace Issues," Reuters, June 22, 2001.
15. Rhina Guidos, "Fashion Checklist: No Blush, No Lipstick . . . No Job," *Christian Science Monitor*, July 17, 2001, p. 1. Martin Griffith, "Nevada Bartender Sues Harrah's over Makeup Policy," Associated Press, July 7, 2001.
16. Drake Witham and Connie Piloto, "Dreadlocks Policy Prompts Complaint," *Dallas Morning News*, May 30, 2001, p. A16. Connie Piloto, "Officer Fired for Not Cutting Dreadlocks," *Dallas Morning News*, June 2, 2001, p. A31. Teresa Gubbins, "Identity Crisis: Police Hairstyle Restrictions Forced Soul-Searching Decisions," *Dallas Morning News*, January 29, 2002, p. C1.
17. Chris Warhurst and Dennis Nickson, *Looking Good, Sounding Right: Style Counselling in the New Economy* (London: The Industrial Society, 2001), p. 15.
18. *U.S. Equal Opportunity Commission v. Ian Schrager Hotels Inc.*, Second Amended Complaint, U.S. District Court, Central District of California, July 20, 2000. U.S. Equal Employment Opportunity Commission, "EEOC and Mondrian Hotel Settle Title VII Lawsuit," press release, August 9, 2000, http://www.eeoc.gov/press/8-9-00.html. The EEOC's suit charged that the hotel discriminated in its recruitment practices, which included "hiring talent agencies to locate prospective hotel employees, searching for prospective employees at a shopping mall, and placing advertisements in entertainment trade publications seeking individuals who are 'high energy, upbeat, handsome/pretty with cool looking individual style.'" Virginia Postrel, "When the 'Cool' Look Is Illegal," *Forbes*, November 27, 2000, p. 90.
19. Eric Steele, interview with the author, September 7, 2000.
20. Michael S. Mitchell, interview with the author, August 16, 2000.
21. Donna Harper, the EEOC's acting assistant general counsel in Mondrian case, interview with the author, September 6, 2000.
22. Elizabeth Fernandez, " 'Teacher Says Fat, Fitness Can Mix; S.F. Mediates Complaint Jazzercise Showed Bias," *San Francisco Chronicle*, February 24, 2002, p. A21. Patricia Leigh Brown, "240 Pounds, Persistent and Jazzercise's Equal," *New York Times*, May 8, 2002, p. A20. City and County of San Francisco Human Rights Commission, "Compliance Guidelines To Prohibit Weight and Height Discrimination," July 26, 2001, http://www.ci.sf.ca.us/sfhumanrights/guidelines_final.htm. Portnick declined Jazzercise's eventual offer of employment.
23. Ellen Goodman, " 'Fat Chance' to Fat Chic," *Boston Globe*, March 31, 2002, p. E7.
24. Elizabeth Fernandez, "Size-16 Aerobics Teacher Gets National Attention," *San Francisco Chronicle*, March 18, 2002, p. A11.
25. "Battle over Fitness," *San Francisco Chronicle*, March 1, 2002, p. A34.
26. Mount Pleasant, South Carolina, Commercial Development Design Review Board minutes, April 24, 2002.
27. Denise Scott Brown, "With the Best of Intentions," *Harvard Design Magazine*, Winter/Spring 1999, pp. 37–42.

28. Brenda Case Scheer, "The Debate on Design Review," p. 2. Despite all the limitations on architects' designs, Scheer also says she found the process "lame," unable to affect the larger-scale features of urban life. Brenda Scheer, interview with the author, July 18, 2002.

29. Brenda Case Scheer, "When Design Is Against the Law," p. 47.

30. Raymond P. Rhinehart, *Princeton University: The Campus Guide* (New York: Princeton University Architectural Press, 2000), p. 123.

31. Robert Venturi, interview with the author, June 9, 2002.

32. Thomas Wright, interview with the author, July 24, 2002.

33. Robert Venturi, "Frist Campus Frieze—Definition and Justification: The Polite (Sort of) Version," memo, March 24, 1998, and "Why the Tasteful Frieze on the Front of the Frist Campus Center Is Not a Vulgar Sign but a Tasteful Frieze—Designed Also by a Highfalutin' Architect," memo, March 23, 1998. Jennifer Potash, "Campus Center Approval Expected," *Princeton Packet*, July 7, 1998, http://www.pacpubserver.com/new/news/7-7-98/center.html. Jonathan Goldberg, "University Receives Approval for Building of Frist Loggia," *Daily Princetonian*, October 14, 1998, http://www.dailyprincetonian.com/Content/1998/10/14/news/goldberg.html. Jim Wallace, Venturi, Scott Brown and Associates, e-mail to the author, June 10, 2002.

34. Pierluigi Zappacosta, interview with the author, September 27, 2000.

35. Zandl Group, "Shopping Attitudes," press release, July 22, 2002.

36. I do not mean to minimize the difficulty of setting environmental standards or the controversies that often swirl around them. The point is that it is not possible *even in theory* to establish objective standards of aesthetic pollution levels. At best, we might be able to measure an effect on real estate prices, which themselves reflect subjective tastes and can thus fluctuate with the fashion cycle or the makeup of the community.

37. Robert Venturi notes that the death or retirement of a design review board member often changes what architectural plans a board will approve. Review boards are not generally elected, and members often hold office indefinitely. Robert Venturi, interview with the author, June 9, 2002.

38. Richard Tseng-yu Lai, "Can the Process of Architectural Design Review Withstand Constitutional Scrutiny?" in Brenda Case Scheer and Wolfgang F. E. Preiser, eds., *Design Review: Challenging Urban Aesthetic Control* (New York: Chapman & Hall, 1994), pp. 31–41. "Given the human nature of all professionals," writes Lai, "expertness can just as easily be a cloak for dogma and subjectivity as a basis for disinterested objectivity."

39. Tracie Rozhon, "From Gehry, a Bilbao on the Hudson," *New York Times*, August 20, 1998, p. F1. Tracie Rozhon, "Bard College Bends on Arts Center," *New York Times*, February 19, 1999, p. B5. The added cost was because the relocated center could no longer share dressing rooms and other facilities with existing buildings.

40. William Baldwin, note to the author, October 6, 1999.

41. The aesthetic ratchet effect may itself be considered an externality—though whether it's positive (because it raises standards) or negative (because it raises costs) depends on who's doing the evaluating. In *Luxury Fever*, Robert Frank treats the effect as a negative externality, ignoring the positive spillovers of a more appealing world.

42. R. H. Coase, "The Problem of Social Cost," in *The Firm, the Market, and the Law* (Chicago: University of Chicago Press, 1988), pp. 95–156. (Reprinted from *The Journal of Law and Economics*, October 1960, pp. 1–44.)

43. Obviously, the final allocation of money does depend on who starts out with the rights and gets paid to transfer them. But to a third party observing only the pollution level, the world looks the same in either case.

44. Even when there are no transaction costs, there can still be problems if the group involved is large enough. Avinash Dixit and Mancur Olson, "Does Voluntary Participation Undermine the Coase Theorem?" *Journal of Public Economics,* June 2000, pp. 309–35.

45. Christine Woodside, "Cell Phone Towers Are Sprouting in Unlikely Places," *New York Times,* January 9, 2000, sec. 14CN (Connecticut Weekly), p. 1.

46. Peter Glen, "Here Comes the Neighborhood," *VM+SD Magazine,* November 1999, http://www.visualstore.com/people/glen/pglen1199.html, "A New Wal-Mart. Custom Fit for Your Neighborhood," Wal-Mart brochure.

47. David Kiser, quoted in Martha Elson, "Family's Dream Home, Neighbors' Nightmare," *Courier-Journal,* April 25, 2002, http://www.courier-journal.com/localnews/2002/04/25/ke042502s194117.htm. Deed restrictions dating to 1925 specified that house exteriors must be of brick, brick veneer, stucco, or stone, but the restrictions hadn't been enforced for decades; many homes in the neighborhood had façades of wood, vinyl, or aluminum siding. Martha Elson, "Judge to Decide Fate of Lakeside House," *Courier-Journal,* April 27, 2002, p. 8-B. Martha Elson, "Contemporary House's Owners Win Court Case," *Courier-Journal,* July 24, 2002, http://www.courier-journal.com/localnews/2002/07/24/ke072402s247377.htm.

48. John Gilderbloom, quoted in Martha Elson, "Family's Dream Home, Neighbors' Nightmare."

49. National boundaries, like the difference between Switzerland and Italy, are obviously drawn way too expansively for this approach. The switching costs are too high.

50. Allison Arieff, "Slugging It Out in Louisville," *Dwell,* April 2002, pp. 42–51. Martha Elson, "Family's Dream Home, Neighbors' Nightmare."

51. Steve Kellenberg, interview with the author, April 19, 2002.

52. Robert H. Nelson, "Local Government as Private Property," mimeo., May 2002.

53. Robert H. Nelson, "Privatizing the Neighborhood: A Proposal to Replace Zoning with Private Collective Property Rights to Existing Neighborhoods," *George Mason Law Review,* Summer 1999, pp. 827–80. William A. Fischel, "Voting, Risk Aversion, and the NIMBY Syndrome: A Comment on Robert Nelson's 'Privatizing the Neighborhood,'" *George Mason Law Review,* Summer 1999, pp. 881–903. Steven J. Eagle, "Privatizing Urban Land Use Regulation: The Problem of Consent," *George Mason Law Review,* Summer 1999, pp. 905–21. These scholars don't seem to have substantially addressed the model provided by existing preservation districts, which tend to be at a similar scale and usually require a supermajority of local residents to petition for district status.

54. Robert Ellickson, "New Institutions for Old Neighborhoods," *Duke Law Journal,* October 1998, pp. 75–110.

55. Los Angeles Municipal Code, Ordinance 174422, effective March 11, 2002.

56. Adriene Biondo, interview with the author, February 20, 2002.

57. Brenda Scheer, interview with the author, July 18, 2002.

58. Stewart Brand, *How Buildings Learn: What Happens After They're Built* (New York: Penguin Books, 1994), pp. 12–23.

59. Barbara Baer Capitman, *Deco Delights: Preserving the Beauty and Joy of Miami Beach Architecture* (New York: Dutton, 1988), pp. 42, 16. Also, see Denise Scott Brown, "My Miami Beach," *Interview*, September 1986, pp. 156–58.

60. Kevin Starr, "Landscape Electric," *Los Angeles Times*, July 4, 1999, pp. M1, M6. Nathan Marsak and Nigel Cox, *Los Angeles Neon* (Atglen, Penn.: Schiffer, 2002).

61. Cited in John J. Costonis, *Icons and Aliens: Law, Aesthetics, and Environmental Change* (Urbana: University of Illinois Press, 1989), frontispiece.

62. Suzanne Stephens, "The Difficulty of Beauty," *Architectural Record*, November 2000, pp. 96–97.

63. "The Twentieth Century's Worst Design Ideas," *Metropolis*, August/September 2002, p. 154. The list is labeled "humor," but is at least partly serious.

64. David Dillon, "Building Debate: Should Towers Go Up Again," *Dallas Morning News*, September 16, 2001, p. 23A. Kari Haskell, "Before & After: Talking of the Towers," *New York Times*, September 16, 2001, sec. 4, p. 4. Michael Fainelli, "Twin Giants: What Will Fill Their Shoes?" *Christian Science Monitor*, October 4, 2001, p. 17.

65. John English, quoted in Scott Timberg, "Modern Love," *New Times Los Angeles*, July 11–17, 2002, p. 13.

66. "Mount Vernon Fact Sheet," http://www.mountvernon.org/press/mv_fact.asp.

67. John J. Costonis, *Icons and Aliens*, p. 37.

68. Gregory Potts, "Protesters Stage Rally To Save Golden Dome," *Daily Oklahoman*, July 24, 2001, p. 1A. Gregory Potts, "Dome Support Spreads; Bank One Plan Meets Protests," *Sunday Oklahoman*, July 29, 2001, sec. 3, p. 1. Gregory Potts, "Bank One To Try Selling Gold Dome; Decision Encourages Preservationists," *Daily Oklahoman*, August 2, 2001, p. 1A. Arnold Hamilton, "Raising the Gold Standard," *Dallas Morning News*, August 16, 2001, p. 23A. Jody Noerdlinger, "Economics, History Weigh in Dome's Fate; Bank One's Bottom Line May Seal Building's Future," *Daily Oklahoman*, December 27, 2001, p. 1C. Arnold Hamilton, "Optometrist's Bid May Save Landmark," *Dallas Morning News*, May 20, 2002, p. 17A.

69. Because of federal and state regulations, the era of convenience came late to banking, while banks in the 1950s and 1960s lavished spending on their buildings, making the industry a notable exception to today's aesthetic imperative. Virginia Postrel, "The New Republic," *D Magazine*, December 2001, pp. 48–52.

70. Charles Crumpley, "Dome Creates Dilemma," *Sunday Oklahoman*, July 22, 2001, p. 1C.

71. Bill Scheihing, president of Bank One Oklahoma, quoted in "Contract Delivered in Bid To Save Landmark Building," Associated Press, May 18, 2002.

72. Jason Hardin, "Row of Houses Spared, But Owner Says Restoration Too Costly," *Post and Courier*, May 23, 2002, p. 3B. Herb Frazier, "Owner of Freedmen's Cottage Receives Demolition Approval," *Post and Courier*, September 22, 1998, p. 1B.

73. A similar approach is to give building owners tax breaks or other compensation, in exchange for agreeing to maintain iconic structures. Unfortunately, in practice such incentives tend to emphasize authenticity-as-purity rather than icons-as-communal-meaning, often selecting buildings for historical details or "living museum" purposes and paying undue attention to aesthetic minutiae.

74. Brenda Case Scheer, "Sympathy with the Devil: Design Review and the Culture of Aesthetic Poverty," *Loeb Fellowship Forum*, Spring/Summer 1996, http://www.scheerandscheer.com/aesthetic.pdf.

Questions for Critical Reading

1. What are aesthetic boundaries, and how does Postrel claim that they can be both positive *and* negative design influences? Define the term using her text and then read her essay critically to determine the ramifications of these boundaries.

2. What role should legislation play in aesthetics? Using Postrel's examples and ideas, suggest the proper function of law in design. Does that function change when the design in question is a matter of personal appearance rather than architecture?

3. According to Postrel, what are "spillovers"? Are they inevitable? Should they help determine aesthetic boundaries? Support your answers with quotations from Postrel's essay.

Exploring Context

1. Postrel discusses the controversy around Princeton University's Frist Campus Center. Visit the Web site for the center at princeton.edu/~frist. How is the center now viewed? Does its Web presence reflect aesthetic boundaries? Are there any remnants of the dispute?

2. Local ordinances play a significant role in Postrel's analysis. Use the Web to research design ordinances for your local community. How is aesthetics regulated where you live? Compare this information to your response on the role of legislation in aesthetics from Question 2 of Questions for Critical Reading.

3. What aesthetic boundaries exist on the Web? Explore MySpace (myspace.com) until you find a page that you think is particularly lacking in aesthetic value. How can you explain this page and its presence in the MySpace community through Postrel's analysis? Relate your answer to your work on aesthetic boundaries from Question 1 of Questions for Critical Reading.

Questions for Connecting

1. What is art? Synthesize Postrel's arguments about aesthetics with Michael Kimmelman's analysis in "The Art of Collecting Lightbulbs" (p. 216). Can we create a definition of art that has a specific boundary? Relate your response to your work with aesthetic boundaries in Question 1 of Questions for Critical Reading.

2. One way to think about Julia Serano's arguments in "Before and After: Class and Body Transformations" (p. 392) is that they are concerned with the boundaries of personal aesthetics. Use Postrel's ideas about design to reconsider Serano's analysis. How can you synthesize their positions?

3. Postrel stresses the fact that people are different. How does that pluralism function in design? Use Kwame Anthony Appiah's ideas in "Making Conversation" (p. 57) and "The Primacy of Practice" (p. 63) to consider aesthetic boundaries. How does the primacy of practice influence the tensions among homogeneity, conformity, and pluralism in design?

Language Matters

1. There is a certain class of grammatical errors often called "sentence boundary" errors, including comma splices, sentence fragments, and run-on or fused sentences. What does *boundary* mean in this context? Are these boundaries at all like the aesthetic boundaries Postrel discusses? How might her essay help us understand the importance of these linguistic boundaries?

2. Editors often use correction symbols; your instructor might use them as well. Design new symbols to represent some common errors you make. How are design and meaning related? Would your symbols make immediate sense to someone else?

3. Narrowing one's topic can be a challenge, even for writers like Postrel. Imagine a "research pyramid" for this essay, with the broadest category at bottom and the most ridiculously specific one at the top point of the pyramid. How many different levels can you find for this essay? Would the essay have been as strong if it were less or more specific? Why did Postrel choose this level of the pyramid for her work?

Assignments for Writing

1. According to Postrel, boundaries work best when the rules are clear and have been voluntarily accepted. Write an essay in which you explore the tension between expressing individual creativity and having others impose their creativity on you. Can a single standard please everyone? Can a design be subjectively harmful? Should we allow trade-offs? Do we have the right to express ourselves if we tell others that they cannot? You might want to consider your work in Questions for Critical Reading, particularly on the issue of spillovers.

2. Postrel states that individuals may expect freedom of expression, but they often feel affronted and victimized by the aesthetic choices of others. Write an essay in which you explore the conflicts between aesthetic expression and aesthetic control. If we accept what others impose on us, are we effectively killing creativity? If we allow others to tell us what they want, are we conforming? In making your argument, consider drawing from your work in Questions for Connecting.

3. Postrel addresses the issues facing a society in which others—from community organizations to government agencies—impose taste on individuals, asking us to consider the proper boundaries of design. Write an essay in which you explore the ethics of allowing government institutions to regulate aesthetics. In making your argument, you may want to draw on your work with legislation concerning aesthetics in Question 2 of Questions for Critical Reading. Also consider: What is design tyranny? Is environmental policy trying to legislate taste? What is the role of lawyers in design?

RICHARD RESTAK

Richard Restak received his M.D. from Georgetown University School of Medicine. He is a clinical professor of neurology at George Washington Hospital University School of Medicine and Health Sciences and president of the American Neuro-psychiatric Association. Known internationally as an expert on the brain, he has written close to twenty books on the human brain and appeared on *Good Morning America, The Today Show,* and *All Things Considered.* Restak's expertise has led to multiple awards, articles in numerous national newspapers, and invitations to write entries for *Encyclopaedia Britannica, Compton's Encyclopedia,* and *World Book Encyclopedia.*

Restak's book *The New Brain: How the Modern Age Is Rewiring Your Mind* (2003) details recent research and technological advances that have provided new insights into the human brain. For example, technologies such as CAT and MRA scans can now prove such things as the harmful effects of television violence, and research on the brain can be leveraged to maximize our capabilities in areas ranging from academics to athletics. Restak suggests that research on the brain has yielded practical applications that we can use every day, from matching drugs to the disorders they can treat to identifying potentially violent individuals before they act out.

"Attention Deficit: The Brain Syndrome of Our Era," a chapter from *The New Brain,* deals with the effects of modern technology on "the plasticity of our brains." Here Restak examines the brain's ability to multitask and the consequences of multitasking—for example, the risks of talking on a cell phone while driving. Our tendency to juggle tasks, Restak warns, may be both unproductive and damaging to our brains. Diagnoses of disorders such as Attention Deficit Disorder (ADD) and Attention Deficit Hyperactivity Disorder (ADHD) have become common in recent years, and Restak suggests that one of the reasons for this might be technology's effect on our evolution.

Multitasking forces our brains to process ever-increasing amounts of information at ever-increasing rates, which raises a question: Is the recent social and cultural trend toward multitasking actually rewiring our brains and causing such problems as ADD and ADHD?

▶ TAGS: *education, feedback, technology, creativity, multitasking*

Attention Deficit: The Brain Syndrome of Our Era

The plasticity of our brains, besides responding to the people and training to which we expose it, also responds, for good or for bad, to the technology all around us: television, movies, cell phones, e-mail, laptop computers, and the Internet. And by responding, I mean that our brain literally changes its organization and functioning to accommodate the abundance of stimulation forced on it by the modern world.

This technologically driven change in the brain is the biggest modification in the last 200,000 years (when the brain volume of *Homo sapiens* reached the modern level). But while biological and social factors, such as tool use, group hunting, and language, drove earlier brain changes, exposure to technology seems to be spurring the current alteration. One consequence of this change is that we face constant challenges to our ability to focus our attention.

For example, I was recently watching a televised interview with Laura Bush. While the interview progressed, the bottom of the screen was active with a "crawler" composed of a line of moving type that provided information on other news items.

Until recently, crawlers were used to provide early warning signs for hurricanes, tornados, and other impending threats. Because of their rarity and implied seriousness, crawlers grabbed our immediate attention no matter how engrossed we were in the television program playing out before our eyes. Crawlers, in short, were intended to capture our attention and forewarn us of the possible need for prompt action. But now, the crawler has become ubiquitous, forcing an ongoing split in our attention, a constant state of distraction and divided focus.

During the First Lady's interview I found my attention shifting back and forth from her remarks to the active stream of short phrases running below. From the crawler I learned that National Airport was expected to be opened in two days since its closure in the wake of the September 11 terrorist attacks; that this season's Super Bowl would be played in New Orleans one week later than usual; and that a home run record was about to be broken by Barry Bonds.

Despite my best efforts to concentrate on Laura Bush's words, I kept looking down at the crawler to find out what else might be happening that was perhaps even more interesting. As a result, at several points I lost the thread of the conversation between the First Lady and the interviewer. Usually, I missed the question and was therefore forced to remain in the dark during the first sentence or so of her response.

On other occasions I've watched split-screen interviews, with each half of the screen displaying images or text of the topic under discussion while the crawler continues with short snippets about subjects totally divorced from the interview and accompanying video or text. In these instances I am being asked to split my visual attention into three components.

One can readily imagine future developments when attention must be divided into four or more components—perhaps an interview done entirely in the form of a voice-over, with the split-screen video illustrating two subjects unrelated to the subject of the interview and accompanied all the while by a crawler at the bottom of the screen dealing with a fourth topic.

Yet we shouldn't think of such developments as unanticipated or surprising. In 1916, prophets of the Futurist Cinema lauded "cinematic simultaneity and interpenetrations of different times and places" and predicted "we shall project two or three different visual episodes at the same time, one next to the other." Yesterday's predictions have become today's reality. And in the course of that makeover we have become more frenetic, more distracted, more fragmented—in a word, more *hyperactive*.

How Many Ways Can Our Attention Be Divided?

Divisions of attention aren't new, of course. People have always been required to do more than one thing at a time or think of more than one thing at a time. But even when engaged in what we now call multitasking, most people maintained a strong sense of unity: They remained fully grounded in terms of what they were doing. Today the sense of unity has been replaced, I believe, by feelings of distraction and difficulty maintaining focus and attention. On a daily basis I encounter otherwise normal people in my neuropsychiatric practice who experience difficulty concentrating. "I no sooner begin thinking of one thing than my mind starts to wander off to another subject and before I know it I'm thinking of yet a third subject," is a typical complaint.

Certainly part of this shift from focus to distraction arises from the many and varied roles we all must now fulfill. But I think the process of personal *dis*-integration is also furthered by our constant exposure to the media, principally television. When watching TV, many of us now routinely flit from one program to another as quickly as our thumb can strike the remote control button. We watch a story for a few minutes and then switch over to a basketball game until we become bored with that, and then move on to Animal Planet. Feeling restless, we may then pick up the phone and talk to a co-worker about topics likely to come up at tomorrow's meeting while simultaneously directing our attention to a weather report on TV or flipping through our mail.

"The demands upon the human brain right now are increasing," according to Todd E. Feinberg, a neurologist at Beth Israel Medical Center in New York City. "For all we know, we're selecting for the capacity to multitask."

Feinberg's comment about "selecting" gets to the meat of the issue. At any given time evolution selects for adaptation and fitness to prevailing environmental conditions. And today the environment demands the capacity to do more than one thing at a time, divide one's attention, and juggle competing, often conflicting, interests. Adolescents have grown up in just such an environment. As a result, some of them can function reasonably efficiently under conditions of distraction. But this ability to multitask often comes at a price—Attention Deficit Disorder (ADD) or Attention Deficit Hyperactivity Disorder (ADHD).

Perhaps the best intuitive understanding of ADD/ADHD comes from the French philosopher Blaise Pascal who said, "Most of the evils in life arise from a man's being unable to sit still in a room." The fourth edition of the *Diagnostic and Statistical Manual of Mental Disorders* (DSM-IV) provides a more contemporary definition. Although ADD/ADHD affects adults as well as children, the DSM-IV describes symptoms as they affect three categories in children: motor control, impulsivity, and difficulties with organization and focus.

The motor patterns include:

(a) often fidgets with hands or feet or squirms in seat

(b) often leaves seat in classroom or in other situations in which remaining seated is expected

(c) is often "on the go" or often acts as if driven by a motor

(d) often runs about or expresses a subjective feeling of restlessness

(e) often has difficulty playing or engaging in leisure activities quietly

(f) often talks excessively

The impulsive difficulties include:

(a) often experiences difficulty awaiting turn

(b) interrupts or intrudes on others (e.g., butts into conversation or games)

(c) often blurts out answers before questions have been completed

To earn the diagnosis of the "inattentive subtype" of ADD/ADHD, the child or adolescent shows any six of the following symptoms:

(a) often does not follow through on instructions and fails to finish school-work, chores, or duties in the workplace

(b) often fails to give close attention to details or makes careless mistakes in schoolwork, work, or other activities

(c) often has difficulty sustaining attention in tasks or play activities

(d) often does not seem to listen when spoken to directly

(e) often avoids, dislikes, or is reluctant to engage in tasks that require sustained mental effort (such as schoolwork or homework)

(f) often loses things necessary for tasks or activities

(g) is often easily distracted by extraneous stimuli

(h) is often forgetful in daily activities

For years doctors assured the parents of an ADD/ADHD child that the condition would disappear as their child grew older. But such reassurances have turned out to be overly optimistic. In the majority of cases, ADD/ADHD continues into adulthood, although the symptoms change.

In their best-selling book, *Driven to Distraction*, psychiatrists Edward Hallowell and John Ratey developed a list of criteria for the diagnosis of Adult Attention Deficit Disorder. Among the most common manifestations are:

1. A sense of underachievement, of not meeting one's goals

2. Difficulty getting organized

3. Chronic procrastination or trouble getting started

4. Many projects going simultaneously; trouble with follow-through

5. A tendency to say whatever comes to mind without necessarily considering the timing or appropriateness of the remark

6. A frequent search for high stimulation

7. Intolerance of boredom

8. Easy distractibility, trouble in focusing attention, a tendency to tune out or drift away in the middle of a page or conversation

9. Impatient; low frustration tolerance

10. A sense of insecurity

Other experts on adult attention disorder would add:

11. Low self-esteem and

12. Emotional lability: sudden and sometimes dramatic mood shifts

A Distinctive Type of Brain Organization

In many instances childhood and adult ADD/ADHD is inherited. Typically, the parents of a child diagnosed with the disorder will be found upon interview to exhibit many of the criteria for adult ADD/ADHD. But many cases of ADD/ADHD in both children and adults occur without any hereditary disposition, suggesting the probability of culturally induced ADD/ADHD.

As a result of increasing demands on our attention and focus, our brains try to adapt by rapidly shifting attention from one activity to another—a strategy that is now almost a requirement for survival. As a consequence, attention deficit disorder is becoming epidemic in both children and adults. This is unlikely to turn out to be a temporary condition. Indeed, some forms of ADD/ADHD have entered the mainstream of acceptable behavior. Many personality characteristics we formerly labeled as dysfunctional, such as hyperactivity, impulsiveness, and easy distractibility, are now almost the norm.

"With so many distracted people running around, we could be becoming the first society with Attention Deficit Disorder," writes Evan Schartz, a cyberspace critic in *Wired* magazine. In Schartz's opinion, ADHD may be "the official brain syndrome of the information age."

"Civilization is revving itself into a pathologically short attention span. The   20
trend might be coming from the acceleration of technology, the short-horizon perspective of market-driven economies, the next-election perspective of democracies,
or the distractions of personal multitasking. All are on the increase," according to
Stewart Brand, a noted commentator on technology and social change.

As ADD expert Paul Wender puts it: "The attention span of the average
adult is greatly exaggerated."

"It's important to note that neuroscientists and experts within the field are
increasingly dissatisfied with ADHD being called a disorder," according to Sam
Horn, author of *Conzentrate: Get Focused and Pay Attention— When Life Is Filled
with Pressures, Distractions, and Multiple Priorities*, which lists forces in the modern world that "induce" ADD/ADHD. "They prefer to see ADHD as a distinctive
type of brain organization."

Such an attitude change toward ADD/ADHD carries practical implications. When creating an optimum environment for learning, for instance, Horn
suggests, "blocking out sounds can hurt. Today's younger generation has become accustomed to cacophony. Street sounds, the screeching of brakes, trucks
changing gears, and the wails of ambulances are their norm. For these people
silence can actually be disconcerting because it's so unusual."

To Horn's list of ADD/ADHD-inducing influences I would add time-compressed
speech, which is now routinely used on radio and TV to inject the maximum
amount of information per unit of time. As a result we have all become accustomed to rapid-fire motormouth commercials spoken at truly incomprehensible
speeds. Think of the last car commer-
cial you saw where all the "fine print"   **The attention span of the average
of the latest deal was read with light-   adult is greatly exaggerated.**
ning speed, or the pharmaceutical
pitch that names a dozen possible side effects in less than five seconds.

"The attitude seems to be one of pushing the limits on the listener as far as   25
'the market will bear' in terms of degrading the auditory signal and increasing the presentation rate of the spoken programming," according to Brandeis
University psychologists Patricia A. Tun and Arthur Wingfield in their paper,
"Slow but Sure in an Age of 'Make it Quick.'"

As these psychologists point out, laptop computers, cell phones, e-mail, and
fax machines keep us in constant touch with the world while simultaneously
exerting tremendous pressures on us to respond quickly and accurately. But
speed and accuracy often operate at cross-purposes in the human brain.

In study after study both young and older listeners recall less from materials told to them at a rapid rate. A similar situation exists in the visual sphere. A
television viewer's memory for information about the weather is actually poorer
after viewing weather segments featuring colored charts and moving graphics
than after viewing straight-forward versions of the same information in which
the weather is simply described.

As Tun and Wingfield put it: "The clutter, noise, and constant barrage of
information that surround us daily contribute to the hectic pace of our modern
lives, in which it is often difficult simply to remain mindful in the moment."

No Time to Listen

As the result of our "make it quick" culture, attention deficit is becoming the paradigmatic disorder of our times. Indeed, ADD/ADHD isn't so much a disorder as it is a cognitive style. In order to be successful in today's workplace you have to incorporate some elements of ADD/ADHD.

You must learn to rapidly process information, function amidst surround- 30 ings your parents would have described as "chaotic," always remain prepared to rapidly shift from one activity to another, and redirect your attention among competing tasks without becoming bogged down or losing time. Such facility in rapid information processing requires profound alterations in our brain. And such alterations come at a cost—a devaluation of the depth and quality of our relationships.

For example, a patient of mine who works as a subway driver was once unfortunate enough to witness a man commit suicide by throwing himself in front of her train. Her ensuing anguish and distress convinced her employers that she needed help, and they sent her to me. The hardest part of her ordeal, as she expressed it, was that no one would give her more than a few minutes to tell her story. They either interrupted her or, in her words, "gradually zoned out."

"I can't seem to talk fast enough about what happened to me," she told me. "Nobody has time to listen anymore."

The absence of the "time to listen" isn't simply the result of increased workloads (although this certainly plays a role) but from a reorganization of our brains. Sensory overload is the psychological term for the process, but you don't have to be a psychologist to understand it. Our brain is being forced to manage increasing amounts of information within shorter and shorter time intervals. Since not everyone is capable of making that transition, experiences like my patient's are becoming increasingly common.

"Don't tell me anything that is going to take more than 30 seconds for you to get out," as one of my adult friends with ADD/ADHD told his wife in response to what he considered her rambling. In fact, she was only taking the time required to explain a complicated matter in appropriate detail.

"The blistering pace of life today, driven by technology and the business 35 imperative to improve efficiency, is something to behold," writes David Shenk in his influential book *Data Smog*. "We often feel life going by much, much faster than we wish, as we are carried forward from meeting to meeting, call to call, errand to errand. We have less time to ourselves, and we are expected to improve our performance and output year after year."

Regarding technology's influence on us, Jacques Barzun, in his bestseller, *From Dawn to Decadence*, comments, "The machine makes us its captive servants—by its rhythm, by its convenience, by the cost of stopping it or the drawbacks of not using it. As captives *we come to resemble it in its pace, rigidity, and uniform expectations*" [emphasis added].

Whether you agree that we're beginning to resemble machines, I'm certain you can readily bring to mind examples of the effect of communication technology on identity and behavior. For instance, cinematography provides us with many of our reference points and a vocabulary for describing and even experiencing our personal reality.

While driving to work in the morning we "fast-forward" a half-hour in our mind to the upcoming office meeting. We reenact in our imagination a series of "scenarios" that could potentially take place. A few minutes later, while entering the garage, we experience a "flashback" of the awkward "scene" that took place during last week's meeting and "dub in" a more pleasing "take."

Of course using the vocabulary of the latest technology in conversation isn't new. Soon after their introduction, railways, telegraphs, and telephone switchboards provided useful metaphors for describing everyday experiences: People spoke of someone "telegraphing" their intentions, or of a person being "plugged in" to the latest fashions.

Modern Nerves

In 1891 the Viennese critic Hermann Bahr predicted the arrival of what he called "new human beings," marked by an increased nervous energy. A person with "modern nerves" was "quick-witted, briskly efficient, rigorously scheduled, doing everything on the double," writes social critic Peter Conrad in *Modern Times, Modern Places.*

In the 1920s, indications of modern nerves were illustrated by both the silent films of the age, with their accelerated movement, and the change in drug use at the time, from sedating agents like opium to the newly synthesized cocaine—a shift that replaced languid immobility with frenetic hyperactivity and "mobility mania."

Josef Breuer, who coauthored *Studies on Hysteria* with Sigmund Freud, compared the modern nervous system to a telephone line made up of nerves in "tonic excitation." If the nerves were overburdened with too much "current," he claimed, the result would be sparks, frazzled insulation, scorched filaments, short circuits—in essence, a model for hysteria. The mind was thus a machine and could best be understood through the employment of machine metaphors. Athletes picked up on this theme and aimed at transforming their bodies into fine-tuned organisms capable, like machines, of instant responsiveness. "The neural pathways by which will is translated into physical movement are trained until they react to the slightest impulse," wrote a commentator in the 1920s on the "cult" of sports.

The Changing Rhythm of Life

In 1931 the historian James Truslow Adams commented, "As the number of sensations increase, the time which we have for reacting to and digesting them becomes less . . . the rhythm of our life becomes quicker, the wave lengths . . . of our mental life grow shorter. Such a life tends to become a mere search for more and more exciting sensations, undermining yet more our power of concentration in thought. Relief from fatigue and ennui is sought in mere excitation of our nerves, as in speeding cars or emotional movies."

In the 60 years since Adams's observation, speed has become an integral component of our lives. According to media critic Todd Gitlin, writing in *Media Unlimited*, "Speed is not incidental to the modern world—speed of production, speed of innovation, speed of investment, speed in the pace of life and the movement of images—but its essence. . . . Is speed a means or an end? If a means, it is so pervasive as to *become* an end."

In our contemporary society speed is the standard applied to almost everything that we do. Media, especially television, is the most striking example of this acceleration. "It is the limitless media torrent that sharpens the sense that all of life is jetting forward—or through—some ultimate speed barrier," according to Gitlin. "The most widespread, most consequential speed-up of our time is the onrush in images—the speed at which they zip through the world, the speed at which they give way to more of the same, the tempo at which they move."

In response to this media torrent, the brain has had to make fundamental adjustments. The demarcation between here and elsewhere has become blurred. Thanks to technology, each of us exists simultaneously in not just one *here* but in several. While talking with a friend over coffee we're scanning e-mail on our Palm Pilot. At such times where are we *really*? In such instances no less is involved than a fundamental change in our concept of time and place.

Where Is Where?

"Modernity is about the acceleration of time and the dispersal of places. The past is available for instant recall in the present," according to Peter Conrad. For example, I was recently sitting in a restaurant in Washington, D.C., while watching a soccer match take place several time zones away. During an interruption in play, the screen displayed action from another match played more than a decade ago. The commentator made a brief point about similarities and differences in the two matches and then returned to the action of the ongoing match. During all of this I was participating in a "present" comprised of two different time zones along with a "past" drawn from an event that occurred twelve years earlier. Such an experience is no longer unusual. Technology routinely places us in ambiguous time and place relationships.

As another example, while recently sitting on the beach at South Beach in Miami I was amazed at the number of people talking on cell phones while ostensibly spending the afternoon with the person who accompanied them to the beach. In this situation the *here* is at least partly influenced by the technology of the cell phone that both links (the caller and the unseen person on the other end of the cell phone) and isolates (the caller and the temporarily neglected person lying beside him or her on the beach blanket). Such technologies are forcing our brains to restructure themselves and accommodate to a world of multiple identity and presence.

Intellectually we have always known that the "reality" of the here and now before our eyes is only one among many. But we never directly experienced this multilevel reality until technology made it possible to reach from one end of the world to another and wipe out differences in time, space, and place. Starting with telephones we became able to experience the "reality" of people in widely dispersed areas of the world. With the cell phone, that process has become even more intimate. Time, distance, night, and day—the rules of the natural and physical world—cease to be limiting factors.

And while some of us may celebrate such experiences and thrive on constantly being connected, others feel the sensation of a giant electronic tentacle that will ensnare us at any moment.

My point here isn't to criticize technology but to emphasize the revolution that technology is causing in our brain's functioning. If, for example, through technology, anyone at any given moment is immediately available, "here" and "there" lose their distinctive meanings. We achieve that "acceleration of time and dispersal of places" referred to by Peter Conrad.

And yet there is an ironic paradox in all this: As a result of technological advances we participate in many different and disparate "realities," yet as a result of our attention and focus problems we can't fully participate in them. We can shift back and forth from a phone conversation with someone in Hong Kong and someone directly in front of our eyes. Yet thanks to our sense of distraction we're not fully focused on either of them. What to do?

The Plastic on the Cheese

"If I can only learn to efficiently carry out several things simultaneously then my time pressures will disappear," we tell ourselves. And at first sight multitasking seems a sensible response to our compressed, overly committed schedules. Instead of limiting ourselves to only one activity, why not do several simultaneously? If you owe your mother a phone call, why not make that call while in the kitchen waiting for the spaghetti to come to a boil? And if Mom should call you first, why not talk to her while glancing down at today's crossword puzzle?

Actually, multitasking is not nearly as efficient as most of us have been led to believe. In fact, doing more than one thing at once or switching back and forth from one task to another involves time-consuming alterations in brain processing that reduce our effectiveness at accomplishing either one.

Whenever you attempt to do "two things at once," your attention at any given moment is directed to one or the other activity rather than to both at once. And, most important, these shifts decrease rather than increase your efficiency; they are time and energy depleting.

With each switch in attention, your frontal lobes—the executive control centers toward the front of your brain—must shift goals and activate new rules of operation. Talking on the phone and doing a crossword puzzle activate different parts of the brain, engage different muscles, and induce different sensory experiences.

In addition, the shift from one activity to another can take up to seven-tenths of a second. We know this because of the research of Joshua Rubinstein, a psychologist at the Federal Aviation Administration's William J. Hughes Technical Center in Atlantic City.

Rubinstein and his colleagues studied patterns of time loss that resulted when volunteers switched from activities of varying complexity and familiarity. Measurements showed that the volunteers lost time during these switches, especially when going from something familiar to something unfamiliar. Further, the time losses increased in direct proportion to the complexity of the tasks. To explain this finding the researchers postulate a "rule-activation" stage, when the prefrontal cortex "disables" or deactivates the rules used for the first activity and then "enables" the rules for the new activity. It's this process of rule deactivation followed by reactivation that takes more than half a second. Under certain circumstances this loss of time due to multitasking can prove not only inefficient but also dangerous.

For example, remember the speculation that cell phone–associated automobile accidents could be eliminated if drivers used hands-free devices? Well, that speculation isn't supported by brain research. The use of cell phones—hands-free or otherwise—divides a driver's attention and increases his or her sense of distraction.

In an important study carried out by psychologist Peter A. Hancock at the University of Central Florida in Orlando and two researchers from the Liberty Mutual Insurance Company, volunteers simulated using a hands-free cell phone while driving. The volunteers were instructed to respond to the ringing of a phone installed on the dashboard of their car. At the instant they heard the ring they had to compare whether the first digit of a number displayed on a computer screen on the dashboard corresponded to the first digit of a number they had previously memorized. If that first digit was the same, the driver was supposed to push a button. In the meantime, they were to obey all traffic rules and, in the test situation, bring the car to a full stop.

While the distracting ring had only a slight effect on the stopping distance of younger drivers (0.61 seconds rather than 0.5 seconds), it had a profound effect on the stopping distance of drivers between 55 and 65 years of age: 0.82 seconds rather than 0.61 seconds, according to the researchers. Distraction, in other words, reduces efficiency.

In another test of the cost of multitasking, volunteers at the Center for Cognitive Brain Imaging at Carnegie Mellon University in Pittsburgh underwent PET scans while simultaneously listening to sentences and mentally rotating pairs of three-dimensional figures. The researchers found a 29 percent reduction in brain activity generated by mental rotation if the subjects were also listening to the test sentences. This decrease in brain activity was linked to an overall decrease in efficiency: It took them longer to do each task.

A reduction in efficiency was also found when the researchers looked at the effect of mental rotation on reading. They discovered that brain activity generated when reading the sentences decreased by 53 percent if the subjects were also trying to mentally rotate the objects.

A similar loss of efficiency occurs when activities are alternated. For instance, David E. Meyer, a professor of mathematical psychology at the University of Michigan in Ann Arbor, recruited young adults to engage in an experiment where they would rapidly switch between working out math problems and identifying shapes. The volunteers took longer for both tasks, and their accuracy took a nosedive compared to their performance when they focused on each task separately.

"Not only the speed of performance, the accuracy of performance, but what   65 I call the fluency of performance, the gracefulness of their performance, was negatively influenced by the overload of multitasking," according to Meyer.

All of which leads to this simple rule: Despite our subjective feelings to the contrary, actually our brain can work on only one thing at a time. Rather than allowing us to efficiently do two things at the same time, multitasking actually results in inefficient shifts in our attention. In short, the brain is designed to work most efficiently when it works on a single task and for sustained rather than intermittent and alternating periods of time. This doesn't mean that we can't perform a certain amount of multitasking. But we do so at decreased efficiency and accuracy.

Thanks to technology, each of us exists simultaneously in not just one *here* but in several.

But despite neuroscientific evidence to the contrary, we are being made to feel that we *must* multitask in order to keep our head above the rising flood of daily demands. Instead of "Be Here Now," we're encouraged to split our attention into several fragments and convinced that multitasking improves mental efficiency.

Instead, multitasking comes at a cost. And it's true that sometimes the cost is trivial, or even amusing, as with the following experience of a young mother: "I had to get dressed for my daughter's middle school choral program, get another child started on homework, and feed another who had to be ready to be driven to soccer practice. Of course, the phone kept ringing, too. I thought I had everything under control when the complaints about the grilled cheese started. Without getting too angry, I growled for her to just eat it so that I could finish getting dressed. What else could I do in such a rush? My daughter then said, 'I can't eat it, Mom. You left the plastic on the cheese.'"

Other times, the cost of multitasking can be much less amusing. Imagine yourself driving in light traffic on a clear day while chatting on a cell phone with a friend. You're having no problem handling your vehicle and also keeping up your end of the conversation. But over the next five minutes you encounter heavier traffic and the onset of a torrential rainstorm. Your impulse is to end the conversation and pay more attention to the road, but your friend on the other end of the line keeps talking. After all, he isn't encountering the same hazardous conditions from the comfort of his office or home. You continue to talk a bit longer, shifting your attention between your friend's patter and the rapidly deteriorating road conditions. As a result, you fail to notice that the tractor-trailer to your right is starting to slide in your direction. . . . Your survivors will never know that your divided attention, with its accompanying decrease in brain efficiency, set you up for that fatal accident.

In essence, the brain has certain limits that we must accept. While it's true 70
that we can train our brain to multitask, our overall performance on each of the
tasks is going to be less efficient than if we performed one thing at a time.

Cerebral Geography

Despite the inefficiency of multitasking, the brain is able to deal with more than
one thing at a time. If that weren't true, we wouldn't be able to "walk and chew
gum at the same time," as a critic once uncharitably described a former U.S.
president. The trick is to avoid activities that interrupt the flow of the main
activity.

For example, listening to music can actually enhance the efficiency among
those who work with their hands. I first learned of this a year or so ago when
a draftsman casually mentioned to me that he felt more relaxed and did better work while listening to background music. Many surgeons make similar
claims. In a study aimed at testing such claims, researchers hooked up 50 male
surgeons between the ages of 31 and 61 to machines that measured blood pressure and pulse. The surgeons then performed mental arithmetic exercises designed to mimic the stress a surgeon would be expected to experience in the
operating room. They then repeated the exercise while the surgeons listened to
musical selections of their own choosing. The performances improved when the
surgeons were listening to the music.

In another study, listening to music enhanced the surgeons' alertness and
concentration. What kind of music worked best? Of 50 instrumental tracks selected, 46 were concertos, with Vivaldi's *Four Seasons* as the top pick, followed
by Beethoven's Violin Concerto op. 61, Bach's Brandenburg Concertos, and
Wagner's "Ride of the Valkyries"—not exactly your standard "easy listening"
repertoire.

But easy listening isn't the purpose, according to one of the surgeons interviewed. "In the O.R. it's very busy with lots of things going on, but if you have
the music on you can operate. The music isn't a distraction but a way of blocking out all of the other distractions."

Music undoubtedly exerts its positive effects on surgical performance at least 75
partially through its kinesthetic effects, an observation made by Socrates in Plato's *Republic*: "More than anything else rhythm and harmony find their way to
the inmost soul and take strongest hold upon it." Thanks to music, the surgeon
is more concentrated, alert, technically efficient, and—most important—in
the frame of mind most conducive to healing. "Take Puccini's *La Bohème*," says
Blake Papsin, an ear, nose, and throat surgeon in Toronto. "It's an absolutely
beautiful piece of music that compels the human spirit to perform, to care, to
love—and that's what surgery is."

Music and skilled manual activities activate different parts of the brain, so
interference and competition are avoided. If the surgeon listened to an audiobook
instead of a musical composition, however, there would likely be interference.
Imagining a scene described by the narrator would interfere with the surgeon's
spatial imaging. Listening to the audiobook would activate similar areas of the

brain and cause competition between the attention needed to efficiently and accurately operate and to comprehend the images and story in the audiobook. We encounter here an example of the principle of *cerebral geography*: The brain works at its best with the activation of different, rather than identical, brain areas. That's why doodling while talking on the telephone isn't a problem for most people, since speaking and drawing use different brain areas. But writing a thank you note while on the phone results in mental strain because speaking and writing share some of the same brain circuitry.

Thanks to new technology, especially procedures like functional MRI scans, neuroscientists will soon be able to compile lists of activities that can be done simultaneously with a minimal lapse in efficiency or accuracy. But, in general, it's wise to keep this in mind: A penalty is almost always paid when two activities are carried out simultaneously rather than separately.

Questions for Critical Reading

1. According to Restak, what are the problems with multitasking? Locate passages where he discusses the impact of this practice. Do you think multitasking is possible? How does it function in your own life?

2. How does culture affect biology? Perform a critical reading of Restak's text in order to describe the ways in which what we do can change what we are.

3. What are "modern nerves"? Define the term through Restak's essay and then provide examples from both his text and your own life.

Exploring Context

1. Take the ADD/ADHD test at psychcentral.com/addquiz.htm. How does your score reflect Restak's argument? Connect your response to your work on multitasking from Question 1 of Questions for Critical Reading.

2. Explore the Web site for Twitter at twitter.com. Is this abbreviated style of blogging a reflection of the problems that Restak explores? Or is staying hyperconnected to your friends a way of combating the demands on attention? Consider the relation between Twitter and your definition of "modern nerves" from Question 3 of Questions for Critical Reading.

3. Play the Multitasking game at itch.com/games/multitasking. How does your performance in the game confirm or complicate Restak's argument? Connect your response to your work on multitasking from Question 1 of Questions for Critical Reading.

Questions for Connecting

1. Kwame Anthony Appiah, in "Making Conversation" (p. 57) and "The Primacy of Practice" (p. 63), explores the persistence of social practices and the possibilities of change. Can we use his ideas to address the problem that Restak

describes? Does multitasking, as a practice, have a kind of primacy? Draw from your work in Questions for Critical Reading in making your argument.

2. In "Ethics and the New Genetics" (p. 76), the Dalai Lama asks us to consider the ethical implications of new technologies. But what are the ethical implications of existing technologies? Is multitasking an ethical issue? Synthesize these two texts to make a larger argument about the ethics of technology.

3. How does culture shape bodies? Consider not only Restak's argument but also Julia Serano's ideas in "Before and After: Class and Body Transformations" (p. 392). You may want to draw from your work in Exploring Context in making your argument.

Language Matters

1. Create a series of presentation slides about this essay using PowerPoint or other software. Since such slides are most effective when they contain only a few key points per slide, you will have to locate the most important elements of Restak's argument; in designing the slides you should also consider how visual elements like color, font, and alignment can enhance an argument.

2. Punctuation marks control the speed of speech: Commas ask us to pause and periods ask us to stop. Given Restak's argument, how can you use punctuation in your writing to guide your reader's attention and combat ADD/ADHD? Which marks might be most helpful, and which might you want to avoid?

3. What's the difference between editing, proofreading, and revising? What would you do to this essay if you were editing it? Revising it? How can you use these different skills in your own writing?

Assignments for Writing

1. Restak examines the way the human brain responds to modern technology, claiming that the changes made in the brain by technology are the biggest changes to that organ in thousands of years. Write an essay that examines the potential benefits of this change at the end of the first decade of the twenty-first century. What is the role of television in the rewiring of the brain? What other technologies have similar effects? Is this change in brain function for the better? Is it possible that technological advances can move faster than is good for humankind? Consider using your work with Restak's concepts from Questions for Connecting in making your argument.

2. Restak looks closely at the role of modern media and communication devices in our daily lives. Write an essay in which you use Restak and your own experience to assess the ways in which current media has created a culture that demands a high-speed, high-efficiency lifestyle. Does media shape our attention? In what ways are we expected to speed up, and in what ways are we urged to slow down? Restak writes about the "crawler" on TV news. What other media features divide our attention?

3. Write an essay that examines the effectiveness of multitasking in the face of modern technologies, synthesizing Restak's text with your own experience. How does the brain multitask? What impedes our ability to multitask? Why is multitasking not as efficient as we may think? What role does modern technology play in our ability to multitask? Do we multitask more than we think? What demands do we place on ourselves when it comes to multitasking? Draw from your experience with Exploring Context in making your argument.

MARY ROACH

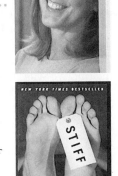

Mary Roach, who holds a B.S. in psychology from Wesleyan University, is a contributing editor for the science magazine *Discover*. She also has contributed to *Vogue*, Salon.com, *Wired*, *Outside*, *GQ*, and the *New York Times Magazine*. Roach is known for her entertaining writing style and unusual subject matter, as illustrated by her best-selling books *Stiff: The Curious Lives of Human Cadavers* (2003) and *Spook: Science Tackles the Afterlife* (2005). Her latest book, *Bonk: The Curious Coupling of Science and Sex*, was published in early 2008.

In *Stiff*, Roach explores the role of the human body once its owner dies. In her research on the uses of human cadavers Roach discovers plastic surgeons who practice new techniques on them, an expert in human decomposition, and real-life human crash test dummies. With these examinations Roach argues that our remains can be a lot more valuable above ground than below.

In "The Cadaver Who Joined the Army," from *Stiff*, Roach focuses on military-related research on corpses. Experiments range from firing bullets into corpses for ballistics research to outfitting severed legs with different types of footwear to see which is most effective in protecting its wearer from a landmine blast. Subjecting cadavers to gunshots and explosions is ethically difficult, though, and Roach explores the complicated moral and ethical questions involved. Particularly tricky is the question of "informed consent" and whether or not families know—or should know—what will be done to the cadavers after they are donated.

Ethics normally provides a set of rules for living, but Roach asks us to extend these considerations to our bodies once we are gone. What role should human bodies play in scientific research, and how do we calculate the trade-off between knowledge and ethics?

▶ TAGS: *research*, *surrogates*, *death*, *ethics*, *morality*

The Cadaver Who Joined the Army

For three days in January of 1893 and again for four days in March, Captain Louis La Garde of the U.S. Army Medical Corps took up arms against a group of extraordinary foes. It was an unprecedented military undertaking, and one for which he would forever after be remembered. Though La Garde served as a surgeon, he was no stranger to armed combat. In the Powder River Expedition of 1876, he had been decorated for gallantry in confronting tribes of hostile Sioux. La Garde had led the charge against Chief Dull Knife, whose name, we can only assume, was no reflection on his intellectual and military acumen or the quality and upkeep of his armaments.

La Garde received his strange and fateful orders in July of 1892. He would be receiving, the letter said, a new, experimental .30-caliber Springfield rifle. He was to take this rifle, along with his standard-issue .45-caliber Springfield, and report to Frankford Arsenal, Pennsylvania, the following winter. Taking shape in the rifles' sights would be men, a series of them, naked and unarmed. That they were naked and unarmed was the less distinctive thing about them. More distinctive was that they were already dead. They had died of natural causes and had been collected—from where is not revealed—as subjects in an Army Ordnance Department experiment. They were to be suspended from a tackle in the ceiling of the firing range, shot at in a dozen places and with a dozen different charges (to simulate different distances), and autopsied. La Garde's mission was to compare the physiological effects of the two different weapons upon the human body's bones and innards.

The United States Army was by no means the first to sanction the experimental plugging of civilian cadavers. The French army, wrote La Garde in his book *Gunshot Injuries,* had been "firing into dead bodies for the purpose of teaching the effects of gunshots in war" since around 1800. Ditto the Germans, who went to the exquisite trouble of propping up their mock victims al fresco, at distances approximating those of an actual battlefield. Even the famously neutral Swiss sanctioned a series of military wound ballistics studies on cadavers in the late 1800s. Theodore Kocher, a Swiss professor of surgery and a member of the Swiss army militia (the Swiss prefer not to fight, but they are armed, and with more than little red pocket knife/can openers), spent a year firing Swiss Vetterli rifles into all manner of targets—bottles, books, water-filled pig intestines, oxen bones, human skulls, and, ultimately, a pair of whole human cadavers—with the aim of understanding the mechanisms of wounding from bullets.

Kocher—and to a certain extent La Garde—expressed a desire that their ballistics work with cadavers would lead to a more humanitarian form of gun battle. Kocher urged that the goal of warfare be to render the enemy not dead, but simply unable to fight. To this end, he advised limiting the size of the bullets and making them from a material of a higher melting point than lead, so that they would deform less and thus destroy less tissue.

Incapacitation—or stopping power, as it is known in munitions circles—became the Holy Grail of ballistics research. How to stop a man in his tracks, preferably without maiming or killing him, but definitely before he maimed or killed you first. Indeed, the next time Captain La Garde and his swinging cadavers took the stage, in 1904, it was in the name of improved stopping power. The topic had been high on the generals' to-do lists following the army's involvement in the Philippines, during the final stage of the Spanish-American War, where its Colt .38s had failed, on numerous occasions, to stop the enemy cold. While the Colt .38 was considered sufficient for "civilized" warfare—"even the stoical Japanese soldier," wrote La Garde in *Gunshot Injuries,* "fell back as a rule when he was hit the first time"—such was apparently not the case with "savage tribes or a fanatical enemy." The Moro tribesman of the Philippines was considered a bit of both: "A fanatic like a Moro, wielding a bolo in each hand who advances with leaps and bounds . . . must be hit with a projectile having a maximum amount of stopping power," wrote La Garde. He related the tale of one battle-enlivened tribesman who charged a U.S. Army guard unit. "When he was within 100 yards, the entire guard opened fire on him." Nonetheless, he managed to advance some ninety-five yards toward them before finally crashing to the ground.

La Garde, at the War Department's urging, undertook an investigation of the army's various guns and bullets and their relative efficacy at putting a rapid halt to enemies. He decided that one way to do this would be to fire at suspended cadavers and take note of the "shock," as estimated by "the disturbance which appeared." In other words, how far back does the hanging torso or arm or leg swing when you shoot it? "It was based on the assumption that the momentum of hanging bodies of various weights could somehow be correlated and measured, and that it actually meant something with regard to stopping power," says Evan Marshall, who wrote the book on handgun stopping power (it's called *Handgun Stopping Power*). "What it actually did was extrapolate questionable data from questionable tests."

Even Captain La Garde came to realize that if you want to find out how likely a gun is to stop someone, you are best off trying it on an entity that isn't already quite permanently stopped. In other words, a live entity. "The animals selected were beeves about to undergo slaughter in the Chicago stock-yards," wrote La Garde, deeply perplexing the ten or fifteen people who would be reading his book later than the 1930s, when the word "beeves," meaning cattle, dropped from everyday discourse. Sixteen beeves later, La Garde had his answer: Whereas the larger-caliber (.45) Colt revolver bullets caused the cattle to drop to the ground after three or four shots, the animals shot with smaller-caliber .38 bullets failed even after ten shots to drop to the ground. And ever since, the U.S. Army has gone confidently into battle, knowing that when cows attack, their men will be ready.

For the most part, it has been the lowly swine that has borne the brunt of munitions trauma research in the United States and Europe. In China—at the No. 3 Military Medical College and the China Ordnance Society, among others—it has been mongrel dogs that get shot at. In Australia, as reported in the Proceedings of the 5th Symposium on Wound Ballistics, the researchers took aim at rabbits. It is tempting to surmise that a culture chooses its most reviled species for ballistics research. China occasionally eats its dogs, but doesn't otherwise have much use or affection for them; in Australia, rabbits are considered a scourge—imported by the British for hunting, they multiplied (like rabbits) and, in a span of twenty years, wiped out two million acres of south Australian brush.

In the case of the U.S. and European research, the theory doesn't hold. Pigs don't get shot at because our culture reviles them as filthy and disgusting. Pigs get shot at because their organs are a lot like ours. The heart of the pig is a particularly close match. Goats were another favorite, because their lungs are like ours. I was told this by Commander Marlene DeMaio, who studies body armor at the Armed Forces Institute of Pathology (AFIP). Talking to DeMaio,

I got the impression that it would be possible to construct an entire functioning nonhuman human from pieces of other species. "The human knee most resembles the brown bear's," she said at one point, following up with a surprising or not so surprising statement: "The human brain most resembles that of Jersey cows at about six months."* I learned elsewhere that emu hips are dead ringers for human hips, a situation that has worked out better for humans than for emus, who, over at Iowa State University, have been lamed in a manner that mimics osteonecrosis and then shuttled in and out of CT scanners by researchers seeking to understand the disease.

Had I been calling the shots back at the War Department, I would have sanctioned a study not on why men sometimes fail to drop to the ground after being shot, but on why they so often *do*. If it takes ten or twelve seconds to lose consciousness from blood loss (and consequent oxygen deprivation to the brain), why, then, do people who have been shot so often collapse on the spot? It doesn't happen just on TV.

I posed this question to Duncan MacPherson, a respected ballistics expert and consultant to the Los Angeles Police Department. MacPherson insists the effect is purely psychological. Whether or not you collapse depends on your state of mind. Animals don't know what it means to be shot, and, accordingly, rarely exhibit the instant stop-and-drop. MacPherson points out that deer shot through the heart often run off for forty or fifty yards before collapsing. "The deer doesn't know anything about what's going on, so he just does his deer thing for ten seconds or so and then he can't do it anymore. An animal with a meaner disposition will use that ten seconds to come at you." On the flip side, there are people who are shot at but not hit—or hit with nonlethal bullets, which don't penetrate, but just smart a lot—who will drop immediately to the ground. "There was an officer I know who took a shot at a guy and the guy just went flat, totally splat, facedown," MacPherson told me. "He said to himself, 'God, I was aiming for center mass like I'm supposed to, but I must have gotten a head shot by mistake. I'd better go back to the shooting range.' Then he went to the guy and there wasn't a mark on him. If there isn't a central nervous system hit, anything that happens fast is all psychological."

MacPherson's theory would explain the difficulties the army had in La Garde's day with the Moro tribesmen, who presumably weren't familiar with the effects of rifles and kept on doing their Moro tribesman thing until they couldn't—owing to blood loss and consequent loss of consciousness—do it anymore. Sometimes it isn't just ignorance as to what bullets do that renders a foe temporarily impervious. It can also be viciousness and sheer determination.

> **And ever since, the U.S. Army has gone confidently into battle, knowing that when cows attack, their men will be ready.**

10

---

*I did not ask DeMaio about sheep and the purported similarity of portions of their reproductive anatomy to that of the human female, lest she be forced to draw conclusions about the similarity of my intellect and manners to that of the, I don't know, boll weevil.

"A lot of guys take pride in their imperviousness to pain," MacPherson said. "They can get a lot of holes in them before they go down. I know an LAPD detective who got shot through the heart with a .357 Magnum and he killed the guy that shot him before he collapsed."

Not everyone agrees with the psychological theory. There are those who feel that some sort of neural overload takes place when a bullet hits. I communicated with a neurologist/avid handgunner/reserve deputy sheriff in Victoria, Texas, named Dennis Tobin, who has a theory about this. Tobin, who wrote the chapter "A Neurologist's View of 'Stopping Power'" in the book *Handgun Stopping Power*, posits that an area of the brain stem called the reticular activating system (RAS) is responsible for the sudden collapse. The RAS can be affected by impulses arising from massive pain sensations in the viscera.* Upon receiving these impulses, the RAS sends out a signal that weakens certain leg muscles, with the result that the person drops to the ground.

Somewhat shaky support for Tobin's neurological theory can be found in animal studies. Deer may keep going, but dogs and pigs seem to react as humans do. The phenomenon was remarked upon in military medical circles as far back as 1893. A wound ballistics experimenter by the name of Griffith, while going about his business documenting the effects of a Krag-Jorgensen rifle upon the viscera of live dogs at two hundred yards, noted that the animals, when shot in the abdomen, "died as promptly as though they had been electrocuted." Griffith found this odd, given that, as he pointed out in the *Transactions of the First Pan-American Medical Congress*, "no vital part was hit which might account for the instantaneous death of the animals." (In fact, the dogs were probably not as promptly dead as Griffith believed. More likely, they had simply collapsed and looked, from two hundred yards, like dead dogs. And by the time Griffith had walked the two hundred yards to get to them, they were in fact dead dogs, having expired from blood loss.)

In 1988, a Swedish neurophysiologist named A. M. Göransson, then of Lund University, took it upon himself to investigate the conundrum. Like Tobin, Göransson figured that something about the bullet's impact was causing a massive overload to the central nervous system. And so, perhaps unaware of the similarities between the human brain and that of Jersey cows at six months, he wired the brains of nine anesthetized pigs to an EEG machine, one at a time, and shot them in the hindquarters. Göransson reports having used a "high-energy missile" for the task, which is less drastic than it suggests. What it suggests is

15

---

*MacPherson counters that bullet wounds are rarely, at the outset, painful. Research by eighteenth-century scientist/philosopher Albrecht von Haller suggests that it depends on what the bullet hits. Experimenting on live dogs, cats, rabbits, and other small unfortunates, Haller systematically catalogued the viscera according to whether or not they register pain. By his reckoning, the stomach, intestines, bladder, ureter, vagina, womb, and heart do, whereas the lungs, liver, spleen, and kidneys "have very little sensation, seeing I have irritated them, thrust a knife into them, and cut them to pieces without the animals' seeming to feel any pain." Haller admitted that the work suffered certain methodological shortcomings, most notably that, as he put it, "an animal whose thorax is opened is in such violent torture that it is hard to distinguish the effect of an additional slight irritation."

that Dr. Göransson got into his car, drove some distance from his laboratory, and launched the Swedish equivalent of Tomahawk missiles at the hapless swine, but in fact, I am told, the term simply means a small, fast-moving bullet.

Instantly upon being hit, all but three of the pigs showed significantly flattened EEGs, the amplitude in some cases having dropped by as much as 50 percent. As the pigs had already been stopped in their tracks by the anesthesia, it is impossible to say whether they would have been rendered so by the shots, and Göransson opted not to speculate. And if they had lost consciousness, Göransson had no way of knowing what the mechanism was. To the deep chagrin of pigs the world over, he encouraged further study.

Proponents of the neural overload theory point to the "temporary stretch cavity" as the source of the effect. All bullets, upon entry into the human form, blow open a cavity in the tissue around them. This cavity shuts back up almost immediately, but in that fraction of a second that it is agape, the nervous system, they believe, issues a Mayday blast—enough of one, it seems, to overload the circuits and cause the whole system to hang a Gone Fishing sign on the door.

These same proponents believe that bullets that create sizable stretch cavities are thus more likely to deliver the necessary shock to achieve the vaunted ballistics goal of "good stopping power." If this is true, then in order to gauge a bullet's stopping power, one needs to be able to view the stretch cavity as it opens up. That is why the good Lord, working in tandem with the Kind & Knox gelatin company, invented human tissue simulant.

I am about to fire a bullet into the closest approximation of a human thigh outside of a human thigh: a six-by-six-by-eighteen-inch block of ballistic gelatin. Ballistic gelatin is essentially a tweaked version of Knox dessert gelatin. It is denser than dessert gelatin, having been formulated to match the average density of human tissue, is less colorful, and, lacking sugar, is even less likely to please dinner guests. Its advantage over a cadaver thigh is that it affords a stop-action view of the temporary stretch cavity. Unlike real tissue, human tissue simulant doesn't snap back: The cavity remains, allowing ballistics types to judge, and preserve a record of, a bullet's performance. Plus, you don't need to autopsy a block of human tissue simulant; because it's clear, you just walk up to it after you've shot it and take a look at the damage. Following which, you can take it home, eat it, and enjoy stronger, healthier nails in thirty days.

Like other gelatin products, ballistic gelatin is made from processed cow bone chips and "freshly chopped" pig hide.* The Kind & Knox Web site does not include human tissue simulant on its list of technical gelatin applications, which rather surprised me, as did the failure of a Knox public relations woman to return my calls. You would think that a company that felt comfortable extolling

———————
*According to the Kind & Knox Web site, other products made with cow-bone-and-pigskin-based gelatin include marshmallows, nougat-type candy bar fillings, liquorice, Gummi Bears, caramels, sports drinks, butter, ice cream, vitamin gel caps, suppositories, and that distasteful whitish peel on the outside of salamis. What I am getting at here is that if you're going to worry about mad cow disease, you probably have more to worry about than you thought. And that if there's any danger, which I like to think there isn't, we're all doomed, so relax and have another Snickers.

the virtues of Number 1 Pigskin Grease on its Web site ("It is a very clean material"; "Available in tanker trucks or railcars") would be okay with talking about ballistic gelatin, but apparently I've got truckloads or railcars to learn about gelatin PR.

Our replicant human thigh was cooked up by Rick Lowden, a freewheeling materials engineer whose area of expertise is bullets. Lowden works at the Department of Energy's Oak Ridge National Laboratory in Oak Ridge, Tennessee. The lab is best known for its plutonium work in the Manhattan (atomic bomb development) Project and now covers a far broader and generally less unpopular range of projects. Lowden, for instance, has lately been involved in the design of an environmentally friendly no-lead bullet that doesn't cost the military an arm and a leg to clean up after. Lowden loves guns, loves to talk about them. Right now he's trying to talk about them with me, a distinctly trying experience, for I keep shepherding the conversation back to dead bodies, which Lowden clearly doesn't enjoy very much. You would think that a man who felt comfortable extolling the virtues of hollow-point bullets ("expands to twice its size and just thumps that person") would be okay talking about dead bodies, but apparently not. "You just cringe," he said, when I mentioned the prospect of shooting into human cadaver tissue. Then he made a noise that I transcribed in my notes as "Olggh."

We are standing under a canopy at the Oak Ridge shooting range, about to set up the first stopping-power test. The "thighs" sit in an open plastic cooler at our feet, sweating mildly. They are consommé-colored and, owing to the cinnamon added to mask the material's mild rendering-plant effluvium, smell like Big Red chewing gum. Rick carries the cooler out to the target table, thirty feet away, and settles an ersatz thigh into the gel cradle. I make conversation with Scottie Dowdell, who is supervising the shooting range today. He is telling me about the pine beetle epidemic in the area. I point to a stand of dead conifers in the woods a quarter mile back behind the target. "Like over there?" Scottie says no. He says they died of bullet wounds, something I never knew pine trees could do.

Rick returns and sets up the gun, which isn't really a gun but a "universal receiver," a tabletop gun housing that can be outfitted with barrels of different calibers. Once it's aimed, you pull a wire to release the bullet. We're testing a couple of new bullets that claim to be frangible, meaning they break apart on impact. The frangible bullet was designed to solve the "overpenetration," or ricochet, problem, i.e., bullets passing through victims, bouncing off walls, and harming bystanders or the police or soldiers who fired them. The side effect of the bullet's breaking apart on impact is that it tends to do this inside your body if you're hit. In other words, it tends to have really, really good stopping power. It basically functions like a tiny bomb inside the victim and is therefore, to date, mainly reserved for "special response" SWAT-type activities, such as hostage rescue.

Rick hands me the trigger string and counts down from three. The gelatin sits on the table, soaking up the sunshine, basking beneath the calm, blue Tennessee skies—*tra la la, life is gay, it's good to be a gelatin block, I* . . . BLAM!

The block flips up into the air, off the table, and onto the grass. As John 25
Wayne said, or would have, had he had the opportunity, this block of gelatin
won't be bothering anyone anytime soon. Rick picks up the block and places it
back in its cradle. You can see the bullet's journey through the "thigh." Rather
than overpenetrating and exiting the back side, the bullet has stopped short
several inches into the block. Rick points to the stretch cavity. "Look at that. A
total dump of energy. Total incapacitation."

I had asked Lowden whether munitions professionals ever concern themselves, as did Kocher and La Garde, with trying to design bullets that will inca-
pacitate without maiming or killing. Lowden's face displayed the sort of look
it displayed earlier when I'd said that armor-piercing bullets were "cute." He
answered that the military chooses weapons more or less by how much damage
they can inflict on a target, "whether the target be a human or a vehicle." This is
another reason ballistic gelatin tends to get used in stopping-power tests, rather
than cadavers. We're not talking about research that will help mankind save
lives; we're talking about research that will help mankind take lives. I suppose
you could argue that policemen's and soldiers' lives may be saved, but only by
taking someone else's life first. Anyway, it's not a use of human tissue for which
you're likely to get broad public support.

Of course, the other big reason munitions people shoot ballistic gelatin is
reproducibility: Provided you follow the recipe, it's always the same. Cadaver
thighs vary in density and thickness, according to the age, gender, and physical condition of their owners when they stopped using them. Still another
reason: Cleanup's a breeze. The remains of this morning's thighs have been
picked up and repacked in the cooler, a tidy, bloodless mass grave of low-calorie
dessert.

Not that a ballistic gelatin shootout is completely devoid of gore. Lowden
points to the toe of my sneaker, at a *Pulp Fiction* fleck of spatter. "You got some
simulant on your shoe."

Rick Lowden never shot a dead man, though he had his chance. He was working on a project, in cooperation with the University of Tennessee's human decay
facility, aimed at developing bullets that would resist corrosion from the acid
breakdown products inside a dead body and help forensics types solve crimes
long after they happen.

Rather than shooting the experimental bullets into his cadavers, Lowden 30
got down on his hands and knees with a scalpel and a pair of tweezers and sur-
gically placed them. He explained that he did this because he wanted the bullets
to end up in specific places: muscle, fatty tissue, the head and chest cavities, the
abdomen. If he'd shot them into the tissue, they might have overpenetrated, as
they say, and wound up in the dirt.

He also did it that way because he felt he had to. "It was always my impression that we couldn't shoot a body." He recalls another project, one in
which he was developing a simulated human bone that could be put inside
blocks of ballistic gelatin, much as banana and pineapple chunks are floated
inside Jell-O. To calibrate the simulated bone, he needed to shoot some actual

bone and compare the two. "I was offered sixteen cadaver legs to shoot at. DOE told me they would terminate my project if I did that. We had to shoot pig femurs instead."

Lowden told me that military munitions professionals even worry about the politics of shooting into freshly killed livestock. "A lot of guys won't do that. They'll go get a ham from the store or a leg from the slaughterhouse. Even then, a lot of them don't openly publish what they do. There's still a stigma."

Ten feet behind us, sniffing the air, is a groundhog who has made unfortunate real estate choices in his life. The animal is half the size of a human thigh. If you shot that groundhog with one of these bullets, I say to Rick, what would happen? Would it completely vaporize? Rick and Scottie exchange a look. I get the feeling that the stigma attached to shooting groundhogs is fairly minimal.

Scottie shuts the ammo case. "Create a lot of paperwork, is what would happen."

Only recently has the military dipped its toes back into the roiling waters of publicly funded cadaveric ballistics research. As one would imagine, the goals are strictly humanitarian. At the Armed Forces Institute of Pathology's Ballistic Missile Trauma Research Lab last year, Commander Marlene DeMaio dressed cadavers in a newly developed body armor vest and fired a range of modern-day munitions at their chests. The idea was to test the manufacturer's claims before outfitting the troops. Apparently body armor manufacturers' effectiveness claims aren't always to be trusted. According to Lester Roane, chief engineer at the independent ballistics and body armor test facility H. P. White Labs, the companies don't do cadaver tests. H. P. White doesn't either. "Anybody looking at it coldly and logically shouldn't have any problem with it," said Roane. "It's dead meat. But for some reason, it's just something that has been politically incorrect from before there was a term for politically correct."

DeMaio's cadaver tests represent a distinct improvement over how vests were originally tested by the military: In Operation Boar, during the Korean War, the Doron vest was tested simply by giving it to six thousand soldiers and seeing how they fared compared to soldiers wearing standard vests. Roane says he once watched a video made by a Central American police department that tested their vests by having officers put them on and then shooting at them.

The trick to designing body armor is to make it thick and unyielding enough to stop bullets without making it so heavy and hot and uncomfortable that officers won't wear it. What you don't want is what the Gilbertese Islanders used to have. While I was in D.C. to see DeMaio, I stopped at the Smithsonian's Museum of Natural History, where I saw a display of body armor from the Gilbert Islands. Battles in Micronesia were so pitched and bloody that Gilbertese warriors would outfit themselves head to foot with doormat-thick armor fashioned from the twisted fibers of coconut hulls. On top of the significant humiliation of making one's entrance onto the battlefield looking like an enormous macramé planter was the fact that the armor was so bulky it required the assistance of several squires to help maneuver you.

As with automotive cadavers, DeMaio's body-armor bodies were instrumented with accelerometers and load cells, in this case on the sternum, to record the impact forces and give researchers a detailed medical rendering of what was happening to the chest inside the armor. With some of the nastier-caliber weapons, the cadavers sustained lung lacerations and rib fractures, but nothing that translated into an injury that—if you weren't already a cadaver—could kill you. More tests are planned, with the goal of making a test dummy along the lines of those used by the automotive industry—so that one day cadavers won't be needed.

Because she had proposed to use human cadavers, DeMaio was advised to proceed with extreme caution. She gathered the blessings of three institutional review boards, a military legal counsel, and a card-carrying ethicist. The project was ultimately approved, with one stipulation: no penetration. The bullets had to stop short of the cadavers' skin.

Did DeMaio roll her eyes in exasperation? She says not. "When I was in medical school I used to think, 'Come on, don't be irrational. They've expired, they've donated their bodies, you know?' When I got into this project I realized that we are part of the public trust, and even if it doesn't make scientific sense, we have to be responsive to people's emotional concerns."

On an institutional level, the caution comes from fear of liability and of unpleasant media reports and withdrawal of funding. I spoke with Colonel John Baker, the legal counsel from one of the institutions that sponsored DeMaio's research. The head of this institution preferred that I refrain from naming it and instead refer to it as simply "a federal institution in Washington." He told me that over the past twenty-some years, Democratic congressmen and budget-minded legislators have tried to close the place down, as have Jimmy Carter, Bill Clinton, and People for the Ethical Treatment of Animals. I got the feeling that my request for an interview had brought this man's day crashing down like so many pine trees behind a DOE shooting range.

"The concern is that some survivor will be so taken aback that they'll bring suit," said Colonel Baker from his desk at a federal institution in Washington. "And there is no body of law in this area, nothing you can look to other than good judgment." He pointed out that although cadavers don't have rights, their family members do. "I could imagine some sort of lawsuit that is based upon emotional distress. . . . You get some of those [cases] in a cemetery situation, where the proprietor has allowed the coffins to rot away and the corpses pop up." I replied that as long as you have informed consent—a signed agreement from the donor stating that he has willed his body to medical research—it would seem that the survivors wouldn't have much of a case.

The sticking point is the word "informed." It's fair to say that when people donate remains, either their own or those of a family member, they usually don't care to know the grisly details of what might be done with them. And that if you did tell them the details, they might change their minds and withdraw consent. Then again, if you're planning to shoot guns at them, it might be good to run that up the flagpole and get the a-okay. "Part of respecting persons is telling them the information that they might have an emotional response to," says Edmund Howe, editor of the *Journal of Clinical Ethics*, who reviewed Marlene DeMaio's research proposal. "Though one could go the other way and spare them that response and therefore ethically not commit that harm. But the downside to withholding information that might be significant to them is that it would violate their dignity to an extent." Howe suggests a third possibility, that of letting the families make the choice: Would they prefer to hear the specifics of what is being done with the donated body—specifics that may be upsetting—or would they prefer not to know?

It's a delicate balance that, in the end, comes down to wording. Observes Baker, "You don't really want to be telling somebody, 'Well, what we'll be doing is dissecting their eyeballs. We take them out and put them on a table and then we dissect them into finer and finer parts and then once we're finished we scrape all that stuff up and put it into a biohazard bag and try to keep it together so we can return whatever's left to you.' That sounds horrible." On the other hand, "medical research" is a tad vague. "Instead, you say, 'One of our principal concerns here at the university is ophthalmology. So we do a lot here with ophthalmological materials.' " If someone cares to think it through, it isn't hard to come to the conclusion that someone in a lab coat will, at the very least, be cutting your eyeball out of your head. But most people don't care to think it through. They focus on the end, rather than the means: Someone's vision may one day be saved.

Ballistics studies are especially problematic. How do you decide it's okay   45
to cut off someone's grandfather's head and shoot it in the face? Even when the reason you are doing that is to gather data to ensure that innocent civilians who are hit in the face with nonlethal bullets won't suffer disfiguring fractures? Moreover, how do you bring yourself to carry out the cutting off and shooting of someone's grandfather's head?

I posed these questions to Cindy Bir, who brought herself to do exactly that, and whom I met while I was at Wayne State. Bir is accustomed to firing projectiles at the dead. In 1993, the National Institute of Justice (NIJ) commissioned her to document the impact effects of various nonlethal munitions: plastic bullets, rubber ones, beanbags, the lot. Police began using nonlethal bullets in the late 1980s, in situations where they need to subdue civilians—mostly rioters and violent psychotics—without putting their lives in danger. In nine instances since that time, "nonlethal" bullets have proved lethal, prompting the NIJ to have Bir look into what was going on with these different bullets, with the aim of its not going on ever again.

As to the question "How do you bring yourself to cut off someone's grandfather's head?" Bir replied, "Thankfully, Ruhan does that for us." (The very same Ruhan who preps the cadavers for automotive impacts.) She added that the nonlethal munitions were not shot from guns but fired from air cannons, because doing so is both more precise and less disturbing. "Still," concedes Bir, "I was glad when that one finished up."

Bir copes like most other cadaver researchers do, with a mix of compassion and emotional remove. "You treat them with dignity, and you kind of separate the fact that . . . I don't want to say that they're not a person, but . . . you think of them as a specimen." Bir was trained as a nurse, and in some ways finds the dead easier to work with. "I know they can't feel it, and I know that I'm not going to hurt them." Even the most practiced cadaver researcher has days when the task at hand presents itself as something other than scientific method. For Bir, it had little to do with the fact that she was directing bullets at her subjects. It is the moments when the specimen steps out of his anonymity, his object-hood, and into his past existence as a human being.

"We received a specimen and I went down to help Ruhan, and this gentle-man must have come directly from the nursing home or hospital," she recalls. "He had on a T-shirt and flannel PJ pants. It hit me like . . . this could be my dad. Then there was one that I went to look at—a lot of times you like to take a look at the specimen to make sure it's not too big [to lift]—and this person was wearing a hospital gown from my hometown."

If you really want to stay up late worrying about lawsuits and bad publicity,   50
explode a bomb near the body of someone who has willed his remains to sci-ence. This is perhaps the most firmly entrenched taboo of the cadaveric research world. Indeed, live, anes-thetized animals have generally been considered preferable, as targets of explosions, to dead human beings.

> **A Central American police department . . . tested their vests by having officers put them on and then shooting at them.**

In a 1968 Defense Atomic Support Agency paper entitled *Estimates of Man's Tolerance to the Direct Effects of Air Blast*—i.e., from bombs—researchers dis-cussed the effects of experimental explosions upon mice, hamsters, rats, guinea pigs, rabbits, cats, dogs, goats, sheep, steers, pigs, burros, and stump-tailed ma-caques, but not upon the actual subject of inquiry. No one had ever strapped a cadaver up against the shock tube to see what might happen.

I called up a man named Aris Makris, who works for a company in Canada called Med-Eng Systems, which engineers protective gear for people who clear land mines. I told him about the DASA paper. Dr. Makris explained that dead people weren't always the best models for gauging living people's tolerance to ex-plosive blasts because of their lungs, which are deflated and not doing the things that lungs normally do. The shock wave from a bomb wreaks the most havoc on the body's most easily compressed tissue, and that is found in the lungs: specifi-cally, the tiny, delicate air sacs where the blood picks up oxygen and drops off carbon dioxide. An explosive shock wave compresses and ruptures these sacs. Blood then seeps into the lungs and drowns their owner, sometimes quickly, in ten or twenty minutes, sometimes over a span of hours.

Makris conceded that, biomedical issues aside, the blast tolerance chaps were probably not highly motivated to work with cadavers. "There are enor-mous ethical or PR challenges with that," he said. "It just hasn't been the habit of blasting cadavers: Please give your body to science so we can blow it up?"

One group recently braved the storm. Lieutenant Colonel Robert Harris and a team of other doctors from the Extremity Trauma Study Branch of the U.S. Army Institute of Surgical Research at Fort Sam Houston, Texas, recruited cadavers to test five types of footwear either commonly used by or being newly marketed for land mine clearance teams. Ever since the Vietnam War, a rumor had persisted that sandals were the safest footwear for land mine clearance, for they minimized injuries caused by fragments of the footwear itself being driven into the foot like shrapnel, compounding the damage and the risk of infection. Yet no one had ever tested the sandal claim on a real foot, nor had anyone done cadaver tests of any of the equipment being touted by manufacturers as offering greater safety than the standard combat boot.

Enter the fearless men of the Lower Extremity Assessment Program. Starting in 1999, twenty cadavers from a Dallas medical school willed body program were strapped, one by one, into a harness hanging from the ceiling of a portable blast shelter. Each cadaver was outfitted with strain gauges and load cells in its heel and ankle, and clad in one of six types of footwear. Some boots claimed to protect by raising the foot up away from the blast, whose forces attenuate quickly; others claimed to protect by absorbing or deflecting the blast's energy. The bodies were posed in standard walking position, heel to the ground, as though striding confidently to their doom. As an added note of verisimilitude, each cadaver was outfitted head to toe in a regulation battle dress uniform. In addition to the added realism, the uniforms conferred a measure of respect, the sort of respect that a powder-blue leotard might not, in the eyes of the U.S. Army anyway, supply.

Harris felt confident that the study's humanitarian benefits outweighed   55
any potential breach of dignity. Nonetheless, he consulted the willed body program administrators about the possibility of informing family members about the specifics of the test. They advised against it, both because of what they called the "revisiting of grief" among families who had made peace with the decision to donate and because, when you get down to the nitty-gritty details of an experiment, virtually any use of a cadaver is potentially upsetting. If willed body program coordinators contacted the families of LEAP cadavers, would they then have to contact the families of the leg-drop-test cadavers down the hall, or, for that matter, the anatomy lab cadavers across campus? As Harris points out, the difference between a blast test and an anatomy class dissection is essentially the time span. One lasts a fraction of a second; the other lasts a year. "In the end," he says, "they look pretty much the same." I asked Harris if he plans to donate his body to research. He sounded downright keen on the prospect. "I'm always saying, 'After I die, just put me out there and blow me up.'"

If Harris could have done his research using surrogate "dummy" legs instead of cadavers, he would have done so. Today there are a couple good ones in the works, developed by the Australian Defence Science & Technology Organisation. (In Australia, as in other Commonwealth nations, ballistics and blast testing on human cadavers is not allowed. And certain words are spelled funny.) The Frangible Surrogate Leg (FSL) is made of materials that react to blast similarly to the way human leg materials do; it has mineralized plastic for bones, for example, and ballistic gelatin for muscle. In March of 2001, Harris exposed the Australian leg to the same land mine blasts that his cadavers had weathered, to see if the results correlated. Disappointingly, the bone fracture patterns were somewhat off. The main problem, at the moment, is cost. Each FSL—they aren't reusable—costs around $5,000; the cost of a cadaver (to cover shipping, HIV and hepatitis C testing, cremation, etc.) is typically under $500.

Harris imagines it's only a matter of time before the kinks are worked out and the price comes down. He looks forward to that time. Surrogates are preferable not only because tests involving land mines and cadavers are ethically (and probably literally) sticky, but because cadavers aren't uniform. The older they are, the thinner their bones and the less elastic their tissue. In the case of land mine work, the ages are an especially poor match, with the average land mine clearer in his twenties and the average donated cadaver in its sixties. It's like market-testing Kid Rock singles on a roomful of Perry Como fans.

Until that time, it'll be rough going for Commonwealth land mine types, who cannot use whole cadavers. Researchers in the UK have resorted to testing boots on amputated legs, a much-criticized practice, owing to the fact that these limbs have typically had gangrene or diabetic complications that render them poor mimics of healthy limbs. Another group tried putting a new type of protective boot onto the hind leg of a mule deer for testing. Given that deer lack toes and heels and people lack hooves, and that no country I know of employs mule deer in land mine clearance, it is hard—though mildly entertaining—to try to imagine what the value of such a study could have been.

LEAP, for its part, turned out to be a valuable study. The sandal myth was mildly vindicated (the injuries were about as severe as they were with a combat boot), and one boot—Med-Eng's Spider Boot—showed itself to be a solid improvement over standard-issue footwear (though a larger sample is needed to be sure). Harris considers the project a success, because with land mines, even a small gain in protection can mean a huge difference in a victim's medical outcome. "If I can save a foot or keep an amputation below the knee," he says, "that's a win."

It is an unfortunate given of human trauma research that the things most likely to accidentally maim or kill people—things we most need to study and understand—are also the things most likely to mutilate research cadavers: car crashes, gunshots, explosions, sporting accidents. There is no need to use cadavers to study stapler injuries or human tolerance to ill-fitting footwear. "In order to be able to protect against a threat, whether it is automotive or a bomb," observes Makris, "you have to put the human to its limits. You've got to get destructive."

I agree with Dr. Makris. Does that mean I would let someone blow up my dead foot to help save the feet of NATO land mine clearers? It does. And would I let someone shoot my dead face with a nonlethal projectile to help prevent accidental fatalities? I suppose I would. . . .

Questions for Critical Reading

1. Should there be publicly funded ballistics research using cadavers? Support your answer using quotations from Roach's text, reading it critically to synthesize her position with your own.

2. What is "informed consent"? Define the term using Roach's text. What are the necessary conditions for it?

3. What are the proper limits for scientific research? Develop an answer through Roach's text. You will need to read her text critically in order to develop an analysis, since she never explicitly states what limits there should be.

Exploring Context

1. Visit the Web site for Bodies . . . The Exhibition (bodiestheexhibition.com), a traveling show of anatomy that uses actual human bodies. You might also use the Web to research the controversy over the cadavers used in this exhibit. How does Bodies . . . The Exhibition complicate Roach's exploration of ethics? What role does ethics — or bodies — have to play in art?

2. Roach discusses work done at the Armed Forces Institute of Pathology (AFIP). Visit the AFIP's Web site at afip.org. Does it convey the kind of work they do? What information can you find about ballistics trauma research? Connect your response to your answers about such research from Questions 1 and 3 of Questions for Critical Reading.

3. According to Roach, the Web site for Kind & Knox minimizes the company's role in the production of ballistics gel. Use the Web to research ballistics gel and gelatin. What information can you find? Is the use of gelatin in ballistics research generally minimized? Why?

Questions for Connecting

1. Is the use of human cadavers in ballistics research consistent with the notion of human dignity as it is explained by Francis Fukuyama (p. 142)? Draw from your work in Questions for Critical Reading in making your argument.

2. What roles can the body play in culture after death? Compare Roach's analysis with Diana Taylor's exploration of death and mourning in "False Identifications: Minority Populations Mourn Diana" (p. 454). How can you synthesize their positions?

3. Daniel Gilbert, in "Reporting Live from Tomorrow" (p. 169), suggests that the best way to determine our future happiness is to ask someone now living our possible future. How can Gilbert's ideas be applied to decisions about donating your body to science? Relate your response to informed consent, as you defined it in Question 2 of Questions for Critical Reading.

Language Matters

1. Imagine you could invite Roach into the discussion in your classroom. What questions would you want to ask her about this essay? What are the limits of written discourse? How might you anticipate your audience's questions when you write?

2. Listen to the latest podcast from Grammar Girl at grammar.quickanddirtytips
.com. How might you apply what she's talking about in the podcast to this essay?

3. Sometimes you can get the best feedback from peers by asking them to review
a key section of your writing—something you know isn't quite there yet. If you
were going to do a target peer revision session for Roach, which section of her
essay would you choose, and what feedback would you give?

Assignments for Writing

1. Roach discusses the use of human cadavers for military testing, suggesting
that the researchers who conduct these tests must approach the cadaver as an
object rather than a human. Find an example in which the body is objectified
and then write a paper using your example as a tool to extend or complicate
Roach's argument about the human body as object. Your work on Bodies . . .
The Exhibition from Question 1 of Exploring Context might serve as a good
starting point in making your argument. Consider: Why does Roach suggest
that body objectification is a necessary step in the experiments she discusses?
Is it possible to conduct scientific experiments on bodies without viewing them
as objects? Is body objectification limited to scientific experimentation? Is
body objectification limited to the dead? What are some of the possible steps
required in order to view a body as an object?

2. Roach explores the complicated ethical, moral, and societal issues that accom-
pany the use of human bodies for research. Using Roach's essay as a framework
for your own, write a paper in which you evaluate the relationship between
scientific experiments and our ethical beliefs. You may want to use your work
on the limits of research from Question 3 of Questions for Critical Reading
in making your argument. Also consider: Must scientific experimentation be
conducted within a system of ethics? What happens when science and ethics
conflict? What are our ethical responsibilities with regard to scientific experimentation? What happens when our personal system of ethics contradicts the
perceived "greater good"?

3. While discussing the ethical questions involved with using human bodies for
research, Roach seems to suggest that the "greater good" of such experiments
should take precedence over ethical concerns. Write a paper in which you extend or complicate Roach's argument in the context of a current conflict or war.
Does such a conflict amplify the ethical issues associated with the use of human
bodies in military testing? What are the needs of a society that is at war? What
happens when the needs or rights of an individual conflict with the needs of
society? How much should we sacrifice in the name of war?

LESLIE SAVAN

Leslie Savan is a former columnist for the *Village Voice* and a three-time Pulitzer Prize finalist. She has written for *Time,* the *New Yorker,* the *New York Times,* the *Los Angeles Times,* and Salon.com. In 1994, she published *The Sponsored Life: Ads, TV, and American Culture.* The following selection, "What's Black, Then White, and Said All Over?" appeared in her book *Slam Dunks and No-Brainers: Language in Your Life, the Media, Business, Politics, and, Like, Whatever* (2005).

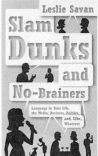

In *Slam Dunks and No-Brainers* Savan examines our everyday language to find out how it originated, what it means, and what it says about our culture. The book explores how a hot new phrase is created and spreads, how media takes advantage of trends in speech, and why we're not sure what pop catchphrases were popular in ancient Rome.

In "What's Black, Then White, and Said All Over?" Savan traces common "pop talk" that has its origins in African American vernacular. "White people," Savan writes, "draw from a black lexicon every day," and in this essay she examines the reasons for and the results of this kind of borrowing. Savan is interested in issues of media appropriation, the "wannabe" phenomenon, the impact of "black talk" on written language, and the idea of "covert prestige" being gained in the process of crossover talk. Ultimately, Savan presents a society that has accepted black vernacular as cool and worthy of imitation yet finds it unacceptable when black students speak it in the classroom.

Language has always been coupled with power. In this piece, Savan helps us to see how language circulates in culture and how its power is used by the media and in advertising.

▶ TAGS: *conversation, diversity, race, media, culture, language, collaboration, creativity*

What's Black, Then White, and Said All Over?

African American vernacular, black English, black talk, Ebonics, hip-hop slang — whatever you want to call it, black-inspired language is all over mainstream pop talk like white on rice.

The talk may be everywhere, but, oddly enough, even during the rabid debate over Ebonics in the late 1990s rarely was there any mention of black English's deep imprint on American English. Yet linguists and other language experts know that America's language wouldn't be what it is—and certainly wouldn't pop as much—without black English.

"In the past, White society has resisted the idea," wrote Robert McCrum, William Cran, and Robert MacNeil in *The Story of English*, "but there is now no escaping the fact that [Blacks' influence] has been one of the most profound contributions to the English language."

"First, one cannot help but be struck by the powerful influence of African American vernacular on the slang of all 20th-century American youth," Tom Dalzell wrote in *Flappers 2 Rappers*. "There were other influences, to be sure, on the slang of America's young, but none as powerful as that of the streets of Harlem and Chicago."

The linguist Connie Eble, author of *Slang and Sociability* and a college and youth slang expert at the University of North Carolina, Chapel Hill, calls the black influence on the American language "overwhelming."   5

White people (and not just the young) draw from a black lexicon every day, sometimes unaware of the words' origins, sometimes using them because of their origins. Here are just some of the words and phrases—born in different decades and now residing at various levels of popdom—that African Americans either coined or popularized, and, in either case, that they created the catchiest meaning of: *all that, back in the day, bling bling, blues, bogus, boogie, bootie, bro, chick, chill, come again, cook, cool, dawg, dig, dis, do your own thing, don't go there, freak, funky, get-go, get it on, get over, gig, give it up, groovy, heavy, hip, homeboy, hot, in your face, kick back, lame, living large, man, my bad, Micky D's, old school, nitty gritty, player, riff, righteous, rip off, rock 'n' roll, soul, tell it like it is, 24/7, up-tight, wannabe, whack, Whassup?/sup?, Whassup with that?, when the shit hits the fan, you know what I'm saying?*

You know what I'm saying. Most of us talk, and all of us hear in the media some of that talk every day. Some phrases are said with an implicit nod to their source (*street cred, chill, You the man*, as well as a fist pound or high five), while others have been so widely adopted that they're beginning to feel sourceless (*24/7, lame, in your face*). *It's a black thang* has become everybody's thing, from *It's a dick thing* to (most offensively, considering who pushed it) "Virginia Slims: It's a Woman Thing."

But black vernacular didn't just add more lively, "colorful" words to the pop vocabulary. Much as marketing has influenced pop language, so black English has changed the American language in more fundamental ways. And that's what we're talking here—not about black talk per se, but about what happens when black talk meets, and transforms, the wider, whiter pop.

First and foremost, this language of outsiders has given us *cool*: the word itself—the preeminent pop word of all time—and quite a sizable chunk of the cool stance that underlies pop culture itself. Pop culture's desire for cool is second only to its desire for money—the two, in fact, are inextricably linked. (Cool may be first and foremost, but more on why it rules later.)

A second way African American vernacular has affected the broader pop   10 is that black talk has operated as a template for what it means to talk pop in the first place. As an often playful, ironic alternative to the official tongue, black slang has prefigured pop language in much the same way that black music has prefigured, and has often become, pop music. While there are important differences, some of the dynamics underlying black talk and pop talk are similar: Like black English, pop language sparks with wordplays and code games; it assumes that certain, often previously unacknowledged experiences deserve their own verbal expression; and it broadcasts the sense that only those who share the experiences can really get the words. For instance, black talk's running commentary on social exclusion is a model for pop talk's running commentary on media experiences.

Why do I say that pop is modeled on black and not the other way around? It's not just because black talk did these things earlier and still does them more intensely than pop, but as the original flipside to the voice of the Man, as the official unofficial speech of America, black talk is the object of pop talk's crush on everything "alternative" and "outsider."

There's an attitude in pop language that it is somehow undermining the stale old ways and sending a wake-up call to anyone who just doesn't get it. You can feel the attitude in everything from advertising's furious but phony rebelliousness to the faintly up-yours, tough-talking phrases **This language of outsiders has given us *cool*.** like *Get a life* and *Don't even* think *about it*. It's not that these particular phrases are black or black-inspired, or that white people aren't perfectly capable of rebelliousness, anger at authority, and clever put-downs on their own. But the black experience, publicized more widely than ever now through hip-hop and its celebrities, has encouraged everyone else to more vigorously adopt the style of fighting the power—at least with the occasional catchphrase.

It may seem twisted, given American history, that general pop language draws from the experience of black exclusion at all. But white attempts to *yo* here and *dis* there are an important piece of identity-and-image building for individuals and corporations alike. Today, the language of an excluded people is repeated by the nonexcluded in order to make themselves sound more included. As the mainstream plays the titillating notes of marginalization, we are collectively creating that ideal mass personality mentioned earlier: We can be part black (the part presumed to be cool and soulful, real and down, jazzy or hip-hop, choose your sound) and be part white (the privileged part, the part that has the luxury to easily reference other parts).

Related to all this imitation and referencing is the most noticeable way that pop talk is affected by black talk: Black talk has openly joined the sales force. At white society's major intersection with black language—that is, in entertainment—white society has gone from mocking black talk, as in minstrel shows, to marketing it, as in hip-hop. In the more than a hundred years between these two forms of entertainment, black language has by and large entered white usage as if it were a sourceless slang or perhaps the latest lingo of some particularly hep white cats, like the fast-talking disc jockeys of the 1950s and 1960s who purveyed black jive to white teenagers. Black language may have been the single most important factor in shaping generations of American slang, primarily through blues, jazz, and rock 'n' roll. But only relatively recently has black talk been used openly, knowingly, and not mockingly to sell products.

This would have been unthinkable once. Even fifteen or twenty years ago, car makers were loath to show black people in commercials for fear that their product would be tainted as inferior or, worse, as "a black car." Although many car companies are still skittish, by 2001 Buick was actually ending its commercials with the rap-popularized phrase "It's all good." (And by 2004, a BMW ad was featuring an interracial couple.) The phrase went from M. C. Hammer's 1994 song "It's All Good" to replacing "I love this game" as the official slogan of the National Basketball Association in 2001. Both Buick and the NBA have since dropped *It's all good*, but with their help the phrase massified, at least for a while. "It's huge" among white "sorority sisters and stoners alike," a twenty-seven-year-old white friend in Chicago told me in 2003.

So it's not all bad, this commercialization of black talk, especially if it can get the auto industry to move from shunning to quoting African Americans. But it comes laden with price tags. To read them, look at MTV, which has to be *the* major force in the sea change from whites-only to black's-da-bomb.

It may be difficult to believe now, but for years MTV wouldn't touch black music videos. The channel relented only under pressure, with videos by Prince and Michael Jackson. Black just wouldn't appeal to its white suburban teen audience, MTV explained. In 1989 with the appearance of the successful *Yo! MTV Raps*, that rationale was turned inside out, and—ka-ching!—black videos began to appear regularly. Since so much of MTV is advertising posing as entertainment (the videos are record company promotions, the parties and other bashes that appear are often visibly sponsored events), MTV has contributed significantly to two marketing trends: To the young, advertising has become an acceptable—nay, desirable—part of the cool life they aspire to; and a black, hip-hop-ish vernacular has become a crucial cog in the youth market machinery.

The outsider style is not solely black or hip-hop, but, at least in the marketing mind, a black package can be the most efficient buy to achieve that style. For corporate purposes, hip-hop in particular is a lucrative formula. Not only does the hip-hop black man represent the ultimate outsider who simultaneously stands at the nexus of cool, but much of hip-hop, created by the kind of people gated communities were meant to exclude, sings the praises of acquiring capitalism's toys. These paradoxes of racism are commercial-ready.

As the critic Greg Tate wrote on the thirtieth anniversary of hip-hop, "globally speaking, hip-hop is money at this point, a valued form of currency where brothers are offered stock options in exchange for letting some corporate entity stand next to their fire. . . . Oh, the selling power of the Black vernacular."

When Sprite realized that teenagers no longer believed its TV commercials telling them that "Image Is Nothing" and that they shouldn't trust commercials or celebrity endorsements (said only half tongue-in-cheek by celebrities like NBA star Grant Hill), the soft drink's marketing department decided to up the ante. So, when you need outsider verisimilitude, who ya gonna call? Why, black rappers, of course, preferably on the hardcore side. Get *them* to testify to the soft drink's beyond-the-bounds, can't-be-bought spirit at Sprite.com launch parties (to be run later on MTV). Or get real kids, looking and sounding ghetto, to rap their own lyrics in TV spots about, say, "a situation that is not too sweet, which is an attribute of Sprite," as a Sprite publicist said. How else to get kids, usually white kids, to understand that you understand that they're sick of commercials telling them what's cool?

And so, while Sprite had long used rappers in its overall "Obey Your Thirst" campaign, now it pumped up the volume. Only by obeying the first commandment that image is everything can you become, as Sprite did by the late nineties, the fastest-growing soft-drink brand in the world. "Sprite has really become an icon," Pina Sciarra, then director of youth brands for Sprite, said on the 2001 PBS documentary *Merchants of Cool.* "It's not just associated with hip-hop, it's really a part of it, as much as baggy jeans and sneakers." Sprite, by the way, is owned by the Coca-Cola Company, the same company that agreed (around the time of the Sprite.com launch in late 2000) to pay $192.5 million to settle a racial discrimination suit by black employees, who accused the company of paying blacks less than whites for the same jobs and of discriminating in promotions and evaluations. (The company denied the allegations, but the settlement was one of the largest of its kind at the time.)

When whites talk black—or, just as commonly, when major corporations do it for them—it makes you wanna shout, *Whassup with that?!*

Terms and Props

Before I address wannabe black talk and other points where black language crosses over into pop, a few words about what "black language" and "black words" are.

I've been using the terms "black English," "black slang," "black talk," and "African American vernacular" rather interchangeably, which, in plain English, seems OK. Yet, at the same time, each term is a bit off the mark.

No one phrase is the perfect vehicle to explain how a people speak, because "a people" don't all speak (or do anything) one way. That's one of the problems with the terms "black English" and "black dialect." "Black English" was more or less booted out of formal linguistic circles, because, as linguist Peter Trudgill wrote in the 1995 revised edition of his book *Sociolinguistics*, "it suggested that all Blacks speak this one variety of English—which is not the case." The newer scholarly term, African American Vernacular English (AAVE), has pros and cons: It "distinguishes those Blacks who do not speak standard American English from those who do," wrote Trudgill, "although it still suggests that only one nonstandard variety, homogeneous through the whole of the USA, is involved, which is hardly likely." The word *Ebonics* was created in 1973 by African American scholars to "define black language from a black perspective," writes Geneva Smitherman, director of the African American Language and Literacy Program at Michigan State University. But the 1997 Ebonics controversy loaded the word with so much baggage (which we'll rummage through later) that, outside of some hip-hop use, it has become nearly immobile.

"Black slang" can't describe black language, because clearly most black language is composed of standard English. However, when referring to actual slang that blacks created (*my bad, dis*), "black slang" is the right term. Personally, I like "black talk" (which is also the title of one of Smitherman's books). Although, like any phrase starting with the adjective "black," it might suggest that all black people talk this way all the time, "black talk" (like "pop talk") is colloquial and flexible, encompassing vocabulary and then some.

In mixing up these terms, I take my cue in part from the Stanford University linguistics professor John Russell Rickford. Rickford's not hung up over what black language is called, though he favors "spoken soul," the title of his book (subtitled *The Story of Black English* and written with his son, Russell John Rickford) and a term coined by Claude Brown, the author of *Manchild in the Promised Land.*

In *Spoken Soul*, the Rickfords spell out the dimensions of the language:

> In homes, schools, and churches, on streets, stages, and the airwaves, you can hear soul spoken every day. Most African Americans—including millions who . . . are fluent speakers of Standard English—still invoke Spoken Soul as we have for hundreds of years, to laugh or cry, to preach and praise, to shuck and jive, to sing, to rap, to shout, to style, to express our individual personas and our ethnic identities . . . to create authentic characters and voices in novels, poems, and plays. . . . The fact is that most African Americans *do* talk differently from whites and Americans of other ethnic groups, or at least most of us can when we want to.

If that approximates a definition of black language, what are "black words"? Word origins in general are difficult to trace, but the origins of black words are particularly so. In the dictionary-style *Black Talk: Words and Phrases from the Hood to the Amen Corner*, Smitherman writes that she did not include etymologies because "these are risky propositions at best when dealing with an oral language such as African American Language." Hampton University professor Margaret Lee, who published "Out of the Hood and into the News: Borrowed Black Verbal Expressions in a Mainstream Newspaper" in the linguistic journal *American Speech* and verified the black origins of each phrase with at least two sources, adds, "The approach Smitherman takes and I take is that these expressions and words were created by African Americans or were circulated in the black community before they went mainstream." In order to define black words that have gone pop, I would only add that a pop word is "black" simply if its most popular meaning or nuance was created by black people—for example, *bad* and *girlfriend* are pop when used with black nuance, but not pop when used conventionally.

Origins tend to get lost in the roaring mainstream. Some words that seem white are black, and vice versa. For instance, until I looked into *24/7*, I would have guessed its roots were cyber or maybe something out of the convenience-store industry. But *24/7* arose from a hip-hop fondness for number phrases. Rapdict.org lists some sixty number phrases, many of which are too obscure or gangsta to cross over; *411* is one of the few others that has gone pop. (A recent Mercedes-Benz magazine ad advised, "Get the 411.")

Bogus, which sounds so surfer, dude, dates back at least as far as 1798, when a glossary defined it as a "spurious coin," write David Barnhart and Allan Metcalf in *America in So Many Words*. "Its origins are obscure, but one guess that is as good as any is that it is from *boko*, meaning 'deceit' or 'fake' in the Hausa language of west central Africa. The word then would have been brought over by Africans sold into slavery here." In addition, some nuances that no one doubts are African American may run deeper in black history than most people, black or white, imagine. When *bad* is used to mean good, the meaning (though obviously not the word itself) is derived, Smitherman writes, from a phrase in the Mandinka language in West Africa, "*a ka nyi ko-jugu*, which means, literally, 'it is good badly,' that is, it is very good, or it is so good that it's bad!"

Meanwhile, some words that most people would identify as black, and that black people did indeed popularize, originated among others. Southern phrases in particular jumped races, "from black to white in the case of *bubba* and *big daddy*, from white to black in the case of *grits* and *chitlins*," write the Rickfords. *Cat*, meaning a hip guy, is a dated piece of slang (though often on the verge of a comeback) that most people attribute to black jazz musicians; Ken Burns's television series *Jazz* states that Louis Armstrong was the first person to have said it. But, as Tom Dalzell writes, in "the late 19th century and early 20th century, *cat* in the slang and jargon of hobos meant an itinerant worker . . . possibly because the migratory worker slunk about like a 'homeless cat.'" However, it did take Armstrong, and then other jazz musicians in the 1920s, to introduce the word into broader usage. That old rap word *fly* (stylish, good-looking, smooth) was flying long before rap. "The most well-established slang meaning of *fly* was in the argot of thieves, where *fly* meant sly, cunning, wide-awake, knowing, or smart," writes Dalzell, who notes those uses of *fly* as early as 1724 and in *Bleak House* by Dickens in 1853. But again, *fly* didn't really buzz until black musicians picked up on it, beginning around 1900, well before *Superfly* in the 1970s and rap in the 1980s.

Wannabe Nation

Whether black-born or black-raised, black words are the ones that many white people are wearing like backwards baseball caps. That brings us to a particularly telling term that went from black to pop. *Wannabe* originally referred to people who wanted to be something they weren't; it was often said of a black person who wanted to be white. In Spike Lee's 1988 film *School Daze*, the conflict was between the dark-skinned, activist "Jigaboos" and the light-skinned sorority sister "Wannabes." Beginning around the time of that movie, *wannabe* was used by just about everybody to mean anybody who wanted to be somebody he or she wasn't—there have been surfer wannabes, Madonna wannabes, and dot.com start-up wannabes. But *wannabe* is not just a blast from decades past. More recently, "podcaster wannabes" have developed, and in just one week on

TV and radio in late 2004, I heard of "artist wannabes," "geek wannabes," and "wannabe homeland security chief" Bernard Kerik.

Racially speaking, *wannabe* has reversed field. Since at least the early nineties, with hip-hop an entrenched, virtually mainstream hit, *wannabe* has been far more likely to refer to whites, especially teenagers, who want to be black or do the style. Sometimes called *wiggers* or *wiggas* (*white* plus *nigger/nigga*), black wannabes try to dance the dance and talk the talk. Even whites who would hate to be black will maintain the right to add the occasional black flourish. Some whites flash a black word or gesture like an honorary badge of cool, to show they're down with black people on certain occasions, usually involving sports or entertainment. Or maybe they do it because some of their best friends and some of the best commercials are flashing it, too. Or maybe they just need to know that black people like them. Take "Johnny and Sally," the fictitious white couple on the very funny Web site BlackPeopleLoveUs.com, which is full of "testimonials" to their racial bigheartedness. As one unnamed black man attested, "Johnny always alters his given name and refers to himself in the third person—for example, 'J-Dog don't play that' or 'J-Dog wants to know wusssaappp.' It comforts me to know that my parlance has such broad appeal."

African Americans aren't the only people whose parlance has broad appeal. Non-Latino blacks dabble in Spanish, Catholics in Yiddish, adults in teenage talk. Cultural skin is always permeable, absorbing any word that has reached a critical mass of usefulness or fun. The human species can't help but borrow—after all, that's how languages develop. 35

But whether we call it wannabe talk or the less derogatory crossover talk, something about white society's sampling of black speech is more loaded than the usual borrowing. Black vernacular's contributions to English are larger in number and run deeper linguistically and psychologically than do any other ethnic group's. And black English, born in slavery, resounds with our society's senses of guilt, fear, identity, and style.

Black-to-white crossover talk, which also began during slavery, is hardly new. But, like most pop talk today, it radiates a new gloss, a veneer in which you can catch the reflection of its increased market value. Black talk comes from something real—"serious as a heart attack," Smitherman says—but, whoop, there it is, sparking out of TV commercials, out of white politicians, out of anyone who has something to promote, spin, or get over.

"Chill, Orrin," the Democratic senator Patrick Leahy told the Republican senator Orrin Hatch when things got a little testy during a Judiciary Committee hearing in 1998. Behind the *chill* was something more than "relax." One white guy was momentarily able to harness and aim some soulful black power at the other white guy. Saying the black word says, I stake myself closer to black people and their righteous anger than you do. You're more afraid of them and their language than I am—so I win this moment.

"Go on, give it up!" the signs throughout Virgin Records implored. *Give it up*'s "it" referred only obliquely to applause. (Used to introduce about every other musical act these days, the black phrase has long been a verbal welcome mat. "Everybody give it up for my very good friend Marion Barry," someone said on the old comedy series *In Living Color* in 1990.) "It" referred even more obliquely to sex. (*Give it up* originally meant "to agree to engage in copulation," according to the *Random House Historical Dictionary of American Slang* [*RHHDAS*].) No, this "it" meant your money—for "The Sacrifice Sale. Hundreds of titles: 3 for $26."

As recently as 2005, McDonald's, like many a corporation trying to sound   40
more "urban," was getting it all wrong. "DOUBLE CHEESEBURGER? I'D HIT IT," read a McDonald's banner ad on ESPN.com. As mocking bloggers pointed out, the hip-hop slang actually meant, "I'd have sex with that cheeseburger."

It's not as if there hasn't been enough time to hit it right. Again, black style's market value jumped around the time *Yo! MTV Raps* debuted in 1989. In a TV spot that same year, the pasty white Pillsbury Doughboy performed a mean rap number. By 1994, Dan Rather (a magnet for every catchy, and uncatchy, turn of phrase that comes along) reported that political candidates were "dissing" each other. In 1999, a hip black guy insisted, for Wendy's, "This sandwich is da bomb."

Three years later, *CNN Headline News* asked the writers responsible for the crawl and other graphics that crowd its screen to inject some hip-hop. "In an effort to be sure we are as cutting-edge as possible with our on-screen persona, please refer to this slang dictionary when looking for just the right phrase," read a *Headline News* memo, according to the New York *Daily News*. "Please use this guide to help all you homeys and honeys add a new flava to your tickers and dekos." Among the phrases mentioned were *fly*, *ill*, and *jimmy hat*, for a condom. (A *Headline News* spokeswoman at the time said a mid-level producer sent the memo without top executives knowing about it.)

"You Go, Girl!" ran a 2004 headline in *Today's Christian Woman* for a story about finding supportive friends.

"She said she'd have more gay people in the White House. I'm like, 'You go, Teresa,'" a gay doctor said of Teresa Heinz Kerry at an Ohio campaign rally. "Women to Heinz Kerry: You Go, Girl," an Associated Press headline read. For a brief moment there, Teresa was the nation's "You go, girl" girl.

You go, girl! is democratic and process-oriented—every girl is presumed to   45
have the strength that can propel her forward. But what's a guy to do? When a man needs an equally exciting, gender-saluting pop phrase that expresses personal recognition, he's almost sure to receive the hierarchical, goal-oriented *You da* (or *the*) *man!* Both black and white men scramble to the top of the heap with this winner-take-all phrase. But in the media and off, it's increasingly white men who adorn one another with this verbal king's crown.

In the 1998 animated movie *Antz*, the ant voiced-over by Sylvester Stallone says to the Woody Allen ant, who has just saved his species' civilization, "You da ant!" And they exchange high-fives.

"You're the man!" Karl ("Bush's Brain") Rove "bellowed back into his cell phone" to Lloyd Smith, who managed Jim Talent's Missouri Senate campaign in the 2002 midterm elections, *Time* magazine reported. Smith had just told Rove that it looked as if Talent was going to beat Democratic senator Jean Carnahan, thereby guaranteeing the Senate to Republicans.

You da man! is now so common that when the sports columnist Frank Deford compiled his 2004 Thanksgiving Day list of things "I wish we still had," he included "golf tournaments that were played without idiots screaming 'you da man.'"

But white men still scream *You da man!* because the words (especially *da*, though it's not required) still suggest a wistful tableau of black folks testifying for white folks. Beyond giving a white man props for smiting a foe, *You da man* gives him authenticity clearance, momentary proof that, at the least, he's not the Man, an oppressive white authority figure.

It's better yet if a white guy can get a real black guy to testify for him (just like in all the movies that star a somehow emotionally stunted white hero who's made to see one light or another by a more soulful black sidekick). An ad campaign a while back made this embarrassingly evident. "The Colonel?" asked what intentionally sounded like a black male voice. "He da man!" The man, of course, was Colonel Sanders of KFC. He's dead, but in the late nineties the Colonel was not only revived as a cartoon character for TV spots, but he also became black (minus a pigment change). "Go, Colonel! Go, Colonel!" the voiceover jived. "The Colonel still has a pink face and white suit," Mark Schone noted on the radio show *This American Life*, "but these days the erstwhile Southern gentleman twirls his cane to . . . old school seventies funk. . . . In an ad campaign that began on his 108th birthday, the Colonel has cabbage patched, tap danced, rapped, and played basketball. . . . What's it mean when a redneck who dressed like a slaveowner comes back from the dead and gets funky?"

And what's it mean when right-wingers take a catchy phrase that points out racism to express their own sense of victimization? "But to you," "Aaron" wrote to "fazz" on rightwingnews.com in 2003, "facts don't matter because Abrams committed the greatest crime of all, he was guilty of BWC (Breathing While Conservative)." (That's Elliott Abrams, who was indicted for giving false testimony to Congress during the Iran-Contra affair, pardoned by Bush I, and recently made Bush II's top White House adviser on global democracy.) "Liberals and their Libertine fellow-travelers accuse Callahan of the one inexcusable crime in America: BWR ('Breathing While Republican')," "Illbay" posted on Freerepublic.com in 2002 about a pork barrel project involving Congressman Sonny Callahan of Alabama.

Breathing while Republican (or *conservative*) is based on the phrase *breathing while black*, the more prominent *voting while black* (which resurfaced during the 2000 and 2004 elections regarding attempts to suppress black votes), and the original *X while black* pop construction, *driving while black* (police using racial profiling to pull black people over on the road or to arrest them chiefly because of their race).

Spelling B

Driving while black, itself twisted from *driving while intoxicated*, is simple, classic wordplay. And DWI to DWB to BWR is classic letterplay and codeplay. Coiled in most pop phrases—and especially in anything compressed further into initials (or numbers, like *24/7* and *411*)—is a Jack-in-the-box meaning that's just waiting to spring out. That is, the energy putting the pop in pop language comes from the power of codes. All language is codes, codes 'R' us and all that, but coded language is an African American art form. The often double meaning of black phrases, the way some words may mean their opposite (*bad, dope, stoopid/ stupid*) developed among slaves who needed to talk to each other in front of the massa without him knowing Jack.

To carry the weight of a twisted meaning not on a word but on a single letter is to pack the code tighter. Altering a letter in an otherwise ordinary word can alter the world outlook. When *boys* went to *boyz*, so went Boyz II Men. The title of the 1991 movie *Boyz N the Hood* declared it was no suburban frolic. Young black musicians and hip-hop-influenced culture in general wear wayward words like visual rap. Hip-hop and R&B singers and groups have long been seizing the Z (Jay-Z, Outlawz, Limp Bizkit), crossing an X (Xscape, Xzibit), or otherwise kurupting the language (Kurupt, OutKast, Fabolous, Ludacris, Shyne, Mystikal).

Hip-hop didn't invent deliberate misspellings as a mild social subversion (remember the left's *Amerika*, the hippies' *freek*?) or as an attention-getting device (way before hip-hop, marketers were messing with the ABCs, from *Beanz Meanz Heinz* and Kool cigarettes to Kwik Save Foodstores and EZLern driving school). Wacky spelling may in fact serve the status quo quite well. In the late 1800s, a loose group of humorists called the Phunny Phellows "fed their Victorian audiences a bland diet of simple gags, sprinkled liberally with malapropisms, terrible puns, comic misspellings, blatant racism, stock characters, and shopworn topical jokes," wrote Kevin MacDonnell in *Firsts* magazine.

But deliberate misspellings have long been used to declare some form of independence, however deep or shallow it might run. In the 1920s, young people "spelled 'rats' as 'rhatz!' and shortened 'that's too bad' to 'stoo bad,'" Dalzell writes, adding that even the famous *phat*, which seems the epitome of hip-hop spelling, has a surprisingly long history. *Fat* meant "rich" back in the seventeenth century, and examples of *fat* meaning "good," "cool," or "living well" have occurred ever since. As for the "ph," in a list of "Negro argot," *Time* magazine listed *phat* "as one of several 'adjectives of approval'" in 1963. But *phat* predated that. Dalzell found that around the turn of the last century "typesetters referred to type that was easily set as being *phat*. . . . Indeed, in 1885, the Post Express Printing Company in Rochester, New York, published the 'Phat Boy's Birds-Eye Map of the Saint Lawrence River' with a drawing of a corpulent boy."

Despite their varied history, creative misspellings today are mostly associated with hip-hop culture. So much so that in his 2000 movie *Bamboozled*, Spike Lee hilariously spoofed the trend. "I respectfully submit," one rapper tells his gangsta crew, "that we from now on, henceforth and whatnot spell black B-L-A-K, not B-L-A-C-K."

Hip-hop misspellings don't just reject select bits of standard white written style; they also reflect a history, beginning in the 1800s, in which standard writers ridiculed Negro speech with exaggerated misspelling. I'm not referring to the sympathetic, if imperfect, attempts at dialect writing in literature, as in *Uncle Tom's Cabin* and *Huckleberry Finn*, but rather to another, contemporary "trend in comic writing where southern speakers, especially blacks, were portrayed as uneducated or as figures of fun," as David Crystal writes in *The Cambridge Encyclopedia of the English Language.* "Dialect vocabulary and grammar (*hain't, saw* for *seen,* etc.) were used as well as misspelling, though it was the spelling which created the impact." Some of the impact of hip-hop's mangled orthography reflects that dis: Do the disapproved thing first; do it aggressively and obviously intentionally, b4 itz dunn 2 U.

And it's that unorthodox, defiant style that larger, nonblack marketing forces are now sucking image off of. If a company abuses the alphabet today, it's usually doing so to look hip-hop fresh, sometimes to look, dare we say . . . outlaw. Customized spellings that developed in part to subvert the Man's words

> **Coded language is an African American art form.**

are now copied by the Man's corporations almost as fast as they'll funnel benjamins to Congress to make them mo' money. (Hey, just like real gangstas!)

In 1999, when Rupert Murdoch's Fox Family Channel launched two new cable channels, it fought the power by naming them the Boyz Channel and the Girlz Channel. (Both were soon zapped.) When it was still running, *Lizzie McGuire* was the most successful show on the Disney Channel lineup called "Zoog Weekendz." The STARZ!, BLACK STARZ!, STARZ! Kids, STARZ! Family digital movie channels add all caps and exclamation marks to convey their over-the-top Zness. Z bumped the old-skool S in DreamWorks' *Antz* (the name of Woody's "You da man!" ant, by the way, was "Z"). One of my favorite stupid attempts of someone to get down is the name of a spammer (apparently now deceased), "BestLoanz.com."

A quick trick to convince children that they're cool and that you, if you're a seller of stuff, are rad, is to call them "kidz" and otherwise buzz their brains with Zs; hence, the glitzoid Trollz dolls and cartoons (based on the 1960s cute-ugly Trolls); Bratz dolls (a massive seller); Nitro Battlerz (cars racing in battle domes and such); Kellogg's Gripz crackers and cookies; Hershey's Koolerz chewing gum, SnackBarz, and Twizzlers Sourz. On the health food side of the aisle, Hain's line of children's products is called Kidz, while EnviroKidz says it makes "The World's First 100% Certified Organic Cereals for Kidz."

Z—the purple of the alphabet, the last in line shall be first, the snap at the tip of the whip (Zorro's?)—is the letter that marketing relies on most to represent childlike fun, diversity, and all things hip-hop.

Z is unconventional, jazzy, but not really dangerous. Like Snoop Dogg's izzle, fo'shizzle ("for sure") pig-Latin-like lingo, Zs can be damn cuddly. (Snoop Dogg has dropped his "shizzolating." "I overdosed on it," he told *MTV News* in 2004. "I'm seeing it everywhere, you know what I'm saying?") For danger, citizens, you gotta get *X.*

X is pornography, the drug ecstasy, a former spouse, the signature of illiteracy, X out, cross out, the cross, an equation's unknown solution, off the charts, extra, extreme, and (in the exception exposing the rule) kisses. Generation X is the somehow canceled-out generation. *The X-Files* were stories of the paranormal too threatening for normals. *X Creatures* was a Discovery Channel

60

show about Loch Ness monsters, giant squids, and other excessive animals. The *X-Men*—whether the original sixties comic book or its later incarnations as animated TV shows and live-action movies—is a parable about "the Other," ethnic hatred, and race relations. (The X-Men have a mutant gene that gives them great powers, but human society reviles them because they're different.)

But now outsiders are in (Outsider Art, by non-art-world, non-art-schooled, often black, and occasionally psychotic artists, draws big bucks). Exy is sexy—it's hardcore, outlaw, a black man, Malcolm X, Brand X. And today brands, rather than running from Xness, practically cut it into their foreheads with razors, probably Schick Xtreme III blades. X is death, like the Slug-X Trap for gardening. In a world of *Survivor, The Sopranos,* and Swift Boat Veterans for Truth, X or be Xed. When NBC and the World Wrestling Federation (now World Wrestling Entertainment) needed a name for their newborn, self-designated "outlaw" (and quickly Xed-out) football league, the choice was obvious: the XFL (and X marked the spot for its teams the Maniax and Xtremes). When Right Guard decided it needed another market for another deodorant, it created Right Guard Xtreme Sport. When Kraft's Jell-O sales declined, the company put the gelatin in push-up packages, named it X-TREME Jell-O Sticks, and took aim at kids: "They're extreme—yeah!" exclaimed the commercial. And when that foxy Fox needed a name for another cable channel, it chose FX. Yes, the name plays nicely on Fox, and if you happen to know that FX is Hollywood for special effects, you might get a goose bump. But more important, *F* looks cooler slapped up against a bad-ass *X,* the naive, open-mouthed *O* squeezed out all together. "Perpleed?" an ad for FX on a commuter train read. "What would life be like without the *X*?"

Well, it might not be quite so easy to sell in. In video games, X marks the spot for Microsoft's Xbox. On TV, the letter has done duty for *The X Show* (about relationships, guy talk, and big breasts), *Maximum EXposure* (about extreme activities—man eats live snakes, ex-wife attacks new wife), and, on the relatively staid History Channel, *Extreme History with Roger Daltrey.* "Beyond AM. Beyond FM. XM" went a slogan for XM Satellite Radio. *XXL* is the name of the hip-hop magazine as well as the extra extra large size. *X* is a ride on the wild side that yet another XXL SUV swears it will deliver: A huge sign over Times Square read, "AS NOT SEEN IN THE HAMPTONS—NISSAN XTERRA."

For pure purchased *X,* look at the Jaguar X-Type, Infiniti's QX or FX45, or any vehicular X. X crosses the chrome on cars, says the automotive writer Phil Patton, because of "its connotations of 'experimental' and 'luxury.'" Or, in the case of XTerra, "Gen X and cross-country," he says. "The S in SE or SX is supposed to suggest 'sport,' but the SX also suggests sex."

OK, so *X* brands products. Earth to me: That's what popular symbols *do.* I guess I shouldn't be surprised to see *X* infiltrate newslike missives from media conglomerates, but when I saw the following, I almost had to slip on some Nike Shox to absorb the blow: A CNBC headline for a segment about international reaction to the U.S. invasion of Iraq was succinct, if not right out of the funnies: "World Reax."

So common is *X,* especially when referring to anything "extreme," that *X* has gone from out there to dead center—or, to restate that in pop, *X* is the new *edge.* Back in 2001, when ESPN's X Games (*X* stands for "extreme sports") were

65

beginning to go global, even ESPN execs paid to propagate *X* were dissing the full *extreme*. "'Extreme' is the old term," Ron Semiao, then in charge of ESPN's Global X division, told *Advertising Age* at the time. "These types of action sports have gone from being an activity of fringe groups to an ingrained part of a generation that influences its fashion, music, entertainment." He helped push for the rather uncatchy term "action sports." (Are there any other kind?) When Heinz's Bagel Bites, which was originally marketed to mothers, revamped to target *X*-attracted "tweens" (kids between childhood and teenhood), a Heinz executive said, "Action sports is a sport that embodies the lifestyle and personality of the Bagel Bites consumer." If true, this proves, finally: Edge is dead, long live the hole in the center.

Obviously, not everything *X* or *Z* is black or black-influenced. Extreme sports, in fact, are pretty darn white. Pornography appears in all colors. *Z* and *X* are mysterious and primal human qualities. But black, according to still-thriving stereotypes, is so often mysterious and primal, so often *Z* and *X*, that the corporate addition of those letters is black pepper for the white sauce. ₇₀

Encouraged by the hip *X* and *Z* hopping around, other letter replacements have gained favor among wannabe companies—that is, they wanna *B*. I'm convinced the whole *B to B* nomenclature (meaning "business to business," the tag of telephone directories and other enterprises in which businesses deal directly with one another rather than with consumers) is a hit because it resonates with the black *B*s: *B-boy, B-ball,* and *B* as a form of address, as in "Yo, B, whassup?" (This last *B* was probably reduced from *blood,* "a positive term, noting the genetic kinship and shared bloodlines of African people," Smitherman writes.) Sure, it makes sense in this abbreviation-loving era that *business to business* would be punched down to *B2B,* as in B2BMarketingTrends.com ("to help marketing professionals stay abreast of B2B marketing trends," according to a press release). But *B2B* has become too popular for brevity to be the only explanation. *B2B* has spawned *B2C, B2B2C, B2G, B2E,* and *P2P*—"business to consumer," "business to business to consumer," "business to government," "business to employee," and "peer to peer" (as in electronic file sharing), respectively. All this B-bop can make any business sound less like it consists of a bunch of suits who bore one another at meetings and more like a crew of B-boys doing some def transactions.

B as short for *be* (along with *U* for *you* and *4* for *for*) has been around for ages (even pre-Prince). But this shading of *B* has been bumped up lately because of its increased use in text messaging as well as in hip-hop. "Now we can b alone," a man writes to a woman on a pager in a noisy concert crowd for a Verizon Wireless spot. A Burger King TV commercial had it both ways, with nods to hip-hop and electronics: "B Real. B Good," voice-overs sang as the lyrics were spelled out on-screen to make sure we C the Bs. "2 Go. BK4U." Bouncy and at the beginning of the alphabet, *B* is on the mild side of businesses that want their bit of blood.

When corporations misspell, they're trying to spell it out: We refuse to put letters together the way the authorities tell us to!

Covert Operations

Wannabe or crossover talk didn't begin with hip-hop, nor is lingo-lending from one group to another confined to blacks and whites in America. Whites talking some black is part of an apparently universal phenomenon that sociolinguists call covert prestige. This means that speakers of a "standard" language (whatever the language) "have favorable attitudes toward lower-class, nonstandard speech forms," explains the linguist Margaret Lee. "However, these attitudes are not always overtly expressed, and they may be subconscious, because they stray from mainstream—or overt—values about the perceived superior status of the standard forms." This occurs, she adds, "for the most part throughout the world—when new forms enter the mainstream, in fact, they usually come from nonstandard speech."

Males are more prone than females to imbibing some of that covert prestige. Perhaps that's because, as some studies indicate, males associate standard speech with femininity. "Females tend to use more 'correct' speech forms," Lee says. On the basis of a study in Norwich, England, Peter Trudgill wrote in *Sociolinguistics*, "A large number of male speakers, it seems, are more concerned with acquiring *covert prestige* than with obtaining social status (as this is more usually defined)." This may be, he wrote, "because working-class speech is associated with the 'toughness' traditionally supposed to be characteristic of working-class life—and 'toughness' is quite widely considered to be a desirable masculine characteristic." 75

Covert or otherwise, black-to-white (and white-to-black) crossover talk in America began during slavery, especially when slave children and white children played together. Most of that language was never recorded, of course, and we have to wait for the development of various media to see how black speech influenced the broader English. "Slavery made its own traditions of speech and vocabulary," McCrum and his coauthors write in *The Story of English*. The entry of black English—an amalgam of Africanisms, the trade English used on slave ships, and plantation English—"into the mainstream of American life began with the Brer Rabbit stories. Later it was to sustain its place there through minstrel shows, vaudeville, music hall, radio, and finally the movies."

By the 1840s, minstrel shows had brought black language to large audiences and in the most overtly covert way possible. White men in blackface sang and told jokes using some variety of black language, often insulting imitations of it, to entertain whites. They were horror shows, "but minstrel shows were also the beginning of influence of African American style on all America," writes Allan Metcalf in *How We Talk: American Regional English Today*.

Black musical forms—spirituals, ragtime, the blues—went on to spread black language to the larger public, but by far the most influential music, until hip-hop, was jazz. Jazz fed generations of slang. Jive, the jokey, mint-cool language that arrived with the swing jazz of the thirties and forties, was slang that went on to become the pop of its time, even spawning a number of dictionaries. Cab Calloway's *Hepster's Dictionary: Language of Jive* (first edition published in 1938) listed jive words like *beat* (exhausted), *chick* (girl), *hip, hype, groovy, in the groove, jam* (improvised swing music), *joint is jumping, mellow, pad, riff, sharp, solid, square, too much,* and *yeah, man.* In *The Original Handbook of Harlem Jive* (1944), Dan Burley wrote: "in the sense that [jive] came into use among Negroes in Chicago about the year 1921, it meant to taunt, scoff, to sneer—an expression of sarcastic comment," and he relates it to the "linguistic procedure which came to be known as 'putting you in the dozens.'"

The whites ("flappers" if they were women) who jammed the Harlem clubs in the 1920s, the jitterbug craze of the 1930s, and influential disc jockeys in the 1940s all contributed to making jive the lingo for black and white youth in the know. Listen, for instance, to this forties DJ: "Hiya cat, wipe ya feet on the mat, let's slap on the fat and dish out some scat. You're a prisoner of wov. W-O-V, 1280 on the dial, New York, and you're picking up the hard spiel and good deal of Fred Robbins, dispensing seven score and ten ticks of ecstatic static and spectacular vernacular from 6:30 to 9."

"A new language has been born," Lou Shelly wrote in 1945 in another jive dictionary, *Hepcats Jive Talk Dictionary,* "and with its usual lustiness youth has made jive talk heard from one end of the land to the other." This meant, as always, that corporate interests were moving in—a process then more likely to signal a phenomenon's demise than it does today. "The end of the jive generation," writes Dalzell, "could be measured by the fact that in 1946 Hallmark cards issued a set of 'Solid Sender' cards, 'groovy as the movie MAKE MINE MUSIC,' based on the 'Disney hepcat scene.'"   80

Though jive began to dive, it kept resurfacing in the slang of later groups. In describing the beat speech of the late-forties hipster, Jack Kerouac called it "a new language, actually spade (Negro) jargon, but you soon learned it." By the 1950s, Kerouac noticed that "even college kids went around hep and cool and using terms I'd heard on Times Square in the early Forties."

Jive, writes Dalzell, "would lay an important foundation for the slang of the hipster/beat movement of the late 1950s, the hippie movement of the 1960s and early 1970s, and to some extent the hip-hop/rap phenomenon of the 1980s and 1990s." "*Cap, fly chick, groovy, homey, hung up, icy, mellow, righteous, sharp, solid,* and *square* all endured quite nicely, playing major roles in the slang of the 1960s and the 1990s."

If the 1960s were the turning point in creating pop language of a different order, that was to a great degree because, simultaneously, black language was undergoing a renaissance and was developing an increased ability to cross over. This black force met up with the big two powers, mass media and marketing, and all three have played with and against one another ever since.

Smitherman describes this blossoming of black language:

> ...perhaps the richest period of linguistic innovation was the last half of the twentieth century, particularly the 1960s and beyond. The emergence of the Black Freedom Struggle marked a fundamental shift in linguistic consciousness as Black intellectuals, scholar-activists, and writer-artists deliberately and consciously engaged in an unprecedented search for a language to express Black identity and the Black condition. This era was in fact the first period in the history of U.S. slave descendants when there was a critical mass of highly educated Blacks.

White people couldn't help but hear the newly invigorated black talk, she continues. "The 1960s was a defining moment in this cultural diffusion process with Motown, on the one hand, crossing racial boundaries with its music, and the Civil Rights Movement, on the other, crossing racial boundaries with its language and rhetoric of protest and moral confrontation, all broadcast live on the eleven o'clock news."

By the 1970s, black was beautiful enough to be in demand in the more liberal circles. As Gerald Boyd, the former managing editor of the *New York Times* and a black man, said in a round-table discussion about race, "When I started out in the early seventies, it was very popular to be black. Every white had to have one." 85

Media Bond

Now, more than a generation later, does every white—or at least every white kid—have to be one?

In the late eighties, the hip-hop movement began to bring black style—music, dance, fashion, language—back harder than anything since the introduction of jive. However, as Dalzell writes, "Unlike the hippie movement where anyone could don a tie-dye shirt and become a weekend hippie, the hip-hop culture did not provide a lifestyle that most American young people could completely embrace. Simply put, white teenagers could not, as much as they might wish to, become black. They could and did, however, listen to the music, dress the dress . . . mirror the hair cuts, adopt the rap vocabulary suitable for their daily lives, mimic the cadence of street speech, and admire from a safe distance the lives of prominent black rappers and athletes."

What made both the mimicking and the distance possible were massive media and marketing, both of which have mushroomed since forties jive. Hip-hop is, for now, the leading culture (followed by various skateboard, drug, and online cultures) that white kids can draw upon to fight the power, be that their parents, their schools, the system, injustice, or the general whateverness of life. Which is why commercial powers want so badly to be associated, however tenuously, with hip-hop. (The truism about "brand loyalty" is, Hook 'em while they're young and you got 'em for life.) For the most part, that rented association is working. If hip-hop weren't commercialized and hadn't hit the pop stage (*stage* in both senses), most of these white kids wouldn't hear or see it enough to wanna be black in the first place.

How easily a word can hop from hep or hippie or hip-hop to shopping pop. In the year 2000, few pop words could compete with *Whassup?!* Perhaps that's because *Whassup?!* (the official Budweiser spelling) was the one phenomenon that most successfully put black style through the marketing processor and coated every particle of implied transgression with a safety seal.

It was advertising, of course, that catapulted the sound into our faces. A 90 Chicago copywriter caught a short movie by filmmaker Charles Stone III in which Stone and some friends, cool black guys all, lay out deep, highly exaggerated *Whassup?!*s for every possible greeting. The ad guy, finding himself mouthing it too, figured, This is exploitable! and signed Stone to transfer his magic word to a client, Budweiser.

Said with tongue hanging out of mouth, the commercial *Whassup?!* was guttural and gross and funny. (Budweiser's spelling was wrong, Stone insisted; since the proper pronunciation is P-less, it should be spelled *Whaazzzaahhh?!* "If you make the P sound, your tongue can't be out," he told me.) After a climactic series of the guys growling *Whaazzzaahhh?!* to one another over phones and intercoms while watching a game on TV, the original spot ended with a sudden calm-down: "What's up, B?" Stone asked one friend over the cordless. "Watching the game. Having a Bud." "True. True," Stone replied. With the spots starring Stone's real-life pals, what emerged through this literally *lingua* franca was a lot of easygoing male bonding among some brotha buds.

(A note on origins: *What's up?* was not originally black. It goes back at least to 1838, Jonathan Lighter, editor of the *RHHDAS*, wrote in a post to the American Dialect Society online discussion group. Nearly a hundred years later, the phrase went mass-pop when Bugs Bunny first uttered a crisp "Eh, what's up, Doc?" in *A Wild Hare* in 1940. But somewhere along the way, African Americans began to unroll *What's up?* into a more all-purpose greeting. By the seventies and eighties, Dalzell writes, long-haired white dudes were saying the blackened *whassup, s'up,* and *z'up.* Stone said he and his pals had been doing the mega *Whaazzzaahhh?!* for sixteen years before selling their shtick to Budweiser. But he feels strongly that it's more of a black thing than Bud's or his own. "Someone suggested to me that I should trademark it," he said. "If it ever came to that, I would hope that someone in the African American community would sue me.")

Whaazzzaahhh?! was just what the nation apparently needed on the eve of a new millennium. The sound instantly became an NBA refrain, a greeting on radio sports shows, the theme of an *SNL* skit (with Brokaw, Koppel, and Shaw *Whaazzzaahhh?!* ing each other), part of another easy question on *Who Wants to Be a Millionaire?*, and the basis of numerous Web site parodies.

Largely because of *Whaazzzaahhh?!*, sales for all Anheuser-Busch beers rose by 2.4 million barrels in 2000. Just as important, *Whaazzzaahhh?!* generated at least $20 million worth of free publicity, according to Bud's ad agency, DDB Worldwide in Chicago. (DDB calls this desirable state "talk value"—it means saturation buzz, a phrase that people use almost involuntarily. But since DDB wanted to reap benefits in case *talk value* acquired talk value, it did what Stone said he wouldn't with *Whaazzzaahhh?!*—it trademarked the term.)

Whaazzzaahhh?! clearly filled a catchphrase/catchgesture void. The Arsenio [95] whoop and the high-five, pop as they still are, had already faded into background pop. The chest bump and the victory dance required actually getting physical. Men, especially sedentary sports-fan men, were ripe for a word that could reinvigorate their manliness, update them multiculturally, and refresh their irony.

And the very sound of the earthy, vomity *Whaazzzaahhh?!* was a perfect counterpoint to the entire high-pitched, beeping wired world. *Whaazzzaahhh?!* was disgusting, low-down, and as analogue as it gets—something to make primal *Fight Club* men out of digital midgets (the 1999 Edward Norton/Brad Pitt movie about wimpy white guys fleeing office cubicles and regaining testosterone by slapping each other around in abandoned buildings came out shortly before Bud's campaign), something to add thick yang to the whiny yin of cell phones and chirping virtuosity and everything eeeeeeeeeeeeeEEEEEEEE. *Whaazzzaahhh?!* was grit thrown onto the computer screen, onto the very TV screen the ads ran on. That is—as racial myths still go—*Whaazzzaahhh?!* could make cool black men out of repressed white males.

But it took another spot of the many in Budweiser's campaign to make that perfectly clear. A bunch of preppie white guys—a sweater is draped over one's shoulders as he watches the "market recap" instead of "the game"—duplicate the plot of the original spot but instead of gutting out *Whaazzzaahhh?!*, they eke out a clunky *What are you doooo-ing?!* By the end, their war cry is very loud but very uncool, and the camera pulls back to show two of Stone's black pals watching these graceless wannabes on TV and looking at each other in disbelief. The spot, which debuted on the 2001 Super Bowl, was really funny. But think about what Budweiser was doooo-ing. It was telling its predominantly white customers that they could better identify with these loose, creative black men than they could with those ghosts-of-men honkies. Pouring on the covert prestige, it flattered white guys by telling them they shared the cool attitude of the black men—though, whew, they didn't have to *live* as black men. Drink Bud and get in touch with your inner black guy.

But not necessarily with an outer one. Because *Whaazzzaahhh?!* was yet another way for white men, and women, to bond with black people without having to actually know any. Knowing *media* black people—actors, athletes, any celebrity will do—is so much easier. If white people can bond with media black people through a phrase or a gesture, we can all "celebrate" an idyllic racial harmony while ignoring real racial politics—assaults on voting rights, racial profiling, income disparities, leaving no African American child behind.

But, hey, this ad's for Bud. Budweiser needed a hit of *Whaazzzaahhh?!* as much as many white people did. Never a big seller to blacks and without an indie bone in its image, the world's largest-selling beer, made by the world's largest brewer, could now say: These hops hip hop. Even though it's not true, true.

The Paying Dues Blues

After just a year or so, *Whaazzzaahhh?!* became mere hall-of-fame pop—no longer "top of mind," as ad people say, but hauled out now and then to fill certain mental slots (like another Budweiser hall-of-famer, "I love you, man"). But within the *Whaazzzaahhh?!* campaign, particularly the preppie spot, lie the seeds of what's wrong with media-enabled crossover talk.

Yes, merging languages is great, and we're better off when "standard" English gets goosed firmly and frequently. Anyway, it simply wouldn't be possible for white people not to use black talk—it's part and parcel of American talk. But whether our national experiments in covert prestige are enriching or exploitative depends on the attitude that insiders bring to outsiders' speech. When white people are too tickled with their ability to reference black talk, when they treat it like exotica, when it's too trendy, too knee-jerk, too associated with the selling of something (including oneself) and dissociated from the politics and history that forged it, then you have to ask, What are the hidden costs, and who reaps the profits?

In his show *You Are All Diseased*, George Carlin started in on theme restaurants like the House of Blues: "Burn down the House of Blues!" he said — it has too many white people playing the blues. "White people ought to understand they *give* people the blues.... A couple of terms used by lame white people: 'happens to be black,' 'openly gay.' When did 'urban' become synonymous with the word black? I don't think white women should be calling each other girlfriend.... 'You go, girl' should probably go along with 'You the man.'"

White people crowing "You the man" does not necessarily flatter black people. "Most black people are not delighted to have aspects of the language borrowed," the linguist John Rickford says. "They think of it as appropriated."

This isn't to say that all imitation of black or hip-hop talk is simply appropriation. Spreading words can spread the word — knowledge, empathy, and certainly the broader hip-hop culture. "It's something to see videos connect white kids in Utah to black kids in South Chicago to Croats and Brazilians," the hip-hop pioneer and former Public Enemy frontman Chuck D. wrote in *Time* magazine's cover story on hip-hop's twentieth anniversary. "This is the sound and style of our young world, the vernacular used in today's speak from scholastics to sports.... It's difficult to stop a cultural revolution that bridges people together." Those words began to sound prescient when, five years later, a rousing rap song, "Razom Nas Bahato" ("Together We Are Many"), became the theme music of Ukraine's pro-Yushchenko "Orange revolution."

Hip-hop truly is the young world's vernacular. But borrowing black language alone doesn't bridge people together. The bridges are often not so much between people as they are between people and the media. The college slang expert Connie Eble puts into perspective, for instance, the white use of the black term of address *girl*. "Well, *girl* is just used and that's all there is to it," she says. "It's one black phrase that has been taken over by white females, middle-aged secretaries around campus," as well as students. Eble once believed that the white use of *girl* and other black slang was a sign of hope. "At first I thought, maybe race relations are improving after all. But I have absolutely no evidence that there is more mixing among the races than there ever has been. After researching it, I found that hardly any black slang entered the white vocabulary because a white student has encountered a black student. They've learned it from MTV, the movies, and rap songs."

What's wrong with whites gaining covert prestige through black talk isn't that it fails to bring the races together (that's too much to ask from any one trend or proclivity). What's wrong is that it usually allows whites to feel good about themselves without having to do anything particularly worthwhile. Such easily picked-up prestige encourages the belief that high-fiving or giving it up are the extent of political commitment that an enlightened person needs nowadays. Whites get to blacken up their act "at bargain-basement prices," as Smitherman writes. "They don't have to PAY NO DUES, but reap the psychological, social, and economic benefits of a language and culture born out of enslavement, neoenslavement, Jim Crow, U.S. apartheid, and twentieth-century hard times."

Dearth of the Cool

The matter of whites reaping benefits from black history brings us to the black-nurtured word and concept that has risen to a status above all others: cool, or rather a dues-free knockoff of it.

Cool is the tent pole of pop culture. Without it, desire flops around; money doesn't know where to put itself. Uttered by folks from two (I've heard it) to seventy, cool is both one of the most expressive concepts of our time and one of the emptiest.

Cool is not just a black thing, by any means. Garbo, Brando, and Eastwood, to name a few obvious cool white symbols, have projected it. Other languages have long had their equivalents—the French royalty displayed *sang-froid*, for instance, on the way to the guillotine. And *cool*, meaning warmer than cold, has been around since the Norman invasion. *Cold, cool, chill, glacier, gelato*, and *Jell-O* all go back to the Latin root *gelare*, meaning to freeze, congeal; by extension, to make rigid, unmoving, with the implication of restraint and control.

Exactly when *cool* jelled into the word we know today is difficult to say. But *cool* as an elixir of composure, detachment, and style is generally thought to have come of age during the era of Count Basie and Duke Ellington. In 1947, Charlie Parker came out with a track called "Cool Blues"; in 1950, Miles Davis, perhaps *the* icon of cool, brought out the album *Birth of the Cool*. 110

But the cool—the stance, the feeling, the vibe—that early jazz musicians exemplified goes back much further. "Cool is all about trying to make a dollar out of 15 cents. It's about living on the cusp, on the periphery, diving for scraps. Essential to cool is being outside looking in," Donnell Alexander writes in the essay "Are Black People Cooler Than White People?" "So in the days when [slaves] were still literally on the plantation they devised a coping strategy called cool, an elusive mellowing strategy designed to master time and space. Cool, the basic reason blacks remain in the American cultural mix, is an industry of style that everyone in the world can use. It's finding the essential soul while being essentially lost."

To pull off such a strategy, you'd have to at times appear unmoving; you'd have to chill. "A wooden-faced model is aristocratic in its roots," says the classicist Margaret Visser, author of *The Way We Are* and *The Geometry of Love*. "Kings and queens perfected an impassive public face as the look of power. If you have no expression on your face, other people interpret *you*—you are all things to all people." While the keeping of a cool public face by nonroyals is a relatively "modern phenomenon," Visser says, it was "adopted by black culture, people who were the opposite of aristocrats, though they knew how to use that to make themselves powerful."

Sometimes that impassive look can be gotten cheaply, by wearing sunglasses. Or by using other symbols—catchphrases, designer labels, a little something to entice other people to interpret you. The more that millions of people have chased the elusive cool, the more the word's meaning has been diluted. Perhaps the seeds of change were there in the sixties, when cool began to shift from a thing to admire to a thing to idolize. But somewhere along the way, *cool* ceased to be primarily a word denoting composure or detachment and became more an all-purpose murmur of approval (where it's sometimes written and pronounced *kewl*—a blend of *cool* and *cute?*). "That's cool," one might say when a cabby suggests taking Thirteenth Street across town instead of Fourteenth. "Cool," I say instead of listening when my son tells me an amazing fact about his Yu-Gi-Oh! cards.

Perhaps, too, *cool*'s cool dissipated as people used it, as they will any fashion, not to cope with life as an outsider, but to enforce a popular-kids-in-class caste system. I used to say *neat*—until 1991, when I saw Madonna's tour movie, *Truth or Dare*. In it, Kevin Costner visited Madonna backstage and told her that her show was "neat." She acidly repeated the word, withering him on the spot for being an outdated creep and a disingenuous suckup. This was not Madonna at her coolest. Cool, as Alexander further defines it, is "about completing the task of living with enough spontaneity to splurge some of it on bystanders." Ten years after *Truth or Dare*, the caste system *cool* got a comeuppance, of sorts, in another movie, *Save the Last Dance*. In this interracial teenage romance, the white heroine compliments a black friend on her clothes: "Cool outfit." "Slammin'," the friend corrects her, "*slammin'* outfit." I'm not sure, but I doubt that *slammin'* still rules. Such words of praise come and go, but in the grand mall of franchised pop, *cool* has outlasted them all.

As *cool* rose in popularity, it needed a chump. "*Square*, a vital word of the 1950s counterculture," Dalzell writes, "became by the dialectic process of slang a vital word of the 1960s predominant youth culture; it is richly paradoxical that kids whom Beats would have found quite square used the word to vilify those who were out of touch with the latest mainstream fashions, styles, and trends." 115

Today *cool* has everything to do with mainstream fashions, styles, and trends and very little to do with originality or art, much less with "trying to make a dollar out of 15 cents." And yet repeating the word's sound—its coo, its ooh, its refreshing pool—still gives the faint impression that the speaker is grooving to something the majority just doesn't get, that maybe he's even slyly artistic or, to veer toward another black-cultivated word of complexity, hip. John Leland, author of *Hip: The History*, says *hip* "refers to an awareness or enlightenment. It's the intelligence behind the mask [of cool's composure]." To that I would just add that cool and hip, as words and as forces, intertwine, overlap, and at times are indistinguishable, but that on the whole cool is central to pop culture, while hip influences it more from the sidelines.

Cool's opposite number among the pop superlatives is not *hip*, but *hot*. Hot and *cool* both convey the utmost in mass desirability, but *hot* doesn't know from detachment; it's all sex, passion, and hubba hubba. Magazine cover lines have hissed *hot* so often that a women's magazine editor once told me his publication had nixed *hot* as being tepid. "Hot is unusable," he said flatly. The moratorium must have lasted all of three months, because the heavy-breathing *hot* is baaack. "What's Hot?" asks a 2005 print ad for (the co-owned) *In Touch* and *Life & Style* magazines. Citing each mag's sales stats, the ad answers: "That's hot!" The lucre-and-loin-driven *hot* is simpleminded, and has none of the paradoxes of *cool* (much less of the way more subtle *hip*).

No rich concept is without paradoxes, real and apparent. Cool is rife with them. Paradox number one is that beneath the frozen face of real cool, you're actually going with the flow (no paradox at all for Buddhist cool). Paradox number two, touched on earlier, is that borrowing from the excluded can make you feel more included. This is less a paradox than a pragmatic tactic for a market that needs outsiders (and even more so, paradox itself) to sex up its merchandise. Even a few years ago, who'd have imagined that GM and Ford would "trick out" their autos with loads of bling to look like the car makeovers on the MTV show *Pimp My Ride?* ("If you had big chrome rims a few years ago, people thought you were a drug dealer or a pimp," Myles Kovacs, the publisher of the hip-hop car magazine *Dub*, told *Newsweek.* "Now you could be a CEO.") Exuding excluded cool can protect a seller from appearing, God help them, boring. So market researchers, like those featured in Malcolm Gladwell's now classic piece "The Coolhunt," stalk the ghetto for music, garb, and slang to process into product.

If white people have made a fetish out of black cool, that too goes back further than the jazz era, as Greg Tate reminds us. In the introduction to the anthology *Everything But the Burden*, he writes: "Capitalism's original commodity fetish was the Africans auctioned here as slaves, whose reduction from subjects to abstracted objects has made them seem larger than life and less than human at the same time." That paradox reverberates today "in a market-driven world where we continue to find ourselves being sold as hunted outsiders and privileged insiders in the same breath."

Anyone who tries to resist the fruit of the coolhunts is bound to fail frequently. There's almost no way not to respond positively, at least momentarily, to marketed cool, whether in the form of a hip-hop Sprite spot or Nike's latest spectacle. We are really responding to presentations of grace—paid, staged, and third-hand though they may be. But in buying the product, we're not honoring cool, we're merely possessing its congealed representation—while the real thing evaporates from our credit-card-bearing hands.   120

"Most think cool is something you can put on and take off at will (like a strap-on goatee)," writes Alexander (ESPN once hired him to help hip-hopify its language). "They think it's some shit you go shopping for. And that taints cool, giving the mutant thing it becomes a deservedly bad name." Found in "advertising agencies, record company artist-development departments, and over-art-directed bars," this "ersatz cool," he adds, "fights real cool at every turn."

When Black Talk Goes to School

White society's fetishization of black cool and black talk might go down easier if that society did not react so virulently when black vernacular left the neighborhood of entertainment and moved to more serious areas, like education. I'm talking, of course, about Ebonics.

In December 1996, the Oakland, California, school board approved a resolution to change how it taught African American students who, the board said, spoke not a dialect of English but a separate, African-based language, Ebonics. On the face of it, which was as far as most of the press went, the resolution sounded like identity politics gone mad: calling a bunch of slang a separate language and proposing to teach it. Indeed, at first many blacks, most notably Jesse Jackson, in addition to most of the media and the larger public, trashed the plan.

Ebonics suddenly became the target of a rash of nasty cartoons, Internet jokes, and fuming commentary. Since the controversy arrived during the holiday season, several "Ebonics translations" of "The Night Before Christmas" began to circulate on the Net, like this one:

> I looked out thru de bars;
> What covered my doe;
> 'spectin' de sheriff;
> Wif a warrent fo sho.

> And what did I see;
> I said, "Lawd, look at dat!"
> Ther' wuz a huge watermellon;
> Pulled by giant warf rats!!

The "Ebonics Lectric Library of Classical Literature" Web site (no longer active) introduced itself thus: "Since the recent decision to make Ebonics (Ebony-Phonics) a second language in our schools it has become obvious that e-bliterations of the classics will be required. We will cover here the greater works of world Literature (Litershure) in the hopes of bridging the gap between English and the new Slanguage." 125

With the general consensus that Ebonics was broken English and teaching it meant the triumph of black special interests, the mockery and stereotypes were suddenly viewed as a healthy dose of politically incorrect humor. "The nationwide roar of laughter over Ebonics is a very good sign," John Leo wrote in *U.S. News Online.*

But most of the outrage against Ebonics was based on the erroneous notion that the Oakland schools had proposed to teach Ebonics and to ignore standard English. Although the resolution was ambiguously and poorly written—a clearer, amended version appeared a few weeks later, partly at the urging of Jackson, who subsequently supported the plan—the idea was never simply to teach Ebonics. Rather it was to compare and contrast the "home language" (Ebonics) of academically failing students with "school English"—that is, to draw on their vernacular to help them master standard English. If teachers ignored the children's home language—or, worse, ridiculed it—the thinking went, the students were less likely to be open to learning the English skills they so desperately needed. The strategy was endorsed by the Linguist Society of America as "linguistically and pedagogically sound."

"The Ebonics controversy confirmed that linguists—whether or not they describe themselves as 'Afrocentric'—are generally united in their respect for the legitimacy and complexity of the language spoken by many African American children," write the Rickfords, who are generally supporters of Ebonics in the classroom. "This perspective clashed with the more widely held public opinion that Ebonics was simply slang and gutter talk, or the product of laziness and carelessness."

Like all languages and dialects, black English follows consistent rules and a system of grammar, most linguists agree. Even vocal opponents of using Ebonics to teach English, like the linguist John McWhorter, say that black English is not simply "bad," "broken," or "inferior" English. Standard English, or the standard version of any language, is but one of many dialects itself. "One of those dialects is chosen as the standard one not because it is somehow 'better' or 'more correct' in the eyes of God, but because it happens to be the one spoken where the center of power coalesces," McWhorter writes in his book *Losing the Race: Self-Sabotage in Black America.* "We have no trouble understanding that a tiger is not a 'degraded version' of a leopard but simply another variation on 'cat'; we do not see house cats' lack of a mane as meaning that they are 'broken' versions of lions. In the same way, Black English is not 'bad standard English' but just another kind of English."

The reason for discussing the Ebonics battle here (in a book that's not about specific dialects themselves) is to look at how conflicts over language and race surface in pop language and the politics that pop can't help but speak of. For whatever you think of Ebonics as an educational tool—and you can find arguments and studies that support or derail it—you have to ask, Why the heat? Why the ridicule at the very mention of Ebonics? 130

Some of the contempt stemmed from ignorance (augmented by the vast majority of the news media, which seemed to willfully ignore the facts, a story the Rickfords detail in *Spoken Soul*). But some of the vehemence was due to a frustrated racism, to prejudices whose outlets of expression had been closing off for years. Condemning Ebonics was a safe way to finally voice anger at and fear of black people and their increasingly confident presence in American culture. Over the last couple of decades, most white people, unless they were outright white supremacists, had been feeling that if they were uncomfortable with black individuals or music or style, they could voice their criticism only gingerly or had to cloak it in disagreements about policies and programs, like affirmative action, welfare, or classroom Ebonics. While I really do believe that you don't have to be racist to oppose any of these programs, if you *are* racist, occasionally have such inclinations, or are just afraid of black people, then mockery of Ebonics can supply convenient cover. (The Ebonics controversy also came, McWhorter reminds us, a few months after the O. J. Simpson verdict in his criminal trial, when white anger at black support for Simpson was at a peak.)

For black opponents of Ebonics, the situation was more complex. For many African Americans the squabble over Ebonics replayed a long-held ambivalence toward their language. The other side of black pride is black shame, something that being treated as subhuman for centuries can engender. "The variously named vernacular of African Americans does have a remarkable capacity to elicit denial and shame from blacks (not to mention others)," write the Rickfords. Arguments among blacks about "talking proper" rise up regularly, they add. "During the Harlem Renaissance of the 1920s," for instance, "debate raged among the black intelligentsia, with Langston Hughes endorsing and exemplifying the use of vernacular, and Alain Locke and others suggesting that African Americans ought to put the quaintness of the idiom behind them and offer the world a more 'refined' view of their culture. These enduring attitudes reflect the attraction-repulsion dynamic, the oscillation between black and white (or mainstream) poles that W. E. B. Du Bois defined a century ago as 'double-consciousness.'"

(If one response to speaking a laughed-at language is to make it bolder and tougher, as hip-hop does, an opposite response might be to brood silently. After the Supreme Court decision against letting Florida recount votes in the 2000 election, during which the Garbo-like Clarence Thomas asked nary a question, the Court's sole black justice discussed his previously unexplained shyness on the bench with a group of high school students. He said his reticence came from fear of being made fun of for speaking his native Gullah, the Creole of the coastal Carolinas, in his otherwise all-white seminary class.)

The attraction-repulsion among blacks toward black English has its parallels among the public at large. "Americans of all types tend to bad-talk soul talk, even though it is the guts of the black music they so relish," write the Rickfords. "Appreciating sung soul is one thing, but appreciating soul as it is spoken is something else entirely. . . . In fact, middle America has quite often jeered those who speak 'jive' in the same breath and with the same enthusiasm that it has grooved to black sounds a la Bessie Smith and Mahalia Jackson and Ray Charles and Lauryn Hill."

There is, however, one other form of black speech as widely grooved to as 135 black song lyrics: individual words and phrases that have evolved from black-only slang into everyone-owns-a-piece-of-it pop. Even middle America holds on to these words as if they were talismans of the soul of a people.

None of this is to say that Ebonics itself is pop. The black talk that turns into pop, whether through the avenues of jive, civil rights, or hip-hop, did indeed begin as Ebonics (or whatever you want to call it), but the pop process has stripped that talk of its other dimensions. "The part of black language that is used by the general public is vocabulary," John Rickford says. "But the core elements of Ebonics or black language, which are the distinct grammar, phonology, and pronunciation patterns—that's not being borrowed to any significant extent, because you have to be living it." Since white people gravitate primarily to the vocabulary—with very occasional pronunciation exceptions as in *You da man* and *gangsta*—Rickford doesn't believe that popularization will be the death knell for black talk: "I don't think it has a powerful effect, at least not on black language itself. Anyway, people are always creating new terms—there's a premium on that in black English."

New terms, dwelling on the periphery, tend to have authenticity cred, and some of them, too, will eventually undergo the media glamour treatment that makes them pop. It might be a drag in real life, but marginalization can be marketable—if it's packaged right. Or, as the writer Khephra Burns put it in 1997, speaking of the students who were supposed to be at the center of the Ebonics brawl: "It can't help our children to be told at every utterance that their mode of expression—which is intimately linked to their identity—is wrong, wrong, wrong, when others who plagiarize them are getting paid."

Questions for Critical Reading

1. What is "covert prestige"? Define the term using Savan's text and provide an additional example from your own experience.

2. Savan discusses "paying the dues." What does that mean? Use Savan's text to develop a definition of the phrase, reading the text critically in order to build your understanding of the term.

3. Savan's primary concern is black talk. Using her text, suggest why other minority or foreign linguistic styles aren't used as prevalently in advertising. You will need to reread her text closely and critically to develop your answer, since she never explicitly addresses this issue.

Exploring Context

1. Savan's argument centers on the use of slang in advertising. Visit some Web sites oriented toward young adults (such as MTV.com, MySpace, Vibe.com). What sort of language is used in the online ads? Does it support or complicate Savan's argument?

2. Savan mentions the Web site Black People Love Us. Visit that Web site at blackpeopleloveus.com and expand her analysis of the site. You might want to use your work on covert prestige and "paying the dues" from Questions for Critical Reading to build your analysis.

3. Savan discusses Ebonics at the end of this selection. Use the Web to locate any initiatives concerning Ebonics in your area. Has it been an issue locally? In what ways? Why or why not?

Questions for Connecting

1. One way to think of Helen Epstein's essay "AIDS, Inc." (p. 106) is that it's about the triumph of language over advertising. How can we apply Epstein's insights about the fight against HIV infection in Africa to the appropriation of black talk by commercial culture? How might conversation defeat lifestyle branding? Synthesize these two essays to make your argument.

2. Julia Alvarez's exploration of the quinceañera in "Selections from *Once Upon a Quinceañera*" (p. 35) includes a discussion of retroculture. How might this phenomenon influence covert prestige? Is retroculture a form of paying the dues? Use the definition of *paying the dues* that you developed in Questions for Critical Reading in making your response.

3. In "The Dell Theory of Conflict Prevention" (p. 121), Thomas Friedman seems to focus primarily on the economic benefits of global supply chains. How does Savan's essay complicate this picture of globalization? What's the price of commercialism in terms of culture?

Language Matters

1. Locate a key sentence from Savan's text and then identify the subject, verb, and object of the sentence. How does the structure of the sentence contribute to Savan's argument? How does it make meaning, and what meaning does it make?

2. How do the headings in Savan's essay contribute to your understanding of it? Devise new headings for this essay. Where would you make the divisions?

3. Select a section of at least four paragraphs in Savan's essay. Find the topic sentence of each paragraph and then copy those sentences together to form a new paragraph. Does the paragraph made out of topic sentences make any sense? Does it reflect the flow of Savan's argument? How can you apply this exercise to your own writing?

Assignments for Writing

1. Savan focuses on the appropriation of black language into pop culture: On the one hand, black talk is fine and acceptable in commercials and ads, but on the other hand, it's seen as unacceptable in education. With this in mind, write a paper in which you evaluate the value of accepted norms for language in education. Should everyone be expected to speak "standard" English? What is the role of education in creating a national identity? How can we balance cultural uniqueness with such norms? You might want to draw from your work on Ebonics from Question 3 of Exploring Context.

2. Write a paper in which you extend Savan's argument using other specific cultural practices or traits that have been appropriated by American society. To help you complete your essay successfully, you may consider pulling from your own life experiences. You may also want to think about the different kinds of cultural practices and traits that have been appropriated in American culture, including art, language, and ceremonies. Is "paying the dues" an issue? Can you find evidence of covert prestige? Use your work on these terms from Questions for Critical Reading to help you make your argument.

3. Using Savan's essay, write a paper in which you determine the possibility of the "melting pot" ideal in America. Is it possible, or will there always be some sort of exploitation of cultures in the process? What gets lost in the melting pot? What do we gain? Can we achieve the goals of such a society without sacrificing the uniqueness of various cultures? How?

JULIA SERANO

Julia Serano lives in Oakland, California, where she works as a researcher in evolutionary and developmental biology at the University of California, Berkeley. She earned her Ph.D. from Columbia University in biochemistry and molecular biophysics. Aside from her scientific research, Serano is also a writer, musician, and spoken word performer as well as a transsexual activist. Serano's writings have appeared in numerous print and online magazines, journals, and anthologies. These published works include excerpts from her book, *Whipping Girl: A Transsexual Woman on Sexism and the Scapegoating of Femininity* (2007), and other works concerning gender and transexual issues. She has also self-published four chapbooks of poetry.

In *Whipping Girl*, Serano takes on issues surrounding transsexualism, sexuality, gender, and feminism. Serano pushes beyond the traditional concepts of gender relations and issues by extending them to the social view and treatment of the transgender community. Drawing on her personal experience with gender reassignment, her professional experience in science, and her knowledge of feminist theories, Serano provides critical arguments surrounding cultural and biological views of transsexuals.

"Before and After: Class and Body Transformations" looks closely at the cultural obsession with human transformation depicted throughout many aspects of culture—most noticeably pop culture. With countless makeover shows and documentaries that focus on bodily alterations airing regularly on television, human transformations have become a popular form of entertainment. Serano approaches the subject from a personal point of view; as a transsexual woman she has experienced people's curiosity about her reassignment surgery and pictures of her as a male. Serano is curious herself and wonders what drives the human interest in transformation. Class, as she points out, factors largely into this interest, for body transformations allow otherwise impenetrable class boundaries to be crossed.

What "classes" exist in our culture? Other than in pop culture, where else are human transformations seen? In what other ways are class boundaries crossed?

▶ TAGS: *technology, gender, objectification, research, class, human dignity*

Before and After: Class and Body Transformations

Transsexual lives are full of obstacles—childhood isolation, denial, depression, coming out, and managing our gender difference in a less than hospitable world. We have to navigate the legal limbo that surrounds what "sex" appears on our driver's licenses and passports, which restrooms we can safely use, and who we are allowed to marry. Many of us face workplace discrimination, police harassment, and the constant threat of violence. Yet the media focuses very little on any of this. Instead, TV shows and documentaries about transsexuals tend to focus rather exclusively on one particular aspect of our lives: our physical transitions.

Such transition-focused programs always seem to follow the same format, which includes rigorous discussions of all of the medical procedures involved (hormones, surgeries, electrolysis, etc.) and plenty of the requisite before-and-after shots. Before I transitioned, I found these programs predictable and formulaic, but I also found them helpful to a certain extent. As someone who had often thought about changing my sex, they gave me a certain understanding of what I might be able to expect if I were to pursue such a path myself. But of course, I was a demographic anomaly. Clearly these shows were being made by and for people who did not identify with the trans person in the program and who were not contemplating sex reassignment themselves. Back then, I never really questioned why a non-trans audience might be so interested in the minutiae of the transitioning process and trans-related medical procedures.

Now, after five years of living as an out transsexual, I have come to realize that these documentaries and TV programs reveal an even deeper underlying compulsion on the part of many cissexual people, one that goes way beyond natural curiosity, to dwell almost exclusively on the physical aspects of the transition process when contemplating transsexuality. Like most transsexuals, I have scores of anecdotes that highlight this tendency: During the question and answer session at a literary event, after reading a piece about the murder of trans woman Gwen Araujo, I was asked by an audience member if I had any electrolysis done on my face; after I did a workshop for college students on binary gender norms and the way we project our ideals about gender onto other people, a young woman asked me several questions about whether or not I'd had a "sex change operation"; after creating switchhitter.net, my coming-out-as-trans website, I received an angry email from a stranger complaining that I did not put any before-and-after pictures up on the site, as if the 3,700-word question and answer section and the 4,500-word mini-autobiography describing my experiences being trans wasn't sufficient for that person to fully grasp my transsexuality—he needed to see the changes firsthand.

Of course, it's not just strangers who ask to see before-and-after shots of me. When friends, colleagues, or acquaintances find out that I am trans, it is not uncommon for them to ask if I have any "before" pictures they can see, as if I just so happen to keep a boy photo of myself handy, you know, just in case.

I usually respond by telling them that before I transitioned I looked exactly like I do now, except that I was a boy. They never seem particularly satisfied with that answer.

The thing that strikes me the most about the desire to see before-and-after pictures, or to hear all of the gory details about sex reassignment procedures, is how bold people often are about it. After all, these people have to know that I felt uncomfortable as male, that it was a difficult and often miserable part of my life. So why on earth would they ask to see pictures of me from that time period? From my perspective, it is as thoughtless as if I had told someone that I was suffering from depression a few years ago and for them to have responded, "Oh, do you have any pictures of yourself from back then?" And really, is there anything more disrespectful and inappropriate than asking someone (in public, no less!) whether they have had any medical procedures performed on their genitals? So what drives these otherwise well-meaning people to want to know about the physical aspects of my transition so badly that they are willing to disregard common courtesy and discretion?

Well, I wasn't quite sure myself until about two years ago, during the height of the reality TV plastic surgery craze, when shows like *Extreme Makeover, The Swan,* and *I Want a Famous Face* filled the airwaves. These shows seemed to be catering to a very similar audience desire: to witness a dramatic physical transformation process replete with before-and-after photos of the subject. Also around that time, gastric bypass surgery began receiving a lot of media attention, and there were numerous programs dedicated to following people who were described as being "morbidly obese" through their surgery and recovery, ending of course with the mandatory before-and-after shots punctuating just how much weight the subjects had lost. On Discovery Health Channel, there is even a series that's called *Plastic Surgery: Before & After,* which often combines conventional plastic surgeries and gastric bypasses in the same episode.

> **Before I transitioned I looked exactly like I do now, except that I was a boy.**

What really impressed me about these shows was how similar they are in format to many of the transsexual documentaries I have seen: They feature subjects who are unhappy with their bodies in some way, sympathetic and able doctors who describe the forthcoming procedures in great detail, hospital shots on the day of surgery and immediately afterward, a final scene after full recovery where the subject talks about how happy they are with the results, and side-by-side before-and-after photos that demonstrate the remarkable transformation in its entirety. Sometimes these shows are even set to slightly disturbing music that, when combined with the narrator's dramatic voice-over, impresses upon the viewer that they are watching something that is simultaneously wondrous and taboo. The only significant difference between many transsexual documentaries and these plastic surgery shows is that the former require a little more background and explanation as to why the subject wants to change their sex in the first place (presumably, the desire to become thinner or more conventionally attractive needs no explanation).

So why do plastic surgeries, gastric bypasses, and sex reassignment procedures receive such similar treatment in these programs? It is not simply because they all portray cutting-edge medical procedures. After all, there are plenty of shows that feature various medical techniques and surgeries, but they are generally far more serious and less sensationalistic in tone. Nor can it be said that the rarity of these procedures leads to the public's fascination with them. While sex reassignment is still fairly rare, 9.2 million cosmetic plastic surgery procedures and an estimated 140,000 gastric bypass surgeries were performed in 2004.[1] It also can't simply be that these shows depict transformations of some kind. After all, one occasionally sees behind-the-scenes programs about Hollywood makeup artists and costume designers who can drastically change an actor's appearance, yet they are never given the sensationalistic spin that these other types of transformations receive. There are also plenty of programs that feature nonsurgical makeovers (for example, *Queer Eye for the Straight Guy* and *What Not to Wear*), but they tend to have a more laid-back and informative feel, seducing the audience with their you-can-do-this-yourself attitude, in contrast to plastic surgery and sex reassignment shows, which have a far more cold and voyeuristic feel to them. And while a woman who changes her hair color and style, or a man who shaves off his beard, undergoes a significant transformation, one that often leaves them looking like a completely different person, the audience is not encouraged to gawk over their before-and-after pictures in the same way they do with the subjects of plastic surgery and sex reassignment programs.

I would argue that the major reason that plastic surgeries, gastric bypasses, and sex reassignments are all given similar sensationalistic treatments is because the subjects cross what is normally considered an impenetrable class boundary: from unattractive to beautiful, from fat to thin, and in the case of transsexuals, from male to female, or from female to male.

Of course, attractiveness as a class issue permeates much of what we see   10
on TV—it determines who gets to be the protagonist or love interest and who ends up being the nerdy next-door neighbor or comic relief. And while TV advertisements may encourage us to buy various beauty products that are supposed to make us look incrementally more attractive, or dieting and exercising programs that are supposed to help us lose that extra ten, twenty, even forty pounds, it is commonly accepted that we each have certain physical limits that we are unable to overcome, limits that generally determine our social status regarding attractiveness. In fact, the large amount of effort that many of us put into attaining the relatively small improvements in our appearance that are achievable by exercising, dieting, and purchasing beauty products is a testament to how much we are judged (and how we judge others) based on conventional standards of beauty and size. So when somebody does cross those supposedly impassable boundaries, essentially changing their social class from not-so-attractive to stunning, or from "morbidly obese" to thin, it can change our thinking about beauty and attraction.

As a transsexual, I find myself dealing with this same phenomenon all the time, only with gender. Whether people realize it or not, most of us value, treat, and relate to women and men very differently, although not necessarily in a conscious or malicious way. Rather, like our attitudes about beauty and attraction, these prejudices are practically invisible to us, as they are woven into our social fabric. So when I tell someone that I used to be male, they are often dumbfounded at first, as if they have difficulty reconciling that someone who seems so naturally female to them could have once been something they consider to be so completely different. The fact that a single individual can be both female and male, or ugly and beautiful, at different points in their life challenges the commonly held belief that these classes are mutually exclusive and naturally distinct from one another.

Coming face-to-face with an individual who has crossed class barriers of gender or attractiveness can help us recognize the extent to which our own biases, assumptions, and stereotypes create those class systems in the first place. But rather than question our own value judgments or notice the ways that we treat people differently based on their size, beauty, or gender, most of us reflexively react to these situations in a way that reinforces class boundaries: We focus on the presumed "artificiality" of the transformation the subject has undergone. Playing up the "artificial" aspects of the transformation process gives one the impression that the class barrier itself is "natural," one that could not have been crossed if it were not for modern medical technology. Of course, it is true that plastic surgeries and sex reassignments are "artificial," but then again so are the exercise bikes we work out on, the antiwrinkle moisturizers we smear on our faces, the dyes we use to color our hair, the clothes we buy to complement our figures, and the TV shows, movies, magazines, and billboards that bombard us with "ideal" images of gender, size, and beauty that set the standards that we try to live up to in the first place. The class systems based on attractiveness and gender are extraordinarily "artificial"—yet only those practices that seem to subvert those classes (rather than reaffirm them) are ever characterized as such.

> **Plastic surgery shows rarely depict people who are conventionally attractive from the outset.**

Shows depicting plastic surgery, gastric bypasses, and sex reassignments are designed (whether consciously or unconsciously) to single out and exaggerate the supposed "artificial" nature of these procedures, thus giving the audience the opportunity to enjoy the spectacle of these dramatic transformations without ever bringing into question the authenticity of the class barrier that is being crossed. The more dramatic the change, the more "artificial" the whole process will inevitably seem. This is why plastic surgery shows rarely depict people who are conventionally attractive from the outset, even though such people certainly represent a significant portion of those who seek out plastic surgery. Nor do they follow subjects who merely want a nose job or a tummy tuck. Rather, these programs almost always depict people of either average or less-than-average attractiveness, and who undergo multiple procedures at once, thus creating the most dramatic and extensive physical change possible.

Similarly, the subjects of sex reassignment programs rarely ever begin the process as very feminine males or as very masculine females, even though many pre-transition trans people fall into these categories. Showing such people transitioning to become trans women and trans men, respectively, would not only make their transformation seem less dramatic; it would give the impression that sex reassignment merely confirms the subject's "natural" gender identity, as opposed to "artificially" altering that person's biological sex.

Perhaps for this reason, the most commonly depicted subject on these programs is a trans woman who starts out as a seemingly masculine male. In addition to the reasons for the media's focus on trans women rather than trans men . . . , there are additional physical reasons to account for this phenomenon. Trans women often have more difficulties "passing" as their identified sex than trans men do, not only because of limitations of the MTF* transition process in reversing some of the irreparable effects of prolonged exposure to testosterone, but because people in our culture predominantly rely on male (rather than female) cues when determining the sex of other people.[2] Therefore, some trans women require more procedures if they wish to be taken seriously as their identified sex. Sex reassignment TV programs I have seen have followed trans women not only through electrolysis, hormone replacement therapy, and bottom surgery (which are all fairly common), but also somewhat less common procedures, such as top surgery to increase the size of their breasts, tracheal shaves to reduce the size of their Adam's apples, and voice lessons to overcome their deep voices. Such shows also frequently depict trans women working with movement coaches and fashion consultants, even though it is safe to say that the overwhelming majority of trans women never engage in such a step.

These programs' concentration on trans people who undergo multiple medical procedures, or who take lessons to help them "pass" as their identified sex, tends to make invisible the many trans men and women who "pass" rather easily after hormone replacement therapy alone, or who choose not to undergo all of the procedures commonly associated with transsexuality. Focusing primarily on those trans people who undergo the most procedures during their transitions not only shows a more dramatic change—one that reinforces the idea that sex reassignment is "artificial"—but also fosters the audience's assumption that trans people are merely mimicking or impersonating the other sex rather than expressing their natural gender identity or subconscious sex.

Perhaps no element in these sex reassignment and plastic surgery shows helps confirm the audience's assumptions about gender and attractiveness more than the before-and-after photos. These pictures are designed to overemphasize stereotypes. In the programs that feature plastic surgery and gastric bypass surgery, the subject is almost always wearing frumpy clothes and frowning in the "before" picture, and dressed smart and smiling in the "after" picture, adding to the perception that they have become more attractive. In the transsexual documentaries, "before" photos of trans women almost always depict them in the most

15

---

*MTF: Male-to-female.

masculine of ways: playing sports as a young boy, with facial hair and wearing a wedding tuxedo or military uniform as a young man. Similarly, "before" shots of trans men often include pictures of them wearing birthday dresses as a child, or high school yearbook photos of them with long hair. The purpose for choosing these more stereotypically female and male images over other potential "before" pictures (for instance, ones where the subject looks more gender-variant or gender-neutral) is to emphasize the "naturalness" of the trans person's assigned sex, thereby exaggerating the "artificiality" of their identified sex.

In real life, before-and-after photos don't always depict such clear-cut gender differences. One time, a friend who has only known me as a woman visited our apartment and saw wedding photos of me and my wife, Dani, for the first time. Despite the fact that I am physically male and wearing a tuxedo in the pictures (as we were married before I physically transitioned), I do not look very masculine; instead, I look like the small, long-haired, androgynous boy that I used to be. My friend seemed a little let down by the photos. She muttered, "It's weird, because it looks just like you in the pictures, except that you're a guy." Similarly, whenever old friends meet up with me for the first time since my transition, they almost invariably comment on how strange it is that I seem like the exact same person to them, except that now I am female. It's as if our compulsion to place women and men into different categories of our brain, to see them as "opposite" sexes, is so intense that we have trouble imagining that it is possible for a person to change their sex without somehow becoming an entirely different person.

These days, whenever people ask me lots of questions about my previous male life and the medical procedures that helped facilitate my transition to female, I realize that they are making a desperate and concerted effort to preserve their own assumptions and stereotypes about gender, rather than opening their minds up to the possibility that women and men do not represent mutually exclusive categories. When they request to see my "before" photos or ask me what my former name was, it is because they are trying to visualize me as male in order to anchor my existence in my assigned sex. And when they focus on my physical transition, it is so they can imagine my femaleness as a product of medical science rather than something that is authentic, that comes from inside me.

I know that many in the trans community believe that these TV shows and documentaries following transsexuals through the transition process serve a purpose, offering us a bit of visibility and the rare chance to be depicted on TV as something other than a joke. But in actuality, they accomplish little more than reducing us to our physical transitions and our anatomically "altered" bodies. In other words, these programs objectify us. And while it has become somewhat customary for trans people to allow the media to use our "before" pictures whenever we appear on TV, this only enables the cissexual public to continue privileging our assigned sex over our subconscious sex and gender identity. If we truly want to be taken seriously in our identified sex, then we must not only refuse to indulge cissexual people's compulsion to pigeonhole us in our assigned sex, but call them out on the way that they continuously objectify our bodies while refusing to take our minds, our persons, and our identities seriously.

20

NOTES

1. American Society of Plastic Surgeons, "9.2 Million Cosmetic Plastic Surgery Procedures in 2004 — Up 5% Growth Paces U.S. Economy Despite Reality TV Fad," press release, March 16, 2005; Nancy Hellmich, "Gastric Bypass Surgery Seeing Big Increase," *USA Today*, December 19, 2005.
2. Suzanne J. Kessler and Wendy McKenna, *Gender: An Ethnomethodological Approach* (Chicago: University of Chicago Press, 1978), 142–53.

Questions for Critical Reading

1. Serano claims that radical body transformations enable people to cross class boundaries, suggesting that physical appearance reflects class. Engage her argument through a critical reading by searching for specific passages where she makes this claim and then responding to them by providing your own examples.

2. What is natural about gender? Using Serano's text, describe those aspects of gender you believe are natural. Does Serano think gender is natural? Why or why not? What does it mean to be "natural"? You will need to read critically to form your response, since you will be drawing from many parts of Serano's text.

3. Why are people fascinated with before-and-after photos of physical transformations? Locate passages that illustrate Serano's answer and then provide your own examples that either confirm or complicate Serano's argument.

Exploring Context

1. Visit Julia Serano's Web site at juliaserano.com. How do the design and content of the site reflect her argument in this essay?

2. According to Serano, people are fascinated by before-and-after pictures of any sort of extreme makeover. Use the Web to locate sites with before-and-after pictures from plastic and cosmetic surgery. Do they reflect the kind of fascination Serano claims? Do class boundaries seem to be involved? Use your responses to Questions 1 and 3 of Questions for Critical Reading in making your argument.

3. Recently the "pregnant man" caused quite a bit of controversy. Research this case on the Web, using Serano's ideas to explore people's interest in this news item. How does this incident reflect what you had to say about gender in Question 2 of Questions for Critical Reading?

Questions for Connecting

1. In "Faith and Diplomacy" (p. 23), Madeleine Albright argues for the importance of taking religion into account when considering diplomacy. In doing so she underscores the vital importance of faith to many people and many political processes around the world while also illustrating the potential of diplomacy to bridge differences and foster peace. What role might faith and diplomacy each

play in the controversial issue of transsexualism? Should faith determine policy when it comes to this matter? Can diplomacy mediate potential conflicts between religious tradition and individual sexual identity?

2. Class is also an issue in the elaborate quinceañeras explored by Julia Alvarez in "Selections from *Once Upon a Quinceañera*" (p. 35). How are class boundaries represented in these two essays? What is the cost of crossing those boundaries? Incorporate your response about class from Question 1 of Questions for Critical Reading.

3. What role might the primacy of practice play in the acceptance of radical body transformations? Apply Kwame Anthony Appiahs's ideas in "Making Conversation" (p. 57) and "The Primacy of Practice" (p. 63) to Serano's analysis, synthesizing their positions.

Language Matters

1. Gender is a primary concern in this essay, and it is also an issue in writing. Writers use a variety of techniques to avoid sexist language, including alternating their use of *he* and *she* or employing the awkward construction *s/he*. Frequently, people use a plural pronoun with a singular antecedent to accomplish this goal—for example, "Someone who wants to avoid sexist language should watch their pronouns." Which method is best, leaving aside the rules of grammar? How might or must language change to accommodate a nonsexist language?

2. What is a hyphen? How is it used? Select a passage of this essay and revise it by adding hyphens. When would you use them in your own writing?

3. Serano claims bodily transformations cross class boundaries. What class boundaries exist in writing? Is slang an issue of class? Can you determine Serano's class from her writing? What class is reflected in academic writing?

Assignments for Writing

1. Serano points out that before-and-after images of physical transformations may be so captivating because they challenge our perception of conventional class boundaries. These images of transformation have been seen in media for years. Think about a television show, documentary, or movie that portrays a transformation. What class boundaries are being crossed? What does this transformation tell us about class values in our culture? Write an essay in which you explore the connection between class and transformation, using Serano and an example of your own. You may want to draw on your work on class from Question 1 of Questions for Critical Reading in making your response.

2. In her essay, Serano points out the many obstacles transsexuals must navigate as well as the threats they face because of conventional ideas concerning gender

and class. Visit the Web site of a national transgender advocacy organization (such as gender.org, nctequality.org, ifge.org, or transgenderlawcenter .org). What issues are being dealt with in the transgender community, and how do these issues illustrate the perception of gender rights in our country? Use Serano's essay and information from your selected site to write a paper in which you examine gender rights in our country today. What rights do such organizations advocate? Are gender rights the same as civil rights?

3. Write a paper in which you use Serano to explore the complex systems through which traditional sex and gender identities are upheld. Using your insights about gender from Question 2 of Questions for Critical Reading, consider what makes gender (and class) natural and what happens when people cross either or both types of boundaries. How are these systems perpetuated, and with what consequences? Why might they be disrupted, and what actions might be taken to do so?

DEBORA L. SPAR

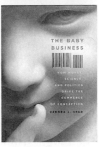

Debora L. Spar is president of Barnard College, a liberal arts college for women in New York City. Previous to her position at Barnard, Spar was the Spangler Family Professor at Harvard Business School. She has consulted for both nongovernmental and governmental organizations as well as for multinational corporations, and she also chairs Making Markets Work, an organization dedicated to leadership development in Africa. Her books include *Cooperative Edge: The Internal Politics of International Cartels* (1994); *Ruling the Waves: Cycles of Discovery, Chaos, and Wealth from the Compass to the Internet* (2001); and *The Baby Business: How Money, Science, and Politics Drive the Commerce of Conception* (2006).

In *The Baby Business,* Spar examines multiple facets of the baby market, ranging from prices and regulations to issues of morality. Reproduction, Spar argues, is a burgeoning industry whose consequences must immediately be considered and whose practices must be governed. The book focuses on the relationships between the economics and technologies of the baby business and the laws of our society.

In "Trading Places: The Practice and Politics of Adoption," a chapter from *The Baby Business*, Spar deals with the concept of "buying" children. As in the other sections of her book, Spar focuses on the ethics of adoption and the role of money in the practice, but she also explains that adoption presents unique differences from other aspects of the baby business, including a thriving black market and contractual agreements between birth and adoptive parents. She details the debates over adoption (particularly international adoption) and the tension between commercial and familial interests.

Globalized economies trouble us little when they lower the prices on goods such as computers, but how should we proceed when the commodity at stake is a human life? At the same time, with children around the world needing parents, how can we ethically meet their needs?

▶ TAGS: *community, family, culture, supply chains, human dignity, ethics, morality*

Trading Places: The Practice and Politics of Adoption

Do not be afraid, for I am with you; I will bring your
children from the east and gather you from the west.

—ISAIAH 43:4–6

The home page for Rainbow Kids is designed to rip your heart out. When you log on to the site—www.rainbowkids.com—you instantly see color photographs of beautiful, usually somber-looking children. There are some babies, some older kids. Most are toddlers, clasping toys or sporting huge bows in their hair. All these children are available—waiting, you quickly learn, for their "forever families."

As you scroll farther, you learn how to search: by country, gender, age. The toughest one is "date added," which shows, in reverse order, how long some children have been waiting. On a recent visit, for example, you could find six-year-old Bulat, who had been on the list for three and a half years. "He is described as quiet and gentle," the site reports, "and really enjoys playing sports." Ten-year-old Yamile "likes to write and draw . . . and dreams of being a doctor when she grows up." At precious.org, another adoption photo listing, you can learn about Sofia—"sweet and smart, sparkly and fun, polite and inquisitive"—or Rafael, an "A+ student" who "is dreaming to have a family." All these children, like all the Rainbow Kids, are orphans. And essentially, they are all for sale.

Officially, of course, baby-selling is illegal. The parents who visit Rainbow Kids aren't looking to *buy* their children; they're hoping to adopt them. In practice, though, adoption is indeed a market, particularly in its international dimension. There is a huge and unsatiated demand for children, the same demand that propels would-be parents to seek out fertility clinics and surrogacy brokers. There is a tragically large supply of "waiting" children and a panoply of intermediaries—adoption agencies, social workers, lawyers—that work to match the two sides.

There are prices, too, in the adoption trade, differentiated "fees" that clearly distinguish one child from another. Little Anita from Eastern Europe, for example, is a "sweet, affectionate girl" who suffers from fetal alcohol syndrome. Her adoption fees are reduced. Yi-Wei of Korea, an eleven-year-old boy found abandoned on the street, comes with a $7,500 private grant.

In purely economic terms, Anita and Yi-Wei are only tiny bits of the global baby trade, substitutes for the genetic offspring that would-be parents can't produce through other means. Although some parents choose adoption instead of (or in addition to) old-fashioned reproduction, many wander onto the Rainbow Kids site after they've exhausted all other channels of child production—after, as one mother wrote, "it felt . . . that we could not succeed at becoming parents."[1] In these cases the market for existing children functions as a nearly perfect substitute for the nonexistent ones, for the children who weren't born as a result of AI, IVF,* or sex. As with the more mechanical forms of reproduction, adoption carries an often hefty price tag, ranging from virtually nothing — the cost of adopting a teenager from the U.S. foster system — to more than $35,000, the fully loaded cost for a healthy white Russian infant.

What separates adoption from other aspects of the baby trade, however, is the obvious difference in "product." In assisted reproduction, the parent is purchasing the *potential* of a child, the hope that technological intervention will lead to the live birth of a baby. The producers, meanwhile, are selling eggs and sperm, services and promises, along with the probability that their high-tech tinkering will create a child. In adoption, by contrast, the child already exists. He or she is a little person, shorn of parents but fully equipped with the rights, dreams, and memories of a human being. Accordingly, the politics and practices of adoption are even more complex than those that surround the more mechanical forms of reproduction. It's one thing (and bad enough, some would say) to sell a sperm or an egg. It's quite another to sell a child.

As a result of this distinction, normative views on adoption split sharply into two camps. On one side are those who see adoption as a purely social interaction: It is about building families and rescuing children and assuaging the pain of missing people. In this view, there is no overlap at all

> **Officially, of course, baby-selling is illegal.**

between adoption and commerce, and no notion of putting prices on children. As Adam Pertman, a well-known adoption advocate, puts it, "Any time we put money and human beings in the same sentence, it is a problem: We denigrate the children and we denigrate the process."[2]

From the other side, however, adoption is not only a market but indeed a market of the worst possible sort. It is a market that sells innocent children, putting a price on their heads without any concern for their well-being or for the toll imposed by being treated as trade. Moreover, opponents also charge that the very possibility of adoption, and particularly of international adoption, raises the stakes for poor, pregnant women. If these women know that they can place their children for adoption, and if they can perhaps receive some payment for their labors, they will be tempted or tricked into choosing adoption — to sell their babies for profit, in the harshest version of this critique, and expand an inherently illicit market.[3] Less dramatically, critics of international adoption also argue that it compromises the human rights of the children involved by thrusting them into a cultural context different from their own.[4]

The debates in this field are passionate, with adoptive families and adoption agencies pitted against those who condemn the process. In the United States, the proponents of adoption have tended to win: U.S. families adopt more than a hundred thousand children each year, roughly 15 percent from abroad and nearly all under the confines of a wide-ranging, state-sanctioned system.[5]

---

* AI, IVF: Artificial insemination, in vitro fertilization.

Most adoptive families are screened by licensed social workers, the FBI (Federal Bureau of Investigation), and a local court. Their homes are evaluated; their finances are reviewed; their friends are enlisted to write letters of recommendation. Indeed, adoption in the United States is regulated far more heavily than any other branch of the baby trade. In Europe, where roughly sixteen thousand children were adopted internationally in 2003, adoption is also subject to a plethora of regulatory controls.[6]

In some respects, the debate over adoption is both small and highly personal. Those who paint adoption as an intimate, admirable, noncommercial activity tend to be either adoptive parents or adoption agencies. Those who scorn it as illicit trade are neither. There is little public attention paid to the world of adoption (aside from the occasional fluff piece or horror story) and little policy overlap with other aspects of the baby business. Yet the questions that surround adoption are both fundamental and far-reaching. Because in adoption, as in surrogacy, IVF, and fertility treatments in general, there is an awkward imbalance between market forces and public perception, between what is happening on the ground and how we choose to describe it.

One look at Rainbow Kids, for example, suggests that something close to commerce is indeed taking place. The same can be said of the seminars that adoption agencies regularly hold to describe their trade, and the stories of "available children" profiled in glossy magazines. Yet such hints of trade need not imply that adoption is illicit or immoral, or that children are being treated as commodities. Instead, market forces could be exactly what makes adoption work in many cases, what allows a vast supply of children to be matched with the equally vast demand for them. And if a little more commerce were injected into this field, more of the waiting Yamiles and Bulats might leave the world of Rainbow Kids and finally head for home.

Finding Families: The Evolution of Adoption

As a method of acquiring children, adoption has a long and fairly reputable past.[7] Historically, it was the only means by which infertile couples could obtain children, the way for them to salve unmet desires and preserve social goals. Childless couples in ancient Greece, for example, often adopted heirs; in Rome, even couples with children frequently adopted, sometimes selecting more attractive children to displace their genetic offspring. In both of these cases, the underlying motivation was largely economic: Parents needed the right kind of descendant to protect their fortunes and preserve their family name. And if they could not produce these descendants on their own, they simply acquired them elsewhere.

During the Middle Ages, this economic relationship assumed a slightly different hue. Because European authorities gave greater sway to bloodlines than the Romans had, families moved away from a formal process of adoption, choosing instead to "take in" children from unrelated families. These children—poor, illegitimate, or simply more numerous than their parents could handle—were frequently installed, or "put out," with wealthier folk as apprentices or servants.

Although some of these wards were treated as children, most assumed a considerably lowlier station, toiling in the stables, workshops, or kitchens of their new-found families. They typically remained in these positions until they reached the age of eighteen or twenty-one, when common law returned them to independence.[8] In some parts of Europe, the putting-out system was vibrant enough to encompass most of society's "surplus" children. Putting out didn't work, however, for some of the toughest cases: the infant children of unwed mothers, the bastards of illicit love, or the orphans of famine or war. Many of these children were quietly killed or abandoned.

Across the Atlantic, meanwhile, economic necessity meant that orphans and other "excess" children were regularly assigned either to their extended families or to unrelated families that could use their labor. As early as 1627, for example, fourteen hundred poor or orphaned children were apprenticed directly to the Virginia Company; in 1740, one wealthy Georgia planter took in sixty-one orphans to join his "family" and work his fields.[9] On a smaller scale, individual families simply assumed the care of their orphaned relatives, sometimes using them as economic assets, sometimes treating them as sons or daughters of their own.[10]

This situation—a haphazard combination of economic necessity and informal family ties—prevailed until the middle decades of the nineteenth century, when adoption slowly became more of an arm's-length transaction. The early signs of this transition were subtle. First, adoption cases began cropping up in state courts, usually involving issues of contested inheritance. In 1858, for example, the nieces and nephews of a recently deceased Louisiana man sued to inherit his property, arguing that his adopted daughter had no legal rights to his estate. The state court disagreed, however, and turned to *Webster's Dictionary* to define adoption as "tak[ing] one who is not a child and treat[ing] him as one, giving him a title to the privileges and rights of a child."[11] Accordingly, the court ruled in favor of the adopted daughter and turned her cousins away. Similar language was used in Pennsylvania statutes at around this same time, clarifying the status of an adopted child as a full and lawful heir.[12]

Second, as adoption became an issue of legal concern, state governments began quietly to envelop it in more explicit legislation. Massachusetts passed the first comprehensive adoption statute in 1851, followed in rapid succession by twenty-four other states. Although there was some variation among the adoption acts, they all shared a common and unprecedented characteristic: They made adoption a legal act and subjected the adoption process to the scrutiny of the state. In Massachusetts, for example, the state retained the right to determine whether the proposed parents were "of sufficient ability to bring up the child."[13] In Washington, D.C., congressional statute laid out the means by which adopted children gained the right of inheritance and gave local judges the authority to transfer custody.[14]

As a result of these laws, adoption in the United States became increasingly accepted. Families took orphaned children into their homes and raised them as their own. Children assumed new sets of parents, and the state put contractual relationships—a couple's commitment to raise a particular child—alongside genetic ones. Yet in most cases, adoption was still occurring within the boundaries of the extended family: Parents were adopting children they already knew and orphans with whom they already felt a familial link.

At the same time, though, social changes rippling across the United States were creating a new class of orphans: children who frequently had no family to support them. These were children born to the immigrants flooding into growing cities like Boston, New York, and Chicago. They were children born into urban poverty, children born out of wedlock or to married parents who succumbed to disease or accident or simply the stress of having too many mouths to feed. In earlier eras, these children had been put out by local authorities or collected into public almshouses. By mid-century, however, the increased concentration of poor urban children had overwhelmed the public houses: Most of their charges received minimal care, and many died alone.[15] As word of their plight spread, these public orphans became an obvious focus for mid-century social reformers, a heart-rending example of the ills wrought by immigration, industrialization, and the era's roller-coaster economy.[16]

Early Experiments

Against this dismal backdrop, one might have expected the reformers to embrace adoption as a nearly perfect solution. Thousands of infertile couples, after all, were aching for children and thousands of children were living without homes. Yet the early reformers did not see this match as feasible, because the available children, they felt, were not the "type" who could ever flourish in typical middle-class homes. And so instead of finding homes, they began to construct private children's agencies, philanthropic institutions that would care for orphaned or abandoned children and offer them what the state did not. All the groups that formed these institutions were passionately devoted to the cause of orphaned children. Few, though, saw formal adoption as a viable option.[17]

The most famous of these early advocates was the Children's Aid Society of New York, founded in 1853 by a Protestant minister named Charles Loring Brace. Like others in the reform movement, Brace was appalled by the squalor and poverty he saw expanding from the nation's urban core. He was particularly aghast at New York City's ranks of homeless children—a "society," he wrote, of "irreclaimable little vagabonds"—and firmly convinced that these children could be saved only by removing them from the streets and sending them instead to "God's Reformatory."[18]

To aid in this transformation, Brace established an unprecedented program of orphan trains. For more than fifty years, he and his associates physically took children (orphaned, abandoned, or simply poor) from New York's roughest neighborhoods and loaded them onto trains bound for the Midwest.[19] Upon arrival, the children were doled out to "healthy" Protestant farm families, destined to spend the rest of their childhoods in a status that hovered between adoption and bound servitude.[20]

Brace's trains made very big news. His Children's Aid Society placed an estimated one hundred thousand children and pioneered the practice of long-distance placement.[21] Brace publicized the dire status of many American orphans and turned reform into a large-scale, well-funded activity. To a large extent, Brace's trains proved that children born to "undesirable" parents could grow and even prosper in newfound homes. He proved, in other words, that adoption by strangers could work. And yet his trains also had an unseemly side, one that would haunt American adoption for years to come. Brace, after all, had done little to check the matches that occurred when his charges disembarked. He never embraced the formal side of adoption, or its potential to make families in any way that wasn't purely functional.[22] Critics have also charged that some of Brace's "orphans" weren't orphans at all, but simply poor children, mostly Roman Catholic, who were taken from their homes without consideration of the parents left behind.[23]

Meanwhile, other agencies were clambering after Brace, trying either to emulate his success or to build a better model. Roman Catholic agencies, for example, tried to provide a religious alternative to Brace's devout Protestantism, and Jewish agencies looked after the growing floods of Jewish immigrants. There were agencies devoted to newsboys and "street arabs" and to the steady stream of infants born to unwed mothers.[24] Most of these agencies, however, conformed to the reformers' underlying suspicions about their charges, and thus to the two core solutions that they offered. Either they provided in-house care for the youngest of children, or, like Brace, they strove to rescue older children by putting them out or assigning them to homes in the Midwest.

Few of these children were ever adopted. In fact, during this period most agencies remained opposed to formal adoption, seeing it as an unnatural intrusion into a family built on blood. Adopting one's relatives, they maintained, was perfectly acceptable. So was taking in an extra farmhand or providing temporary foster care to an orphaned toddler. But unrelated children were dangerous baggage, rightful objects of pity, perhaps, but not the stuff of which families were made.[25]

Over time, however, a handful of well-placed intermediaries began to consider more direct options. In large urban centers like New York and Boston, for example, a small circle of upper-class women took it upon themselves to "save" the babies born to unwed mothers.[26] Quietly, they took these children and delivered them to friends or acquaintances looking for a child. These newborns would subsequently be adopted under state law, joining families as if, in common parlance, "they were their own."

Other brokers soon joined the trade as well: hospital nurses, private maternity homes, local court officials. These brokers operated out of commercial interest and beyond the reach of the law.[27] In 1907, a popular women's magazine took this trade one step further, launching a "child rescue campaign" that featured profiles of dependent children and offered them to interested readers. After its very first installment, the magazine received three hundred requests for the two children profiled; it subsequently found homes for nearly two thousand others — "rescued" as one adoptive mother opined, "from miserable lives and disgrace."[28]

The larger agencies, of course, disdained such matches. They fretted about the dangers of hasty or sentimental placements and warned that children born to poor or unmarried women were likely to be scarred for life. As the director of Boston's Bureau of Illegitimacy noted in 1920, "The children of unmarried parents, who doubtless make up a large number of adoptions, may turn out to show an undue proportion of abnormal mentality."[29] The best hope for such children, most agencies insisted, was to educate them outside the family environment and prepare them for a life of labor. But despite the agencies' pleas to this effect, and despite a growing chorus of experts who insisted that heredity did indeed shape destiny, childless couples besieged the few agencies willing to place infants. By 1919 a judge from the Boston probate court publicly announced that "the woods are full of people eager to adopt children—the number appearing to be in the increase."[30]

At this point, therefore, the major child welfare agencies found themselves in a quandary. On the one hand, the agencies truly believed that many of their charges were unsuitable for adoption. They believed that these children needed institutional care and the kind of treatment only professionals were suited to provide. The market, on the other hand, was revealing something very different. Comfortable families wanted these "unadoptable" children so much that they were running to less professional agencies or to shady intermediaries with no standing in the world of child reform. By standing on the sidelines, therefore, the professional agencies were losing ground.

In retrospect, it's difficult to tell whether the agencies' eventual change in attitude was due to shifting mores, better science, or fear of competition from unsavory upstarts. In any case, between roughly 1920 and 1935, most of the country's largest child service organizations began to offer and eventually promote adoption.[31] Although many of the most prominent reformers continued to insist that "bad heredity" put an adopted child at risk, they now reversed this logic, arguing that because adoption was such a risky business, it was best handled by competent professionals—namely, by the social workers who ran and managed the country's child welfare agencies. Accordingly, as these professionals moved into the adoption business, they endorsed, and then helped to enforce, an ostensibly sharp distinction between "licensed" agencies and "independent" providers, between those that were recognized by the state and those that operated apart from its control.

The Evolution of Adoption

Over the next several decades, adoption in the United States became both more regulated and more regular.[32] The U.S. Children's Bureau began to collect and publish statistics regarding adoption practices in the United States, and many states passed adoption statutes of their own, typically focusing on the procedures involved in matching available children with suitable homes. State governments also began to regulate adoption more formally, issuing licenses to approved child-placing agencies and instituting procedures for examining both agencies and parents.[33]

Under Minnesota's 1917 law, for example, prospective parents had to undergo a "social investigation" before being granted custody of a minor child. In Delaware, the law also provided for a two-year probationary period before an adoption could be finalized, and allowed for social workers or other experts to make recommendations to the finalizing court.[34] Note that in both instances—and indeed in nearly all adoption legislation passed during this period—social workers and state-licensed agencies were knit integrally into the adoption process, serving as ostensible guardians for both the child and the state.[35] By contrast, independent practitioners were excluded, relegated to a shadowy area that was generally regarded as baby-selling rather than adoption.

Yet the market, it appears, did not care. Instead, by the 1930s, the soaring demand for babies had bestowed a newfound prominence on independent adoption agencies. Unlike their state-linked peers, these agencies now openly recruited birth mothers, advertised their services to prospective parents, and charged handsomely for their work. They also guaranteed birth mothers that their identities would remain secret, and they often took—and placed—babies who were only weeks old. This relaxed attitude stood in sharp contrast with the rules of most licensed agencies.[36] But it made the private "homes" exceedingly attractive to birth mothers, many of whom wanted to relinquish their infants as quickly and as quietly as they could, and to prospective parents, who wanted children "as young as possible" and generally preferred *not* to know the mother's identity.[37] By offering something to both sides of the equation, therefore, independent providers could charge for their services and turn adoption into a profitable venture. At the upper end, the going price for a privately placed baby—a little girl, ideally, with blonde hair and blue eyes—was an estimated $1,000 in the 1930s, rising to $5,000 by the 1940s.[38]

Repeatedly, the licensed adoption agencies railed against this trade, arguing that "baby farms" and baby-selling rings harmed the children they served and exploited the parents involved. This they almost certainly did. At one Montreal home, for example, the proprietor regularly took in pregnant women, kept them in squalor, and then transferred their babies—filthy and unfed— to wealthy Americans who were willing to pay.[39] In New York, an attorney named Marcus Siegel placed more than ninety infants for adoption, paying the birth mothers in each case between $1,500 and $2,500 to relinquish their children.[40] Even public reports of such scandals, however, did little to stanch the demand. Instead, as one contemporary article exclaimed, "The baby market is booming. . . . We behold an amazing phenomenon: a country-wide scramble on the part of childless couples to adopt a child."[41] Estimates compiled by the Children's Bureau suggested that roughly half of American adoptions in the 1940s occurred outside the purview of licensed adoption agencies.[42]

So again the agencies were caught. They didn't want to replicate such explicitly commercial practices, because their stated purpose was to serve the child. At the same time, though, they realized that their model was under attack. As a 1937 report by the Children's Welfare League of America woefully put it, "The fact that such a large amount of adoption work is going on beyond the reach of the organized social agencies seems to indicate that in some way we have failed to meet the community's need—why has the stream passed us by?"[43]

It took some time for the agencies to respond to this query, but within a de- 35 cade they had worked through a compromise of sorts, responding to the market without actually joining it.

Publicly, the agencies and their political allies maintained a drumbeat of criticism against the abuses of independent adoption.[44] There were stories in the mainstream media, angry denunciations when scandals broke, and even an eventual congressional investigation. Quietly, however, the agencies also began to change the way they did business. First, they essentially reversed their deep-seated distrust of heredity. Rather than suspect abandoned or illegitimate children of bearing inherently "bad genes," and rather than subject even the tiniest of children to batteries of emotional and intelligence tests, adoption agencies started assuming, for the most part, that their charges were perfectly normal. To some extent, this change in attitude was part of a larger intellectual shift, a movement away from the rigid view of genetic determinism (or "nature") in favor of environment (or "nurture").[45] But it was also deeply strategic. Because if most children were destined to fare well in their adoptive homes, then agencies no longer had to worry about finding the perfect child for a given couple; they didn't need to place "average" or "inferior" babies only in "average" or "inferior" homes. In other words, by changing their own theories of adoption, agencies were able to expand the pool of potential matches.[46]

> **But for adoption, the combination of contraception and abortion was disastrous.**

A second change focused on the agencies' relationship with young and unmarried mothers. In earlier decades, most licensed agencies had disdained unwed mothers as criminal, feebleminded, or simply bad. Insofar as they concerned themselves with the mothers' welfare, it was typically to urge these young women to keep the children they bore, either because motherhood would redeem the fallen woman or because the bond between mother and child was considered too precious to sunder.

In the aftermath of World War II, however, out-of-wedlock births soared from 88,000 in 1938 to 201,000 by 1958.[47] Illegitimacy no longer carried quite the stigma it once had, and the development of infant formula meant that women could relinquish even tiny babies without necessarily fearing for their health.[48] As a result, mainstream agencies began to deal more directly with pregnant women, in many instances offering them care and counseling as well as a safe place in which to relinquish their child. Arguably, this change in attitude offered unwed mothers a more compassionate alternative.* It also, though, allowed the agencies to expand their rosters of available children, competing head-on with the baby farms that had long sold their services to "women in need."

Finally, during the postwar period the adoption community began to redefine its notion of the adoptable child. No longer obsessed with genetics,

---

*To woo these mothers, increasing numbers of whom came from "good" families, the agencies also began to promise that their identities would be kept secret. It was this move that led, by the 1950s, to the "closing" of most adoption records.

agencies became considerably more open-minded about placing children across religious or cultural lines. They started to place older and handicapped children, and then — slowly and controversially — to encourage adoption across racial lines.[49] As with the agencies' embrace of "bad" genes and unwed mothers, the move to interracial adoption reflected in large part the changing mores of the postwar period: Scientists were debunking eugenic theories, middle-class teens were having sex, and racial divisions were finally starting to soften. But they also allowed the licensed adoption agencies to address the threat of independent adoption. For by expanding their definition of adoptable children, by sheltering unwed mothers, and by placing babies across a broader racial spectrum, the agencies were also engaging in a sensible market realignment, expanding the supply of children to meet the soaring demand.[50] Between 1938 and 1965, the number of adoptions in the United States skyrocketed, from 16,000 a year to 142,000.[51]

Supply-Side Shocks and the Global Search

In retrospect, this period soon proved to be the heyday of domestic adoption in the United States. The postwar years brought a new prosperity to the country and a renewed focus on domestic life. As soldiers returned from war and women left the factories they had staffed during the wartime years, Americans embraced a domestic ideal that nearly always included a working husband, a stay-at-home wife, and a couple of kids running through the suburban yard. Because children were an inherent part of this ideal, childless couples turned to infertility treatments with unprecedented fervor. And when these treatments proved futile or too expensive, they moved rapidly on to adoption.[52] Meanwhile, extramarital relations were also on the rise during this period, leading to more unplanned births and more young women willing to place their children for adoption. For the first time, supply and demand reached a fragile balance, and most infertile couples were eventually able to find children of their own.[53]

In 1955, the U.S. Congress launched its first investigation into the illicit baby trade, eventually finding evidence of an interstate market generating as much as $15 million a year. Aghast, Senator Estes Kefauver (D-TN), who led the investigation, wrote legislation that would make it illegal for any commercial entity to place children across state lines.[54] Only licensed agencies were exempt. But the bill never passed the House of Representatives, in part because several influential representatives knew that their constituents preferred independent adoption.[55]

As a result, U.S. adoption law remained deliberately vague. There were no federal statutes regarding adoption, and no legal distinctions between legitimate and illegitimate practice. Instead, adoption remained almost entirely under the jurisdiction of individual states, most of which maintained a relatively laissez-faire attitude. Adoption was legal in all fifty states; adoptions were finalized before local courts; and prospective parents were generally required to undergo the social investigations imposed in the 1920s. Only a handful of states, however, drew a distinction between licensed adoption agencies and independent practitioners.[56] Elsewhere, a range of intermediaries — lawyers, doctors, brokers—were free to arrange adoptive matches. Baby-selling was explicitly illegal in most states, but few of them bothered to define the limits of associated fees, consulting services, or reimbursement for a mother's pregnancy.[57]

Between roughly 1946 and 1970, therefore, the adoption market in the United States worked relatively well. More than two million children were adopted during this time, through a combination of licensed agencies and independent providers.[58] Although adoption records were increasingly shrouded in secrecy, adoption itself was a fairly public phenomenon, widely accepted as the ideal way of matching children with homes.

Abortion, the Pill, and Adoption

Very quickly, however, this situation dissolved. In 1960, the birth control pill became widely available. Then in 1973, the landmark case of *Roe v. Wade* legalized abortion across the United States. The impact of these events was complicated and sweeping: the liberation of women, the freeing of traditional mores, the separation between procreation and its recreational forms.

But for adoption, the combination of contraception and abortion was disastrous. First, the mechanics of contraception, along with the sexual freedom they entailed, appear to have contributed to a higher incidence of infertility. Women were waiting longer to bear children, and they were increasing their number of sexual partners, a practice that could lead over time to pelvic inflammatory disease and resulting difficulties with conception. More directly, the availability of safe and legal abortion meant a sharp decline in the number of unplanned births, and thus in the number of infants relinquished for adoption.

Between 1970 and 1975, the number of unrelated adoptions in the United States fell precipitously, from more than 89,000 a year to only 50,000.[59] Young women were having abortions in record numbers and relying increasingly on birth control.[60] Women who did choose to give birth were also deciding more frequently to keep their babies, in part because the ease of abortion meant that proceeding with an unwanted pregnancy had become a conscious, public choice. As one manual explained, "If the girl has decided to have the baby rather than having an abortion, there is a sense that she is obligated to care for the child."[61] Before 1973, 20 percent of white unwed mothers relinquished their infants for adoption; by 1982, only 12 percent of these women made the same choice.[62]

For the first time in the postwar period the supply of available children —particularly healthy white infants—was no longer even close to satisfying the persistent demand. And parents, emboldened now by a generation of relatively easy adoption, were incensed. By 1975, many licensed agencies had stopped accepting applications for healthy white babies, and others informed applicants that the likely waiting time for such a child was three to five years.[63]

As the adoptive market evaporated, frustrated parents began to search for new sources of supply. Some white families pushed to adopt black or biracial children, reigniting a vicious debate about the merits of adoption across racial lines.[64] Some fought for changes in the foster care system, arguing that it kept too many adoptable children in a state of nearly permanent limbo. Most, though, began to look toward the developing world, where the supply of excess children stood sadly undiminished.

Adoptions from Abroad

By this point, a small number of overseas adoptions were already taking place. In the immediate aftermath of World War II, for example, Americans had adopted some of the orphans created by war: some German children, some Greek children, and about fifteen hundred orphaned survivors of Hiroshima and Nagasaki. After these countries stabilized, prospective adopters turned to Korea, where the ravages of civil war had created thousands of orphaned and homeless children.

Between 1953 and 1962, Americans adopted an estimated fifteen thousand children from abroad, creating, for the first time, a considerable population of foreign-born adoptees.[65] They also pushed for subtle changes in the legal structure of adoption, changes that permitted these foreign-born children to enter the United States and eventually become citizens.[66] By 1984, Americans were adopting roughly ninety-five hundred foreign children a year. [67]

The next great wave of international adoptions began in the early 1990s, when the fall of communism opened a vast new supply of available children. In Romania, for example, nearly one hundred thousand babies and toddlers were languishing in horrific orphanages. In China, thousands of infant girls were abandoned each year, left by mothers struggling to comply with their nation's one-child policy.[68] And in Russia, thousands of children were living in state-run baby hospitals or aging children's homes. To their local governments, these children were a political embarrassment, evidence of what communism had not been able to provide. To Western parents, though, they were an odd source of hope—and a new supply of potential adoptees.

The first country to open fully was Romania. In December 1989, the country's brutal dictator, Nicolae Ceauçescu, was executed along with his wife. As camera crews streamed in to film the aftermath, they broadcast haunting pictures of tiny children tied to beds or neglected by their ostensible caregivers.[69] Shocked by these images, international aid agencies rushed into Romania in 1990, followed in short order by parents eager to whisk these children away. Initially, many of these parents were connected to the aid agencies or church groups that had come to volunteer in the country. They hadn't necessarily considered adoption before and were simply responding to the tragedy they saw around them.

As word of their adoptions spread, however, the broader adoption community saw the attractions of Romania: thousands of children in need of homes, fees of only around $2,000, and a legal system that was essentially collapsing. By 1991, a legion of facilitators, brokers, and adoption agencies had descended upon Romania, placing 2,594 children with American families and pushing the cost of a Romanian adoption in some cases to more than $11,000.[70]

At around this time, China and Russia also began to open their orphanages to potential foreign parents. In 1991, China modified laws that had previously forbidden foreigners from adopting; in 1992, Russia established a separate

50

division in its Ministry of Education for foreign adoption and created a database of all potentially adoptable children. With these systems in place, adoption agencies streamed into both countries and children started flowing out. By 1996, Americans alone were adopting more than 2,400 Russian and 3,300 Chinese children each year.[71]

Meanwhile, the agencies that served this global marketplace had also begun to multiply, morphing from the handful of charitable groups that once dominated the field to include a much wider and more diverse set of agencies. By 1999, about eighty U.S. agencies devoted themselves to Russian adoptions, and one hundred fifty had programs in China.[72] Others worked in Vietnam, Guatemala, or Peru; many offered a range of countries from which prospective parents could choose.

All these agencies existed under the hybrid regulatory structure that had grown around international adoption, a structure that essentially vetted parents at both ends of an international transaction. All of them also worked with counterparts in their home countries who handled local regulations and identified available children. Together, these two tiers had come to constitute a vast and growing business in international adoption: In 2003, more than 42,000 children were adopted internationally, 21,616 in the United States alone.[73]

Structure of a Trade

In purely economic terms, adoption is the most rational aspect of the baby trade. There is a vast unmet demand for children and a ready supply of them scattered across the world. By matching demand with supply, adoption would appear to be the ideal solution to infertility, a match of immeasurable value on both sides of the transaction.

Yet the problems with this market are clear. The "buyers" don't *really* want to purchase their babies. The "suppliers" don't want to sell. And governments around the world consistently condemn baby-selling as a crime akin to slavery. But still there are surplus children in the world, and would-be parents who want to adopt them. And so adoption has generated an ersatz market of sorts, a system of structured trades in which the supply of children is channeled to the waiting demand. In this trading system, regulation replaces commerce and prices morph into fees, facilitations, and charity.

Money changes hands in this market-without-a-name, but the money is rarely buying children per se and the system is subject to a labyrinth of formal controls—far more, in fact, than exist in nearly any other sector of the baby business. The system is global and marked by significant national variation, and it sports both a (large) legal sector and a (small) illegal sector. In the United States alone, the adoption system places more than 120,000 children a year, for a cost that typically ranges between zero and $35,000.[74]

These children fall generally into one of three categories: they are older or have special needs, they are healthy newborns, or they are foreign.[75] Although some agencies deal with all three types of adoption, most are increasingly focused on a particular niche.

Domestic Trade

The first of these niches, for older or special-needs kids, resembles most closely the original model of U.S. adoption. The children here are almost entirely the product of the U.S. foster care system; they have been abandoned by their parents or taken from them by law. Sadly, this is the one area of adoption that does not suffer from a lack of supply: On the contrary, there were 534,000 children in the U.S. foster care system as of 2002, roughly 126,000 of whom were formally eligible for adoption.[76] Because these children are legally wards of the state, only state agencies can handle their adoptive placements. And the process typically is exasperating: Parental rights must be legally terminated, extended relatives contacted, and, frequently, racial considerations weighed. In the meantime, the children get older and their needs often increase.[77]

Financially, the market for foster adoption is quite different from that for either newborns or foreign children. First, because the children are wards of the state and are placed by the state, adoptive parents pay nothing. Instead, the state pays foster parents a minimal fee to care for these children until they are adopted or reunited with their birth families. In some cases, the foster parents subsequently decide to adopt their charges, getting, in effect, a free adoption. In economic terms, then, foster adoption is both a purely nonprofit venture for the agencies involved and a relative bargain for adoptive parents.

The second distinction, though, is a much harsher one, a distinction that points unambiguously to the variable price of children. Because the children who come out of foster care are simply not deemed as desirable as others: They are older, often scarred by difficult pasts, and frequently children of color. In 2002, 73 percent of the children in U.S. foster care were over the age of five, and 37 percent were African American.[78] Historically, the demand for these children has been stunted, squeezed initially by social workers who refused to place black children with white parents, and then by parents wary of adopting kids whom most would describe as having special needs.[79]

Between the mid-1980s and the mid-1990s, the number of children adopted each year from the U.S. foster system stayed stubbornly in the range of 17,000 to 21,000, accounting for only about 10 percent of the number available in any given year.[80] In 1997, however, Congress passed the Adoption and Safe Families Act, a legislative package designed to move children more quickly from foster care to adoption.[81] As the act's provisions worked their way through the foster system, adoption rates began to rise: Roughly 46,000 children were placed in adoptive homes in 2000, 47,000 in 2001, and 53,000 in 2002. These numbers suggest that the demand for foster kids is substantially higher than placement figures once indicated and that the market in this area could well increase over time. For now, however, the placement of older and special-needs kids remains quiet and noncommercial, the province of public agencies that tend only to wards of the state.

The market for newborns, by contrast, is more vigorous and commercial. Currently, an estimated twenty thousand to forty thousand U.S.-born infants are placed each year for adoption; the figures vary widely because there is no central reporting mechanism.[82] Nearly all these adoptions are handled privately,

65

with an estimated two-thirds managed by independent (that is, unlicensed) intermediaries.[83] In a typical domestic adoption, the prospective parents pay an up-front adoption fee (usually between $100 and $500) to the agency of their choice. They then pay between $700 and $3,000 to cover the cost of a home study, the social investigation that determines whether the would-be parents are suitable adopters. If a child is found, the parents then pay a placement fee that varies widely—from $6,500, as indicated in Table 1, to more than $50,000. They also generally cover the birth mother's medical expenses and her costs of living during the pregnancy.[84]

What complicates the financial picture of infant adoption is the basic calculus of supply: the understandable fear that the dearth of (healthy white) babies means that a given couple will wait months, or even years, before finding their child. For some people—particularly singles, older couples, or homosexuals—the wait could well prove infinite, because many agencies impose criteria that explicitly work against them. As a result, prospective adopters are increasingly trying to beat the odds, usually through procedures with a decidedly commercial cast.

Some parents, for example, place ads directly in newspapers or college magazines, offering upbeat descriptions of their desire to adopt. "Devoted happily married couple wishes very much to adopt white newborn," states one typical ad. "We will give your baby a warm, loving home with strong family values and financial security." Others troll online, visiting sites such as

TABLE 1 Typical domestic adoption placement fees, 2004

Agency	Adoption fee
Children's Home and Aid Society of Illinois www.chasi.org	15% of income (minimum of $10,000 and maximum of $25,000)
Beacon House Adoption Service (Florida) www.beaconhouseadoption.com	$10,000 placement fee, $2,500 advertising fee
Adoptions from the Heart (New Jersey) www.adoptionsfromtheheart.org	$18,000
Christian Child Placement Services (New Mexico) www.nmcch.org	$12,000
Jewish Family Service, Inc. (Tennessee) www.jewishfamilyservicememphis.org	$15,000
American Adoptions (Kansas) www.americanadoptions.com	$12,000–$19,000 (African American or biracial) $20,000–$25,000 (traditional, Caucasian) $27,000–$35,000 (traditional, expedited)
Family Service Agency (Arizona) www.fsaphoenix.org	20% of gross income; minimum $6,500
Adoption Services (Pennsylvania) www.adoptionservices.org	$40,000–$52,000

Source: Agency Web sites.

www.adoptionnetwork.com or www.parentprofiles.com, where they join lists of waiting families and broadcast their credentials to potential birth mothers. "We have visions of a life that includes late nights reading books," writes one earnest couple, "eating ice cream on hot summer days, finger painting at the kitchen table and snowball fights."

Many couples also work with adoption attorneys or independent brokers, who endeavor to link them directly with birth parents.[85] In a typical case, the couple provides the broker with a file of materials about themselves and their desired child. The broker then presents these materials to a birth mother, allowing her to choose from several prospective families. In the interim, the broker frequently coaches families through the art of presentation, advising them, for example, about what color of paper to use or what kinds of photos to select.[86] Most brokers charge separately for these services, applying an hourly rate of $200 to $350.[87]

Open Adoption

Recently, some brokers and independent adoption agencies have also begun to offer a more radical version of adoption, one that arguably takes the matching of unrelated families to its logical extreme. In "open adoption," the birth mother (and occasionally the birth father) chooses the child's parents in person. Birth parents submit their personal information to a broker who specializes in open services; they review the binders and photographs of potential parents that the broker provides for them; and then they typically meet with the couples they've selected, ensuring that the fit is right. In this process, the historical veil of secrecy is almost completely removed: The adoptive parents know the birth parents, the birth parents actually choose the adoptive parents, and the child is fully informed about the details of his or her origins.

This level of transparency, according to the proponents of open adoption, ensures that the old stigmas of adoption are forever discarded. In theory, the child never has to search for his or her identity, and the birth mother is spared the lifelong burden of wondering what became of her child.[88]

All this may well be true. At a commercial level, however, open adoption also rearranges the fundamental patterns of business. In standard adoption, the adoptive parents are always the "buyers." They are the ones who historically have searched for available children, the ones who pay intermediaries to find and acquire a child. In open adoption, the adoptive parents still pay for the process, but only after the birth parents have found and selected them. It is the birth parents, then, who engage in the initial round of "buying," assuming most of the functions that once belonged solely to the agencies themselves.

In open adoption, in other words, it is the birth parents who select from the dozens of couples clamoring for their child. As a result, the agencies are thrust into a very different role: mediating transactions rather than making them. Not surprisingly, then, the largest players in open adoption are not traditional agencies, but rather a growing hodgepodge of lawyers and well-connected brokers, people who have begun to specialize in the niche of matching, not babies and parents, but birth parents and their adoptive successors.

As of 2004, the typical cost of an infant adoption in the United States ranged between $10,000 and $40,000.[89] In a handful of cases, prices as high as $100,000 were reported.[90]

International Trade

The third major segment of the adoption industry consists of cross-border transactions, the placement of children from one country into families in another. Once a tiny sliver of the baby business, international adoption has rapidly become a major enterprise, accounting for roughly 15 percent of total nonrelative adoptions in the United States.[91]

Three aspects of international adoption differentiate it from its domestic counterpart. First, because the children are moved across international borders, the legal regime is proportionately more complex. International adoptions effectively happen twice: once in the country of the child's origin, and again in his or her new home.

Second, internationally adopted children are by definition more diverse than their counterparts in any single country. They come in many colors, from many cultures, speaking a range of languages. Accordingly, they raise a host of social issues that rarely occur with domestic adoption and create a more differentiated market.

Finally, because these children almost always come from poorer countries, their adoption raises a heightened concern about exploitation and human trade. Some see the flow of foreign-born children as a combination of humanitarianism and family-building. But for others, it is simply trafficking in lives.

Legally, the regime for cross-border adoption is vast and sophisticated. It encompasses the major child-importing and -exporting nations and is embedded in a formal international treaty known as the Hague Convention.[92] Under the convention's terms, both sending and receiving countries are required to establish a central authority governing adoption, an authority that provides protection for the children involved, tracks and reviews prospective parents, and ensures that no baby-selling occurs.[93]

In commercial terms, compliance with the Hague makes international adoption a fairly cumbersome procedure. Would-be parents need to undergo a home study (as they would with domestic adoption), an immigration clearance and FBI background check, and whatever requirements are imposed by authorities in the child's home country. They typically must provide police reports and medical records and then have all the documents notarized and translated. The paperwork is mammoth, as are the opportunities for error.

As a result, the incentives for independent adoption are considerably reduced. Most would-be parents in the United States rely on licensed agencies to handle overseas adoptions, and agencies have considerable leeway in pricing their foreign packages. Typically, they charge an application fee, a home study fee, and a program fee. Overseas charges are figured separately and generally include a set "donation" to the child's orphanage or baby home in addition to fees to the agency's local facilitator, driver, and interpreters. In exchange for these fees, most agencies can provide prospective parents with a child of their choice, usually within a year.

In international adoption, however, the notion of choice is complicated by the variety available. In domestic adoption, after all, supply essentially controls demand: There are so few (healthy white) babies that parents almost never choose among them. In assisted reproduction, choice is a factor of the components available: the egg, sperm, womb, and embryo that will mix together in an unpredictable way. Parents can choose the basic physical characteristics their child is likely to inherit, but they cannot pick a particular kid. With international adoption, however, choice is simultaneously multiplied and made concrete. When parents adopt abroad, they are almost always choosing to adopt a child who is already born.* They are adopting a particular child, in other words, and one who usually is old enough to have displayed both physical characteristics and a certain personality type. In international adoption, therefore, much more so than in domestic infant adoption or assisted reproduction, parents are literally choosing their child.

This process of selection is deeply embedded in the structure of international adoption. To begin with, parents choose the country from which they would like to adopt. For U.S. adopters, this means choosing from thirty-nine possible nations, ranging, as of 2005, from Belarus to Vietnam. All these countries have available children, but the options they offer are different. In China, for example, nearly all the available children are girls, typically between the ages of ten months and seventeen months. In Russia, there are boys and girls, with some infants and a huge supply of older, institutionalized children. In Guatemala, most of the children are very young, subtly classified as either "Latino" or "Mayan."

When parents choose a country, then, they are also choosing a particular type of child. In many cases, they are also choosing a particular price structure, one that implicitly reveals preferences as well. For example, white children are almost always more expensive than black ones; as Table 2 indicates, the typical cost of adopting a (white) Russian child in 2004 (in addition to travel costs and agency fees) was about $15,000, whereas the cost of a (black) child from Ethiopia was between $6,700 and $8,000. Children of other colors fall somewhere in the middle, ranging from about $6,000 for a Filipino child to about $7,000 for a Chinese and $8,900 for a Colombian.[94] Guatemala stands as a bit of a pricey exception, because children in this heavily Roman Catholic country are frequently placed directly after birth and birth mothers are commonly assumed to be "good girls" forced by cultural constraints to relinquish any child born out of wedlock. Costs also vary sharply by age and degree of handicap. In Russia, for example, the cost of adopting an infant through one prominent agency is $7,000 more than the cost of adopting a school-age child. Handicapped children are frequently offered with some kind of "scholarship" or financial assistance.

At the level of the individual child, meanwhile, international adoption also offers a sometimes shocking array of choices. When parents begin the adoptive

---

*There are some exceptions. In Guatemala, for example, parents occasionally identify a pregnant woman and agree to adopt her child.

TABLE 2 Sample foreign adoption fees, 2004

Agency	Application and agency fees	Program fee: Russia	Program fee: Guatemala	Program fee: China	Program fee: India	Program fee: Ethiopia
Wide Horizons for Children	$5,700	$15,000	$18,240	$7,165	$5,000	$6,700
Holt International	$2,995	NA	$8,690	$9,360	$8,190 (healthy) $5,325 (with health needs)	NA
Angels' Haven	$4,500	$11,000	$17,500	$6,000	NA	$8,000
MAPS International	$2,000	$15,650	$19,000	$12,250	$14,500	NA
Families Thru International Adoption	$4,800	$13,978	$19,000	$3,000	$12,000	NA
Commonwealth Adoptions	$200	$17,000	$26,900	$12,000	$12,000	NA

Sources: Agency Web sites (www.whfc.org; www.holtintl.org; www.angelshaven.org; www. mapsadopt.org, www.ftia.org; www.commonwealthadoption.org) and conversations with author.

process, they usually inform their selected agency of their preferences: whether they want an infant or a younger child, a girl or a boy. They describe the kind of child they feel competent to parent and the kind of family they are hoping to build. Sometimes, the selection ends there. The agency works with its counterpart in the chosen country, identifies a child, and presents him to the prospective parents, usually in the form of a photograph or short video. The parents can choose to accept the child (most do) or wait for a second referral. In other cases, however, parents play a much more active role in the selection process. They actually choose a particular child—from photos or in person—and then begin the process of adopting her.

The most extreme examples of such selection are the online photo listings mentioned earlier. On Web sites like Rainbow Kids or precious.org, agencies regularly list their available charges, organized by country, gender, or age. At any given time, the lists may contain as many as five hundred kids, all of whom are officially eligible for adoption. Many agencies also have their own online lists of waiting children, complete with photos and brief, often heart-wrenching descriptions. Interested parents are urged to contact the agency for more information and to begin the process that will "bring their child home." Although precise numbers are not available, the director of Rainbow Kids estimates that more than six thousand children have been adopted since 1997 from her site alone.[95] Hundreds more are adopted each year through various summer camps or hosting programs that bring older children to the United States to meet prospective families.

There are several ways of viewing these selective arrangements. On the one hand, photo listings and summer camps provide a crucial matching function. They relay information about some of the world's hardest-to-place children: older kids, sibling groups, and babies born with handicaps. They get this information to a wide group of prospective parents, enabling them to find—or pick—their particular child.[96] On the other hand, critics note that such arrangements operate uncomfortably like global bazaars, with well-heeled customers choosing merchandise from a glossy and sentimental catalog.

This brings us to the third distinguishing facet of cross-border adoption. In families that are forged between the first and third worlds it is consistently the parents who come from the wealthier states and the children who migrate out of poverty. It is the poor states that produce children, and the rich that consume them. In the process, poor parents are left behind, serving only as the initial fabricators of other people's children.

This essential equation has caused critics to cast international adoption in a particularly evil light: as a commercial process that both thrives off global poverty and perpetuates it. As Twila Perry, an American legal scholar, argues, "The imbalance in the circumstances . . . involved in international adoption presents a troubling dilemma: In a sense, the access of affluent white Western women to children of color for adoption is often dependent upon the continued desperate circumstances of women in third world nations."[97] Similarly, feminist critics like Janice Raymond assert that international adoption involves trafficking in *both* women and children; like surrogacy, she writes, adoption "encourages *throw-away women* who are discarded after fulfilling their breeding role."[98]

Such criticism, of course, rankles adoption proponents, who insist that international adoption has nothing to do with exploitation or global inequities.[99] Instead it is humanitarianism of the most intimate sort, humanitarianism that literally transplants some of the world's poorest and most vulnerable inhabitants into the homes and hearts of the most privileged. Through international adoption, supporters insist, surplus children are delivered to parents who want them, and surplus capital (via local fees and donations) flows to impoverished states.[100]

And so they do. Yet the claim that international adoption is a virtuous market does not negate the fact that it is nevertheless a market. Adoption agencies hold regular seminars to describe their trade. They list their children online (in some cases) and profile them in glossy magazines. They also charge clearly differentiated prices. It's hard to argue that this isn't commerce, because it is.

The Black Market

It is in the final tier of the baby market, however, that commerce becomes most explicit and extreme. This is the part of the market in which adoption agencies are replaced by baby brokers and money unabashedly changes hands. This is the unsavory but persistent realm of black market babies, a realm populated by infamous intermediaries like Georgia Tann of the Tennessee Children's Home Society, who placed more than one thousand children between 1930 and 1950 and personally reaped more than $1 million in profit. Or Ron Silverton, a California attorney indicted in 1974 for arranging unauthorized adoptions and attempting to sell a person.[101]

It is a world that has recently gone global, too, as evidenced by well-publicized stories of brokers who place attractive children with eager parents and profit handsomely from the exchange.[102] It is difficult to estimate how large this illicit market is or how deeply it affects the broader flow of adoption. In 1975, a congressional hearing estimated that more than five thousand babies were sold each year in the United States, for prices that ranged between $10,000 and $15,000.[103] Today, industry experts estimate that less than 1 percent of domestic adoptions go through implicitly illegal channels, as do perhaps 5 percent of international adoptions.[104] Accusations vary widely across exporting countries, with a handful—Cambodia, Vietnam, India, Guatemala—accounting for the bulk of alleged illegal activity.

Defining this black market, though, is tricky, because nearly all adoptions (aside from those in the foster care system) involve some transfer of money. Indeed, it is this very transfer of money that makes adoption's critics quick to deride it. But black market adoptions have a distinctive set of characteristics, a pattern of trade and behavior that sets them sharply, if subtly, apart.

First, black market adoptions occur by definition outside the boundaries of licensed trade. They are conducted by independent brokers or unlicensed intermediaries who cater exclusively to parents' demands and don't perform the home studies required by state law. The prices involved are often secretive, and key documents are frequently forged. Legitimate adoption is a hugely transparent procedure, involving social workers, judges, and local recording clerks. Black market adoption, by contrast, is quiet and covert, which helps to explain its persistent appeal.

Second, in black market adoption, the prohibition on payment breaks down. Instead of covering only the birth mother's costs for pregnancy and childbirth, baby brokers pay extra, "reimbursing" the mother for relinquishing her child. The monies involved here may be minimal—$180 for a Cambodian infant, according to a 2002 scandal, $20 for an Indian girl—but the principle is key.[105] Under legitimate circumstances, mothers relinquish their children because they cannot, or choose not to, raise them by themselves. These mothers either place their newborns through a court-sanctioned process (the norm in U.S. domestic adoption) or leave them quietly in a baby hospital or public marketplace (the typical route in China). Sometimes, mothers are also judged incapable of parenting and are forced to cede their children to the state. This is a common pattern for children placed in the U.S. foster care system and for many so-called

95

Russian "orphans." Note, however, that none of the relinquishing mothers in these cases was *paid* to place her children. In black market adoption, by contrast, the transaction is explicitly commercial: A mother (or occasionally a father) receives money in exchange for the child.

A third characteristic of black market adoption takes this phenomenon to its logical and egregious extreme. Once children are explicitly purchased and their sale occurs outside formal and transparent channels, it is only a small step toward the outright theft and subsequent resale of children. Thankfully, such cases are rare.[106] But they do occur. In 2001, for example, the United States suspended adoptions from Cambodia, citing allegations of both baby-selling and baby-stealing.[107]

These horrific examples constitute only a tiny fraction of the overall adoptive market. Yet because the extreme end of adoption is so sinister and because even legitimate adoption entails a fair measure of commerce, it is easy to conflate adoption with theft, and for critics to paint all adoptions as thinly veiled versions of baby-selling. As one critic writes, "Adoption in America today is a lucrative industry operating on greed and exploitation, with white babies its precious commodity and prices determined by desperation. Those in the white-baby business are no longer philanthropic individuals . . . but a small group of private entrepreneurs, dealers, and middlemen who have turned a placement into a deal."[108]

What complicates matters even further is that the legal distinction between legitimate and illegitimate adoption is not clear. Following state law, for example, any birth mother can legally arrange for her own child's adoption. In theory, this provision simply allows mothers to decide what is best for their children. In practice, though, it creates a massive loophole: As long as the birth mother agrees, any adoption is technically legal. And any intermediary who "helped" the birth mother or the adoptive parents can reasonably claim to have provided counseling services, legal advice, or any other innocuous service that is difficult to define as illegal. As a result, very few Americans have ever been convicted of baby-selling.[109] Laws are somewhat tighter in Europe, where all the major countries have ratified the Hague Convention and many have laws that explicitly ban baby-selling or child trafficking. Still, even with the toughest legal regime, it remains difficult to determine the provenance of an adopted child or the circumstances that surrounded his or her adoption.[110]

Black market adoption *is* different from legitimate adoption. It occurs furtively and often with forged documents; it involves payment for the child herself; and it occasionally descends into the realm of either kidnapping or theft. But these distinctions are not always obvious, and wily brokers can squeeze rather easily through the loopholes of the law. Moreover, even though legitimate adoption providers despise the black market and the shadow it casts upon all adoption, the legitimate market is itself sharply divided: between public agencies and private, between faith-based nonprofits and independent attorneys. These entities do not like to admit that they are competing among themselves, but they are.

And the terms of competition make it even more difficult to establish any lines. Because if all payment were banished from the world of adoption—a policy often espoused by adoption's foes—then all adoptions would revert to state-run agencies, putting even licensed providers out of business. Similarly, if it were illegal to transport any adopted child across state or national boundaries (another frequent proposal), then scores of intermediaries would lose their commercial niche. In the process, market efficiencies would also vanish, because state-run agencies cannot provide the speed and service of their private counterparts, and state-specific adoption would mean segregating thousands of children far from the parents most likely to adopt them.

This brings us to the central question posed by black market adoption, and indeed by adoption in general. Most people agree that it is inherently wrong to sell a child, that we can never treat babies or the parents who produced them as marketplace commodities.[111] But does this moral prohibition imply that we can never transfer children from one set of parents to another? That we can never allow any form of payment to enter into such a transfer? Does our revulsion for the black market in babies mean that parents can never pay an intermediary to get Yamile or Bulat off the Rainbow Kids list and into their homes? In the contemporary world, adoption undeniably operates as a market. The question is whether this market is necessarily bad.

Selling Souls or Saving Lives? Prospects for the Adoption Market

If one looks at adoption by itself, it's tempting to say yes across the board, to say that money should never enter the relationship between parent and child.[112] It is certainly plausible to suggest that adoption be taken out of private hands and returned fully to governments. It is possible to express deep sympathy for Yamile's and Bulat's plight while still arguing against their adoption. Indeed, on moral grounds, one can argue that the prohibition against selling children is so deep and so crucial that nothing—not even the fate of these children themselves—can violate it.[113]

If one sees adoption as part of a broader baby trade, however, such sweeping pronouncements are more difficult to make. Clearly, profits are being made in other parts of the trade: in infertility treatments, in sperm sales, in surrogacy. By what logic can we argue that the Fertility Institute of Las Vegas can charge its clients $44,800 for a gestational surrogate cycle, but Angels' Haven can't charge $8,000 to place a war orphan from Ethiopia?

Perhaps one can draw a hard and fast line at the child himself, distinguishing between the components of conception and the *product* of that conception. In other words, one can say that from the moment the child is born, he or she can no longer be traded or treated as part of a market transaction. This is a legitimate position. It also, however, often runs contrary to the interests of the child at hand. Because it takes money to bring a little boy from Sierra Leone to Milwaukee; it takes money to care for that little boy in a local orphanage and to ensure that his prospective parents can raise him in an appropriate manner. If this money does not change hands—if, in other words, the market for international adoption were to disappear—that little boy would almost certainly spend his childhood in an institution and without a family.[114] And only a tiny handful of sociologists and child welfare advocates would still maintain that any child is better served by institutional life.[115]

Alternatively, one could allow the transaction to occur but insist that it re-   105 main apart from any market influence. Practically, such a position would mean ceding adoption entirely to the state. It would mean expending state resources and replacing market structures with government bureaucracies. This kind of system is eminently possible; indeed, government agencies control the adoption process in most exporting countries (China, Russia, Guatemala, Peru) and several importing ones (the Netherlands, Australia).

In the United States, however, state-based adoption would clash head-on with a deeply seated preference for choice. It would thrust family-making into bureaucratic hands and would likely engender the kinds of delays and ineffi- ciencies that currently cloud the foster system. In the United States, moreover, a state-based adoption system would stand in even sharper contrast with other elements of the baby market. In Australia, after all, adoption sits closer to the state, but so do IVF, egg donation, and surrogacy. If the United States were somehow to bring adoption out of the market entirely, it would mean creating a sharp dichotomy between reproductive options that can be purchased (eggs, embryos, PGD,* IVF) and those that cannot. It would mean, in practical terms, allowing the rich to purchase procreation while pushing the poor to adopt.

Such a system is indeed possible, and if we take the moment of conception as a clear dividing line then it may be the best we can do. But taking adoption out of the market would lessen the efficiencies that now exist. It would reduce the number of children available for adoption and increase the amount of time involved. It would also impose older-era guidelines on parenting, leaving gov- ernment agencies to determine who is suitable to form a family, and how.

Once again, the trade-offs of such a system become most evident when compared to other means of baby-making. At a societal level, adoption almost certainly provides a better option than assisted reproduction. It draws upon the existing supply of children rather than creates new ones. It conserves financial resources that would otherwise be spent on foster care or institutional arrange- ments, and it avoids the cost of new, higher-tech children.

Admittedly, one wouldn't want childless couples to bear sole responsibility —or indeed any real responsibility—for solving the problem of parentless chil- dren.[116] By the same token, though, it also seems foolhardy to put adoption at a relative *disadvantage* to assisted reproduction. If we let people donate eggs and sperm and embryos, how can we insist that infants be handed to the state? If we let an unmarried fifty-two-year-old woman pay $100,000 for the IVF treat- ment that will provide her with newborn twins, why should we prevent that same woman from paying, say, $25,000 to adopt Sofia or Rafael?[117]

The funny thing about the adoption market is that it works. It doesn't work   110 in every case, of course, and it works better for some kids and parents than

---

*PGD: Preimplantation Genetic Diagnosis.

others. Yet the history of adoption provides a surprisingly consistent picture of success. Whether they adopt through public agencies or private, through friends or foreign lawyers, and whether they adopt infants who look "just like them" or distant toddlers of a different race, most adoptive parents subsequently assess their experiences in rather glowing terms.[118] They embrace their adopted children as theirs and don't seem to harbor any lingering doubts about the nature of the original transaction. The only prevalent complaints revolve around shortages and bureaucratic delays: too few children, too much red tape.

For adopted children and birth parents, the picture is murkier, but not for reasons that relate directly to commerce. Some limited evidence suggests, for example, that adult adoptees resent the transactions that surrounded their placement.[119] Some studies argue that adoptees bear the lingering pain of their birth mother's "rejection" or that they face a lifelong quest to discover their genetic origins.[120] Most adoption experts currently argue that open adoption is better than closed and that adoptees have a right to know the circumstances of their birth.[121] None of these complaints, however, has anything to do with the *business* of adoption. On the contrary, critics reserve their sharpest bile for the old model of state-based or licensed agency adoption, where all transactions were secret and power rested with a handful of social workers.

Similar complaints are voiced by, or on behalf of, birth mothers, now commonly regarded as the most vulnerable element in the adoption triad. During adoption's heyday in the middle of the twentieth century, birth mothers were routinely denied any say in their child's destiny, or even their own. They were routed into unsavory maternity homes by parents or boyfriends, where their children were frequently taken before they even awoke after the birth. For many birth mothers, placing their child for adoption remains a harrowing memory, a loss from which they never fully recover.[122]

Yet again, the tragedy of adoption in these cases has little or nothing to do with the market. Women didn't relinquish their children in the 1950s and 1960s because they had a financial incentive to do so; they relinquished them because they didn't have the means or social standing to raise them on their own. Circumstances changed somewhat after the advent of birth control and abortion, because the sudden dearth of adoptable infants made brokers more willing to offer enticements, and birth mothers more ready to accept them. A far more important change, though, was that birth mothers began to exercise choice and discretion, deciding whether to place their children and, increasingly, with whom.

Again, therefore, the introduction of market forces actually enhanced the options that birth mothers faced. At the extreme, as noted earlier, market forces have put birth mothers into the buyer's position, enabling them, literally, to select from a catalog of potential parents. Such options do not imply that the decision to relinquish a child has become easy, or that birth mothers see their choices as representing some kind of pleasant parental supermarket. By the same token, though, it is difficult to argue that market forces have worsened the plight of birth parents.

Those who do advance accusations along these lines generally focus on [115] the less-developed world, where, they contend, women are coerced by their own poverty to relinquish children they would prefer to raise.[123] But again, it is hard to blame the market for *causing* these women's undeniable pain, or to believe that halting cross-border adoption would do anything to alleviate their situation. Instead, the adoption market sends capital flowing in precisely the direction that adoption's opponents desire: from rich countries to poor, from wealthy parents to abandoned, neglected, or relinquished kids.

The market for adoption isn't always pretty. There are children who come from abusive backgrounds and never recover. There are children who yearn for their genetic origins or cultural roots, children who ache for an identity that eludes them. There are children who go to bad homes, and children, like Anita and Yi-Wei, who may never find homes. It is tempting in this market to focus on the nasty underside and on the abusive practices that will always scar adoption's edges.

But setting adoption within the larger baby business presents a starkly different view. For there are children created by IVF who will also grow up to be abused, children born by sperm or egg donation who will also eventually yearn for their own genetic roots. All these children are also created through market transactions, none of which operate under the regulatory apparatus that has long hovered over adoption.

In fact, the U.S. adoption market—clunky and cumbersome as it may be—could even offer a model of how a modified baby business might function. It is a model where money undeniably changes hands, and where some intermediaries profit from transacting in children. Yet it is also a market that combines a relatively small for-profit segment with a much larger nonprofit one. It is a market where government agencies provide oversight and regulation, and private entities compete to provide service. It is a market where parents have to prove that they are suited to parent, but also where most parents—be they gay or straight, single or married, rich or working class—can hope to find "their" child. And it is a market that essentially works.

In September 2005, just before this book went to press, I returned to the Rainbow Kids and precious.org sites to check on the children I had chosen at random some nine months before. Bulat had found his forever family. Yamile, Sofia, and Rafael were still waiting.

NOTES

1. From a post at www.frua.org, a chat room for parents interested in adopting from Russia and Ukraine.
2. Quoted on "Internet Adoptions," *CNN: The Point with Greta Van Susteren,* January 22, 2001.
3. For critiques along these lines, see, for example, Jacqueline Bhabha, "Moving Babies: Globalization, Markets, and Transnational Adoption," *Fletcher Forum of World Affairs* 28 (Summer 2004): 181–96; Anne L. Babb, *Ethics in American Adoption* (Westport, CT: Bergin & Garvey, 1999); and Christine Gailey, "Seeking

'Baby Right': Race, Class, and Gender in US International Adoption," in *Yours, Mine, Ours . . . and Theirs: International Adoption*, eds. Anne-Lise Rygvold et al. (Oslo: University of Oslo, 2000).

4. See Drucilla Cornell, *At the Heart of Freedom: Feminism, Sex and Equality* (Princeton, NJ: Princeton University Press, 1998); and Emma Nicholson, "Red Light on Human Traffic," *Guardian Unlimited*, July 1, 2004, available at www.guardian.co.uk/child/story/0,7369,1250908,00.html. For a critical response, see Carra E. Greenberg and Diane B. Kunz, "Enemies of Intercountry Adoption," mimeo, Center for Adoption Policy, 2005.

5. Adoption data are surprisingly difficult to find, since they are no longer collected in the United States by a single organization. For recent statistics, see National Adoption Information Clearinghouse, "How Many Children Were Adopted in 2000 and 2001?" (Washington, DC: National Adoption Information Clearinghouse, August 2004).

6. Peter Selman, "Trends in Intercountry Adoption 1998–2003: A Review of Recent Statistics for Receiving States," Adoption Working Paper 1, School of Geography, Politics and Sociology, University of Newcastle upon Tyne, work in progress, March 22, 2005.

7. For descriptions of adoption's long history, see E. Wayne Carp, *Family Matters: Secrecy and Disclosure in the History of Adoption* (Cambridge, MA: Harvard University Press, 1998); Leo Albert Huard, "The Law of Adoption: Ancient and Modern," *Vanderbilt Law Review* 9 (1956): 743–63; and Stephen B. Presser, "The Historical Background of the American Law of Adoption," *Journal of Family Law* 11 (1971): 443–516.

8. For more on the apprentice system, see Philippe Ariès, *Centuries of Childhood*, trans. Robert Baldick (London: Pimlico, 1996).

9. Arthur Wallace Calhoun, *A Social History of the American Family from Colonial Times to the Present* (New York: Arno Press, 1973), 306–7, 232.

10. See the description in John Demos, *A Little Commonwealth: Family Life in Plymouth County* (New York: Oxford University Press, 1970), 73–75; see also Margaret Marsh and Wanda Ronner, *The Empty Cradle: Infertility in America from Colonial Times to the Present* (Baltimore: Johns Hopkins University Press, 1996), 17–20.

11. *Vidal v. Commagere*, 13 La. Ann. 516 (1858). Cited in Presser, "Historical Background of the American Law of Adoption," 461.

12. See the discussion in Presser, "Historical Background of the American Law of Adoption," 463–64.

13. "An Act to Provide for the Adoption of Children," Acts and Resolves passed by the General Court of Massachusetts, Chapter 324 (1851).

14. Julie Berebitsky, *Like Our Very Own: Adoption and the Changing Culture of Motherhood, 1851–1950* (Lawrence: University Press of Kansas, 2000), 23. For other state laws during this period, see William H. Whitmore, *The Law of Adoption in the United States and Especially Massachusetts* (Albany, NY: Joel Munsell, 1876), 79–83; and Jamil S. Zainaldin, "The Emergence of a Modern American Family Law: Child Custody, Adoption, and the Courts, 1796–1851," *Northwestern University Law Review* 73, no. 6 (1979): 1038–89.

15. In 1849, for example, Folks reports the following statistics for one New York public almshouse: "514 children were cared for . . . 280 died." See Homer Folks, *The Care of Destitute, Neglected and Delinquent Children* (New York: Macmillan Co., 1902), 21; see also Peter C. English, "Pediatrics and the Unwanted Child in History: Foundling Homes, Disease and the Origins of Foster Care in New York City, 1860–1920," *Pediatrics* 73 (1984): 699–711.

16. For more on the movement to reform orphanages and the care of abandoned children, see David M. Rothman, *The Discovery of the Asylum: Social Order and Disorder in the New Republic* (Boston: Little, Brown, 1971), especially 206–36; and William I. Trattner, *From Poor Law to Welfare State: A History of Social Welfare in America,* 5th ed. (New York: Free Press, 1994), 112–27.

17. For example, in the first forty-five years of operation, the Boston Female Asylum, an orphanage in Boston, placed only 4.9 percent of its charges for adoption. See Susan Lynne Porter, "The Benevolent Asylum—Image and Reality: The Care and Training of Female Orphans in Boston, 1800–1840" (Ph.D. diss., Boston University, 1984). See also E. Wayne Carp, "Orphanages vs. Adoption: The Triumph of Biological Kinship, 1800–1933," in *With Us Always: A History of Private Charity and Public Welfare,* eds. Donald T. Chritchlow and Charles H. Parker (New York: Rowman & Littlefield Publishers, Inc., 1998), 123–44; and Peter Romanofsky, "The Early History of Adoption Practices, 1870–1930" (Ph.D. diss., University of Missouri at Columbia, 1969). Some charitable institutions did rely on adoption, but they were few in number and generally under attack. See Marsh and Ronner, *The Empty Cradle,* 106–7.

18. From Charles Loring Brace, *The Dangerous Classes of New York,* quoted in Miriam Z. Langsam, *Children West: A History of the Placing-Out System of the New York Children's Aid Society, 1853–1890* (Madison: State Historical Society of Wisconsin, 1964), v.

19. The bulk of the orphan trains ran from 1854 to 1904, although a handful traveled as late as 1929. See Burton Z. Sokoloff, "Antecedents of American Adoption," *Adoption* 3, no. 1 (Spring 1993): 20.

20. For more on Brace and the orphan trains, see also Marilyn Irvin Holt, *The Orphan Trains: Placing Out in America* (Lincoln: University of Nebraska Press, 1992); Langsam, *Children West;* and Henry Thurston, *The Dependent Child: A Story of Changing Aims and Methods in the Care of Dependent Children* (New York: Columbia University Press, 1930).

21. Sokoloff, "Antecedents of American Adoption," 20.

22. Brace himself argued that "very many" of his charges were adopted. Yet the historical record strongly suggests otherwise. See Joan Heifetz Hollinger, "Introduction to Adoption Law and Practice," in *Adoption Law and Practice,* ed. Hollinger (New York: Matthew Bender & Co., Inc., 1991), 1–32. For Brace's account, see Charles L. Brace, "The 'Placing Out' Plan for Homeless and Vagrant Children," *Proceedings of the Conference of Charities and Correction* (Albany, NY: Joel Munsell, 1876), 140.

23. See the discussion in Carp, *Family Matters,* 10–11; Bruce Bellingham, "Institution and Family: An Alternative View of Nineteenth-Century Child Saving," *Social Problems* 33 (December 1986): S33–S57; and Langsam, *Children West,* 45–67.

24. For a description of this proliferation, see Folks, *The Care of Destitute, Neglected, and Delinquent Children,* 64–71, 179–97; LeRoy Ashby, *Saving the Waifs: Reformers and Dependent Children, 1890–1917* (Philadelphia: Temple University Press, 1984); and Holt, *The Orphan Trains,* 106–17.

25. See, for example, Katherine P. Hewins and L. Josephine Webster, "The Work of Child-Placing Agencies," Children's Bureau publication 171 (Washington, DC: Government Printing Office, 1927); W. H. Slingerland, *Child-Placing in Families: A Manual for Students and Social Workers* (New York: Russell Sage Foundation, 1919); and Romanofsky, "The Early History of Adoption Practices," 66–104. For a description of the growing role of sentiment in child placement and the

eventual embrace of foster care, see Viviana Zelizer, *Pricing the Priceless Child: The Changing Social Value of Children* (Princeton, NJ: Princeton University Press, 1985), 177–84; and Susan Tiffin, *In Whose Best Interest? Child Welfare Reform in the Progressive Era* (Westport, CT: Greenwood Press, 1982), 61–109.

26. See Berebitsky, *Like Our Very Own,* 130; and Romanofsky, "The Early History of Adoption Practices," 117–23.

27. See the description in Carp, "Orphanages vs. Adoption," 134.

28. From *Delineator,* May 1908, 808, quoted in Berebitsky, *Like Our Very Own,* 62.

29. Ada Elliot Sheffield, quoted in Carp, *Family Matters,* 18.

30. Robert Grant, "Domestic Relations and the Child," *Scribner's Magazine* 65, May 1919, 527; cited in Zelizer, *Pricing the Priceless Child,* 190.

31. For a description of this shift, see Elizabeth S. Cole and Kathryn S. Donley, "History, Values, and Placement Policy Issues in Adoption," in *The Psychology of Adoption,* eds. David M. Brodzinsky and Marshall D. Schecter (New York: Oxford University Press, 1990), 276–78; and E. Wayne Carp, ed., *Adoption in America: Historical Perspectives* (Ann Arbor: University of Michigan Press, 2002), 199.

32. A similar process occurred in Great Britain, where adoption was legalized in 1926. See Margaret Kornitzer, *Child Adoption in the Modern World* (New York: Philosophical Library, 1952), xi–xiii.

33. See Tiffin, *In Whose Best Interest?* 207–8.

34. Barbara Melosh, *Strangers and Kin: The American Way of Adoption* (Cambridge, MA: Harvard University Press, 2002), 26.

35. For more on the more general embrace of professional social work during this period, see Tiffin, *In Whose Best Interest?* 253–80.

36. During most of this period, professional social workers were adamant about not separating infants from their mothers for at least several months. See E. Wayne Carp, "Professional Social Workers, Adoption, and the Problem of Illegitimacy, 1915–1945," *Journal of Policy History* 6, no. 3 (1994): 161–84. For an alternative view, see Regina Kunzel, "The Professionalization of Benevolence: Evangelicals and Social Workers in the Florence Crittenton Homes, 1915 to 1945," *Journal of Social History* 22 (1988): 21–43.

37. See Melosh, *Strangers and Kin,* 36–38; and Zelizer, *Pricing the Priceless Child,* 169–207.

38. Zelizer, *Pricing the Priceless Child,* 199. For a related picture but lower estimated prices, see Frederick G. Brownell, "Why You Can't Adopt a Baby," *Reader's Digest,* September 1948, 55–59.

39. See *Hearings Before the Subcommittee to Investigate Juvenile Delinquency of the Committee on the Judiciary,* United States Senate, 84th Congress, 1st session, July 15 and 16, 1955 (hereafter cited as Kefauver Commission), 50–71.

40. Kefauver Commission, 10, 110; and "Adoption Tale Told by Unwed Mother," *New York Times,* July 17, 1955, 32.

41. Vera Connolly, "Bargain-Counter Babies," *Pictorial Review* 38 (March 1937), quoted in Zelizer, *Pricing the Priceless Child,* 192–93.

42. Cited in Carp, *Family Matters,* 26. For similar estimates in the late 1940s and early 1950s, see Huard, "The Law of Adoption," 761; and Richard Perlman and Jack Wiener, "Adoption of Children, 1953: A Statistical Analysis," *Iowa Law Review* 40 (1955): 339–40.

43. "Regarding Adoptions," Children's Welfare League of America, Special Bulletin (March 1937), 8, cited in Carp, *Family Matters,* 31.

44. See, for example, "Moppets on the Market: The Problem of Unregulated Adoption," *Yale Law Review* 59 (1950), 715–36. Although not written by a social worker, this article lays out the standard argument that many social workers and licensed agencies put forth.

45. Much of this shift was driven by postwar embarrassment over Nazi atrocities committed under the banner of eugenics. . . .

46. They also began charging for their services. See Zelizer, *Pricing the Priceless Child*, 201–7.

47. Clark Vincent, "Illegitimacy in the Next Decade: Trends and Implications," *Child Welfare* 43 (December 1964): 515.

48. In the days before infant formula, removing a baby from her mother also often meant condemning the child to death.

49. See, for example, Alice Lake, "Babies for the Brave," *Saturday Evening Post*, July 31, 1954, 26–27, 65; and Michael Schapiro, *A Study of Adoption Practice: Adoption of Children with Special Needs* (New York: Child Welfare League of America, 1957).

50. Because out-of-wedlock births have historically been higher among African Americans, and because African American couples have tended to be less interested than whites in adoption, adoption agencies in the United States typically have had trouble finding a sufficient number of black families to adopt all the available black children.

51. Carp, *Family Matters*, 28.

52. For more on changing views toward childlessness during this period, see Elaine Tyler May, *Barren in the Promised Land: Childless Americans and the Pursuit of Happiness* (Cambridge, MA: Harvard University Press, 1997), 127–79.

53. See Arthur D. Sorosky, Annette Baran, and Reuben Pannor, *The Adoption Triangle: The Effects of the Sealed Record on Adoptees, Birth Parents and Adoptive Parents* (Garden City, NY: Anchor Books, 1979), 35.

54. See Kefauver Commission; and Linda Tollett Austin, *Babies for Sale: The Tennessee Children's Home Adoption Scandal* (Westport, CT: Praeger, 1993), 109–27.

55. Lincoln Caplan, *An Open Adoption* (New York: Farrar, Straus & Giroux, 1990), 87; and Austin, *Babies for Sale*, 152–53.

56. By 1976, only four states—Connecticut, Delaware, Massachusetts, and Minnesota—explicitly prohibited private placement. See Margaret V. Turano, "Black-Market Adoptions," *Catholic Lawyer* 22 (Winter 1976): 54.

57. Generally, statutes against baby-selling are expressed as prohibitions against receiving compensation for relinquishing maternal legal rights. For an overview of the relevant statutes, see Avi Katz, "Surrogate Motherhood and the Baby-Selling Laws," *Columbia Journal of Law and Social Problems* 20, no. 1 (1986): 1–53; Turano, "Black-Market Adoptions"; and Daniel G. Grove, "Independent Adoption: The Case for the Gray Market," *Villanova Law Review* 13 (Fall 1967): 116–36.

58. These are very rough estimates based on voluntary disclosure. No data exists for 1945–1950, 1952–1954, or 1956. See Penelope L. Manza, "Adoption Trends: 1944–1975," *Child Welfare Research Notes* #9 (U.S. Children's Bureau, August 1984), 1–4.

59. Berebitsky, *Like Our Very Own*, 173. Kathy S. Stolley, "Statistics on Adoption in the United States," *Future of Children* 3 (Spring 1993): 30–33.

60. Between 1973 and 1983, the number of abortions performed on teenaged girls rose from 244,000 to 412,000. See Alfred Kadushin and Judith A. Martin, *Child Welfare Services* (New York: Macmillan Publishing Co., 1988), 471.

61. Kadushin and Martin, *Child Welfare Services*, 495.
62. Christine Bachrach, "Adoption Plans, Adopted Children and Adoptive Mothers," *Journal of Marriage and the Family* 48 (May 1986): 243–53.
63. Kadushin and Martin, *Child Welfare Services*, 539.
64. This debate became one of the most contested issues in the history of U.S. adoption. For a discussion, see Andrew Billingsly and Jeanne M. Giovannoni, *Children of the Storm: Black Children and American Child Welfare* (New York: Harcourt Brace Jovanovich, 1972); Elizabeth Bartholet, *Nobody's Children: Abuse and Neglect, Foster Drift, and the Adoption Alternative* (Boston: Beacon, 1999); Randall Kennedy, "Orphans of Separatism: The Painful Politics of Transracial Adoption," *American Prospect* 17 (Spring 1994): 38–45; and Lucille J. Grow and Deborah Shapiro, *Black Children—White Parents: A Study of Transracial Adoption* (New York: Child Welfare League of America, 1974).
65. Carp, *Family Matters*, 34; Howard Altstein and Rita J. Simon, *Intercountry Adoption: A Multinational Perspective* (New York: Praeger, 1990), 3.
66. The process was not necessarily simple, because adoptive parents had to document, first, that they satisfied federal criteria for parental fitness; second, that they had fulfilled all requirements of their child's home country; and third, that their child fit a narrow definition of "orphan." For a review and critique of these requirements, see Elizabeth Bartholet, "International Adoption: Current Status and Future Prospects," *The Future of Children: Adoption* 3, no. 1 (Spring 1993): 89–103.
67. INS data, as reported in Adam Pertman, *Adoption Nation: How the Adoption Revolution Is Transforming America* (New York: Basic Books, 2000), 23.
68. In 1979, China instituted a draconian "one child" policy that prohibited couples from bearing more than a single child. Although there were some exceptions, couples were generally required to receive birth permits prior to attempting to conceive, and women either had to be sterilized or use an IUD after the birth of their child. For a discussion of how this policy has affected both adoption and China's own demographics, see Valerie M. Hudson and Andrea M. den Boer, *Bare Branches: Security Implications of Asia's Surplus Male Population* (Cambridge, MA: MIT Press, 2004); and Karin Evans, *The Lost Daughters of China: Abandoned Girls, Their Journey to America and the Search for a Missing Past* (New York: J.P. Tarcher/Putnam, 2000).
69. See Carol Sisco, "Strict Romanian Birth Rules Bred Orphanages, Says Expert," *Salt Lake City Tribune*, November 14, 1991, B1; and Bill Snead, "The Abandoned Children of Romania's Orphanages," *Washington Post*, September 17, 1991, 6.
70. Pertman, *Adoption Nation*, 73; and John Taylor, "Romania's Lost Children . . . Omahans Challenge System, Bring Home Maria," *Omaha World-Herald*, July 2, 1991, 29.
71. *Immigrant Visas Issued to Orphans Coming to the U.S.*, available at http://travel.state.gov/family/adoption/stat/stats_451.html.
72. W. Tyree, "The Business of International Adoption," *Japan Times*, June 9, 1999, 1–2; and Madelyn Freundlich, *The Market Forces in Adoption* (New York: Child Welfare League of America, 2000), 43.
73. Statistics on intercountry adoption are notoriously difficult to find. No international institution collects them, and researchers have thus been forced to cobble together estimates from sending and receiving countries, many of which also have no central collection mechanism. For a discussion of this problem, see R. H. Weil, "International Adoptions: The Quiet Migration," *International Migration*

Review 18, no. 2 (1984): 276–93; and S. Kane, "The Movement of Children for International Adoption: An Epidemiological Perspective," *Social Science Journal* 30, no. 4 (1993): 323–39. For the best recent estimates, see Peter Selman, "The Movement of Children for Intercountry Adoption: A Demographic Perspective," Poster Presentation P275, at XXIVth IUSSP General Population Conference, Salvador, Bahia, Brazil, August 18–24, 2001. Figures for 2003 come directly from Selman, personal conversation with author, February 9, 2005. See also Selman, "Trends in Intercountry Adoption 1998–2003."

74. Precise data are unavailable, because no U.S. agency collects adoption statistics regularly. See *How Many Children Were Adopted in 2000 and 2001?* (Washington, DC: National Adoption Information Clearinghouse, 2004).

75. A fourth category—adoption by a relative or stepparent—is not considered here.

76. Susan Freivalds, "What's New in Adoption?" in "2005 Adoption Guide," special issue, *Adoptive Families* (2005): 11.

77. Complaints about the U.S. foster care system are voluminous. See, for example, Carole A. McKelvey and JoEllen Stevens, *Adoption Crisis: The Truth behind Adoption and Foster Care* (Golden, CO: Fulcrum Publishing, 1994); and "Health Care of Young Children in Foster Care," *Pediatrics* 109, no. 3 (March 2002): 536–41.

78. The Adoption and Foster Care Analysis and Reporting System (AFCARS), estimated as of August 2004, available at http://www.acf.hhs.gov/programs/cb/publications/afcars/report9.htm.

79. For more on parental preferences, see Mark E. Courtney, "The Politics and Realities of Transracial Adoption," *Child Welfare* 76, no. 6 (1997): 749–80.

80. Freundlich, *Market Forces in Adoption*, 68–73.

81. Adoption and Safe Families Act (ASFA) of 1997, P.L. 105–89, November 19, 1997.

82. See Hollinger, "Introduction to Adoption Law and Practice," 1–56; and *How Many Children Were Adopted in 2000 and 2001?* (Washington, DC: National Adoption Information Clearinghouse, 2004).

83. Hollinger, "Introduction to Adoption Law and Practice," 1–68.

84. These costs vary widely. For estimates, see http://costs.adoption.com.

85. For the growth of independent adoption and an argument for its merits, see Mark T. McDermott, "Agency Versus Independent Adoption: The Case for Independent Adoption, *Adoption* 3, no. 1 (Spring 1993): 146–51.

86. See the description in Caplan, *An Open Adoption*, 14–15; and Laura Mansnerus, "Market Puts Price Tags on the Priceless," *New York Times*, October 26, 1998, A1.

87. Interview with Mark T. McDermott, Washington, DC, January 7, 2005. The rate of $350 is at the very high end of the market.

88. See Annette Baran and Reuben Pannor, "Open Adoption," in *The Psychology of Adoption*, eds. Brodzinsky and Schecter, 316–31; and Annette Baran, Reuben Pannor, and Arthur D. Sorosky, "Open Adoption," *Social Work* 21 (1976): 97–105.

89. *2005 Adoption Guide*, 40; *Costs of Adopting: A Factsheet for Families* (Washington, DC: National Adoption Information Clearinghouse, June 2004).

90. Mansnerus, "Market Puts Price Tags on the Priceless," A1.

91. See William L. Pierce, "Accreditation of Those Who Arrange Adoptions Under the Hague Convention on Intercountry Adoption as a Means of Protecting,

Through Private International Law, the Rights of Children," *Journal of Contemporary Health Law and Policy* 12 (1996): 535–59.

92. Formally, the Hague Convention on the Protection of Children and Cooperation in Respect of Intercountry Adoption. See Ethan B. Kapstein, "The Baby Trade," *Foreign Affairs*, November 1, 2003, 115–25; and Peter Selman, "Intercountry Adoption in Europe after the Hague Convention," in *Developments in European Social Policy: Convergence and Diversity*, eds. Rob Sykes and Pete Alcock (Bristol: The Policy Press, 1998), 147–69.

93. The United States has approved the treaty but has yet to formally ratify it.

94. These particular fees are from Wide Horizons for Children, available at www.whfc.org. Other agencies' fees vary but follow a similar pattern.

95. Conversation with author, April 2005.

96. In economic terms, they reduce the information asymmetries that would otherwise exist. For a critical examination of this process, see Lisa Cartwright, "Photographs of 'Waiting Children': The Transnational Adoption Market," *Social Text* 74, vol. 21, no. 1 (Spring 2003): 83–109.

97. Twila L. Perry, "Transracial and International Adoption: Mothers, Hierarchy, Race and Feminist Legal Theory," *Yale Journal of Law and Feminism* 10 (1998): 105.

98. Janice G. Raymond, "The International Traffic in Women: Women Used in Systems of Surrogacy and Reproduction," in *Reconstructing Babylon: Essays on Women and Technology*, ed. H. Patricia Hynes (Bloomington: Indiana University Press, 1991), 97. Italics in original. For similar arguments, see Raymond, *Women as Wombs* (North Melbourne, Australia: Spinifex Press, 1995), 144–54; and Kenneth J. Herrmann Jr. and Barbara Kasper, "International Adoption: The Exploitation of Women and Children," *Affilia* 7, no. 1 (Spring 1992): 45–58.

99. For a balanced argument along these lines, see Madelyn Freundlich, "Families without Borders—I," *UN Chronicle* no. 2 (1999): 88.

100. See, for example, Bartholet, "International Adoption."

101. For Tann, see Zelizer, *Pricing the Priceless Child*, 199; and Austin, *Babies for Sale*. For Silverton and similar cases, see Lynne McTaggart, *The Baby Brokers: The Marketing of White Babies in America* (New York: The Dial Press, 1980); and Nancy C. Baker, *Babyselling: The Scandal of Black Market Adoption* (New York: Vanguard Press, 1978).

102. See, for example, Holly C. Kennard, "Curtailing the Sale and Trafficking of Children: A Discussion of the Hague Conference Convention in Respect of Intercountry Adoptions," *University of Pennsylvania Journal of International Business Law* 14, no. 4 (1994): 623–49.

103. Hearings before the Subcommittee on Children and Youth of the Committee on Labor and Public Welfare, 94th Congress, 1st session (1975), 141–45.

104. Author interviews with Mark T. McDermott, past president of American Academy of Adoption Attorneys; and Thomas C. Atwood, president and CEO, National Council for Adoption, Washington, DC, January 7, 2005.

105. For Cambodia, see Sara Corbett, "Where Do Babies Come From?" *New York Times Sunday Magazine*, June 16, 2002, 42; for India, see Raymond Bonner, "For Poor Families, Selling Baby Girls was Economic Boon," *New York Times*, June 23, 2003, A3; and Gregory Katz, "The £18 Babies," *FT Magazine*, June 19, 2004, 20–23.

106. Even groups critical of international adoption tend to agree that cases of outright kidnapping are extremely rare. See, for example, Marie-Françoise

Lucker-Bubel, "Inter-Country Adoption and Trafficking in Children: An Initial Assessment of the Adequacy of the International Protection of Children and Their Rights" (Geneva: Defense for Children International, 1990), 2. For a discussion of how trafficking allegations skew the debate over international adoption, see Elizabeth Bartholet, *Family Bonds: Adoption and the Politics of Parenting* (Boston: Houghton Mifflin Company, 1993), 150–60.

107. See Corbett, "Where Do Babies Come From?" and Thomas Fields-Meyer et al., "Whose Kids Are They?" *People*, January 19, 2004, 74–78. For earlier allegations, see Marlise Simons, "Abductions in Salvador Fill a Demand: Adoption," *New York Times*, December 17, 1985; and *International Children's Rights Monitor* 5, no. 4 (1988).

108. McTaggart, *The Baby Brokers*, 1. See also the discussion in Daniel G. Grove, "Independent Adoption: The Case for the Gray Market," *Villanova Law Review* 13 (Fall 1967): 116–36.

109. For individual cases, see McTaggart, *The Baby Brokers*; and Robert D. McFadden, "Adoption Lawyer Throws a Party," *New York Times*, March 3, 1979, 26.

110. For a legal discussion of these ambiguities, see James B. Boskey and Joan Heifetz Hollinger, "Placing Children for Adoption," in *Adoption Law and Practice*, ed. Hollinger, 3–26, 3–39.

111. For a classic argument along these lines, see Margaret Jane Radin, "Market Inalienability," *Harvard Law Review* 100 (June 1987): 1849–1937. For a rare and extremely controversial argument in favor of the marketplace, see Elisabeth M. Landes and Richard A. Posner, "The Economics of the Baby Shortage," *Journal of Legal Studies* 7, no. 2 (June 1978): 323–48.

112. For arguments that baby markets are inherently bad, see J. Robert S. Prichard, "A Market for Babies?" *University of Toronto Law Journal* 34 (1984): 341–57; Robin West, "Submission, Choice and Ethics: A Rejoinder to Judge Posner," *Harvard Law Review* 99 (1986): 1449–56; and Tamar Frankel and Francis H. Miller, "The Inapplicability of Market Theory to Adoptions," *Boston University Law Review* 67 (1987): 99–103.

113. See, for example, Perry, "Transracial and International Adoption," 147.

114. Of course, theoretically it is possible that funds and efforts could be devoted to helping the child's relatives or neighbors care for him. This is the option offered by many critics of international adoption. Under current circumstances, however, it seems highly improbable that sufficient monies will flow in this direction.

115. For a discussion, see E. Wayne Carp, "Two Cheers for Orphanages," *Reviews in American History* 24, no. 2 (1996); and Deborah A. Frank et al., "Infants and Young Children in Orphanages: One View from Pediatrics and Child Psychiatry," *Pediatrics* 97 (April 1996): 569–78.

116. As Posner asks rhetorically, "Are the infertile to be blamed for a glut of unwanted children?" See Richard A. Posner, "The Ethics and Economics of Enforcing Contracts of Surrogate Motherhood," *Journal of Contemporary Health Law and Policy* 21 (April 1989): 21–31.

117. For a compelling argument along these lines, see Bartholet, *Family Bonds*.

118. There is a voluminous literature evaluating the success of adoptive placements. See, for example, Rita J. Simon and Howard Altstein, *Transracial Adoptees and Their Families: A Study of Identity and Commitment* (New York: Praeger, 1987); Barbara Tizard, "Intercountry Adoption: A Review of the Evidence," *Journal of Child Psychology and Psychiatry* 32, no. 5 (1991): 743–56; William

Feigelman and Arnold R. Silverman, *Chosen Children* (Westport, CT: Praeger Publishers, 1983); Janet L. Hoopes, "Adoption and Identity Formation," in *The Psychology of Adoption*, eds. Brodzinsky and Schecter, 144–66; and James A. Rosenthal, "Outcomes of Adoption of Children with Special Needs," *The Future of Children: Adoption* 3, no. 1 (Spring 1993): 77–88.

119. For one argument along these lines, see Hearings before the Subcommittee on Children and Youth (1975), 579–81.

120. See Betty Jean Lifton, *Lost and Found: The Adoption Experience* (New York: Dial Press, 1979); and Arthur D. Sorosky, Annette Baran, and Reuben Pannor, "Identity Conflicts in Adoptees," *American Journal of Orthopsychiatry* 45, no. 1 (1975): 18–27.

121. For the classic argument in favor of open adoption, see Annette Baran and Reuben Pannor, "Open Adoption," in *The Psychology of Adoption*, eds. Brodzinsky and Schecter, 316–31; and Annette Baran, Reuben Pannor, and Arthur D. Sorosky, "Open Adoption," *Social Work* 21 (1976): 97–105. For a discussion of the politics behind the open adoption movement, see E. Wayne Carp, *Adoption Politics: Bastard Nation and Ballot Initiative* 58 (Lawrence: University Press of Kansas, 2004).

122. See Anne B. Brodzinsky, "Surrendering an Infant for Adoption: The Birth-mother Experience," in *The Psychology of Adoption*, eds. Brodzinsky and Schecter, 295–315.

123. See, for example, the arguments made in Bhabha, "Moving Babies"; and Perry, "Transracial and International Adoption," 101–64.

Questions for Critical Reading

1. Is adoption a compassionate social practice, a troubling economic market, or both? Analyze Spar's essay and select quotations that support your position.

2. Spar spends a great deal of time detailing the history and evolution of adoption. Why do you think she provides this information? In what ways does it support her argument? Perform a critical reading of the structure of her argument using that section of her essay.

3. According to Spar, what role does race play in adoption? Does this reflect the economic function of race in general?

Exploring Context

1. Spar opens this essay talking about the Rainbow Kids Web site at rainbowkids .com. Explore the site. Is her description of it accurate? What can you find on the site to further support or complicate Spar's argument? Are Yamile, Sofia, and Rafael still waiting to be adopted? How does your exploration relate to your response to Question 3 of Questions for Critical Reading about the role of race in adoption?

2. Visit Adoption.com (adoption.com). Does the site suggest that adoption is a humanitarian endeavor or an economic one? What evidence can you find for each perspective? Use your response on these issues from Question 1 of Questions for Critical Reading in your answer.

3. Spar is currently president of Barnard College. Visit her page on Barnard's site at barnard.edu/president. How does this essay reflect Spar's body of work as an academic and as a leader?

Questions for Connecting

1. Is there a global baby supply chain? Apply Thomas Friedman's ideas about global economics in "The Dell Theory of Conflict Prevention" (p. 121) to Spar's discussion of international adoption, connecting your response to your work on adoptions and economics from Question 1 of Questions for Critical Reading.

2. The Dalai Lama calls for a new ethics for biotechnology in "Ethics and the New Genetics" (p. 76). How do his insights apply to the practice of adoption? Can we use those insights to separate the social and economic aspects of adoption? What ethical guidelines should we follow in this practice?

3. Is adoption consistent with human dignity? Use Francis Fukuyama's understanding of the concept in his essay of that name (p. 142) to explore Spar's analysis. How might Factor X enable us to draw a line between ethical and unethical adoptions?

Language Matters

1. Apostrophes indicate possession. Go through Spar's text and locate some examples of the apostrophe, which is perhaps one of the most frequently misunderstood marks of punctuation. Can you use Spar's ideas about the complexities of adoption to think about why people don't use the apostrophe when they should? What are the complexities of "possession" in today's world, in writing and in reality?

2. Locate the strongest transition in Spar's essay. What makes it strong or effective? How can you use this strategy in your own writing?

3. What are higher and lower order concerns in writing? Apply these concepts to Spar's writing. What are the higher order concerns of the essay? Are there any?

Assignments for Writing

1. Spar states that what separates adoption from the rest of the baby trade is the difference in product: purchasing an existing child through adoption rather than a potential one through assisted reproduction. Write an essay in which you explore the risks, costs, and benefits of assisted reproduction versus adoption. You might want to use your response about the ethics of adoption from Question 2 of Questions for Connecting. Also consider: In which situations is one option better than the other? Why do adoption agencies put potential parents through rigorous testing before they are allowed to adopt? Why, in assisted reproduction, are potential parents not put through the same kind of testing? What are the dangers of adoption or of assisted reproduction?

2. Spar explains that adoption presents unique differences from other aspects of the baby business, including a thriving international black market and contractual agreements between birth and adoptive parents. Write an essay in which you evaluate the ethics of international adoption. You may want to begin with the work you did in Question 1 of Exploring Context and Question 2 of Questions for Connecting. How can we differentiate between children in need and children being sold? Is international adoption a humanitarian or an economic industry?

3. Much of Spar's essay lays out the complications of domestic and international adoptions. Write an essay in which you propose the best means of regulating adoption. Consider: Should governments oversee adoptions, or are they best handled by private agencies? Should domestic adoption be a free market? How can we best regulate international adoptions?

JAMES SUROWIECKI

James **Surowiecki** writes the business column "The Financial
Page" for the *New Yorker* and has contributed to publications
such as *Slate*, the *Wall Street Journal*, and *Wired*. Surowiecki
was also a writer for the Motley Fool Web site and editor-in-
chief for the Fool's "Rogue" column. Surowiecki edited the
anthology *Best Business Crime Fighting of the Year* (2002) before publishing his book *The Wisdom of Crowds: Why the Many
Are Smarter than the Few and How Collective Wisdom Shapes
Business, Economies, Societies, and Nations* (2004).

THE WISDOM
OF CROWDS

JAMES
SUROWIECKI

Surowiecki's argument in *The Wisdom of Crowds* is that
even when the few are elite, brilliant, or successful, the many
are generally smarter. Whether guessing the weight of an ox
at a country fair or the answer to a question on *Who Wants to
Be a Millionaire?* the crowd tends to be remarkably correct. Though the thought is
counterintuitive, a large and largely inexpert group can come up with answers that
are often more accurate than those of any of the smartest individuals in the group.
Surowiecki shows how group wisdom can predict everything from elections to the
location of a lost submarine more accurately than individual experts. This technique,
Surowiecki argues, can be as effective in the worlds of business, economics, and
science as it is in our daily life.

In "Committees, Juries, and Teams: The *Columbia* Disaster and How Small
Groups Can Be Made to Work," from *The Wisdom of Crowds*, Surowiecki acknowledges that sometimes collective knowledge can fail—with disastrous consequences.
However, these exceptions, including "verdict-based" juries and the Mission Management Team of the space shuttle *Columbia* during its final mission, prove the rule
while underscoring that it's not sufficient simply to seek the advice of the crowd.
Surowiecki suggests that groups are correct only under specific circumstances.
Understanding how to foster those circumstances is part of Surowiecki's goal in this
excerpt.

Group work is frequently a requirement of college, and it is also a common
working practice across an array of professions and careers. Knowing how small
groups can fail and, more important, knowing how to make them succeed can offer
you valuable insights for your future.

▶ TAGS: *collaboration*, *education*, *diversity*, *knowledge*, *groups*

Committees, Juries, and Teams: The *Columbia* Disaster and How Small Groups Can Be Made to Work

On the morning of January 21, 2003, the Mission Management Team (MMT) for NASA mission STS-107—the twenty-eighth flight of the space shuttle *Columbia*—held a teleconference, its second since the *Columbia*'s launch on January 16. An hour before the meeting, Don McCormack had been briefed by members of the Debris Assessment Team (DAT), a group of engineers from NASA, Boeing, and Lockheed Martin, who had spent much of the previous five days evaluating the possible consequences of a large-debris strike on the *Columbia*. During the shuttle's ascent into the atmosphere, a large piece of foam had broken off the left bipod area of the shuttle's external fuel tank and had smashed into the ship's left wing. None of the cameras that were tracking the shuttle's launch had provided a clear picture of the impact, so it was difficult to tell how much damage the foam might have caused. And although by January 21 a request had been made for on-orbit pictures of the *Columbia*, they had not been approved. So the DAT had done what it could with the information it had, first estimating the size of the foam and the speed at which it had struck the *Columbia*, and then using an algorithm called Crater to predict how deep a piece of debris that size and traveling at that speed would penetrate into the thermal-protection tiles that covered the shuttle's wings.

The DAT had reached no conclusions, but they made it clear to McCormack that there was reason to be concerned. McCormack did not transmit that sense of concern to the MMT during its teleconference. The foam strike was not mentioned until two-thirds of the way through the meeting, and was brought up only after discussions of, among other things, a jammed camera, the scientific experiments on the shuttle, and a leaky water separator. Then Linda Ham, who was the MMT leader, asked McCormack for an update. He simply said that people were investigating the possible damage and what could potentially be done to fix it, and added that when the *Columbia* had been hit by a similar strike during mission STS-87, five years earlier, it had suffered "fairly significant damage." This is how Ham answered: "And I really don't think there is much we can do so it's not really a factor during the flight because there is not much we can do about it."

Ham, in other words, had already decided that the foam strike was inconsequential. More important, she decided for everyone else in the meeting that it was inconsequential, too. This was the first time the MMT had heard any details about the foam strike. It would have been logical for McCormack to outline the possible consequences and talk about what the evidence from past shuttles that had been struck with debris showed. But instead the meeting moved on.

Hindsight is, of course, twenty-twenty, and just as with the critiques of the U.S. intelligence community after September 11, it's perhaps too easy to fault the MMT at NASA for its failure to see what would happen to the *Columbia* when it reentered the Earth's atmosphere on February 1. Even those who have been exceptionally critical of NASA have suggested that focusing on this one team is a mistake because it obscures the deep institutional and cultural problems that plague the agency (which happen to be many of the same problems that plagued the agency in 1986, when the *Challenger* exploded). But while NASA clearly is an object lesson in organizational dysfunction, that doesn't fully explain just why the MMT handled the *Columbia* crisis so badly. Sifting through the evidence collected by the Columbia Accident Investigation Board (CAIB), there is no way to evade the conclusion that the team had an opportunity to make different choices that could have dramatically improved the chances of the crew surviving. The team members were urged on many different occasions to collect the information they needed to make a reasonable estimate of the shuttle's safety. They were advised that the foam might, in fact, have inflicted enough damage to cause "burn-through"—heat burning through the protective tiles and into the shuttle's fuselage—when the shuttle reentered the Earth's atmosphere. The team's leaders themselves raised the possibility that the debris damage might have been severe. And yet the MMT as a whole never came close to making the right decision on what to do about the *Columbia*.

In fact, the performance of the MMT is an object lesson in how not to run a   5
small group, and a powerful demonstration of the way in which, instead of making people wiser, being in a group can actually make them dumber. This is important for two reasons. First, small groups are ubiquitous in American life, and their decisions are consequential. Juries decide whether or not people will go to prison. Boards of directors shape, at least in theory, corporate strategy. And more and more of our work lives are spent on teams or, at the very least, in meetings. Whether small groups can do a good job of solving complex problems is hardly an academic question.

Second, small groups are different in important ways from groups such as markets or betting pools or television audiences. Those groups are as much statistical realities as experiential ones. Bettors do get feedback from each other in the form of the point spread, and investors get feedback from each other in the stock market, but the nature of the relationship between people in a small group is qualitatively different. Investors do not think of themselves as members of the market. People on the MMT thought of themselves as members of that team. And the collective wisdom that something like the Iowa Electronic Markets produces is, at least when it's working well, the result of many different independent judgments, rather than something that the group as a whole has consciously come up with. In a small group, by contrast, the group—even if it is an ad hoc group formed for the sake of a single project or experiment—has an identity of its own. And the influence of the people in the group on each other's judgment is inescapable.

What we'll see is that this has two consequences. On the one hand, it means small groups can make very bad decisions, because influence is more direct and immediate and small-group judgments tend to be more volatile and extreme. On the other hand, it also means that small groups have the opportunity to be more than just the sum of their parts. A successful face-to-face group is more than just collectively intelligent. It makes everyone work harder, think smarter, and reach better conclusions than they would have on their own. In his 1985 book about Olympic rowing, *The Amateurs*, David Halberstam writes: "When most oarsmen talked about their perfect moments in a boat, they referred not so much to winning a race but to the feel of the boat, all eight oars in the water together, the synchronization almost perfect. In moments like that, the boat seemed to lift right out of the water. Oarsmen called that the moment of *swing*." When a boat has swing, its motion seems almost effortless. Although there are eight oarsmen in the boat, it's as if there's only one person—with perfect timing and perfect strength—rowing. So you might say that a small group which works well has intellectual swing.

Swing, though, is hard to come by. In fact, few organizations have figured out how to make groups work consistently well. For all the lip service paid, particularly in corporate America, to the importance of teams and the need to make meetings more productive, it's still unusual for a small group to be more than just the sum of its parts. Much of the time, far from adding value to their members, groups seem to subtract it. Too often, it's easy to agree with Ralph Cordiner, the former chairman of General Electric, who once said, "If you can name for me one great discovery or decision that was made by a committee, I will find you the one man in that committee who had the lonely insight—while he was shaving or on his way to work, or maybe while the rest of the committee was chattering away—the lonely insight that solved the problem and was the basis for the decision." On this account, groups are nothing but obstacles, cluttering the way of people whose time would be better spent alone.

> **Instead of making people wiser, being in a group can actually make them dumber.**

The performance of the MMT helps explain why. First, the team started not with an open mind but from the assumption that the question of whether a foam strike could seriously damage the shuttle had already been answered. This was, to be fair, partly a matter of bad luck, since one of the team's technical advisers was convinced from the beginning that foam simply could do no serious damage, and kept saying so to anyone who would listen. But there was plenty of evidence to suggest otherwise. Rather than begin with the evidence and work toward a conclusion, the team members worked in the opposite direction. More egregiously, their skepticism about the possibility that something might really be wrong made them dismiss the need to gather more information, especially in the form of pictures, leading to the DAT's requests for on-orbit images being rejected. Even when MMT members dealt with the possibility that there might be a real problem with *Columbia*, their conviction that nothing was wrong limited discussion and made them discount evidence to the contrary. In that sense, the team succumbed to what psychologists call "confirmation bias," which causes decision makers to unconsciously seek those bits of information that confirm their underlying intuitions.

These problems were also exacerbated by the team's belief that it knew more than it did. For instance, when the shuttle managers turned down the request for pictures, one of the justifications they offered was that the resolution

10

of the images would not be good enough to detect the small area where the foam struck. In fact, as the CAIB noted, none of the managers had the necessary security clearances to know how good the resolution of the photos would be, nor did any of them ask the Department of Defense—which would have taken the pictures—about picture quality. In other words, they were "making critical decisions about imagery capabilities based on little or no knowledge," and doing so with an air of complete assurance.

Social scientists who study juries often differentiate between two approaches juries take. Evidence-based juries usually don't even take a vote until after they've spent some time talking over the case, sifting through the evidence, and explicitly contemplating alternative explanations. Verdict-based juries, by contrast, see their mission as reaching a decision as quickly and decisively as possible. They take a vote before any discussion, and the debate after that tends to concentrate on getting those who don't agree to agree. The MMT's approach was practically, though not intentionally, verdict-based. You can see this especially clearly in the way Linda Ham asked questions. On January 22, for instance, the day after the meeting where the foam was first mentioned, Ham e-mailed two members of the team about whether the foam strike might, in fact, pose a threat to the shuttle's safety. "Can we say that for any ET [external tank] foam lost," she wrote, "no 'safety of flight' damage can occur to the Orbiter because of the density?" The answer that Ham wanted was built into the question. It was a way of deflecting genuine inquiry even while seeming to pursue it. As it happens, one of the members of the team did not give Ham the answer she was looking for. Lambert Austin answered her question by writing, "NO," in capital letters, and then went on to explain that there was no way at that point to "PRECLUDE" the possibility that the foam might have seriously damaged the tiles. Yet Austin's cautionary note garnered little attention.

One reason for the team's lack of follow-through may have been its implicit assumption that if something was wrong, there was no possibility of fixing it. At that January 21 meeting, you'll remember, Ham said, "And I really don't think there is much we can do so it's not really a factor during the flight because there is not much we can do about it." Two days later, Calvin Schomburg, the technical expert who insisted throughout that the foam could not seriously damage the tiles, met with Rodney Rocha, a NASA engineer who had become the unofficial representative of the DAT. By this point, the DAT was increasingly concerned that the damage inflicted by the foam could potentially lead to burn-through on reentry, and Rocha and Schomburg argued over the question. At the end of the discussion, Schomburg said that if the tiles had been severely damaged, "Nothing could be done."

The idea that nothing could have been done if the damage to the tiles had been uncovered in time was wrong. In fact, as part of the CAIB investigation, NASA engineers came up with two different strategies that might have brought the *Columbia* crew back to Earth safely (though the shuttle itself was doomed from the moment the foam struck). There was no reason for the MMT to know what those strategies were, of course. But here again, the team had made a decision before looking at the evidence. And that decision—which roughly amounted to saying, "If there is a problem, we won't be able to find a solution"—undoubtedly shaped the team's approach to figuring out whether there was a problem at all. In fact, the CAIB report includes personal notes from an unnamed NASA source that say that when Ham canceled the DAT's request for pictures of the *Columbia*'s wing, "[she] said it was no longer being pursued since even if we saw something, we couldn't do anything about it." This was not exactly the ethos that brought *Apollo 13* safely back to Earth.

One of the real dangers that small groups face is emphasizing consensus over dissent. The extreme version of this, . . . is the kind of groupthink that Irving Janis described in his account of the planning of the Bay of Pigs, where the members of the group become so identified with the group that the possibility of dissent seems practically unthinkable. But in a more subtle way small groups can exacerbate our tendency to prefer the illusion of certainty to the reality of doubt. On January 24, the DAT engineers met again with Don McCormack, who had become their unofficial liaison to the MMT, to present the findings of their foam-strike study. The briefing room where the presentation took place was so crowded that engineers ended up out in the hallway, which said a lot about how worried people were. In any case, the DAT offered five different scenarios of what might have happened. The team's conclusion was that it was likely that the shuttle was safe. But they qualified their conclusion by saying that their analysis was profoundly limited by their tools and their lack of good information. Because the MMT had refused to authorize on-orbit images, the engineers did not know where exactly the foam had struck. And the Crater algorithm they were using had been designed to measure the impact of pieces of debris hundreds of times smaller than the one that hit *Columbia*, so there was no way to be sure that its results were accurate. The engineers stressed, in other words, how uncertain their analysis was. But NASA management focused instead on their conclusion.

An hour after the briefing, the MMT met, and McCormack summarized   15 what the DAT had said. "They do show obviously there's potential for significant damage here, but thermal analysis does not indicate that there is potential for a burn-through," he said. "Obviously there is a lot of uncertainty in all this in terms of the size of the debris and where it hit and the angle of incidence and it's difficult." This was a relatively obscure way of explaining that the engineers' analysis was built on a lot of untested assumptions, but it was at least an attempt at caution. Ham responded by again asking a question that answered itself: "No burn-through, means no catastrophic damage and the localized heating damage would mean a tile replacement?" McCormack said, "We do not see any kind of safety of flight issue here yet in anything that we've looked at." Ham came back with another nothing-is-wrong question: "No safety of flight and no issue for this mission nothing that we're going to do different, there may be a turnaround?" Then, after a short interchange between Ham and McCormack and Calvin Schomburg, one of the other team members on the conference call said that they hadn't been able to hear what McCormack had said. Ham summarized neatly: "He was just reiterating with Calvin that he doesn't believe that there is any burn-through so no safety of flight kind of issue, it's more of a turnaround issue similar to what we've had on other flights. That's it? Alright, any questions on that?" For all intents and purposes, when that meeting ended, the *Columbia*'s fate had been sealed.

What's most striking about that January 24 meeting is the utter absence of debate and minority opinions. As the CAIB noted, when McCormack summarized the DAT's findings, he included none of its supporting analysis nor any discussion of whether there was a division of opinion on the team about its conclusions. More strikingly, not one member of the MMT asked a question. Not one member expressed any interest in seeing the DAT study. One would have thought that when McCormack mentioned the uncertainties in the analysis, someone would have asked him to explain and perhaps even quantify those uncertainties. But no one did. In part, that may have been because Ham was so obviously anxious for the problem to be resolved, and so convinced that there was nothing to talk about. Her attempts to briskly summarize McCormack's conclusions — "No burn-through, means no catastrophic damage" — effectively shut off discussion. And anyone who's ever been in a business meeting knows that "Alright, any questions on that?" really means "There are no questions on that, right?"

The MMT failed to make the right decision in part because of problems that are specific to the culture of NASA. Although we think of NASA as a fundamentally meritocratic, bottom-up culture, it is in fact deeply hierarchical. This meant that even though the DAT engineers had serious qualms from the beginning about the foam strike, their concerns — and, in particular, their insistence that they needed images of the Orbiter's wing before they could make a truly informed analysis — never received a serious hearing from the MMT. At the same time, the MMT violated nearly every rule of good group decision making. To begin with, the team's discussions were simultaneously too structured and not structured enough. They were too structured because most of the discussions — not just about the debris strike, but about everything — consisted of Ham asking a question and someone else answering it. They were not structured enough because no effort was made to ask other team members to comment on particular questions. This is almost always a mistake, because it means that decisions are made based on a very limited supply of analysis and information. One of the consistent findings from decades of small-group research is that group deliberations are more successful when they have a clear agenda and when leaders take an active role in making sure that everyone gets a chance to speak.

The team also, as I've mentioned, started with its conclusion. As a result, every new piece of information that came in was reinterpreted to fit that conclusion. This is a recurring problem with small groups that have a hard time incorporating new information. Social psychologist Garold Stasser, for instance, ran an experiment in which a group of eight people was asked to rate the performance of thirty-two psychology students. Each member of the group was given two relevant pieces of information about the students (say, their grades and their test scores), while two members of the group were given two extra pieces of information (say, their performance in class, etc.), and one member of the group received another two. Although the group as a whole therefore had six pieces of useful information, their ratings were based almost entirely on the two pieces of information that they all shared. The new information was discounted as either unimportant or unreliable. Stasser has also shown that in unstructured, free-flowing discussions, the information that tends to be talked about the most is, paradoxically, the information that everyone already knows. More curiously, information can be presented and listened to and still make little difference, because its contents are misinterpreted. New messages are often modified so that they fit old messages, which is especially dangerous since unusual messages often add the most value. (If people are just saying what you expect them to say, they're hardly likely to change your thinking.) Or they are modified to suit a preexisting picture of the situation.

What was missing most from the MMT, of course, was diversity, by which I mean not sociological diversity but rather cognitive diversity. James Oberg, a former Mission Control operator and now NBC News correspondent, has made the counterintuitive point that the NASA teams that presided over the *Apollo* missions were actually more diverse than the MMT. This seems hard to believe, since every engineer at Mission Control in the late 1960s had the same crew cut and wore the same short-sleeved white shirt. But as Oberg points out, most of those men had worked outside of NASA in many different industries before coming to the agency. NASA employees today are far more likely to have come to the agency directly out of graduate school, which means they are also far less likely to have divergent opinions. That matters because, in small groups, diversity of opinion is the single best guarantee that the group will reap benefits from face-to-face discussion. Berkeley political scientist Chandra Nemeth has shown in a host of studies of mock juries that the presence of a minority viewpoint, all by itself, makes a group's decisions more nuanced and its decision-making process more rigorous. This is true even when the minority viewpoint turns out to be ill conceived. The confrontation with a dissenting view, logically enough, forces the majority to interrogate its own positions more seriously. This doesn't mean that the ideal jury will follow the plot of *Twelve Angry Men*, where a single holdout convinces eleven men who are ready to convict that they're all wrong. But it does mean that having even a single different opinion can make a group wiser. One suspects that, had there been a single devil's advocate pushing the idea that the foam strike might have seriously damaged the wing, the MMT's conclusion would have been very different.

> **When that meeting ended, the *Columbia*'s fate had been sealed.**

Without the devil's advocate, though, it's likely that the group's meetings actually made its judgment about the possible problem worse. That's because of a phenomenon called "group polarization." Usually, when we think of deliberation, we imagine that it's a kind of recipe for rationality and moderation, and assume that the more people talk about an issue, the less likely they will be to adopt extreme positions. But evidence from juries and three decades of experimental studies suggests that much of the time, the opposite is true. 20

Group polarization is still a phenomenon that is not well understood, and there are clearly cases where it has little or no effect. But since the 1960s, sociologists have documented how, under certain circumstances, deliberation does not moderate but rather radicalizes people's point of view. The first studies of the phenomenon tried to elicit people's attitudes toward risk, by asking them what they would do in specific situations. For instance, they were asked, "If a man with a severe heart illness is told that he must either change his way of life completely or have an operation that will either cure him or kill him, what should he do?" Or, "If an electrical engineer who has a safe job at a small salary is given the chance to take a new job that pays much better but is also less secure, should he move?" Individuals answered these questions privately at first, then gathered into groups to reach collective decisions. At first, researchers thought that group discussions made people more likely to advocate risky positions, and they termed this the "risky shift." But as time went on, it became clear that the shift could be in either direction. If a group was made up of people who were generally risk averse, discussion would make the group even more cautious, while groups of risk takers found themselves advocating riskier positions. Other studies showed that people who had a pessimistic view of the future became even more pessimistic after deliberations. Similarly, civil juries that are inclined to give large awards to plaintiffs generally give even larger awards after talking it over.

More recently, University of Chicago law professor Cass Sunstein has devoted a great deal of attention to polarization, and in his book *Why Societies Need Dissent*, he shows both that the phenomenon is more ubiquitous than was once thought and that it can have major consequences. As a general rule, discussions tend to move both the group as a whole and the individuals within it toward more extreme positions than the ones they entered the discussion with.

Why does polarization occur? One reason is because of people's reliance on "social comparison." This means more than that people are constantly comparing themselves to everyone else (which, of course, they are). It means that people are constantly comparing themselves to everyone else with an eye toward maintaining their relative position within the group. In other words, if you start out in the middle of the group and you believe the group has moved, as it were, to the right, you're inclined to shift your position to the right as well, so that relative to everyone else you're standing still. Of course, by moving to the right you're moving the group to the right, making social comparison something of a self-fulfilling prophecy. What's assumed to be real eventually becomes real.

It's important to see, though, that polarization isn't just the result of people trying to stay in tune with the group. It also results, strangely, from people doing their best to figure out what the right answer is. As we saw in our discussion of social proof—remember the passersby who ended up staring into an empty sky—people who are uncertain about what they believe will look to other members of the group for help. That's the point of deliberating, after all. But if a majority of the group already supports one position, then most of the arguments that will be made will be in support of that position. So the uncertain people are likely to be swayed in that direction, in part simply because that's more of what they'll hear. Similarly, people who have more extreme positions are more likely to have strong, coherent arguments in favor of their positions and are also more likely to voice them.

This matters because all the evidence suggests that the order in which   25
people speak has a profound effect on the course of a discussion. Earlier comments are more influential, and they tend to provide a framework within which the discussion occurs. As in an information cascade, once that framework is in place, it's difficult for a dissenter to break it down. This wouldn't be a problem if the people who spoke earliest were also more likely to know what they were talking about. But the truth is that, especially when it comes to problems where there is no obvious right answer, there's no guarantee that the most-informed speaker will also be the most influential. On juries, for instance, two-thirds of all foremen—who lead and structure deliberations—are men, and during deliberations men talk far more than women do, even though no one has ever suggested that men as a gender have better insight into questions of guilt and innocence. In groups where the members know each other, status tends to shape speaking patterns, with higher-status people talking more and more often than lower-status people. Again, this wouldn't matter as much if the authority of higher-status people was derived from their greater knowledge. But oftentimes it doesn't. Even when higher-status people don't really know what they're talking about, they're more likely to speak. A series of experiments with military fliers who were asked to solve a logic problem, for instance, found that pilots were far more likely to speak convincingly in defense of their solution than navigators were, even when the pilots were wrong and the navigators were right. The navigators deferred to the pilots—even when they had never met the pilots before—because they assumed that their rank meant they were more likely to be right.

That kind of deference is important, because in small groups ideas often do not succeed simply on their own merits. Even when its virtues may seem self-evident, an idea needs a champion in order to be adopted by the group as a whole. That's another reason why a popular position tends to become more popular in the course of deliberations: It has more potential champions to begin with. In a market or even a democracy, champions are far less important because of the sheer number of potential decision makers. But in a small group, having a strong advocate for an idea, no matter how good it is, is essential. And when advocates are chosen, as it were, on the basis of status or talkativeness, rather than perceptiveness or keenness of insight, then the group's chance of making a smart decision shrinks.

Talkativeness may seem like a curious thing to worry about, but in fact talkativeness has a major impact on the kinds of decisions small groups reach. If you talk a lot in a group, people will tend to think of you as influential almost by default. Talkative people are not necessarily well liked by other members of the group, but they are listened to. And talkativeness feeds on itself. Studies of group dynamics almost always show that the more someone talks, the more he is talked to by others in the group. So people at the center of the group tend to become more important over the course of a discussion.

This might be okay if people only spoke when they had expertise in a particular matter. And in many cases, if someone's talking a lot, it's a good sign that they have something valuable to add. But the truth is that there is no clear correlation between talkativeness and expertise. In fact, as the military-flier studies suggest, people who imagine themselves as leaders will often overestimate their own knowledge and project an air of confidence and expertise that is unjustified. And since, as political scientists Brock Blomberg and Joseph Harrington suggest, extremists tend to be more rigid and more convinced of their own rightness than moderates, discussion tends to pull groups away from the middle. Of course, sometimes truth lies at the extreme. And if the people who spoke first and most often were consistently the people with the best information or the keenest analysis, then polarization might not be much of a problem. But it is.

The obvious temptation is to do away with or at least minimize the role that small groups play in shaping policy or making decisions. Better to entrust one reliable person—who at least we know will not become more extreme in his views—with responsibility than trust a group of ten or twelve people who at any moment, it seems, may suddenly decide to run off a cliff. It would be a mistake to succumb to that temptation. First of all, groups can be, as it were, depolarized. In a study that divided people into groups of six while making sure that each group composed two smaller groups of three who had strongly opposed views, it was found that discussion moved the groups from the extremes and toward each other. That same study found that as groups became less polarized, they also became more accurate when they were tested on matters of fact.

More important, as solid as the evidence demonstrating group polarization 30 is, so too is the evidence demonstrating that nonpolarized groups consistently make better decisions and come up with better answers than most of their members, and surprisingly often the group outperforms even its best member. What makes this surprising is that one would think that in a small group, one or two confused people could skew the group's collective verdict in the wrong direction. (The small group can't, in that sense, rely on errors canceling themselves out.) But there's little evidence of that happening.

One of the more impressive studies of small-group performance was done in 2000 by Princeton economists Alan S. Blinder and John Morgan. Blinder had been vice chairman of the Federal Reserve Board during the mid-1990s, and the experience had made him deeply skeptical of decision making by committee. (Interest-rate changes are set by the Federal Open Market Committee, which consists of twelve members, including the seven members of the Federal Reserve Board and five presidents of regional Federal Reserve banks.) So he and Morgan designed a study that was meant to find out if groups could make intelligent decisions and if they make decisions as a group quickly, since one of the familiar complaints about committees is that they are inefficient.

The study consisted of two experiments that were meant to mimic, crudely, the challenges faced by the Fed. In the first experiment, students were given urns that held equal numbers of blue balls and red balls. They started to draw the balls from the urns, having been told that sometime after the first ten draws, the proportions in the urn would shift, so that 70 percent of the balls would be red and 30 percent blue (or vice versa). The goal was to identify, as soon as possible, which color had become more prevalent. This was roughly analogous to the Fed's job of recognizing when economic conditions have changed and whether a shift in monetary policy is needed. To place a premium on making the right decision quickly, students were penalized for every draw they made after the changeover had happened. The students played the game by themselves first, then played together as a group with free discussion, played as individuals again, and finally once more as a group. (This was to control for the effect of learning.) The group's decisions were both faster and more accurate (the group got the direction right 89 percent of the time, versus 84 percent for individuals), and outperformed even the best individual.

The second experiment demanded more of the students. Essentially, they were asked to play the role of central bankers, and to set interest rates in response to changes in inflation and unemployment. What the experiment was really asking was whether they could detect when the economy had started to slow or was picking up steam, and whether they would move interest rates in the right direction in response. Once again, the group made better decisions than the individuals, who moved interest rates in the wrong direction far more often, and made them as quickly as the individuals. Most strikingly, there was no correlation between the performance of the smartest person in a group and the performance of that group. In other words, the groups were not just piggybacking on really smart individuals. They genuinely were smarter than the smartest people within them. A Bank of England study modeled on Blinder and Morgan's experiment reached identical conclusions: Groups could make intelligent decisions quickly, and could do better than their smartest members.

Given what we've already seen, this is not shocking news. But there are two important things about these studies. The first is that group decisions are not inherently inefficient. This suggests that deliberation can be valuable when done well, even if after a certain point its marginal benefits are outweighed by the costs. The second point is probably obvious, although a surprising number of groups ignore it, and that is that there is no point in making small groups part of a leadership structure if you do not give the group a method of aggregating the opinions of its members. If small groups are included in the decision-making process, then they should be allowed to make decisions. If an organization sets up teams and then uses them for purely advisory purposes, it loses the true advantage that a team has: namely, collective wisdom. One of the more frustrating aspects of the Columbia story is the fact that the MMT never voted on anything. The different members of the team would report on different aspects of the mission, but their real opinions were never aggregated. This was a mistake, and it would have been a mistake even had the Columbia made it home safely.

Questions for Critical Reading

1. Much of Surowiecki's essay is about the many ways in which small groups can fail. Working from his argument, what are some elements essential to the success of small groups? Use quotations from the text to develop your answer. You will need to read his text critically to compose your response, since it will depend on abstracting those factors essential to the success rather than the failure of small groups.

2. What is "group polarization"? Define the concept using Surowiecki's text and then provide an example from your own experience.

3. Are the benefits of small groups worth the risk? What does Surowiecki think? Begin by critically rereading Surowiecki's text and then support your position by using quotations from the text.

Exploring Context

1. At the center of Surowiecki's analysis is the *Columbia* disaster. Visit NASA's Web site at nasa.gov. Can you find any evidence of change in NASA's culture that might prevent such a disaster from happening again? How are missions handled? Who seems to work there?

2. Visit the Web site for the Advocates, a jury consulting firm, at theadvocates.com. How might such a service influence the small group dynamics of a jury? How do they represent themselves in terms of Surowiecki's argument? You may want to draw from your work on group polarization in Question 2 of Questions for Critical Reading.

3. How do small groups work together online? Explore an online collaboration tool such as Google Docs (docs.google.com). How does the interface promote collaboration? How does it open that collaboration to the pitfalls of small groups documented by Surowiecki? You may want to draw from your work on small groups from Question 1 of Questions for Critical Reading.

Questions for Connecting

1. Can the failure of small groups help explain the challenges of cultivating community and diversity on college campuses? Synthesize Surowiecki's ideas and Rebekah Nathan's analysis in "Community and Diversity" (p. 228).

2. Michael Pollan discusses a different kind of small group in "The Animals: Practicing Complexity" (p. 281). In what ways are organic farming ecosystems like the small groups that Surowiecki discusses? How does the success of organic farming point to strategies for small group success? Relate your response to your answer to Question 1 of Questions for Critical Reading.

3. What is the economical potential—and risk—of small groups? Synthesize Surowiecki's ideas and Thomas Friedman's discussion of global supply chains in "The Dell Theory of Conflict Prevention" (p. 121).

Language Matters

1. Indexes help you locate important information quickly. Create a simple index for Surowiecki's essay. What terms or entries would you include? How often do they appear in the text?

2. Surowiecki ultimately believes in the power of small groups. Working in small groups in class, debate a common grammatical issue or error, such as the run-on sentence. Should it be an error? How important is it? How does your discussion reflect Surowiecki's ideas?

3. Why is "*Columbia*" italicized in this essay? What are the rules for using italics? Develop a system to help you remember when to use them.

Assignments for Writing

1. Surowiecki discusses ways in which group dynamics contributed to the failure of the *Columbia*'s Mission Management Team. Using Surowiecki's observations, write a paper that determines the best practices for organizing and running a small group. In composing your response, consider these questions: What makes a small group more than just the sum of its parts? How can group identity be made to serve the purpose of the group? What is the ideal structure for a group? How important is cognitive diversity, and why? How can "group polarization" be avoided? In what ways could "talkativeness" be regulated to ensure equal participation?

2. Although the Mission Management Team's decisions were made as a group, Surowiecki pays particular attention to the actions of a few individual members. Using Surowiecki's observations, write a paper that evaluates the influence of an individual person in a group setting. To what extent can an individual voice influence a group? Is a small group more than just the sum of its parts? How does individual identity exist in the larger group identity? How is dissent productive to a group decision? In what ways could an individual voice dissolve group polarization? How do the studies Surowiecki mentions support your evaluation? You may want to use your work from Questions for Critical Reading and from Question 2 of Questions for Connecting.

3. Surowiecki describes the pitfalls of logic that await a small group, paying particular attention to the effects of flawed reasoning on group decisions. Using Surowiecki's observations, write an analysis of the error in reasoning that played the biggest role in the Mission Management Team's failure: Describe all instances of the error, identify its origin in flawed reasoning, and trace its consequences for the group's decision-making process. Consider these questions: Could the Mission Management Team's errors be seen only in hindsight? In what way did the Mission Management Team's small group dynamics affect its decisions? Does the fundamental error belong to one person, several people, or the group as a whole? Why? Whose influence was most powerful within the group? Whose influence should have been the most powerful within the group?

DIANA TAYLOR

Diana Taylor holds a B.A. in creative writing from the University of the Americas, a Certificat d'Études Supérieures from the Université Aix-Marseille, an M.A. in comparative literature from the National University of Mexico, and a Ph.D. in comparative literature from the University of Washington. As a professor of performance studies and Spanish at New York University, her areas of research are varied, ranging from Latin American performance to trauma studies. Taylor is also the founding director of the Hemispheric Institute of Performance and Politics. She is the editor of several collections and has won multiple awards for three books of her own: *Theatre of Crisis: Drama and Politics in Latin America* (1991), *Disappearing Acts: Spectacles of Gender and Nationalism in Argentina's Dirty War* (1997), and *The Archive and the Repertoire: Performing Cultural Memory in the Americas* (2003). In 2005, she was awarded the John Simon Guggenheim Fellowship.

Taylor's *The Archive and the Repertoire* deals with performances in the Western hemisphere, particularly in response to tragedies such as the terrorist attacks of September 11, 2001. The book examines cultural performances and the part they play in making political statements, memorializing tragic events, and creating cultural identities.

In "False Identifications: Minority Populations Mourn Diana," from *The Archive and the Repertoire,* Taylor addresses various performances in response to the death of Princess Diana. It is curious that minority populations in New York City would design murals in memory of a former member of the British Royal Family, and the effect is made even more perplexing when murals of Diana share space with depictions of Mother Teresa and Mike Tyson. Taylor tracks these performances, the gradual alterations made to them, and the worldwide responses to this "universal" tragedy. Taylor also tracks the parallels between the responses to Diana's death and those of more "local" figures, such as Selena and Evita, to examine the "virtual act of identification" and individuals' "need for active participation" in such situations.

We usually think of responses to death as intensely personal, but in an age of global celebrity, how do we collectively mourn the famous? And what do those performances of grief tell us about ourselves and our emerging global culture?

▶ TAGS: *mourning, community, diversity, religion, identity, aesthetic boundaries, culture*

False Identifications: Minority Populations Mourn Diana

We sat on the sofa—my young daughter, Marina, on my lap—lamenting the death of a woman we didn't know. As the coffin slowly made its way toward Westminster Abbey, the commentators reverentially droned on about the silence, the mood, the dramatic demonstration of public emotion. But there were so many publics, it seemed, participating in what looked like one and the same theatre of mourning. The exclusive, well-behaved public of dignitaries and movie stars inside the Abbey, the charged "popular" audience on the meadows outside, the two billion people watching each other watching around the world. Everywhere the camera rested, people were sobbing silently. The emotion was contagious: the pity for Diana and her boys, the terror of sudden death, the rage at the ungiving queen, the contempt for the unloving husband. As in theatre, emotion gave way to applause. It erupted outside the Abbey following the Earl Spencer's eulogy and pushed its way inside, back to front, uninvited, disrupting the solemnity and reminding the high and mighty that this was, after all, the public's command performance. Then, as the hearse carrying the remains made its way out of London, the public threw its last bouquets at the departing diva. The incessant repeats of the coverage assured us we were watching "live." What does live mean, I wondered out loud, watching as we were across the Atlantic? "It means we're live and she's dead," Marina explains. Then, "You won't die, will you, Mummy?" punctuated by crying. "No, darling, no, I promise," suddenly crying too, but embarrassed. Our tears were of a different kind—hers about pity and fear; mine complicated by my determination to resist this kind of identification which I found coercive and humiliating.

What's Diana to me, that I should weep for her? This was an odd mirroring effect—one Diana crying for another.

Once again, I was that awkward, chubby child in Parral, Chihuahua—my hair pulled back in pigtails so tight that my eyes wouldn't shut, my skirt pinned together because I'd popped my button, wearing my cowgirl boots, my fringed suede jacket, and my beloved little gold scissors earrings that opened and closed. My Anglo-Canadian grandmother said I looked like a savage. Princess Anne, she reminded me, didn't wear suede jackets, to say nothing of the scissors earrings. I certainly was not her "little princess" and I would never grow up and marry the Prince if I didn't shape up and act like a good girl. Every holiday brought a new corrective for my savage condition: a royal calendar, a commemorative teacup. Now, there she was, the other Diana, the one who had been tall and blonde and beautiful, the one who would never be caught dead without a button, the one who would sooner have died than be chubby; the one who had married the Prince. And look what happened to her. Here, once more, I was caught in a drama that had unexpectedly become my own. I felt a shudder, sensed the ghost.

Downloading Grief

Whose fantasy was this, I kept wondering during the weeks following the death and funeral of Diana, Princess of Wales? Or, rather, how did so many disparate fantasies come to converge on this rather ordinary human being? The disparity between the accident-as-incident and the spectacularity of the worldwide reaction demanded reflection. Diana's ghost, I suspected, had more to tell us about international relations than did Madeleine Albright. What was the basis of such seemingly widespread identification? Were we watching a hodge-podge of funerary traditions, or was this really a case of multicultural mourning styles coalescing before our eyes? What were the politics of such memorializing energy and the mimetic performances of grief being enacted simultaneously in various parts of the world, the synchronized moments of silence, the condolence book signings, the floral shrines? In Argentina, a magazine ran a drawing of Santa Evita and Santa Diana sitting side by side in heaven. There she was, "the most beloved lady of our time," gracing the stamps of the Togolese Republic. The Trinidadian carnival featured a number, "Paparazzi Is Hell," as a "Tribute to the Queen of Hearts." Memorial walls on the Lower East Side of Manhattan were painted by U.S. artists of color. One mural, by Chico, places her next to other female Latina victims: Selena and Elisa (Figures 1–3), both murdered by people close to them. Was this a conspiracy mural? On another, Diana is a savior, along with Mother Teresa, in "royalty and holiness" (Figure 4). And here, in an admonishing mural by A. Charles that covers a synagogue on Houston Street, Diana's death is depicted as media overkill (Figures 5–7). She's placed next to fallen African American icons Tupac Shakur and Mike Tyson. "Live by the gun, die by the gun." The murals made visible the versions of the saint, victim, and media object circulating in the public sphere. How did these global images get downloaded onto these neighborhood walls? Why would minority populations care about her, when their own icons—from Evita to Selena to Tupac—had fared so poorly in the media? By what mechanism did Diana's popularity get construed as "the popular"? The world willingly suspended its disbelief as this most aristocratic of women, married to a prince and future king, the mother of princes and future kings, who socialized with billionaires and celebrities, was transformed before our eyes into the "people's princess" and "queen of people's hearts."

Diana's life, death, funeral, and afterlife as quasi-sacred relic on display illuminates the way multiple, intersecting social dramas play both globally and locally. All sorts of issues, ranging from eating disorders, to unhappy marriages, to AIDS, to the workings of the media, to neocolonialism, to globalization, seem magically incarnated in her image. The tragic emplotment of the events surrounding Diana and the theatricality of the staging, transmitted internationally, create the illusion of a cohesive, "universal" audience. But is this not perhaps an international spectacle, in the Debordian sense, that "presents itself simultaneously as all of society, as part of society and as an instrument of unification" as it "concentrates all gazing and all consciousness"?[1] There is a difference between playing to a global audience and claiming that the drama has a

Figures 1, 2, 3   Murals by Chico on East Houston Street in New York City: Diana, Selena, Elisa.

Photos by Diana Taylor, 1997.

Figures 4, 5 (*top*) Mural by Chico, "In Memory of Royalty and Holiness," on 11th Street and Avenue A, New York City. (*bottom*) Murals by A. Charles on Houston Street and First Avenue, New York City.

Photos by Diana Taylor, 1997.

Figures 6, 7   Murals by A. Charles on Houston Street and First Avenue, New York City: Overkill, Diana, Tupac Shakur.

Photos by Diana Taylor, 1997.

universal appeal. By looking at the nature and staging of these social dramas, I explore how globalization gets cast as "universality" and how this "universality" gets downloaded strategically and reconfigured on the local level.

Social Drama

If we follow Victor Turner's model of the "social drama" for a minute, a model he claims to be universally valid, we can easily recognize the four phases he identifies: (1) the breach, or social rupture and flouting of the norm; (2) crisis, in which the breach widens and escalates; (3) redressive action, which seeks to contain the spread of the crisis; and (4) the reintegration, the reordering of social norms.[2] Each of the four stages unfolds in a different dramatic mode, each rivaling the last in pushing the limits of theatricality.

The breach—her divorce from Charles and her estrangement from the Royal family—was pure melodrama. Played in the shrill key of interrogatives, declaratives, and denunciations, the drama unfolded in explosive, sporadic cries and whispers. Almost everyone could (and apparently did) tune in to the latest episodes featuring the insensitive husband, the other woman, the disapproving mother-in-law. The boundaries of the "appropriate" were repeatedly emphasized and transgressed. This private drama so publicly enacted situated protagonists and spectators alike on, and often over, the very brink of the admissible. I, like millions of others, lived the traumas of the infidelities and the self-destructive behaviors, eavesdropped on conversations, and shared the thrill of revelations and denials. When she wasn't struggling to hold back the tears, the captions pointed at the evidence of vulnerability. Her pain became the spectacle, played out in a hide-and-seek mode of strategic self-exposure on her part and unrepentant voyeurism on mine. What made it all so thrilling, of course, was not its originality but its predictability: Her story, played out so glamorously in the here and now, was basically the same old story. I, like many, many others, had lived it or seen it all before.

> She's placed next to fallen African American icons Tupac Shakur and Mike Tyson.

Her death—the crisis—was tragic drama. The fateful crash, which I (like those before me) will replay at length later, moved Diana out of the "same-old" and cast her as the "one." We're alive and she's dead—she's left the anonymity of the "we" to inhabit the singularity of the "she." She crystallized into the original, quintessential, tragic lover, beautiful princess, angel of mercy, and doting mother. Her sudden uniqueness, her tragic magnitude, allowed us to forget for a moment that she was also very much the product of a long history of collective imaginings that have normalized heterosexuality, glorified maternity, fetishized youth and femininity, glamorized whiteness, eroticized imperialism, and promoted a discourse of volunteerism. Live? Or one more repeat of the live?

The redressive action—the funeral—was a theatrical performance. Following in the tradition of other state funerals, this event was one more repetition, only the latest but never the first or the last of such spectacles. Eleanor of Castile, apparently, had a sumptuous send-off in 1290. Evita's funeral in 1952 was a magnificent spectacle, as massive and stately as Diana's. It was a performance, orchestrated with a beginning, middle, and end. The theatricality emanated from the careful choreographing of color, movement, sound, space, and regalia. Theatricality, commonly thought to be an attribute of theatre, clearly precedes and extends beyond it. Communities without theatre (such as non-Western cultures like the Mexica) understood, and were ruled by, theatricality. And issues concerning theatricality lay at the center of many of the tensions between the Queen and the British population. How much or how little theatricality should the country demand in honoring the passing of their Princess?

The theatricality of the event, as state spectacle, claimed visual power   10
through layering, the addition and augmentation of traditional and nontraditional elements. Diana's funeral, weighed down in splendor, outdid those that had come before. But repetition was not simply a mimetic return to former displays of pomp and circumstance. Rather, the pomp associated with the past served to monumentalize the present. Each *reincarnation* gains power through accumulation. Citationality thus was put to the service of originality, enhancing the "new," nontraditional touches, such as Elton John singing his pop hit "Candle in the Wind," in itself recalling an earlier death. Yet, the prescribed, twice-behaved nature of funerals also has another, ritual function. The formal handling of painful or dangerous transitions, or passings, helps regulate the expenditure of emotion. Funerals have long served to channel and control grief. But this televised funeral, with its insistence on participation, seemed to provoke the very emotions it was designed to channel. The spectators, as much as the casket and the visible Royals, became the spectacle for a global audience brought together, perhaps by grief but most certainly by television, newspapers, journals, and the Web. Unlike these earlier events, the media and communications systems performed the identification they claimed to report, assuring us that the loss, like the Princess, was ours.

The phase of reintegration, the period of reordering social norms, played itself out in multiple, less cohesive, less centralized dramas. After the initial phase of virtual participation through frantic memorialization, Diana's ghost became a site of intense renegotiating among various communities. Would the status quo ruptured by the breach be restored? Would the monarchy be reinvigorated, or permanently outmoded? Was Diana the new face of Tony Blair's kinder, gentler, more modern England? Did the burial site constructed by her brother emblematize England's "image in the world [as] a low tech 'theme park of royal pageantry'"?[3] Or had she been transformed into a thoroughly non-British relic in a pay-per-view shrine out of Disney? Are the ruptures and divides made visible by her death overcome in this moment of reintegration, or are the divides more starkly visible than before?

The Hauntology of Performance

Various modalities of expressive culture are made visible through the social drama paradigm outlined by Turner. And he is probably correct in affirming that this four-stage model illuminates all types of social conflict, ranging from office disputes to national conflicts. However, I am less convinced that these dramas play internationally and cross-culturally in any clear-cut way. The "drama" of Diana's death and the "theatricality" of her funeral elide rather than clarify the "trauma" of border crossings as specters traverse ethnic or national boundaries. What counts as a drama in one context gets demoted to a mere incident elsewhere. The Diana specter becomes visible and meaningful as it dances within various scopic, political, and economic repertoires—and vice versa. England's rose occludes Norma Jean as the new candle dancing in the wind. The dance performs more plays of substitution or, in Joseph Roach's term, surrogation: England's rose crowds out Selena, the Rose of Texas; her funeral outdoes Evita's as the most overproduced funeral of the century for a woman.[4] The specter, the spectacle, and the spectator are all dancing at this funeral. Maybe because it's so hard to get a handle on, *spec-ere* (to see) that phantoms, fantasy, and performance have traditionally been placed on the opposite side of the "real" and "historical." The fantasies in play may be linked to so-called universal and eternal anxieties about a glorious life, an unexpected death, and the fall of the great. The iterative and highly stylized nature of this stately display should not suggest that it is not, at the same time, deeply political and historically specific. What conditions allow these fantasies to become visibly incarnated in a woman no one cares much about? Though the specter may come in and out of time, and though performances make visible the conflicts that otherwise remain diffuse, both specters and performances are very live. "Haunting," Derrida notes, "is historical . . . but not dated."[5] The fantasies converging around the figure of Diana, I suggest, require certain conditions of visibility and bring various histories, ontologies, and hauntologies of performance into focus.

In *Unmarked*, Peggy Phelan outlines the "ontology of performance," stressing the liveness of the performative event, the *now* in which that performance takes place: "Performance's only life is in the present. Performance cannot be saved, recorded, documented, or otherwise participate in the circulation of representations of representation."[6] An event such as Diana's death and funeral, however, also begs us to look at the flip side of performance's ontology, at what Derrida has called its "hauntology." Many cultures are grounded on the notion of a second coming: the Mexica, the Christian, the Jewish, the Marxist, to name a few. The ghost is, by definition, a repetition, Derrida's *revenant*. This is the moment of postdisappearance, rather than the moment preceding it that Phelan points to. The sumptuousness of the ceremony performs the sacralization of the *remains*, theoretically antithetical to performance. The remains, in this spectacle, take on a life of their own—so much so that one tabloid photo montage has Di looking on at her own funeral from the corner with a bittersweet smile, one more witness to an event that has overtaken her. The body we assume lies in the coffin is all that we have to assure us that Diana was real. It provides the authenticating materiality that sustains the performance of resuscitation. In spirit, she was present at her funeral, as perhaps, inversely, we could argue that she was absent from her life. The shrine housing her remains will continue to guarantee the materiality of the global phenomenon that is Diana, the massive reappearance of the revenant. Politically and symbolically, we haven't seen the end of her. The caption of a recent photograph of a London newsstand states that "one might be forgiven for imagining that Diana never died last August. The Princess of Wales still keeps the presses roaring."[7] The February 2, 1998, cover of *People* depicts Diana as active in death as she was in life: "In death as in life, she has raised millions for charity."

My view of performance rests on the notion of ghosting, that visualization that continues to act politically even as it exceeds the live. Like Phelan's definition, it hinges on the relationship between visibility and invisibility, or appearance and disappearance, but comes at it from a different angle. For Phelan, the defining feature of performance—that which separates it from all other phenomena—is that it is live and disappears without a trace. The way I see it, performance makes visible (for an instant, live, now) that which is always already there: the ghosts, the tropes, the scenarios that structure our individual and collective life. These specters, made manifest through performance, alter future phantoms, future fantasies. Diana may have been the product of one way of envisioning royalty, but she has changed the look, style, and scope in which royalty will be performed, and desired, in the future. Her enactment left a trace. Every woman running for political office in Argentina today wears the obligatory dyed blonde bun and Dior suit associated with Evita. In one sense, of course, the live performance eludes the "economy of reproduction," as Phelan puts it.[8] But I would argue that its efficacy, whether as art or as politics, stems from the way performances tap into public fantasies and leave a trace, reproducing and at times altering cultural repertoires. Performance, then, involves more than an object (as in performance art), more than an accomplishment or a carrying through. It constitutes a (quasi-magical) invocational practice. It provokes emotions it claims only to represent, evokes memories and grief that belong to some other body. It conjures up and makes visible not just the live but the powerful army of the always already living. The power of seeing through performance is the recognition that we've seen it all before—the fantasies that shape our sense of self, of community, that organize our scenarios of interaction, conflict, and resolution.

What conditions of visibility are needed to conjure up the ghost? Of all the many potential specters, why do certain ones gain such power? Why Diana and not somebody else? Why, as Michael Taussig asks in *Mimesis and Alterity*, does the spirit (and, I would add, the ghost) need embodiment at all?[9] Evita's corpse, perhaps, can shed some light on the need to give material shape to a political force. The most politically powerful woman in the world in the early 1950s, Evita has the world's most expensive corpse. It cost $200,000 to embalm her and three wax copies were produced to trick all the would-be body snatchers. The copies were so authentic that Dr. Ara removed the tip of her little finger to distinguish her real body from its replications. The original, here as elsewhere, is never as whole as its representation. Her body, the most politically charged fetish of the twentieth century, is key because it anchors the "other Eva," the more powerful one, the one whose ghost continues to dominate Argentine politics. *Spec-ere*, to see, is possible only through a history of spectacles and ghosts. Performance, be it artistic or political, accomplishes a moment of revisualization. It

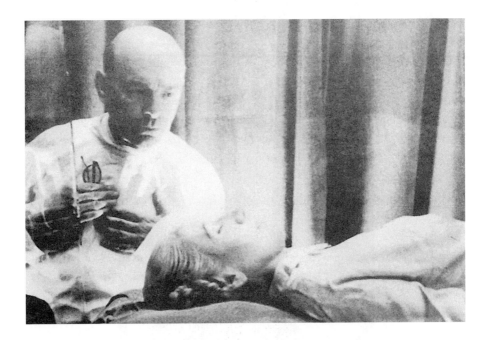

Figure 8   Dr. Ara and Evita's corpse. From *Página 12*, September 22, 1996.
Photo courtesy of Diana Taylor.

disappears only to hover; it promises or threatens to reappear, albeit in another shape or form.

Performance becomes visible, meaningful, within the context of a phantasmagoric repertoire of repeats. But there is a double mechanism at work. On the one hand, we see only what we have been conditioned to see: that which we have seen before. So part of the grief we feel surrounding Diana's death is that she is so familiar to us. She represents the most general, undifferentiated version of the death of the beautiful woman, a scenario so powerful, so naturalized that it underwrites the Western imaginary and seems always to have been there.[10] On the other hand, the spectacle presents itself as a universal and unifying event. But spectacle, to conjure up Debord for a minute, "is not a collection of images, but a social relation among people, mediated by images."[11] The spectacle, then, is that which we do *not* see, the invisible that "appears" only through mediation. Diana's specter unites the spectators in the fantasy of loving and losing a woman no one really knows even as it hides the social relations among the very people who, theoretically, participate in the fantasy. Diana's death looks more like one more repetition of the same. Her death (singular and sudden) represents both the instant of her passing ("real," not-performative) *and* the reappearance of another death: Evita, Selena, Marilyn Monroe, Mother Teresa. As Elisabeth Bronfen argues, "The death of a beautiful woman emerges as the requirement for a preservation of existing cultural norms and values. . . .

Figure 9   "La Otra Eva," *Página 12***, Radar section, September 22, 1996.**
Photo courtesy of Diana Taylor.

Over her dead body, cultural norms are reconfigured or secured, whether because the sacrifice of the virtuous, innocent woman serves a social critique and
transformation or because a sacrifice of the dangerous woman reestablishes an
order that was momentarily suspended due to her presence."[12] This seemingly
universal scenario elides the politics of cultural transmission. What we don't
see, as the world mourns Diana, is that these women (judged innocent or dangerous, and usually both) form part of profoundly different imaginaries, and the
borders of these imaginaries are policed. The specter hides the spectacle. The
mourning rituals may be similar; they may even encourage fantasies that they
are communicable to different populations. But the politics are untranslatable.

Policing the Imaginary

Chicanas and Chicanos, as well as other Latinos, mourned Selena en masse, covered her coffin with thousands of roses, gathered tens of thousands of signatures
in commemorative books, declared an official Selena Day, and attempted to in-
scribe her name and face on everything from Web sites to memorial walls to
Coca-Cola bottles. The similarity of the rituals highlights the lack of empathetic
reciprocity; theatricality blinds even as it makes visible. The redressive moment

of one social drama (Selena's funeral) signals the moment of breach in another. A few hours before her funeral, Howard Stern had already shipped her back to Mexico: "Selena? Her music is awful. I don't know what Mexicans are into. If you're going to sing about what's going on in Mexico, what can you say? . . . You can't grow crops, you got a cardboard house, your eleven-year-old daughter is a prostitute. . . . This is music to perform abortions to!"[13] According to Stern, this death proves too lowly to constitute a drama. It's reduced to an incident— no drama, no breach. These nondramas don't travel. How, then, do some ghosts dance over cultural boundaries while others are stopped, strip-searched, and denied entry?

The specter is as visible and powerful as the cultural scenarios surrounding it. Stern's "What can you say?" relegates Selena to the ignominy of particularism: poverty, deviance, genocide. Stern sets himself up as the *migra* of the imaginary, the border police who ensure that certain identifications don't sneak into dominant culture. There are no fictions of the reciprocity that Walter Benjamin ascribes to translation here, no lip service to communication, no invitation to make meaning in this puzzling affair—we don't understand you, what are Mexicans into?[14] Punto. The performance of explicit noncaring performs the breach even as it denies the drama. By refusing to acknowledge a loss, it forecloses the possibility of redressive action and reintegration. The contempt of mourning rite denies the ghost its afterlife: This is about aborting. Diana, on the other hand, is invoked in hushed, reverential terms. She is assured an afterlife either as saint, as mother of the future king, or as a fund-raiser for charities. Guaranteed a visa, her face crosses borders on stamps, calendars, magazines. Her image serves as the occasion for bringing artists together in the service of disenfranchised communities, even as members of those communities are denied the stage. Yet everyone, it seems, is invited to participate and conjecture—to participate by conjecturing. The staging of her death ricochets between twin poles of singularity and universality; Diana's life and death, though utterly unique and one of a kind, nonetheless sheds light on misery, suffering, and stoicism everywhere. The coverage relished each detail, including what she ate for dinner on that fateful night! Yet it shunned particularism, stressing that this death was also about everything and everyone. Immediately, the death was aestheticized as drama and cast in the most powerful and universalizing paradigm available to meaning-making culture: tragedy.

Tragedy

Diana's death and funeral is the clearest example I have ever witnessed of an Aristotelian tragedy of international magnitude, "made sensuously attractive . . . enacted by the persons themselves," provoking pity and fear in millions of spectators. True, Aristotle insists that tragedy is the "imitation" of an action, rather than the real action itself.[15] And in a sense, of course, the distinction between art and life is a vital one. But there is also a way in which life imitates or is constructed through art, and not the other way around, that allows us to think of life as performative in the early Butlerian usage of the term as "a stylized repetition of acts."[16] The "Diana" we knew was a performative construct, the product of stylized acts—royal protocol, fairy tales, designer styles, and Hollywood fantasy—a real princess, a royal model as well as a new model for royalty. Her wedding provided the role and inserted her into a script shaped by tradition. She temporarily fit the bill (a young, aristocratic, malleable, good-looking virgin), the way an actor might be typecast for a role. What, one wonders, is real about this live performance?

Diana's death seemed similarly scripted, not by royal protocol this time but by "fate" and the media. Everything about it was "impossibly tragic." It was significant and of Aristotelian "magnitude" due to the nobility and beauty (heroic stature) of the woman, the struggle to shape her own destiny, the tricks to ward off fate (the real driver leaving the Ritz as decoy). Diana's *hamartia* (tragic flaw) was so simple, so human according to the media/chorus: She merely wanted to be happy. The *peripeteia*, or reversal of fortune, was abrupt. The inevitability of the *catastrophe* was almost a given, considering the persistent mad chase by the paparazzi and the equally mad attempts at flight. The identification, as always in tragedy, was written into the performance. We don't have to know these great figures in order to weep for them.

And the timing couldn't be more tragically ironic. Just as she was starting her new life, which she had attained against all odds, she died on the very night he gave her "the ring." Not only that, she died with her lover—the latest version of the "star-crossed lovers," as one tabloid called them. Even the names played into the tragedy as Dodi, meaning "my beloved," and Di raced off to their "destiny" (as the accident is repeatedly alluded to by the tabloids). It was already written—not just in Aristotle but in the *Song of Songs*: "Dodí li va-aní lo" (My beloved is mine and I am his). Others find her death already coded in Genesis. The spectacle of the death elicits the specters of the already there. We're moved because we already know the story: the dark tunnel, the frantic chase, Diana the huntress hunted down. The paparazzi, who dedicated their lives to "doing Di," to banging, blitzing, hosing, ripping, smudging, and whacking her (all words, we learn, for taking pictures rapidly), finally got their prey.[17] The pace of the drama was fast, the tunnel tomblike in its dark enclosure; the plot revolved around sex and love; the reversal from supreme happiness to sudden death was precipitous; the end unexpected, shocking. And there was even a whiff of conspiracy about this end to a life that was otherwise so transparent, so devoid of mystery. Was the thought of Diana marrying an Egyptian playboy with a purportedly mafioso background too much for the royal family? The innocent woman had little by little become the dangerous woman—the woman whose bulimia, suicide attempts, and infidelities threatened the image of the royal body, and now, its ethnic purity and exclusivity. Or was her accident contrived by the royal family to elicit popular support for itself? Project Interflora, an online site warning of royal conspiracy, had also seen it all before and warned its audience, "REMEMBER! Awaken!!!!" It reads the "Di thing" as a way of assuring the "continuance of the Monarchy." The floral tributes are an example of "Flower Power . . . an MI5 mind control program aimed at mass manipulation of the hearts and minds of the people of Britain. . . . These floral tributes are NOT spontaneous!" Even

Aristotle could not have envisioned a more perfectly crafted plot. While one tabloid headline screams out "She didn't have to die!" the way that the media "made sense" of her death stressed the tragic inevitability of "the love she died for."[18] Anyone who has grown up with *Romeo and Juliet* or *West Side Story*, not to mention Agatha Christie and the Old Testament, might find something to relate to in this drama.

Diana's death precipitated a process of transformation and resolution on multiple levels. Diana, the dangerous and transgressive woman, "died a lover."[19] However, she was buried a mother, an innocent victim, a model of humanitarianism, a quasi-saintly do-gooder, and a member of the royal family. Once again, her image was transposed from one economy to another: The fairy tale princess in the heavy gown of the wedding photos and the formally attired, motherly wife of the early years had already given way to the casual, lightly clad, jet-setting image of her final years. Her death weighted her down again with the heavy brocade of the royal colors. She was back in the fold, center stage in the state's (polyvalent) self-imaging. After her wedding to Dodi, a sumptuous state funeral would have been unthinkable. Even as it was, the Queen initially demanded that "Diana's body should not be placed in any of the royal palaces and should be taken to a private mortuary."[20] The body, now saturated with the sacred/abject power of the transgressor, had to be kept away from the royal. It was "private" now, exiled to the mundane sphere of the ordinary. But the non-Royals wouldn't have it, not for "their" Princess. It was the Queen's turn to undergo public shaming. The "people" forced her to perform her emotions, whether she felt them or not. "Show Us You Care," demanded the *Express*; "Your People are Suffering: SPEAK TO US MA'AM," the *Mirror* shouted from the stands. "Where is Our Queen? Where is Her Flag?" the *Sun* wanted to know. "Let the Flag Fly at Half Mast," the *Daily Mail* insisted, giving the Queen her own little lesson in protocol.

> **The coverage relished each detail, including what she ate for dinner on that fateful night!**

The funeral was equally dramatic, though in a different way. This was imperial theatre, theoretically brokered by the "people" and elaborately negotiated by all parties. The behind-the-scenes bickering of how much or how little (whether in terms of spectacle, emotion, or viewers) was suspended by the splendor of the affair. The lavishness of the funeral made visible that the feuding, like the body, could be laid to rest; now that Diana was dead, rivalries and contentions could be forgotten. The country was once more united in tragedy, and the overwhelming sensual experience (the smell of the flowers, the echoing sound of the horses' hooves, the trembling bodies of sobbing spectators) rekindled the erotic, though ambivalent, attraction to the state. So the funeral was an act of national conflict and resolution, an act of remembering one Diana by forgetting the others, of celebrating a life and transcending (obscuring) it with claims to a higher purpose and a sanctity it never had. The transgressive, casual Diana was now thoroughly snuffed out, in part, by the very people who claimed to love her.

The funeral as imperial theatre was the opposite of the death as drama. As in theatre, a word that refers both to the physical, institutional frame and the intentional action that takes place within its limits, the theatricality of the funeral elided issues of Diana's relationship to the monarchy by normalizing the rite of passage within the demarcations of historical tradition. Tensions disappeared behind the sensuousness, the ceremony of it all. The route, the lines of spectators, the choreography of the funeral party: This was a deliberate staging of the restoration of order, carefully modeled on previous, orderly funerals. It was about the "again," "now," and "as always" of royal self-representation. It disappears only to reappear. The achingly slow procession signaled the seemingly eternal and stable quality of a royal order now so openly up for grabs. The monarchy on show was very different from the one that waved at the world during the wedding. But the physical staging was also an act of restoration; it bracketed and emplotted the event, the first and last act of the Princess of Wales. After the abrupt crisis caused by the crash, the funeral provided aesthetic closure and emotional resolution. As in ritual, this final stage promised to be deeply conservative. The restitution of the social order, disrupted but probably not profoundly altered by the crisis, meant that Diana once more returned to the official body she tried so hard to elude. As Charles, the two young Princes, Prince Philip, and Earl Spencer followed the coffin on foot, it was clear that the procession was as much about possession and control as about emotion and empathy.

What do "the people" have to do with this imperial theatre, with the struggles between the Queen and the Prince, the Windsors and the Spencers, the Tories and Tony Blair's Labour Party? Que vela tenemos nosotros en este entierro? How do "the people" get constructed? The "staging of the popular," as Néstor García Canclini argues in *Hybrid Cultures,* "has been a mix of participation and simulacrum."[21] Newspapers around the world ran the same article, extending the reach of the we as it extended its audience. The same picture of Diana would appear, often with the same text, reporting on our reaction to the devastating turn of events. One Web site instructed the user to "send your feelings, condolences, or memorial regarding Princess Diana by *clicking here.*" The "Princess Diana fax poll" (set up by the *Post*) asked people to define what she meant to them.[22]

In England, the event was interpreted as a "revolution" (of sorts) because it showed "the people" their new power. The *New York Times* reported the "remarkable confrontation between the British people and Buckingham Palace and . . . an even more remarkable royal retreat."[23] "The people" won their show-down with the Queen. They had demanded the pomp and ceremony of empire self-fashioning. The ritual, traditional to the extreme, could be read as a subversive reversal, for it was the public, not the Crown, who ordered it. Now, Tony Blair would have us believe, the old aristocratic ways vanished in one more act of surrogation: The Queen is dead, Long live Diana, the Queen of the people's hearts. Diana was the new face of the new England: stylish, youthful, and compassionate. Hegemony now enjoyed a more casual, photogenic look. Diana, like England, was coming out of a depression. She would be the goodwill ambassador, the kinder, gentler, post-Thatcher face of England. Instead of politics, style. Instead of bitter ideological divides, consensus and national unity. "The people" were featured as actors, rather than spectators, in the national drama.

The drama, then, is not just about Diana's tragic death, her regal funeral, or the current political situation in England. The event, commentators insist, is performative; it is about changing structures of feeling. It changed the way the English performed their emotions: Out with stiff upper lips and mean-spirited politics; in with touching, smiling, and generous public displays of spontaneity. Diana touching AIDS patients, or dying children, signaled a new mode of being (British).

Loss

Loss. A ghost is about loss, loss made manifest, the vision of that which is no longer there. But what, I wonder, has been lost? Diana's candles, like Evita's and Mother Teresa's, provided the thousand points of light that corporate governments no longer feel compelled to provide. Lost, too, were both a working-class and a feminist agenda. Unlike Evita, who came from a working-class background and wielded unprecedented political power in Argentina, Diana and Mother Teresa had no political aspirations. Evita's popularity, channeled into a formidable populism, exceeded her death to the point that her ghost is still the most politically powerful player in Argentine politics today. This world is not ready for another Evita. The female powerhouse of the 1940s and early 1950s becomes the apolitical, unthreatening sophisticate of the 1990s. Evita too is denied a visa. When she was resuscitated in the movie *Evita*, Madonna was a style, a "look." The passionate public of political actors who maintained Evita in power melted into teary-eyed spectators and consumers. Evita's prophecy of her revenance, "I will return, and I will be millions," seemed ironically fulfilled. For here she was, incarnated by Madonna, of all people. Even the walls cried out in protest: "Out Madonna, Evita lives." Evita lives, but only in Argentina. In the United States, she is a lipstick, a fascist, a whore, and an oddity. What next, Frank Rich asks? Maybe "Barbie-like Evita dolls laid out in little clear plastic caskets."[24] The conjuring act accomplishes one more disappearance by repetition — one face for another, one name for another, Evita dissolves in Madonna, while Madonna gains visibility through Evita.

So the choices were not, and never could be, between Diana and Evita, but about Diana and Mother Teresa. A 1998 *New Yorker* cartoon by Frank Cotham showed winged inhabitants of heaven moving along Princess Di Way and Mother Teresa Blvd. The way of the Empire and the way of the Church each take their ambassadors on the clearly one-way journey across borders, unsolicited yet living proof that the First World cares. In the language of love rather than power, these women claim to relinquish their enormous political, economic, and symbolic capital to the have-nots. As with all overloaded icons, these women looked so transparent. It's all so simple, this love talk. One could love Diana and love Mother Teresa and still hate politics, as if the naturalized act of charitable

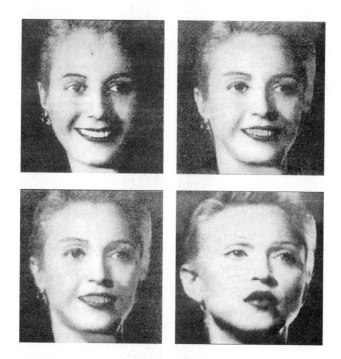

Figure 10.   Evita fades into Madonna on the cover of *La Maga*, January 31, 1996.
Photo courtesy of Diana Taylor.

giving had nothing to do with the expansionism of imperialism, Catholicism, and late capitalism.

Lost too, perhaps, is the colonial nostalgia for the Royal Love. For viewers in the former colonies, Diana also embodied a love-hate relationship with empire and imperialism, which she simultaneously represented and transcended. Her estrangement from the Royals allowed for the ambiguous positioning, the nepantla of Latin American postcolonialism, or the "ambivalence" stemming from what Homi Bhabha refers to as the "double articulation" (the like, but not quite) of the colonial predicament.[25] What options do colonials have but to juggle the complicated play of identification/disidentification? She was living proof that the Royal Love had failed. Yet the love of the Royal could continue through our love of her. And our love for her led us to the possibility of transcending the racism at the heart of colonialism through her new romantic attachment to Dodi. This dark, sexy, playboy Other, the ultimate consumer, was the antithesis of Charles, the ultimate, old fashioned, nerdy "one of them." It made her, supposedly, "one of us" — one of those left out or betrayed by an atrociously uptight establishment. Okay, Dodi was a billionaire jet-setter, maybe not quite one of us, and in our heart of hearts we wonder if they would have been happy, but the beauty of fairy tales depends precisely on the suddenness and untimeliness of their endings.

30

In another way, of course, Diana's death was about the loss of another form of materiality. Her image gave a "universal" face to the disembodied globalism facilitated by satellites and the World Wide Web. A product of intercommunication systems, the Diana we saw was never and always live. Never live because, as one publication put it, "No Pix, No Di."[26] Her liveness was a product of mediation. Susan Stewart, in *TV Guide*, writes, "I know for a fact that Diana existed apart from television: I once shook her hand. It was exciting—she was already an international icon—but almost meaningless. All I remember is a blur of blond hair, a purr of a greeting. There are at least a dozen film clips of Diana more vivid in my mind than our actual off-screen meeting."[27] Her physical existence, redundant even in life, served merely to authenticate her more complete, real, and ubiquitous image that continues to defy the limits of space and time.

Thus, she was never (but is always) live and here everywhere, haunting our present. A Virtual Di, her image outlives her death; the signifier has no need of the signified, except as authenticating remains. She existed; that's enough to hang our dramas on. The Web asks us to light a candle for her, expanding the simulacrum of participation. She is a fetish, a sacred image whose meaning emanates not from within but is assigned to it from without. As a fetish (whether in psychoanalytic terms or as commodity fetishism), her success stems both from the facility with which anxieties and fears are displaced onto her and the process of disavowal whereby the public can admire the image while ignoring the violence that contributed to its making. Her vulnerability, unhappiness, and physical distress only contributed to her popularity, for as someone noted, the unhappier she was, the better she looked. After her death, a new (and improved) generation of commodities circulate with her image on them: commemorative stamps, plates, and dolls. The music and books she inspired reached the top of the charts and grossed millions of dollars. Her name is invoked in the war against drunken driving, land mines, AIDS, bulimia, and other assorted social ills. A new army of designers will take charge of dressing and tutoring the ghost. Sightings have been reported. New performances, political, artistic, or entrepreneurial, rise out of these archival remains. Other women will dance in that space of impossibility made visible by her performance.

Negotiating the Local

After the orgy of promiscuous identification has passed, do communities feel the abandonment and exploitation of the one-night stand? When we look in that colonial mirror, does her reflection look back at us, or do we see ourselves, complete with pigtails and popped buttons? The murals in Figures 1–7, as spaces of communal, public mourning, show signs of ongoing debate. Rather than simply reiterate the universal show of love and loss, the murals make the events local, bringing them right into the heart of the community. "Why do we care about Diana?" they seem to ask. By honoring her untimely death, the memorial walls situate her squarely in the long, unacknowledged history of untimely deaths in these neighborhoods. They call attention to the gang and police violence in New York City that people prefer to overlook. But the walls also manifest the anger of the unrequited, the "why should we care about her when no one cares about us?" The Latino murals to Princess Di now have "Die" written all over them. Someone has written "NO MORE SPECTACLES AT ALL LADY DIE" in yellow paint on the admonishing mural that had warned about media overkill (Figure 11). The mural that had declared its love for Diana, announcing that she would be missed worldwide, now has a consciously postcolonial message on it: "We spent years of toil to break from the tyranny of British rule. NO SAINTS, NO SINNERS" (Figure 12). The Holiness and Royalty mural featuring Diana and Mother Teresa not only screams "DIE! DIE! DIE!" but participates in another form of circulation (Figure 13). This mural shows more than the displaced images of transnational globalization. It captures, too, the flip side of that same economy that leaves people out in the cold: the displaced people, poverty, and homelessness that volunteerism does not dissipate on the Lower East Side. The homeless man places himself, like an offering, at this "altar" to holiness.

Diana's ghost keeps dancing, tracing the convergence of preexisting phantoms and the latest crisis—always a rewriting, an updating, a making actual, of something that is already. Because we are all caught in transnational

Figure 11   "No More Spectacles," graffiti-altered mural by A. Charles, on Houston Street and First Avenue, New York City.
Photo by Diana Taylor, 1997.

Figures 12, 13 (*top*) "No Saints, No Sinners," graffiti on the Diana mural by Chico, on East Houston Street, New York City. (*bottom*) "Die, Die, Die," graffiti on "In Memory of Royalty and Holiness" mural by Chico.

Photos by Diana Taylor, 1997.

economic and iconographic systems, we have no choice, it seems, but to participate in the circulation of capital, symbolic as well as economic. How we download these images and engage with them, however, reflects the power of the local community in framing the terms of the debates. On one level, of course, Diana's death and funeral constitute a global drama of mass appeal. Here are all the ingredients of a successful tearjerker: the death of a noble, beautiful, and misunderstood princess. Thus, it is both a first and a repetition, a ghosting, a performatic reappearance. In this particular staging, "the people" are not only the consumers but also the constructed of this death. The spectacle of the specter makes the spectator. Instead of mourning, the undifferentiated multitudes consume grief—the recipients, not the agents, of an emotion that is not their own. "The people" light imaginary candles for Diana on the Web in a virtual act of identification. But, on another level, the event has also staged the need for active participation. Is it so strange that we may want to act in a drama we know full well is not our own? If we must engage, as it seems we must, these muralists show that people will establish the terms of conversation. Rather than constitute one more space for a downloading of the global, it opens one more strategic site for the negotiation of the local. Maybe it's not so odd that we, like the artists of the memorial walls, may wish to insert our own version of events by placing her next to our victims, next to other icons of caring, knowing full well that the gesture will never be reciprocated. But as always, there is the ambivalent push-pull of the imperial fantasy. The DI erupts in DIE. These rituals of passing insist that we forget that we don't belong, even as we remember.

We walk around the streets of the Lower East Side, Marina and I, taking photographs. The walls change constantly, reflecting new social interests and concerns. The synagogue, later converted into a Yiddish musical theatre venue, on which A. Charles painted Tupac, Tyson, and Diana, was boarded up for a year. It recently opened as a posh movie theatre, showing excellent alternative films (Figure 14). After September 11, Chico used the wall on which he painted "In Memory of Royalty and Holiness" to commemorate those lost in the attack. I had forgotten that he had long since painted over the faces of Diana and Mother Teresa. He had clearly wanted to blot out his bout with false identification. "What was here before?" I asked Marina. She too has forgotten. Later we remember: a huge, banal "Wouldn't it be beautiful?" had been written on an equally banal image of the sun setting over the peaceful sea. It had nothing to do with anything—very unusual for mural art. No wonder we didn't recall. On Houston, the three large walls dedicated to Diana, Elisa, and Selena had also undergone change. Chico had repainted Selena and Elisa, whose faces are still up today. Diana was gone, surrogated by the image of a cat and a dog against the New York skyscape. "Overpopulation is killing us: Please spay or neuter," and below it the name of a clinic. Even Selena had an arrow over her head, pointing to a pharmacy around the corner (Figure 15). Lots of disappearances, lots of forms of forgetting. Soon, we will forget that we have forgotten.

Figure 14   The facade that A. Charles painted on Houston Street undergoes gentrification.
Photo by Diana Taylor, 2000.

Figure 15   "Overpopulation Is Killing Us," mural by Chico on East Houston Street.
Photo by Diana Taylor, 2000.

NOTES

1. Guy Debord, *Society of the Spectacle* (Detroit: Black and Red, 1983), 3.
2. Victor Turner, *Dramas, Fields, and Metaphors: Symbolic Action in Human Society* (Ithaca: Cornell UP, 1974), 37–42.
3. Winston S. Churchill, "Modernizing Britain, the Tony Blair Way," *New York Times*, January 2, 1998, A17.
4. Joseph Roach, *Cities of the Dead: Circum-Atlantic Performance* (New York: Columbia UP, 1996), 2.
5. Jacques Derrida, *Specters of Marx* (London: Routledge, 1994), 4.
6. Peggy Phelan, *Unmarked: The Politics of Performance* (London: Routledge, 1993), 146.
7. Warren Hoge, "Diana's Hereafter, an Eternity of Newsstand Life," *New York Times*, February 9, 1998, A4.
8. Phelan, *Unmarked*, 146.
9. Michael Taussig, *Mimesis and Alterity* (New York: Routledge, 1993), 10.
10. See Elisabeth Bronfen, *Over Her Dead Body: Death, Femininity and the Aesthetic* (New York: Routledge, 1992), 181.
11. Debord, *Society of the Spectacle*, 4.
12. Bronfen, *Over Her Dead Body*, 181.
13. Quoted in Maria Celeste Arraras, *Selena's Secret* (New York: Simon and Schuster, 1997), 24.
14. Walter Benjamin, *Illuminations: Essays and Reflections* (New York: Harcourt, Brace and World, 1955), 72.
15. Aristotle, *Poetics*, trans. Gerald F. Else (Ann Arbor: U of Michigan P, 1973), 25.
16. Judith Butler, "Performative Acts and Gender Constitution: An Essay in Phenomenology and Feminist Theory," in *Performing Feminisms: Feminist Critical Theory and Theatre*, ed. Sue-Ellen Case (Baltimore: Johns Hopkins UP, 1990), 270.
17. Sarah Lyall, "Diana's Hunters: How Quarry Was Stalked," *New York Times*, September 10, 1997, A1.
18. "She Didn't Have to Die!" *Globe*, September 16, 1997, cover; "The Love She Died For," *Globe*, September 16, 1997, 22.
19. Barbara Kirshenblatt-Gimblett, "Issues and Methods" class, Performance Studies, New York University, September 1997.
20. Kamal Ahmed, "Charles and the Queen at War over Diana," *Guardian*, International ed., September 9, 1997, 1.
21. Néstor García Canclini, *Hybrid Cultures: Strategies for Entering and Leaving Modernity*, trans. Christopher L. Chiappari and Silvia L. López (Minneapolis: U of Minnesota P, 1995), 11, n. 1.
22. "Princess Diana Fax Poll," *New York Post*, September 4, 1997, 5.
23. Warren Hoge, "Flower Power," *New York Times*, September 9, 1997, A1.
24. Frank Rich, "101 Evitas," *New York Times*, December 11, 1996, A27.
25. Homi Bhabha, *The Location of Culture* (New York: Routledge, 1994), 86.
26. Max Frankel, "No Pix, No Di," *New York Times Magazine*, September 21, 1997, 53.
27. Susan Stewart, "TV Bids Farewell to Its Princess," *TV Guide*, September 20, 1997, 24.

Questions for Critical Reading

1. What is "social drama"? Define the term using Taylor's text and then provide your own example.

2. Taylor uses the term *ghosting*. What does she mean by this term? How does she use it in this essay? Define the term using her text and then perform a critical reading of the role it plays in her overall argument.

3. Why do minority populations mourn figures like Princess Diana? What's the social function of mourning? Perform a critical reading of the essay to formulate your response, and support your position with quotations from Taylor's essay.

Exploring Context

1. Visit princess-diana.com. How does this tribute site reflect Taylor's argument? What other populations continue to mourn Princess Diana? Connect your response to your work on mourning from Question 3 of Questions for Critical Reading.

2. Using the Web, research another celebrity or political figure who has recently died. How are they mourned? Who mourns them? How does mourning take place online? Is there any social drama or ghosting involved? Draw from the definitions of these terms you created for Questions 1 and 2 of Questions for Critical Reading.

3. Google Fight (googlefight.com) lets you compare the results from two different search terms. Stage a Google fight between Selena and Princess Diana or between two other objects of mourning such as Evita and Mother Teresa. How do the results confirm or complicate Taylor's argument?

Questions for Connecting

1. Taylor is interested in the social function of mourning and the identifications of racialized and colonial subjects. Use her ideas to further explain the appropriation of black talk as explored by Leslie Savan in "What's Black, Then White, and Said All Over?" (p. 363). Does slang partake in social drama? Does black talk work as a form of ghosting? Use your definitions of Taylor's terms from Questions for Critical Reading to compose your response.

2. What role might the primacy of practice play in mourning? Apply Kwame Anthony Appiah's ideas in "Making Conversation" (p. 57) and "The Primacy of Practice" (p. 63) to Taylor's argument. Is cosmopolitanism evident in the identifications that Taylor examines? How can you synthesize their positions?

3. Taylor's essay focuses on the end of life. In contrast, Debora L. Spar's "Trading Places: The Practice and Politics of Adoption" (p. 402) focuses on the beginning of life. Use Taylor's ideas about hauntology and social drama—drawing from

your work in Questions for Critical Reading—to examine Spar's essay. Is the baby market a kind of social drama? Do international adoptions represent a kind of false identification?

Language Matters

1. How do foreign languages affect our understanding of language in general? Use your experience with a foreign language, learned at school or at home, to think about your own writing. Does understanding the grammar of another language help you in your writing?

2. Wikipedia is an increasingly popular resource, though one that usually plays little role in academic writing. Start by reading Wikipedia's entry for Diana Taylor. Then write a short piece that could serve as the entry for this essay. What information would you include? Before writing, you might want to check out Wikipedia's style manual at en.wikipedia.org/wiki/wikipedia:Manual_of_Style. What grammatical issues seem most important in a Wikipedia entry, and why? How does writing for this online encyclopedia differ from academic writing? Why might that influence the usefulness of this source in research?

3. What's the social function of grammar? Why do we even have grammar? Connect your answers to Taylor's concepts.

Assignments for Writing

1. Engage Taylor's text by assessing the relationship between culture and politics, and then write an essay in which you examine the role of popular culture in political discourse. How do societies construe their politicians? Does "popularity" matter in political discourse? Why or why not? What is the appeal of foreign political figures to other cultures? What is the role of performance in culture and politics? You might want to begin your response with your work from Question 2 of Exploring Context.

2. Taylor examines the reactions of people around the world to the death of Princess Diana. Analyze the role of celebrity in today's society, and then write an essay in which you examine the power of celebrity in our society. What effect does the cult of celebrity have on society? Is the mirroring of style, appearance, and actions positive or negative? Do things like location, religion, nationality, gender, or race factor into an individual's or a society's reaction to celebrity?

3. Explore the specific reactions people have to universal tragedy throughout Taylor's essay, and then write an essay in which you evaluate the function of individual tragedy for groups. What function does the press have in the shaping of universal tragedy? How does the concept of social drama interact with this widespread identification? What is the role of collective imagining?

KENJI YOSHINO

Kenji Yoshino is the Chief Justice Earl Warren Professor of Constitutional Law at New York University. Previously, Yoshino was a professor of law and the deputy dean of intellectual life at Yale Law School, where he earned a J.D. after graduating from Harvard and Oxford universities. His articles have appeared in various law journals as well as the *New York Times*, the *Village Voice*, the *Boston Globe*, and the *Nation*. His book *Covering: The Hidden Assault on Our Civil Rights* was published in 2006.

Covering offers a unique perspective on the familiar concepts of assimilation and passing, utilizing Yoshino's background experience as both a law scholar and a gay Asian American. Yoshino combines personal narrative and legal argument to lay out a new definition of civil rights. The term *covering*, as Yoshino uses it, means "to tone down a disfavored identity to fit into the mainstream," and Yoshino argues that though Americans value the idea of the melting pot as a model for our culture, that ideal can have unintended negative consequences. Despite our avowed appreciation for multiculturalism, the unstated public expectation is still for people of all genders, sexual orientations, and races to conform to rigid expectations.

The selections here, "Preface" and "The New Civil Rights," form something close to a set of bookends for Yoshino's argument in *Covering*. After defining the concept of covering and the problems caused by it in the "Preface" and investigating the issue of a distinct "True Self" and "False Self" in the second excerpt, Yoshino moves on to propose a new paradigm for civil rights. Questioning the idea of legislating civil rights, Yoshino suggests that the next step may have to occur in bars, restaurants, and Internet chat rooms; he also suggests that in order to accommodate an increasingly diverse population, the model of civil rights itself must change. Yoshino points the way by helping us to rethink our model of civil rights and the mechanisms used to bring those rights into existence.

The United States is more diverse than ever. How can we balance the rights of diverse groups with the demands of individuals and the nation?

▶ TAGS: *community, identity, social change, diversity, civil rights, human dignity*

Preface

Everyone covers. To cover is to tone down a disfavored identity to fit into the mainstream. In our increasingly diverse society, all of us are outside the mainstream in some way. Nonetheless, being deemed mainstream is still often a necessity of social life. For this reason, every reader of this book has covered, whether consciously or not, and sometimes at significant personal cost.

Famous examples of covering abound. Ramón Estévez covered his ethnicity when he changed his name to Martin Sheen, as did Krishna Bhanji when he changed his name to Ben Kingsley. Margaret Thatcher covered her status as a woman when she trained with a voice coach to lower the timbre of her voice. Long after they came out as lesbians, Rosie O'Donnell and Mary Cheney still covered, keeping their same-sex partners out of the public eye. Issur Danielovitch Demsky covered his Judaism when he became Kirk Douglas, as did Joseph Levitch when he became Jerry Lewis. Franklin Delano Roosevelt covered his disability by ensuring his wheelchair was always hidden behind a desk before his Cabinet entered.

I doubt any of these people covered willingly. I suspect they were all bowing to an unjust reality that required them to tone down their stigmatized identities to get along in life. Sheen says he needed to "get a name people could pronounce and connect with" if he "wanted to work commercially." Yet he now regrets having done so, and has exhorted his sons—Emilio and Charlie—to use the family name. One of them has not done so, signaling the enduring force of the covering demand.

In a supposedly enlightened age, the persistence of the covering demand presents a puzzle. Today, race, national origin, sex, religion, and disability are all protected by federal civil rights laws. An increasing number of states and localities include sexual orientation in civil rights laws as well. Albeit with varying degrees of conviction, Americans have come to a consensus that people should not be penalized for being different along these dimensions. That consensus, however, does not protect individuals against demands that they mute those differences. We need an explanation for why the civil rights revolution has stalled on covering.

Covering has enjoyed such a robust and stubborn life because it is a form of assimilation. At least since Hector St. John de Crèvecoeur's 1782 *Letters from an American Farmer,* this country has touted assimilation as the way Americans of different backgrounds would be "melted into a new race of men." By the time Israel Zangwill's play of that name was performed in 1908, the "melting pot" had acquired the burnish of an American ideal. Only with the civil rights movement of the 1960s was this ideal challenged in any systematic way, with calls to move "beyond the melting pot" and to "celebrate diversity." And not withstanding that challenge, assimilation has never lost its hold on the American imagination. Indeed, as our country grows more pluralistic, we have seen a renaissance of the melting pot ideal. Fearful that we are spinning apart into balkanized groups, even liberals like Arthur Schlesinger have called for a recommitment to that ethic. In the United States, as in other industrialized democracies, we are seeing the "return of assimilation."

I recognize the value of assimilation, which is often necessary to fluid social interaction, to peaceful coexistence, and even to the dialogue through which difference is valued. For that reason, this is no simple screed against conformity. What I urge here is that we approach the renaissance of assimilation in this country critically. We must be willing to see the dark side of assimilation, and specifically of covering, which is the most widespread form of assimilation required of us today.

Covering is a hidden assault on our civil rights. We have not been able to see it as such because it has swaddled itself in the benign language of assimilation.

But if we look closely, we will see that covering is the way many groups are being held back today. The reason racial minorities are pressured to "act white" is because of white supremacy. The reason women are told to downplay their child-care responsibilities in the workplace is because of patriarchy. And the reason gays are asked not to "flaunt" is because of homophobia. So long as such covering demands persist, American civil rights will not have completed its work.

Unfortunately, the law has yet to perceive covering as a threat. Contemporary civil rights law generally only protects traits that individuals cannot change, like their skin color, chromosomes, or innate sexual orientations. This means that current law will not protect us against most covering demands, because such demands direct themselves at the behavioral aspects of our personhood. This is so despite the fact that covering imposes costs on us all.

The universality of the covering demand, however, is also a potential boon for civil rights advocates. I, too, worry about our current practice of fracturing into groups, each clamoring for state and social solicitude. For this reason, I do not think we can move forward by focusing on old-fashioned group-based identity politics. We must instead build a new civil rights paradigm on what draws us together rather than on what drives us apart. Because covering applies to us all, it provides an issue around which we can make common cause. This is the desire for authenticity, our common human wish to express ourselves without being impeded by unreasoning demands for conformity.

> **We must instead build a new civil rights paradigm on what draws us together rather than on what drives us apart.**

I thought I would make this argument in purely political terms. As a law professor, I have become accustomed to the tones of legal impersonality. But I came to see that I could not compose an argument about the importance of human authenticity without risking such authenticity myself. So I have written this . . . in a more intimate voice, blending memoir with argument. In trying to make the stakes of assimilation vivid, I draw on my attempts to elaborate my identity as a gay man, and, to a lesser extent, my identity as an Asian-American.

Yet this is not a standard "coming out" narrative or racial memoir. I follow the Romantics here in their belief that if a human life is described with enough particularity, the universal will begin to speak through it. What interests me about my story, and the stories of others, is how similar they are in revealing the bones of our common human endeavor, the yearning for human emancipation that stirs within us all.

The New Civil Rights

To describe the new civil rights, I return to the source of my argument. What most excited me about gay civil rights was its universal resonance. Unlike other civil rights groups, gays must articulate invisible selves without the initial support of our immediate communities. That makes the gay project of self-elaboration emblematic of the search for authenticity all of us engage in as human beings. It is work each of us must do for ourselves, and it is the most important work we can do.

In looking for a vocabulary for this quest for authenticity, I found psychoanalysts more helpful than lawyers. The object-relations theorist D. W. Winnicott makes a distinction between a True Self and a False Self that usefully tracks the distinction between the uncovered and covered selves. The True Self is the self that gives an individual the feeling of being real, which is "more than existing; it is finding a way to exist as oneself, and to relate to objects as oneself, and to have a self into which to retreat for relaxation." The True Self is associated with human spontaneity and authenticity: "Only the True Self can be creative and only the True Self can feel real." The False Self, in contrast, gives an individual a sense of being unreal, a sense of futility. It mediates the relationship between the True Self and the world.

What I love about Winnicott is that he does not demonize the False Self. To the contrary, Winnicott believes the False Self protects the True Self: "The False Self has one positive and very important function: to hide the True Self, which it does by compliance with environmental demands." Like a king castling behind a rook in chess, the more valuable but less powerful piece retreats behind the less valuable but more powerful one. Because the relationship between the True Self and the False Self is symbiotic, Winnicott believes both selves will exist even in the healthy individual.

Nonetheless, Winnicott defines health according to the degree of ascendancy the True Self gains over the False one. At the negative extreme, the False Self completely obscures the True Self, perhaps even from the individual herself. In a less extreme case, the False Self permits the True Self "a secret life." The individual approaches health only when the False Self has "as its main concern a search for conditions which will make it possible for the True Self to come into its own." Finally, in the healthy individual, the False Self is reduced to a "polite and mannered social attitude," a tool available to the fully realized True Self. 15

This paradigm captures my coming-out experience. My gay self, the True Self, was hidden behind an ostensibly straight False Self. Yet it would be wrong to cast the closeted self as purely inimical to the gay one. In my adolescence, this False Self protected the True Self until its survival was assured. Only at this point did the False Self switch from being a help to being a hindrance. And even after I came out, the False Self never disappeared. It was reduced to the minimum necessary to regulate relations between the True Self and the world.

I could slot other civil rights identities into Winnicott's paradigm. The importance of the paradigm, however, lies in its self-conscious universality. Winnicott posits that each of us has a True Self that must be expressed for us to have the feeling of being switched on, of being alive. And if the True Self embodies the importance of authenticity, the False Self embodies our ambivalence about assimilation, which is both necessary to survival and obstructive of life. The goal is not to eliminate assimilation altogether, but to reduce it to the necessary minimum. This is what the reason-forcing conversation seeks to do.

When I describe the uncovered self in Winnicott's terms, many people respond immediately with stories that attest to the concept's universality. Most of these have little to do with conventional civil rights categories. They often pertain to choices about people's careers or personal lives, like the woman who left a career in law to write plays, or the man who left his fiancée at the altar to pursue his first childhood love. I nonetheless hear the same themes threading through these stories as I do through the traditional civil rights cases. These individuals cannot articulate what authenticity is, but know an existence lived outside its imperative would be a substitute for life.

Parents often respond to the concept of the True Self by speaking of their children. Based on extensive clinical research, psychologist Carol Gilligan argues that children have an authentic voice they lose as they mature, with girls retaining it longer than boys. (The breaking of this emotional voice mirrors the breaking of the physical voice, as the voices of boys break earlier and more dramatically than those of girls.) Gilligan's work is replete with instances of parents awed by the directness and realness of their children. These parents suggest that one of the most agonizing dilemmas of parenting is how much they should require their children to cover in the world.

This psychological discourse about authentic selves sounds distant from current civil rights discourse. We must close that gap. The new civil rights must harness this universal impulse toward authenticity. That impulse should press us toward thinking of civil rights less in terms of groups than in terms of our common humanity.

Two recent cases show that the Supreme Court is sympathetic to that shift. In the 2003 case of *Lawrence v. Texas* . . . the Supreme Court struck down a Texas statute that criminalized same-sex sodomy. Many assumed the Court would use this case to decide whether to give gays the judicial protections currently accorded to racial minorities and women. But while the Court struck down the statute (and overruled *Bowers v. Hardwick* in the process), it did not do so based on the equality rights of gays. Rather, it held that the statute violated the fundamental right of all persons—straight, gay, or otherwise—to control our intimate sexual relations.

Similarly, in the 2004 case of *Tennessee v. Lane*, the Supreme Court considered the question of whether two paraplegic individuals could sue Tennessee for failing to make its courthouses wheelchair accessible. (One plaintiff was forced to crawl up the courthouse steps to answer criminal charges against him; the other, a certified court reporter, alleged she had lost job opportunities because some county courthouses were inaccessible.) Again, the Court ruled in favor of the minority group without framing its ruling in group-based equality rhetoric. Rather, it held that all persons—disabled or otherwise—have a "right of access to the courts," which had been denied in this case.

In an era when the Supreme Court has closed many civil rights doors, it has left this one wide open. It is much more sympathetic to "liberty" claims about freedoms we all hold than to "equality" claims asserted by a subset of the population. It is easy to see why. Equality claims—such as group-based accommodation claims—inevitably involve the Court in picking favorites among groups.

In an increasingly pluralistic society, the Court understandably wishes to steer clear of that enterprise. Liberty claims, on the other hand, emphasize what all Americans (or more precisely, all persons within the jurisdiction of the United States) have in common. The claim that we all have a right to sexual intimacy, or that we all have a right to access the courts, will hold no matter how many new groups proliferate in this country.

The Supreme Court's shift toward a more universal register can also be seen in its nascent acceptance of human rights. I worked on a friend-of-the-court brief in the *Lawrence* case produced by a team centered at Yale Law School. With the former President of Ireland and U.N. High Commissioner Mary Robinson as our client, we argued that decisions by international tribunals and courts in other Western democracies had recognized the fundamentality of the right to adult consensual sexual intimacy. We knew this argument would be resisted by some justices on the Court, who do not take kindly to arguments that decisions outside the United States should guide their jurisprudence. But to our surprise, the majority opinion cited our brief for the proposition that *Bowers* violated "values we share with a wider civilization."

At the end of their lives, both Martin Luther King Jr. and Malcolm X argued 25 for this transition from civil rights to human rights. Both believed that civil rights unduly focused on what distinguished individuals from one another, rather than emphasizing what they had in common. As Stewart Burns, one of the editors of the King papers at Stanford, observes, King "grasped that 'civil rights' carried too much baggage of the dominant tradition of American individualism and not enough counterweight from a tradition of communitarian impulses, collective striving, and common good." Similarly, Malcolm X exhorted Americans to "expand the civil-rights struggle to the level of human rights," so that the "jurisdiction of Uncle Sam" would not prevent us from allying with our "brothers" of other nations.

The universal rights of persons will probably be the way the Court will protect difference in the future. I predict that if the Court ever recognizes language rights, it will protect them as a liberty to which we are all entitled, rather than as an equality right attached to a particular national-origin group. And if the Court recognizes rights to grooming, such as the right to wear cornrows or not to wear makeup, I believe it will do so under something more akin to the German Constitution's right to personality rather than as a right attached to groups like racial minorities or women.

One of the great benefits of analyzing civil rights in terms of universal liberty rather than in terms of group-based equality is that it avoids making assumptions about group cultures. I've touched on the problem that the covering concept might assume too quickly that individuals behaving in "mainstream" ways are hiding some true identity, when in fact they might just be "being themselves." A female colleague of mine gave me a powerful version of this critique: "Here is what I dislike about your project. When I do something stereotypically masculine—like fixing my bike—your project makes it more likely people will think I'm putting on a gender performance rather than accepting the most straightforward explanation for what I'm doing. I don't fix my bike because I'm trying to downplay the fact that I'm a woman. I fix it because it's broken."

She gave another example: "When I was in graduate school, there was an African-American man who studied German Romantic poetry. Under your model, I could easily see someone saying he was 'covering' his African-American identity by studying something so esoteric and highbrow. But it was clear to me he was studying Romantic poetry because he was seized by it. And if someone had assumed he was studying it to 'act white,' they would have diminished him as a human being."

The coup de grâce: "Your commitment is to help people 'be themselves' — to resist demands to conform that take away their ability to be the individuals they are. But the covering idea could perpetuate the stereotypes you want to eliminate. One way minorities break stereotypes is by acting against them. If every time they do so, people assume they are 'covering' some essential stereotypical identity, the stereotypes will never go away."

I have literally lost sleep over this criticism. But in my waking hours, I take it more as a caution than as a wholesale indictment. I agree that we must not assume that individuals behaving in "mainstream" ways are necessarily covering. My ultimate commitment is to autonomy as a means of achieving authenticity, rather than to a fixed conception of what authenticity might be. (Here I follow Winnicott, who observes the True Self is not susceptible to specific definition, as its nature differs for each of us.) In talking about classic civil rights groups, I have focused on the demand to conform to the mainstream because I think that for most groups (except women) these are the demands that most threaten our authenticity. But I am equally opposed to demands that individuals reverse cover, because such demands are also impingements on our autonomy, and therefore on our authenticity.

> **I have literally lost sleep over this criticism.**

In practice, I expect the liberty paradigm to protect the authentic self better than the equality paradigm. While it need not do so, the equality paradigm is prone to essentializing the identities it protects. Under an equality paradigm, if a woman who wore a lot of makeup were protected by a court because makeup is an "essential" part of being a woman, this could reinforce the stereotype that women wear makeup. But if the same woman were given the liberty right to elaborate her own gender identity in ways that did not impinge on her job performance, she would be protected from demands to be either more "masculine" or more "feminine." Marsha Wislocki-Goin would be protected for wearing "too much makeup" and Darlene Jespersen would be protected for not wearing it at all. Each woman would then have the full panoply of options from which she could fashion her gender identity. And in protecting that range, the law would not articulate any presupposition about what an "authentic" or "essential" woman would look like. Authenticity would be something these women, and not the state or employer, would find for themselves.

Group-based identity politics is not dead. As I have argued, I still believe in a group-based accommodation model for existing civil rights groups. This is in part because I believe we have made a commitment to those groups to protect them from such covering demands. The statutory language of the Civil Rights Act and the Americans with Disabilities Act already protects racial minorities, religious minorities, women, and individuals with disabilities *as groups* against covering demands. It has been the courts that have erroneously limited the ambit of those protections. Such a group-based equality paradigm is completely consistent with the individual liberty paradigm. In fact, the equality and liberty strands of antidiscrimination law are inextricably intertwined.

Moreover, even if we shift the focus of civil rights law away from equality to liberty, identity politics will still be crucial. If it weren't for the gay rights movement, or the disability rights movement, cases like *Lawrence* or *Lane* would never have made it to the Court. But I'm sympathetic to the Court's desire to frame these cases not as "gay" or "disability" cases, but as cases touching on rights that, like a rising tide, will lift the boat of every person in America. Ironically, it may be the explosion of diversity in this country that will finally make us realize what we have in common. Multiculturalism has forced us to vary and vary the human being in the imagination until we discover what is invariable about her.

While I have great hopes for this new legal paradigm, I also believe law will be a relatively trivial part of the new civil rights. A doctor friend told me that in his first year of medical school, his dean described how doctors were powerless to cure the vast majority of human ills. People would get better, or they would not, but it would not be doctors who would cure them. Part of becoming a doctor, the dean said, was to surrender a layperson's awe for medical authority. I wished then that someone would give an analogous lecture to law students, and to Americans at large. My education in law has been in part an education in its limitations.

For starters, many covering demands are made by actors the law does not—and in my view should not—hold accountable, such as friends, family, neighbors, or people themselves. When I hesitate before engaging in a public display of same-sex affection, I am not thinking of the state or my employer, but of the strangers around me and my own internal censor. And while I am often tempted to sue myself, this is not my healthiest impulse.

Law is also an incomplete solution to coerced assimilation because it has yet to recognize the myriad groups subjected to covering demands outside traditional civil rights classifications like race, sex, orientation, religion, and disability. Whenever I speak about covering, I receive new instances of identities that can be covered. This is Winnicott's point—each one of us has a False Self that hides a True one. The law may someday move to protect some of these identities. But it will never protect them all.

Most important, law is incomplete in the qualitative remedies it provides. I confronted this recently when I became a plaintiff in a lawsuit against the Department of Defense. Under a congressional statute called the Solomon Amendment, the department threatened to cut off $350 million of federal funding from Yale University if the law school did not exempt the military from the law school's policy of protecting gays against discrimination by employers. Our suit argues that the statute is unconstitutional. I believe in this lawsuit, and was heartened that the vast majority of my law school colleagues signed on as plaintiffs. I was also elated when the district court judge, Judge Janet Hall, granted summary judgment in our favor. (As the government has taken an appeal, the case is still pending.) But there is nothing like being a plaintiff to realize that lawsuits occur between people who have no better way of talking to each other.

When I think about the elaboration of my gay identity, I am grateful to see litigation has had little to do with it. The department is the only entity I have ever wanted to sue. Even when I encountered demands for assimilation, my best response was to draw my interlocutor into a conversation. Just as important, framing the project of self-elaboration in purely legal—and therefore adversarial—terms would fail to honor all those who were not adversaries. I have described in these pages many individuals who helped me toward myself. But there were many more. I think here of my law professor Charles Reich, who wrote a memoir about coming out in 1976, when it was an act of real courage to do so, and who let me write the essay that begins this book in his class, though its relationship to the law was then entirely unclear. I think of the chair of my midtenure review committee, who sat me down when I was the only untenured member of the faculty and, unsurprisingly, a mass of nerves, to give me the verdict of the committee. He told me his only advice for the coming years was that I should be more myself, that instead of reasoning within the law as it existed, I should speak my truth and make the law shape itself around me. And I think of my parents, whose response to this manuscript was to say, with calm and conviction, that they were proud of the man I have become.

For these reasons, I am troubled that Americans seem increasingly to turn toward the law to do the work of civil rights precisely when they should be turning away from it. The real solution lies in all of us as citizens, not in the tiny subset of us who are lawyers. People who are not lawyers should have reason-forcing conversations outside the law. They should pull Goffman's term "covering" out of academic obscurity and press it into the popular lexicon, so that it has the same currency as terms like "passing" or "the closet." People confronted with demands to cover should feel emboldened to seek a reason for that demand, even if the law does not reach the actors making the demand, or recognize the group burdened by it. These reason-forcing conversations should happen outside courtrooms—in workplaces and restaurants, schools and playgrounds, chat rooms and living rooms, public squares and bars. They should occur informally and intimately, where tolerance is made and unmade.

What will constitute a good enough reason to justify assimilation will ⁴⁰ obviously be controversial. But I want to underscore that we have come to some consensus that certain reasons are illegitimate—like white supremacy, patriarchy, homophobia, religious intolerance, and animus toward the disabled. I ask us to be true to the commitments we have made by never accepting such biases as legitimate grounds for covering demands. Beyond that, I have sought to engender a series of conversations, rather than a series of results—what reasons count, and for what purposes, will be for us to decide by facing one another as individuals. My personal inclination is always to privilege the claims of the individual against countervailing interests like "neatness" or "workplace harmony." But we should have that conversation.

Such conversations are the best—and perhaps the only—way to give both assimilation and authenticity their proper due. These conversations will help us chart and stay the course between the monocultural America suggested by conservative alarmists and the balkanized America suggested by the radical multiculturalists. They will reveal the true dimension of civil rights. The aspiration of civil rights has always been to permit people to pursue their human flourishing without limitations based on bias. Focusing on law prevents us from seeing the revolutionary breadth of that aspiration, as law has limited civil rights to particular groups. I am not faulting that limitation, as I think prioritization is necessary, and that the law's priorities are correct. But civil rights, which has always extended far beyond the law, may now need to do so more than ever. It is only when we leave the law that civil rights suddenly stops being about particular groups and starts to become a project of human flourishing in which we all have a stake.

We must use the relative freedom of adulthood to integrate the many selves we hold. This includes uncovering the selves we buried long ago because they were inconvenient, impractical, or even hated. Because they must pass the test of survival, most of the selves we hold, like most of our lives, are ordinary. Yet sometimes, what is consequential in us begins to shine.

Questions for Critical Reading

1. What does Yoshino mean by the "new" civil rights? Define the term by locating passages from his text. What makes it new? How does it differ from "old" civil rights? Use Yoshino's text to define liberty and equality paradigms as part of your response.

2. What is "covering"? Define the concept using Yoshino's text and then offer your own example.

3. How does Yoshino think we can achieve the new civil rights? Provide passages that show his position and then respond to it. Do you think his vision is possible? Is it something we should strive for? In making your response, reread Yoshino's text critically to locate points of connection between his position and yours.

Exploring Context

1. Explore the Web site for the U.S. Commission on Civil Rights (usccr.gov). Which paradigm does it reflect, liberty or equality? Use your definition of these terms from Question 1 of Questions for Critical Reading.

2. Yoshino uses recent Supreme Court decisions to make his argument. Visit the Web site for the Supreme Court at supremecourtus.gov. What recent cases have concerned civil rights? What impact do these cases (or the lack of such cases) have on Yoshino's argument?

3. According to Yoshino, changes in civil rights should come not from legislation but through conversation. Visit BlogPulse's trend tool (blogpulse.com/trend) and search for *civil rights* and related terms. Are people talking about these issues online? What does this say about Yoshino's argument? Connect your exploration to your response to Question 3 of Questions for Critical Reading.

Questions for Connecting

1. Kwame Anthony Appiah also extols the power of conversation in "Making Conversation" (p. 57) and "The Primacy of Practice" (p. 63). Place his ideas in conversation with Yoshino's essay, synthesizing their ideas about the power of conversation. Is Yoshino also calling for cosmopolitanism? How do civil rights function like other social practices?

2. Though explicitly concerned with aesthetics, Virginia Postrel's "The Boundaries of Design" (p. 296) might also be considered as an essay on civil rights and individual liberties. How do Postrel's arguments affect Yoshino's? How are the challenges of locating aesthetic boundaries similar to the challenges of civil rights? Can Postrel's insights help us achieve a new civil rights, or do they point to the difficulty of such a project? Use your understanding of the new civil rights from Question 1 of Questions for Critical Reading in your response.

3. Francis Fukuyama argues for the necessity of a concept of human dignity in his essay of the same name (p. 142). What role might human dignity play in civil rights? Is Factor X an essential component of a new civil rights? Synthesize the ideas of Fukuyama and Yoshino into an argument about human rights.

Language Matters

1. Every part of speech and every punctuation mark has certain "rights"; for example, the period has the right to end a sentence and the comma does not. How can we describe the rules of grammar using Yoshino's ideas of liberty and equality paradigms?

2. Defining terms is an important part of academic writing. Locate a passage where Yoshino defines a term. What strategies does he use? Does he offer a dictionary definition? An example? An authority? How should you define terms in your own text?

3. Is there a form of covering that takes place in peer revision? Are people tempted to tone down unfavorable comments? How does Yoshino's discussion of covering offer advice for more effective peer revision?

Assignments for Writing

1. Yoshino discusses the concept of groups and individuals covering in order to conform to the mainstream. Locate your own example of covering and then write an essay that extends or complicates Yoshino's argument through your example. Does your example reinforce or refute Yoshino's ideas about covering? Are any civil rights at stake in your example? What relation is there between covering and civil rights? You will want to use your definition of the term *covering* from Question 2 of Questions for Critical Reading.

2. Yoshino discusses the challenges to civil rights posed by the proliferation of groups engendered by a diverse society; he offers his own vision of how to transform civil rights to account for these groups. Write a paper in which you suggest what changes we should make to civil rights and how we might achieve those changes. Draw from your work in Questions for Critical Reading and Questions for Connecting in making your argument. Consider, too: Should we use a liberty paradigm or an equality paradigm? Would you propose a different paradigm of your own? Is legislation the best way to achieve your vision for civil rights? Is conversation?

3. In Question 3 of Exploring Context you examined current online conversations about civil rights. Yoshino suggests that such conversations are the best means of achieving a new civil rights. Write a paper in which you argue for the role of conversation in social change. Is talking about an issue enough to engender change? Does it matter who is doing the talking? How does change happen in society?

Rites/Rights of Passage: Identifying the Self

JULIA ALVAREZ

MADELEINE ALBRIGHT

JOAN DIDION

DEBORA L. SPAR

In this sequence, you will examine the connection between rites that help us form our identities and the larger rights of our communities. You'll begin by using Julia Alvarez to consider the role of quinceañeras in the development of self-identity. Building on that analysis, you will use Madeleine Albright to explore the ways in which national as well as personal identities can be shaped by forces such as religion. Then you'll turn to a difficult and very personal rite of passage — the death of a loved one — using Joan Didion to consider the ways in which death changes those who are left behind. The final assignments of this sequence turn to the family, first by synthesizing Didion's and Alvarez's ideas and then by using Debora L. Spar to determine what rights should be allowed in the creation of families through international adoption.

▶ TAGS: kinship, *family*, change, *tradition*, loss, *religion*, community, mourning, *culture*, death, *identity*

Assignment 1. ALVAREZ

How do quinceañeras help to define self-identity in the Hispanic community? Write a paper in which you define the relationship between these rituals and self-identity. In making your argument you may want to use the other rituals you explored in Question 3 of Exploring Context (p. 53) or some of the concepts you synthesized in Questions for Connecting, such as super-replicators or cultural performance.

   To help you begin your critical thinking on this assignment, consider these questions: How do traditions, both native and acquired, contribute to the development of identity? How does gender determine self-identity in the Hispanic community? Why do only girls receive quinceañeras? What part does retroculturation play in the establishing of self-identity? Is this rite of passage similar to or different from rites of passage in other cultures? Does the commercialization of the quinceañera affect its overall value in establishing a girl's self-worth and self-identity? If so, how?

Assignment 2. ALVAREZ AND ALBRIGHT

Quinceañeras often have a religious component. And, as Albright's essay makes clear, religion is often a significant force in shaping identities, both personal and national. Write a paper in which you explore the ways in which personal and national identities are shaped by faith. You might begin by revisiting your work on the relationship between religion and diplomacy in Question 1 of Questions for Critical Reading for Albright (p. 31).

To help you begin your critical thinking on this assignment, reflect on these questions: What role does religion play in shaping personal and national identities? Can retroculturation assist in creating a faith-based diplomacy? How do quinceañeras transcend national borders? In what sense are they a kind of international diplomacy? Do girls have a right to a quinceañera or to other rites of passage?

Assignment 3. DIDION

One of the more difficult rites of passage we must face is dealing with the loss of a loved one. Write a paper in which you analyze the effect death has on an individual. You might want to start by using the definition of *grief* you created in Questions for Critical Reading (p. 102) as well as your arguments on the ways in which Didion's essay is concerned with creating meaning in life.

To help you begin your critical thinking on this assignment, consider these questions: How does grief inform self-identity? How does Didion change as a person because of this experience? How does an unexpected death have a greater effect on an individual? Is a distant encounter with death, such as knowledge of a national disaster, as much a rite of passage as an intimate encounter is? How so?

Assignment 4. ALVAREZ AND DIDION

Both Alvarez's and Didion's essays are centrally concerned with families. Both, too, consider the ways in which families, whether immediate or extended, influence who and what we are. Using both Alvarez and Didion to support your argument, write a paper in which you examine the role that family plays in shaping self-identity.

To help you begin your critical thinking on this assignment, ask yourself these questions: Does a sense of cultural identity come from the home or the culture as a whole? How do families change when a loved one is lost? Do rites of passage such as quinces or mourning make families grow closer? Where is the boundary between an individual and the family? Do we find that boundary in the ordinary instant?

Assignment 5. SPAR AND ONE OTHER

Write a paper in which you identify and analyze the challenges that emerge when children are raised outside of their native culture. Utilize the ideas of Spar and one other author in this sequence to assist. Consider starting with your analysis of the role race plays in adoption in Question 3 of Questions for Critical Reading for Spar (p. 436). You might also want to use the Rainbow Kids or Adoption.com Web sites in supporting your argument.

Also think about these questions: Do parents have a responsibility to educate an adopted child in the culture of his or her heritage? Should race or ethnicity play a role in the adoption process? How might retroculturation help in adoption? What role should faith or religion play in adoption? Does adoption involve a kind of mourning?

SEQUENCE 2

Surviving Alone, Surviving Together: Ethical Conflict in a Global Economy

KWAME ANTHONY APPIAH

HELEN EPSTEIN

THOMAS FRIEDMAN

DEBORA L. SPAR

This sequence asks you to examine how we can survive and indeed thrive in an interconnected and diverse world. The first assignment, with Kwame Anthony Appiah, asks you to develop a set of conceptual tools for creating social change. You will extend these tools using the work of Helen Epstein, considering how they can be used to create change on a global scale. The third assignment more specifically asks you to apply that work to the global fight against terrorism, drawing additionally from Thomas Friedman's work on mutant supply chains. In the final assignment, you will use Debora L. Spar to consider the limits of global cooperation and the boundaries between surviving together and surviving alone.

▶ TAGS: *international policy*, *globalization*, *ethics*, *terrorism*, *community*, *social change*

Assignment 1. APPIAH

Appiah discusses his choice of cosmopolitanism as a rubric for moving forward. At the same time, he also discusses the problems of realizing social change. Based on his discussion of the primacy of practice, how can we advocate for change in social practices? Write a paper in which you identify the best tools for achieving social change. You may wish to build on the cultural practice you explored in Question 2 of Exploring Context (p. 73) in constructing and supporting your argument.

Assignment 2. APPIAH AND EPSTEIN

Epstein describes two very different approaches to HIV/AIDS prevention in Africa. She points out that in South Africa, where open discussion of the epidemic is taboo, prevention programs that avoid the harsh realities of the AIDS epidemic are popular but less successful than their counterparts in Uganda, where the realities of the disease are openly acknowledged. To what extent can Appiah's primacy of practice be applied to AIDS prevention in countries with stringent social taboos? Drawing on Epstein's and Appiah's ideas, write a paper in which you determine how individuals acting locally can create global change. You may want to draw from your definition of *social cohesion* from Question 2 of Questions for Critical Reading for Epstein (p. 117).

Ask yourself these questions: How can we overcome the primacy of practice when such practices put lives at risk from disease? What role does conversation have in creating change locally or globally? How can we take action to solve problems like HIV/AIDS even when we hold different values? Is social cohesion an effect of cosmopolitanism, or do these two concepts work against each other? What role might global companies and advertising play in social change?

Assignment 3. EPSTEIN AND FRIEDMAN

Friedman argues that countries participating in global supply chains become economically interdependent and are thus less likely to be involved in political conflicts. At the same time he warns that terrorists are using similar supply chains to spread violence around the world. Given that both terrorism and HIV/AIDS threaten lives without respect for borders, how can we mitigate terrorist supply chains? Write an essay in which you use Epstein's insights about HIV/AIDS prevention in Africa to propose strategies for fighting terrorism globally. Use your work on the role of collaboration as well as your analysis of mutant supply chains from Questions for Critical Reading for Friedman (p. 138).

Also think about: How can we promote collaboration while minimizing its destructive potential? How can social cohesion play a role in the fight against terrorism? What about lifestyle brands? What role do supply chains play in the transmission of and fight against HIV/AIDS in Africa?

Assignment 4. SPAR AND ONE OTHER

Spar focuses on the ethical questions concerning international adoption, a practice that can be seen as either a humanitarian endeavor or as a global black market in babies. Using Spar and one of the other authors in this sequence, write a paper in which you determine the limits of international policy on individuals.

Should international adoptions be more closely regulated? Are babies part of a global supply chain? Should governments mandate individual behavior? When health is at stake, as in HIV/AIDS, does that make a difference? How do we work together while retaining our rights as individuals?

SEQUENCE 3

Yes We Can, But Should We?
The Politics of Science

THE DALAI LAMA

KENJI YOSHINO

FRANCIS FUKUYAMA

MADELEINE ALBRIGHT

How can we develop an ethical system to guide us in scientific and technological progress? In this sequence of assignments, you will begin to answer that question first by working with the Dalai Lama's examination of genetic technologies, considering the ramifications of these technologies for economic and political stability. Then you will turn to Kenji Yoshino's discussion of civil rights, synthesizing his ideas with the Dalai Lama's to argue for the best balance between progress and rights. In the third assignment, you will discuss all of these issues specifically in the context of stem cell research, folding Francis Fukuyama's ideas about biotechnology and human dignity into your analysis. Finally, you will use Madeleine Albright to look at the role of religion in science. If our ethics are not based in faith, then what system can we develop to guide us in the search for new knowledge?

▶ TAGS: *diplomacy,* **morality,** *biotechnology,* knowledge and responsibility, *human dignity,* **ethics,** civil rights

Assignment 1. THE DALAI LAMA

The possible consequences of genetic manipulation reach far beyond the sphere of science. Consider, for example, the role of national and global politics in relation to scientific breakthroughs that have the potential to literally change the face of humanity but will almost certainly not be available to everyone. Write a paper in which you examine the consequences of technology in terms of social and economic stability. How does the Dalai Lama characterize the relationship between knowledge and responsibility? In what ways does genetic engineering have the potential to perpetuate our disparities on social, political, and ethical levels? Should new technologies be available to everyone?

Assignment 2. THE DALAI LAMA AND YOSHINO

According to the Dalai Lama, rapid advances in technology demand new ethical standards. Yoshino makes a similar argument in claiming that the proliferation of groups in a diverse society necessitates a new civil rights. Synthesizing the positions of these two authors, write an essay in which you determine the best means of balancing political rights and technological progress. You might want to use the understanding of Yoshino's concept of civil rights that you developed in Questions for Critical Reading (p. 488) in making your argument.

And consider: Are scientists just another group demanding rights? Should we use a liberty paradigm or an equality paradigm in considering the ethical quandaries raised by biotechnology? Are reason-forcing conversations the best means of achieving the Dalai Lama's vision for ethics, or is legislation? What role does a moral compass play in both science and civil rights?

Assignment 3. THE DALAI LAMA, YOSHINO, AND FUKUYAMA

In the first two assignments of this sequence you were asked to consider the impact of science and technology on social and economic stability as well as on political rights. Fukuyama addresses some of these same concerns in his discussion of biotechnology and human dignity. Synthesize the ideas of these three authors to write a paper in which you determine the ethics of stem cell research. Your goal in writing this paper is not to argue for or against this particular field of scientific inquiry. Instead, you will want to propose how we can make decisions about such difficult matters.

Reflect on the Dalai Lama's moral compass. Does human dignity help us find that moral compass? Is human dignity part of the True Self or the False Self? How do the needs for both a moral compass and human dignity limit any claims to a liberty paradigm for civil rights?

Assignment 4. ALBRIGHT AND ONE OTHER

The authors you've examined so far have largely separated ethics from the question of religion, even though faith serves as the foundation for many people's ethical systems. Albright suggests that we should take faith into consideration when it comes to foreign policy. Should we do the same for science? Working with Albright and one of the authors from this sequence, write an essay in which you determine the role faith should play in science. You might want to begin by revisiting your response to Question 1 of Questions for Critical Reading for Albright (p. 31), in which you explored whether faith was ultimately a help or a hindrance to diplomacy.

Also ponder: How can we create an ethical system apart from religion? Should faith play a role in determining research agendas? How can we accommodate religious concerns while still pursuing technological and scientific progress?

SEQUENCE 4

The Talking Cure: Conversation as Social Medicine

DANIEL GILBERT

HELEN EPSTEIN

JAMES SUROWIECKI

STEVEN JOHNSON

In this sequence you will analyze the role conversations can play in creating social change. To start, you will explore Daniel Gilbert's concept of a surrogate, a way of predicting your own future happiness through conversations with someone experiencing the future you would like to have. Then you will extend Gilbert's idea using Helen Epstein's analysis of HIV/AIDS prevention in Africa in order to consider the potential for conversation to create social and not just personal change. Yet conversation is not without its risks, and so you will turn to James Surowiecki's analysis of the failure of small groups in order to determine the limits of conversation as a social medicine. Finally, with Steven Johnson, you will synthesize these positions to consider technologies that can harness conversation as social medicine.

▶ TAGS: *conversation*, *social change*, *technology*, *surrogates*

Assignment 1. GILBERT

According to Gilbert, surrogates can offer us an accurate sense of our future happiness. Write a paper in which you assess the potential of the kind of surrogates that Gilbert describes. You will want to extend, complicate, or refute Gilbert's argument for surrogates and their reliability in predicting the future. Consider these questions: What role does individuality have in determining our future happiness? Is Gilbert correct in claiming that we are not as unique as we believe? Can surrogates be used to examine all future events? How can surrogates be used to control social processes? If we are not unique, why do we see ourselves as individuals? Use your definition of *surrogate* from Question 2 of Questions for Critical Reading (p. 187) as well as your work with Yahoo! Answers from Questions 3 of Exploring Context (p. 188).

Assignment 2. GILBERT AND EPSTEIN

In the last assignment you considered the power of conversation—specifically conversations with surrogates—to help people shape their futures. Epstein, however, is concerned with the future of more than just individuals. Her analysis of HIV/AIDS prevention programs concerns the future of that disease on the African continent. Using Gilbert's and Epstein's ideas, write a paper in which you determine the power of conversation to change people's behavior. Consider drawing from your work with Epstein, particularly your analysis of how social networking sites like Facebook can facilitate conversations around HIV/AIDS, from Question 3 of Exploring Context (p. 118).

Contemplate these questions to help you in formulating your argument: Could surrogates play a role in the fight against HIV/AIDS? What role does imagination play in social cohesion? How might Gilbert explain the failure of the loveLife campaign? Can conversation about the disease function as a kind of super-replicator?

Assignment 3. SUROWIECKI AND ONE OTHER

To some extent, Surowiecki's essay is centrally concerned with the failure of conversations—for example, the conversation of the Mission Management Team concerning *Columbia*. You've already explored the potential of conversation to create change, but what are the risks of conversation in group or social settings? Write a paper in which you explore the failures of conversation using the work of Surowiecki and one or more of the other authors you've read. Recall your determination of whether or not small groups are worth the risk from Question 3 of Questions for Critical Reading for Surowiecki (p. 451).

Consider, too: What are the risks involved when conversation fails? Given those risks, is conversation a good choice as social medicine? Given Surowiecki's analysis, how might surrogates fail to predict your future? Does group polarization threaten social cohesion?

Assignment 4. JOHNSON AND TWO OTHERS

Johnson explains that by altering the type of feedback given to a system, the public can alter the response of that system. Specifically, he demonstrates this power through his analysis of Slashdot. Using the work of Johnson and two of the other authors you've read in this sequence, write a paper in which you determine how technology can harness the power of conversation in creating social change. Draw from your own analysis of Slashdot in Question 3 of Questions for Critical Reading (p. 214) as well as Question 1 of Exploring Context (p. 214). What other technologies can enable this transformative power of conversation?

Ask yourself: How does technology enable the spread of super-replicators? How does it enable greater access to surrogates? What role might technology play in the prevention of HIV/AIDS? How can it be used to expand Uganda's success at that task? Can technology mitigate the factors that cause small groups to fail?

SEQUENCE 5

Wonderful Displays: Revelations of Art and Culture

MICHAEL KIMMELMAN

DIANA TAYLOR

VIRGINIA POSTREL

RICHARD RESTAK

In this sequence you will evaluate the role that art plays in shaping culture as well as the boundaries for creative expression. First you will explore Michael Kimmelman's argument by locating your own example of a "wonder cabinet." Then you will read more generally about the role that performance plays in culture by examining Diana Taylor's argument. With that base of understanding, you will then turn to the limits of artistic expression by exploring the rights of individuals and of communities using the work of Virginia Postrel and by exploring, more abstractly, the roles of chaos and order in both art and society. In the next assignment of the sequence, you will apply your ideas to the question of censorship as a way of making your understandings of the boundaries of art concrete. In the final assignment of the sequence, you will use Richard Restak to think about the future of art and aesthetics in a technological culture.

▶ TAGS: *culture*, *art*, *performance*, *aesthetic boundaries*, *censorship*, *creativity*, *technology*

Assignment 1. KIMMELMAN

Kimmelman states that the great collector is touched to the core by the confusion and the dispersal in which things are found in this world. Locate your own example of a wonder cabinet and write an essay in which you extend or complicate Kimmelman's argument through this example. Does your example participate in finding order out of chaos? Can a collection of dissimilar objects in itself be considered ordered? What is the purpose of collecting? Does collecting make sense of a senseless world? In making your argument, consider using your exploration of eBay in Question 1 of Exploring Context (p. 226).

Assignment 2. TAYLOR

Taylor examines cultural performances and the part they play in making political statements, memorializing tragic events, and creating cultural identities.
In suggesting that Princess Diana's funeral was a performance, she asks us to
consider what *performance* means as well as the relevance of performances to
culture. Using Taylor's argument, write an essay in which you determine the
effect of performance on a culture. Can performances create social change, or
are they just "play"? You might want to begin with your analysis of the social
function of mourning from Question 3 of Questions for Critical Reading as well
as your definitions of *social drama* and *ghosting* (p. 477).

Consider these questions too: Did Princess Diana's funeral unite cultures?
Why or why not? How does art bring cultures together? Can the expression of
art help to form a cultural identity? What makes the funeral of a celebrity or
political figure a "performance" and not just a funeral?

Assignment 3. TAYLOR AND POSTREL

Taylor and Postrel are both concerned with the role of aesthetics and performance within a culture. Postrel, however, specifically considers the boundaries
of individual aesthetic expression within a community. Drawing from Postrel's
analysis and Taylor's ideas, write a paper in which you argue how best to
balance the rights of the community and those of the individual in terms of art
and aesthetics. You might want to begin with your answers to the Questions for
Critical Reading for Postrel (p. 329), particularly your response to spillovers and
legislation in relation to aesthetics.

What role should artistic creativity have in a community? What is expressive freedom? What is visual pollution? Are murals a form of visual pollution?
Why or why not? Does social drama play a role in aesthetic boundaries? What
spillovers are caused by community expressions of mourning? What is the
hauntology of aesthetics?

Assignment 4. KIMMELMAN AND POSTREL

Art and aesthetics, Kimmelman and Postrel seem to suggest, have in part to do
with organizing the world as a means of both creative expression and community formation. Write a paper in which you examine the functions of order and
chaos in art, aesthetics, and community. Your examination of local design ordinances from Question 2 of Exploring Context for Postrel (p. 329) might serve as
a specific foundation for your analysis.

But also think about: Is art simply the ordering of chaos? How do we determine the best balance of order and chaos? Do aesthetic boundaries represent
that balance? Does a wonder cabinet constrain disorder? Are wonder cabinets
a kind of aesthetic boundary? Is chaos a spillover of art or collecting? Is order?

Do communities need art? How do communities negotiate order and chaos, and what role does art play in that negotiation?

Assignment 5. KIMMELMAN, TAYLOR, AND POSTREL

All of the authors you've read so far are centrally concerned with the impact of art and aesthetics on culture. Examine the intersection of aesthetics and culture more closely by writing a paper in which you use all three of these authors to make an argument about the ethics of censorship.

Weigh these questions: Does a community have the right to regulate artistic expression? What about when that expression threatens to cause disorder? What role does censorship play in social drama? Are collections a kind of ghosting? How does the reaction of minority communities to Princess Diana's death suggest the limits of any form of censorship?

Assignment 6. RESTAK AND ONE OTHER

Restak asks us how technology affects the way we perform everyday tasks. On the one hand, technology enables us to perform many tasks at once; on the other hand, none of the tasks is done well because of the competing demands on our brains. Using Restak and one of the other authors from this sequence, write a paper in which you determine the impact of technology on creative expression. Draw from your discussion of the relation between culture and biology from Question 2 of Questions for Critical Reading for Restak (p. 344).

Also ask yourself these questions: Is multitasking a form of performance? Can multitasking be tragic? Are we moving so fast that we are unable to appreciate art? Are we moving into a future that will make the arts unnecessary in culture? How might the rewiring of our brains change our understanding of art and aesthetics?

SEQUENCE 6

Trouble with a Capital "C": Communities and Integration

REBEKAH NATHAN

KWAME ANTHONY APPIAH

THOMAS FRIEDMAN

MARSHALL POE

In this sequence you will explore the role of diversity in forming successful communities. You'll begin by using Rebekah Nathan's work to consider the possibility of a fully integrated community. You will then expand that analysis using Kwame Anthony Appiah's, suggesting the tools we can use to form successful and diverse communities. Such communities are not without risk, and so you will turn to an analysis of Thomas Friedman to examine the dangers of community both in general and, more specifically, through an analysis of ethnic conflicts in the world today. Finally, you will use Marshall Poe's examination of Wikipedia's success to imagine an open, collaborative world. In completing these assignments, you will gain an understanding of the challenges facing community formation, the risks of diversity, and the possibilities of integration in the world today.

▶ TAGS: community, globalization, diversity, education, supply chains, ethnic conflict, integration, cosmopolitanism

Assignment 1. NATHAN

Nathan notes that despite AnyU's best efforts to unite the university's population, students who make up the different communities within the school would rather bond within their own social groups than venture outside of them. Assess the situation Nathan talks about in her essay. Thinking beyond Nathan's findings, write a paper in which you examine the possibilities of communities becoming fully integrated. Is such integration even possible in a world made up of so many diverse and differing communities? The purpose of this essay is for you to apply the concepts in Nathan's essay to your own specific observations and experiences. Rather than simply writing a story about your own opinions, you should instead use your experiences among and observations of diverse communities, on an academic campus or elsewhere, to explore the possibilities of a truly integrated community. You may also want to use your responses to Questions for Critical Reading and Exploring Context (pp. 246–247) in supporting your argument.

Assignment 2. NATHAN AND APPIAH

In the last assignment you considered the possibility of integrating communities and the challenges inherent in such a task. Appiah's ideas about cosmopolitanism and the processes of changes in practice offer additional insight on this topic. Using both Appiah and Nathan, write a paper in which you determine the key tools necessary for successfully forming diverse communities. You might build your argument from the work you did in Question 2 of Questions for Critical Reading for Appiah (p. 73), in which you explored the tools needed to enact cosmopolitanism.

Also consider: Can we form diverse communities in practice without agreeing on the values behind such communities? How does the challenge of accomplishing diversity on college campuses reflect the challenge of embracing community on a global scale? Can conversation overcome ego-centered networks?

Assignment 3. FRIEDMAN AND APPIAH

Appiah argues for the need for cosmopolitanism among world citizens; in Friedman's essay we see how companies and nations also benefit from "world citizen" attitudes. Yet Friedman also illustrates how such networks can have undesirable effects and consequences. Use Friedman's examination of global networks and mutant supply chains to complicate Appiah's discussion about the importance of interconnected social networks, writing a paper in which you explore the dangers of a connected, flattened world. In the end, is a completely interconnected world really the ideal world? You might begin your critical thinking by revisiting your discussion of collaboration and mutant supply chains from Questions for Critical Reading for Friedman (p. 138).

Also contemplate: Can cosmopolitanism mitigate mutant supply chains? Is terrorism a consequence of the lack of diversity? How can we agree on practices for global peace while holding different values? Can businesses contribute to cosmopolitanism?

Assignment 4. FRIEDMAN, NATHAN, AND APPIAH

All three authors you've read so far discuss collaboration in one form or another, extolling its virtues while also warning of its dangers. Write a paper in which you use all three of these authors to propose strategies for minimizing ethnic conflicts in the world today. You might consider choosing a specific contemporary ethnic war, such as the one in Darfur.

Ask yourself: How does the experience of community and diversity on college campuses play out in the larger world? What are the limits of cosmopolitanism? Though the Dell Theory of Conflict Prevention seems to promote peace between nations, what tools are there for promoting peace *within* nations?

Assignment 5. POE AND ONE OTHER

Poe explores how the collaborative construction of knowledge plays out on the Internet, but the ideas and problems he touches on have much wider implications. Using Poe's work and at least one other reading from this sequence, consider the possibility of a world that is completely "open," without any rules aside from those agreed upon by a majority. Examine the lessons that could be learned from entities like Wikipedia and use these lessons to write a paper in which you argue how our world would differ if it were left completely "open."

In making your argument, respond to these questions: What would happen to minority groups in such a society? Would groups form more diverse connections between each other, or would there be greater segregation? What chance would cosmopolitanism have in such a world? Would global supply chains be possible? Would they be necessary? Is such a world possible or even desirable?

SEQUENCE 7

Deep Impact: Technology and Our World

MARSHALL POE

THOMAS FRIEDMAN

RICHARD RESTAK

FRANCIS FUKUYAMA

In this sequence you will explore the impact of technology on ourselves, on our world, and on what it means to be human. You'll begin by looking at the ways in which technology has changed our understanding of "experts," specifically using Marshall Poe's analysis of Wikipedia and the collaborative creation of knowledge. In the next assignment you will turn to Thomas Friedman's examination of the globalized, "flattened" world to determine the economic and political effects of technology. In the final assignments of this sequence, you will use first Richard Restak's work and then Francis Fukuyama's to assess technology's impact on biology and our concepts of the human race. In performing these analyses, you will gain a new understanding of the ways in which technology permeates our lives. You will also gain conceptual tools for assessing and perhaps mitigating technology's impact on humanity.

▶ TAGS: *politics*, *technology*, *knowledge*, *human dignity*, *multitasking*, *collaboration*, *economics*

Assignment 1. POE

What is the power of experts? Does a consensus determine the truth? Poe's essay asks us to consider these questions, since the collaborative authorship of Wikipedia suggests that experts are not vital in the creation of knowledge. Write a paper in which you suggest the proper boundaries between experts and nonexperts in relation to knowledge.

Also think about: What role does technology play in this process? Should experts be granted special status in relation to knowledge? What makes an expert "expert" anyway?

Assignment 2. FRIEDMAN

In the first assignment of this sequence you were asked to consider the impact technology has had on our concept of what an "expert" is. Friedman is also concerned with how technology has changed our world, addressing this topic both directly, through his opening narrative about the construction of his laptop, and more generally, through a discussion of the complex networks of supply chains around the world. Write a paper in which you consider the ways in which technology has influenced both economics and politics.

Consider: How did social networking sites affect the 2008 presidential election? How did television determine the outcome of the 1960 election? How do supply chains determine international or domestic politics? How did the economic crisis or "financiapocalypse" of 2008 reflect the dangers of a technologically interconnected world? In what specific ways has technology connected economics and politics?

Assignment 3. RESTAK AND ONE OTHER

Through your analyses of Poe and Friedman you've considered the impact of technology on knowledge, economics, and politics. But Restak raises a far more fundamental question: How is technology rewiring our brains? How can the strategies described by Poe or Friedman mitigate these effects? Write a paper in which you use the work of Restak and one of the other authors from this sequence to explore the ways in which collaboration can counteract the detrimental effects of multitasking. You might want to begin with your examination of multitasking from Question 1 of Questions for Critical Reading for Restak (p. 344).

In thinking critically about this assignment, ask: How does Wikipedia represent the benefits of collaborative attention to a subject? Does it represent a kind of antidote to "modern nerves"? Do mutant supply chains represent the potential for a kind of hyperfocus? Does global interconnection through supply chains minimize the effects of ADD?

Assignment 4. FUKUYAMA AND ONE OTHER

Fukuyama is centrally concerned with what it means to be human, particularly in relation to emerging genetic technologies. Throughout this sequence you've considered the impact of technology on ourselves and on our world. Now, using the work of Fukuyama and one of the other authors from this sequence, write a paper in which you determine the point at which science, financial wealth, and access to technology will be, or is already, intrinsic to the development of the human race. Your definition of Factor X from Question 1 of Questions for Critical Reading (p. 166) will be a critical starting point for thinking about your argument.

Ask yourself: What makes us human? Are we overreaching the ethical boundaries of science? What are the benefits of genetic manipulation to our development, and what are the possible pitfalls? Will genetic engineering level the playing field between people, or will it merely reinforce the economic stratification present today?

SEQUENCE 8

Every Body's Right: Buying Bodies

MARY ROACH

DANIEL GILBERT

DEBORA L. SPAR

JULIA SERANO

In this sequence you will explore the implications of the human body as object and commodity. That exploration will begin with Mary Roach, as you locate your own example of the human body as object in order to extend or complicate her discussion of human cadaver research. Then, by using Daniel Gilbert's ideas about predicting future happiness, you will consider how to best make decisions about the use of our bodies after death. The next assignment turns from the end of life to its beginning, as you use Debora L. Spar's analysis of the global adoption market to determine the role that economics should play in adoption. Finally, with Julia Serano, you will examine the function of the media in objectifying the body. As you complete this sequence you will have a better understanding of the complex issues at play when the body is treated as a commodity, to be given, bought, sold, or transformed.

▶ TAGS: *research*, **body**, *economics*, *media*, *adoption*, *objectification*, *makeovers*

Assignment 1. ROACH

Roach discusses the use of human cadavers for military testing, suggesting that the researchers who conduct these tests must approach the cadaver as an object rather than a human. Find an example in which the body is objectified and then write a paper using your example as a tool to extend or complicate Roach's argument about the human body as object. Your work on the Bodies . . . The Exhibition from Question 1 of Exploring Context (p. 361) might serve as a good starting point in making your argument.

Reflect on: Why does Roach consider body objectification a necessary step in the experiments she discusses? Is it possible to conduct scientific experiments on bodies without viewing them as objects? Is body objectification limited to scientific experimentation? Is body objectification limited to the dead? What are some of the possible steps required in order to view a body as an object?

Assignment 2. ROACH AND GILBERT

Gilbert suggests that our imaginations cannot reliably predict our future happiness. Given that argument, the question of informed consent regarding the donation of our bodies to research becomes somewhat problematic. How can we know if we're making the right decision about our future? Write a paper in which you propose the key factors in making the best decisions about the use of our bodies after death. Begin with your discussion of informed consent from Question 2 of Questions for Critical Reading for Roach (p. 361); also consider the definitions of *surrogate* and *happiness* that you created in the Questions for Critical Reading for Gilbert's essay (p. 187).

In formulating your argument, think about these questions as well: Does informed consent represent the limit of surrogates' usefulness? What role might super-replicators play in the process of body donation? Does such a decision have more to do with our future happiness or our current happiness?

Assignment 3. SPAR AND ONE OTHER

In the previous assignments in this sequence you've explored the idea of the human body as an object after death, but Spar raises questions about newborn bodies as commodities. Using Spar and one of the other authors you've read for this sequence, write a paper in which you determine the role that economics should play in international adoption. You may wish to begin with your discussion of adoption from Question 1 of Questions for Critical Reading for Spar (p. 436).

Also think about these questions: Do ethical standards in the area of human commerce shift when the bodies in question are living instead of dead? What processes of informed consent might be used in international adoptions? Do the benefits of adoption outweigh any concerns about a black market? How might Gilbert's understanding of surrogates aid in limiting the role of economics in adoption? How could a super-replicator transform the economics of adoption?

Assignment 4. SERANO AND ONE OTHER

So far in this sequence you've viewed the human body as an object in research and in adoption and considered the questions of ethics and economics involved. Serano's essay also discusses the objectification of the body, in this case through a media-driven public fascination with extreme transformations of the body. Using the work of Serano and at least one other author from this sequence, write a paper in which you explore the consequences of the body's objectification in the media. Start with your work in Questions for Critical Reading and Exploring Context for Serano (p. 398), particularly your examinations of before-and-after photos and their effects.

Give consideration to: What role do adoption Web sites play in fueling the black market for babies? How do they promote a kind of fascination? Are class boundaries also at issue in adoption? How does the media's treatment of transsexuals act as a kind of super-replicator? Can media representations of extreme body makeovers serve as a kind of surrogate?

SEQUENCE 9

The Melting Not: One American Culture?

LESLIE SAVAN

STEVE OLSON

REBEKAH NATHAN

MADELEINE ALBRIGHT

In this sequence you will explore the problems and potential of community and diversity. You will begin by using Leslie Savan's analysis of the appropriation of black talk by pop talk to consider the possibility of achieving a melting pot ideal in America. Then you will turn to Steve Olson's argument about genetics and race to further explore why ethnicity persists in society, despite the lack of any genetic basis for conceptions of race. Rebekah Nathan's exploration of these issues on college campuses will provide you with an opportunity to ground them in very specific and very local examples. Finally, with Madeleine Albright's essay, you will explore the role that faith might have in achieving the goal of a melting pot society. At the end of this sequence, you will have a greater understanding of the challenges of community and diversity. But you will also have a set of conceptual tools for describing and perhaps solving this challenge.

▶ TAGS: *melting pot*, **diversity**, religion, *faith*, *diplomacy*, community of descent, *ethnicity*, **race**, education

Assignment 1. SAVAN

Using Savan's essay, write a paper in which you determine the possibility of actualizing the melting pot ideal in America. Is it possible to achieve that ideal, or will there always be some sort of exploitation of cultures in the process? What gets lost in the melting pot? What do we gain? Can we achieve the goals of such a society without sacrificing the uniqueness of various cultures? How?

Assignment 2. OLSON AND SAVAN

According to Olson, there is no longer any genetic basis for race, yet he also makes it clear that concepts of race and ethnicity in Hawaii and elsewhere continue to persist. Synthesizing Olson's and Savan's arguments, write a paper in which you explain the reasons for the persistence of ethnic divisions in America and in which you consider the possibility of a solution to these divisions. Begin with your response to Question 3 of Questions for Critical Reading for Olson (p. 277), in which you located reasons for the persistence of race. Incorporate Savan's ideas in making your argument.

Ask yourself: What role do the media and advertising play in the persistence of race and ethnicity? Does covert prestige promote the end of race, or does it further entrench racial divisions? Does one need to "pay the dues" in order to join a community of descent? What role does education play in the persistence of race and ethnicity, according to both authors?

Assignment 3. NATHAN AND ONE OTHER

Nathan examines the challenges to achieving community and diversity on college campuses, bringing issues from the essays you've read so far down to a specific and local level. Using the work of Nathan and one other author from this sequence, write a paper in which you propose strategies for achieving community on college campuses. You might want to use your experience at your school as an example to support your argument. You could also draw from your work in Question 3 of Questions for Critical Reading for Nathan (p. 246), in which you identified the tools needed to reach this goal; synthesize these tools with the concepts from the second author you've chosen to work with.

To further help you think critically about your argument, ponder these questions: How does Savan's discussion of the controversy over Ebonics suggest the challenges of forming community on college campuses? How might paying the dues suggest a solution? Does covert prestige contribute to the problem? How might communities of descent function on campus? How does Olson's discussion of schools in Hawaii also emphasize the challenges of such a project?

Assignment 4. ALBRIGHT AND ONE OTHER

So far in this sequence you've examined some of the challenges of achieving an integrated community. And though Albright's explicit concern is the role of faith in diplomacy, she does have a lot to say about the role of religion in integrating communities. For this last assignment, use ideas from Albright and one other author from this sequence to write a paper in which you propose what role religion and faith might play in achieving the vision of a melting pot in the United States. You might decide that such a vision is impossible, in which case your argument should work with Albright and another author in order to argue that point.

In crafting your argument, reflect: Could faith play a role in mediating appropriations of ethnic languages? Could religion provide a neutral language through which groups might communicate? Does faith function as a community of descent? Can it transcend race? What role might religion play on college campuses? Could it enhance community, or would it be divisive?

Putting the "I" in Team: The Practices of Collaboration

JAMES SUROWIECKI

MARSHALL POE

THOMAS FRIEDMAN

MICHAEL POLLAN

In this sequence you will explore the practices of collaboration. You will begin by using James Surowiecki's exploration of the failure of small groups in order to deduce the best practices for making such groups successful. Then you will extend those ideas by using Marshall Poe's analysis of Wikipedia to determine what role the size of a group has in its success. In the third assignment of this sequence you will use your understanding of collaborative practices to propose strategies for minimizing their dangers, as represented in the mutant supply chains examined by Thomas Friedman. In the last assignment of this sequence, you will use Michael Pollan's idea of the holon to argue for the role of the individual in collaboration. At the end of this sequence you will have an understanding of what makes groups succeed or fail. You will also understand the dangers of collaborative processes and the strategies you can use to avoid those dangers, all the while preserving the individual within the group.

▶ TAGS: *holons,* **technology**, *groups*, Wikipedia, *knowledge,* **collaboration**, *supply chains*

Assignment 1. SUROWIECKI

Surowiecki discusses ways in which group dynamics contributed to the failure of the *Columbia*'s Mission Management Team. Using Surowiecki's observations, write a paper that determines the best practices for organizing and running a small group. In composing your response, consider these questions: What makes a small group more than just the sum of its parts? How can group identity be made to serve the purpose of the group? What is the ideal structure for a group? How important is cognitive diversity, and why? How can group polarization be avoided? In what ways could "talkativeness" be regulated to ensure equal participation by all members of the group?

Assignment 2. POE AND SUROWIECKI

While Surowiecki explores the failure of groups, Poe focuses on the success of the group effort behind Wikipedia. One way to account for the vastly different results of the collaborative efforts in these two essays is to consider the size of each group. Write a paper in which you use both Surowiecki and Poe to explore how the dangers, advantages, and strategies change as the size of a group collaboration increases.

In composing your response, ask yourself these questions: Would the small group practices you identified in the first assignment of this sequence work for Wikipedia? Would a bottom-up organization work for a small group? Does the cathedral model or the bazaar model have an optimal size? Could the "Cunctator" have succeeded as a member of the Mission Management Team? Could group polarization and talkativeness plague Wikipedia? How is the sense of community altered by the size of the community?

Assignment 3. FRIEDMAN AND POE

Friedman's essay is largely concerned with the benefits of collaboration represented by global supply chains. But in turning to mutant supply chains, he reveals the dangers that collaboration can pose as well. Using Friedman and Poe, write a paper in which you propose a solution to mitigate these dangers that incorporates Wikipedia's strategies of collaborative knowledge. You might want to begin with your discussion of collaboration in Question 1 of Questions for Critical Reading for Friedman (p. 138).

In formulating your argument you might also think about these questions: How could Nupedia's neutral point of view work for the Internet at large? How could it mitigate terrorist propaganda? What significance does the aphorism "given enough eyeballs, all bugs are shallow" have for this situation? How can your solution avoid the fear of centralized authority that the Cunctator worried about?

Assignment 4. POLLAN AND ONE OTHER

So far in this sequence you've considered practices of collaboration, practices which are also at work on Polyface farm, as Pollan makes clear. Yet in introducing the concept of the holon, Pollan also suggests the role that individuals play in group processes. For this final assignment, use the work of Pollan and one other author from this sequence to write a paper in which you determine the importance of the individual in collaboration. You might draw on the definition of *holon* that you developed for Question 2 of Questions for Critical Reading for Pollan (p. 292).

Also consider: Does the individual hurt or hinder the small group processes that Surowiecki describes? Could an individual have made a difference on the Mission Management Team? Are Wikipedia's contributors holons? How are supply chains similar to Polyface?

Acknowledgments (continued from page iv)

Julia Alvarez, selections from *Once Upon a Quinceañera: Coming of Age in the USA* by Julia Alvarez. Copyright © 2007 by Julia Alvarez. Published by Plume, a member of the Penguin Group (USA) Inc., and originally in hardcover by Viking. By permission of Susan Bergholz Literary Services, New York, NY, and Lamy, NM. All rights reserved.

Kwame Anthony Appiah, "Making Conversation" and "The Primacy of Practice." From *Cosmopolitanism: Ethics in a World of Strangers* by Kwame Anthony Appiah. Copyright © 2006 by Kwame Anthony Appiah. Used by permission of W. W. Norton & Company, Inc.

The Dalai Lama, "Ethics and the New Genetics." From *The Universe in a Single Atom: The Convergence of Science and Spirituality* by His Holiness The Dalai Lama. Copyright © 2005 by the Dalai Lama. Used by permission of Morgan Road Books, an imprint of the Doubleday Broadway Publishing, a division of Random House, Inc.

Joan Didion, "After Life." From *The Year of Magical Thinking* by Joan Didion. Copyright © 2005 by Joan Didion. Used by permission of Alfred A. Knopf, a division of Random House, Inc.

Helen Epstein, "AIDS, Inc." From *The Invisible Cure: Africa, the West, and the Fight against AIDS* by Helen Epstein. Copyright © 2007 by Helen Epstein. Reprinted by permission of Farrar, Straus and Giroux, LLC.

Thomas L. Friedman, "The Dell Theory of Conflict Prevention." From *The World Is Flat: A Brief History of the Twenty-first Century* by Thomas L. Friedman. Copyright © 2005, 2006 by Thomas L. Friedman. Reprinted by permission of Farrar, Straus and Giroux, LLC.

Francis Fukuyama, "Human Dignity." From *Our Posthuman Future: Consequences of the Biotechnology Revolution* by Francis Fukuyama. Copyright © 2002 by Francis Fukuyama. Reprinted by permission of Farrar, Straus and Giroux, LLC.

Daniel Gilbert, "Reporting Live from Tomorrow." From *Stumbling on Happiness* by Daniel Gilbert. Copyright © 2006 by Daniel Gilbert. Used by permission of Alfred A. Knopf, a division of Random House, Inc.

Steven Johnson, "Listening to Feedback." From *Emergence: The Connected Lives of Ants, Brains, Cities, and Software* by Steven Johnson. Copyright © 2001 by Steven Johnson. Reprinted with the permission of Scribner, a division of Simon & Schuster, Inc. All rights reserved.

Michael Kimmelman, "The Art of Collecting Lightbulbs." From *The Accidental Masterpiece: On the Art of Life and Vice Versa* by Michael Kimmelman. Copyright © 2005 by Michael Kimmelman. Used by permission of the Penguin Press, a division of Penguin Group (USA) Inc.

Rebekah Nathan, "Community and Diversity." From *My Freshman Year: What a Professor Learned by Becoming a Student* by Rebekah Nathan. Copyright © 2005 by Rebekah Nathan. Used by permission of the publisher, Cornell University Press.

Steve Olson, "The End of Race: Hawaii and the Mixing of Peoples." From *Mapping Human History* by Steve Olson. Copyright © 2002 by Steve Olson. Reprinted by permission of Houghton Mifflin Harcourt Publishing Company. All rights reserved.

Marshall Poe, "The Hive." From the *Atlantic Monthly*, September 2006. Copyright © 2006 by Marshall Poe. Reprinted by permission of Marshall Poe.

Michael Pollan, "The Animals: Practicing Complexity." From *The Omnivore's Dilemma* by Michael Pollan. Copyright © 2006 by Michael Pollan. Used by permission of the Penguin Press, a division of Penguin Group (USA) Inc.

Virginia Postrel, "The Boundaries of Design." Chap. 5 from *The Substance of Style* by Virginia Postrel, pp. 122–63. Copyright © 2003 by Virginia Postrel. Reprinted by permission of HarperCollins Publishers.

515

Art Credits

Alvarez: Cover design by Roseanne J. Serra; cover photo by Trujillo-Paumier/Getty Images. Courtesy of Penguin Group.

Appiah: From *Cosmopolitanism: Ethics in a World of Strangers* by Kwame Anthony Appiah. Used by permission of W. W. Norton and Company, Inc.

The Dalai Lama: Jacket cover from *The Universe in a Single Atom: The Convergence of Science and Spirituality* by His Holiness The Dalai Lama. Used by permission of Morgan Road Books, an imprint of the Doubleday Broadway Publishing Group, a division of Random House, Inc.

Didion: Book cover copyright © 2005 by Alfred A. Knopf, from *The Year of Magical Thinking* by Joan Didion. Used by permission of Alfred A. Knopf, a division of Random House, Inc.

Epstein: Courtesy of Picador Press.

Friedman: Courtesy of Picador Press.

Fukuyama: Courtesy of Picador Press.

Gilbert: Book cover copyright © 2006 by Alfred A. Knopf, from *Stumbling on Happiness* by Daniel Gilbert. Used by permission of Alfred A. Knopf, a division of Random House, Inc.

Johnson: Reproduced with the permission of Scribner, a division of Simon and Schuster, Inc., from *Emergence: The Connected Lives of Ants, Brains, Cities, and Software* by Steven Johnson. All rights reserved.

Kimmelman: Courtesy of Penguin Group.

Nathan: Courtesy of Penguin Group.

Olson: Cover of *Mapping Human History* by Steve Olson (Boston: Mariner Books, 2003).

Poe: Courtesy of the *Atlantic Monthly*.

Pollan: Courtesy of Penguin Group.

Postrel: Book cover from *The Substance of Style* by Virginia Postrel. Reprinted by permission of HarperCollins Publishers.

Restak: Courtesy of Rodale Press.

Roach: From *Stiff: The Curious Lives of Human Cadavers* by Mary Roach. Used by permission of W. W. Norton and Company, Inc.

Savan: Book cover copyright © 2005 by Alfred A. Knopf, from *Slam Dunks and No-Brainers* by Leslie Savan. Used by permission of Alfred A. Knopf, a division of Random House, Inc.

Serano: Courtesy of Perseus Books Group.

Spar: Courtesy of Harvard Business School Publishing.

Surowiecki: Jacket cover from *The Wisdom of Crowds: Why the Many Are Smarter Than the Few and How Collective Wisdom Shapes Business, Economies, Societies, and Nations* by James Surowiecki. Used by permission of Doubleday, a division of Random House, Inc.

Taylor: Diana Taylor, "cover image," *The Archive and the Repertoire*. Copyright 2003, Duke University Press. All rights reserved. Used by permission of the publisher.

Yoshino: Book cover, copyright © 2006 by Random House, Inc., from *Covering* by Kenji Yoshino. Used by permission of Random House, Inc.

Interior Images

Kimmelman: *Charles Willson Peale*, courtesy of the Pennsylvania Academy of the Fine Arts, Philadelphia. Gift of Sarah Harrison (The Joseph Harrison Jr. Collection). *J. Dennis Welsch*, courtesy of the Mütter Museum/The College of Physicians of Philadelphia.

Olson: Map of Hawaii, *Mapping Human History* by Steve Olson (Boston, Mariner Books, 2003).

Taylor: All photos by Diana Taylor.